# SOCIAL NORMS

# SOCIAL NORMS

*Michael Hechter*
*AND*
*Karl-Dieter Opp*

*Editors*

RUSSELL SAGE FOUNDATION / NEW YORK

## The Russell Sage Foundation

The Russell Sage Foundation, one of the oldest of America's general purpose foundations, was established in 1907 by Mrs. Margaret Olivia Sage for "the improvement of social and living conditions in the United States." The Foundation seeks to fulfill this mandate by fostering the development and dissemination of knowledge about the country's political, social, and economic problems. While the Foundation endeavors to assure the accuracy and objectivity of each book it publishes, the conclusions and interpretations in Russell Sage Foundation publications are those of the authors and not of the Foundation, its Trustees, or its staff. Publication by Russell Sage, therefore, does not imply Foundation endorsement.

**Library of Congress Cataloging-in-Publication Data**

Social norms / Michael Hechter and Karl-Dieter Opp, editors.
    p. cm.
  Includes bibliographical references and index.
  ISBN 0-87154-354-0
    1. Social norms.  I. Hechter, Michael.  II. Opp, Karl-Dieter.

HM676.S63 2001
306—dc21                                                  00-051000

Text design by Suzanne Nichols.

RUSSELL SAGE FOUNDATION
112 East 64th Street, New York, New York 10021
10 9 8 7 6 5 4 3 2 1

For Joshua
—M.H.


For Elisabeth
—K.D.O.

# Contents

# Contributors

MICHAEL HECHTER is professor of sociology at the University of Washington in Seattle.

KARL-DIETER OPP is professor of sociology at the University of Leipzig, Germany.

ELIZABETH BORLAND is doctoral candidate in sociology at the University of Arizona.

KAREN S. COOK is Ray Lyman Wilbur Professor of Sociology at Stanford University.

THRÁINN EGGERTSSON is professor of economics at the University of Iceland in Reykjavík and visiting Olin Fellow at the Columbia University School of Law.

ROBERT C. ELLICKSON is Walter E. Meyer Professor of Property and Urban Law at Yale Law School.

GARY ALAN FINE is professor of sociology at Northwestern University.

RUSSELL HARDIN is professor of politics at New York University.

CHRISTINE HORNE is assistant professor of sociology at Brigham Young University.

GUILLERMINA JASSO is professor of sociology at New York University.

SATOSHI KANAZAWA is assistant professor of sociology at Indiana University of Pennsylvania.

MICHAEL SCHUDSON is professor of communication and adjunct professor of sociology at the University of California, San Diego.

MARY C. STILL is doctoral candidate in sociology at Cornell University.

THOMAS VOSS is professor of sociology at the University of Leipzig.

# Introduction

*Michael Hechter and Karl-Dieter Opp*

N ORMS are cultural phenomena that prescribe and proscribe behavior in specific circumstances. As such, they have long been considered to be at least partly responsible for regulating social behavior. Without norms, it is hard to imagine how interaction and exchange between strangers could take place at all (this was a main point in Émile Durkheim's *The Division of Labor in Society* [1893] 1933). Among other things, they instruct people not to kill, not to injure others, to keep their promises, to abide by the Golden Rule, and so forth. That foundation of Judeo-Christian ethics, the Ten Commandments, is neither more nor less than an enumeration of norms. Just as sets of mutually consistent norms help regulate behavior, so sets of inconsistent or rapidly shifting norms—a state of affairs leading to Durkheim's famous anomie—are often regarded as a symptom, if not a cause, of social unrest (Berger 1998).

This is not to claim that norms must do all the heavy lifting. The state, of course, is also responsible for regulating behavior in modern society. Its principal instrument in this respect is the law. Although the law, too, relies on norms, legal norms are different from social norms. Legal norms are created by design—usually through some kind of deliberative process, precisely specified in written texts, linked to particular sanctions, and enforced by a specialized bureaucracy. Social norms, by contrast, often are spontaneous rather than deliberately planned (hence, of uncertain origin), unwritten (hence, their content and rules for application are often imprecise), and enforced informally (although the resulting sanctions can sometimes be a matter of life and death).

Despite their regulative role, the attention afforded to social norms has varied notably in the social sciences. In sociology and anthropology, social norms were celebrated by classical theorists of the late nineteenth and early twentieth centuries and by functionalist theorists of the 1950s. Moreover, a famous series of social psychological experiments carried out by Solomon Asch (1951), Stanley Milgram (1974), and Philip Zimbardo (Haney, Banks, and Zimbardo 1973) revealed, at least in part, the power of norms to affect individual behavior.

Once functionalism began to lose popularity in sociology, however, explicit discussion of social norms began to wane. Ironically, just when sociologists were losing interest in social norms, other social scientists were becoming intrigued with them. The growing influence of rational choice and game theory brought increasing attention to social norms in economics, political science, international relations, law, and philosophy.

The reason for this growing attention to norms is easy to discern. Phenomena like cooperation, collective action, and social order cannot readily be explained on the basis of the rational egoistic behavioral assumptions that are typically countenanced by rational choice theorists (see Hechter 1994). Hence, rational choice theorists have regarded these kinds of outcomes (or equilibria), however rare they may be, as a major challenge to their theoretical commitments. In their quest for explanations of these ostensibly problematic outcomes, social norms have come to occupy pride of place. Indeed, a large body of research suggests that social norms regulate such diverse phenomena as queuing (MacCormick 1998), fertility (Simons 1999), cooperation (Axelrod 1984; Taylor 1987), crime (Sampson, Raudenbush, and Earls 1997), government effectiveness (Putnam 1994), and social order (Hechter and Kanazawa 1993).

Given this rekindling of interest in social norms, we felt that it was a propitious time to take stock of what is currently known about them.[1] Fortunately, the Russell Sage Foundation generously agreed to sponsor a series of workshops on the topic. As much less is known about the emergence of social norms than about their effects, these workshops were designed to emphasize the problem of normative emergence.

To this end, we convened participants employing different methodologies and theoretical perspectives from a variety of social science disciplines. Because research on social norms, such as it is, is scattered across different disciplines and substantive topics, we assumed that no one scholar could possibly be apprised of the current state of knowledge. It was therefore decided that the book should begin with critical reviews of existing theory and research on the emergence of social norms. Chapters were sought on the current status of norms in sociology, law, economics, and game theory, for the role of social norms is particularly central in these fields.[2] The authors of the chapters in part I of the volume were given a mandate to comprehensively survey recent research on social norms in their respective disciplines, to systematize existing theory, and to provide new insights. Thus the volume begins with critical reviews of the current state of knowledge about social norms in sociology (Christine Horne), law (Robert Ellickson), economics (Thráinn Eggertsson), and game theory (Thomas Voss).

These chapters suggest that consensus about social norms is limited both across disciplines and within them. To begin, the concept of social norm clearly means different things to different scholars. Basically, two types of definitions can be distinguished in these chapters.[3] According to the first, social norms entail a moral imperative—that is, a sense of oughtness. From this point of view, we identify as a social norm behavior that people believe ought (or ought not) to be performed regardless of its outcome for the agent. Dueling offers an example: a man who engaged in a duel was prepared to give up his life to salvage his honor.

The second definition is much less restrictive. According to it, norms are merely behavioral regularities that generate social expectations without any moral obligations. From this point of view, we identify certain behavior as a social norm if deviation from that practice results in costs being imposed on an agent (see chapter 4). For example, a person apprehended by a police officer is expected to behave respectfully. If he or she deviates from this expectation—by running away, for example, or by reaching for what the police suspect might be a concealed weapon—the police are likely to react with force (Dan Barry, "What to Do If You're Stopped by the Police," *New York Times*, February, 27, 2000).

Violating any kind of social norm makes one vulnerable to sanctioning. Norms of the first type—what could be called "oughtness norms"—however, differ from regularity norms in one important respect. Because the violator is likely to have internalized this kind of norm, sanctioning is not contingent on detection. Violation of an oughtness norm is likely to entail some internal sanctioning—the experience of guilt or shame. Clearly, then, oughtness norms do a better job of controlling behavior than regularity norms.

As there is no common definition of social norms, there can be little agreement about how to measure them. Part II of this volume contains most of the measurement procedures currently being employed in the empirical analysis of social norms, as well as some novel ones. Evidence about norms is provided by ethnographic methods (chapter 5), content analysis (chapter 6), questions from factorial surveys (chapter 8), historical analysis (chapter 7), and experiments (chapter 8).

Despite this definitional and methodological diversity, a good deal is known about the effects of social norms. Much less clear, however, are the conditions responsible for their emergence.[4] Because of the dearth of empirical research on the emergence of social norms, much of the relevant literature is speculative.[5] In this regard, one speculation in particular—the instrumental theory of normative emergence (chapter 8)—has gained wide currency. According to the instrumental theory, norms tend to emerge to satisfy demands to mitigate negative externalities or to promote positive ones. Instrumental theorists certainly do not maintain that all imaginable socially desirable norms will emerge, however. Their claim is much more limited—to wit, that the norms that actually do emerge are likely to be socially beneficial.

Although the instrumental theory is increasingly popular, it has come under attack. Critics (Rawls 1971; Elster 1999) argue that it is too rosy, on the one hand, and too bloodless, on the other: too rosy because it fails to anticipate the existence of malign norms like the duel, the feud, and the vendetta, too bloodless because it ignores the emotional bedrock that gives norms what the critics regard as their exceptional regulatory power.

By analyzing the emergence of a number of specific real-world norms, the chapters in part II shed considerable light on the adequacy of the instrumental theory. Gary Alan Fine begins this section of the volume with an ethnographic analysis of the social norms that have emerged among members of the Minnesota Mycological Society. This is a voluntary association made up of a variety of different kinds of nature lovers—amateur mycologists, photographers, and people who enjoy collecting mushrooms to eat them. Among other things, Fine asks how these naturalists can engage in activities that damage the environment they are ostensibly committed to protecting from human depredation. He argues that they do so by minimizing the extent of the harm they cause the environment and by distinguishing themselves from others who do more damage. In this way, Fine explains how a social norm becomes modified. In Fine's view, social norms are part of a negotiated order in which meanings are context bound rather than fixed. Hence, to a greater or lesser degree, social norms are ambiguous; they are inherently subject to modification and instrumental manipulation.

Michael Schudson then provides a historical account of the emergence of the norm of objectivity among American journalists. Journalists play a key role in democratic societies, for more than people in other professions they can provide the information that makes it possible for the electorate to hold their elected representatives accountable. Schudson argues that this norm—which obliges reporters to separate facts from values and to report on the facts alone—is most highly developed in American journalism. The norm did not suddenly appear; rather, it emerged gradually, beginning in the late nineteenth century. The story of the development of this norm is far from straightforward, however; as Schudson shows, the history of the norm is shrouded in mystery. (The chapter leads one to suspect that much the same is true about the emergence of many other social norms.) Schudson seeks to explain why the norm of objectivity is so much more salient in this country than in the European democracies. He contrasts the relative merits of technological explanations of the emergence of the objectivity norm—which claim that new developments in communications technology made it easier for stories to be checked and hence increased reporters' accountability to editors—and institutional explanations of its emergence, finding greater merit in the latter perspective.

Michael Hechter and Elizabeth Borland next consider the merits of an institutional explanation of the emergence of another norm—national self-determination—relative to an instrumental alternative. National self-determination as a norm has two parts: it holds that citizens should have the right to choose their own government and also to determine their own collective identity. Although norms that emerge among journalists and mushroom collectors usually do not have life-or-death consequences, the same cannot be said for the norm of national self-determination. Indeed, instantiation of this norm—in the form of current secessionist conflicts—is responsible for much of the political violence occurring in the world today (Gurr 1993; Gurr and Harff 1994). Hechter and Borland trace the emergence of this norm from the American and French Revolutions, showing how it has been applied in the wake of the dismantling of territorial (Austro-Hungarian, Ottoman, and Soviet) and colonial (British, French, and Portuguese) empires. Although the norm has a quasi-legal status—it is enunciated in the charter of the United Nations—key elements of the norm are ambiguous, as Hechter and Borland demonstrate. This ambiguity is revealed in the empirical record: for the most part, application of the norm has been restricted to external colonies rather than to internal ones or national minorities. In opposition to an institutionalist view that sees the diffusion of norms regarding human rights occurring universally, driven by processes of legitimation, Hechter and Borland argue that this ambiguity enables the most powerful actors in the international system to employ the norm of national self-determination for their own strategic purposes.

Karl-Dieter Opp then discusses the role social networks play in the emergence of norms that oblige people to participate in protest events. He suggests a two-step explanation of normative emergence. The first step provides propositions about conditions that increase the likelihood of the emergence of a given norm. The second explains the mechanisms chosen by actors interested in establishing the norm. Opp regards social norms as second-order public goods that are most likely to emerge when they are instrumental for the attainment of group goals. In his view, a given norm tends to emerge when individuals' perceived efficacy is high and when establishment of the norm is supported by strong positive selective incentives. This view suggests that social networks have no necessary implications for the emergence of norms. Instead, the relation between networks and norms is mediated by positive incentives that are often by-products of social networks. Moreover, norms often arise spontaneously from the informal enunciation of normative statements and sanctioning in the course of organizing collective action. These propositions are then subjected to a test on the basis of evidence drawn from a panel study conducted in East Germany in 1993 and 1996. Many of Opp's propositions are confirmed in the subsequent analysis.

Satoshi Kanazawa and Mary Still apply evolutionary psychology to the analysis of marriage norms—in particular, those mandating monogamous as against polygynous marriage. Although evolutionary psychology aims to explain individual cognition and behavior, the authors argue that it can also serve as a foundation for a macro-level theory of the emergence of regularity norms. Kanazawa and Still make a distinction between consensual norms (those that prescribe behavior that people are likely to engage in anyway) and imposed norms (those that prescribe behavior that people would not otherwise engage in), arguing that evolutionary psychology can explain the emergence only of the former. Their analysis of international data suggests that marriage norms at the macro level reflect the choices that women make independently to marry either monogamously (when resource inequality among men is small) or polygynously (when such inequality is large).

Next, Christine Horne seeks to determine the relative merits of two general approaches to explaining the emergence of social norms. Behavior-based explanations suggest that norms essentially ratify preexisting behavioral regularities. Externality-based explanations, in contrast, suggest that norms largely arise to overcome negative externalities or to promote positive ones in well-defined groups. She applies these theoretical perspectives to explain norms that regulate female sexual behavior in parts of Africa and concludes that an externality-based approach can best explain the very different norms that obtain there. Horne then uses these two general perspectives to develop contrasting predictions regarding controller-selection norms and then tests them experimentally.

Although the chapters are substantively diverse, most of them advert, either positively or negatively, to the instrumental theory of the emergence of norms. The view that norms are created to prevent negative externalities, or to promote positive ones, is virtually canonical in the rational choice literature. Hechter and Borland treat states as collective actors, and the instrumental interests of these states are a factor—if not the sole factor—responsible for application of the norm of national self-determination. Horne's behavior-based approach assumes that a behavior may lead to a norm in part "because individuals value consistency and prefer that others behave in predictable ways." Kanazawa and Still argue that one factor, among others, responsible for the emergence of marriage norms is women's interest in increasing their material welfare.

Although Fine and Schudson can hardly be considered advocates of rational choice, much of the material in their chapters also suggests that social norms are, at least in part, instrumental. Fine's mycologists are intensely interested in mushrooms and understand full well that this interest conflicts with norms they also hold about the sanctity of the environment. This conflict leads to social pressure, cognitive dissonance, and the search for justifications.

Fine also discusses another norm that keeps the mushroomers from maximizing their haul. He notes that mushrooming is competitive: "The mushroom that I pick, you cannot." This suggests that the mycologists are faced with a negative externality. In this instance, the norm "First come, first serve" might be applied; however, this solution is likely to breed strain in the mushroomers' community; thus emerges a "need to tame competition." Why? Their desire to maintain good personal relations is inconsistent with untrammeled competition. Thus, the emergence of a norm about constraining the collection of mushrooms arises from the group's conflicting interests.

Schudson argues that the objectivity norm in American journalism also depends on the interests of individual actors. For example, one such interest is the group's desire to "celebrate itself" and to define itself in relation to other groups. In exploring why the norm of objectivity is less accepted in Europe than in the United States, Schudson finds that American journalists were motivated by a "desire to distinguish themselves from public relations practitioners [that] was absent in Europe." If that is the case, then the objectivity norm served the interests of journalists. Note, however, that this is not the only factor that accounts for the emergence of the norm.

The contributions in part II do not refer to anything like a representative sample of all important social norms. Only a few of these case studies concern norms of the highest salience—such as dueling, honor killing, foot binding, and genital mutilation. Such norms impose the greatest costs on the individuals who are subject to them. In comparison, some of the norms discussed in this section (those regarding mushrooming, political protest, and objectivity in journalism) have much less salience. Others, however—norms about marriage and national self-determination—are indeed highly salient. Although we would have welcomed more studies of high-salience norms, the study of such extreme norms in a disciplined fashion presents grave obstacles to academic researchers (see, however, Cohen and Nisbett 1997).

Part III moves from case studies to theory construction. Two chapters outline new theoretical perspectives on norm emergence. Karen Cook and Russell Hardin (chapter 11) discuss how social norms and social networks work together to resolve the problem of mutual assistance. They argue that the small community works through quasi-universal norms that cover many different aspects of potential cooperation. In contrast, urban society works through networks of ongoing relationships embedded within a much larger context. Because any given urban network is partial—in that it covers only a particular realm of potential cooperation—participants are each involved in many quite different networks. Cook and Hardin focus on the norm of communal cooperativeness, arguing that it does not appear to generalize to more diffuse urban contexts.

Guillermina Jasso argues that human beings are, by nature, rule makers, and that the characteristics of their norms grow out of the operation of basic social processes. She shows how comparison theory—a general, axiomatic theory—can be used to study the emergence of norms concerning theft. The theft illustration yields a variety of testable predictions. A small sample of these includes the following:

1. The rule, "Thou shalt not steal," is not likely to arise in homogeneous societies because most of the population is indifferent to theft. Nor is it likely to emerge in heterogeneous societies because there are strong factions both in support and in opposition.

2. A homogeneous society quickly embraces the rules, "Never steal from someone poorer than yourself," and "When stealing from someone richer than yourself, never leave him or her poorer than you were before the theft."

   This volume concentrates on social norms, not on law and lawmaking. There is no question that law is a kind of norm, as indicated above; and the emergence of law is a highly controversial subject (see n. 3). This volume confines its attention to social norms largely out of practical considerations. The emergence of law is treated in a number of far-flung literatures—including jurisprudence, the sociology of law, public administration, and rational choice theory, among others. To do the topic justice would require an entirely new volume and quite a different set of contributors. For all these reasons, we limited the scope of the volume to social norms alone.

   When this volume was initially planned, it was hoped that the case studies in part III would systematically relate to the general theoretical chapters in part I by applying, extending, or modifying the theories presented therein. In retrospect, this appears to have been a utopian objective. For better or worse, the literature on social norms consists of a loose collection of mostly independent propositions that are scattered in the literatures of various disciplines. As the chapters in part I indicate, no adequate theory of the emergence of social norms can be said to exist at this juncture. Given the present state of the art, the best that could be hoped for is a set of rather loose connections between the theoretical chapters and the case studies. Moreover, these case studies are substantively informative in their own right. It is interesting to learn how the norm of objectivity arose in American journalism and how the right of self-determination emerged as an international norm. Thus, the case studies represent the current state of interdisciplinary knowledge about a number of specific norms.

   The volume as a whole comprises a set of literature reviews, empirical studies, and theories about the emergence of social norms. As such, it probably offers the most comprehensive critical overview currently available of this complex and multifaceted subject. Even so, many questions remain unclear. In the conclusion, we highlight the principal points of agreement and contention in the preceding chapters, paying particular attention to the status of the instrumental theory. In addition, we discuss some of the fundamental issues that have to be faced in explaining normative phenomena and point toward an agenda for future research.

# Notes

1.  Another indication of the increasing centrality of social norms can be found in the many "new institutionalisms" that are presently flourishing in economics, political science, international relations, and sociology.

2.  Our attempts to find an anthropologist willing to participate in this enterprise came to naught. Although the working group had one political scientist (Russell Hardin), reviews were not solicited in either political science or international relations. Interest in norms is also strong in philosophy, but we purposely confined our attention to the more empirical social science disciplines.

3.  It is notable that a similar distinction has been made about legal norms. Legal positivists have argued that legal norms need have no moral foundations, whereas the advocates of natural law have taken the opposing view. Recently, the distinctions have become much more complex; see, for example, *Legal Theory* 6, no. 1 (2000).

4.  This point can be illustrated by considering some of the reactions to Robert Putnam's (1994) highly influential book, *Making Democracy Work*. Building on themes first explored in Edward Banfield's *The Moral Basis of a Backward Society* (1958), Putnam provides extensive documentation that civic norms in northern and southern Italy are as distinct from one another as night from day, and that these normative differences are associated with striking variations in economic development and government performance (northern Italy clearly outstrips the Mezzogiorno with respect to each). Like Banfield before him, Putnam argues that civic norms are responsible, at least in part, for the starkly varying fates of these two Italian regions. Yet the origins of these norms are as mysterious for Putnam, writing in the 1990s, as they were for Banfield in the 1950s (Goldberg 1996; Levi 1996; Tarrow 1996).

5.  Jon Elster (1999, 405) argues that the regulatory power of norms is fundamentally emotional. Consequently, the best evidence about emotions, he claims, is to be found in works of history, anthropology, fiction, and philosophy. It is doubtful, however, that these sources of evidence can contribute much to an analysis of social norms. More likely, the kinds of evidence that can be garnered from anthropologists' and novelists' thick description lead to the "just-so stories" that Elster so frequently disparages in many of his other writings.

# References

Asch, S. E. 1951. "Effects of Group Pressure upon the Modification and Distortion of Judgments." In *Groups, Leadership, and Men*, edited by Harold Guetzkow. Pittsburgh: Carnegie Press.

Axelrod, Robert. 1984. *The Evolution of Cooperation*. New York: Basic Books.

Banfield, Edward C. 1958. *The Moral Basis of a Backward Society*. Glencoe, Ill.: Free Press.

Berger, Peter L., ed. 1998. *The Limits of Social Cohesion: Conflict and Mediation in Pluralist Societies*. Boulder: Westview Press.

Cohen, Dov, and Richard E. Nisbett. 1997. "Field Experiments Examining the Culture of Honor: The Role of Institutions in Perpetuating Norms About Violence." *Personality and Social Psychology Bulletin* 23(1): 1188–99.

Durkheim, Émile. [1893] 1933. *The Division of Labor in Society.* Translated by George Simpson. Glencoe, Ill.: Free Press.

Elster, Jon. 1999. *Alchemies of the Mind: Rationality and the Emotions.* New York: Cambridge University Press.

Goldberg, Ellis. 1996. "Thinking About How Democracy Works." *Politics and Society* 24(1): 7–18.

Gurr, Ted Robert. 1993. *Minorities at Risk: A Global View of Ethnopolitical Conflicts.* Washington, D.C.: U.S. Institute of Peace Press.

Gurr, Ted Robert, and Barbara Harff. 1994. *Ethnic Conflict in World Politics.* Boulder: Westview Press.

Haney, Craig, Curtis Banks, and Philip Zimbardo. 1973. "Interpersonal Dynamics in a Simulated Prison." *International Journal of Criminology and Penology* 1(1): 69–97.

Hechter, Michael. 1994. "The Role of Values in Rational Choice Theory." *Rationality and Society* 6(3): 318–33.

Hechter, Michael, and Satoshi Kanazawa. 1993. "Group Solidarity and Social Order in Japan." *Journal of Theoretical Politics* 5(4): 455–93.

Levi, Margaret. 1996. "Social and Unsocial Capital: A Review-Essay of *Making Democracy Work.*" *Politics and Society* 24(1): 45–55.

MacCormick, Neil. 1998. "Norms, Institutions, and Institutional Facts." *Law and Philosophy* 17(3): 301–45.

Milgram, Stanley. 1974. *Obedience to Authority: An Experimental View.* New York: Harper and Row.

Putnam, Robert. 1994. *Making Democracy Work.* Princeton: Princeton University Press.

Rawls, John. 1971. *A Theory of Justice.* Cambridge: Harvard University Press, Belknap Press.

Sampson, Robert J., Stephen W. Raudenbush, and Felton Earls. 1997. "Neighborhoods and Violent Crime: A Multilevel Study of Collective Efficacy." *Science* 277: 918–24.

Simons, John. 1999. "The Cultural Significance of Western Fertility Trends in the 1980s." In *Dynamics of Values in Fertility Change,* edited by Richard Leete. Oxford: Oxford University Press

Tarrow, Sidney. 1996. "Making Social Science Work Across Space and Time: A Critical Reflection on Robert Putnam's *Making Democracy Work.*" *American Political Science Review* 90(2): 389–98.

Taylor, Michael. 1987. *The Possibility of Cooperation.* New York: Cambridge University Press.

# Part I

Disciplinary Perspectives on Social Norms

# SOCIOLOGICAL PERSPECTIVES ON THE EMERGENCE OF SOCIAL NORMS

*Christine Horne*

N O CONCEPT is invoked more often by social scientists in the explanation of human behavior than 'norm'" (Sills 1968, 208). Particularly for sociologists, norms are fundamental. Despite their importance, however, there is little consensus about them—what they are, how they are enforced, and how they emerge. Because of this disagreement and confusion, it is difficult to know just what the contribution of sociology has been to the study of norm emergence. Outsiders criticize the discipline for having produced little that is useful (Ellickson 1998), and sociologists themselves are unsure of the state of research on the issue. Part of the difficulty is that sociology is a diverse discipline made up of many subfields in which researchers ask different questions, rely on inconsistent assumptions, and have contradictory views of the research enterprise. The study of norms, unfortunately, does not fit neatly into any of these established areas. Rather, relevant work can be found in a variety of subfields. This chapter culls out of the literature some of the common themes. It seeks not to provide a comprehensive summary of the relevant research, but rather to develop a framework with which to organize thinking about norms.

## What Are Norms?

The study of norms is a difficult undertaking, as is the evaluation of existing work, in part because scholars disagree about what norms are. To complicate matters, they use a variety of terms—custom, convention, role, identity, institution, culture, and so forth—to refer to concepts that are similar to or overlap with notions about norms. Furthermore, the word has various meanings depending on the focus of the researcher. On some occasions it is used as an umbrella term that refers to a variety of controls, including formal organizational rules and laws as well as informal social controls, whereas at other times it is used more narrowly.

Even when viewed simply as informal social controls, definitions vary. For some, norms are a system of meaning. According to Gary Alan Fine, they "constitute a 'frame' within which individuals interpret a given situation and from which they take direction for their responsibilities as actors in that domain" (chapter 5, this volume). For these scholars, the problem of order is solved by mutual understanding—which norms provide (Durkheim 1915, 30). For others, norms are patterns of action. Game theorists, for example, view cooperative behavior as a general equivalent to any norm. Self-interested individuals act in their own interests rather than those of others. Norms encourage them to behave prosocially instead of merely for themselves. Therefore, cooperative behavior is normative, and by studying the emergence of patterns of cooperative behavior, scholars explain how norms emerge.

Probably the most widely accepted view of norms, however, is that they are statements that regulate behavior. For some, these statements identify expectations.[1] Such "expectations that arise concerning habits emerging and crystallizing in the course of repeated interactions might be regarded as latent norms" (Wrong 1994, 48; see also Bicchieri 1997, 25, 27). More frequently, these rules are seen as "ought" statements (Homans 1961, 12). They are "verbal description[s] of a concrete course of action . . . regarded as desirable, combined with an injunction to make certain future actions conform to this course. An instance of a norm is the statement 'Soldiers should obey the orders of their commanding officers'" (Parsons 1937, 75; see also Williams 1970, 413; LaPiere 1954, 118; and Blake and Davis 1964, 456). Norms may give permission, proscribe, prescribe, discourage, and so forth.

Norms are not, however, simply rules. Without some means of enforcement, rules serve merely as assertions of ideals. Scholars differ in their views on exactly what it is that makes norms effective. For some, norms must be internalized (see Durkheim 1915, 236–45, for a discussion of internalization). Individuals apply sanctions to their own behavior and respond to these internally generated rewards or punishments (Coleman 1990, 243; Elster 1989; Durkheim 1951). Norms also may be internalized when individuals come to value the behavior specified by a norm for its own sake: that is, they follow social norms because they want to. When seen in this way, the concept of internalized norms is consistent with the term "values" as used by others (for example, Hechter et al. 1999).

Whereas some focus on internalization as an enforcement mechanism, the majority of scholars emphasize the role of external sanctions. On this view, "norms are ordinarily enforced by sanctions, which are either rewards for carrying out those actions regarded as correct or punishments for carrying out those actions regarded as incorrect" (Coleman 1990, 242; see also Scott 1971; MacIver 1937; Blake and Davis 1964). Even those who rely heavily on the idea of internalization still recognize the importance of additional sources of enforcement. Talcott Parsons, for example, typically is associated with the view that social norms are internalized and, once internalized, control individual behavior. Yet he also acknowledges the role of external sanctions.

> There is always a double aspect of the expectation system. . . . On the one hand there are the expectations which concern and in part set standards for the behavior of the actor, ego, who is taken as the point of reference. . . . On the other hand there is a set of expectations relative to the contingently probable reactions of others ("alters")—these will be called sanctions, which in turn may be subdivided into positive and negative according to whether they are felt by ego to be gratification-promoting or depriving. The relation between role-expectations and sanctions then is clearly reciprocal. (Parsons 1952, 38; see also Durkheim [1903] 1953, 36, 43)[2]

For Parsons, as for most sociologists, social enforcement is an essential component of norms.

In addition to enforcement, for a norm to exist there must be agreement among group members regarding the validity of the rule and the right of group members to enforce it. A rule advocated only by an individual is not a norm at all but merely a personal idiosyncrasy. Although the amount of acceptance is unspecified, it is generally argued that at least some level of consensus is necessary.

This brief discussion illustrates some of the disagreement and lack of clarity over precisely what norms are. Several key elements, however, are widely acknowledged as essential. Based on these elements I define norms as rules, about which there is at least some degree of consensus, that are enforced through social sanctions. Understanding the emergence of norms, then, requires explanations of norm content, enforcement, and distribution.

# The Content of Norms

Three general approaches to explaining the content of normative rules can be identified: those that focus on the actions of ego, those that emphasize ego's reactions to alter's behavior, and those that address negotiation between ego and alter. Standing alone, each of these approaches fails to completely explain emergence; each, nonetheless, provides important insights.

## Model 1: Focus on the Actions of Ego

One widely held view of norms is that they reflect existing patterns of action. Arguments of this kind begin by identifying or predicting ego's behavior. "An individual may change his behavior, especially his social actions, either to protect his interests under new external conditions or simply to promote them more effectively under existing conditions" (Weber

1978, 755; see also Opp 1982). Actors may actively calculate the course of action that is most likely to produce desired ends at the lowest cost; or they may more passively simply imitate those around them (Asch 1956; Sherif [1936] 1973).[3] Thus, for example, American car manufacturers imitate the strategies of Japanese companies, activists adopt successful methods of earlier exemplars (Clemens 1993), and educational institutions worldwide exhibit striking similarities (Meyer, Ramirez, and Soysal 1992; Meyer, Scott, and Deal 1992).[4] In addition to imitating others, actors may engage in trial and error, repeating those strategies that appear to produce positive outcomes (Macy 1993; Sumner 1979).[5] Finally, individuals may recall norms successfully applied in other situations and behave similarly under new conditions (Dobbin 1994).

Whatever the reason for the initial action, when many people engage in the same behavior, that behavior comes to be associated with a sense of oughtness. Thus patterns of action emerge that then become normative (Opp 1982; Homans 1950, 266; Sumner 1979; Weber 1978, 754–55). Individuals, in turn, comply with the new norm both for the original reason that the behavior was appealing, and also because it is now socially enforced (Homans 1950, 266, 320). If conditions change so that compliance with the norm becomes excessively costly, actors explore new strategies, and the emergence process begins once again. On this view, Jewish restrictions on eating pork, for example, are seen as the result of individuals making the association between pork and trichinosis and changing their dietary habits. When many people make this change, these new practices presumably become normative and therefore continue even when the original danger— trichinosis—is no longer a threat.

Research on teenage pregnancy provides an illustration of this process (Fernandez-Kelly 1995). In poor inner-city neighborhoods in which residents have few ties outside of the community, girls do not have access to conventional means of achieving adulthood—educational opportunities, good jobs, and marriage. Motherhood is the most readily available route. Girls, therefore, have good reasons to want to have babies, and, as one might expect, rates of pregnancy among unwed teens are high. When babies are born, young mothers receive positive attention from family and friends. Thus individual choices about motherhood produce high pregnancy rates among teens, and in turn childbearing on the part of unwed girls is generally accepted.

At least on their face, arguments such as this are appealing. There are, however, at least two difficulties with this kind of approach. How does behavior that is merely habitual becomes normative? How are changes in normative behavior brought about?

*How Do Patterns of Behavior Become Normative?* It has been argued that once certain behaviors are adopted they become associated with a sense of oughtness (Homans 1950, 122, 266, 412; see also Hardin 1995, 60–65, for a discussion of the is-ought relationship); but which behaviors? In his study of religion, Émile Durkheim (1915) attempts to explain why a group comes to identify an emblem as being sacred. He suggests that "it is by uttering the same cry, pronouncing the same word, or performing the same gesture in regard to some object that [individuals] become and feel themselves to be in unison. . . . It is the homogeneity of these movements that [makes the group] exist" (262–63). Durkheim's discussion emphasizes the importance of commonality but has little to say about why particular behaviors and objects, rather than others, become imbued with sacredness. Thus, it is not clear why some behaviors become normative and others do not. Are all activities that are widespread supported by social sanctions?

One possibility is that, indeed, any action that is observed comes to be expected. Because individuals value certainty, they will be upset by deviation from what is usual (Opp 1982). Thus all behaviors that are reasonably frequent or consistent will become normative. If this is the case, then norms are synonymous with what is typical—there is no distinction between the term as referring to patterns of behavior and as referring to a rule. To the extent that this is so, one might reasonably wonder whether the concept is useful. Surely it would be more straightforward simply to focus on behavior rather than complicate matters by bringing in notions of norms.

It may be, however, that there is something different about behavior that is merely typical and that which has an additional normative component. For example, one takes off one's winter hat upon coming into the house because it is warm. One may remove one's hat in church, however, because one is expected to do so. "Taking off your hat to escape the heat is different from taking off your hat to satisfy an obligation. The former is a regularity and the latter is a norm" (Cooter 1996, 1656; see also Weber 1978, 34). There seems to be at least an intuitive distinction between behavior that is merely habitual and that which is normative.

Why is it that some behaviors are associated with a stronger sense of oughtness than others? One possibility is that the salience of a behavior—for example, the frequency with which it is observed—matters. Another is that actions that have greater effects on others may be more likely to be subject to disapproval than those that create only minimal externalities. Thus a co-worker who has to perform the tasks of tardy colleagues will respond more strongly to their lateness than to their clothing style. Finally, it may be that when individuals have a more intense personal preference for a behavior, the perceived negative consequences of others' deviance are greater (Opp 1982).

Scholars have suggested at least some potential mechanisms through which behavior that is typical may be distinguished from that which is normative. Although explanations have been proposed, however, they have not been fully developed. The ego-centered approach, does not enable us to distinguish between those behaviors that become normative and those that do not.

*At What Point Do Individuals Engage in New Behaviors?*    This weakness in the argument points to another challenge—identifying the points at which, and the reasons that, norms change. How do individuals weigh the oughtness of an existing norm against the interests that motivate new behaviors? Many arguments of the structure described here predict initial behaviors based on the assumption that individuals try to advance their own welfare. In seeking to explain continued obedience, they then shift to the assumption either that individuals internalize notions of oughtness or that they act from a desire for social approval. New norms are thought to emerge when the costs of compliance with existing norms become too high relative to the rewards. There often, however, is no explanation of how to weigh concerns about the costliness of the normative action (which encourages experimentation with new strategies) against concerns with morality or social opinion (which reinforce the status quo) (see Montgomery 1998 for a relevant discussion). Presumably, this balance shifts when social change occurs. Without further specification, however, we have no means of determining the circumstances under which individuals will simply follow the existing norm or will begin to explore other possibilities. Thus we are left to wonder when new norms will emerge and how long they will persist.

   One possible solution to this problem is to change the assumptions about individual motivation so that they are consistent throughout the argument. Under the assumption that actors always desire social approval, individual motivation will remain constant, and there will be no shift to be accounted for. However, this assumption will then require an argument to explain why social opinion sometimes favors the status quo and at other times encourages innovation. Perhaps, for example, when compliance with norms becomes costly, individuals who may want to change their behavior are unwilling to risk disapproval. They might, however, give positive feedback to those who do take such risks; and once some have tested the new strategy, others are likely to follow with less fear of social sanction. This explanation requires that at least some individuals are willing to violate norms. Another possibility is that innovators receive social approval. When behaviors become widespread, they are taken for granted and no longer merit such attention. Therefore actors, to gain recognition, must repeatedly engage in new strategies.

   Alternatively, explanations might assume that individuals care only about instrumental consequences and not about social approval per se. Under this assumption, norms presumably will reflect individual self-interest. Because, as an empirical matter, this clearly is not true, such an explanation would have to account for the persistence of behaviors past the point of usefulness for the individual and also identify the point at which they do change.

Another possible solution is to assume that although motivations remain constant over time, they vary across actors. Because people have different motivations, they will respond differently to changed circumstances. Some individuals will be innovators; others will adopt only those new behaviors that appear to be growing in popularity (Schelling 1978; see also Kuran 1991 on protest in Eastern Europe; and Laitin 1998 for an explanation of ethnic identity).

Approaches focusing on ego's behavior give little guidance as to how individuals might balance the obligation to obey norms against their interests in engaging in new non-normative behavior. This difficulty reflects an underlying weakness in arguments of this type—namely, that they say little about why behavior that is common becomes associated with a sense of oughtness, and therefore they cannot distinguish between those behaviors that become normative and those that do not.

## Model 2: Focus on Ego's Reactions to Actions of Alter

A second approach to explaining the emergence of normative rules to a large extent overcomes this problem. These arguments focus on actors' concerns with the behavior of others (Demsetz 1967). On this view, individuals must do more than consider the consequences of their own actions; they also must pay attention to the behavior of other people. Individuals are likely to approve of actions that benefit them and to dislike those that bring them harm.[6] Under certain conditions, actors develop strategies to encourage others to engage in desirable behavior (Coleman 1990, 243–44, 266). Norms thus emerge when behavior produces externalities, when people recognize a right to sanction such externality-producing behaviors, and when the group has the ability to enforce its decisions (see Horne forthcoming for experimental evidence supporting this view).

Gerry Mackie's (1996) explanation of foot binding and female genital mutilation is consistent with this approach. He begins by assuming that individuals want to have and raise children and that, therefore, men desire assurances of paternity and women seek assurances of support. Men want to know that their wives can be trusted to be faithful and that the children they raise carry on their bloodlines. In stratified polygamous societies, wealthy men have difficulty keeping track of their many wives, and monitoring costs are, therefore, high. Foot binding and female genital mutilation reduce these costs by providing a signal of a woman's reliability. Because women want good husbands, they are willing to engage in behaviors that establish that reliability and increase the likelihood that successful men will choose them as marriage partners. Thus part of the argument is that men's interest in female behavior, and their ability to make and enforce demands for assurances of fidelity, have contributed to the emergence of norms constraining women—in this case, requiring the binding of young women's feet in China and the mutilation of their genitals in parts of Africa.

For scholars taking this approach, norms emerge in response to externalities produced by the behaviors of others (Coleman 1990). Thus people will approve of actions that result in positive outcomes for them and disapprove of those that have negative consequences. To the extent that people are damaged by others, they will favor norms that discourage antisocial behaviors; and to the extent that they benefit from others' behaviors, they will want norms that institutionalize those behaviors. The mere existence of externalities does not necessarily lead to the emergence of a normative rule, however.

If individuals are to object to behavior of others that produces negative effects, they must be able to link that behavior with the resulting damage. Dissemination of information, therefore, is likely to matter. Widespread disapproval of drunk driving, for example, emerged only after research was made public showing that alcohol-related car accidents were preventable. This knowledge led the public to make the link between the behavior and the resulting harm (McCarthy 1994). Connections of this sort, however, are not always obvious. In parts of Malawi, for example, puberty rites for girls include an initiation into sex. They are instructed to practice with the threat that if they do not, they will lose the ability. Malawi has the youngest population of any country in the world and has high rates of acquired immunodeficiency syndrome (AIDS). Yet the tradition continues. Apparently the negative consequences of sexual activity are not salient. In many situations, it seems, causal relations are not clear because actors do not have adequate information or do not receive it within an appropriate time frame.

Even if people are able to link consequences to underlying causes, however, their responses will be affected by the extent to which they perceive those consequences as harmful or beneficial; and unfortunately, their evaluations may be different from those of the researcher. What appears obviously harmful to an outside observer may be seen by group members as beneficial. In other words, discrepancies between what may be objectively identified as a cost and what is subjectively experienced as such may create difficulties for predicting the content of norms.

Focusing on the consequences of alter's behavior solves some of the problems of the first argument presented. Here it is clear which behaviors will become normative: those that create externalities will be evaluated by the group, and those that produce only personal consequences will not. Thus once researchers identify the externalities experienced by the group, norm content ought to be predictable. This approach is useful, however, only in situations in which costs and benefits of externalities are determinative; and, of course, this is not always the case. Costs and benefits may be uncertain or unknown. In situations in which they are not predictive, how is the appropriateness of a behavior determined?

## Model 3: Focus on Negotiation Between Ego and Alter

The third general approach to explaining norm content suggests a way of answering this question. It focuses on meanings produced through negotiation. For people to interact successfully, they must share common understandings of the situation they are in, their behaviors, and their roles—for example, it is helpful for both parties to speak the same language. Typically, these commonalities have been developed during previous encounters. When individuals are placed in new situations, they are able to draw on their past experience to evaluate what is happening and to assess what they ought to do (chapter 5, this volume). Sometimes, however, a situation is problematic. Participants may have different or conflicting understandings, or old definitions learned from past experience may not apply (Becker 1982; Heiss 1981, 116–26). Under such conditions actors must negotiate mutually agreed-upon understandings for their interaction to flow smoothly. This negotiation involves "interpretation, or ascertaining the meaning of the actions or remarks of the other person, and definition, or conveying indications to another person as to how he is to act. Human association consists of a process of such interpretation and definition. Through this process the participants fit their own acts to the ongoing acts of one another and guide others in doing so" (Blumer 1966, 537–38).

Arlie Hochschild's (1989) analysis of relationships between spouses provides an example of the importance of negotiating common understandings. She describes the tensions that arise when husbands and wives attach different meanings to a behavior. If one gives what he or she perceives as a gift (for example, a husband offers to watch the children) that the other perceives as an entitlement (his wife believes that fathers are supposed to participate in child rearing), then both parties feel unloved and unappreciated. To maintain a mutually rewarding relationship, spouses must negotiate common meanings for their actions (see LaRossa 1988 for another example of work on gender roles).

What triggers these negotiations? Fine (chapter 5, this volume) describes the emergence of new common meanings among mushroom gatherers. He argues that when individuals engage in behavior that conflicts with existing norms to which they adhere, a problematic situation is created. For example, mushroom gatherers accept norms advocating respect for wilderness, but they are themselves altering natural settings and must justify their behavior. Conflicts of interest also create potential difficulties. Mushroom gatherers compete with one another and therefore must negotiate rules governing who is entitled to what. Finally, potential danger gives rise to narratives regarding how to engage safely in the activity—providing protection from ingestion of potentially deadly mushrooms. Thus a variety of circumstances lead to the negotiation of new, commonly accepted meanings.

Many scholars pay attention to these negotiation processes. Research suggests that children learn the meaning of friendship in the course of interacting with playmates (Davies 1982; Rizzo 1989, 105), and adolescents develop interpretations of events and establish routines unique to their group (Everhart 1983; Fine 1987; Willis 1981). Scholars of social movements describe framing processes and the negotiation of common identities (Cohen 1985, 707; Hunt, Benford, and Snow 1994; Johnston, Larana, and Gusfield 1994; McAdam, McCarthy, and Zald 1996, 6). Others have examined crime control (Manning 1977), favor seeking and career advancement (McLean 1998), and a variety of other social phenomena. Thus negotiation processes are widely seen as important.

*How Do Individuals Determine How to Interpret and Send Signals?*   One challenge for scholars taking this approach is to develop general predictive theories regarding the relation between behavior and meaning. Individuals are thought to pay attention to the signals they send by engaging in certain behaviors as well as to the meaning of the actions of others. Thus students who study experience instrumental consequences—they increase the likelihood that they will get good grades; but they also are sending messages about themselves—in some settings, that they are ambitious and disciplined, and in other situations, that they are boring and antisocial. The messages that one sends through studying, drinking alcohol, or carrying a gun can vary depending on who one is with and where the interaction occurs. Behavior thus has symbolic as well as instrumental consequences. The question is, how do symbols or meanings come to be attached to particular actions?

Because much work of this type lacks empirically testable propositions, this question does not lend itself to an easy answer. Research is often descriptive, explaining particular norms at specified times and places. This specificity, in fact, frequently is seen as desirable. In principle, more general theories regarding the content of meaning and value could be developed. Similarly, generalizations regarding the processes through which individuals attach meaning to their environment could be proposed.[7] Work by Randall Collins (Collins and Hanneman 1998) provides one example of an attempt to develop a general, abstract theory. He builds on the work of Erving Goffman and Emile Durkheim to propose an argument regarding the way in which actions, events, and so forth become associated with meaning. Like others, he suggests that the salience of an act matters, but he also emphasizes the importance of emotional stimulus. Salience, in conjunction with the strength of emotional stimuli, leads to interaction, during which awareness of the shared emotion grows. Over time, as interaction continues, symbols of group membership develop. For Collins, increasing the salience of an act, as well as the intensity of group emotion, contributes to the likelihood that respect for cultural symbols will emerge.

Whereas some scholars develop general, abstract theories, many of those who emphasize interaction and negotiation processes do not attempt such generalizations. In practice, this means that the more that scholars rely on the assumption that individuals actively interpret their environment, rather than respond in predictable ways to external stimuli, the less likely it is that testable hypotheses will be proposed. Thus the same view of human actors that results in insight regarding the importance of symbols also frequently limits predictions.

*What Is the Relation Between Meaning and Interests?*    A second challenge for explanations of this type is to identify the relative importance of meaning and interest. The recognition that human beings are symbolic creatures raises the question of the relation between the two. The approach emphasizes agreement—the negotiation of mutually held understandings. It also recognizes, however, that individuals are purposive and have interests of their own that they want to pursue. Thus it is possible that desires for agreement and for other ends are incompatible. It is unclear how these different motivations are weighed. How much do individuals care about the symbolic meaning, or oughtness, of their acts compared with the instrumental consequences? Scholars suggest that the outcome of negotiation affects behavior: "A group finds itself sharing a common situation and common problems. . . . In the course of their collective discussion, the members of the group arrive at a definition of the situation, its problems and possibilities, and develop a consensus as to the most appropriate and efficient ways of behaving. This consensus thenceforth constrains the activities of individual members of the group" (Becker 1982, 520). Although the literature draws our attention to symbols as well as to interests, however, it tells us little about their relative importance.

One way to approach this problem is to assume that individuals are concerned about meaning to the extent that it affects their instrumental outcomes. Thus if actors value social interaction for its own sake, then their desire for agreement about definitions will be high, because consensus will facilitate interaction. By contrast, if actors value status, then they will seek agreement only to the extent that it enhances that status. For example, if a master and servant both care about ease of interaction, then agreement between them about their relative status is likely. If, on the other hand, the servant sees herself or himself as the master's equal and values equality, consensus is problematic and interactions will be more conflictual.

One also might assume that individuals value meaning and ignore the role of interests. Presumably, agreement then is likely to center around that which is most salient. Taking this approach, the challenge becomes to identify the factors that determine salience—frequency, visibility, and so forth—in other than an ad hoc way.

## Unified Model of Norm Content

What are we to make of these three general approaches to explaining the emergence of normative rules? Each seems to identify important processes, yet each also misses essential elements. I propose a unified model of the emergence of normative rules that draws on the strengths of these different arguments—recognizing the importance of individuals' interests in their own behavior and that of others as well as the role of negotiation. This model is illustrated in figure 1.1.

*The Role of Interests*   Explanations of norm emergence should not rely exclusively either on ego's interest in its own behavior or on ego's interest in the behavior of others. Instead, it is important to recognize that people receive benefits (and experience costs) as a result of both their own behavior and that of group members.[8] That is, an individual's behavior produces consequences for them, and the actions of others also have effects.

In some instances, these two sets of interests will be consistent (figure 1.1, quadrants 2 and 4). Arguably, incest, for example, produces harmful consequences both for the individuals on whom it is perpetrated and for the group as a whole. In addition, individuals may naturally be averse to it (Fox 1983). Thus incest is contrary to both the interests of the individual and those of the group (figure 1.1, quadrant 4). Similarly, a member of a sports team personally benefits from practice (improving her skills), and she also benefits when other players work hard (improving the team's game). Practice contributes to the welfare of the individual and the group (figure 1.1, quadrant 2). These illustrations provide examples of conditions in which interests in one's own behaviors and those of others are consistent (figure 1.1, quadrants 2 and 4). Thus in some situations, the benefits to an individual of not engaging in a behavior are consistent with the benefits they receive when others also abjure the same activity, and the benefits of engaging in a behavior may be compatible with the benefits they receive when others do so as well. When the interests of the individual and the group are consistent it does not much matter which theoretical argument one uses. Either will produce accurate predictions.

Under other conditions, however, interests in one's own and others' behaviors conflict—that is, people prefer to engage in activities themselves that they would rather others not perform, or they might wish to avoid personally costly actions yet approve of others engaging in them. For example, a thief benefits from stealing but experiences costs if others steal from him or her (quadrant 3). Individuals might not want to bear the costs

FIGURE 1.1     *A Unified Approach to Explaining Norm Content*

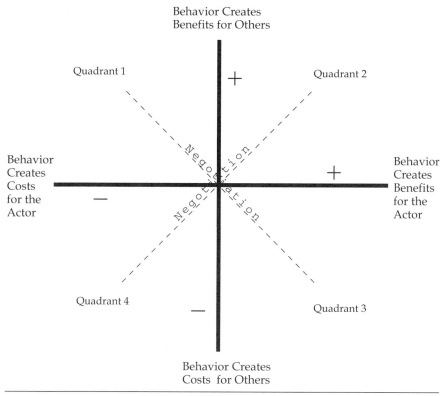

*Source:* Author's compilation.

of contributing to public radio, yet approve of, and benefit from, others doing so (quadrant 1). In situations such as these, individual and group interests conflict. Under these conditions it becomes important to know which kind of approach will best explain outcomes.

One way to address this issue is to compare the interests of individuals in their own behavior against their interests in the actions of others. The relative weight and direction of these interests will affect the content of normative rules. In addition, they will affect the extent to which norms forbid or merely discourage, require or simply permit. Perhaps, for example, people prefer that others engage in a certain behavior. If they personally experience great costs when they engage in this behavior themselves, and those costs outweigh the benefits to them if others participate in the activity, they will be less supportive of a norm prescribing such actions. For example, individuals being mugged in a New York subway station might well appreciate the intervention of bystanders. The costs to them of stepping in to help another are so high, however, that they are unlikely to demand a norm requiring intervention. In this case, although people might be grateful if others risk death or serious injury to help them, they do not expect such behavior.

On the other hand, people may enjoy particular activities for themselves but experience great costs when others engage in similar behaviors. In these situations, they will prefer a norm constraining such actions. Although they would like to engage in the activity, the benefits to them of doing so are less than the costs they experience if other group members do so. As a result, norms discouraging the behavior will emerge. For example, any individual might prefer to litter—it is more convenient than taking trash home. If everyone leaves garbage in public places, however, the physical environment is much less attractive (at least for people who value clean surroundings). One would expect, therefore, the existence of norms that discourage littering.[9]

Thus when group and individual interests conflict, weighing the direction and magnitude of the two sets of interests will allow accurate predictions of norm content.[10] In other words, both approaches focusing on the behavior of ego and those focusing on reactions to alter's behavior are a part of the explanation of norm emergence. Norms will reflect the goals of group members—taking into account the consequences of their own actions as well as those of others. This argument implies that, in some situations, norms will appear to reflect behavior, whereas in others, they will constrain actions that produce externalities.

Some scholars are pessimistic regarding the ability of social scientists to produce general theories of norm emergence. They point out that arguments predicting that norms benefit individuals cannot be right, because numerous contradictory examples can be observed. In many instances norms prevent individuals from doing what they would otherwise want to do. In addition, researchers argue, many norms are inconsistent with the interests of the group (Elster 1989). Because none of the available approaches seems to be adequate, some scholars lose hope in the entire enterprise. The unified argument proposed here helps to explain the anomalies upon which they base their pessimism. It helps to show why norms sometimes appear to be inconsistent with the interests of individuals in their own behavior and, at other times, with the well-being of group members. Norms that are harmful to the group may emerge and survive because each individual's interest in performing a behavior is greater than the cost to them of others engaging in that behavior. Similarly, norms that are harmful to individuals may emerge because they encourage behaviors producing positive externalities whose benefits outweigh the costs to the individual.

Consider, for example, norms that discourage the individual advancement of group members, thus serving to maintain a group's disadvantaged position. Numerous researchers describe such norms. Puerto Ricans in the Bronx are described as discouraging individuals from seeking jobs outside the community. "When you see someone go downtown and get a good job, if they be Puerto Rican, you see them fix up their hair and put some contact lenses in their eyes. They fit in and they do it! I have seen it! . . . Look at all the people in that building, they all turn-overs. They people who want to be white" (quoted in Portes 1998, 17). Mexican and African Americans similarly may be discouraged from achieving academically (Matute-Bianchi 1986, 1991; Fordham and Ogbu 1986). Gypsy (Rom) culture often creates conflicts with mainstream norms and law (Sutherland 1998). In these situations, norms seem to conflict with both individual and group interests. These apparent anomalies can be explained by looking more closely at the interests at stake under these particular circumstances. Individuals have interests in the outcome of their own behavior, but as members of the group, they also may receive collective benefits. Thus they have a personal interest in the community's survival. Under conditions of uncertainty and risk, when the prospects for individual achievement are not clear, the benefits of group membership become even more important. Individuals, therefore, will not want others to engage in activities—such as obtaining jobs outside the community—that may weaken the group. Thus norms that maintain solidarity emerge even if they inhibit the advancement of both the individual and the community (see Hardin 1995 for additional relevant discussion).

In this example, all group members have similar interests. The same individuals are both targets and beneficiaries of a norm. Norms are conjoint (Coleman 1990). It often is the case, however, that group members have different interests—that is, the costs and benefits for one person or set of people are different from those for another (see, for example, Ermakoff 1997). In these situations, norms are disjoint (Coleman 1990, 247). Some group members want to impose their preferences on others, and there are disagreements among subgroups about what norms ought to be. Under such conditions, contradictory norms will emerge, or the group with the strongest interest will succeed in having norms that benefit it prevail.

*The Role of Meaning and Negotiation*    Although a purely interest-based approach often will produce accurate predictions, in some situations recognizing meaning and incorporating negotiation processes may be necessary as well. For example, the benefits to an individual of engaging in a behavior may be equivalent to, but in the opposite direction from, their interests in others engaging in that same behavior. Individuals may not much care what the norm is, as long as people agree. Alternatively, group members may be unsure as to the costs and benefits of a particular behavior, either because they lack information or because society is in a state of flux. Under such conditions, where interests are irrelevant or unhelpful, attention to negotiation becomes important (see figure 1.1, the dotted diagonal lines).

Of course, meaning also may matter when interests do predict outcomes; but researchers may be able to do quite well relying on costs and benefits alone without turning to messier (and potentially harder to measure empirically) issues of meaning. When interests alone are not predictive, however, then understanding the processes through which negotiation produces shared meanings, and predicting the content of those meanings, becomes crucial.

*Conditions Conducive to Changes in Norm Content*   What does this unified model suggest about the conditions under which new normative rules are likely to emerge? Two factors that impact norm content—costs and benefits and exposure to alternatives—are particularly significant. For interest-based arguments, changes in costs and benefits associated with a behavior, and information regarding those new outcomes, produce changes in the norms regulating the behavior. A variety of social and technological innovations may affect these material conditions. For example, the balance between individuals' interests in their own behavior and the behavior of others may be affected by the dependence of the individual on the group for collective goods (see Hechter 1987 for a related discussion). Thus, if work teams, rather than individuals, are held responsible for completion of a task, then colleagues will be more likely to agree that they have a right to control one another's actions (see Hechter and Kanazawa 1993, 483, for discussion of Japanese and American work organization). If, however, each person has little need for the group, then such an agreement is less likely to emerge. Changes in structural factors produce a shift in costs and benefits leading, in turn, to a new rule. In addition to social structure, technology also can have an important impact. It can change costs and benefits, or provide new information affecting people's perceptions of those costs and benefits.

For meaning-based arguments, changes that expose individuals to alternative possibilities are likely to result in negotiation and, in turn, new norms. New material circumstances may create uncertainty about the best course of action, or desire for exceptions to an existing rule (Edgerton 1985, 205), and new agreements about what is appropriate emerge. Exposure to other people who adhere to different norms leads to negotiation. Conflicting norms—such as those that arise when individuals find themselves obligated to behave according to different role demands—also may lead to reassessment (Ridgeway and Smith-Lovin 1994). Social and technological changes not only affect the costs and benefits of behaviors but also create a recognition that other normative arrangements are possible. All of these changes set the stage for new normative rules to emerge.

# The Enforcement of Norms

Of course, for norms to exist, the group must have the ability to enforce its rules. To the extent that normative rules are consistent with individual interests, little if any enforcement is necessary. When individual and group interests conflict, however, enforcement is crucial. In addition, when meaning encourages one action and interests another, then enforcement is necessary to encourage people to act in appropriate symbolic ways, even if such behaviors are not in their personal interest. Thus for norms to be effective, there must be some mechanism that translates rules into action.

The principal source of enforcement of social norms is informal sanctioning by group members (Coleman 1990; Hechter 1984; Scott 1971). Much sociological research focuses on the ways in which structures of interaction produce incentives encouraging compliance (the contributions of game theorists are particularly important here) and the conditions that increase the likelihood that individuals will affirmatively sanction deviance.

## Social Sanctioning

Why do people punish deviance or reward exceptional behavior? Some scholars argue that individuals punish others unconsciously without necessarily being aware that they are doing so—thus, control is cheap (Pettit 1993, 327–31). In addition, under certain conditions, sanctioning occurs as a by-product of other self-interested behavior.

Most explanations, however, assume that sanctioning is costly (see, for example, Axelrod 1986; Heckathorn 1989; Yamagishi 1986, 1995; Yamagishi and Takahashi 1994). Costs associated with punishing others include the risk of retaliation or at least the potential loss of relationship, the loss of time or money, emotional discomfort, and so forth. In the face of these costs, people are, arguably, more likely to sanction if they receive compensating benefits as a result. One source of benefit is the change in deviant behavior that results from the punishment. In other words, to the extent that another's behavior produces externalities, discouraging that behavior will reduce those externalities. For some people the benefits of this reduction outweigh the costs of sanctioning, and they will punish such behavior. Often, however, this incentive is too small to motivate individuals to sanction.

Scholars, therefore, identify another possible source of benefits—the reactions of others. These reactions constitute metanorms that encourage sanctioning (Axelrod 1986). This solution to the problem gives rise to the additional question of why individuals reward punishers. Again, two answers are possible. Rewarders may be interested in the benefits resulting from sanctioning (Coleman 1990)—that is, like sanctioners, they may pay attention to the benefits resulting from a change in the rate of externality-producing behavior. Alternatively, they may be motivated by the potential reactions of others, including the person imposing the punishment (Horne 2000). Here the focus is not on giving rewards to sanctioners to change rates of deviance but, rather, on the potential rewarder's relationships. Variation in these relationships—for example, the distribution of resources and people's dependence on one another—affects willingness to punish or reward. Thus sanctioning is motivated not just by norm content (an interest in a share of the benefit) but also by an interest in exchange relationships and the rewards that can be obtained from them. Structural factors like interdependency, therefore, affect reactions to norm-violating behavior (Horne forthcoming).

The ability of groups to organize themselves to respond to deviance can have an effect as well (see Coleman 1990 for an argument that the structure of network ties matters; also see Sampson, Raudenbush, and Earls 1997; Sampson and Groves 1989; Shaw and McKay [1942] 1969 for evidence that social disorganization decreases informal control). For example, actors may need to engage in collective action in order to enforce a particular norm. That is, if one group benefits from a norm and others are constrained by it, the extent to which that norm will be accepted and enforced will be affected not only by the relative power of the two groups, but also by their ability to organize. Those in disadvantaged positions will benefit if they can unite to enforce their demands against a more powerful actor (Emerson 1962). They are unlikely to be successful in enforcing the norm they prefer, however, if they lack resources or the ability to organize (Coleman 1990, 266; McAdam, McCarthy, and Zald 1996, 8). Arguably, when a potential norm benefits some and constrains others, it will not be reinforced if the beneficiaries are weak, few in number, or unorganized relative to the targets of the potential norm.

## Other Types of Control

Of course, other kinds of control mechanisms exist alongside informal sanctioning. The legal system, for example, provides formal responses to deviance that may directly affect the extent to which behavior complies with social norms. It also may have an indirect influence through its effect on informal control processes. Because institutions such as the legal system exist side by side with normative controls, we need to explain how social conditions that contribute to informal sanctioning are related to it. My previous experimental research (Horne 2000), for example, finds that the existence of a strong legal system inhibits informal sanctioning and weakens the social relations that facilitate the exercise of such control. Thus although law has a direct effect on compliance, it also reduces the likelihood that group members will impose social sanctions (see also Posner 1996).

Whereas under some conditions alternative sources of control weaken informal sanctioning, under other conditions they may supplement it. That is, other social processes can make up for the inadequacies of weak social controls. Thus when informal sanctions are inadequate to produce compliance, other processes may encourage cooperative behavior. Some argue, for example, that when informal controls are ineffective, group members develop a sense of trust that allows them to engage in profitable interactions even in the absence of assurances that controls may provide. They simply act on the assumption that others will behave appropriately and treat them that way—initiating cooperative exchanges (Yamagishi, Cook, and Watabe 1998; see also Axelrod 1984). In situations in which control mechanisms are in place (as in Japan), those controls will discourage antisocial behavior. If such sanctions are lacking, however, then individuals must exercise trust if they are to enter into profitable exchanges. Thus in societies like that of the United States, a desire that others behave prosocially translates into trust, which in turn increases the likelihood that individuals will initiate cooperative interactions. Apparently, the existence of risk resulting from the lack of informal control creates the need for trust, which leads in turn to higher levels of cooperative behavior (Kollock 1994). According to this argument, trust emerges when controls are lacking, and encourages cooperative behavior which otherwise might not occur.

Internalization of norms also has the potential to increase compliance. The contribution of internalization is unclear, however. To the extent that individuals constrain their own behavior, they will follow norms even without external social pressures. In many situations, however, even deeply ingrained values are violated.[11] Despite research on the subject, questions remain to be answered. We still have much to learn about the factors that contribute to the persistence of internalized notions of oughtness, the relative weights of internal and external enforcement mechanisms, and so forth.

## The Distribution of Norms

For a rule to be a norm, it must be accepted by group members. Research relevant to explaining the emergence of consensus—in other words, the distribution of norms—often emphasizes structural elements, such as network ties and position in the social structure or impersonal selection mechanisms. Rather than explaining why an individual might adopt a particular norm, such theories predict the pattern of norm distribution across a group or groups. Of course, discussions of individual acceptance of norms are relevant to the group-level emergence of norms, and group-level processes are relevant to individual-level explanations. The two approaches are not mutually exclusive. Nevertheless, they can be distinguished in terms of their focus (for a related discussion see Ensminger and Knight 1997). Scholars identify several key group-level processes. Innovations may spread across networks through diffusion from one actor to another;[12] group members in similar social structural positions may independently develop similar strategies; or the survival of a norm may be determined by selection processes.

## Diffusion

Norms may become widespread as a result of diffusion (for a review of diffusion literature, see Strang and Soule 1998). Sociological research contributes much to our understanding of the distribution of innovations within a group. Michael Macy and John Skvoretz (1998), for example, use computer simulations to explore the conditions under which cooperation spreads.[13] They begin by identifying decision rules (or norms) that actors might follow during interaction. Certain combinations of these rules are more successful—that is, produce better outcomes for the actor—than others. Actors using inferior combinations randomly adopt strategies from the superior outcome combination.[14] Over time, successful combinations spread across the group. As this process unfolds, norms favoring cooperation develop first in small, embedded groups and then diffuse outward as group members have contact with strangers.

Ronald Burt's (1987) analysis of the diffusion of new medical practices—that is, the acceptance of a new procedure as appropriate and normative—proposes a different mechanism. He finds that physicians adopt innovations not as a result of interaction but in response to what others in similar structural positions do (see also Mark 1998; Shibutani 1962; Strang and Meyer 1993, 491; Strang and Soule 1998). Thus norms spread among people in the same role positions, not necessarily among those who have personal contact. Other research addresses a variety of factors, finding that diffusion increases with physical proximity (see Petras and Zeitlin 1967 for a study of the spread of radical ideology in Chile), has a direction (see Schreiber 1978 for an analysis of the willingness to vote for a woman president; and Labov 1980 on dialect change), and is facilitated by the media and other authorities (Ericson, Baranek, and Chan 1987; Gitlin 1980; McCarthy 1994).

Diffusion research varies in its treatment of the individual. Some researchers make no assumptions about actors or treat them as behaving randomly. Others rely implicitly on notions of human motivation but do not explicitly state them. These structural arguments contribute to the understanding of norm distribution. To the extent that human beings make choices about their actions, however, these explanations potentially could benefit from incorporating assumptions about actors.

## Structural Equivalence

A second approach to explaining how group members come to adopt the same norms focuses on the similarities of their structural positions. People in these positions have access to the same information, face the same constraints, and are likely to develop similar understandings of their situations.[15] According to William Graham Sumner, "The operation by which folkways are produced consists in the frequent repetition of petty acts, often by great numbers . . . acting in the same way when face to face with the same need. . . . It produces habit in the individual and custom in the group" (Park and Burgess 1924, 101).

Melvin Kohn's (1977) well-known research provides an example of work of this type. He argues that parents' expectations of and reactions to their children's behavior vary with social position. Working-class parents are more likely to value obedience, whereas middle-class adults value self-direction. These differences are associated with variation in disciplinary practices. Working-class parents sanction children based on the consequences of misbehavior. Middle-class parents, by contrast, punish based on the child's intention. Thus social structural position affects values, as well as the norms people accept and enforce.

Much sociological research emphasizes the correlation between social structure and norms (for examples in social exchange, see Ekeh 1974; Homans 1950, 362; in organizations, Hannan and Freeman 1977, 946; in social structure and personality, Beniger 1984; Inkeles and Smith 1974; Robinson and Bell 1978). Studies suggest that structural factors such as occupation may affect many facets of psychological functioning, including anxiety, self-esteem, resistance to change, conservatism, and alienation. Thus position in the social structure acts on individuals, affecting the values they hold and the norms to which they adhere (Miller-Loessi 1995).

As with work on diffusion, this research also could benefit from the insights of individual-level theories. Scholars focusing on social structure vary in the extent to which they explain the mechanisms responsible for identified correlations. Arguments lacking such explanations could be improved by incorporating an understanding of ego's behavior, ego's reaction to alter, and communication between ego and alter. Clearly, individuals do not simply exist in a nonresponsive environment. Rather, they live in a social world in which they look to and interact with others. Understanding these interactions, as well as the context within which they occur, may improve predictions.

## Selection

A third approach to explaining group-level distribution of norms is to focus on selection processes. Groups that have adaptive norms persist, whereas those that do not fail (Romanelli 1991). Proponents of this approach argue that "groups with belief systems that cause individuals within the group to cooperate effectively survive longer and produce more cultural propagules. Eventually this process would cause self-sacrificial belief systems to predominate" (Boyd and Richerson 1985, 205). Others point out that although these between-group pressures may be operating, within the group itself other forces favor self-interested rather than prosocial behavior (Boyd and Richerson 1985). Therefore selection will occur only if it is stronger across, rather than within, groups.

This may be the case for some kinds of groups—for example, formal organizations. Thus organizational ecologists are able to use this type of model. These scholars attempt to account for the diversity of organizational forms. They suggest that in some kinds of situations, actors (organizations) cannot adapt—that is, they cannot change in response to their environment. This might happen, for example, if the organization has invested in equipment that cannot be easily transferred, if it lacks complete information, or if it has internal political processes that produce pressures to maintain the status quo. Under these conditions, when actors cannot adopt new strategies, selection occurs. In competitive markets, organizations that have inefficient forms will fail, and superior norms will be selected for (Hannan and Freeman 1977). Many social groups, however, have less control over their members and engage in little competition. Under these conditions, the model is not likely to apply.

Other scholars suggest a different mechanism. They argue that cultural forms survive or fail based on their ability to attract members: just as people are resources for which groups compete, they also are resources for which norms compete (Mark 1998). Those norms that attract a large number of adherents will spread, whereas less successful norms will dwindle and disappear. The weakness of these arguments is that they do not identify the types of norms that are likely to be appealing. Which ones will be successful? Which types of norms will attract more people? Why do norms with a particular content attract individuals with certain sociodemographic characteristics? Explanations of this kind predict the spread of norms based on specified group characteristics such as age, socioeconomic status, and so forth but fail to identify the reasons that those characteristics matter. Thus such arguments predict the distribution of norms but not their content.

Selection-based arguments that actually do focus on content tend to be functional. They predict efficient norms, explaining their emergence by the mere fact of their existence. Efficient norms persist, and those norms that are observed must be efficient, since they survived. Such explanations cannot be empirically tested unless the characteristics of a superior, or adaptive, norm are determined a priori. Paul Allison's (1992) work provides an example. He attempts to explain the emergence of norms encouraging altruistic behavior. The key to his argument is that "self-sacrificing behavior that is differentially directed toward other organisms that are likely to propagate the same behavior may experience positive selection pressures" (Allison 1992, 282). He uses this notion to make predictions about the kinds of norms that are likely to flourish.

Selection arguments explain the distribution of norms. To the extent that they address content, they tend to predict simply that adaptive norms will survive (but see Allison 1992). Theories often make no assumptions about motivation and treat individual behavior as random. Thus, again, incorporating insights from individual-level explanations of norm emergence could be of benefit—contributing to our understanding of the mechanisms through which norms with particular contents emerge and are distributed across social space.

## Evaluating the Three Group-Level Models

Understanding distribution processes is essential, but the problem of explaining norm content remains a weakness of group-level approaches. To the extent that distribution arguments ignore the individual-level mechanisms through which people come to accept and enforce norms, they say little about the content of normative rules or the conditions under which they are enforced. They predict, in a generic way, the patterns of diffusion of norms specific, but they do not allow one to say much about the norms that might be appealing to a particular group. Because norms have different effects on people in different positions, arguments that focus solely on structural position without taking interests into account are likely to be less accurate than they could be. Thus structural arguments would be strengthened by incorporating individual-level mechanisms.

How can interests be incorporated? Social structure often is seen in terms of socioeconomic status, race, age, and so forth. People of the same race with the same income are more likely to interact and to engage in similar behaviors than are people of different races or different incomes (Mark 1998). Thus interaction networks ought to correspond with demographic variable. Another way to conceptualize structure is to see it in terms of constraints—that is, the costs and benefits of behaviors provide incentive structures that arguably also correspond with network ties. Whether through diffusion or structural equivalence, we, therefore, would expect norms to spread across social space in ways that reflect these network (or incentive) structures. Norms will be more consistent among those who experience similar costs and benefits (and therefore are in similar social positions) than among those who experience different costs and are less likely to interact. Conceptualizing structure in terms of the costs and benefits of behavior is one way of integrating individual-level concerns with structural characteristics. Thus identifying the distribution of these costs and benefits across a group will facilitate prediction of the spread of norms with particular contents.

# A General Framework for Explaining Norm Emergence

Based on the literature described above, I propose a general, simplified framework for thinking about norm emergence, outlined in figure 1.2. This

FIGURE 1.2     *An Integrated Framework for Explaining the Emergence*
                *of Norms*

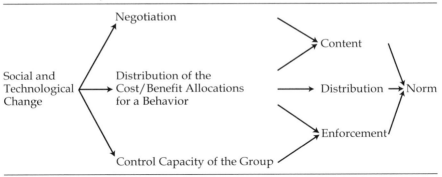

*Source:* Author's compilation.

framework recognizes that three essential elements must be explained: norm content, norm enforcement, and norm distribution.

What explanations exist regarding the content of norms? Examining the costs and benefits individuals experience when they engage in a behavior, compared with the consequences if others do so, allows prediction of norm content (see figure 1.1). Social and technological changes that affect the distribution of the costs and benefits associated with a behavior, therefore, affect the content of the norm that individuals adopt. Such changes also affect the likelihood that people will engage in negotiations that lead to new norms. When costs and benefits alone are an inadequate basis for prediction, then negotiation processes determine normative rules.

Like norm content, norm enforcement also is a function of people's interests in the behavior targeted by a norm. The more that people benefit from a norm, the more likely they will be to sanction deviance. Enforcement also is affected, however, by structural factors such as the interdependencies of group members. Therefore, the distribution of the costs and benefits of behaviors as well as characteristics of the group, such as cohesion, that increase control capacity affect the likelihood of social sanctioning. Social change leads to new norms by affecting the interests that people have in a norm and the characteristics of the group. These factors, in turn, affect the extent to which norms are enforced.

Finally, group-level models help to explain the distribution of norms across a group. I advocate incorporating individual-level interests into structural arguments relevant to the emergence of consensus about norms, arguing that costs and benefits provide a measure of the social structure within which norms travel. Thus the distribution of these costs and benefits determines the distribution of normative rules.

The costs and benefits of behaviors and their distribution, negotiation processes, and the control capacity of the group taken together explain the emergence of the essential elements of norms—content, enforcement, and distribution. Much research on norm emergence considers only one component. The framework presented here treats all three elements as essential and suggests a way of organizing the diverse studies found in the literature.

## Sociology's Contribution to the Study of Norm Emergence

What has sociology contributed to our understanding? What has it failed to do? Sociologists have long been interested in social norms, and much sociological research focuses on relevant issues. Sociology, more than other disciplines, has produced work contributing to understanding the distribution of norms. This is, perhaps, not surprising, given its traditional emphasis on social structure. Scholars have produced cumulative research addressing a variety of important questions: Do norms diffuse through interpersonal interaction or across social position? How is the distribution of social structural characteristics such as age, race, and gender related to the distribution of norms? Does physical proximity matter? If we want to understand changes in norms regarding sexual behavior, career aspirations, and any number of other phenomena, answers to these questions will be essential. However, group-level approaches alone are not likely to be satisfying, because they often say little about norm content or enforcement mechanisms. As I have suggested here, an adequate framework with which to think about norm emergence requires consideration of both group- and individual-level explanations.

In addition, sociologists have contributed to research on the social processes through which norms are enforced. Scholars interested in criminology, social psychology, game theory, and other areas explore these processes. They have produced a large body of work that identifies key conditions under which social sanctioning and cooperative behavior are likely to be observed.

Finally, sociological research suggests approaches to explaining norm content. This is the area in which there is the least amount of consensus and cumulative work. In fact, scholars disagree over whether predictions are possible or even desirable (Elster 1989; Blumer 1956). Nevertheless, as described above, three general kinds of approaches can be identified. I argue that these approaches can be integrated—producing an argument that considers individuals' interests in both their own behaviors and the behavior of others, as well as the role of negotiation in situations in which interests alone are not dispositive.

So what has sociology contributed? Sociologists have been criticized for saying little of use about norm emergence. The literature described in this chapter suggests that at least some of this criticism can be attributed to the difficulty of recognizing and organizing relevant work, not to the lack of it. Although the level of diversity within sociology has discouraged the unified, systematic study of emergence, it also has resulted in a breadth of substantive area and approach. Sociologists have studied a variety of phenomena from etiquette to railways in fields as diverse as social psychology, crime, organizations, and social movements. In the process, they have identified key factors and processes that contribute to the emergence of norms—their content, enforcement, and distribution. Thus sociology has produced theoretical and empirical scholarship that sheds light on norm emergence and suggests directions for further research. The challenge now is to develop a more unified approach—including at a minimum, explicit statements of the underlying assumptions regarding actors and clarity about the aspect of norm emergence being explained—so that a cumulative theoretical and empirical research program may flourish.

# Notes

1. Norms also are seen as statements describing behavior performed by a person with a certain identity. Francesca Cancian (1975), for example, suggests that "norms [are] 'is' statements that define what identities exist and what actions and attributes validate them" (142). From this point of view, statements such as "good professors publish" and "good students study" are norms. Gerry Mackie's (1996) study of foot binding in China and female genital mutilation in Africa uses the term "convention" in a similar way. Foot binding was, and female genital mutilation continues to be, behavior that desirable (marriageable) women engage in.

2. Durkheim (1915) suggests that "the man who has done his duty finds, in the manifestations of every sort expressing the sympathy, esteem or affection which his fellows have for him, a feeling of comfort." (242). In other words, individuals are not entirely internally motivated; the reactions of others also matter.

3. There is a large social psychological literature on imitation (see for example, Bandura and Walters 1963; Miller and Dollard 1941).

4. Who do actors imitate? Sociologists have emphasized factors such as the degree to which individuals are attached to others and the status of potential models (Homans 1950, 417; Elias 1983). The answer may depend on assumptions about whether individual motivations are instrumental or moral. Those who are concerned with outcomes of their behaviors, for example, will seek information about the most efficient strategies. They, therefore, are likely to follow the examples of those who are successful. On the other hand, individuals who want to do what is appropriate may be more likely to look to others who are similar to them or to whom they feel an attachment (Cain 1968; Shibutani 1962).

5. The idea that people change their behavior in response to trial and error is rooted in learning theory. For an overview, see Schwartz and Reisberg (1991).

6. Most work in this area assumes that people are purposive, but some research focuses on the moral nature of human beings. Tom Tyler and Robert Boeckmann (1997), for example, compare instrumental and moral explanations of Californians' support for "three-strikes" laws. They argue that people are punitive not because they are concerned about the potential dangers of crime but because they perceive the moral fabric of society to be breaking down. Demands for severe legal sanctions are a way of reaffirming the moral order.

7. Affect control and expectation states theory are two bodies of work that focus on the connections between social structure, interaction, and meaning (Ridgeway and Smith-Lovin 1994).

8. Of course, determining what those interests are may in itself be a difficult task. One approach is to make assumptions about what they might be. It is reasonable to assume, for example, that those goods such as money and status that are highly fungible are likely to be widely valued. Another approach is to measure values (Hechter et al. 1999) and rely on empirical data as a base from which to develop theories about the consequences of individual values for social life.

9. Of course, people may still attempt to do what they want despite the norm. The extent to which they do so will be affected by the degree to which the norm is enforced.

10. In addition, even when interests are consistent, comparing them may be useful. In some circumstances, for example, individuals may prefer a behavior for themselves that they also prefer for others, though it may be that they benefit much more if others engage in the activity than if they themselves do so. Under such conditions, comparing the size of the benefits for the group and the individual would provide an indication of the strength of the norm. Of course, it is not quite this simple. People making "mistakes," for example. They may initiate the wrong behavior, or draw illogical and inaccurate conclusions about the effectiveness of various courses of action (see, for example, Kahneman 1997).

11. See, for example, Read 1974 and Gregg 1955.

12. Of course, diffusion is an element of the ego-centered approach to explaining norm emergence. There, however, the focus is on the importance of imitation. Here the emphasis is on who imitates whom, who is connected through network ties, and so forth. Thus, Macy and Skvoretz (1998) describe how norms spread from a small group throughout the larger encompassing group, and Burt (1987) argues that norms diffuse across people in similar structural positions.

13. For some scholars, game theorists, for example, explaining cooperation is the same thing as explaining norm emergence. Because they view norms as constraining antisocial behavior, any prosocial behavior is seen as equivalent to a norm. For these researchers, explaining norm emergence means explaining cooperative behavior.

14. Macy and Skvoretz make no explicit assumptions about actors. Their assumption that actors adopt superior strategies, however, plays an equivalent role in their argument.

15. The classic structuralist, of course, is Karl Marx (see Tucker 1978).

# References

Allison, Paul D. 1992. "The Cultural Evolution of Beneficent Norms." *Social Forces* 71(2): 279–301.

Asch, Solomon E. 1956. "Studies of Independence and Conformity: I, A Minority of One Against a Unanimous Majority." *Psychological Monographs* 70(9): 1–70.

Axelrod, Robert. 1984. *The Evolution of Cooperation.* New York: Basic Books.

———. 1986. "An Evolutionary Approach to Norms." *American Political Science Review* 80(4): 1095–1111.

Bandura, Albert, and Richard H. Walters. 1963. *Social Learning and Personality Development.* New York: Holt, Rinehart and Winston.

Becker, Howard S. 1982. "Culture: A Sociological View." *Yale Review* 71(4): 513–27.

Beniger, James R. 1984. "Mass Media, Contraceptive Behavior, and Attitudes on Abortion: Toward a Comprehensive Model of Subjective Social Change." In vol. 2 of *Surveying Subjective Phenomena,* edited by Charles F. Turner and Elizabeth Martin. New York: Russell Sage Foundation.

Bicchieri, Cristina. 1997. "Learning to Cooperate." In *The Dynamics of Norms,* edited by Cristina Bicchieri, Richard Jeffry, and Brian Skyrms. New York: Cambridge University Press.

Blake, Judith, and Kingsley Davis. 1964. "Norms, Values, and Sanctions." In *Handbook of Modern Sociology,* edited by R. E. L. Faris. Skokie, Ill.: Rand McNally.

Blumer, Herbert. 1956. "Sociological Analysis and the 'Variable.'" *American Sociological Review* 21(6): 683–90.

———. 1966. "Sociological Implications of the Thought of George Herbert Mead." *American Journal of Sociology* 71(5):535–44.

Boyd, Robert, and Peter J. Richerson. 1985. *Culture and the Evolutionary Process.* Chicago: University of Chicago Press.

Burt, Ronald S. 1987. "Social Contagion and Innovation: Cohesion Versus Structural Equivalence." *American Journal of Sociology* 92(6): 1287–1335.

Cain, Maureen E. 1968. "Some Suggested Developments for Role and Reference Group Analysis." *British Journal of Sociology* 19(2): 191–208.

Cancian, Francesca M. 1975. *What Are Norms? A Study of Belief and Action in a Maya Community.* New York: Cambridge University Press.

Clemens, Elisabeth S. 1993. "Organizational Repertoires and Institutional Change: Women's Groups and the Transformation of U.S. Politics, 1890–1920." *American Journal of Sociology* 98(4): 755–98.

Cohen, Jean L. 1985. "Strategy or Identity: New Theoretical Paradigms and Contemporary Social Movements." *Social Research* 52(4): 663–716.

Coleman, James S. 1990. *Foundations of Social Theory.* Cambridge: Harvard University Press, Belknap Press.

Collins, Randall, and Robert Hanneman. 1998. "Modeling the Interaction Ritual Theory of Solidarity." In *The Problem of Solidarity: Theories and Models,* edited by Patrick Doreian and Thomas Fararo. Amsterdam: Gordon and Breach.

Cooter, Robert D. 1996. "Decentralized Law for a Complex Economy: The Structural Approach to Adjudicating the New Law Merchant." *University of Pennsylvania Law Review* 144(5): 1643–96.

Davies, Bronwyn. 1982. *Life in the Classroom and Playground: The Accounts of Primary School Children.* London: Routledge and Kegan Paul.

Demsetz, Harold. 1967. "Toward a Theory of Property Rights." *American Economic Review* 57(2): 347–59.

Dobbin, Frank. 1994. *Forging Industrial Policy: The United States, Britain, and France in the Railway Age.* Cambridge: Cambridge University Press.

Durkheim, Émile. 1915. *The Elementary Forms of the Religious Life.* New York: Free Press.

———. 1951. *Suicide.* New York: Free Press.

———. [1903] 1953. "The Determination of Moral Facts." In *Sociology and Philosophy,* translated by D. F. Pocock. London: Cohen and West.

Edgerton, Robert B. 1985. *Rules, Exceptions, and Social Order.* Berkeley: University of California Press.

Ekeh, Peter P. 1974. *Social Exchange Theory: The Two Traditions.* Cambridge, Mass.: Harvard University Press.

Elias, Norbert S. 1983. *The Court Society.* New York: Pantheon Books.

Ellickson, Robert C. 1998. "Law and Economics Discovers Social Norms." *Journal of Legal Studies* 27(2): 5375–52.

Elster, Jon. 1989. *The Cement of Society: A Study of Social Order.* New York: Cambridge University Press.

Emerson, Richard. 1962. "Power-Dependence Relations." *American Sociological Review* 27(1): 31–41.

Ensminger, Jean, and Jack Knight. 1997. "Changing Social Norms: Common Property, Bridewealth, and Clan Exogamy." *Current Anthropology* 38(1): 1–24.

Ericson, Richard V., Patricia M. Baranek, and Janet B. L. Chan. 1987. *Visualizing Deviance: A Study of News Organization.* Toronto: University of Toronto Press.

Ermakoff, Ivan. 1997. "Prelates and Princes: Aristocratic Marriages, Canon Law Prohibitions, and Shifts in Norms and Patterns of Domination in the Central Middle Ages." *American Sociological Review* 62(3): 405–22.

Everhart, Robert B. 1983. *Reading, Writing, and Resistance: Adolescence and Labor in a Junior High School.* Boston: Routledge and Kegan Paul.

Fernandez-Kelly, M. P. 1995. "Social and Cultural Capital in the Urban Ghetto: Implications for the Economic Sociology of Immigration." In *The Economic Sociology of Immigration,* edited by Alejandro Portes. New York: Russell Sage Foundation.

Fine, Gary Alan. 1987. *With the Boys: Little League Baseball and Preadolescent Culture.* Chicago: University of Chicago Press.

Fordham, Signithia, and John U. Ogbu. 1986. "Black Students' School Success: Coping with the Burden of 'Acting White.'" *Urban Review* 18(3): 176–206.

Fox, Robin. 1983. *The Red Lamp of Incest: An Enquiry into the Origins of Mind and Society.* Notre Dame: University of Notre Dame Press.

Gitlin, Todd. 1980. *The Whole World Is Watching: Mass Media in the Making and Unmaking of the New Left.* Berkeley: University of California Press.

Goodwin, M. H. 1982. "Processes of Dispute Management Among Urban Black Children." *American Ethnology* 9: 760–96.

Gregg, Jacob Ray. 1955. *A History of the Oregon Trail, Santa Fe Trail, and Other Trails.* Portland, Oreg.: Binsfords and Mort.

Hannan, Michael T., and John Freeman. 1977. "The Population Ecology of Organizations." *American Journal of Sociology* 82(5): 929–64.

Hardin, Russell. 1995. *One for All: The Logic of Group Conflict.* Princeton: Princeton University Press.

Hechter, Michael. 1984. "When Actors Comply: Monitoring Costs and the Production of Social Order." *Acta Sociologica* 27(3): 161–83.

———. 1987. *Principles of Group Solidarity.* Berkeley: University of California Press.

Hechter, Michael, and Satoshi Kanazawa. 1993. "Group Solidarity and Social Order in Japan." *Journal of Theoretical Politics* 5(4): 455–93.

Hechter, Michael, James Ranger-Moore, Guillermina Jasso, and Christine Horne. 1999. "Do Values Matter? An Analysis of Advance Directive for Medical Treatment." *European Sociological Review* 15(4): 405–30.

Heckathorn, Douglas D. 1989. "Collective Action and the Second-Order Free Rider Problem." *Rationality and Society* 1(1): 78–100.

Heiss, Jerold. 1981. "Social Roles." In *Social Psychology: Sociological Perspectives,* edited by Morris Rosenberg and Ralph H. Turner. New York: Basic Books.

Hochschild, Arlie. 1989. "The Economy of Gratitude." In *The Sociology of Emotions: Original Essays and Research Papers,* edited by David D. Franks and E. Doyle McCarthy. Greenwich, Conn.: JAI Press.

Homans, George C. 1950. *The Human Group.* New York: Harcourt, Brace.

———. 1961. *Social Behavior: Its Elementary Forms.* New York: Harcourt, Brace.

Horne, Christine. 2000. "Community and the State: The Relationship Between Normative and Legal Controls." *European Sociological Review* 16(3).

———. Forthcoming. "The Contribution of Norms to Social Welfare: Grounds for Hope or Pessimism?" *Legal Theory* 7(2).

Hunt, Scott A., Robert D. Benford, and David A. Snow. 1994. "Identity Fields: Framing Processes and the Social Construction of Movement Identities." In *New Social Movements: From Ideology to Identity,* edited by Enrique Larana, Hank Johnston, and Joseph R. Gusfield. Philadelphia: Temple University Press.

Inkeles, Alex, and David H. Smith. 1974. *Becoming Modern: Individual Change in Six Developing Countries.* Cambridge: Harvard University Press.

Johnston, Hank, Enrique Larana, and Joseph R. Gusfield. 1994. "Identities, Grievances, and New Social Movements." In *New Social Movements: From Ideology to Identity,* edited by Enrique Larana, Hank Johnston, and Joseph R. Gusfield. Philadelphia: Temple University Press.

Kahneman, Daniel. 1997. "New Challenges to the Rationality Assumption." *Legal Theory* 3(2): 105–24.

Kohn, Melvin L. 1977. *Class and Conformity: A Study in Values.* 2d ed. Chicago: University of Chicago Press.

Kollock, Peter. 1994. "The Emergence of Exchange Structures: An Experimental Study of Uncertainty, Commitment, and Trust." *American Journal of Sociology* 100(2): 313–45.

Kuran, Timur. 1991. "Now Out of Never: The Element of Surprise in the East European Revolution of 1989." *World Politics* 44(1): 7–48.

Labov, William. 1980. "The Social Origins of Sound Change." In *Locating Language in Time and Space,* edited by William Labov. New York: Academic Press.

Laitin, David D. 1998. *Identity in Formation: The Russian Speaking Populations in the Near Abroad.* Ithaca, N.Y.: Cornell University Press.

LaPiere, Richard. 1954. *A Theory of Social Control.* New York: McGraw-Hill.

Larana, Enrique, Hank Johnston, and Joseph R. Gusfield, eds. 1994. *New Social Movements: From Ideology to Identity.* Philadelphia: Temple University Press.

LaRossa, Ralph. 1988. "Fatherhood and Social Change." *Family Relations* 37(4): 451–57.

MacIver, Robert M. 1937. *Society: A Textbook of Sociology.* New York: Farrar and Rinehart.

Mackie, Gerry. 1996. "Ending Footbinding and Infibulation: A Convention Account." *American Sociological Review* 61(6): 999–1017.

Macy, Michael W. 1993. "Backward-Looking Social Control." *American Sociological Review* 58(6): 819–36.

Macy, Michael W., and John Skvoretz. 1998. "The Evolution of Trust and Cooperation Between Strangers: A Computational Model." *American Sociological Review* 63(5): 638–60.

Manning, Peter K. 1977. *Police Work: The Social Organization of Policing.* Cambridge: MIT Press.

Mark, Noah. 1998. "Birds of a Feather Sing Together." *Social Forces* 77(2): 453–85.

Matute-Bianchi, Maria Eugenia. 1986. "Ethnic Identities and Patterns of School Success and Failure Among Mexican-Descent and Japanese-American Students in a California High School: An Ethnographic Analysis." *American Journal of Education* 95(1): 233–55.

———. 1991. "Situational Ethnicity and Patterns of School Performance Among Immigrant and Non-immigrant Mexican-Descent Students." In *Minority Status and Schooling: A Comparative Study of Immigrant and Involuntary Minorities,* edited by M. A. Gibson and J. U. Ogbu. New York: Garland.

McAdam, Doug, John D. McCarthy, and Mayer N. Zald. 1996. *Comparative Perspectives on Social Movements: Political Opportunities, Mobilizing Structures, and Cultural Framings.* New York: Cambridge University Press.

McCarthy, John D. 1994. "Activists, Authorities, and Media Framing of Drunk Driving." In *New Social Movements: From Ideology to Identity,* edited by Enrique Larana, Hank Johnston, and Joseph R. Gusfield. Philadelphia: Temple University Press.

McLean, Paul D. 1998. "A Frame Analysis of Favor Seeking in the Renaissance: Agency, Networks, and Political Culture." *American Journal of Sociology* 104(1): 51–91.

Meyer, John, Francisco O. Ramirez, and Yasemin Nuhoglu Soysal. 1992. "World Expansion of Mass Education, 1870–1980." *Sociology of Education* 65(2): 128–49.

Meyer, John, W. Richard Scott, and Terrence E. Deal. 1992. "Institutional and Technical Sources of Organizational Structure: Explaining the Structure of Educational Organizations." In *Organizational Environments: Ritual and Rationality,* edited by John Meyer and W. Richard Scott. Newbury Park, Calif.: Sage Publications.

Miller, Neal E., and John Dollard. 1941. *Social Learning and Imitation.* New Haven: Yale University Press.

Miller-Loessi, Karen. 1995. "Comparative Social Psychology: Cross-Cultural and Cross-National." In *Sociological Perspectives on Social Psychology,* edited by Karen S. Cook, Gary Alan Fine, and James S. House. Boston: Allyn and Bacon.

Montgomery, James D. 1998. "Toward a Role-Theoretic Conception of Embeddedness." *American Journal of Sociology* 104(1): 92–125.

Opp, Karl-Dieter. 1982. "The Evolutionary Emergence of Norms." *British Journal of Social Psychology* 21(2): 139–49.

Park, Robert E., and Ernest W. Burgess. 1924. *Introduction to The Science of Sociology.* Chicago: University of Chicago Press.

Parsons, Talcott. 1937. *The Structure of Social Action.* New York: McGraw-Hill.

———. 1952. *The Social System.* New York: Free Press.

Petras, James, and Maurice Zeitlin. 1967. "Miners and Agrarian Radicalism." *American Sociological Review* 32(4): 578–86.

Pettit, Philip. 1993. *The Common Mind: An Essay on Psychology, Society, and Politics.* New York: Oxford University Press.

Portes, Alejandro. 1998. "Social Capital: Its Origins and Applications in Modern Sociology." *Annual Review of Sociology* 24: 1–24.

Posner, Eric. 1996. "The Regulation of Solidary Groups: The Influence of Legal and Nonlegal Sanctions on Collective Action." *University of Chicago Law Review* 63(1): 133–97.

Read, Piers Paul. 1974. *Alive: The Story of the Andes Survivors.* Philadelphia: Lippincott.

Ridgeway, Cecelia, and Lynn Smith-Lovin. 1994. "Structure, Culture, and Interaction: Comparing Two Generative Theories." *Advances in Group Processes* 11: 213–39.

Rizzo, Thomas A. 1989. *Friendship Development Among Children in School.* Norwood, N.J.: Ablex.

Robinson, Robert V., and Wendell Bell. 1978. "Equality, Success, and Social Justice in England and the United States." *American Sociological Review* 43(2): 125–43

Romanelli, Elaine. 1991. "The Evolution of New Organizational Forms." *Annual Review of Sociology* 17: 79–103.

Sampson, Robert J., and W. Byron Groves. 1989. "Community Structure and Crime: Testing Social Disorganization Theory." *American Journal of Sociology* 94(4): 774–802.

Sampson, Robert J., Stephen W. Raudenbush, and Felton Earls. 1997. "Neighborhoods and Violent Crime: A Multilevel Study of Collective Efficacy." *Science* 277(August 15, 1997): 918–24.

Schelling, Thomas. 1978. *Micromotives and Macrobehavior.* New York: W. W. Norton.

Schreiber, E. M. 1978. "Education and Change in American Opinions on a Woman for President." *Public Opinion Quarterly* 42(2): 171–82.

Schwartz, Barry, and Daniel Reisberg. 1991. *Learning and Memory.* New York: W. W. Norton.

Scott, John Finley. 1971. *Internalization of Norms: A Sociological Theory of Moral Commitment.* Englewood Cliffs, N.J.: Prentice-Hall.

Shaw, Clifford, and Henry D. McKay. [1942] 1969. *Juvenile Delinquency and Urban Areas.* Chicago: University of Chicago Press.

Sherif, Muzafer. [1936] 1973. *The Psychology of Social Norms.* New York: Octagon Books.

Shibutani, Tamotsu. 1962. "Reference Groups and Social Control." In *Human Behavior and Social Processes,* edited by Arnold M. Rose. Boston: Houghton Mifflin.

Sills, David L., ed. 1968. *International Encyclopedia of the Social Sciences.* New York: Macmillan.

Strang, David, and John W. Meyer. 1993. "Institutional Conditions for Diffusion." *Theory and Society* 22(4): 487–511.

Strang, David, and Sarah A. Soule. 1998. "Diffusion in Organizations and Social Movements: From Hybrid Corn to Poison Pills." *Annual Review of Sociology* 24: 265–90.

Sumner, William Graham. 1979. *Folkways.* New York: Arno Press.

Sutherland, Anne. 1998. "Gypsy Identity, Names, and Social Security Numbers." In *Applying Cultural Anthropology,* edited by Gary Ferraro. Belmont, Calif.: Wadsworth.

Tucker, Robert C., ed. 1978. *The Marx-Engels Reader.* 2d ed. New York: W. W. Norton.

Tyler, Tom R., and Robert J. Boeckmann. 1997. "Three Strikes and You Are Out, But Why? The Psychology of Public Support for Punishing Rule Breakers." *Law and Society Review* 31(2): 237–65.

Weber, Max. 1978. *Economy and Society.* Edited by Guenther Roth and Claus Wittich. Berkeley: University of California Press.

Willis, Paul E. 1981. *Learning to Labour: How Working-Class Kids Get Working-Class Jobs.* New York: Columbia University Press.

Williams, Robin M., Jr. 1970. *American Society: A Sociological Interpretation.* New York: Alfred A. Knopf.

Wrong, Dennis. 1994. *The Problem of Order: What Unites and Divides a Society.* New York: Free Press.

Yamagishi, Toshio. 1986. "The Provision of a Sanctioning System as a Public Good." *Journal of Personality and Social Psychology* 51(1): 110–16.

———. 1995. "Social Dilemmas." In *Sociological Perspectives on Social Psychology,* edited by Karen S. Cook, Gary Alan Fine, and James S. House. Boston: Allyn and Bacon.

Yamagishi, Toshio, Karen S. Cook, and Motoki Watabe. 1998. "Uncertainty, Trust, and Commitment Formation in the United States and Japan." *American Journal of Sociology* 104(1): 165–94.

Yamagishi, Toshio, and Nobuyuki Takahashi. 1994. "Evolution of Norms Without Meta-Norms." In *Social Dilemmas and Cooperation,* edited by Ulrich Schulz, Wulf Albers, and Ulrich Mueller, N.Y.: Springer-Verlag.

# 2

## THE EVOLUTION OF SOCIAL NORMS: A PERSPECTIVE FROM THE LEGAL ACADEMY

*Robert C. Ellickson*

I N A classic article that helped launch the field of law and economics, Harold Demsetz (1967) described how members of a tribe of Labradorian Amerindians had privatized their hunting territories in order to exploit new opportunities to sell fur pelts to Europeans. Demsetz offered no explanation, however, of how the Labradorians had succeeded in altering their ways. In effect, he relegated the inner workings of the tribe to a black box. In this chapter I look inside that black box and suggest how a "market for norms" might enable the individual members of a social group to adjust their informal rules to suit changing conditions.[1] Although the theory rests on several simplifying assumptions, it may offer some insights into social changes such as the decreasing tolerance of smoking, racist jokes, and dueling, and the increasing acceptance of out-of-wedlock births. Although the proffered theory focuses only on the evolution of specific norms (microsociology, if you will), this endeavor is an essential prelude to a better understanding of changes in cultures and other clusters of norms (macrosociology).

Law obviously is intertwined with custom. Nevertheless, scholars influenced by the law-and-economics approach paid scant attention to how social norms arise and evolve until the mid-1990s, when dozens of them contributed to the boomlet of interest in the issue. The theory offered here builds on the contributions of the "new" norms scholars such as Lisa Bernstein, Robert Cooter, Dan Kahan, Lawrence Lessig, Richard McAdams, Randal Picker, Eric Posner, and Cass Sunstein.[2] Although these commentators differ on many points, they generally share a common conception of norms and a common methodological approach. They regard a social norm as a rule governing an individual's behavior that is diffusely enforced by third parties other than state agents by means of social sanctions.[3] A person who violates a norm risks becoming the target of punishments such as negative gossip and ostracism. Conversely, someone who honors a norm may reap informal rewards such as enhanced esteem and greater future opportunities for beneficial exchanges. A person who has internalized a norm as a result of socialization enforces the norm against himself, perhaps by feeling guilt after violating it or a warm glow after complying with it (especially if the norm had been burdensome to honor).[4] A norm can exist even if no one has internalized it, however, as long as third parties provide an adequate level of informal enforcement.[5]

The new norms scholars all hew to a rational choice model of human behavior. This methodological individualism—also dominant in economics, evolutionary biology, and public choice theory—supposes that each individual generally is both rational and self-interested.[6] As a result, the new norms scholars have been influenced more by game theorists, who examine the dynamic interactions of purposive actors, than by traditional sociologists, who employ a methodological holism that views aggregations such as cultures and social classes as operative agents in the generation of norms.

An understanding of social norms can illuminate an issue at the core of both political theory and public economics. According to the view classically associated with Thomas Hobbes, people are unable to coordinate with one another without significant assistance from a coercive central authority. According to this Hobbesian conception, the basic problem is that public order is a public good. Each individual seemingly has an incentive to take a free ride on the efforts of anyone who volunteers to serve as a member of the social police.[7] According to the standard theory of public goods, only a Leviathan able to tax and regulate can succeed in countering this tendency. Echoes of this Hobbesian view surface in the work of the new norms scholars associated with the "New Chicago School" (Lessig 1998).[8] Recognizing the centrality of norms, these scholars advocate intentional governmental interventions to manipulate the norm-making process. By contrast, some Burkean and libertarian theorists insist that a social group commonly can succeed in using informal methods to deter crime and provide other sorts of public goods (for example, Morriss 1998). According to this perspective, social traditions winnowed through natural selection tend to be wiser than the ratiocinated policies of the most brilliant policy makers.[9] All commentators, whether they aim to shrink or expand the role of the state, can benefit from a better understanding of how norms arise, persist, and change.

What follows is a modest contribution in that direction. I begin by presenting some stylized assumptions about individuals and their motivations. I then explore the supply side of the norms market, in particular the role of change agents, such as norm entrepreneurs and opinion leaders, who either act in new ways and or provide new patterns of social sanctions. Next, I present analysis of the demand side of the market, especially the roles of members of the social audience, the most detached evaluators of others' social behavior. In brief, members of the audience can compensate worthy suppliers of new norms by conferring esteem (or, in the alternative, trading opportunities) upon them. I then describe the two events that may trigger a change in norms: an alteration in the economic conditions that a stably constituted social group faces; or an external event that reconfigures who belongs to a group. After either sort of event, the model suggests how a cascade toward a new norm might occur. The final portions of the chapter investigate social failures, that is, potential defects in the market for norms, and the comparative advantages that an organization, in particular the state, may have when it participates in the norm-making process.

I develop the theory at an intermediate level of rigor. Although the market analogy is strained in some respects, it does serve to reveal how individuals have varying incentives to participate in norm making. Given prevailing academic norms, my inclusion of various simplifying assumptions is likely to offend humanists, and my failure to include a formal mathematical model is likely to offend economic theorists. But, as the theory itself explains, a would-be change agent has to expect to take some heat.

## Norm-Maker's Roles: Actors, Enforcers, and Members of the Audience

In the model, an individual may belong to one or more social groups, which may vary in size. Individuals qualify as members of a group if they are situated in a way that enables them, first, to learn about what the other members do when they interact (that is, to obtain historical information) and, second, to bestow punishments and rewards on other members by means of gossip, ostracism, adjustment of exchange relationships, and other self-help methods. In turn, a member of a group is vulnerable to the informal punishments and rewards that the group's other members might mete out.

At various times each member assumes three distinct roles within the group: as an *actor*, as an *enforcer*, and as a *member of the audience*. A person is an actor when engaging in behavior unrelated to norm enforcement—for example, lighting a cigar, driving a car, or giving a lecture on mathematics. This sort of primary behavior may affect the welfare of the group's other members for better or worse. Smoke from a cigar at a dinner party, for instance, may be injurious to other guests. In the model, the demand for norms springs primarily from the desires of the members of a group to have informal rules designed to make actors take into account the external costs and benefits of their primary behaviors.[10]

An enforcer is on the frontline of the system of informal social control. Enforcers observe what actors do and respond by meting out calibrated social rewards and punishments. These social sanctions can range from doing nothing, to making a comment or facial gesture, to administering a weightier response, such as a gift or a punch to the jaw. A host who chastises a guest who smokes at a dinner party is acting as an enforcer, as is a student who openly compliments a mathematics professor after a guest lecture or a parent who grounds a teenager for using drugs.

Although it is possible to envision further tiers of participants, for the sake of simplicity the model adds only one more, the members of the audience. Each member of the audience observes what both actors and enforcers do but can respond only by conferring esteem or opprobrium (negative esteem) on enforcers.[11] (In this instance and others, devotees of Eric Posner's signaling theory of norms are invited to substitute *future exchange opportunities* for *esteem*.)[12] In the illustrative situations presented in the previous paragraph, the audiences would consist of, at a minimum, the other dinner guests, the other attendees at the lecture, and the parents' friends and neighbors. In brief, norms arise when enforcers, to please their audiences, administer informal sanctions to influence the behavior of actors. A major objective of this chapter is to indicate why rational and self-interested actors might choose to participate in all stages of this market for norms.

To keep the analysis tractable, the model makes some simplifying assumptions about a person's knowledge, desires, and capabilities. In some respects individuals are assumed to be homogeneous.

- Perfect historical knowledge: As noted, all members of a group are assumed to know, either by direct observation or receipt of gossip, what all members previously have done in their various roles.

- Power to levy social sanctions: Each member is assumed to be capable of rendering rewards and punishments. An enforcer may choose among an unlimited panoply of sanctions, including material and violent ones. A member of the audience, however, can only confer esteem (positive or negative). As explained later, a member incurs no net personal costs when rendering an esteem sanction.

- Utilitarian bias: A model of norm change presupposes an understanding of participants' objectives. These determine not only who contributes to norm reform but also what events provoke reformers to act. Because human affairs are complex and conflict ridden, a simplifying heuristic about participants' objectives can serve to help reveal processes of norm change that otherwise would remain obscure. To that end, I reductively assume that each member of a social group, when acting in the role of a member of the audience,[13] has a utilitarian bias—that is, a selfless preference for norm changes that satisfy the criteria of Kaldor-Hicks efficiency.[14] This means that each member of the audience would favor a norm change if the members who would be beneficiaries of the change would gain enough to be potentially able to compensate the members who would lose from the change. As long as members of the group would gain in the aggregate, audience members would not object to a norm on the ground that it would disadvantage them individually. Audience members, in other words, would not insist on Pareto superiority. According to the assumption of a utilitarian bias, a new antismoking norm, for example, would win unanimous support from the audience if it would be cost effective for the group in the aggregate, even though it might be detrimental to individuals who smoked.[15]

If a reductive assumption is to be made about human motivation, why should it be utilitarianism? The choice has a number of things to commend it. First, anthropologists and other investigators commonly have induced from field studies that human groups indeed tend to make cost-effective improvements in rules (Ellickson 1991, 184–264; see also Sober and Wilson 1998). Second, some theoretical models predict a drift toward more efficient norms (Bendor and Swistak 1998).[16]

Third, the rules of a group with a utilitarian bias in the long run may comport with distributive justice, the goal most commonly regarded as in tension with utilitarianism.[17] Because of the transaction costs of securing unanimity, a group can increase its aggregate wealth if it can force selected members to bear isolated losses for the good of the whole. If, conversely, every member had the power to veto a change, a group either would have to forgo many reforms that would satisfy Kaldor-Hicks criteria or else incur the onerous administrative costs involved in compensating the myriad potential losers from a reform. Given that unappealing choice, a rational person should see that it is generally in his long-run interest to entitle his group to follow Kaldor-Hicks (as opposed to Paretian) criteria—that is, to refrain from compensating losers from an efficient change.[18] Over the long haul the member gains from this utilitarian ethic as long as his share of the transaction-cost savings that it generates are sufficient to offset the losses he incurs when reforms do deserve his interests. In sum, in a group in which the fabric of social interactions is thick, a rational member should be able to see the advantage of having a utilitarian bias when appraising a proposed norm change.

That said, I should reemphasize that I assume a utilitarian bias only to have a simplifying heuristic. No doubt the objectives of individuals cannot be so neatly packaged. Moreover, to assume as I do that audience members apply Kaldor-Hicks criteria is to assume that they transcend self-interest when performing in that role. This is optimistic, to put the point gently. It is necessary, however, to stipulate some substantive objective that members seek in order to predict how they will act. One of the model's central results is that the audience will tend to get what it wants, whatever that happens to be. If audience members were to prefer norms that would be consistent with Rawlsian justice, or that would be congruent with their religion, or that would make them poorer, they will be able to employ esteem rewards to induce norm suppliers to serve those other ends.

## Heterogeneous Attributes of Individuals

In several dimensions other than those just listed, people are assumed to be heterogeneous. As a result, some members of a group have sharper incentives to lead the process of norm change. Among the heterogeneous attributes my model assumes of actors are the following:

- Variable endowments: Individuals are assumed to differ in endowments such as physique, wealth, and human capital.[19] As a result, they may obtain different levels of tangible benefits when a new norm is adopted. For example, a person suffering from emphysema receives more benefits than most when an antismoking norm is put into effect.
- Variable discount rates: Discount rates vary among group members.
- Variable technical intelligence: Although members observe everything (have perfect historical knowledge), they differ in their ability to assess the aggregate costs and benefits that an act or enforcement effort generates for group members in the aggregate. For example, some individuals know more than others about the dangers of secondhand smoke or about the topic of a lecture on mathematics.
- Variable social intelligence: Apart from differences in technical intelligence, individuals vary in their ability to forecast group social dynamics. Some, as astute as Thomas Schelling (1960, 1978), know when existing social conditions are ripe for a cascade to a new norm. Others lack this social intelligence and have a relatively poor sense of how one person's decision can influence that of another.
- Variable leadership skills: People vary in their ease of organizing and inspiring those around them.[20] As a result of these variations, as well as differences in technical and social intelligence, work for social innovations is more effortless for some than for others. These low-cost suppliers can be expected to be disproportionately successful in the market for norms.[21]

# The Supply Side of the Market for Norms: Change Agents

Legal scholars have used a variety of labels to describe an individual who promotes a change in norms. The traditional sociological designation is "moral entrepreneur" (for example, Becker 1963, 147–48; see also R. Posner 1998a, 1638, 1664–68). Cass Sunstein has devised the notion of a "norm entrepreneur" (Sunstein 1996b, 909), a phrase that many legal scholars have since embraced (for example, E. Posner 1998).[22]

Both actors and enforcers may supply new norms. Actors participate on the supply side when they adopt new patterns of behavior. An example is a smoker who tests the limits of propriety at a dinner party. Enforcers serve as suppliers when they react in new ways to the behavior of actors. An example is a dinner guest who creatively responds to smoking on the part of another guest, perhaps either by lauding the smoker's courage or, conversely, by throwing a glassful of wine toward the smoker's cigarette. Those on the demand side of the market for norms then react to these stimuli.

Figure 2.1 depicts the operation of both the supply and demand sides of the market for norms. The supply side is indicated by the solid arrows pointing toward the right; these identify flows of evidence of behavior on the part of both actors and enforcers. The demand side of the market is indicated by the solid arrows that point to the left; these indicate the responses of enforcers and members of the audience to the social evidence they receive from norm suppliers. (In this model, it must be stressed, an enforcer's behavior simultaneously both expresses demand to actors and also supplies a norm to audience members.)[23]

I refer to an actor or enforcer who is relatively early in supplying a new norm as a *change agent*. According to the rational-actor perspective, a change agent offers new norms because he anticipates that over time he will receive a flow of benefits that will outweigh (in present-value terms) the various costs he will incur while acting in that role. A change agent moves earlier than others because his expected net benefits from acting in that role are unusually large. This may be so either because his expected costs are lower or his expected benefits greater, or both.[24]

Change agents tend to have attributes that make them relatively low-cost suppliers of new norms. In general, they possess superior technical intelligence, social intelligence, and leadership skills. These attributes reduce the opportunity costs they incur when they work for norm reform. Change agents also tend to face favorable conditions on the benefit side of the ledger. Successful promoters of a new norm receive two distinguishable sorts of benefits. First, each garners a personal share of the *tangible benefits* that the new norm creates for the group. Change agents tend to have special personal endowments conducive to their receipt of above-normal tangible benefits. Second, as a special reward for helping bring about social reform, change agents receive *esteem* and other social rewards when group members widely accept a new norm. Individuals embedded in subgroup social networks consisting of persons prone to esteem them are prime candidates to become change agents.

These factors help explain the prominence of black religious leaders in the civil rights movement. Being black, they had much to gain from dismantling racial segregation. Being religious leaders, they were ideally positioned to receive early esteem from members of their immediate social groups (that is, members of their congregations) and also relatively immune to social opprobrium, economic retaliation, and physical violence on the part of racist whites.

FIGURE 2.1      *The Market for Norms*

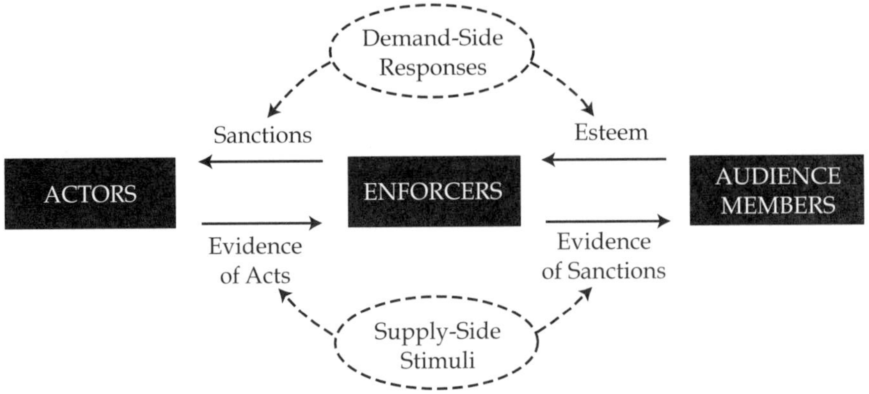

*Source:* Author's compilation.

Apart from costs and benefits, change agents tend to have relatively low discount rates and long time horizons. The stigma and other personal costs of attempting to change a norm generally are incurred early, whereas the esteem and tangible benefits generally are reaped late. The more future-oriented a person is, the more rational it is to pursue social reform.

In an effort to clarify the dynamics of norm change, I distinguish between three subcategories of change agents: self-motivated leaders, norm entrepreneurs, and opinion leaders.[25] Although all three types respond relatively early to a shift in cost-benefit opportunities, they lead for different reasons. Figure 2.2 depicts in a general way the chronological sequence in which a series of successful change agents participates in supplying a new norm.[26]

## Self-Motivated Leaders

Self-motivated leaders move early to change a norm because, owing to their special endowments and talents, they anticipate receiving unusually high levels of net tangible benefit from challenging the existing norm. Indeed, these net tangible benefits are sufficiently large to motivate them to favor change even in the absence of potential esteem rewards.[27] Hence the adjective "self-motivated."[28] To illustrate: A charismatic person faces lower costs of working for social change. A lessening of smoke especially benefits persons with emphysema or other lung disease. Therefore a charismatic person suffering from emphysema would be an ideal candidate to become a self-motivated leader of an antismoking campaign.

Self-motivated leaders commonly spark changes in the network norms that facilitate communication and coordination. For example, in 1833, Augustine Taylor invented the balloon-frame method of wood construction, a system lighter in weight and more flexible than the traditional post-and-

FIGURE 2.2    *The Involvement of Change Agents in the Supply of a*
              *New Norm*

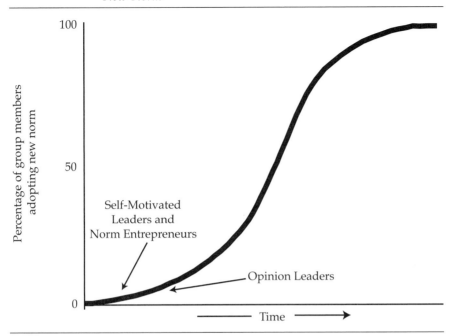

*Source:* Author's compilation.

beam system, for use in the construction of St. Mary's Roman Catholic Church in Chicago. Other builders rapidly switched to the balloon frame, and it remains the dominant system of light construction in the United States (Davis, Easterlin, and Parker 1972, 621).[29] The self-motivated change agents in this instance were Taylor, the actor, and the head of the church, the enforcer who snubbed traditional mores and permitted Taylor to proceed with his unorthodox design. Both parties most likely possessed superior technical intelligence and also anticipated reaping unusually large tangible benefits, given the nature of their current and future building projects.

When a new norm suddenly becomes manifestly advantageous for a group, many self-motivated individuals with unexceptional leadership abilities may supply it simultaneously. When this happens, historians will have difficulty attributing the new norm to particular change agents. For instance, dueling fast became extinct in the South once the Civil War had shattered the social networks of the southern aristocracy. Although anti-dueling societies had been active in the South before the war (Picker 1997,

1285 n. 88), esteem rewards apparently were not needed to motivate the rejection of dueling after Appomattox.

A technical innovation may diffuse across space from its place of invention as neighbors copy the best practices of those around them. A pivotal historical example is the slow diffusion of agriculture outward from its birthplace in the Fertile Crescent ten thousand years ago (Diamond 1997, 180–91).[30] The earliest inventors and copiers in this instance are likely to have had endowments that gave them special tangible benefits from engaging in farming. Many millennia later, Zvi Griliches (1957) found that the American farmers who pioneered the planting of hybrid corn tended to be the ones who profited most from that innovation. In the late 1970s in China, the rapid repudiation of Maoist communal agriculture was partly triggered by a successful (and illegal) return to family farming by residents of the village of Xiaogang (Erik Eckholm, "Village of Small Farmers Marks Own Great Leap," *New York Times,* September 19, 1998, A4). Although these villagers later were esteemed in China for having helped provoke Deng Xiaoping to adopt legal reforms, their original motivation was most likely the relatively high levels of tangible benefits they stood to gain from privatizing their fields.

## Norm Entrepreneurs

For the remaining two types of change agents—norm entrepreneurs and opinion leaders—external rewards provide an essential carrot. Although leaders of both types are likely to garner some tangible benefits from a norm change, they also need to gain esteem to cover their full costs of supplying a new norm. Norm entrepreneurs are specialists who campaign to change particular norms, whereas opinion leaders are generalists. Ward Connerly, Martin Luther King Jr., Catharine MacKinnon, Joseph McCarthy, and Carry Nation are norm entrepreneurs. Jimmy Carter, Walter Cronkite, Doris Kearns Goodwin, and Billy Graham are opinion leaders. Both types tend to be endowed with personal attributes, such as charisma and skill in communication, that reduce their costs of serving in these capacities.

What special traits distinguish a successful norm entrepreneur? First, a norm entrepreneur tends to possess a relatively high level of technical knowledge relevant to the norms within his specialty.[31] This knowledge enables the entrepreneur to respond early to a change in cost-benefit conditions. Entrepreneurs who favor antismoking norms tend to know a lot about lung diseases. Joseph McCarthy rose to prominence when he appeared to have inside information about communist infiltration of government and then foundered when it seemed that much of his specific information was bogus. Second, a norm entrepreneur is likely to be cognizant that there are appreciative experts (often, close associates in a social subgroup) who are likely immediately to esteem the norm entrepreneur for trying to change the social practice at issue. In other words, a norm entre-preneur faces unusually favorable conditions on the demand side of the norms market.

## Opinion Leaders

Unlike the self-motivated leader and the norm entrepreneur, the opinion leader is not at the forefront of norm change but instead is located one position back from the front (see figure 2.2).[32] An opinion leader evaluates the initiatives of these other change agents (the true catalysts) and then decides which of their causes to endorse. Opinion leaders therefore play a pivotal role in determining whether change agents succeed in triggering a cascade toward a new norm (Rogers 1983, 27–28, 281–88).[33]

A successful opinion leader tends to have two exceptional characteris-tics. The first is an usually high level of social intelligence, which helps the opinion leader anticipate better than most which social innovations will end up attracting bandwagon support. An adept opinion leader, for exam-ple, may be aware that many people have been disguising their true opin-ions about the merits of current norms (Sunstein 1996b, 929–30). Opinion leaders involved in the Velvet Revolutions in Eastern Europe, for instance, best sensed that support for communism was less genuine than it seemed. Second, an opinion leader is likely to be a person to whom other members of the group are unusually prone to defer to avoid being socially out of step.[34] An opinion leader may have earned this trust through prior accom-plishments in the arena of norm enforcement and change. A village elder is a generic example. The costs of supplying a new norm fall when someone expects to be followed. A norm entrepreneur who commands little trust is wise to recruit to his crusade an opinion leader whom the audience regards as more credible. Thus, in 1786, James Madison, the political entrepreneur spearheading the nascent movement to replace the Articles of Confedera-tion, recognized the monumental advantage of enlisting George Washing-ton in the cause.[35]

# The Demand Side of the Market for Norms: The Role of a Social Audience

Individuals indicate their demand for various norms by levying informal rewards (or punishments) to indicate their approval (or disapproval) of what norm suppliers are doing. I refer to persons who provide early sup-port to suppliers of a new norm as *cheerleaders*. Enforcers function as cheer-leaders when they reward actors who are engaging in new forms of pri-mary behavior. Members of the audience function as cheerleaders when they confer esteem on innovative enforcers. These relationships are por-trayed in figure 2.1.

Possession of special information is for the most part what sets a cheerleader apart from the crowd on the demand side. *Appreciative experts* are enforcers or audience members who have unusually good technical intelligence about the cost-benefit trade-offs that competing norms pose. In timing, the role of appreciative experts is like that of a writer of newspaper editorials, a critic in the arts, or a peer reviewer in academic life. They are among the first to recognize that suppliers of a cost-effective new norm are doing something worthy of reward. During the civil rights movement in the South, the observers most aware of the high costs of segregation to blacks were likely to be among the first to esteem civil rights activists. Barbara Dafoe Whitehead's influential article, "Dan Quayle Was Right," helped encourage the change agents who had been seeking to reestablish the norm against out-of-wedlock births (Whitehead 1993).[36]

Opinion leaders—persons with an extraordinary level of social intelligence—are important on the demand side as well as on the supply side. Opinion leaders join the esteeming bandwagon at an early stage after noticing that appreciative experts have been jumping on board. Hollywood stars, magazine journalists, and leaders of prize-granting organizations commonly aspire to serve in this role.

## How Costlessly Conferred Audience Rewards Can Induce Norm Enforcement

It is easy to understand why an actor would choose to conform to a norm that is systematically enforced. If it is considered gauche to smoke at a dinner party, lighting a cigar will damage a cigar smoker's reputation. It is harder to understand why a rational onlooker would make the effort to administer punishments on wrongdoers and rewards on rightdoers.[37] Why would a host care to enforce an antismoking norm?[38] One reason might be tangible benefits; if secondhand smoke is either carcinogenic or unpleasant, the host obtains environmental benefits by suppressing it. The host's enforcement also would help the other guests, however, and to that extent would be a public good. Much norm enforcement, that, for instance, against acts of littering or bearing a child out of wedlock, mainly generate public benefits, not benefits to the enforcer personally. When the private costs of enforcement would seem to exceed the tangible benefits, what might motivate an enforcer to act as a member of the social police instead of as a free rider? Although many legal scholars intuitively reject the Hobbesian view that order is never possible without a central authority, they have struggled to come up with a plausible explanation of how people ever are able to solve this second-order collective action problem. In 1998, however, two of the new norms scholars—Richard McAdams and Eric Posner—independently proposed rival theories that suggest how members of an audience could, in some contexts, costlessly confer rewards to spur enforcers to function as informal police officers.[39]

*Richard McAdams's Esteem Theory of Norms*   McAdams (1997, 355–75) postulates that an individual values the esteem of others for its own sake.[40] Just as eating a tasty dessert is a source of pleasure, so is receiving kudos. Esteem sanctions, either positive or negative, therefore can influence the behavior of a change agent.

McAdams's more provocative idea is that an individual incurs no net costs when conferring esteem on another.[41] This assumption of zero esteeming costs is plausible in some contexts. The historical information needed to accord esteem tends to be readily at hand. A dinner guest with adequate technical and social knowledge instantaneously can evaluate the propriety of a host's enforcement actions against a smoker. In many contexts conferring esteem also is virtually effortless. To smile or to frown, to bow or to snub, to praise or to rebuke—all require little more effort than taking a breath.

To be sure, conferring negative esteem can be costly if the target is able to retaliate in some way. McAdams (1995, 1024–25) notes, however, that a person actually may reap offsetting benefits by participating as a member of the social police. For instance, an audience member who had internalized norms governing performance in that role might feel a warm glow after performing well in that capacity.[42] Indeed, appreciative members of live audiences at entertainment events appear to enjoy conferring applause. Any benefits derived from esteeming would reduce, and perhaps outweigh, an audience member's conceivable costs of conferring esteem.

McAdams's conception of the demand side for norms suggests the following scenario: Members of the audience survey the behaviors that various norm suppliers are offering. Audience members then costlessly confer positive esteem on enforcers who are serving the aggregate welfare of the members of the group and negative esteem on those enforcers who are not. Because enforcers value receiving esteem, they are led to supply norms that satisfy the audience's utilitarian bias. Some historical episodes indicate that this scenario is not far-fetched. Diffusely situated observers conferred esteem to reward change agents who had incurred high risks during the civil rights movement in the South (Chong 1991, 100–1, 191–92).

*Eric Posner's Signaling Theory of Norms*   In an article (1998) and a book (2000), Posner has developed a more limited, but potentially more testable, theory of norms. Drawing on the work of Michael Spence (1974), Posner views norms as conventions that govern the behaviors a person employs to signal that he is a "good type."[43] By wearing the "right" clothes, for instance, an actor advertises that he is likely to be a good person to hire or marry. Transported into the present model, Posner's analysis suggests that an enforcer might be tempted to function as a member of the social police in situations in which that service would signal his general trustworthiness to the members of the audience. To an audience with a utilitarian bias, the more efficient the norm an enforcer has supplied, the more favorable the signal. Audience members would later reward a meritorious enforcer by entering into additional cooperative exchanges with him. To illustrate, a host signals that he is a "good type" by enforcing a norm against smoking; a week later, an appreciative dinner guest invites the host to serve as a trustee for a trust, an exchange that will benefit the former guest because he is more confident than before that his former host is a "good type."

*McAdams's and Posner's Theories Compared*   Posner's theory is similar to McAdams's in important respects. First, both theories anticipate a strong correlation between social rewards and an enforcer's net private costs. Posner asserts that the favorability of an audience's response to a signal increases with the cost of the signal to the signaler. An audience that confers esteem similarly is likely to correlate its aggregate reward with the size of an enforcer's sacrifice. Superheroes win more plaudits than ordinary heroes do.

Second and more important, under both theories members of a social audience can, at no net cost, provide valuable carrots to the enforcers who create norms. McAdams views esteem as costlessly conveyed. When a signal results in additional exchanges, as Posner anticipates, the members of an audience similarly incur no net costs. A trade generally generates gains for all participants. As a result, audience members benefit from receiving and responding to signals because they are able to make more discerning choices among trading partners.[44]

Under ideal conditions both theories anticipate that audience members have no incentive to free ride on the efforts of others to reward an enforcer who had supplied a public good. In developing my model, I adopt only this common denominator of the two theories and have no need to endorse either of them as such.[45] Throughout this chapter I consistently refer to audience rewards as "esteem," but only to keep the exposition compact. Whenever "esteem" appears, a reader who prefers Posner's theory to McAdams's is invited mentally to substitute "enhanced opportunities for cooperative interactions" and to ponder whether the analysis still holds.

The two theories also vary in important respects. First, Posner's theory promises to be more testable than that of McAdams (see also E. Posner 1998, 786 n. 32, 797–98). In most contexts, it is easier to observe an exchange transaction than a conferral of esteem. Second, the two theories have different implications about the timing of a meritorious enforcer's rewards from an audience. McAdams seems to envisage an immediate conferral of esteem. Posner, by contrast, foresees rewards as delayed until subsequent periods of play, when mutually favorable transactions are executed. Posner's theory therefore more strongly implies that a person with a high discount rate or a person in endgame would perform unreliably in the role of enforcer. For instance, Posner's theory suggests that the contemporary jury is an ill-advised legal institution, at least if the major function of a jury is to bring contemporary social norms to bear in a legal proceeding. In an urban setting today, jurors are strangers with scant prospects of further interaction once the group has disbanded. Posner's theory predicts jurors therefore have weak incentives to signal that they are "good types" by enforcing prevailing norms. If jurors in fact perform well, they either must bring internalized norms of civic duty into the jury room or (as McAdams supposes) must hunger for esteem from fellow jurors. Third, an audience must appropriately aggregate its total rewards to get enforcers' incentives right. Both McAdams's and Posner's theories suggest difficulties of proper aggregation, but difficulties of different sorts.[46]

# How Norms Change

The model rests on the reductive assumption that members of a group have a utilitarian bias. An upshot of this assumption is that norms can be expected to evolve when underlying supply and demand conditions change. What kinds of events might provoke shifts in economic conditions? Which sorts of change agents and cheerleaders are likely to respond first when an old norm is under stress?

## Events That Can Trigger a Change in Norms

*An Exogenous Shock Creates New Economic Conditions Within a Stable Group*    In a social group with static membership, a new trading opportunity, technology, or environmental event may alter cost-benefit conditions.[47] As mentioned at the outset, Demsetz (1967) has described the response of a Labradorian tribe to the arrival of Europeans eager to exchange goods for pelts. In earlier times, the tribe's norms had supported communal hunting rights within its forests, a system that creates few incentives for an individual hunter to conserve the stock of game. Once the European traders had come on the scene the tribe shifted to a system of exclusive hunting territories.[48] This system is more efficient when game is scarce because the sole owner of a territory inhabited by nonmigratory wild animals has a much sharper incentive than a communal owner to avoid overhunting.[49]

New scientific or technical information, similarly, can alter social practices.[50] Rain dancing is apt to become less common after members of a tribe

have learned some meteorology. In the 1940s, pediatricians routinely prescribed tonsillectomies; they later dropped this norm after wholesale use of
the procedure was shown to be inadvisable.[51] In the 1950s in the United
States, the increasing military threat posed by the Soviet Union help support the rise of norms against association with communists (E. Posner 1998,
775).

An environmental shock also can alter endowments and hence cost-
benefit conditions. A drought, for example, may give rise to norms supporting conservation of water. The devastation of a war or natural disaster
is apt to trigger norms of mutual support in part because people who have
lost wealth see more benefit in having an informal system of social insurance. Relatedly, a stable group that migrates may vary its norms as it confronts changing environmental conditions. High-seas whalers, for example,
appear to have efficiently adapted their informal rules of capture to the
characteristics of the species of whales present in a particular fishery
(Ellickson 1991, 191–206).

*A Group Adds or Loses Members*   Because individuals vary in their endowments, a change in group composition can alter internal cost-benefit
conditions.[52] New blood is likely to be a source of new informal arrangements. A university can reinvigorate a fading academic department by hir-
ing a cluster of established but youthful scholars; because their time horizons are longer, these young scholars have more to gain from the
emergence of norms of scholarly output that would enhance the department's reputation. The subtraction of certain members from a group similarly may have an effect on which norms are cost-justified in the aggregate.[53] The exclusion of children from an apartment building, for example,
would lessen the costs of the building's residents having a norm against
noisemaking because fewer children would have to bear the burden of
suppressing their high spirits.

A war or natural disaster may shatter the outer boundaries of a group
and thereby change its norms. Defeat in the Civil War ended the insulation
and cohesion of the southern aristocracy, thereby decimating the aristo-
crats' gains from the constitutive ritual of dueling. The events of World
War II helped break down ethnic and (to a lesser degree) racial barriers in
American life. Conversely, the destruction of a group's unifying forces may
lead to a balkanization of norms. Indeed, the passing of Josip Broz Tito
weakened pan-Slavic nationalism in Yugoslavia and enabled more parochial ethnic groups to reassert their norms.

A government may provide the exogenous shock that alters group
composition. Before the 1960s, southern whites and blacks were socially (if
not necessarily physically) segregated. In that environment, whites were
likely not only to tolerate racist jokes but even, at least according to

McAdams's analysis, to encourage that form of humor in order to enhance the status of whites as a group (McAdams 1995). The civil rights acts of the 1960s helped bring about significant integration of workplaces and schools in the South, with the result that many whites there began to belong to reference groups that included significant numbers of blacks. Blacks now had leverage to administer informal sanctions and confer esteem. After these changes in social structure, whites became far less likely to engage in racist humor.

Innovations in transportation and communication technologies make new concatenations of human interactions possible. In general, these tend to widen social relations and erode parochial norms. The expansion of trade, for example, fosters cooperation by expanding the compass of merchants' reputational stakes.[54] On the other hand, innovations such as web pages, e-mail, and cheap long-distance flights can enable geographically scattered persons with common narrow interests to maintain a group that previously could not have been sustained. For instance, these new technologies may help both universities to knit together their alumni and international terrorists to knit together their sympathizers.

## The Process of Norm Change

Either sort of exogenous shock—a shift in internal cost-benefit conditions or an alteration of group membership—can spur a group to change its informal rules. However, it is not groups, as such, that act but, rather, individuals. As previously discussed, individuals possess different attributes that incline them to play specialized roles in the process of norm change.

Legal commentators interested in the dynamics of norm change have borrowed from theories put forward by game theorists, evolutionary biologists, and economists of information. According to the new norms scholars, in the paradigm case an upstart norm starts slowly, gains momentum, and culminates in a triumphant rush. Various authors refer to a tipping point being passed (Cooter 1998; McAdams 1997, 365–72), an equilibrium changing not gradually but in punctuated fashion (Roe 1996, 663–65), or a cascade being triggered (Sunstein 1996b, 909).[55]

The literature on cascades suggests why people follow leaders. Works in this genre distinguish between two relevant phenomena: informational cascades and reputational cascades. According to the foundational article, "An informational cascade occurs when it is optimal for an individual, having observed the actions of those ahead of him, to follow the behavior of the preceding individual without regard to his own information" (Bikhchandani, Hirshleifer, and Welch 1992, 994).[56] One goes along with the crowd on the ground that the crowd is probably right. A person joins a reputational cascade, by contrast, to avoid the social disapproval that may be visited on those who are out of step (Kuran 1998; Kuran and Sunstein 1999, 685–87). One goes along with the crowd to be with the crowd, even if one knows that the crowd is wrong.[57]

Cascade theory helps reveal how change agents and cheerleaders become so influential. The basic scenario of a successful bandwagon is this: An exogenous change creates new cost-benefit conditions that favor a switch to a new norm. Various change agents, employing advocacy or exemplary acts or enforcements, offer up competing norms to govern the new conditions. The first change agents to supply new norms are self-motivated leaders, who will attain net tangible benefits from a shift, and norm entrepreneurs, who have the best technical information about the aggregate advantages of possible changes.[58] Over time, members of the audience assess these competing offerings and confer esteem on worthy change agents. Because the first change agents to move are challenging traditional ways, for a time ordinary members of the audience may accord them less esteem than previously. The change agents' early losses tend to be mitigated, however, by their relatively low supply costs (arising from their low discount rates and special knowledge and skill) and by their awareness of the existence of appreciative experts who soon will be according them higher esteem. Opinion leaders—those with the best social intelligence—then play a key role. They notice that the technical experts have been gravitating toward the new norm, a sign that it is one that other audience members eventually will learn to appreciate. Hopping on the bandwagon, the opinion leaders begin to supply the new norm and to esteem the change agents who have been pushing it. An ordinary member of the group observes all these moves and for a number of reasons eventually infers that it would be prudent to join the cascade. First, because technical experts are approving the change, it is likely to be good for the group. Second, social experts, those who best understand where the crowd will end up, also are on board, and it is socially risky not to follow them. The mass of ordinary members ultimately conforms to what their respected leaders have been doing. The informational and reputational cascades both crash to completion.

The speed of norm evolution is determined by the rates at which the members of the group acquire the technical and social knowledge necessary to appreciate that a new norm is more utilitarian than the old one. The entire process may proceed briskly. Sunstein gives as examples the rise of feminism, the abandonment of communism in Eastern Europe and of apartheid in South Africa, and the collapse of reflexive political correctness on American campuses (Sunstein 1996b, 929–30). Even more rapid was Jesse Jackson's successful campaign to substitute, within the reference group for which he is an opinion leader, "African American" for "black."

## The Rise of the Norm Against Smoking

For a more extended illustration, consider the evolution of norms governing smoking. Informal pressure against smoking in a social setting increased markedly, at least in North America, during the last third of the
twentieth century.[59] Statistics on declines in the adult smoking population
can serve as a rough proxy for the rise of this antismoking norm.[60] Although there is little empirical evidence on some points, the following stylized scenario is plausible.

The triggering event is the gradual amassing of new scientific information about health risks associated with firsthand and secondhand smoke.[61]
Medical researchers and public health officials, who have a superior command of this technical information, soon emerge as the norm entrepreneurs
in the antismoking cause.[62] Nonsmokers who suffer from lung diseases join
in as self-motivated leaders. These early change agents receive plaudits
from appreciative medical experts. Key opinion leaders then increasingly
join the cause. Whereas in the 1950s, Edward R. Murrow smoked conspicu-
ously on camera, television executives now make sure that successor news
anchors do not. The general public, taking its cues from these leaders,
starts directing opprobrium at smokers and those who encourage them. As
the bandwagon grows, social hosts increasingly decline to set out ashtrays
for guests. Surgeon General Everett Koop, David Kessler, commissioner of
the Food and Drug Administration, and the other norm entrepreneurs in
the antismoking cause come to be broadly esteemed.

The actual story, of course, is more complicated. The norm against
public smoking has diffused at different rates within different demographic
groups. In the United States, college graduates are much less likely than
high school dropouts to smoke (Kagan and Vogel 1993, 22, 47 n. 20, 48 n.
25). This is understandable because college graduates are likely to have
lower discount rates, better technical information about the risks of smoking, and a lower likelihood of belonging to an oppositional subculture in
which smoking is fashionable because mainstream norms have been shifting against it (Gusfield 1993, 66).

A man in France is considerably more likely to smoke than is a man in
North America.[63] It is implausible to chalk this up to differences in technical
information in the hands of health experts in the two nations. Legal variations may account for some of the difference. Although France heavily
taxes tobacco products and tightly controls their advertising, it has relatively lax laws on smoking in workplaces and public accommodations (Kagan and Vogel 1993). However, differences in norms may matter as well.
Partly because opinion leaders in France have been somewhat slower than
their counterparts in North America to quit smoking,[64] the French public is
less likely to be supportive of antismoking norms. Why would French
opinion leaders be relatively slow to act? Some observers might be tempted

to resort to an ad hoc cultural explanation, such as that smoking serves as a more potent signal of sophistication in France than it does in North America.[65] Data on trends in smoking in France, Canada, and the United States, however, suggest that the direction and pace of norm change actually has been rather similar in the three nations. In each of the three, about 20 percent fewer members of the total adult male population were smoking in the early 1980s than in the mid-1960s.[66] This suggests the main reason that France has more smokers and weaker antismoking norms today is that a larger fraction of its population happened to be smoking when the new information about the dangers of tobacco surfaced. Cultural variations among the three nations may have affected their baseline smoking rates but not the basic thrust of their social responses to the new medical evidence.

## Social Failures: The Limitations of Norms

Up to this point, I have been generally upbeat about the ability of members of a social group to adapt their norms to new conditions. This tone is generally consistent with my prior work (Ellickson 1991) and the views of Robert Cooter (1996, 1677–78), Demsetz (1967), and the other "optimists" about norms.[67] There are also, however, many "pessimists" among the scholars, including Eric Posner (1996a, 1706–10) and, in important respects, McAdams (1997, 409–24; see also Basu, Jones, and Schlicht 1987, 8–12; Kraus 1997; Roe 1996, 651–52). The pessimists repeatedly indicate that the norm-making process may fail to serve utilitarian ends, even in a group whose members have a utilitarian bias. I contend that the scholars in these opposing camps may disagree less about the nature of norm making than about the likelihood that government officials can outperform norm makers.

Conventional transaction-cost economics helps lay bare the ways in which social processes may fail. In Ronald Coase's hypothetical world of zero transaction costs, a norm could not be the source of a deadweight loss because, if it were, all affected persons instantly would contract to reform it (Coase 1960). Nonutilitarian norms therefore can arise only in contexts in which transactions costs are high.[68] The details of social contexts, such as the number of members involved, thus matter a great deal. Transaction costs are especially likely to impede correction of an inefficient norm in cases in which: the costs of the norms are mostly deflected to outsiders; a group has difficulty coordinating the aggregate amounts of its rewards to worthy change agents; a group's esteem awards are likely to be insufficient to overcome various forms of inertia favoring the status quo; and social conditions make a group vulnerable to reputational cascades toward inefficient fashions.

## The Slighting of Interests of Outsiders

All of the new norms scholars, even the optimists, agree that a closely knit group may generate a norm that injures outsiders more than it helps insiders (for example, Cooter 1996, 1684–85). McAdams's (1995, 1033–82) analysis of southern traditions of racial segregation, for example, indicates that the norms southern whites developed to enhance their own status had horrific effects on blacks. A legislature therefore may be wise to enact a statute, such as, in this case, a civil rights act, that attends to the external costs a parochial norm has been inflicting. For the same reason, a common-law judge should not elevate a custom of an industry to the status of law in a context in which the custom affects the welfare of outsiders who have no practical capacity to bargain.[69] The customs of the tugboat industry, for example, which may well serve the needs of shippers, cannot be expected to serve the interests of owners of oceanfront improvements that a wayward barge might strike.[70]

## The Difficulty of Coordinating Aggregate Awards to Worthy Change Agents

To get the incentives of enforcers right, an audience must dispense its rewards in the appropriate total amounts. If all your other neighbors already have praised you for chastising a smoker, perhaps I should refrain from doing so, or else you might start devoting too much time to antismoking campaigns. More precisely, in present-value terms, an audience's expected aggregate rewards ideally should equal the value of the social benefits that an enforcer produces. Coordinating total laurels to accomplish that equivalency is a collective action problem of the highest degree of difficulty.

Although neither McAdams's nor Eric Posner's theory provides much hope that a group could aggregate its rewards well, McAdams's is somewhat more encouraging. Esteem rewards do seem to be carefully calibrated in practice. Newspapers vary the lengths of obituaries, writers vary the heartiness of congratulatory messages, and live audiences vary the enthusiasm of their applause.[71] Rosa Parks, who challenged the segregation of public facilities in the South, and Joseph Welch, who took on Joseph McCarthy at his height, were seen as particularly heroic and accordingly received especially high levels of esteem.

If rewards take the form of future exchanges, however, as Posner's theory supposes, an enforcer's aggregate rewards invariably are poorly calibrated to induce behavior that serves the group in the aggregate. Although accomplishing a great deed is likely to signal that one is a "good type" better than merely accomplishing a good deed, trading partners still have little or no incentive to appropriately aggregate their bestowals on signalers. They act as seekers of gains from trade, not as rewarders of producers of public goods.

Under both McAdams's and Posner's theories, then, audiences are capable only of creating crude aggregate incentives. Whether this crudeness results in too much norm change, or too little, will depend on the social context.

## Sources of Inertia: Why Custom May Lag

For a variety of other reasons, however, aggregate audience rewards to worthy change agents generally tend to be too low, not too high. As a result, inefficient social norms are weeded out more slowly than they would be if transaction costs were zero.

*Cognitive Bias in Favor of the Status Quo*   An individual tends to regard the prospective loss of a given amount as more momentous than the prospective gain of an equivalent amount.[72] This loss aversion would incline audience members to withhold esteem from a challenger of the status quo in a circumstance in which they later would discover that they were pleased that the norm in dispute had been challenged. Other forces, however, may work to soften this effect. For instance, a person might earn the status of an opinion leader by showing skill in helping others overcome their status quo biases.

*The Costliness of Displacing Internalized Norms*   Internalization of a norm retards a person's receptiveness to new technical information after the norm has become obsolete. As a result, enforcers and audience members who have internalized an old norm take a longer time to appreciate the deeds of a supplier of a new and better norm.[73] When the audience has been socialized to favor the status quo, would-be change agents therefore are more cautious about challenging it.

Southern norms of dueling can serve to illustrate this point. Before the end of the Civil War, an upper-class southern male was honor bound to follow dueling rituals to resolve a dispute over a slight to his dignity.[74] Rich white southerners, fearing that black slaves might rebel against them, had more need than northerners to maintain their solidarity. Dueling rituals were constitutive norms that generally served that end.[75] The freeing of slaves after the South's loss of the Civil War eliminated many of the benefits of maintaining upper-class solidarity. This profound change triggered a norm cascade that quickly obliterated the ritual of dueling (Schwartz, Baker, and Ryan 1984, 349). It is likely, however, that dueling had become obsolete long before that time but that high transaction costs had prevented members of the southern elites from coordinating to eliminate the practice (McAdams 1997, 423–24; Schwartz, Baker, and Ryan 1984, 328–29). One reason may have been that most members of older generations had internalized the norm and therefore resisted the sporadic efforts of reform-minded legislators and members of antidueling societies to extirpate the custom (Hasen 1996, 2150).

*The Costliness of Moving Away from a Local Optimum*    The new norms scholars seem to be most concerned about are another potential source of inertia. Game theorists have established that a group may settle on an equilibrium that is less utilitarian than another because it is not in the interest of any person to be the first to move away from it.[76] In more technical language, a group may become stuck at a local optimum as opposed to the global optimum.[77] In an instance in which members of a group are aware that they have a bad norm, of course, they may be able to coordinate a move to a better norm if they can cheaply communicate and contract with one another. However, transaction costs, which presumably grow with group size, can keep a group glued to an inefficient norm.[78] In particular, if there are too few appreciative experts with the technical knowledge to recognize that the time for change has arrived, change agents may not have adequate esteem incentives to embark on the hard work of trying to trigger a cascade from the status quo.

## Perverse Reputational Cascades

To complicate matters further, another body of theory suggests that in some social circumstances norms governing fashions may not only shift too quickly but may also produce poor outcomes. The length of skirts and the width of neckties are standard examples. Eric Posner and others who view norms as signals contend that people can succumb to a negative-sum game when they jockey for status. When individuals are unable to coordinate a truce, norms may push them to engage in conspicuous consumption, to undergo cosmetic surgery, and to excessively manicure their front lawns. In these instances, change agents pursuing ephemeral personal gains promote a new fashion, and others are forced to join the bandwagon to avoid being out of step. These sorts of reputational cascades not only consume resources but also may result in fashions that are less efficient than their predecessors (E. Posner 2000 40–42).[79]

## The Debate Between the Norm Pessimists and Norm Optimists

Drawing on these potential sources of social failure, pessimistic scholars delight in putting forward examples of norms that support seemingly wasteful practices, such as dueling, foot binding, and female circumcision. None of the optimistic scholars appear to deny the possibility of social failure; rather, they stress the presence of corrective forces, such as the market for norms, that tend to spring into action after a social group has gone off track (Cooter 1994, 224–26).[80] Optimists point out that all the wasteful norms listed at the beginning of this paragraph are either dead or in decline.[81]

Debates over the efficiency of network norms further illuminate the differences between the camps. Pessimistic economists assert the obsolescence of the QWERTY keyboard, which originally was designed in part to prevent typewriter keys from colliding (David 1985). Optimistic economists, by contrast, claim that QWERTY's disadvantages are slight and that it has survived in the face of powerful corrective pressures (Liebowitz and Margolis 1990).[82] Pessimists might point to the persistence of the English system of weights and measures in the United States; optimists, to the widespread inroads of the metric system in scientific laboratories and other venues in which its advantages are greatest.

I sense that the differences between the pessimists and optimists are not as profound as they first appear. Optimists should admit that transaction costs can immunize an inefficient norm from change and that a reputational cascade at times will generate an inefficient norm. For their part, pessimists should admit that corrective social forces such as the market for norms generally tend to erode norms that are suboptimal for a group's insiders. Indeed, the more inefficient a current norm, the greater the incentives of change agents to attack it.[83]

In the end, the key difference between the two camps appears to be that the optimists have less confidence than the pessimists that a government can outperform social forces in reforming inefficient norms. It is worth reemphasizing, as well, that both optimists and pessimists generally applaud a government that uses its laws to counter group norms that are injurious to outsiders.

## Organizations and Governments as Change Agents

An individual concerned about norms need not act singly but can, rather, coordinate on either the supply or demand side through an organization such as a household, a private association, or a government. A vast social scientific literature is devoted to the comparative advantages of these various institutions (for example, Komesar 1994; Williamson 1975).

One advantage of an organization is its ability to exploit economies of scale. It also can spread risks—for example, by coordinating a number of early moves to lower the amount of opprobrium heaped on a first mover. In addition, by shortening lines of communication between the organization's members who are appreciative experts and those who are norm entrepreneurs, it can help assure the entrepreneurs that they will receive some esteem from the outset of their campaigns. A norm-change organization with prior successes may earn a reputation as a credible source of technical and social information, strengthening its social power. These advantages, taken together, may explain why organizations such as the National Association for the Advancement of Colored People, the Student Nonviolent Coordinating Committee, and the Southern Christian Leadership Conference were central in the fight against norms of racial segregation in the South.[84]

Organizations have disadvantages as well. There is the familiar risk that an agent may pursue personal, not organizational, interests. An individual's incentives when acting through an organization are especially likely to be dulled if the external rewards for successful norm innovation are uniformly spread among all organization members. An organization that pushes new norms therefore is likely to provide internal incentives to reward the agents who have done the most work. These might take the form of promotions, higher compensation, or internal esteem.[85]

## Nongovernmental Organizations as Change Agents

Many nonprofit organizations devote themselves to norm change. In one dramatic instance, sects of Christian missionaries played a central role in triggering the decline of foot binding, a custom that Chinese parents once followed to make their daughters more desirable marriage partners. In 1889, 99 percent of parents in Tinghsien were still honoring this practice. The missionaries helped create self-sustaining anti-foot-binding societies, whose ideas spread so rapidly that by 1919, foot binding had practically ceased (Picker 1997, 1284–85). Note that two different sorts of nongovernmental organizations were active in the process: the Western missionary organizations and the Chinese anti-foot-binding societies.

For-profit organizations generally are less involved in the production of public goods such as norms. Nevertheless, a business may influence informal rules when it spreads technical or social information through its advertising. An ad for a nicotine skin patch helps communicate that smoking is addictive; an ad for Virginia Slims signals that smoking is "in" among young women. Corporate measures also may influence the identity of social groups to which employees belong. A firm may sponsor a softball team and resist organization of a union. A company may pay for an executive's fee to join a local country club, a membership that would help bind the executive to local commercial society and its attendant norms.

## Governments as Change Agents

According to the Hobbesian conception, a government exercises its unrivaled power to coerce in an effort to quell free riding. This enables it not only to administer punishments that other institutions cannot but also to bestow rewards financed by compulsory taxes. These tools enable a government to provide public goods, including a legal system that enhances social order. Legal scholars traditionally have focused on the way specialized government agents produce and enforce legal rules. The new norms scholars reject this legal centralism, however, and emphasize that a state commonly also seeks to influence the norm-making process at work in civil society. At times government agents may do this directly, as various surgeons general have done in serving as norm entrepreneurs in the campaign against smoking. Alternatively, a government may act indirectly, perhaps by altering the incentives of private norm makers.

Kahan (1997), Lessig (1998), Sunstein (1996b), and the other members of the New Chicago School warm to the possibilities of government norm shaping.[86] Although cognizant of the risks of totalitarianism (Lessig 1995, 949–50 n. 19, 1016–19, 1034–44; Sunstein 1996b, 965–67), they believe that in a pluralistic society government interventions readily can be restrained to prevent excesses. The agenda of the New Chicago School invites a preliminary examination of the comparative advantages of governments in the norm-making process. It is implausible that government agents inherently possess better technical intelligence than members of "civil society."[87] Rather, the case for state involvement must rest either on the state's special capabilities as a moral educator or on its unmatched capacity to exercise force. How plausible are these arguments?

*A Government's Comparative Advantage in Changing Norms*   A normative statement by a government agent or institution might carry more inherent weight than an equivalent statement by a nongovernmental change agent. Nancy Reagan used to urge teenagers to "Just Say No" to drugs. Is there reason to believe that her views were more influential than an equivalent statement by an equally famous nongovernmental celebrity would have been? Do citizens give any deference to merely hortatory language in a statute? The new norms scholars have begun to investigate this question, which conventionally is articulated as whether law can serve an "expressive function" when it is not backed by sanctions.[88]

Cooter (1996, 1675) offers a scenario in which he anticipates that a legislature's embrace of a norm would carry special expressive weight. He supposes that a municipality has enacted a pooper-scooper ordinance that no one expects it to enforce. He argues the ordinance nevertheless might embolden a pedestrian to chastise an irresponsible dog owner because the pedestrian now could say, "Clean up. It's the law."

Members of a group are likely to follow the lead of norm makers whom they think possess more and better information than they do. On what dimensions of the pooper-scooper issue might a city resident perceive that members of the city council have superior information? It is implausible that citizens would especially respect the moral intelligence of city politicians. Indeed, opinion polls indicate that the public has a relatively low opinion of the ethics of those who hold public office.[89]

In some contexts, an ordinary person might defer to a government official's hortatory statement on the ground that the official has superior technical knowledge. A surgeon general therefore is better positioned to speak out on the dangers of cigarette smoking than a first lady is on the dangers of drugs. Informational asymmetries are hardly present, however, when the issue at hand is the removal of canine waste.

Nevertheless, Cooter's scenario is plausible because a city resident is apt to sense that local elected officials possess better social knowledge than ordinary citizens do. As McAdams (1997, 397–407) ably explains, a person who knows that a norm enjoys widespread social acceptance is more likely to be willing to support it.[90] Politicians specialize in discerning public opinion. A democratic legislature is a superior—indeed, on many issues, an unsurpassed—forum for revealing the presence or absence of a social consensus. The enactment of a pooper-scooper ordinance therefore strongly signals that there has been a norm cascade in favor of cleaning up after dogs, and this signal might embolden a pedestrian to join the bandwagon. It follows that a law that citizens perceive to be the product of special-interest lobbying (for instance, a ban on ticket scalping) would not influence the evolution of norms because it would not convey credible evidence of an underlying social consensus.

A government has a comparative advantage in norm making only in contexts in which individuals are concerned with their status among all or most members of the polity. For instance, a teenager is likely to be more responsive to a rock star's opinions about drugs than to Nancy Reagan's. A president's spouse caters to the entire national electorate, whereas a rock star caters to antiestablishment youth, a more potent reference group for most teenagers.

*How a Government Can Use Its Coercive Powers to Influence Norm Making* A government's basic norm-shaping tools are readily discerned.[91] First, government can augment the payoffs of private change agents who share its agenda and lessen the payoffs of those who do not. For instance, a government can use subsidies or tax benefits to give a financial boost to antismoking activists. Conversely, it could impose a ban or a time-place-manner regulation, backed by criminal or civil sanctions, on cigarette advertising.[92] By altering the level of tangible benefits that change agents expect to receive, these sorts of policies influence change agents' willingness to supply new norms.

Second, to speed the rate of norm change, a government can subsidize the provision of favorable technical and social information in order to influence opinion leaders and appreciative experts. Notable instances are the surgeon general's reports of 1964 and 1986, which respectively reported scientific evidence on the dangers of firsthand and secondhand smoke (Gusfield 1993, 54–60, 79).

Third, government can attempt to regulate groups as such.[93] For example, it can attempt to lessen the efficacy of an existing group, such as a youth gang, whose norm-making activity it generally disfavors. This might involve an attack on the constitutive norms (such as gang symbols) that maintain the solidarity of the group,[94] rewarding informers who divulge group strategies, enforcing legal rights of privacy that impede a group's ability to monitor its members (McAdams 1997, 424–32), and conditioning other government benefits on nonmembership in the group. Conversely, a government can strengthen a group whose norms it generally favors—for example, by funneling subsidies to individuals through it. The social influence of a religious institution grows when a government subsidizes its soup kitchens.

Finally, instead of passively accepting the boundaries of existing groups, a government can attempt to alter those boundaries to achieve its goals. As noted earlier, the enactment of the civil rights acts of the 1960s lessened the parochialism of southern whites and changed their norms. A government that engages in ethnic cleansing, by contrast, enhances both the homogeneity of its demographic groups and the parochialism of their norms.

The ethnic cleansing example should serve as a caution to the members of the New Chicago School. Even if informal norm-making is vulnerable to the social failures described earlier, it does not follow that an activist government would improve matters. Government actions commonly have unanticipated consequences. The Bolsheviks aggressively attempted to inculcate norms of selflessness and ended up dissipating Russia's scarce social capital. As Robert Clark (1989, 1732) has noted, a society that relies on norms encounters fewer risks than a society that empowers technocrats to rule by force. The basic point is that a narrow interest group cannot capture the diffuse forces of "civil society" as easily as it can the state.[95] The most serious atrocities of the Nazis, Bolsheviks, and Balkan ethnic cleansers began only after those groups had attained political power. In sum, although the state does have some special capabilities in norm making, it is also by far the most dangerous participant in that process.[96]

## Conclusion

Aware that law and social norms are complexly intertwined, legal scholars have begun to peek inside the black box of cultural change. Methodological individualists see a social norm as emerging not from a collective decision by an informal group but rather from the purposive interactions of the group's individual members. This chapter has presented a semirigorous model in which a new norm arises out of the workings of a market for norms. Change is triggered by a shift in either cost-benefit conditions or group composition. Because individuals are heterogeneous in important respects, they respond differently to these triggering events. The first persons to supply new norms generally are individuals who have either superior technical knowledge of cost-benefit conditions, superior social knowledge of group dynamics, or special endowments that provide them with unusually high tangible benefits from norm reform. Members of the social audience observe the competing efforts of these norm suppliers and reward the most meritorious ones by conferring either esteem or, according to a rival theory, new exchange opportunities. Under ideal conditions, members of the audience—the demand side of the market for norms—have no incentive to free ride in rewarding a worthy norm innovator because they incur no net costs when conferring their rewards.

The model incorporates numerous simplifying assumptions in order to render complex social phenomena more tractable. Two of the most heroic assumptions are that members of a social audience selflessly prefer utilitarian outcomes and that they can successfully coordinate the aggregate rewards they confer. Critics are invited to exploit these and other weaknesses. More broadly, it is not obvious that modeling norm making as a market process enlightens more than it distorts. I am firmly convinced, however, of the value of a theory that links norm changes with heterogeneities among individuals.

Many of the results of this chapter's analysis may seem obvious: leaders lead, followers follow, group composition matters, and so on. The reason is simple. Because each of us spends much of each day swimming in social waters, we each have a deep intuitive understanding of social phenomena. Common-law judges similarly appear to have had a good intuitive understanding of microeconomics before the time of Adam Smith. However, just as economic theory has served to deepen economic understandings, a more powerful theory of social norms should serve to sharpen social intelligence.

In particular, theory can stimulate valuable empirical work. As Ronald Coase (1960, 18–19) stresses in the foundational article in the field of law and economics, a better understanding of the human condition ultimately depends on the study of actual practices. Legal scholars, although eager to draw on others' studies of norms governing smoking, dueling, foot binding, and so on, themselves rarely undertake primary research on norms. I esteem the few, such as Lisa Bernstein, who have broken the mold and urge you to do the same.[97]

# Notes

1. There is a large literature, much of it by sociologists, on the diffusion of new ideas and practices. See, for example, Coleman, Katz, and Menzel 1966 (discussing the spread of medical innovations); Lionberger 1960 (analyzing diffusion of farm practices); Rogers 1983 (reviewing the field). Although the schol-

ars who contribute to this literature use many of the same terms that I employ ("change agent," "opinion leader," and so on), to my knowledge none of them conceives of the process as a set of interactions between a supply side and a demand side. However, compare Chong 1991, 141–64 (developing a supply-and-demand model of collective action).

2.  For a concise overview of the new norms scholarship, see McAdams 1997.

3.  On the roles of norms and law in the overall system of social control, see Ellickson 1991, 123–36. This chapter focuses on norms that constrain the actions of single individuals. No attention is given to norms that bear on the conduct of organizations of individuals—for instance, customary international law and the norms governing the internal labor markets of corporations. The new norms scholarship has had some influence on scholars investigating these complex issues. See, for example, Koh 1997; Goldsmith and Posner 1999; Rock and Wachter 1996. The dynamics of organizational behavior of course may differ from the dynamics of individual behavior; see, for example, McAdams 1995, 1014 (marshaling evidence that a team of individuals is more likely than a single individual to defect in games in an iterated prisoner's dilemma tournament).

4.  For a hypothesis that might lead to a neurobiological account of the internalization process, see Damasio 1994, 173–80.

5.  In my view, these patterns of external sanctions are the best evidence of the existence of a norm (Ellickson 1991, 128–30). However, compare Cooter 1996, 1661–66 (viewing internalization as a necessary condition for the existence of a norm).

6.  Some scholars devoted to methodological individualism have sought to enrich the simplest rational choice models of human behavior to account for limits on an individual's rationality, will power, and self-interestedness. These efforts are synthesized in Jolls, Sunstein, and Thaler 1998.

    The new norms scholars' unbending devotion to methodological individualism distinguishes them from Émile Durkheim, Karl Marx, Max Weber, and other predecessors in sociology. However, compare Tushnet 1998 (asserting that the new norms scholarship is old sociological wine in new bottles).

7.  A classic analysis is Olson 1965.

8.  Representative contributions are Kahan 1997; Lessig 1998; Sunstein 1996b.

9.  See Clark 1989, 1729 n. 58 (associating Cicero, Edmund Burke, and Friedrich Hayek with this view).

10. Norms appear in as many varieties as legal rules do (Ellickson 1991, 132–36, 184–264). This chapter mainly focuses on substantive norms, the informal rules that govern the primary behavior of actors. Procedural, remedial, and controller-selecting (jurisdictional) norms govern how enforcers carry out the process of informal sanctioning. Particularly intriguing are the constitutive norms that govern the obligations of members of a group to communicate with one another and to engage in ritual activities. Members may especially esteem persons adept at supplying their group with an ideology, that is, an account that justifies its system of norms and thereby enhances group solidarity (McAdams 1995, 1059–62).

11. Someone who confers esteem or opprobrium directly upon an actor is playing the role of an enforcer, not that of a member of the audience.

12. See text accompanying notes 43 and 44.

13. For evidence that individuals are inclined to don public-spirited hats under conducive circumstances, see Lewinsohn-Zamir 1998 and sources cited therein. See also Margolis 1982 (hypothesizing that an individual has preferences for group outcomes that are distinct from his preferences for personal outcomes).

14. By forcing an actor to take externalities into account, an enforcer may reduce the deadweight losses (unexploited gains from trade) that a group's members sustain. A new norm, however, is likely to entail transaction costs different from those of the old one. An audience with a utilitarian bias therefore would esteem an enforcer who supplied norms that served to minimize the sum of all members' deadweight losses and transaction costs. See also Roe 1996, 643–52 (discussing when path dependency leads to inefficiency).

15. See Ellickson 1991, 170–74 (inducing a hypothesis that norms tend to advance Kaldor-Hicks efficiency); Dau-Schmidt 1990, 19–22 (arguing that intentional norm shapers can pursue only Kaldor-Hicks efficiency); see also Lessig 1995, 1002–4 (discussing application of Kaldor-Hicks and Paretian criteria to norms); Sunstein 1996b, 955–56 (analyzing situations in which some gain and some lose).

16. Employing evolutionary game theory, Jonathan Bendor and Piotr Swistak (1998) assert that Pareto-deficient norms, although perhaps stable enough to survive, are less stable than Pareto-efficient norms.

17. Many norms that superficially appear to be distributive are reconcilable with utilitarian ethics. For example, norms that support selective giving of alms to the poor create an informal social insurance system that can enhance efficiency in an environment in which people are risk averse; see Ridley 1996, 85–102 (describing the universal hunter-gatherer custom of sharing meat after the successful pursuit of large game); Binmore 1998, 285–98 (offering a model that supports sharing by preliterate hunters); compare Lessig 1995, 1004–7 (discussing distributive norms).

18. The seminal analysis is Michelman 1967.

19. I have declined to allow for variations in tastes as such. However, compare Bernheim 1994, 844 (viewing nonconformists as people with extreme preferences).

20. Compare Weber 1947, 358–63 (on "charismatic authority").

21. I assume that an analyst can obtain evidence of individuals' discount rates, special intelligences, and leadership abilities by observing their behavior in domains other than the market for norms. If not, many propositions in the theory could not be tested.

22. Christine Jolls, Cass Sunstein, and Richard Thaler (1998, 1519–22) introduce the notion of an "availability entrepreneur" who seizes upon a recent event (such as toxic wastes at Love Canal) to mobilize support for a cause (such as enactment of Superfund legislation dealing with toxic wastes).

23. To illustrate: a dinner guest who has upbraided another for smoking has both expressed demand to that smoker and also supplied a norm for the other guests at the dinner table to appraise.

24. I ignore special psychological attributes and developmental histories that change agents are likely to possess. On that front, see, for example, Sulloway

1996 (demonstrating that later-born children tend to challenge the status quo more than first-borns do).

25. These distinctions cut across the distinction between actors and enforcers. For instance, a norm entrepreneur can pioneer either new patterns of behavior or new patterns of sanctioning.

    For a sampling of others' efforts to distinguish among change agents, see Lionberger 1960, 52–66 (distinguishing among "innovators," "communicators," and "influentials"); Rogers 1983, 241–346 (distinguishing among contributors according to both timing ["innovators," "early adopters," and so on] and function ["opinion leaders," "change agents," and so on]). The authors' empirical evidence about the characteristics of persons who fit these categories is largely consistent with my analysis.

26. Figure 2.2 mimics the structure of a graph appearing in Rogers 1983, 11.

27. This notion can be restated in game-theoretic terms. A self-motivated leader faces a payoff structure that encourages the leader to play cooperatively, that is, to supply the new norm; see Chong 1991, 131 (referring to an "unconditional cooperator"). An ordinary player, by contrast, faces a payoff structure that invites uncooperative play.

28. Compare the notion of a "passive leader," developed in Kuran 1998, 654.

29. Business customs, such as this one, are shaped not only by the informal exchanges but also by explicit price signals.

30. See also Picker 1997 (presenting a model in which actors are influenced by events in their "information neighborhoods").

31. This may stem either from special intellectual abilities or from special experiences, such as the travels of Marco Polo or Alexis de Tocqueville.

32. The term "opinion leader" apparently derives from Bernard Berelson, Paul Lazarsfeld, and William McPhee (1954, 109–14), who define the phrase more broadly than I do. Compare Bikhchandani, Hirshleifer, and Welch 1992, 1002–3 (stressing the role of opinion leaders in triggering changes in social practices); McAdams (1997, 416).

33. See text accompanying notes 55 to 66.

34. See also Clark 1989, 1730 nn. 59–60 (discussing the possibility that humans have an evolved biological instinct to conform to the behavior of others, particularly persons of high status).

35. See Wills 1984, 147–58 (describing Madison's recruitment efforts). Washington was not only the paramount opinion leader of the postrevolutionary era but also, on account of his wide-ranging experiences, something of a technical expert in the field of governmental structure.

36. Note that a critic such as Whitehead simultaneously both expresses demand for certain norms and also supplies evidence of enforcement behavior for audience members located at the next higher tier of social control to appraise; see text at note 23.

37. It is frequently argued that norms tend to be undersupplied because enforcers are unable to capture all the benefits of enforcement activity; see, for example, Katz 1996, 1749–50; E. Posner 1998, 792–95.

38. Some scholars have explored the way in which socialization or evolutionary processes might generate internalized norms that would induce meritorious

enforcers to reward themselves after they had served the public weal; see, for example, Bowles and Gintis 1998 (offering a model in which an enforcer obtains utility simply by enforcing a norm). My model, by contrast, generally assumes that enforcers need external rewards but that audience members do not. On the plausibility of the notion that either enforcers or audience members could be selfless, see sources cited in note 13 and text accompanying note 42.

39. "Audience" is my term, not either of theirs.

40. See also McAdams 1995; Smith [1759] 1982, 116. Compare Ridley 1996, 109–14 (describing debate among anthropologists over whether a hunter-gatherer gives food to others to obtain esteem or reciprocal gifts).

41. Apparently a number of scholars hatched this idea independently. Besides McAdams, see Sober and Wilson 1998, 144–46, 151, 166–68; Pettit 1990, 738–42; compare Cooter 1996, 1668–69 (asserting that enforcers can cheaply engage in negative gossip and ostracism).

42. Social psychologists find that most people believe that rewards should be apportioned according to the merit of individuals—the essence of so-called equity theory; see Binmore 1998, 277–78 (explaining this notion). If equity theory is sound, an audience member, in order to maintain his self-conception as a moral person, would have to esteem others who had been conferring public goods.

43. Other legal scholars have indicated a receptivity to the notion that some norms can be regarded as signals; see McAdams 1995, 1066–67; R. Posner 1998b, 553–54.

44. This statement assumes that signals in fact convey valuable information, which, under Spence's theory, they do only when there are separating (as opposed to a pooling) equilibria. It also assumes that most transactions take place in markets in which the elasticities of supply and demand enable both producers and consumers to garner some surplus.

45. Indeed, I regard both theories as highly reductive, as a beginning theory has to be.

46. See text accompanying note 71.

47. An economic change can affect the costs and benefits associated not only with primary behavior but also with the operation of the system of social control itself. The Internet might enhance, for example, an enforcer's capacity to obtain social information and an audience member's capacity to confer esteem.

48. However, compare E. Posner 1996a, 1712–13 (asserting that the tribe members may have taken two centuries to adjust their norms regarding land tenure).

49. In a related vein, economic historians partly attribute the enclosure (privatization) of medieval open fields to improvements in farm technologies and to increased demand for labor and wool; see Ellickson 1993, 1388–92. Most enclosures cannot be characterized as pure instances of norm change, however, because they were backed by governmental force.

50. Because norms themselves can affect the rate of innovation, in a more ambitious model technological change would be endogenous. However, any model must keep some variables independent. For a succinct analysis of this methodological point, see Basu, Jones, and Schlicht 1987, 3.

51. See also Bikhchandani, Hirshleifer, and Welch 1992, 1011–12 (putting the tonsillectomy example to somewhat different use).

52. I treat a change in group composition as an exogenous event. In reality, concerns about norms may affect the makeup of a group; see Sunstein 1996b, 919–20 (discussing how disgruntled persons may use the power of exit to form their own norm communities).

53. In an influential empirical study of commercial practices, Lisa Bernstein (1996) found that merchants apply end-game norms when they do not foresee the possibility of further interactions but apply more cooperative relationship-preserving norms to resolve midgame disputes.

54. See Bernstein 1992, 140, 143–44 (reporting how advances in communications can broaden the domain in which a person has reputational stakes) and Hirschman 1982 (describing the seventeenth-century view that commerce is a civilizing agent).

55. See, generally, Picker 1997, 1250–51 (illustrating the possibility of rapid norm change).

56. See also Bikhchandani, Hirshleifer, and Welch 1998 (updating the theory).

57. Some scholars suppose that humans have a hard-wired instinct to conform to the behavior of persons of high status; see note 34. If so, this instinct toward conformity could serve both as a method of cheaply acquiring information and as a way of protecting one's reputation.

58. Although all the characters in this scenario are presented as if they were distinct individuals, a person with the requisite attributes could simultaneously assume a number of these roles.

59. The evolution of norms governing smoking has received extensive attention in the legal literature; see, for example, Rabin and Sugarman 1993; Lessig 1995, 1025–34; McAdams 1997, 404–7; Sunstein 1996b, 905–6, 930, 950–51.

60. The proportion of American adults who smoke fell from 42 percent in 1955 to 26 percent in 1991 (McAdams 1997, 404 n. 219).

61. There is broad agreement that the new information about health risks arising from smoking precipitated its decline; see, for example, Gusfield 1993, 54–60; Zimring 1993, 96–99. On the history of the diffusion of scientific information about the risks of smoking, see Hanson and Logue 1998, 1181–1223 (asserting, among other things, that consumers still underestimate the risks of addiction to tobacco).

62. This is an instance of individuals coordinating to make a governmental institution into a change agent. On this topic, see text at notes 86 to 97.

63. In the early to mid-1980s, about two-thirds of men in Japan smoked, as did one-half of the men in France, and one-third of Canadian and American men (Zimring 1993, 98).

64. See Kagan and Vogel 1993, 34 (comparing smoking behavior of elites in France, Canada, and the United States); see also Kagan and Skolnick 1993, 79 (describing how "visible elites" in the United States dropped smoking).

65. Compare Lessig 1995, 1030 (playing down the impact of new scientific information on smoking norms, on the ground that smoking has a different "social meaning" in Europe from that in North America).

66. See Zimring 1993, 98 (presenting a graph depicting a drop in France from 72 to 50 percent; in the United States, from 53 to 35 percent; and in Canada, from 54 to 32 percent).

67. See also Schwartz, Baker, and Ryan 1984, 330–31 (arguing that a convention survives only if it serves a group's instrumental and symbolic goals). Sober and Wilson (1998, 10–11, 170–73) refer to this perspective, with which they largely agree, as "group functionalism."

68. See, generally, McAdams 1997, 355–75, 393–94 (analyzing how changes in information and enforcement costs would affect the evolution of norms).

69. Cooter (1996, 1655) argues, more generally, that the law's willingness to defer to a group's custom should depend on the soundness, from a lawmaker's perspective, of the incentive structures that the group's members face.

70. The tugboat example is drawn from Judge Learned Hand's famous decision in *The T. J. Hooper*, 60 F. 2d 737 (2d Cir. 1932) (holding that evidence that a firm had complied with industry custom did not conclusively prove that it had not been negligent). On the possibility that maritime customs will disserve outsiders, see *Rodi Yachts, Inc. v. National Marine, Inc.*, 984 F. 2d 880, 888 (7th Cir. 1993) (R. Posner, Judge); Epstein 1992, 4; Landes and R. Posner 1987, 132–33 (articulating the more general proposition that custom is apt to be efficient in situations in which transaction costs are low but not those in which transactions costs are high).

71. If esteem is costless to confer, as McAdams supposes, an audience conceivably could provide it in infinite quantities, which would make its receipt valueless. Any esteem theory of norms therefore has to include a conception of how members of an audience budget esteem.

72. See Rabin 1998 (reviewing evidence on this point.).

73. As McAdams (1995, 394–97) points out, a rapid cascade toward a new norm indicates that the old norm was not effectively internalized. Cascades thus are hard to square with the notion, mentioned in note 5, that internalization is a necessary condition for the existence of a norm.

74. Many of the new norms scholars have addressed dueling. Besides the sources cited in this paragraph, see, for example, Lessig 1995, 968–72; E. Posner 1996a, 1736–40.

75. This resembles the theory developed in Schwartz, Baker, and Ryan 1984. However, compare Cohen and Vandello 1998, 570 (attributing the white South's enduring "culture of honor" [which excuses self-help violence to remedy an insult] to its origins as a herding society remote from law enforcers).

76. Game theorists use the term "folk theorem" to refer to the proposition that virtually any outcome is a Nash equilibrium under conditions of repeat play. For an accessible introduction, see Rutten 1997, 1158–62. On the possibility of multiple stable equilibria in the context of norms, see Akerlof 1976; Kuran 1998, 641–46.

77. This possibility commands a wide consensus in the legal literature; see, for example, Cooter 1996, 1687–88; McAdams 1997, 409–24; E. Posner 1996a, 1711–25 (discussing a variety of reasons that norms may lag behind technological change); R. Posner 1997, 366. For an elegant demonstration of this risk when automatons engage in repeat play, see Picker 1997, 1248.

78. Note that a global optimum is more efficient than the status quo only if the reduction in deadweight losses attained by getting to the global optimum would exceed the incremental transaction costs incurred in making the move; see note 14.

79. See also Kahan 1997, 352–61 (on risks of herd behavior toward tax cheating, juvenile delinquency, and the like); Kraus 1997, 403 (drawing on Boyd and Richerson 1985, a theory of the evolution of norms); McAdams 1997, 412–24 (on this and other varieties of inefficient norms); Pesendorfer 1995 (developing a model in which cycling of fashions is wasteful); Picker 1997, 1275 (on the risk of perverse herd behaviors).

80. See, generally, McAdams 1997, 410 (describing how self-interest, voice, and exit all create pressures toward norm efficiency).

81. On the decline of female circumcision, see Barbara Crossette, "A Uganda Tribe Fights Genital Cutting," *New York Times*, July 16, 1998, A8.

82. As an optimist, I point to the rapid evolution in network norms in the recorded music industry—from 78 rpm records, to 33 rpm records, to tapes, to compact disks, to whatever the future brings.

83. My analysis implies that the sum of a change agent's tangible benefits and esteem rewards would be positively correlated with his contributions to aggregate efficiency. As noted in Cooter 1996, 1649, 1690–94, the notion that change agents disproportionately attack inefficient norms brings to mind the hypothesis, familiar to law-and-economics scholars, that litigants disproportionately challenge inefficient common-law rules.

84. In his stimulating article on norm evolution, Randal Picker (1997) envisions institutions as having a special role in "seeding" experimental norms. This conclusion, however, flows entirely from the stylized structure of Picker's computerized tournament, not from any demonstrated advantages of institutions as change agents. In Picker's tournament, enforcers are unable to invent new norms; instead, they simply mimic the best strategy that they observe at work in their "information neighborhoods" (1247). Therefore, Picker's recommendation that institutions have a special role in seeding norms rests solely on his artificial assumption that individuals are incapable of supplying new norms; compare Picker 1997, 1235 (agreeing that he has not provided a theory of the generation of new norms).

85. Jerry Rohacek (1998) analyzes the ways in which a private organization that generates public goods can provide material incentives to its activists.

86. Members of the New Chicago School share other common characteristics— notably, an appreciation of the empirical significance of norms and also an interest in behavioral economics (the approach outlined in Jolls, Sunstein, and Thaler 1998).

87. For example, when externalities are not present, tugboat operators and their shippers are better than judges and jurors at determining the safety equipment a tug should carry. See sources cited in note 70.

88. See, for example, Dau-Schmidt 1990 (primarily discussing how legal expressions can assist internalization of norms); Sunstein 1996a (primarily exploring the influence of law on behavior of actors and enforcers); see also E. Posner 1998, 793–97.

89. See The American Enterprise 1999 (reporting that in 1998 about 20 percent of Gallup poll respondents regarded the honesty and ethical standards of elected officials at all levels of government as "high" or "very high"; these ratings were above those for lawyers [14 percent] but well below those for bankers [30 percent], policemen [49 percent], and college teachers [53 percent]).

Tom Tyler (1990, 45–46) asserts that people tend to respect the law as such, even when they disagree with the morality that underlies it. Tyler's respondents, however, made highly favorable moral assessments of all six laws featured in his survey instrument (Tyler 1990, 44). Tyler's inclusion of several immoral laws might have altered his findings.

90. See also text accompanying notes 56 and 57 (sources on informational and reputational cascades).

91. For a variety of views on the appropriate scope of state regulation of norms, see McAdams 1997, 351–432; E. Posner 1996a, 1725–36; Sunstein 1996b, 948–50.

92. Some commentators urge government action to prevent wasteful arms races in signaling behavior. See Pesendorfer 1995, 786 (asserting that sumptuary legislation regulating clothing styles may enhance efficiency). However, compare E. Posner 2000, 176 (skeptically assessing proposals to tax consumption of positional goods).

93. The definitive discussion is E. Posner 1996b; see also Picker 1997, 1265–81, 1285–86.

94. See Kahan 1998, 612–15 (recommending curfews and antiloitering laws that would make it harder for a gang to signal power to teenagers); Kuran 1998 (discussing production of norms that sustain ethnic groups).

95. Some observers do suppose that powerful factions can manipulate social norms in their favor. Marx saw the "ruling class" as able to inculcate a false consciousness in the masses. Some feminist scholars see males as having dominated the norm-making process to the detriment of women. On the possibility of interest-group capture of norms, see McAdams 1997, 416; E. Posner 1996a, 1719.

96. Most law-and-economics scholars seem not to share the New Chicago School's relative confidence in the state. See, for example, Bernstein 1996, 157 (concluding that merchants' norms are superior to legal rules); Macey 1997, 1137–49; Picker 1997, 1284–88 (favoring government seeding of experimental norms but not grander governmental interventions); E. Posner 1998, 795–98 (seemingly retreating from a rosier view of state intervention expressed in E. Posner 1996a); Roe 1996, 665–66; compare Tushnet 1998, 587–88 (stating that "culture is rather resistant to conscious manipulation, particularly by law").

97. See also, for example, West 1997.

# References

Akerlof, George. 1976. "The Economics of Caste and of the Rat Race and Other Woeful Tales." *Quarterly Journal of Economics* 90(4): 599–617.

The American Enterprise. 1999. "Opinion Pulse." March–April 1999, 90.

Basu, Kaushik, Eric Jones, and Ekkehart Schlicht. 1987. "The Growth and Decay of Custom: The Role of the New Institutional Economics in Economic History." *Explorations in Economic History* 24: 1–21.

Becker, Howard S. 1963. *Outsiders: Studies in the Sociology of Deviance.* New York: Free Press.

Bendor, Jonathan, and Piotr Swistak. 1998. "The Evolution of Norms." Unpublished paper. Stanford University.

Berelson, Bernard R., Paul F. Lazarsfeld, and William N. McPhee. 1954. *Voting.* Chicago: University of Chicago Press.

Bernheim, B. Douglas. 1994. "A Theory of Conformity." *Journal of Political Economy* 102(5): 841–77.

Bernstein, Lisa. 1992. "Opting Out of the Legal System: Extralegal Contractual Relations in the Diamond Industry." *Journal of Legal Studies* 21(1): 115–57.

———. 1996. "Merchant Law in a Merchant Court." *University of Pennsylvania Law Review* 144(5): 1796–1821.

Bikhchandani, Sushil, David Hirshleifer, and Ivo Welch. 1992. "A Theory of Fads, Fashions, Custom, and Cultural Change as Informational Cascades." *Journal of Political Economy* 100: 992–1026.

———. 1998. "Learning from the Behavior of Others: Conformity, Fads, and Informational Cascades." *Journal of Economic Perspectives* 12(3): 151–70.

Binmore, Ken G. 1998. "The Evolution of Fairness Norms." *Rationality and Society* 10: 275–301.

Bowles, Samuel, and Herbert Gintis. 1998. "The Evolution of Strong Reciprocity." Unpublished paper. University of Massachusetts, Amherst.

Boyd, Robert, and Peter J. Richerson. 1985. *Culture and the Evolutionary Process.* Chicago: University of Chicago Press.

Chong, Dennis. 1991. *Collective Action and the Civil Rights Movement.* Chicago: University of Chicago Press.

Clark, Robert C. 1989. "Contracts, Elites, and Traditions in the Making of Corporate Law." *Columbia Law Review* 89: 1703–47.

Coase, Ronald H. 1960. "The Problem of Social Cost." *Journal of Law and Economics* 3: 1–44.

Cohen, Dov, and Joe Vandello. 1998. "Meanings of Violence." *Journal of Legal Studies* 27(2): 567–84.

Coleman, James S., Elihu Katz, and Herbert Menzel. 1966. *Medical Innovation: A Diffusion Study.* Indianapolis: Bobbs-Merrill.

Cooter, Robert D. 1994. "Structural Adjudication and the New Law Merchant: A Model of Decentralized Law." *International Review of Law and Economics* 14(2): 215–31.

———. 1996. "Decentralized Law for a Complex Economy: The Structural Approach to Adjudicating the New Law Merchant." *University of Pennsylvania Law Review* 144(5): 1643–96.

———. 1998. "Expressive Law and Economics." *Journal of Legal Studies* 27(2): 585–608.

Damasio, Antonio R. 1994. *Descartes' Error: Emotion, Reason, and the Human Brain.* New York: G. P. Putnam.

Dau-Schmidt, Kenneth G. 1990. "An Economic Analysis of Criminal Law as a Preference-Shaping Policy." *Duke Law Journal* 1990(1): 1–38.

David, Paul A. 1985. "Clio and the Economics of QWERTY." *American Economic Review* 75(2): 332–37.

Davis, Lance E., Richard A. Easterlin, and William N. Parker. 1972. *American Economic Growth: An Economist's History of the United States.* New York: Harper and Row.

Demsetz, Harold. 1967. "Toward a Theory of Property Rights." *American Economic Review* 57(2): 347–59.

Diamond, Jared. 1997. *Guns, Germs, and Steel.* New York: W. W. Norton.

Ellickson, Robert C. 1991. *Order Without Law.* Cambridge, Mass.: Harvard University Press.

———. 1993. "Property in Land." *Yale Law Journal* 102(6): 1315–1400.

Epstein, Richard A. 1992. "The Path to *The T. J. Hooper:* The Theory and History of Custom in the Law of Tort." *Journal of Legal Studies* 21(1): 1–38.

Goldsmith, Jack L., and Eric A. Posner. 1999. "A Theory of Customary International Law." *University of Chicago Law Review* 66(4): 1113–77.

Griliches, Zvi. 1957. "Hybrid Corn: An Exploration in the Economics of Technological Change." *Econometrica* 25(4): 501–22.

Gusfield, Joseph R. 1993. "The Social Symbolism of Smoking and Health." In *Smoking Policy: Law, Politics, and Culture*, edited by Robert L. Rabin and Stephen D. Sugarman. New York: Oxford University Press.

Hanson, John D., and Kyle D. Logue. 1998. "The Costs of Cigarettes: The Economic Case for Ex Post Incentive Regulation." *Yale Law Journal* 107(5): 1163–1361.

Hasen, Richard L. 1996. "Voting Without Law." *University of Pennsylvania Law Review* 144(5): 2135–79.

Hirschman, Albert O. 1982. "Rival Interpretations of Market Society: Civilizing, Destructive, or Feeble?" *Journal of Economic Literature* 20(4): 1463–84.

Jolls, Christine, Cass R. Sunstein, and Richard Thaler. 1998. "A Behavioral Approach to Law and Economics." *Stanford Law Review* 50(5): 1471–1550.

Kagan, Robert A., and Jerome H. Skolnick. 1993. "Banning Smoking: Compliance Without Enforcement." In *Smoking Policy: Law, Politics, and Culture*, edited by Robert L. Rabin and Stephen D. Sugarman. New York: Oxford University Press.

Kagan, Robert A., and David Vogel. 1993. "The Politics of Smoking Regulation: Canada, France, the United States." In *Smoking Policy: Law, Politics, and Culture*, edited by Robert L. Rabin and Stephen D. Sugarman. New York: Oxford University Press.

Kahan, Dan M. 1997. "Social Influence, Social Meaning, and Deterrence." *Virginia Law Review* 83(2): 349–95.

———. 1998. "Social Meaning and the Economic Analysis of Crime." *Journal of Legal Studies* 27(2): 609–22.

Katz, Avery. 1996. "Taking Private Ordering Seriously." *University of Pennsylvania Law Review* 144(5): 1745–63.

Koh, Harold. 1997. "Why Do Nations Obey International Law?" *Yale Law Journal* 106(8): 2599–2659.

Komesar, Neil K. 1994. *Imperfect Alternatives*. Chicago: University of Chicago Press.

Kraus, Jody S. 1997. "Legal Design and the Evolution of Commercial Norms." *Journal of Legal Studies* 26(2): 377–411.

Kuran, Timur. 1998. "Ethnic Norms and Their Transformation Through Reputational Cascades." *Journal of Legal Studies* 27(2): 623–59.

Kuran, Timur, and Cass R. Sunstein. 1999. "Availability Cascades and Risk Regulation." *Stanford Law Review* 51(4): 683–768.

Landes, William M., and Richard A. Posner. 1987. *The Economic Structure of Tort Law*. Cambridge, Mass.: Harvard University Press.

Lessig, Lawrence. 1995. "The Regulation of Social Meaning." *University of Chicago Law Review* 62(3): 943–1045.

———. 1998. "The New Chicago School." *Journal of Legal Studies* 27(2): 661–91.

Lewinsohn-Zamir, Daphna. 1998. "Consumer Preferences, Citizen Preferences, and the Provision of Public Goods." *Yale Law Journal* 108(2): 377–405.

Liebowitz, S. J., and Stephen E. Margolis. 1990. "The Fable of the Keys." *Journal of Law and Economics* 33(1): 1–25.

Lionberger, Herbert F. 1960. *Adoption of New Ideas and Practices*. Ames: Iowa State University Press.

Macey, Jonathon R. 1997. "Public and Private Ordering and the Production of Legitimate and Illegitimate Rules." *Cornell Law Review* 82(5): 1123–49.

Margolis, Howard. 1982. *Selfishness, Altruism, and Rationality*. New York: Cambridge University Press.

McAdams, Richard H. 1995. "Cooperation and Conflict: The Economics of Group Status Production and Race Discrimination." *Harvard Law Review* 108(5): 1003–84.

———. 1997. "The Origin, Development, and Regulation of Norms." *Michigan Law Review* 96(2): 338–433.

Michelman, Frank I. 1967. "Property, Utility, and Fairness: Comments on the Ethical Foundations of 'Just Compensation' Law." *Harvard Law Review* 80: 1165–1258.

Morriss, Andrew P. 1998. "Miners, Vigilantes, and Cattlemen: Overcoming Free Rider Problems in the Private Provision of Law." *Land and Water Law Review* 33(2): 581–696.

Olson, Mancur. 1965. *The Logic of Collective Action*. Cambridge, Mass.: Harvard University Press.

Pesendorfer, Wolfgang. 1995. "Design Innovations and Fashion Cycles." *American Economic Review* 85: 771–92.

Pettit, Philip. 1990. "*Virtus Normativa:* Rational Choice Perspectives." *Ethics* 100(4): 725–55.

Picker, Randal C. 1997. "Simple Games in a Complex World: A Generative Approach to the Adoption of Norms." *University of Chicago Law Review* 64(4): 1225–88.

Posner, Eric A. 1996a. "Law, Economics, and Inefficient Norms." *University of Pennsylvania Law Review* 144(5): 1697–1744.

———. 1996b. "The Regulation of Groups: The Influence of Legal and Non-Legal Sanctions on Collective Action." *University of Chicago Law Review* 63(1): 133–97.

———. 1998. "Symbols, Signals, and Social Norms in Politics and the Law." *Journal of Legal Studies* 27(2): 765–98.

———. 2000. *Law and Social Norms*. Cambridge, Mass.: Harvard University Press.

Posner, Richard A. 1997. "Social Norms and the Law: An Economic Approach." *American Economic Review* 87(2): 365–69.

———. 1998a. "The Problematics of Moral and Legal Theory." *Harvard Law Review* 111(7): 1637–1717.

———. 1998b. "Social Norms, Social Meaning, and Economic Analysis of Law: A Comment." *Journal of Legal Studies* 27(2): 553–65.

Rabin, Matthew. 1998. "Psychology and Economics." *Journal of Economic Literature* 36(1): 11–46.

Rabin, Robert L., and Stephen D. Sugarman, eds. 1993. *Smoking Policy: Law, Politics, and Culture*. New York: Oxford University Press.

Ridley, Matt. 1996. *The Origins of Virtue*. London: Viking.

Rock, Edward B., and Michael L. Wachter. 1996. "The Enforceability of Norms and the Employment Relationship." *University of Pennsylvania Law Review* 144(5): 1913–52.

Roe, Mark J. 1996. "Chaos and Evolution in Law and Economics." *Harvard Law Review* 109(3): 641–68.

Rogers, Everett M. 1983. *Diffusion of Innovations*. 3d ed. New York: Free Press.

Rohacek, Jerry K. 1998. "Revolutionary Armies, Labor Unions, and Free-Riders: Organization, Power, and In-Kind Benefits." *Independent Review* 3(2): 229–41.

Rutten, Andrew. 1997. "Anarchy, Order, and the Law: A Post-Hobbesian View." *Cornell Law Review* 82(5): 1150–64.

Schelling, Thomas C. 1960. *The Strategy of Conflict*. Cambridge, Mass.: Harvard University Press.

———. 1978. *Micromotives and Macrobehavior*. New York: W. W. Norton.

Schwartz, Warren F., Keith Baker, and David Ryan. 1984. "The Duel: Can These Gentlement Be Acting Efficiently." *Journal of Legal Studies* 13: 321–55.

Smith, Adam. [1759] 1982. *The Theory of Moral Sentiments,* edited by D. D. Raphael and A. L. Macfie. New York: Oxford University Press.

Sober, Elliott, and David Sloan Wilson. 1998. *Unto Others: The Evolution and Psychology of Unselfish Behavior.* Cambridge, Mass.: Harvard University Press.

Spence, A. M. 1974. *Market Signaling.* Cambridge, Mass.: Harvard University Press.

Sulloway, Frank J. 1996. *Born to Rebel: Birth Order, Family Dynamics, and Creative Lives.* New York: Pantheon Books.

Sunstein, Cass R. 1996a. "On the Expressive Function of Law." *University of Pennsylvania Law Review* 144(5): 2021–53.

———. 1996b. "Social Norms and Social Roles." *Columbia Law Review* 96(4): 903–68.

Tushnet, Mark. 1998. "'Everything Old is New Again': Early Reflections on the 'New Chicago School'" *Wisconsin Law Review* 1998(2): 579–90.

Tyler, Tom R. 1990. *Why People Obey the Law.* New Haven, Conn.: Yale University Press.

Weber, Max. 1947. *The Theory of Social and Economic Organization,* edited by Talcott Parsons, translated by A. M. Henderson and Talcott Parsons. New York: Oxford University Press.

West, Mark D. 1997. "Legal Rules and Social Norms in Japan's Secret World of Sumo." *Journal of Legal Studies* 26(1): 165–201.

Whitehead, Barbara Dafoe. 1993. "Dan Quayle Was Right: Harmful Effects of Divorce on Children." *Atlantic,* April 1993, 47–84.

Williamson, Oliver E. 1975. *Markets and Hierarchies.* New York: Free Press.

Wills, Garry. 1984. *Cincinnatus: George Washington and the Enlightenment.* Garden City, N.Y.: Doubleday.

Zimring, Franklin E. 1993. "Comparing Cigarette Policy and Illicit Drug and Alcohol Control." In *Smoking Policy: Law, Politics, and Culture,* edited by Robert L. Rabin and Stephen D. Sugarman. New York: Oxford University Press.

# 3

# NORMS IN ECONOMICS, WITH SPECIAL REFERENCE TO ECONOMIC DEVELOPMENT

*Thráinn Eggertsson*

A CULTURE, whether it is a national culture, a corporate culture, or the culture of academic economists, guides behavior through both formal rules and informal norms. Just like laws, norms reflect shared beliefs and ideas about various facets of society. Norms specify what behavior is required or, less stringently, what behavior is not allowed; and they sanction illegitimate behavior. Specialized agents of the state, such as police officials and judges, enforce laws and regulations, but norms rely on decentralized enforcement. A person who violates a norm can receive punishment in three different ways: from an actor who directly is affected by the violation, from a third party who acts to uphold community standards, and from the violator's own consciousness.

Traditional economics builds its theories on a particular model of mankind in which the actor is a rational egoist with fixed or stationary values and preferences. The economic approach is not well suited to deal with theoretical concepts such as internalization, guilt, spontaneous enforcement of community standards, and the emergence and development of social values. Although economists have mastered specialized skills for analyzing social beliefs and norms within their own framework and without relying on concepts and theories from other fields such as modern psychology, they have, in general, avoided the subject of norms. Socialization in graduate departments of economics in the United States and in many other countries imprints on young economists a norm against norms, which states that social norms are not a particularly interesting topic and, if studied at all, should be analyzed in terms of the rational egoist model. The economics profession uses efficiency arguments to justify this strategy: any softening of the hard core of economic methodology undermines research in economics, not unlike the way soft budget constraints (subsidies) undermine the economic health of enterprises and industries. A critical mass of academic economists is available to spontaneously sanction violators of the norm. The sanctions vary: the violators may receive a gentle rebuke, lose respect as serious scientists, fail to get their papers into mainstream journals, or be denied tenure.

These circumstances are changing. Two recent developments have raised the interest of the academic world in the study of norms: a renaissance of game theory and a new emphasis on the role of social institutions in structuring incentives (Coase 1937, 1960; Nelson and Winter 1982; Axelrod 1984; Williamson 1985; North 1990; Eggertsson 1990; Binmore 1994; Furubotn and Richter 1997; Drobak and Nye 1997). Traditional microeconomics, which models actors as adjusting to fixed parameters, has little to say about interactive behavior in social groups. Game theory, which studies human interactions, provides economists with tools to study various interesting aspects of norms, without violating the norm against norms. The new institutionalism in economics primarily is concerned with the role of effective rules in shaping economic behavior and emphasizes formal rules of the state and social organizations as well as social values and norms. One can say, therefore, that norms are one of the legs on which the new institutionalism stands. Furthermore, the literature is slowly trying to make a theoretical and empirical case for the importance of norms in economic growth and development. Vernon Ruttan's (1991, 276) statement that "it would be hard to find a leading scholar in the field of developmental economics who would commit herself or himself in print to the proposition that in explaining different patterns of political and economic development . . . a central variable is culture" is no longer entirely accurate.

Recent studies of economic performance increasingly go beyond the traditional focus of economics and now pay attention to norms and related social issues. Douglass North (1990) explores the linkages among ideas, institutions, and economic performance; Avner Greif (1994) analyzes the way the social structure of individualist and collectivist societies affects economic performance; Barry Weingast (1997a, 1997b) studies the contribution of the coordination of ideas about legitimate roles for the state to self-enforcing constitutional rules and to stable markets; Robert Bates, Rui de Figueiredo, and Weingast (1998) show how leaders can transform the policy agenda from economic reforms to ethnic strife by exploiting latent beliefs; Mancur Olson (1997) examines the way the environment of rulers determines their support for property rights; Robert Putnam (1993), digging deep, finds the roots of economic progress in the historical social capital of a community; Robert Barro (1997) and other pioneers of the new growth accounting literature now add various political and cultural variables to their regressions; and law-and-economics scholars are preoccupied with the relationship among laws, norms, and behavior (see "Law, Economics, and Norms" 1996).

Modern economics lacks a comprehensive theory of economic systems, but recent contributions to the "new institutional economics," or new institutional theory, may constitute the initial stage of such a research program. The new approach gives norms a central role in organizing social activities, particularly in production and exchange, and in political action. In this chapter, I review the life and death of norms from two related angles. One perspective is the struggle of scholars to account for the life cycle of norms without violating the assumptions of the rational egoist model. The other perspective concerns the place of norms in the new institutional view of the process of economic development.

If norms appear always to emerge spontaneously in social groups and efficiently solve the various problems of social interaction, economists will have little incentive to modify their theories and develop new methods of analysis to study norms. Similarly, norms are of limited interest in the study of economic development if they cannot be influenced directly or indirectly by public policy. However, economists have good reason to reconsider their theories and methods if they are unable to explain the existence and persistence of inefficient norms: norms that seem to interfere with the solutions of social problems or even block the development process. Economists need to understand such norms and examine whether policy can influence these social structures. In this chapter, I discuss a number of studies involving both efficient and inefficient norms, but running through the chapter are empirical examples from my own work on the economic history of Iceland, as well. In particular I discuss at some length a possibly inefficient "Good Samaritan" norm, which required Icelandic farmers to share hay with their neighbors, when needed, in a bad year. The norm may have been inefficient, as it probably created a strong incentive for farmers to follow a costly high-risk strategy in managing their livestock.

## Norms in the New Institutional Theory

Until recently price theory or microeconomics, the standard method of economics for analyzing market behavior, did not formally incorporate the notion that information is scarce and transactions are costly. In a world of costly information, traders need to verify (measure) the quality of the commodities they exchange and also discover their partners' motives and standards of honesty. In addition to direct transaction costs of measurement and enforcement, traders may fail to protect themselves against opportunistic behavior and outright loss of resources. If an entrepreneur who faces high probability of losses or high costs of protection decides not to invest in a particular project, then the value of an opportunity lost in this manner also is a transaction cost. Explicit recognition of the costs of information and transactions, a distinguishing feature of the new institutional analysis, directs our attention not only to problems of measurement and enforcement but also to social constructs such as reputation, trust, social values, and norms.

The new assumptions about information and transaction costs complicate previous attempts by economists to explain various norm-driven social actions, such as people's observation of religious norms, as rational behavior by calculating egotists.[1] Consider early attempts in economics to model religious behavior simply as one more item of consumption: the demand for afterlife consumption (Azzi and Ehrenberg 1975). The marketing of afterlife consumption involves high transaction costs because rational actors must verify or form rational expectations about the quality of the commodity. Afterlife consumption is not a "search good," with qualities that consumers easily can verify at the time of purchase or investment, but rather an "experience good," with high measurement costs. The proof of experience goods is in the pudding (Nelson 1970). Unless information about afterlife consumption can pass from actual users to potential buyers here on earth, rational actors cannot build up trust in the product, and the selling of afterlife consumption (and corresponding norms) should disappear from the market, according to the transaction costs approach and the rational egoist model.[2] Economists who want to be faithful to standard economic methodology but also have a strong interest in understanding the life and death of norms face a dilemma, which we can call the "materialist's dilemma." Neither of their two choices is good. Faithful economists have either to ignore important aspects of norms or to violate a norm that they internalized in graduate school: to be faithful to the rational egoist model. Of course, the preferred way to solve dilemmas is to have it both ways, and much of the discussion that follows is concerned with various creative attempts by rational choice social scientists to do just that.

In the new institutional economics the definition of norms and other institutions falls into two categories. Richard Nelson and Bhaven Sampat (forthcoming) characterize the two as the bottom-up and top-down definitions. According to the bottom-up version, norms (and other institutions) are social constraints that influence social outcomes by affecting the incentives and behavior of individuals.[3] This version defines institutions as made up of rules and their enforcement mechanisms. Formal institutions (laws and rules of private organizations) rely on specialized enforcement, but norms depend on decentralized enforcement that often is the by-product of social interaction. The top-down version begins at the level of social outcomes and defines institutions as regularities of behavior that follow from a particular structure of rules (and incentives) in some area of frequent social interaction.

The bottom-up and top-down definitions are two sides of the same coin, but their uses are different. Logically, the new institutional theory begins by defining a set of institutions and then proceeds to analyze how the corresponding set of incentives generates social outcomes. Nelson and Sampat (forthcoming) make the important point that a set of rules is a skeleton without flesh and blood—or brain. Given people's initial endowment of resources (land, labor, and capital), social outcomes are driven not only by individual preferences and rules but by the technologies known and available to the community. Furthermore, communities rely on two types of technologies: the usual production technologies, which standard economic theory discusses, that are employed to transform physical inputs into output, and social technology or social models that are used to order social relations. The corporation, the democratic state, and the tribe are products of particular social (and production) technology that reflects the available stock of knowledge. The study of how norms affect social outcomes, therefore, must be interpreted in the context of available transformation technologies and social models.

Finally, in the context of institutional analysis, it is useful to distinguish between the institutional environments of actors and social groups and their institutional arrangements. Institutional arrangements, such as market practices or organizational forms, are nested in institutional environments. Actors can, by definition, influence their institutional arrangements, but institutional environments cannot be changed; they are exogenous. The higher they are placed in the social hierarchy, the more powerful are individuals and social groups, and the greater the control they have of social institutions. The institutional environment of groups influences the type of solutions they seek to solve problems of social interaction and the effectiveness of their solutions. Norms seem to be less malleable than formal rules, and recently many economists have concluded that inefficient norms can create formidable obstacles to economic reform—for instance, in Eastern Europe and the former Soviet Union.

We are now ready to discuss different approaches that institutional analysis follows in exploring norms. The new institutional economics sees norms as often playing an important role in the process of economic development and growth, and the following discussion reflects this concern.

## Introduction to Functionalism

Perhaps the most conventional approach of economists who examine social values and norms is to interpret these phenomena in functional terms. Functionalism, which many scholars frown on as a disreputable scientific method, claims that social problems create incentives for their own solutions, and social arrangements, such as norms, then arise to satisfy this need. The sensible notion that people persist in improving their circumstances, even when they are constrained by limited information and imperfect knowledge, gives credence to functionalism. Functionalism implies that norms tend to be efficient, and the case for efficiency is relatively strong if the scholar can point to some force, such as nature or economic competition, that filters out inefficient social arrangements (Demsetz 1980).

Economic theory talks about "external effects," those that arise when actors, making a decision in a social setting, fail to consider all social costs and benefits of their actions. For instance, entrepreneurs who are not liable for whatever pollution they cause will ignore pollution costs when they make production plans. If entrepreneurs are somehow forced to bear the full cost of the pollution they cause, then, according to the jargon, producers "internalize" the external effects. Either laws or norms can be used to compel producers to internalize external effects. Perhaps the most important contribution of economics to the study of norms is the idea that norms emerge when an activity creates rising external effects. The new norms are said to have the function of internalizing these effects. The original insight usually is attributed to Harold Demsetz (1967). Demsetz's influential study uses as an illustration the case of Labradorian indigenous peoples who adopted norms of exclusive property rights in land when an external demand for furs had created incentives for individuals to wastefully exploit the beaver population in their region.[4]

In short, functional analysis explains how an exogenous impulse (foreign trade or new technology, for example) can destabilize efficient social arrangements and create new social problems. Norms somehow emerge to solve these problems. Institutional analysis has a strong interest in understanding how societies solve the basic problem of social cooperation and create enough stability to encourage various types of investments. In addition to laws, or even instead of laws, religious values and corresponding social norms may play an important role in creating order. Arguing in a classic functionalist mode, Brooks Hull and Frederick Bold (1994) theorize about the nature of societies that are likely to rely extensively on social control through religious beliefs and norms. They conclude that these are societies that have left the stage at which order is best established through personal interactions in small and relatively isolated groups but have not yet reached a social stage at which complex bureaucracies are the least-cost enforcers of order. The authors go even further, offering an explanation of why some cultures rely on both the promise of afterlife in heaven and threats of torture in hell to enforce norms of socially useful behavior, whereas other cultures emphasize only afterlife in heaven. The answer is simple. In societies in which norms based on religion carry the main burden of social control, microeconomic reasoning and the criterion of maximum effectiveness indicate that efficiency requires the use of both the carrot and the stick.[5]

## Static and Dynamic Institutional Analysis

Although functional explanations lack behavioral foundations, they can be tested empirically. In their imaginative study, Hull and Bold (1994) present the results of an empirical test of the heaven-and-hell hypothesis, in which they find support for the hypothesis.

The Hull and Bold study of religious beliefs and norms is an example of static institutional analysis because the study does not seek to explain how individuals acquire their beliefs and values and internalized norms. Instead, the authors assume, in apparent contradiction to the rational part of the rational egoist model, that actors readily take on a variety of beliefs about hell and heaven depending on how their communities want to enforce public order. Instead of presenting a theory of learning, the study, for instance, cites an author who claims that "no purely religious urge can run counter to economics and ecology for a long time" (Hull and Bold 1994, 451).

The new institutionalism spans a wide spectrum of theoretical approaches, which is likely to bewilder scholars who are used to neat paradigms.[6] These studies can be interpreted as challenges of differing intensity to functionalism and, especially, to the standard economic assumptions of rational egoistic actors with fixed preferences.[7] If we use the standard model of rational choice as a point of reference, the alternative approaches involve new assumptions about the information available to actors, the ability of actors to process information and make (optimal) decisions, the level of analysis, methods for aggregating individual decisions, and the evolution of tastes, preferences, and knowledge. These new approaches have obvious implications for studying the formation of norms, the variety of norms, and the existence and persistence of inefficient norms.

For the present purposes, I simplify and divide institutional theories into only two categories. Static institutional theory is a relatively homogeneous approach that assumes stable preferences, maximization rationality, and equilibrium—or, alternatively, relies on functionalism with "as if" maximization, or bounded rationality.[8] Dynamic institutional theory consists of a portfolio of approaches that explicitly model social learning and knowledge and employ various cognitive approaches and models of rule-governed (procedural) rationality (Knudsen 1995, 183).

Static institutional theory is unable to explain the internalization of norms, but it can analyze norms as decision rules, exogenous preferences, or external constraints. Static institutional theory usually draws on the theoretical apparatus of microeconomics and game theory and has a relative advantage in analyzing parametric or strategic decisions of actors. Dynamic theory has on its agenda the analysis of changes in knowledge, beliefs, perception, preferences, and identities but does not emphasize choice. To fully understand social outcomes we need theories that help us both to understand common knowledge and to provide ways for analyzing strategies, but such a general theory for analyzing norms and formal institutions is lacking (Katzenstein, Keohane, and Krasner 1998, 687–79).[9] Furthermore, dynamic institutional theories, although they provide important insights, have not converged on any single theory of preferences and beliefs that is appropriate for analyzing the evolution of norms and the process of economic development. A possible future for the new institutional theory may involve a division of labor between the static and dynamic branches. Dynamic analysis would seek "to understand how preferences are formed and knowledge is generated, before the exercise of instrumental rationality," which is the proper domain of static analysis (Katzenstein, Keohane, and Krasner 1998, 681).

# Thinking About Inefficient Norms: The Institutional Framework

A number of cases from the economic history of Iceland serve to illustrate my argument. Before introducing these, however, some background is required.[10] Premodern Iceland was almost entirely a rural community of farmers and their servants, who raised livestock, mostly sheep. Some 160 local communes (each consisting of about between one hundred and five hundred individuals) provided social security in a decentralized manner through a mixture of social norms and formal rules, but public order and enforcement of rules depended on norms to a high degree. The settlers of Iceland, most of whom came from Norway, colonized the country around A.D. 900, adapting regional Norwegian laws to create an unusual form of government involving the private enforcement of law (Jóhannesson 1974; Friedman 1979; Byock 1982; Miller 1990). Following a civil war, the country lost its independence in 1262, and after a relatively brief association with Norway, Iceland became a Danish dependency or colony, a status it maintained until the twentieth century. During the years of foreign rule, the Icelanders kept most of their ancient laws and local courts but were allowed to appeal cases to a higher authority in Copenhagen. Denmark did not maintain a military presence in Iceland but relied instead on a handful of (usually native) regional administrators, and the country did not have a police force.[11]

The literature generally is optimistic about the efficiency of norms and social arrangements that emerge in stable institutional environments that provide secure basic property rights. If the foundation is solid, Oliver Williamson's (1985) governance structures, Yoram Barzel's (1997) organization of markets, the informal institutions of Robert Ellickson's (1991) ranchers and farmers, and Elinor Ostrom's (1990) common pool regimes, such as those governing communal pastures or forests, tend to be wealth enhancing. For instance, in her study of small and medium-size social groups, Ostrom finds that such groups, particularly when they are stable and fairly homogeneous, have a high rate of success in maintaining efficient use of common property resources. Inefficiency is likely when a (distant) central government distorts the institutional environment of a group—either because of ignorance or because the interests of the group and the interests of the state do not coincide.

The small premodern Icelandic farming community of roughly fifty thousand individuals was an ideal setting for the emergence of efficient norms, according to most strands of institutional theory. The communes provided face-to-face interactions for small groups, the country's technology of production changed little until the nineteenth century, there was virtually no in- or out-migration, and nature was a hard taskmaster. Climatic conditions made Icelandic farming marginal, and the cost of inefficient social arrangements was high.

The new institutional literature has always recognized inefficient forms of economic organization but has usually traced such outcomes to the constraints that an institutional framework imposes on local economic actors. Typically, the search for the sources of inefficient social arrangements begins in the political domain, on the theory that political struggles or outright inability to impose political order are the major source of economic inefficiency and inefficient social norms. There is general agreement in the literature that secure property rights are a necessary condition for economic development.[12]

Attempts to explain the social foundations of secure property rights, however, test static institutional analysis to the limit. The problem concerns the inability of static analysis to explain the emergence of social values and internalized norms. Various studies, often analyzing historical cases such as the Glorious Revolution in England (North and Weingast 1989), have demonstrated, usually in the language of game theory, that secure property rights (efficient constitutional equilibrium) involve balancing the respective powers of the elite, the public, and the state. A careful look at studies that employ the rational egoist model to analyze efficient constitutional equilibrium reveals that most of these studies implicitly or explicitly rely on a prior condition. The equilibrium requires that a critical mass of the actors internalize appropriate constitutional norms, norms that define legitimate political behavior by the state. Actors must be willing to sanction the state when it violates the norms of legitimacy, even when the rights of others than themselves are under attack. Static theory is not able to explain why such norms are internalized in one community and not in another. Empirically, however, we seem to observe more constitutional stability than the theory predicts.[13]

Even in countries that achieve constitutional stability and succeed in providing a general foundation for secure property rights, the economies often are burdened with distorted institutional frameworks that give rise to inefficient economic organization and inefficient norms. I have argued elsewhere (Eggertsson 1996) that in historical Iceland the country's institutional framework blocked the development of a prosperous specialized fishing industry. To develop a full-scale fishing industry using the best contempo-rary technology, the Icelanders had no choice but to cooperate with other European nations, both to acquire capital assets and to market the output. Denmark, however, put Iceland off limits to foreigners after almost losing control of the country to English and German fishing interests in the fif-teenth and sixteenth centuries. From 1602 to 1787, the Danish Crown en-forced a royal trade monopoly with Iceland and purchased fish from Ice-landic farmers, who fished in small open boats in the winter season when the labor needs of farming were low. For various reasons, Nordic entrepre-neurs did not have an interest in exploiting the famous fishing banks off Iceland, although several other European nations maintained large fishing fleets in the area. However, foreign fishermen were not permitted to come close to the island or go ashore.[14] Rather than engage in high-productivity (and high-wage) fisheries, the Icelanders concentrated on marginal, subarc-tic farming and suffered recurrent episodes of mass starvation, some of the worst in the European experience.

The isolation of the country from contacts with outsiders suited local landowners, who feared competition for the country's labor force from a strong fishing industry. To prevent the development of coastal villages, throughout the premodern period all individuals were required to live on farms, and court records show that local leaders sought to ban technologi-cal innovations, such as lines with many hooks (setlines), in the primitive coastal fisheries. Beliefs and social values that portrayed life off the farm as dangerous and immoral nourished the inefficient profarming norms that supported this order.

The Crown abolished the royal trade monopoly in 1787 and permitted the Icelanders to trade with all citizens in the Danish kingdom, but it was not until after 1855, when Denmark lifted all restrictions on foreign trade, that a modern fishing industry took off, rapidly becoming the country's engine of growth. For the study of norms and institutional change, it is interesting to note that these adjustments in the institutional framework generated economic incentives that were strong enough to encourage norm (and law) violators to bring about structural change by moving out of agri-culture.[15] Some of the laws and regulations requiring people to live on the farm remained in effect into the early twentieth century. Although already in the nineteenth century there were enough norm violators in the country to initiate the modernization phase, the internal sanctions of prorural norms had not lost all their bite. For instance, in the first half of the twen-tieth century, Icelandic literature was preoccupied with the struggle be-tween farm and urban values and the guilt of those who betrayed the countryside—and the extreme poverty of Icelandic farming.

The history of antiurban norms in Iceland illustrates well why static analysis based on the rational egoist model has survived competition with other modes of analysis. The static approach explains the origin and demise of the norms in terms of the material interests of the powerful land-owners and their tenants. There is no need to appeal to changing values and individual preferences. The antiurban norms are informal rules imposed by landlords on tenants and farm laborers to secure cheap labor. Furthermore, the ban on trading with foreigners (other than representatives of the Danish Crown) prevented free riding among the landlords, who otherwise might have been tempted to invest in full-time fishing operations and use state-of-the-art technology. The introduction of free trade sharply increased the gains from violating antiurban norms, which became soft constraints that norm violators ignored in their search for material gains.

## Thinking About Inefficient Norms: Inefficient Institutional Arrangements

I have already mentioned the presumption in institutional analysis that small, homogeneous groups and competitive business environments usually are able to develop efficient private rules and norms to organize their affairs (Cooter 1996). The implication for policy is that the state should provide communities with secure property rights and let social groups develop their own detailed rules. Later, perhaps, the state can solidify such private institutions by enacting them into law.

There are exceptions to this view. Joseph Stiglitz (1994) has argued that information problems (such as moral hazard and adverse selection) sometimes undermine the ability of private groups to organize their affairs efficiently. Information problems can even push certain activities, such as some insurance services, off the market. When the market does not supply them, these services and commodities sometimes are provided in a relatively costly manner in small social groups, which activate norms and social sanctions, for instance, to deal with people's propensity to cheat. Stiglitz contends that the state either should organize these troubled activities or regulate them through industry-specific rules. Of course, the state's success in improving the provision of a commodity or a service depends on its capacity to cope with the relevant information problems, which now also include problems with perverse incentives in state agencies.

Eric Posner (1996a) discusses the relative capacity of norms, statutes, and customary law in solving social dilemmas of cooperation and coordination and vigorously argues that norms often produce less efficient outcomes than statutes and customary law. Using game theory analogies, he suggests, for instance, that social groups that rely on norms rather than laws often depend on appropriate focal points to reach efficient outcomes. In other words, the strategies chosen by the actors depend on various cultural factors, and such points of coordination are historical accidents. Laws need not depend on the existence of appropriate focal points. Posner also points out that dispersed social groups, although they may be well informed about local conditions, are often poorly prepared to evaluate changes in external circumstances, such as technological change. The groups therefore may fail to adjust their norms to the new conditions. Judges and legislators have better access to specialists and to aggregate sources of information than various social groups. Furthermore, in some circumstances social sanctions are less efficient methods of enforcement than the police and the courts. Finally, a closely knit social group is likely to ignore various costs and benefits (external effects) that its activities create for other groups, whereas courts and legislatures usually take a more inclusive view.

No matter which side we take in this debate, it is clear that the mix of norms, statutes, and judicial laws affect economic outcomes. Furthermore, it is by no means obvious that social forces always adjust the mix of institutions to ensure maximum welfare for the affected social groups. Avery Katz (1996, 1754) notes that Ronald Coase (1937, 1960) casts institutional policy as a search for a second-best solution in a world of transaction costs in which policy makers choose between markets, business firms, and government agencies.[16] Katz argues that reliance on private groups and their norms is a fourth way to allocate resources: "Such groups are structurally different from markets, business firms, and government agencies; they face different constraints and use different procedures for making rules. Thus they will have different transaction costs and will be better suited to solving certain sorts of allocation problems and worse suited to solving others" (Katz 1996, 1774–75).

This new dimension of social organization further complicates the study of norms and institutional analysis, and there is yet another complication. Evaluations should not focus on individual institutions or rules but ought instead to compare interrelated bundles of arrangements, such as a set of norms, laws, and enforcement mechanisms. In the case of norms, Ellickson (1994) points out that systems of norms mimic legal systems (or vice versa): some norms govern substantive entitlements, other norms govern remedies and procedures; and there are controller-selecting rules that specify for each type of activity how to achieve social order. In some circumstances control-selecting norms even forbid a grievant from using the legal system (Ellickson 1994, 98).

In a previous study (Eggertsson 1998b), I have tried to evaluate the effectiveness of the system of social security in premodern Iceland, which, although based on ancient laws, relied on norms of mutual help. Under these arrangements, individuals or families who had suffered some misfortune could appeal to the leaders of their communes for help. The members of the commune would share food and housing with the needy, the degree of support determined by the wealth of each contributing household. The system, which was a primitive farming society's substitute for an insurance market or a welfare state, generally appears to have functioned well, often under difficult circumstances. This welfare system, however, could not cope with nationwide or regional catastrophes that required central coordination, which did not exist. Furthermore, the historical evidence reveals, perhaps not surprisingly, that well-off heads of households were preoccupied with the possibility of free riding by the poor. They feared that the system might give some people an incentive not to work or even motivate them to undertake risky ventures and count on help from the commune when their projects failed.

In evaluating the Icelandic communal system, I consulted the theoretical and empirical literature on risk management in traditional agricultural and farm communities (Eggertsson 1998b). The Icelandic solution was in many ways similar to methods used at present in some developing countries. The literature explains the structures of these informal insurance arrangements in functional terms, relating the arrangements to the type of risks involved and to the nature of measurement and enforcement required to control cheating. However, complex interactions between components of a social system make it difficult to account for the full effects of particular institutional arrangements. Particularly suspect in the Icelandic case was a Good Samaritan norm of sharing, which required farmers to share surplus fodder (hay) with their neighbors.

From early on, the Icelandic system created disincentives for storing hay. The law that introduced the tithe in 1096, and was the first substantive instance of taxation in the country, treated hay reserves as taxable wealth if the reserves were more than one year old. A law dating from 1281 gave farmers no choice but to sell surplus hay to their neighbors on request, at a fixed price. Those who resisted selling their hay had virtually no rights.[17] The evidence does not tell us whether the law simply codified an already prevailing norm of sharing or whether the law created such a norm, but it is hard to believe that the law was out of touch with current values and practices. Evidence from the centuries that followed the legislation show clearly that the farming community observed a strong hay-sharing norm.

In historical Iceland fluctuations in temperatures were a major source of risk. Relative cooling of the climate, a random event, could merge winter and summer, shorten the maximum period of outdoor grazing, and result in meager crops of hay in the fall. The farmers could self-insure against such events through a long-term strategy of storing hay and by planning for not one but several annual farming cycles. It is clear, however, that the norm of sharing deprived farmers of exclusive property rights in surplus hay. Those who were relatively well supplied with fodder could be forced to share their hay in late winter and early spring, even before it was clear whether they themselves would have enough fodder that year, if summer were to come much later than the community expected. Furthermore, they were deprived of stores for future years. Whatever the reason, it is clear from the evidence that Icelandic farmers did not self-insure against temperature fluctuations through long-term storage of fodder. In hard years, even as late as the beginning of the twentieth century, a substantial portion of the country's livestock periodically starved to death.[18]

Already in the seventeenth century reformers strenuously argued in writing that failure to store fodder was an important cause of recurrent crisis in the Icelandic community. I have not found any record of actual enforcement through the legal system of the law of 1281, but there is much evidence of a strong Good Samaritan norm. For instance, in 1806, when a royal decree abolished the hay-sharing law, the farmers did not change their behavior and introduce storage and long-term livestock management. In the nineteenth century, as in previous centuries, farmers who needed fodder turned to their neighbors. Contemporary accounts of exchanges of hay show that late or no payment was a relatively mild offense that did not cause serious loss of reputation, but breach of contract in the purchase of sheep and horses was considered a major offense (Eggertsson 1998b, 22).

The effort to undermine the hay-sharing norm and introduce long-term storage of fodder was led by Icelandic experts and intellectuals who had taken their education abroad, especially in Denmark, and by agents of the government—in 1770 and 1771, for instance, by a high-level royal commission. Copenhagen appointed the commission to find solutions to the country's economic ills following a near collapse of the country's economy. Some of the commission's many recommendations aimed at improving livestock management by requiring public control of the size of livestock herds on each farm, punishment for farmers whose flocks exceeded prescribed numbers, and central stores of hays managed by community leaders.[19] When Denmark gave the Icelandic national assembly the right to pass laws concerning internal affairs, in 1874, several bills dealing with the provision of fodder and prudent management of livestock were almost immediately introduced and passed into law (Eggertsson 1998b, 19). These laws had no impact, and the evidence shows that local authorities did not enforce them. The farming community's lack of interest in new forms of livestock management is a puzzling issue and raises questions both about the durability of the hay-sharing norm and about the ability of reformers and governments to undermine norms. Many of my readers probably refuse to believe that generations of Icelandic farmers—after living in the country for hundreds of years, using the same technology and engaging in the same type of farming—failed to remedy a critical source of inefficiency in farm management. In my earlier study (Eggertsson 1998b), I was able to establish that experts and higher authorities in Iceland and Denmark favored long-term livestock management and storage;[20] in a technical sense, the farming community was capable of stabilizing herd size through storage; and farmers and local communes favored the status quo and ignored attempts to impose storage plans from the top down. Assuming that the farmers desired greater output and more security, I can think of four possible reasons why Icelandic farmers generally refused to trim their livestock and store hay to meet the demands of hard years.

First, because of bounded rationality or lack of information, the farmers wrongly evaluated their circumstances and followed an inefficient decision rule. Second, although the farmers recognized that their livestock strategy was inefficient, they could not find ways to cooperate and set up an alternative approach; that is, the problem involved a failure of collective action. Third, the values behind the general norm of sharing, which supported the country's system of social security and made possible the sharing of food and housing for the human population, could not be truncated to exclude the sharing of animal fodder. Sharing of hay may have been inefficient, but human psychology excludes segmentation of closely related values, and the hay-sharing norm can be interpreted as a cost or an undesirable side effect of the country's overall system of social security. Given that superior forms of organizing social security were not available to premodern Iceland, the system as a whole was efficient. Fourth, the livestock-hay strategy of the farmers was efficient in itself. In Iceland's unstable environment, the best economic strategy for farmers was to live for the moment rather than engage in long-term planning of livestock. Farmers maximized their wealth and welfare by raising the largest possible flocks of sheep in good years, relying on neighbors for fodder in individual emergencies such as fires.[21] The high-risk strategy involved losing most of the flock in hard years, but the farmers then would start the cycle again or, in the worst case, give up farming and become farm laborers. The strategy was a risk worth taking.

As it turns out, static institutional theory and the available historical evidence do not allow us decisively to select any one of these possible explanations, but according to the static view the last explanation is the most likely or acceptable one. Static institutional analysis based on the rational egoist model does not recognize decision errors, limits on rationality, or indivisible or lumpy moral values as valid explanations. The notion that the farmers were trapped in an inefficient equilibrium and unable to find a better solution because of problems with collective action is implausible: the state repeatedly tried to provide the necessary leadership, but the community did not cooperate. This fourth possibility, namely that periodic mass losses of livestock through starvation was economically efficient for the farmers, is not convincing to me, however, and it was not convincing to many of the best-educated contemporaries and specialists of the premodern period. However, I have not found a way to refute the hypothesis statistically—for instance, by calculating the rates of returns associated with storage and nonstorage strategies. In my mind, the most likely explanations seem to require modification of the rational egoist model. I am inclined to see the farmers' behavior either as reflecting bounded rationality and an inability or unwillingness to experiment with new strategies or (not unrelated) as an undesirable side-effect of the informal social security system, which was based on sharing.

Consider now some of the methods that the government of a country can use to promote public policy by undermining undesirable norms. The success of such measures depends on their impact on what Eric Posner (1996b, 137–44) calls the "cooperation-defection differential" of potential norm violators. The differential compares the net gains from observing a norm and the net gains from violating the norm. If the net gains from violating a norm become greater than the net gains from observing it, then a rational actor will abandon the norm. In a rational calculus the net gains from observing a norm include all benefits from social cooperation that the actor attributes to the norm less the actor's costs of helping to enforce the norm. Net gains from violating a norm include the value of the best available alternative but allow for the punishment costs that a violator should expect. When a positive cooperation-defection differential begins to shrink, actors initially may attempt to restore the differential by no longer participating in costly enforcement of the norm, though they themselves still observe the substantive norm. When the differential becomes negative, rational actors no longer observe the norm, and the social routines that the norm supports no longer are sustainable.

The cooperation-defection differential illustrates the possible directions that government policy can take when the authorities want to uproot an inefficient norm (Posner 1996a, 1728–36). The aim of such policy is to turn a positive differential into a negative one. For this purpose the policy can seek to lower perceptions of direct benefits from the social routine that the norm supports; raise the costs to norm followers of enforcing the norm in their group; lower punishment costs for those who violate the norm; or provide attractive alternative social arrangements to compete with those supported by the norm.

In the Icelandic case the social routine that the authorities sought to encourage was a strategy of long-term storage of fodder and systematic livestock management over several agricultural cycles. To undermine the norm that appeared to interfere with storage, the government and reformers explored almost every possible dimension.[22] To lower punishment costs for norm violators, the authorities tried to make individual farmers legally responsible for satisfactorily feeding their animals. If lack of hay in midwinter officially is defined as negligence, the cost of refusing to honor the norm of sharing might be reduced somewhat. A royal decree issued in Copenhagen in 1746 instructed local authorities to monitor their farmers' hay reserves and ensure that their supplies were adequate. In fact, official recommendations, rules, and laws going back at least to 1702 and extending to the end of the nineteenth century followed a similar line. Probably the best known of these attempts is the so-called Starvation Act of 1884, which imposed fines on farmers if they ignored recommendations by communal authorities concerning appropriate hay reserves and starved their animals. An 1889 revision of the Starvation Act provided for imprisonment of offenders in extreme cases. Historians agree that all these attempts, spanning at least two centuries, were ignored by farmers and local enforcement officials alike (Eggertsson 1998b, 19–20).

In addition to trying to lower the cost of violating the norm, the authorities and reformers used propaganda and publicity campaigns in an attempt to make the farmers reevaluate the net benefits of their high-risk strategy and follow an alternative strategy. These attempts also did not succeed; the farmers showed no signs of wanting to give up their game against nature.

Finally, government policy can make the cooperation-defection differential negative by creating (perhaps through subsidies) social arrangements that are superior to the old norm-supported arrangements. If successful, the new system can make the old norm immaterial. The Icelandic solution, which in the first part of the twentieth century both stabilized the country's livestock and undermined the hay-sharing norm, belongs to this category. The new system was one of a centralized (rather than individual or local) storage arrangement, and the initiative came from the national legislature, the central government, and a new national association of farmers. The program received substantial financial support from the central government and relied on new technology and new industrial organization in Iceland. The country's system of communications—on land, in the air, and on sea—had improved, a modern fishing industry provided fishmeal as fodder, and imported supplies now were available on short notice.

## Building Bridges Between Static and Dynamic Theories of Norms

In the discussion of the hay-sharing norm in Iceland, I mentioned two explanations of its existence that are not consistent with the rational egoist version of static institutional theory. One of these explanations implies lack of knowledge about the best farming strategy; the other involves the psychological dimensions of altruism.

Altruism is consistent with the rational part of the rational egoist model, although many economists argue that the unconstrained addition of new preferences makes it possible to explain almost any form of behavior, but at the cost of draining the theory of any substance. The hypothesis that some unspecified behavioral laws made it impossible for farmers in premodern Iceland to be egoistic about sharing fodder, once they had become altruistic about sharing food and housing with their neighbors, is a prime example of the ad hoc speculations that these critics abhor. Such criticism would not be valid if the conjecture were supported by a theory of prefer-ence formation with testable empirical content—supported, that is, by a sound dynamic theory.

The hypothesis that Icelandic farmers lacked knowledge about appro-priate farming methods immediately takes us outside the rational choice framework. Static institutional analysis readily recognizes that information is scarce, that agents invest in costly acts of measurement and other collec-tion of data but usually do not acquire full information, and that they adapt norms and other social arrangements to lower the costs of transact-ing. Static analysis, however, does not recognize that the actors lack knowl-edge of the structure of their environment—for instance, that lack of knowledge about their environment led Icelandic farmers to engage in a high-risk strategy of livestock management.

Dynamic institutional theory is concerned with the question of how actors acquire knowledge, both normative and positive knowledge, about their social and technical environments. A dynamic approach attempts to do one or more of the following: modify the extreme rational choice model and, for instance, allow for rule-following behavior and learning; explain how actors form preferences and adopt norms; and develop a theory of knowledge that allows for variation in people's subjective models of reality. The lines of demarcation between information and knowledge and be-tween static and dynamic theory are fuzzy, but roughly we can associate knowledge with theoretical models that actors use to interpret information. Different models can give different interpretations of the same data or in-formation. In terms of classical game theory, dynamic analysis attempts to explain the structure of the game, whereas static analysis takes the struc-ture of the game as given and studies how actors play within the given structure.[23]

The search for a dynamic social theory that is based on individual behavior is a diverse, multidisciplinary, and often uncoordinated research program, which still has not produced a generally accepted approach. Many scholars who believe that moral force is an essential feature of most norms and that ideas often drive social action claim that dynamic institu-tional analysis has not produced a psychological theory that explains why people sometimes feel an emotional or psychological compulsion to follow norms (Posner 1996a, 1709–10).[24] Other scholars argue that psychologists and cognitive scientists have developed rich and useful theories of mental models, internalization of norms, and learning (Denzau and North 1994; Cooter 1996, 1661–62; Clark 1998).

Perhaps the most obvious explanation of limited interactions between dynamic and static analysis is that the two approaches typically use differ-ent time frames or different levels of analysis. Evolutionary theories (espe-cially biology-based theories) frequently take a very long view that usually does not overlap with the time frame of problems that interest economists.

To specialists in economic development, psychological and cognitive theories that emphasize misperceptions, addictions, rules of thumb, and routines seem to operate at a level of analysis that is not helpful for explaining why some countries are rich and others are poor.[25] Finally, even if we grant that ideas are a driving force in human affairs, new ideas flow from human imagination and creativity and appear to be of unpredictable magnitudes. In that case, the best we can do is to study the impact of new ideas and their dissemination in society. For instance in the Icelandic case we might want to study why new (and foreign) ideas about storage and livestock planning failed to take root.

The most urgent task in this area is to build bridges between static and dynamic theory. Perhaps the most obvious way to begin such a task is to work on the fuzzy interface between static and dynamic approaches: the interface between information and knowledge. The study of economic development would benefit if we would direct our attention to the variation among social groups in their models of social arrangements and to the processes that update these models. Norms, being rules of conduct, clearly must depend on the way people model both their world and the consequences of alternative rules of conduct. Static analysis usually proceeds by assuming that variations in social arrangements, ranging from laissez-faire markets, through African socialism, to soviet central management, reflect different material interests and the relative power of key players. All actors have common knowledge of the proper structure of the economic and social world, which usually corresponds to the worldview of the analysts themselves. The history of the twentieth century, however, leaves little doubt that the evolution of normative and positive ideas about social relationships and social technologies are independent forces in economic development. In modern history, there have been genuine doubts and changes of heart about issues such as the effectiveness of the gold standard, central planning, state enterprise, free international trade, unregulated industries, and the causes of corruption and crimes (Eggertsson 1997).

Again, consider the case of Iceland, and now the early modern period. The early modern period saw gradual erosion of the norms of sharing in farming, as well as norms against specializing in nonfarming activities, but still there is evidence that lingering farm values and norms delayed the process of modernization in the late nineteenth and early twentieth centuries (Eggertsson 1998a). When Iceland eventually gained independence from Denmark, the political parties adopted and fought over three contrasting social models: the capitalist-entrepreneurial model, the socialist (including the Marxist) model, and the traditionalist model, or so it appears. The traditionalist model saw the Industrial Revolution as a perverse historical development that might bring a temporary increase in wealth. In the long run, industrialization, with concomitant factory work and city living, would undermine the social fabric and lead to economic decline. Traditionalists called for an agricultural rather than industrial revolution, rural rather than urban living, regulated international trade, and strict control of foreign investments. Traditionalists approved of small-scale manufacturing only in rural areas, particularly if the activities, like the old fisheries, somehow were integrated with large-scale farming.

Recent studies of the political history of Iceland in the last quarter of the nineteenth century and the first half of the twentieth century show that traditionalism influenced not only parties that explicitly were farm oriented but also all parties, from left to right, across the political spectrum. Ólafur Ásgeirsson (1988) suggests that the fundamental divide in Icelandic politics was not the usual divide between capitalists and socialists but rather the one that set capitalists and socialists against traditionalists. All the political parties were split along traditionalist and nontraditionalist lines, and traditionalists in all parties cooperated, sometimes by reaching across political parties to join in coalition governments, in an effort to delay urbanization and industrialization.[26] The traditionalists, building on rural values and norms, succeeded in retarding the development process by several decades—for instance, by blocking investments in large hydroelectric power plants, aluminum smelters, and railways.[27]

How do elites acquire or choose particular models of economic development and the various related norms? Sun-Ki Chai (1998, 282) takes a step toward answering this question by attempting to explain the "striking relationship between an experience with Western colonialism and a tendency toward state economic intervention" in countries that recently have broken away from colonial rule. Just as in Iceland, leaders of newly independent countries faced a range of foreign models of social and economic development. Tests of contending social models are seldom unambiguous, and ambiguity permits different interpretations. Fundamental choice of policy depends not only on political processes and the power of organized interests but also on the appeal of alternative social models. Chai argues that in the former Western colonies, well-understood psychological processes, which he discusses, led to internalization of "opposition ideologies" and motivated the rulers' initial choice of social models. The opposition ideologies were attempts at homegrown policies that differed from those of the former masters. According to Chai's study, developing countries that had not experienced colonial rule did not go through a similar phase of opposition ideologies and policies in the postwar period.

Whether or not one agrees with his theory and conclusions, Chai's study is an interesting attempt to bridge dynamic and static analysis and combine the analytical levels of personality and society. Theories that recognize a psychological base for social models, values, and norms suggest that knowledge of these psychological mechanisms could be used to manipulate norms and social values for the purposes of public policy. Rulers, of course, regularly make such attempts but with varying success, as can be seen in the case of the hay-sharing norm in Iceland. In social groups, prevailing models, values, and norms often have deep historical roots, and these constructs filter information in a particular way, creating a corresponding set of incentives and behavior. Knowledge of the social structures can enable a ruler to change behavior by manipulating events and the flow of information to the group. The study of such manipulation of events and information explores what I refer to as the fuzzy interface between information and knowledge. Even if scholars cannot explain how subjective beliefs and social models emerge, they may be able to analyze how leaders exploit these social structures.

Bates, de Figueiredo and Weingast (1998) attempt this task by analyzing political manipulation of events in terms of rational choice theory under risk and by portraying the updating of prior beliefs as being consistent with Bayes' rule.[28] Their study uses two cases as illustration: the overthrow of the United Independence Party in Zambia in 1991 and the outbreak of ethnic tension and violence in the former Yugoslavia. The study describes President Slobodan Milosevic's attempt to save his political skin by playing on latent beliefs, ethnic values, and norms in the former Yugoslavia and shifting preferences around from postcommunist economic reforms to ethnification.

The Bates, de Figueiredo, and Weingast study provides fascinating insights, but, as the authors recognize, their story is not complete because of the static (that is, rational choice) nature of their analysis. In the Yugoslavian case, for instance, the players observe only actual events—and corresponding pieces of information for updating their beliefs—that are associated with the equilibrium path. Yet equilibrium behavior depends also on expected values of outcomes that never happen. Behavior along the equilibrium path can be analyzed using Bayes' rule, whereas behavior off the equilibrium path cannot (Bates, de Figueiredo, and Weingast 1998, 627). In other words, according to Bayes' rule, rational actors adjust their beliefs after observing what they consider to be actual events or actions but not "perception, debates, persuasion, influence, and rhetoric: these processes rather than rational decision making and experience, govern the calculations that inform the choice of strategies off the equilibrium path" (628).

One of the most important unfinished tasks of dynamic analysis is to begin to employ the concept of rule-following behavior. The Bates, de Figueiredo, and Weingast study can be seen as a valiant but not entirely successful contribution toward that task. Viktor Vanberg has sought to reconcile rational choice and rule-following behavior; citing work by Friedrich Hayek, Karl Popper, Ronald Heiner, and Brian Arthur, he reinterprets rational action as rule following. Learning and rule following are two sides of the same coin. In a complex world, actors "do not, and cannot, respond to the full complexity of each and every particular problem situation they confront. Instead they rely on simplifying mental models that reflect past experience and are adjusted in response to new experience" (Vanberg 1998, 432). Vanberg's rule-following behavior also is consistent with Nelson and Sampat's (1998) concept of routinized social technologies, which are procedures that knowledgeable actors undertake—channeled choices, behavioral patterns that reflect both applied knowledge and, in the background, social rules (institutions). The notion of social technologies is an attempt to make institutions an integral part of economic growth theory and thereby to go beyond the concept of institutions as rules or constraints.

The well-known empirical studies by Geert Hofstede (1980, 1991, 1998) nicely support the concept of social technologies and illustrate how variation in social technology affects behavior and outcomes. Hofstede identifies five dimensions of cultural differences (values and norms) among business personnel of different nationalities and defines the social models of these groups as the collective programming of the mind. A considerable literature has emerged that examines the way business organization varies with national character (for example, Folta and Ferrier 1996). Hofstede sees a particular way of doing business as reflecting both the constraints of local rules and the social knowledge of a community. The high-risk strategy that farmers in premodern Iceland followed in livestock management was set in a context of local rules and particular social knowledge. Their strategy was a Hofstede business organization structured by the local culture. Following Nelson and Sampat (forthcoming), we also can characterize the strategy as a (sticky) social technology. These concepts make us aware of the importance of variation in social models; they do not, however, help us understand change, which returns us to the task of building bridges between static and dynamic analysis.

# Notes

1. The economics of religion is a small but interesting field within economics (Iannaccone 1998; Hardin 1997). These studies, which dig into religion with market metaphors and analyze churches as firms or clubs, show that factors such as the opportunity cost of time explain differences in religious observance by age and sex, timing of religious switches, and the frequency of same-religion marriages. The approach explicitly or implicitly recognizes the prior existence of religious norms but treats them as any other preferences, such as preferences for tea or coffee. People respond to changes in the relative prices (and costs) of observing religious norms by changing their religious behavior. Although this approach has had considerable success in explaining differences in the average religious behavior of various social groups, the approach apparently is not well suited to explain surges of religious activity. Laurence Iannaccone (1998, 1467) concludes that narrow economic analysis has problems explaining "the resurgence of evangelical Christianity in the United States, the rise of Islamic fundamentalism in the Middle East, the explosive growth of Protestantism in Latin America, the religious ferment in Eastern Europe and the former Soviet Union, [and] the role of religion in political conflict world wide."

2. The theory says that all experience goods will disappear from the market unless producers make a credible commitment to the quality of the products. For instance, if producers have invested large sums in developing a brand name for an experience good, the brand-name capital is lost if experience shows that the product is of a much lower quality than that advertised. If rational buyers calculate that a producer's gains from cheating are less than the associated loss of brand-name capital, they trust the advertised quality of the commodity and are ready to buy it. Such an argument does not apply to afterlife consumption, unless disappointed buyers are somehow able to pass on their experience to prospective buyers.

3. Essentially there are three types of institutional constraints: rules of the state, rules of private organizations, and informal rules or norms.

4. Posner (1996a, 1712–13) maintains that Eleanor Leacock's data, which Demsetz uses, suggest that property rights emerged in the middle of the eighteenth century and fur trading "had reached significant proportions by the middle of the 1500s. Thus the efficient norm may have lagged by *two centuries.*"

5. Maximum effectiveness in using religion to encourage socially efficient behavior requires that the promises of heaven be increased and the tortures of hell modified until a balance is struck. The balance requires that the last embellishment of heaven and the last addition to the tortures of hell have equal corrective impact on behavior. In other words, society invests in both forms of control until the last block of investment in each method gives the same rate of return. The analysis assumes that additional threats or additional promises have a decreasing impact on behavior, and it further assumes that people give finite (rather than infinite) values to prospects of eternal afterlife pain or pleasure.

6. In economics, the current revival of interest in norms and other institutions emerged as a response to the lack of a theory of business and market organization in mainstream economics (Coase 1937). The new institutionalism has generated approaches that have strong, weak, or nonexistent ties to the standard paradigm of economics (Putterman 1988). Knudsen (1995), studying different approaches to business organization, identifies the following approaches: traditional microeconomics, modern industrial organization analysis, managerialism, principal-agent models, behavioralism, the nexus-of-contract view, Williamson's transaction-cost economics, Nelson and Winter's evolutionary paradigm, and knowledge-based theories.

7. Although the new institutionalism in economics borrows from the other social science disciplines, it is also a source of ideas for them. See Miller 1997 and "Views and Comments on the 'New Institutionalism'" 1998.

8. Scholars often use the concept of "as if" maximization to avoid explaining individual decisions and collective choice. They simply claim that certain social outcomes occur "as if" purposive individual maximization has taken place. According to this approach, efficient selection mechanisms (nature or some type of competition) might have produced these outcomes.

9. Katzenstein and colleagues, in a thoughtful review of research in *International Political Economy,* identify the same basic dichotomy in that field. The field of international political economy emerged in the 1970s and introduced economic methods to the study of international politics (see Katzenstein, Keohane, and Krasner 1998, 673). The school of static analysis in international political econ-

omy has been criticized for taking preferences and identities for granted and ignoring nationalism and other (partly) norm-driven concerns, such as increased interest in human rights and environmental issues (673–74). See "Research on International Political Economy" 1998. Additionally, Hechter and Kanazawa (1997), in a review of rational choice sociology, recognize a similar need for a dynamic theory.

10. See Eggertsson 1996 and 1998b for more details and references.

11. In the eighteenth century, until 1770, the governor over Iceland resided in Copenhagen. A deputy governor was positioned in Iceland, and under him served eighteen magistrates. In all, the royal administration in Iceland numbered only some thirty individuals (excluding a few inspectors of Crown property and the servants of the church, who became servants of the Crown after the Protestant Reformation) (Eggertsson 1996, 7–8).

12. Freeman and Lindauer (1999) survey recent empirical work on causes of economic decline in sub-Saharan Africa to look for fundamental explanations of the problem. After rejecting various candidates—low investment in education, isolation from the international economy, inequality, urban bias, and geography, the authors state, "We hypothesize that there is a lexicographic ordering of the determinants of growth and that first and foremost is political stability and security of property" (20) and then add, "There is no simple nor single recipe for achieving economic growth, but there is one way to prevent growth: through instability and absence of property rights" (21).

13. In a world of rational egoists, if social values and internalized norms are not a necessary prior condition for solving the constitutional dilemma, two alternative solutions come to mind. Constitutional stability is achieved by applying appropriate social technology (such as the democratic model), which, like production technology, can be borrowed from abroad or imitated. Alternatively, constitutional equilibrium reflects a real balance of power or fortuitous convergence of interest among social groups spontaneously created by historical circumstances. The three explanations need not be mutually exclusive.

14. Foreign fishermen often violated the ban on contacts with the Icelanders, but such illegal relationships were ephemeral and could not support long-term commercial relations.

15. Some 15 percent of the population actually left the country for North America in the first and only large-scale out-migration in the country's history.

16. First-best solutions are found in perfect markets with full information and no transaction costs. The perfect market is, of course, a theoretical construct.

17. "According to the law, farmers who were short of hay could request public search for surplus hay in their general area, both in their own and neighboring communes. Appointed agents (farmers) would then estimate whether any farmers in the area had stored more fodder than they required for the winter. Surplus hay was to be sold and first offered to farmers in the same commune as the source. The law prescribed severe punishment for those who . . . refused to comply with the redistribution scheme: Their reserves should be confiscated and the offenders receive a fine. The law permitted use of force to remove surplus hay, and farmers who received injury while defending their surplus could not claim compensation, but the crown would decide in each case whether compensation was justified, if those resisting were killed. The law created an incentive for people to expose stubborn neighbors who hid their

reserves. If the neighbors refused to trade, those who first requested the hay could buy it at half price and also receive half the fine" (Eggertsson 1998b, 22).

18. A cold spell from 1800 to 1802 reduced the sheep population by 171,000 animals (60 percent). In the cold spell from 1881 to 1883, the loss was 187,000 sheep, and from 1881 to 1908 the combined loss of grown sheep, lambs, and horses and reduction in quality of survivors was equivalent to 884,000 sheep, or about 13 sheep on average for each person in the farming community (Eggertsson 1998b, 18–19).

19. Conditions in premodern Iceland did not make central storage of hay a good economic proposition. There were no scale advantages in storage that justified such an arrangement. Icelandic farms were not grouped into agricultural villages but were scattered throughout each district.

20. In the late nineteenth and early twentieth centuries, the most visible individual proponent of the storage strategy was Torfi Bjarnason, a farmer, an agronomist educated in Scotland, and the founder, in 1880, of Iceland's first agricultural school (Eggertsson 1998b, 21).

21. In exceptionally hard times, of course, the farmers had nowhere to turn to obtain fodder.

22. Posner (1996a, 1736) mentions that sometimes the weight of sanctions for norm violators can be reduced if the circumvention of a norm is partly hidden. For instance, governments can provide legal support for actors who attempt to circumvent usury laws by structuring loans as sales or leases. Posner describes a market in tradable emission rights, which was authorized in the United States in 1990, as norm circumvention—circumvention of a norm that permits firms to pollute, as long as they do not pollute too much (1735–36). The norm was inefficient because it did not distinguish between high-value and low-value polluters—between differences in the opportunity costs to firms of cleaning up. As for the Icelandic case, I have found no cases in which the authorities sought to help violators of the hay-sharing norm to hide their circumvention.

23. In the words of Katzenstein, Keohane, and Krasner (1998, 679), static analysis assumes "that actors have common knowledge. They all share the same view of the game, including the payoff matrix, the strategic choice points, the types of actors they are playing against, and the probability of each type. Players know the options from which they can choose. If they are uncertain about the nature of their opponents, they may have the opportunity to update their probability assessment as the game progresses because of the information that is revealed by moves taken in the game."

24. The editors of a recent conference volume, which includes nineteen essays by leading scholars who summarize the current state of dynamic analysis, reach a pessimistic conclusion: "The subject of norms, values, and preference formation is increasingly attracting the attention of economists. . . . Yet this field of inquiry, now in its initial stages, still lacks a unified analytical framework and . . . a common set of conclusions. In particular, there is little empirical evidence to support or refute various theoretical claims made in this volume" (Ben-Ner and Putterman 1998, xxiii–xxiv).

25. Efforts by Putnam (1993) and others to resurrect Tocqueville's idea of civil society come close to linking the economics of underdevelopment to the study of cognitive structures and norms. Yet these studies generally are static and

emphasize only the economic and social impact of social structures, not their origins and development. Static analysis is best at explaining the way various features of civicness, such as norms of reciprocity, trust, and accountability, lower transaction costs and facilitate enforcement of laws and the organization of markets. Putnam's work, which originally sought to explain variation in economic development between the regions of Italy, emphasizes the stability (measured in hundreds of years) of norms that are inefficient in terms of economic development. The problems of transition to markets in former soviet-type economies have created extensive interest in sticky norms and civic culture.

26. Apparently, the membership of the country's Marxist Party was less divided than that of the other parties over the merits of farm and rural versus industrial and urban life, perhaps because they saw industrialism as an inevitable historical stage.

27. The country is still entirely without railways.

28. Bayes' rule is a statistical formula for updating prior beliefs in light of new information. This rule is the formal rational way to update beliefs.

# References

Ásgeirsson, Ólafur. 1988. *Idnbylting hugarfarsins: Átök um atvinnuthróun á Íslandi, 1900–1940* (Industrialization of the mind: Confrontation over industrial development in Iceland, 1900–1940). Reykjavík: Menningarsjódur.

Axelrod, Robert. 1984. *The Evolution of Cooperation.* New York: Basic Books.

Azzi, Corry, and Ronald D. Ehrenberg. 1975. "Household Allocation of Time and Church Attendance." *Journal of Political Economy* 83(1): 27–56.

Barro, Robert J. 1997. *Determinants of Economic Growth: A Cross-Country Empirical Study.* Cambridge, Mass.: MIT Press.

Barzel, Yoram. 1997. *Economic Analysis of Property Rights.* 2d ed. Cambridge: Cambridge University Press.

Bates, Robert H., Rui J. P. de Figueiredo Jr., and Barry R. Weingast. 1998. "The Politics of Interpretation: Rationality, Culture, and Transition." *Politics and Society* 26(4): 603–42.

Ben-Ner, Avner, and Louis Putterman, eds. 1998. *Economics, Values, and Organization.* Cambridge: Cambridge University Press.

Binmore, Ken. 1994. *Game Theory and the Social Contract.* Vol. 1, *Playing Fair.* Cambridge: MIT Press.

Byock, Jesse L. 1982. *Feud in the Icelandic Saga.* Berkeley: University of California Press.

Chai, Sun-Ki. 1998. "Endogenous Ideology Formation and Economic Policy in Former Colonies." *Economic Development and Cultural Change* 46(2): 263–90.

Clark, Andy. 1998. *Being There: Putting Brain, Body, and the World Together Again.* Cambridge: MIT Press.

Coase, Ronald H. 1937. "The Nature of the Firm." *Economica* 4 (November): 386–405.

———. 1960. "The Problem of Social Cost." *Journal of Law and Economics* 3(1): 1–44.

Cooter, Robert D. 1996. "Decentralized Law for a Complex Economy: The Structural Approach to Adjudicating the New Law Merchant." *University of Pennsylvania Law Review* 144(5): 1643–96.

Demsetz, Harold. 1967. "Toward a Theory of Property Rights." *American Economic Review* 57(2): 347–59.

———. 1980. *Economic, Legal, and Political Dimensions of Competition.* Amsterdam: North-Holland.

Denzau, Arthur, and Douglass C. North. 1994. "Shared Mental Models: Ideologies and Institutions." *Kyklos* 47(1): 3–31.

Drobak, John N., and John V. C. Nye, eds. 1997. *The Frontiers of the New Institutional Economics.* San Diego: Academic Press.

Eggertsson, Thráinn. 1990. *Economic Behavior and Institutions.* Cambridge: Cambridge University Press.

———. 1996. "No Experiments, Monumental Disasters: Why It Took a Thousand Years to Develop a Specialized Fishing Industry in Iceland." *Journal of Economic Behavior and Organization* 20(1): 1–23.

———. 1997. "When the State Changes Its Mind: Discontinuity in State Control of Economic Activity." In *Privatization at the Turn of the Century,* edited by Herbert Giersch. Berlin: Springer.

———. 1998a. "National Culture and International Transactions." Unpublished paper. Max Planck Institute for Research into Economic Systems, Jena, Germany.

———. 1998b. "Sources of Risk, Institutions for Survival, and a Game Against Nature in Premodern Iceland." *Explorations in Economic History* 35(1): 1–30.

Ellickson, Robert C. 1991. *Order Without Law: How Neighbors Settle Disputes.* Cambridge, Mass.: Harvard University Press.

———. 1994. "The Aim of Order Without Law." *Journal of Institutional and Theoretical Economics* 150(1): 97–100.

Folta, Timothy B., and Walter J. Ferrier. 1996. "International Expansion Through Sequential Investment: The Effects of National Culture on Buyouts and Dissolutions in Biotechnology Relationships." Unpublished paper. University of Kentucky, Lexington.

Freeman, Richard B., and David L. Lindauer. 1999. "Why Not Africa." Working paper 6942. Cambridge, Mass.: National Bureau of Economic Research.

Friedman, David. 1979. "Private Enforcement and Creation of Law: A Historical Case." *Journal of Legal Studies* 8(2): 399–415.

Furubotn, Eirik G., and Rudolf Richter. 1997. *Institutions and Economic Theory: The Contribution of the New Institutional Economics.* Ann Arbor: University of Michigan Press.

Greif, Avner. 1994. "Cultural Beliefs and the Organization of Society: A Historical and Theoretical Reflection of Collectivist and Individualist Societies." *Journal of Political Economy* 102(5): 912–50.

Hardin, Russell. 1997. "The Economics of Religious Belief." *Journal of Institutional and Theoretical Economics* 153(1): 259–78.

Hechter, Michael, and Satoshi Kanazawa. 1997. "Sociological Rational Choice Theory." *Annual Review of Sociology* 23:191–214.

Hofstede, Geert. 1980. *Culture's Consequences: International Differences in Work-Related Values.* Beverly Hills, Calif.: Sage.

———. 1991. *Cultures and Organizations: Software of the Mind.* London: McGraw-Hill.

———. 1998. "Attitudes, Values, and Organizational Culture: Disentangling the Concepts." *Organizational Studies* 19(3): 477–92.

Hull, Brooks B., and Frederick Bold. 1994. "Hell, Religion, and Cultural Change." *Journal of Institutional and Theoretical Economics* 150(3): 447–64.

Iannaccone, Laurence R. 1998. "Introduction to the Economics of Religion." *Journal of Economic Literature* 36 (3): 1465–95.

Jóhannesson, Jón. 1974. *The History of the Icelandic Commonwealth.* Translated by Haraldur Bessasson. Winnipeg: University of Manitoba Press.

Katz, Avery. 1996. "Taking Private Ordering Seriously." *University of Pennsylvania Law Review* 144(5): 1745–64.

Katzenstein, Peter J., Robert O. Keohane, and Stephen D. Krasner. 1998. "International Organization and the Study of World Politics." *International Organization* 52(4): 645–85.

Knudsen, Christian. 1995. "Theories of the Firm, Strategic Management, and Leadership." In *Resource-Based and Evolutionary Theories of the Firm*, edited by C. P. Montgomery. Norwell, Mass.: Kluwer Academic.

"Law, Economics, and Norms." 1996. Special issue of *University of Pennsylvania Law Review* 144(4).

Miller, Gary J. 1997. "The Impact of Economics on Contemporary Political Science." *Journal of Economic Literature* 35(3): 1173–1204.

Miller, William Ian. 1990. *Bloodtaking and Peacemaking: Feud, Law, and Society in Saga Iceland*. Chicago: University of Chicago Press.

Nelson, Phillip. 1970. "Information and Consumer Behavior." *Journal of Political Economy* 78(2): 311–29.

Nelson, Richard R., and Bhaven N. Sampat. Forthcoming. "Making Sense of Institutions as a Factor Shaping Economic Performance." *Journal of Economic Behavior and Organization*.

Nelson, Richard R., and Sidney A. Winter. 1982. *An Evolutionary Theory of Economic Change*. Cambridge: Harvard University Press.

North, Douglass C. 1990. *Institutions, Institutional Change, and Economic Performance*. Cambridge: Cambridge University Press.

North, Douglass C., and Barry R. Weingast. 1989. "Constitutions and Commitment: The Evolution of Institutions Governing Public Choice in Seventeenth-Century England." *Journal of Economic History* 49(4): 803–32.

Olson, Mancur. 1997. "The New Institutional Economics: The Collective Choice Approach to Economic Development." In *Institutions and Economic Development: Growth and Governance in Less-Developed and Post-Socialist Countries*, edited by Christopher Clague. Baltimore: Johns Hopkins University Press.

Ostrom, Elinor. 1990. *Governing the Commons: The Evolution of Institutions for Collective Action*. Cambridge: Cambridge University Press.

Posner, Eric A. 1996a. "Law, Economics, and Inefficient Norms." *University of Pennsylvania Law Review* 144(5): 1697–1744.

———. 1996b. "The Regulation of Groups: The Influence of Legal and Nonlegal Sanctions on Collective Action." *University of Chicago Law Review* 63(5): 133–97.

Putnam, Robert. 1993. *Making Democracy Work: Civic Traditions in Modern Italy*. Princeton: Princeton University Press.

Putterman, Louis, ed. 1988. *The Economic Nature of the Firm: A Reader*. Cambridge: Cambridge University Press.

"Research on International Political Economy." 1998. Special Issue of *International Organization* 52(4).

Ruttan, Vernon. 1991. "What Happened to Economic Development." *Economic Development and Cultural Change* 39(2): 265–92.

Stiglitz, Joseph E. 1994. *Whither Socialism?* Cambridge, Mass.: MIT Press.

Vanberg, Viktor J. 1998. "Rule Following." In *The Handbook of Economic Methodology*, edited by John B. Davis, Wade D. Hands, and Uskali Mäki. Cheltenham, Eng.: Edward Elgar.

"Views and Comments on the 'New Institutionalism' in Sociology, Political Science, and Anthropology." 1998. *Journal of Theoretical and Institutional Economics* 154(4): 695–789.

Weingast, Barry R. 1997a. "The Political Foundation of Limited Government: Parliament and Sovereign Debt in Seventeenth- and Eighteenth-Century England." In *Frontiers of the New Institutional Economics*, edited by John N. Drobak and V. C. Nye. New York: Academic Press.

———. 1997b. "The Political Foundations of Democracy and the Rule of Law." *American Political Science Review* 91(2): 245–63.

Williamson, Oliver E. 1985. *The Economic Institutions of Capitalism*. New York: Free Press.

# 4

# GAME-THEORETICAL PERSPECTIVES ON THE EMERGENCE OF SOCIAL NORMS

*Thomas Voss*

R ATIONAL choice theory argues that social norms emerge because the norms' content yields benefits for some agents. Game theory is that branch of rational choice theory that deals with social interactions among rational actors. The subject of game theory is therefore social action and social relations among rational agents (in Max Weber's sense). The emergence of social norms is closely related to the Hobbesian problem of social order, and its explanation is among the most important issues of social theory. In this chapter I discuss game theoretical approaches to social norms.

A core concept of game theory is the Nash equilibrium, a profile of actions in which no actor has a positive incentive to unilaterally deviate from those actions. Most game theoretical approaches use the basic idea that a social norm will be enforced if the actions that are compatible with that norm are supported by a Nash equilibrium. Hence, one task of game theoretical analysis is to point out those conditions or social mechanisms that lead to those equilibria.

When adopting a rational choice approach, as I do here, two questions are usefully distinguished (see, for example, Coleman 1990, chapters 10 and 11): What are the structural features of social situations that generate a "demand" for social norms? and What mechanisms contribute to the enforcement, or "effective realization," of norms? These two problems must be addressed separately, because not every social norm that potentially provides benefits to a certain class of agents will actually come into existence.

The effective realization of norms depends on mechanisms that render norm conformity self-enforcing. Self-enforcement means that rational target actors of a norm accept a norm because the norm beneficiaries have created certain incentives that make norm conformity consistent with a Nash equilibrium. The incentives may vary but often include some form of sanction. The analyses in the literature thus far rest on the assumption that the actors employ certain types of endogenously created sanctions, what may be called "indirect sanctions," but many real-world descriptions of social norms refer to other, more active types of sanction in this chapter.

## What Are Social Norms?

To understand the form and function of social norms, we might begin by considering the following examples of human behavior:

1. Every morning, Roberta practices Mozart sonatas on her piano.
2. During the late winter, many people in some Catholic countries (for example, southern Germany) celebrate carnival.
3. In the Leipzig concerto house, Gewandhaus, the audience applauds a performance of Schubert's *Winterreise* after the final song, rather than between songs.
4. In many high school classes, those students who learn eagerly are not popular. Similarly, in working groups in large organizations, workers regularly restrict their output (see, for example, Homans 1951), and overperformers are targets of informal sanctions.
5. Some business people act in accordance with the principle that commitments are to be honored (Macaulay 1963; see also Ellickson 1991, 189–91).
6. In the community of Internet users, a rule prohibiting the use of e-mail for commercial advertising is widely respected (Fukuyama 1995, 196).
7. In sports contests (for example, the Tour de France), athletes are expected to respect the rule prohibiting the use of drugs that enhance athletic performance and thus might improve their chances of winning a prize. Apparently, many athletes systematically break this rule.

The first example describes a personal rule or individual regularity in the behavior of a single actor. Personal rules may be of interest, in principle, in the context of norm formation because of their relation to individual self-control processes, "character planning" and the like (see Loewenstein and Elster 1992). For purposes of this exposition, personal rules are dismissed as irrelevant. The second example describes a regularity in the behavior of some population of agents, a behavior that might be called a social custom. However, it is a theoretically uninteresting case. Prima facie, this case can be explained by the assumption that within a population of actors certain preferences are shared. These agents share an interest in the joint production of a consumption good. There are—at least at a first glance—no non-trivial strategic interaction problems involved in this social custom: Those people who like carnival join the activities, those who do not stay at home.

The third case, though substantially trivial, describes an interesting problem. Consider a woman who visits a performance of classical music for the first time. From the very beginning, she enjoys the presentation and wants to express her admiration and approval. Should she break into applause after the first song of the cycle? If she were to do so, and no other person joined her, she would probably be embarrassed. If she does not know the proper rule, she will probably wait until others start to clap. This scenario describes a coordination problem. Coordination situations are strategic social interactions with multiple equilibria—for example, to clap after each piece, not to clap at all, to wait until others begin to clap, and so forth. Most people would be uncomfortable being the only person or among the few persons who applaud. Were this circumstance to be realized, even if by accident, the people involved would feel that they had committed an error. The last four examples (4 through 7) are of a different kind. In each of these cases, there exist social norms (informal or formal) that prescribe or proscribe certain actions. The content of each norm is such that the interests of the participants are met. The norm encouraging restricted effort in a working situation, for example, serves the interests of the average group member. If the norm were enforced, every group member—according to the group members' perception of the situation—would be better off, at least in comparison with the outcome if no members were to respect the norm. The norm eliminates competition. However, many group members may perceive a temptation to contradict the norm: it might be advantageous for an individual to put in effort above the group standard because it would improve the worker's chance of receiving higher rewards (increased income, career opportunities, and the like).

These last four cases illustrate incentive problems. They resemble prisoner's dilemma situations. The prisoner's cooperation will benefit him (or her) if all others cooperate but will harm him (or her) if he (or she) cooperates and others do not. If an actor unilaterally cooperates he (or she) will receive the worst possible payoff. In a coordination problem, like that described in example (3), rational interacting agents completely share the interests of their interaction partners: thus, they have an interest in coordinating their choices. If coordination is successful, there will be no incentive for individuals to deviate from a behavioral regularity, commonly called a convention (Lewis 1969). A convention is self-stabilizing or self-enforcing, and, once realized, conformity serves the interests of both the group and its individual members. Thus, in the case of a coordination problem, there is no need to impose sanctions to achieve universal cooperation. In a prisoner's dilemma, however, there is an incentive to deviate from a norm that prescribes cooperation; in such a case, sanctions are generally needed to coordinate behavior to achieve a universally advantageous outcome.

The content of a norm may be expressed as an imperative—that is, a statement that some kind of action ought to be done or ought not to be done under appropriate circumstances. Some sociologists (Homans 1951;

Opp 1983) use this criterion as a core definiens of the concept of a norm. However, from a sociological perspective, norms are more than imperatives that are approved or not approved by people. To use Émile Durkheim's (1895) phrase, norms are social facts ("faits sociaux"), outcomes of actions, and, as such, they are collective phenomena. Norms exist, in a sense, independently from the consciousness of individuals: they are objective and causally relevant if they are enforced within a community or group of actors. If I deviate from a norm that is perfectly realized and monitored, even if I am unaware of the norm's content, I am likely to become the target of more or less severe sanctions.

Norms are more than imperatives in another sense: Even if agents are informed about the norm's content and accept the norm as valid, they do not necessarily conform to the norm. Consider the example of the no-drugs norm in sports. It may be realistic to assume that most—if not all—athletes think that this norm prescribes "right," "valid," or "fair" behavior. Nevertheless, the same people will systematically break the norm because of the temptation—as in the prisoner's dilemma—to achieve a better position in the contest. Hence, it is important to focus on actions, especially regularities in the actions of a population.

Rational choice theory may explain many ingredients of social norms. First, it is possible to express the demand for certain norms in terms of statements about desirable or obligatory actions in certain situations. This can be an important explanatory task. Second, and perhaps more difficult, it can point out those conditions that lead to an enforcement of norms. In fact, most game theoretical explanations focus mainly on this problem of norm enforcement. With the emphasis on enforcement, social norms can be defined as behavioral regularities in a population of actors. For the purposes of this exposition a social norm may be defined as a regularity $R$ in a population $P$ of actors such that

1.  $R$ arises in recurrent interactions among the agents of population $P$
2.  almost every member of $P$ prefers to conform to $R$ on the condition that almost every other member of $P$ also conforms to $R$
3.  almost every member of $P$ believes that almost every other member of $P$ conforms to $R$
4.  $R$ is a Nash equilibrium of the recurrent interaction (Lewis 1969; Bicchieri 1993, 232; see also, for example, Schotter 1981; Sugden 1986; Leibenstein 1987. Robert Axelrod 1986, 1097, uses a simplified version of such a definition)

This concept may be expressed more strictly by distinguishing between social norms (in the proper sense of examples 4 through 7 at the beginning of the chapter) and conventions. A social norm proper is a regularity *R* such that members of *P* expect that nonconformity will (with positive probability) be punished with (negative) sanctions, and these expectations are a reason for the fact that conditions (2) and (3) hold true. A convention, on the other hand, is a regularity *R* such that *R* is a coordination equilibrium in a recurrent coordination situation. Hence, social norms are closely related to, though distinct from, conventions. One might even argue that social norms accompanied by sanctions are a subset of the class of conventions (see Young 1998, 144–45).

This concept of a social norm may serve as an explication of some intuitions that have been expressed within the sociological tradition.[1] Norms (and conventions) are treated as social facts. In Max Weber's (1976) sense they are regularities in the behavior of agents who are involved in a "social relation." Theodor Geiger (1970, 43–91) has pointed out that norms arise from social interdependence (see also Popitz 1980; Ziegler 1984; Baurmann 1996). They are regularities that are generally stabilized by threats of negative sanctions. From a game theoretical point of view, this "stabilization" results from a Nash equilibrium.

There are many classes of social norms that may be of interest. Max Weber (1976) distinguishes legal norms (law) from informal norms. The underlying dimension that generates this typology is the kind of sanctioning abuse of the norm engenders. Law is enforced by a specialized "staff" of agents who monitor the target actors of a norm and punish deviant behavior. Other norms are enforced by sanctions that are created within the community of agents who are targets of the norm. These norms are, so to speak, norms of self-help. More recently, James S. Coleman (1990) has proposed a typology based on the relation between the set of norm beneficiaries and the set of target actors (that is, those agents whose actions are regulated by a norm). If these two sets are identical, that is, if the targets and the beneficiaries of a norm are the same individuals, the norm is "conjoint"; if the targets and beneficiaries are different, or if their interests do not converge, it is "disjoint" (Coleman 1990, 247–48). Conjoint norms are particularly important because they are among the most elementary yet also the most fundamental norms. Examples for those norms are all those regularities of behavior that arise in situations of a Hobbesian anarchy, if any. Hobbesian anarchy is a situation in which cooperation, although profitable, is difficult to achieve. There is no external agency (such as the state) that could enforce mutually advantageous rules. Therefore, every actor represents a threat to every other actor. All actors prefer the universal recognition of certain rules, for instance with respect to property rights, to the war of every man against every man. However, everyone perceives that there is a temptation to defect. Concrete cases are those norms mentioned in examples (4) through (7). The explanation of the emergence of conjoint norms is a difficult task, in particular in prisoner's dilemma situations, because it has to be demonstrated that rational agents create sanctions that are severe enough to enforce a socially optimal equilibrium.

## Conditions That Generate a Demand for Social Norms

Focusing on conjoint norms, rational choice theory offers a general hypothesis: Social norms develop and are maintained in such a way that their content serves to improve the aggregate welfare of the norm beneficiaries (this hypothesis is adopted, in a slightly modified form, from Ellickson 1991, 167; see also Ullmann-Margalit 1977; Opp 1979; Coleman 1990, chapter 10, for similar hypotheses). In other words, norms emerge when they promise to bring about efficiency gains to the beneficiaries. Efficiency gains may be interpreted as Pareto improvements (although other gains may be possible) in game theoretical terms. Norms help beneficiaries avoid or escape social dilemmas.[2] A social dilemma is defined as a situation of (strategic) interdependence in which rational agents fail to achieve an efficient outcome. This means that there exists an outcome (which is not realized) in which the situation of every agent would improve or they all would at least receive the same payoff.

Figures 4.1 through 4.4 illustrate several types of social dilemmas that may arise among rational agents (see Harsanyi 1977; Voss 1985).[3] In a classic prisoner's dilemma (figure 4.1), there is no Pareto-optimal equilibrium. Consequently, rational action (defection) yields a collectively irrational outcome that could (physically) be improved by universal cooperation. In a noncooperative bargaining game, there are several pure Pareto-optimal Nash equilibria, but there is also a "bargaining deadlock," owing to the conflict of interest among the players. In the battle-of-the-sexes game, for example (figure 4.2), two equilibria are in pure strategies ([A, A] and [B, B]) (see, for example, Young 1998, 25). However, these equilibria are not eligible, according to classic game theory, because the agents' preferences are in conflict. A mixed strategy equilibrium would arise if the row player were to play A with a probability of two in three and B with a probability of one in three. The column player's mixed equilibrium strategy is to play A with a probability of one in three and B with a probability two in three. This yields a payoff of 2/3 to both players, which is strictly less than the payoff of each player's worst pure strategy equilibrium. Rational agents will hence realize a suboptimal outcome. Both players would be better off if any of the pure equilibria had been selected.

Another prominent bargaining scenario is known as the chicken game (figure 4.3). Consider two agents who can contribute to a collective good. The production function is such that any player's contribution is sufficient to produce the good. There are no economies of scale. As a concrete example one may think of help in emergency situations (compare the n-person

FIGURE 4.1      *Prisoner's Dilemma Game*

|   | C | D |
|---|---|---|
| C | 3,3 | −1,5 |
| D | 5,−1 | 0,0 |

*Source:* Author's compilation.
*Note:* The entries of each cell of a matrix represent the actors' payoffs as ordered pairs. The first number is the payoff of the row player, the second is the payoff of the column player.

variant of this game, called the Volunteer's Dilemma, in Diekmann 1985). The two asymmetric Nash equilibria, (C, D) and (D, C), generate a bargaining problem. There is also a mixed equilibrium, namely, cooperation with a probability of three in five. This mixed equilibrium gives an expected payoff of three. Any of the two pure equilibria would yield a Pareto-superior payoff—that is, it would make one player better off without altering the payoffs of the other player.

A pure coordination game (see figure 4.4) has at least two efficient Nash equilibria. However, if there is no preplay communication among the players, they will have to choose the mixed equilibrium of playing each pure strategy with a probability of one in two. This gives an expected payoff of one to each player, which is strictly less than the payoff of any pure strategy equilibrium.

All of these social dilemmas generate a "demand" for a social norm, or—in the case of the coordination problem—for a convention.[4] This norm's content includes an imperative to choose the action that is consistent with an efficiency gain to the actors. The "function" of the norm or convention would be a Pareto improvement. For example, in the prisoner's

FIGURE 4.2      *Battle of the Sexes Game*

|   | A | B |
|---|---|---|
| A | 1,2 | 0,0 |
| B | 0,0 | 2,1 |

*Source:* Author's compilation.
*Note:* The entries of each cell of a matrix represent the actors' payoffs as ordered pairs. The first number is the payoff of the row player, the second is the payoff of the column player.

FIGURE 4.3    *Chicken Game*

|   | C | D |
|---|---|---|
| C | 3,3 | 3,5 |
| D | 5,3 | 0,0 |

*Source:* Author's compilation.
*Note:* The entries of each cell of a matrix represent the actors' payoffs as ordered pairs. The first number is the payoff of the row player, the second is the payoff of the column player.

dilemma, there is no efficient equilibrium at all. A norm prescribing cooperation would make every player better off. Similarly, common knowledge of a rule that one should choose A would make the players better off in a coordination situation.

There is one core problem with such an approach that is apparently most severe in the case of the prisoner's dilemma. Given the fact that a social norm of cooperation would improve the situation, it is obvious that the beneficiaries of the norm will have an interest in creating the norm. The inefficient outcome generates a demand for a norm (Coleman 1990, chapter 10). If that norm were to be realized or enforced, the beneficiaries would be better off; but how can the norm be realized? Answers to this question can broadly be classified as exogenous and endogenous solutions. Exogenous solutions draw on the involvement of third parties in the process of norm creation and enforcement. Another type of exogenous argument refers to an internal sanctioning system or internalized sentiments, such as guilt. The problem with exogenous solutions is, of course, their incompleteness. They are probably heuristically fruitful but need to be complemented by arguments that explain the emergence and stability of third-party interventions or an internalized sanctioning system by explicitly using the assumption of rational action. Endogenous explanations require arguments dem-

FIGURE 4.4    *Coordination Game*

|   | A | B |
|---|---|---|
| A | 2,2 | 0,0 |
| B | 0,0 | 2,2 |

*Source:* Author's compilation.
*Note:* The entries of each cell of a matrix represent the actors' payoffs as ordered pairs. The first number is the payoff of the row player, the second is the payoff of the column player.

onstrating that rational self-interested agents in a social dilemma situation conform to social norms of cooperation in response to incentives created by these actors themselves. Because in an ordinary prisoner's dilemma situation there is no cooperation among rational actors, the emergence of norms may depend on threats of negative sanctions that are created by the target actors of the norms themselves. In the case of coordination problems, it has to be demonstrated how the members of the population that recurrently encounters coordination problems achieve common knowledge of a unique focal point (in Schelling's [1960] sense) and, in this way, endogenously create a rule that becomes the basis of a convention.

## The Effective Enforcement of Social Norms

Consider conjoint social norms that may regulate generalized prisoner's dilemma situations. It is well known that with respect to a norm of universal cooperation a free-riding problem will arise: Every actor will profit from the collective good that is produced by cooperative collective action (norm conformity). Yet there will be an incentive for an individual to avoid contributing to the costs of cooperation because the good can be consumed by any member of the group, independently of that individual's contribution. A social norm of cooperation would be enforceable if the actors used appropriate sanctions (negative or positive). However, the threat (or promise) to provide norm deviators (or norm conformers) with sanctions (or rewards) apparently involves a "second-order" collective good problem (see Oliver 1980; Axelrod 1986; Heckathorn 1989; Coleman 1990, 270–73 and passim). This problem results from the fact that agents who apply sanctions must be compensated for their costs, assuming that the provision of sanctions is not a generally costless activity.

Although the problem situation is often framed in game theoretical terms, a thorough game theoretical analysis of the "effective realization" of social norms is quite rare. Most analyses of the first- and second-order problems of cooperation implicitly use the assumption of parametric (that is, nonstrategic) behavior. Using a parametric analysis, Coleman, for example, conjectures that the second-order problem may be solved if the norm beneficiaries are "able to share appropriately the costs of sanctioning the target actors or will be able to generate second-order sanctions among the set of beneficiaries that are sufficient to induce effective sanctions of the target actors by one or more of the beneficiaries. This condition depends on the existence of social relationships among the beneficiaries" (1990, 273). By and large, this proposition may be right, but Coleman's arguments for it are mostly unconvincing (for a more detailed discussion, see Voss 1998a, 122–24) because Coleman, as well as others, dispenses with an explicit game theoretical analysis of both levels of individual decision with regard to norm conformity: the first-order problem of norm conformity and the second-order problem of conformity to a "metanorm" of sanctioning target actors (Axelrod 1986). These two levels are treated separately by making use of arguments that do not focus on the strategic feature of the interactions.

In contrast, a game theoretical approach has to deal with a number of desiderata. Regularities of behavior conforming to a social norm are self-enforcing if they result, to speak technically, from a Nash equilibrium. Hence, a first requirement corresponds to answering the question, What are the conditions for an efficient equilibrium of universal cooperation in a social dilemma situation (in particular, of the generalized prisoner's dilemma type)? Providing a satisfactory answer to this question is at least a necessary condition of a potential endogenous explanation of conjoint norms in prisoner's dilemma situations. Cooperation depends on sanctions created by the norm beneficiaries themselves. This leads to a second question: What are the conditions for the emergence of threats of sanctions that are not only consistent with Nash equilibrium behavior but also credible? It is well known that threats and promises in strategic interactions will be effective in changing incentives only if the agents who offer them actually apply them when the appropriate circumstances are reached (Schelling 1960; Selten 1965). Even in cases—in which—contrafactually—a path out of an equilibrium of a game were to be realized, the relevant actor should have no positive incentive to deviate from the implementation of a threat. Technically speaking, a minimum requirement for Nash equilibria, which include certain threats or promises as moves of the equilibrium strategy, is that they be subgame perfect (Selten 1965).[5]

## The Endogenous Emergence of Social Norms with Sanctions: Some Mechanisms

One important mechanism that may change actors' incentives in a social dilemma is repeated interactions (see, for example, Taylor 1976, 1987; Axelrod 1984, for treatments of iterated prisoner's dilemmas). Repeated interactions allow for the implementation of a special type of endogenous sanctions, that is, sanctions created by the agents themselves. For purposes of illustration, but without loss of generality, I choose the classic two-person prisoner's dilemma. Figure 4.5 displays the payoff matrix of the prisoner's dilemma in normal form.

Assuming a standard infinitely repeated game means roughly that (1) the prisoner's dilemma game is repeated infinitely often among the same players; (2) players discount their future payoffs with a constant discount factor $a$ $(1 > a > 0)$; and (3) there is (almost) complete information about the moves of the players in the past.[6] As is well known (Friedman 1971; Fudenberg and Maskin 1986), there may exist Pareto-optimal Nash equi-

FIGURE 4.5      *The Classic Prisoner's Dilemma Game*

|       | C     | D   |
|-------|-------|-----|
| C     | R,R   | S,T |
| D     | T,S   | 0,0 |

$$T > R > 0 > S$$

*Source:* Author's compilation.
*Note:* The entries of each cell of a matrix represent the actors' payoffs as ordered pairs. The first number is the payoff of the row player, the second is the payoff of the column player.

libria in which both players cooperate if the "shadow of the future" (Axelrod 1984) is large enough. The shadow of the future corresponds to the actors' discount parameters $a$ and can also be interpreted as the actors' (conditional subjective) probabilities that the iteration of the game will be continued for another period.

If the payoffs of the prisoner's dilemma are represented by the inequality $(T > R > 0 > S)$, the payoffs of the repeated game can be represented as weighted sums of the payoffs in each period. Because it is assumed that the discount factor $a$ is constant in each period, future payoffs will be discounted exponentially. For example, assuming that both players cooperate forever, every player will expect to receive the payoff

$$R + aR + a^2R + \ldots = R/(1 - a)$$

in the repeated game.

Cooperation in the repeated game can be enforced by trigger strategies (Friedman 1971). These demand conditional cooperation, that is, cooperation that lasts as long as the other actors cooperate. Otherwise, the strategy prescribes defection. I call this type of punishment "indirect punishment." The simplest variant of a trigger strategy responds with "eternal damnation" (that is, defection) to the first defection. Unilateral deviations from a profile of trigger strategies yield a payoff of $T$ at maximum in the iterated game. Consequently, a pair of trigger strategies is in equilibrium if and only if,

$$a \geq a^* : = (T - R)/(T - 0) = 1 - (R/T).$$

This equilibrium depends on credible threats of punishment. A single defection triggers the partner's "eternal" defection. This means that the trigger-strategy player uses the threat to implement the unique equilibrium action of the prisoner's dilemma. There is clearly no positive incentive to deviate from those threats out of equilibrium. The profile of trigger strategies is hence a subgame perfect equilibrium if $a \geq a^*$. Note, however, that not every strategy of conditional cooperation is subgame perfect. The celebrated tit-for-tat strategy (Axelrod 1984) is subgame perfect only for one particular value of the discount factor. It can easily be demonstrated that conditions for tit-for-tat to be in subgame equilibrium with itself are

$$2R > T + S,$$

$$a \geq a^* := 1 - R / T,$$

and

$$a = a^{**} := (T - R) / (R - S).^{7}$$

If only the second inequality, $a > a^{**}$, holds, tit-for-tat employs threats and promises that are not credible for particular histories of the game (out of equilibrium), namely, for histories with an alternation of Cs and Ds. The "forgiving" tit-for-tat is therefore—from the point of view of analytical game theory—a strategy in the iterated game that does not generally pass the rationality criteria. Substantially, one could argue that tit-for-tat does not successfully surmount the second-order dilemma.

Under appropriate conditions, repeated interactions generate endogenous indirect sanctions that can enforce conjoint social norms of conditional cooperation. One should, however, notice that there exists a large number of equilibria in a repeated game if the shadow of the future (the discount factor) approaches one (see the folk theorems in Fudenberg and Maskin 1986). There is always the equilibrium of universal defection, which is obviously subgame perfect; but there are also many efficient (Pareto-optimal) subgame perfect equilibria—for example, different kinds of trigger strategies. This means that there is an equilibrium selection problem. In game theoretical terms this selection problem can be expressed as a coordination or (noncooperative) bargaining problem. We encounter a bargaining problem if an outcome is profitable to one of the players at the disavantage of his partner.

The equilibrium selection problem has often been overdramatized in critiques of the game theoretic approach (for example, Hechter 1992). It is clearly a major difficulty of the repeated-games program. Contemporary evolutionary game theory (see also the remarks at the end of this chapter) aims to provide models that show how coordination equilibria are determined endogenously. The traditional game theory approach treats this selection problem exogenously.

Obviously, these coordination problems are "solved" in groups with a common history. Any equilibrium that is realized at some point in history will be a focal point for the process of a convergence of reciprocal expectations that a particular equilibrium will be chosen. Moreover, the content of social norms of cooperation may be interpreted in such a way that it points out particular equilibria. There may be equilibria that are consistent with egalitarian Pareto-optimal divisions of the cake and others with more unequal divisions (see, for example, Binmore and Samuelson 1994; Binmore 1994). Given the coordination and bargaining problems in repeated games, an important lesson emerges: different cultures (groups, communities) may have enforced different social norms (or no efficient social norms at all) in structurally similar recurrent situations. It seems likely, in other words, that path dependencies exist (for general discussions of path dependency, see North 1990, 92–104; Greif 1994; Young 1996).

It could perhaps be argued that path dependency makes the theory untestable. However, this impression is wrong. First, the game theoretical approach suggests that in cases of a low discount factor (smaller than the critical threshold value to support cooperation), no Pareto-improving social norms can be enforced. This statement can clearly be falsified. Second, in cases of a large discount parameter, path dependency is relevant. Even in this context, however, hypotheses with empirical content about the emergence of different norms in structurally similar social systems can be derived, and thus it is important to include information on historical data in this context. Third, adopting an evolutionary approach (Young 1998), the structure of resulting "long-run" equilibria of a dynamic may be described quite precisely. Under particular circumstances, there may even exist equilibria with no path dependencies or efficient "long-run" path-dependent equilibria.

Some critics of the rational choice approach to norms point out that there are many norms with no associated efficiency gains. Some norms would even stabilize Pareto-inferior states (Elster 1989). Yet this observation is consistent with the traditional as well as the evolutionary game theoretical approach. Owing to historical accidents or for other reasons, there may be instances of norms or conventions that are stable but suboptimal.

The analysis of repeated games suggests the general idea that social norms emerge endogenously in recurrent dilemma situations if the population is a close-knit community (Ellickson 1991, 167). A close-knit community is "defined as a social network whose members have credible and reciprocal prospects for the application of power against one another and good supply of information on past and present internal events" (Ellickson 1991, 181).[8] Notice that it is assumed that the "application of power against one another" is based on particular types of sanctions, namely, trigger strategies. Other types of sanctions will be discussed soon.

Many concrete examples illustrate this mechanism of norm emergence. Among the most prominent are norms of reciprocity in social exchange (Axelrod 1984; Voss 1985) and—in n-actor interactions—norms of collusion in oligopolistic industries (Phlips 1995). Another example is norms of privacy with regard to political actors. In the United States, the media heavily investigate the private lives of politicians. In Germany, there is an informal norm that mass media should not report delicate or other private details of politicians' lives without their consent. This may be a conjoint norm because enforcement may be in the interests of most journalists and publishers. The norm may foster politicians' willingness to cooperate with regard to the transfer of information on political issues. Also, most high-quality journalists would not want to investigate private affairs but would prefer to research important political issues. On the other hand, there is a clear temptation to disclose private affairs because any newspaper (or other medium) that acted as a prime mover in this respect would sell more copies (and would thereby improve short-run profits). Apparently, this conjoint norm is in part enforced by trigger strategies among the press. A leading German journalist, commenting on the Monica Lewinsky affair of 1998, has remarked that the German press respects the ethical code as long as everybody conforms to the norm.[9] Otherwise, norm conformity rapidly collapses: one deviation immediately triggers nearly universal defection.

The repeated-games approach, in principle, helps to construct empirical (qualitative) hypotheses about social conditions of norm emergence. It can be used in two ways. First, the core theoretical parameters, like the "shadow of the future" (discount factor $a$) and quotients of payoff differences ($a^*$), directly suggest a number of hypotheses:

- Cooperation increases with the shadow of the future ($a$)
- Cooperation decreases with the "costs of cooperation" ($T - R$)
- Cooperation increases with the "cost of conflict" ($T - 0$)

Other hypotheses can be derived by making use of "bridge assumptions" (in Lindenberg's 1985 sense) that link variables of the game theoretical model to exogenous factors describing social conditions. For example, with regard to multiperson dilemma situations, such as the n-person prisoner's dilemma, one might argue that there will be a "large-numbers" dilemma (Buchanan 1965; Olson 1965) in the repeated game (Raub 1988): The requirements of cooperative equilibria in the repeated game are less likely to be met as the size of the group of norm beneficiaries increases. Increasing group size will, in turn, decrease the actors' monitoring opportunities (Hardin 1982, 40, 170–71). Another aspect of the large-numbers dilemma is related to the agents' shadow of the future. A large group will most likely consist of a heterogeneous group of actors—that is, there will be some members with discount factors that are too low to support universal cooperation.

Moreover, the repeated-games approach can be used to inquire as to structural effects on norm emergence in a more direct way. Werner Raub and Jeroen Weesie (1990) explicitly analyze a mechanism that generally fosters cooperation in dilemma situations, namely, multilateral reputation. Consider two actors, A and B, who are involved in an exchange (or other) social relationship that is associated with a prisoner's dilemma. If these agents A and B were embedded into a larger social network consisting of potential (structurally similar) partners C, D, . . . , information about the behavior of A and B may spread to these third agents, C, D, . . . . In this case, the threshold of the discount factor supporting an equilibrium of cooperation is lower than it would be in an isolated (socially atomized) interaction.

Another aspect of embeddedness is multiplexity. Consider two agents A and B who are not only in one relation, $R_1$, but also in a second relation, $R_2$, with each other. In this case, the agents may cognitively connect these relations. They cooperate in any of these relations $R_i$ on the condition that the partner likewise has cooperated in all relations $R_1, R_2, . . . .$ It has been shown that the critical value of the discount factor that is necessary to support cooperation is—under certain conditions—lower if there is multiplexity (Voss 1998b, 106–7, 125–26). (These applications of repeated games correspond to analyses of "multimarket" contact in industrial organization; see Bernheim and Whinston 1990; Hughes and Oughton 1993.) Other work combines repeated-games theory with social network analysis by investigating the effects of various network parameters (Buskens 1999).

Research on structural effects in this sense largely supports the intuitive hypothesis that norms of cooperation are enforceable in small, stable, and culturally homogeneous communities. In such communities, multilateral reputation is very effective because of the high degree of network connectedness. The role specialization is typically low, or, in other words, social relations are "diffuse" and multiplex (see Taylor 1982, 76, and the references therein). Much ethnographic and historical evidence corroborates this intuition (see, for example, Greif 1994, 1998; Macaulay 1963; Ellickson 1991).

## Direct (Retributive) Sanctions

The trigger strategy with the implicit threat of defection ("Nash threat," with respect to the prisoner's dilemma) is not the only kind of sanctioning mechanism we encounter in real-life interactions. Numerous examples from the sociological literature (for example, Homans 1951, 123 and passim) refer to norms that seem to be effective because of the imposition of more active and possibly more severe sanctions. Another mechanism is the application of exit threats: norm deviation is punished by ostracizing the deviators from future interactions. There are many empirical descriptions of this sanctioning mechanism (for example, Ostrom 1990) and somewhat fewer theoretical analyses (Tullock 1985; Hirshleifer and Rasmusen 1989; Schüssler 1989; Vanberg and Congleton 1992).

Norms supported by exit threats can be considered as cases of decentralized outcomes of market processes. These norms may be enforced even in cases of large numbers of actors under conditions of anonymity (Tullock 1985; Schüssler 1989). The basic point is that defectors can be crowded out under certain structural conditions (if a large pool of cooperators is available and exit and searching costs are minimal). These processes are, however, not easily described analytically. They are best illustrated by intuitive ideas or by simulation studies (Schüssler 1989; Vanberg and Congleton 1992).

In Coleman's discussion of norm enforcement, "incremental" sanctions are important (Coleman 1990, chapter 11). These sanctions are more active than the threat to defect. Incremental sanctions are applied by members of a group. Every individual provides a small "increment" of a sanction that is apparently not very costly to the punisher. The sum of these sanctions may, on the other hand, be a severe punishment to the norm deviator. An example may be so-called mobbing (horizontal violence, bullying) in working groups. The person who deviates from a group norm is punished by social disapproval of the other group members.

The following example, borrowed from Francis Fukuyama (1995, 196), may illuminate the distinction between indirect and direct sanctions more clearly: The community of Internet users was initially (in the 1970s and 1980s) quite small. Among the net's informal conjoint norms was a rule prohibiting the use of e-mail for commercial advertising. Using electronic mail for advertising could clog the net and would be a potential threat to the viability of the system as a whole. The informal norm was broken in 1994 by a pair of lawyers who advertised for their services. Other users reacted not by advertising for their own services (which would have been a plausible response, at least for commercial users) but by sending hate e-mail to the deviators and to the service provider. The provider eventually canceled the account. The example illustrates incremental sanctions by e-mail users and the application of the sanction of social exclusion by a third party. Both of these sanctions are clearly different from the Nash threat of defection.

A simple game theoretical model, inspired by Robert Boyd and Peter Richerson's (1992) evolutionary analysis, can be useful in analyzing retributive and other direct sanctions. Figure 4.6 illustrates an enlarged variant of the classic prisoner's dilemma presented in figure 4.5. This enlarged game is in fact a modification, rather than an example, of the classic prisoner's dilemma. I call this game the norm game (actually, it is a simplified version

FIGURE 4.6    *The Norm Game in Extensive Form*

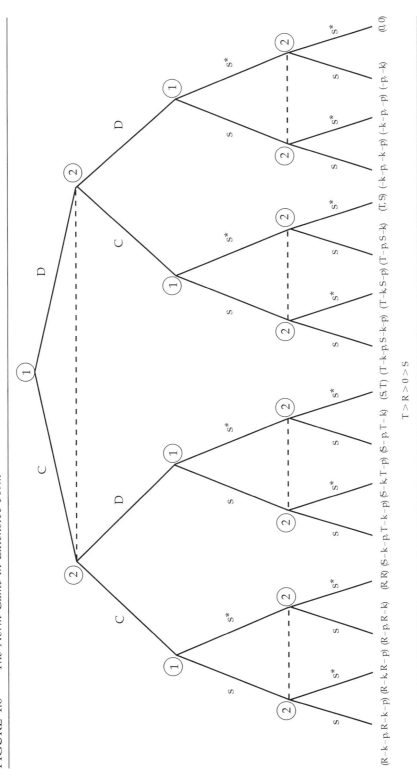

*Source:* Author's compilation.

of Axelrod's [1986] norms game). In the norm game there are two stages. In the first stage, both players simultaneously choose between the alternative responses—cooperation (C) and defection (D)—to the prisoner's dilemma. The second phase is a sanctioning or punishment stage. In this stage, both players can react on the decisions of the first stage (which are disclosed at the end of the prisoner's dilemma phase). Both players can punish their partners by selecting a negative sanction, $s$. Alternatively, they can select $s*$—that is, they can chose not to employ a sanction. Using this sanction yields a punishment cost of $-p$ to the target actor and a cost of (actively) sanctioning of $-k$. I assume that the payoffs in the norm game are sums of the payoffs in both stages of the game, namely, the payoffs of the prisoner's dilemma ($T$, $R$, $0$, or $S$) and payoffs of the sanctioning phase ($-k$, $-p$, or $[-k - p]$).

In the norm game, an actor who defects vis-à-vis a cooperating partner receives a payoff of $T$. The actor who is punished by his or her partner receives the payoff $T - p$. The partner's payoff is $S - k$.

As played out in figure 4.6, there are three results of the norm game that indicate circumstances in which there is no second-order dilemma.

- Proposition 1: In the norm game there is a Nash equilibrium of mutual cooperation if and only if $p \geq (T - R)$.

- Proposition 2: A Nash equilibrium of mutual cooperation is subgame perfect if and only if $k \geq 0$.

- Proposition 3: In an infinitely repeated norm game with discounting, there exist subgame perfect equilibria of universal cooperation even for $k > 0$, if the shadow of the future (discount factor) is large enough.

Proposition 1 is based on the idea that the players use strategies of the following kind: "Play C; if your partner has chosen D, play $s$, otherwise select $s*$." A pair of those strategies is an equilibrium if and only if the cost of cooperation ($T - R$) is not larger than the punishment $p$. Intuitively, the enlargement of the original prisoner's dilemma by means of sanctions transforms the prisoner's dilemma into a game that has affinities with an assurance game (in Sen's sense). In an assurance game, mutual cooperation is an equilibrium because both players hold the preferences $R > T > 0 > S$.

Proposition 2 says that the threat to punish a defection is credible if and only if the cost of punishing the partner is $k \leq 0$. If $k > 0$, a rational player would not have an incentive to implement the threat to punish a defection because the punisher would not only sanction the partner's norm deviation but would also punish himself or herself. Assuming that a partner has defected, this defection is irreversible. Punishing this defection will not increase the punisher's payoffs; in fact, it will even decrease the payoffs if $k > 0$. To reiterate, these results demonstrate conditions of rational mutual conditional cooperation in a norm game that is not repeated. Under the conditions stated in the propositions, there is no second-order dilemma.

However, the requirement that $k \leq 0$ seems to be quite strong. Yet it has been observed that the application of sanctions is generally not very costly—in particular, in comparison with the harm that sanctions may cause (Hardin 1995, 52–53). How could an assumption of costless sanctioning ($k \leq 0$) be justified? First, in the case of interactions involving social approval—for instance, social exchange relations in small-group contexts—the refusal to provide social approval to a group member may be a negative sanction that is not costly. Moreover, it may even be the case that this action is a positive reward ($k < 0$) to the punisher if the provision of social approval is costly. Second, emotional dispositions may serve as commitment devices (Frank 1988). If one has observed a partner's defection, sanctioning may provide emotional, "psychic" rewards that outweigh the material costs of punishing. Strictly speaking, elaborating this idea means that the payoffs of the norm game must be specified in such a way that these rewards are represented in addition to the other components of utility. Third, the norm game may be embedded into a larger game that represents social networks. An actor in those networks might have an interest in acquiring a personal reputation as a bully. Such an actor would be willing to apply sanctions even in cases in which the material costs are large. The basic reason is that such a reputation will be profitable in future interactions with third partners. This idea could be modeled explicitly in game theoretical terms (see Eaton and Engers 1999 for hints on such an analysis in the context of international relations). However, I will not pursue this or other defensive approaches here, because there is another entirely plausible scenario in which no second-order dilemma emerges even for large ($k > 0$) costs of sanctioning.

Proposition 3 addresses the norm game that is repeated indefinitely. The actors have expectations with regard to the chances of another repetition, given that the game has already been played for a number of periods. These expectations are measured by the discount factor (the shadow of the future). The standard repeated-games assumptions apply.

The proof of proposition 3 follows from the findings of Drew Fudenberg and Eric Maskin (1986) on folk theorems and on optimal punishment.[10] Intuitively, infinitely repeated games ensure that punishment costs to the punisher will be outweighed by the target's cooperation in the future. Therefore, even for positive costs ($k > 0$) of sanctioning, the threat to punish defection may be optimal. To illustrate, consider an $n$-person variant of the norm game—for instance, Hardin's (1971, 1982) $n$-prisoner's dilemma game with an additional phase of direct punishment in each period of the iterated game (see Boyd and Richerson 1992). It is assumed that

1. Every actor can sanction every other actor by direct punishment.
2. The level of punishment is independent of the number of punishers.
3. There may be positive costs of punishing, $k > 0$. These costs are not shared and are independent of the number of punishers.

The repeated norm game makes it possible to use conditional strategies that are in fact a mixture of direct and indirect punishments. These strategies require that actors be "friendly," that is, that they cooperate in the first period of the game. Moreover, they demand that a defector be punished for a number—say, $t$—of periods by implementing direct and indirect sanctions. Furthermore, an agent who fails to punish a norm deviator will be similarly punished for a number of periods by direct and indirect sanctions, and so forth. Such a pattern of punishments may be individually optimal because severe and costly sanctioning today may ensure perpetual universal cooperation in the future (see, for example, Osborne and Rubinstein 1994, chapter 8, for a detailed exposition).

This punishment regime may look very complicated. Yet one should note that in equilibrium these sanctions need not be implemented. What in equilibrium will be observed is universal conformity. The enforcement of the social norm is based on the agents' self-fulfilling expectations that every deviation from the norm and the metanorm will be sanctioned.

In conclusion, there is no second-order dilemma for a sufficiently large shadow of the future, even if the agents implicitly use the threat to implement costly punishments (provided the punishment costs are not too large). In addition, one should note not only that this mechanism of enforcement may sustain Pareto-optimal ("good") social norms but also that a population of rational agents may realize a "bad" (that is, inefficient) social norm by using these sanctions (as is also argued by Hirshleifer and Rasmusen 1989; Boyd and Richerson 1992).

## Discussion

The results of this exposition may be summarized as follows. Conjoint social norms emerge among rational actors in situations of a prisoner's dilemma under the following conditions:

1. norm deviations are detected easily and immediately
2. the beneficiaries use appropriate indirect or direct sanctions
3. either sanctioning is costless ($k \leq 0$), or there is a sufficiently large shadow of the future
4. appropriate "cultural beliefs" are held in the population of norm beneficiaries

The first condition seems trivial, but it is substantively very important. For example, conformity to the no-drugs norm in sports probably would yield efficiency gains to the group of competing athletes. One could argue that in principle many conditions of a repeated prisoner's dilemma are present in this case. The same athletes repeatedly meet each other in matches indefinitely often. However, the informational requirements of almost perfect information on the other agents' past moves in the game are obviously not fulfilled. An athlete cannot observe whether or not a competitor has taken proscribed drugs. Therefore, the beneficiaries of the norm will not be able to enforce the norm without the assistance of a third party.

Enforcement of norms also requires the use of appropriate sanctions—both direct and indirect—on the part of beneficiaries (condition [2]). Indirect sanctions are similar to trigger or tit-for-tat strategies. They react to a partner's defection by selecting a responding defection. Indirect sanctions can be very effective, but under many circumstances, they have disadvantages. In large groups, trigger strategies punish not only those agents who deviate from a norm but also the members of the group who have conformed to the norm. A single defection triggers universal defection within the whole group. Direct sanctions, on the other hand, are applicable more precisely toward those actors who have defected. They can also be implemented in situations that are not repeated. Hence, it is not surprising that the bulk of sociological and ethnographic descriptions of informal norm enforcement contains statements on this type of sanctions.

Moreover, with regard to endogenously created sanctioning, it is important to note that the condition of costless sanctioning (condition [3]) is crucial if one accepts the rationality criterion of the credibility of threats (or, technically, subgame perfection). The critical threshold value of the shadow of the future (discount factor) depends on certain variables, namely, the embeddedness of the recurrent interaction in social networks. In general, it can be argued that denser and more "closed" social networks are more effective in promoting norms of cooperation than more "open" social structures (Coleman 1990, chapter 11). Game theoretical analyses may give a rationale for this intuition by pointing out that structural embeddedness reduces—ceteris paribus—the critical value of the discount factor, which is necessary to sustain a Nash equilibrium of cooperation. Note, however, that there are exceptions to this rule of the strength of cohesive groups (see Flache 1996; Flache and Macy 1996). Another aspect of the discount factor's critical value is its (logical) dependence on the payoff differences in the original game: The larger the costs of cooperation $(T - R)$, the larger the critical value of the shadow of the future, $a^*$. (A similar relationship holds for the required level of direct punishment: the larger the costs of cooperation, the more severe must be the punishment.)

None of the Nash equilibria in repeated games (for a sufficiently large shadow of the future) and in a norm game are unique—that is, there is a coordination or a bargaining problem of selecting one specific equilibrium. The enforcement of norms therefore is based on the assumption of jointly held "cultural beliefs." Appropriate cultural beliefs are those rational beliefs "that capture individuals' expectations with respect to actions that others will take in various contingencies" (Greif 1994, 915). It is important that these rational cultural beliefs are restricted to those expectations that are self-enforcing—that is, every player is expected to play his or her best response, given identical and commonly known beliefs (see Greif 1994, 914–17). This is a crucial property of cultural beliefs in game theoretic terms: They will not be stable determinants of behavior if they are not focused on a Nash equilibrium. In contrast, certain culturalist explanations are based on the idea that cultural ideas directly affect behavior. The rational choice and game theory approach, however, suggests that cultural beliefs per se cannot provide incentives that change behavior, although they may help to select a more or less efficient equilibrium profile of actions.

Cultural beliefs are, for example, formed and transmitted in socialization processes. Once established, they become focal points that determine what type of behavioral regularity or norm will be enforced in a given population. It is obviously possible that two societies exhibit similar social structures (that is, similar incentives to cooperate or conform to a norm) but have huge differences with regard to social institutions and social norms. Norms are typically dependent on the paths taken by history. In this way, besides the shadow of the future, a "shadow of the past" comes into play.

The importance of cultural beliefs can hardly be overestimated. However, classical game theory cannot contribute much toward an explanation of cultural beliefs. Cultural beliefs have to be treated as given, exogenous variables. The main exception arises in some Bayesian games with incomplete information such that certain beliefs are rationally adapted or learned by rational agents.

Learning processes with respect to cultural beliefs are at the center of some recent developments within evolutionary game theory. These evolutionary approaches are sociologically relevant if they dispense with the assumption of genetically determined behavior. As one of the pioneers of the evolutionary approach has noted, "Game-theoretical ideas originated within sociology. Naturally enough, the solution concepts which developed were based on the idea of rational calculation. The ideas were borrowed by evolutionary biologists, who introduced a new concept of a solution, based on selection and heredity operating in a population. If, as seems likely, the idea of evolutionary stability is now to be reintroduced into sociology, it is crucial that this should be done only when a suitable mechanism of cultural heredity exists" (Maynard Smith 1982, 172). There are many seminal contributions to specify sociologically meaningful ideas on mechanisms of cultural heredity (for example, Boyd and Richerson 1985). Most of these works use the assumption of boundedly rational behavior and try to elaborate analytically tractable and empirically meaningful assumptions about individual and social learning processes.

The core features of some recent approaches (Fudenberg and Levine 1998; Samuelson 1997; Young 1998) are summarized as follows:

- A population of boundedly rational agents who are recurrently engaged in social interactions is represented as a stochastic dynamical system.

- Bounded rationality means that only limited data, not perfect information about the others' past behavior, is required.

- Agents do not select with certainty best replies toward their expectations about others' behavior; there is some small probability of an erroneous response.

- There are possibly stochastic shocks corresponding to mutations within biological evolution.

The basic research question of those models concerns the long-run behavior in these interactions. Consider a game in normal form with multiple strict Nash equilibria (for example, a coordination game). It is of interest, then, to inquire which equilibria will more frequently persist in the long run—under conditions of stochastic shocks. For example, in a two-by-two (matrix) coordination game with two equilibria, one of them being Pareto dominant, certain kinds of learning processes (which are described and illustrated in Young 1998) will realize the efficient equilibrium, provided that this equilibrium is consistent with the risk-dominance criterion, as stated by John Harsanyi and Reinhard Selten (1988). However, depending on properties of the payoff structure, it need not be the case that the "most efficient" equilibria will be "stochastically stable" long-run equilibria of the dynamic (Kandori, Mailath, and Rob 1993; Young 1998).

With regard to the repeated prisoner's dilemma, consideration of the long-run dynamics implies an assumption that there is a nonzero probability that any particular strategy will become extinct. This contrasts with Robert Axelrod's (1984) approach, which studies only the short-run dynamic. In the Axelrod approach, it is assumed that the contest of strategies yields states in which the less successful strategies become successively extinct. It can be shown that the evolutionary dynamic may dramatically change if one adopts the long-run dynamic perspective. In particular, tit-for-tat will be much less viable in the long run than in the short run (Young and Foster 1991).

The new evolutionary approach provides several important results that are, in principle, empirically testable (Young 1998, chapters 4 and 5):

For certain simple games in normal form (coordination and noncooperative bargaining games in Harsanyi's 1977 sense), learning processes within a population of boundedly rational agents in fact lead to the evolution of stable conventions. However, I am not aware of any empirical work that employs this approach. One difficulty in the application of the new concepts of stochastically stable equilibria and so forth is that it is not easy to determine what the long-run behavior perspective means empirically. Long-run behavior certainly does not always correspond with a long distance on a physical or historical timescale (Young 1998, 14–19). Most empirical studies on norm emergence use a short-run perspective.

The new evolutionary approach is important because it sheds new light on an issue that has up to now generally been treated as an exogenous problem, the evolution of conventions. As has been argued, any social norm is based on conventions or cultural beliefs that there is a stable regularity of behavior in a population of recurrently interacting agents. In the case of social norms, there are rational reciprocal expectations that certain actions are forbidden or allowed and that there will be punishment in cases of deviant behavior. The new approach may be particularly fruitful because it links evolutionary and bounded rationality ideas to more traditional game theoretic concepts, especially the Nash equilibrium. It may also be understood as a rationalization of the more traditional concepts that have been developed from a hyperrationalistic perspective of perfectly rational players. Some of the results of traditional game theory, in fact, apparently are robust if more "realistic" ideas about individuals' behavior are introduced.

The sketch of a game theoretical explanation of conjoint social norms demonstrates that those norms emerge among self-interested actors if appropriate social conditions are met. However, this approach to social norms is incomplete. People sometimes follow social norms in the absence of credible external sanctions: for instance, it is difficult to understand why people conform to the norm of tipping in restaurants they are sure they will never visit again. There is ample evidence of cooperation in situations with external incentives to free ride. The level of cooperation observed in social dilemma and public goods situations is significantly higher than predicted by game theoretical rationality standards (see, for example, Thaler 1992, chapter 2; Green and Shapiro 1994, chapter 5; and Kagel and Roth 1995 for surveys of the research results). This does not mean that the variables fostering or inhibiting cooperation—according to game theory—such as group size, shadow of the future, and the like, do not have marginal effects.

Two possible mechanisms may be relevant. First, it may be important to incorporate internal incentives into a rational choice analysis of social norms. (Robert Frank [1992, 150–52], for example, critically comments on Coleman's approach). In contrast to the traditional sociological approach, internalized norms should not be treated as given, exogenous factors. It seems, however, difficult to give a consistent explanation of the adoption of preferences in which (conditional) cooperation is valued per se. Only quite recently have some ideas emerged that attempt to tackle this problem. One important observation in this context is that intrinsic motives may play an instrumental role in an actor's ability to achieve rewards that are material or social (such as social approval). For example, considering a standard (single-shot) prisoner's dilemma situation, individual agents would be better off in terms of their "natural" (material and social) preferences ($T > R > 0 > S$) if they were endowed with internalized "moral" preferences prescribing conditional cooperation ($R^m > T^m > 0 > S^m$) instead of unconditional defection. Moral preferences may result from an internalized sanctioning system that provides negative sanctions (in the form of a guilty conscience), vis-à-vis a cooperating partner, to an actor who unilaterally defects. For example, if the cost of defecting is $m$, an actor will receive ($T^m$: $= T - m$) instead of a payoff $T$. If ($m > [T - R]$), then the strength of the internal sanctions would change the incentive structure of the game, provided both actors had adopted moral preferences and there were some transparency (common knowledge) with respect to these moral preferences. These moral preferences would transform a prisoner's dilemma into an assurance game. In an assurance game, mutual cooperation is a Nash equilibrium. Under these circumstances, an actor with moral preferences will cooperate with a partner who is similarly endowed with moral preferences. The resulting outcome would be superior even in terms of the actors' natural preferences (see Sen 1974, 80).

Another scenario is related to the norm game. Consider two or more agents who are involved in such a prisoner's dilemma with a possibility to use threats of negative sanctions. These agents would be better off in terms of their nonmoral or "natural" preferences if internalization meant that an agent would feel obliged to employ sanctions even if they violated his or her material interests. Such an agent who is committed to punishing an opportunistic partner would use a credible threat even if this threat would not be a credible one in terms of the agent's material interests. Some contributions to the literature attempt to demonstrate that rational actors would choose such moral preferences if they had an opportunity to modify their preferences.[11]

Another body of work is based on the assumption of bounded rationality. First of all, the notion of action frames as used in "interpretative" sociology and cognitive psychology may be relevant in this context. The basic idea is that actors use situation-specific decision rules. If a situation is framed to be governed by a social norm, the individual will use a normative decision rule.[12] The main desideratum of such an analysis is that ad hoc explanations should be strictly avoided. Every behavior could, in principle, be "explained" by postulating specific preferences or a specific frame or decision rule. Still another body of work is based on the idea that boundedly rational actors are endowed with preferences that are subject to evolutionary forces (Frank 1988; Güth and Kliemt 1993). An argument that bears some family resemblance to this follows from the recent evolutionary approach (Samuelson 1997, chapter 5). It can be argued that Nash equilibria that are not subgame perfect may, nevertheless, be stable long-run equilibria of evolutionary processes. Also, certain norms of fairness—for example, the norm to leave money for the waitperson on the table—may be stable because "the amounts involved and the frequency with which the situation arises are too small to provide sufficient evolutionary pressure to eliminate the phenomenon in a noisy environment" (Samuelson 1997, 164).

## Appendix

There are many excellent introductions and comprehensive textbooks on game theory that may be consulted, including Eric Rasmusen (1994), Avinash Dixit and Susan Skeath (1999), and, more advanced, Ken Binmore (1992) and Martin Osborne and Ariel Rubinstein (1994). Binmore's (1994, 1998) treatise gives an illuminating game theoretical analysis of moral norms in the spirit of David Hume. The core concepts of game theory are introduced informally and in the context of a discussion of philosophical topics.

The most important concept of game theory is the Nash equilibrium. A Nash equilibrium of a game with complete information in strategic or normal form (such as the games in figures 4.1 through 4.5) is a profile of actions such that no player has a positive incentive to unilaterally deviate from that profile. That there is no positive incentive to deviate means that no player would be (strictly) better off if he or she deviated (unilaterally) from the equilibrium, provided all other players choose their equilibrium actions.

For example, in the battle-of-the-sexes game charted in figure 4.2, there are two Nash equilibria, namely (A, A) and (B, B). These are equilibria in pure strategies, which means that an action of the equilibrium profile is chosen with a probability of one. There is also a mixed equilibrium in this game. A mixed equilibrium represents circumstances under which the player's behavior is influenced by probabilistic rules.

The mixed equilibrium can be calculated easily using the theorem that any pure strategy is a best reply to the mixed equilibrium strategies of the other player or players. This means that any pure strategy of an actor against the mixed equilibrium strategies chosen by other players yields the same payoff to this actor. To illustrate, consider the battle-of-the-sexes game. Denote $q$ the row player's probability of choosing A. This player, then, will choose B with $(1 - q)$. Denote $p$ the column player's probability of choosing A. Then it must be the case that the column player is indifferent between A and B if the row player uses his or her mixed equilibrium action. This means that the column player's expected utility (*EU*) of using A equals his or her payoff of using B against the row player's mixed strategy:

$$EU_A(\text{column}) = q = EU_B(\text{column}) = 2(1 - q).$$

Solving for *q* gives the equilibrium value of *q*, namely, $q = 2/3$ (that is, a probability of two in three). By similar reasoning, one gets the probability *p* for the column player's mixed strategy, $p = 1/3$ (that is, a probability of one in three). It can easily be seen that the expected payoff of this mixed equilibrium is a 2/3 for both players. In extensive games with perfect information (for example, the norm game shown in figure 4.6) including a detailed description of the players' sequential decisions, not all Nash equilibria may be sensible. Consider two actors, E and W. E has the first move and proposes a contract A to W, yielding a payoff of two to E and one to W. Alternatively, he could propose a different contract B, yielding one to E and two to W. W can accept or refuse either contract. If W refuses a contract, both players receive a payoff of zero. There are two equilibria in this game, namely (1) player E proposes contract A, and player W is willing to accept either contract A or B; and (2) player E proposes contract B, and player W is willing to accept contract B and rejects contract A. The second equilibrium contains a threat by player W to refuse the undesirable contract. However, is this threat credible? Assume that player E had, in fact, chosen to propose contract A. W would not, then, employ his threat to refuse because this refusal would hurt not only player E but also player W; thus threat is not a credible one. Formally, the criterion of subgame perfection (Selten 1965) rules out those Nash equilibria that use threats or promises that are not credible. Subgame perfect equilibria are strategy profiles that are Nash equilibria for any history of the game, including histories out of the equilibrium path. A subgame is roughly defined as a history of the game that starts with a single node (decision point) and includes all of its successors. This node is a singleton within the player's information set, that is, the player knows that he or she has to choose at this particular node. For example, one subgame of the bargaining game between players E and W originates with the node at which player W has to choose as the second mover (after player E has decided which contract to propose). The criterion of subgame perfection requires that a player's strategy choices must be optimal given any history of the game, that is, player W has to choose his or her best reply in the subgame that starts after E has chosen contract A. In this case, W's best response will be to accept the (undesirable) contract. Hence, the strategy profile (If contract B is proposed, accept proposal; if contract A is proposed, reject proposal) cannot be subgame perfect because it prescribes suboptimal behavior in a particular history of the game.

# Notes

1. There are other well-known definitions of social norms that prima facie do not coincide with the definition given here. Coleman 1990, 243, states that "a norm concerning a specific action exists when the socially defined right to control the action is held not by the actor but by others. . . . This implies a consensus in the social system or subsystem that the right to control the action is held by others." Yet this concept is roughly equivalent with the game theoretical definition, if Coleman's words "rights" and "consensus" are linked to the equilibrium concept. A right can be said to exist whenever an actor is free to determine an action such that there will be no punishment in equilibrium (see, for example, Binmore 1994, 129 and passim).

2. Some authors in the rational choice tradition argue that a demand for a social norm arises if a population is in a situation with externalities (Coleman 1990, 249–51; see also Opp 1983). Coleman's examples make it clear that the meaning of the term "externality" corresponds to social dilemmas. Coleman's usage of the term is clearly more general than in welfare economics.

3. See the appendix for an explanation of some technical game theoretical concepts.

4. Note that a typology of social dilemma situations that generate a "demand" for norms may depend on what has been called a general "solution theory" for noncooperative games (Harsanyi 1977; Harsanyi and Selten 1988). This is particularly relevant for certain coordination and noncooperative bargaining games, that is, games with multiple equilibrium points. In those games considerations about the "risk dominance" of equilibria are of central importance. Interestingly, this normative concept of Harsanyi and Selten seems to be relevant even for evolutionary game theory and the "theory of learning in games" (Fudenberg and Levine 1998, chapter 5; Young 1998), which certainly can be understood as empirical research programs. Moreover, it is of interest to notice that risk dominance and payoff or Pareto dominance do not necessarily coincide (Fudenberg and Levine 1998, 138). There will result a different typology of norm-generating situations if one uses risk dominance criteria rather than some other solution theory (for example, Harsanyi's [1977] earlier theory).

5. See the appendix for an explanation of the concept of credible threats.

6. For a more rigorous treatment, see, for example, Friedman 1986 and Myerson 1991.

7. Compare the prisoner's dilemma with payoffs as in figure 4.5.

8. See also Taylor 1982 and Raub and Voss 1986 for similar arguments and for hints on the correspondence between game theoretical conditions of cooperation and social conditions of a close-knit community.

9. Herbert Riehl-Heyse, of *Süddeutsche Zeitung,* in a German television talk show (ARD) on February 1, 1998 ("Sabine Christiansen").

10. For a convenient exposition, see Osborne and Rubinstein 1994, in particular proposition 151.1.

11. See, in particular, Gauthier 1986 and, for a short game theoretical explication of Gauthier's program, Bicchieri 1993, 202–13; other works in this direction are Hegselmann, Raub, and Voss 1986 and Raub and Voss 1990.

12. See, for example, Lindenberg 1988; for an approach that is closely related to game theory, see Montgomery 1998.

# References

Axelrod, Robert. 1984. *The Evolution of Cooperation.* New York: Basic Books.

———. 1986. "An Evolutionary Approach to Norms." *American Political Science Review* 80: 1095–111.

Baurmann, Michael. 1996. *Der Markt der Tugend.* Tübingen, Germany: Mohr.

Bernheim, B. Douglas, and Michael D. Whinston. 1990. "Multimarket Contact and Collusive Behavior." *Rand Journal of Economics* 21: 1–26.

Bicchieri, Cristina. 1993. *Rationality and Coordination.* Cambridge: Cambridge University Press.

Binmore, Ken. 1992. *Fun and Games.* Lexington, Mass.: D. C. Heath.

———. 1994. *Game Theory and the Social Contract.* Vol. 1, *Playing Fair.* Cambridge, Mass.: MIT Press.

———. 1998. *Game Theory and the Social Contract.* Vol. 2, *Just Playing.* Cambridge, Mass.: MIT Press

Binmore, Ken, and Larry Samuelson. 1994. "An Economist's Perspective on the Evolution of Norms." *Journal of Institutional and Theoretical Economics* 150: 43–63.

Boyd, Robert, and Peter J. Richerson. 1985. *Culture and the Evolutionary Process.* Chicago: University of Chicago Press.

———. 1992. "Punishment Allows the Evolution of Cooperation (or Anything Else) in Sizable Groups." *Ethnology and Sociobiology* 13: 171–95.

Buchanan, James M. 1965. "Ethical Rules, Expected Values, and Large Numbers." *Ethics* 76: 1–13.

Buskens, Vincent. 1999. *Social Networks and Trust.* Ph.D. diss., Universiteit Utrecht.

Coleman, James S. 1990. *Foundations of Social Theory.* Cambridge, Mass.: Harvard University Press, Belknap Press.

Diekmann, Andreas. 1985. "Volunteer's Dilemma." *Journal of Conflict Resolution* 29: 605–10.

Dixit, Avinash, and Susan Skeath. 1999. *Games of Strategy.* New York: Norton.

Durkheim, Émile. [1895] 1973. *Les règles de la méthode sociologique.* 18th ed. Paris: Presses Universitaires de France.

Eaton, Jonathan, and Maxim Engers. 1999. "Sanctions: Some Simple Analytics." *American Economic Review Papers and Proceedings* 89(2): 409–14.

Ellickson, Robert C. 1991. *Order Without Law.* Cambridge, Mass.: Harvard University Press.

Elster, Jon. 1989. "Social Norms and Economic Theory." *Journal of Economic Perspectives* 3: 99–117.

Flache, Andreas. 1996. *The Double Edge of Networks: An Analysis of the Effect of Informal Networks on Cooperation in Social Dilemmas.* Amsterdam: Thesis Publications.

Flache, Andreas, and Michael W. Macy. 1996. "The Weakness of Strong Ties: Collective Action Failure in Highly Cohesive Groups." *Journal of Mathematical Sociology* 21: 3–28.

Frank, Robert H. 1988. *Passions within Reason.* New York: Norton.

———. 1992. "Melding Sociology and Economics: James Coleman's Foundations of Social Theory." *Journal of Economic Literature* 30: 147–70.

Friedman, James W. 1971. "A Non-Cooperative Equilibrium for Supergames." *Review of Economic Studies* 38: 1–12.

———. 1986. *Game Theory with Applications to Economics*. New York: Oxford University Press.

Fudenberg, Drew, and David Levine. 1998. *The Theory of Learning in Games*. Cambridge, Mass.: MIT Press.

Fudenberg, Drew, and Eric Maskin. 1986. "The Folk Theorem in Repeated Games with Discounting or with Incomplete Information." *Econometrica* 54: 533–54.

Fukuyama, Francis. 1995. *Trust*. New York: Free Press.

Gauthier, David. 1986. *Morals by Agreement*. Oxford: Clarendon.

Geiger, Theodor. [1947] 1970. *Vorstudien zu einer Soziologie des Rechts*. 2d ed., Neuwied: Luchterhand.

Green, Donald P., and Ian Shapiro. 1994. *Pathologies of Rational Choice: A Critique of Applications in Political Science*. New Haven, Conn.: Yale University Press.

Greif, Avner. 1994. "Cultural Beliefs and the Organization of Society." *Journal of Political Economy* 102: 912–50.

———. 1998. "Self-Enforcing Political Systems and Economic Growth: Late Medieval Genoa." In *Analytic Narratives,* edited by Robert H. Bates, Avner Greif, Barry R. Weingast, and Jean-Laurent Rosenthal. Princeton, N.J.: Princeton University Press.

Güth, Werner, and Hartmut Kliemt. 1993. "Competition or Co-operation: on the Evolutionary Economics of Trust, Exploitation and Moral Attitudes." *Metroeconomica* 45: 155–87.

Hardin, Russell. 1971. "Collective Action as an Agreeable *n*-Prisoners' Dilemma." *Behavioral Science* 16: 472–81.

———. 1982. *Collective Action*. Baltimore, Md.: Johns Hopkins University Press.

———. 1995. *One for All*. Princeton, N.J.: Princeton University Press.

Harsanyi, John C. 1977. *Rational Behavior and Bargaining Equilibrium in Games and Social Situations*. Cambridge: Cambridge University Press.

Harsanyi, John C., and Reinhard Selten. 1988. *A General Theory of Equilibrium Selection in Games*. Cambridge, Mass.: MIT Press.

Hechter, Michael. 1992. "The Insufficiency of Game Theory for the Resolution of Real-World Collective Action Problems." *Rationality and Society* 4: 33–40.

Heckathorn, Douglas D. 1989. "Collective Action and the Second Order Free-Rider Problem." *Rationality and Society* 1: 78–100.

Hegselmann, Rainer, Werner Raub, and Thomas Voss. 1986. "Zur Entstehung der Moral aus natürlichen Neigungen." *Analyse und Kritik* 8: 150–77.

Hirshleifer, David, and Eric Rasmusen. 1989. "Cooperation in a Repeated Prisoner's Dilemma with Ostracism." *Journal of Economic Behavior and Organization* 12: 87–106.

Homans, George C. 1951. *The Human Group*. London: RKP.

Hughes, Kirsty, and Christine Oughton. 1993. "Diversification, Multi-market Contact and Profitability." *Economica* 60: 203–24.

Kagel, John H., and Alvin E. Roth, eds. 1995. *The Handbook of Experimental Economics*. Princeton, N.J.: Princeton University Press.

Kandori, Michihiro, George J. Mailath, and Rafael Rob. 1993. "Learning, Mutation, and Long Run Equilibria in Games." *Econometrica* 61: 29–56.

Leibenstein, Harvey. 1987. *Inside the Firm. The Inefficiencies of Hierarchy*. Cambridge, Mass.: Harvard University Press.

Lewis, David K. 1969. *Convention*. Cambridge, Mass.: Harvard University Press.

Lindenberg, Siegwart. 1985. "An Assessment of the New Political Economy: Its Potential for the Social Sciences and for Sociology in Particular." *Sociological Theory* 3: 99–113.

———. 1988. "Contractual Relations and Weak Solidarity." *Journal of Institutional and Theoretical Economics* 144: 39–58.

Loewenstein, George, and Jon Elster, eds. 1992. *Choice over Time*. New York: Russell Sage Foundation.

Macaulay, Stewart. 1963. "Non-Contractual Relations in Business: A Preliminary Study." *American Sociological Review* 28: 55–67.

Maynard Smith, John. 1982. *Evolution and the Theory of Games*. Cambridge: Cambridge University Press.

Montgomery, James D. 1998. "Toward a Role-Theoretic Conception of Embeddedness." *American Journal of Sociology* 104(1): 92–125.

Myerson, Roger. 1991. *Game Theory*. Cambridge, Mass.: Harvard University Press.

North, Douglass C. 1990. *Institutions, Institutional Change and Economic Performance*. Cambridge: Cambridge University Press.

Oliver, Pamela. 1980. "Rewards and Punishments as Selective Incentives for Collective Action." *American Journal of Sociology* 85: 1356–75.

Olson, Mancur. 1965. *The Logic of Collective Action*. Cambridge, Mass.: Harvard University Press.

Opp, Karl-Dieter. 1979. "The Emergence and Effects of Social Norms." *Kyklos* 32: 775–801.

———. 1983. *Die Entstehung sozialer Normen*. Tübingen, Germany: Mohr.

Osborne, Martin, and Ariel Rubinstein. 1994. *A Course in Game Theory*. Cambridge, Mass.: MIT Press.

Ostrom, Elinor. 1990. *Governing the Commons*. Cambridge: Cambridge University Press.

Phlips, Louis. 1995. *Competition Policy: A Game-theoretic Perspective*. Cambridge: Cambridge University Press.

Popitz, Heinrich. 1980. *Die normative Konstruktion von Gesellschaft*. Tübingen, Germany: Mohr.

Rasmusen, Eric. 1994. *Games and Information*. 2d, rev. ed., Cambridge, Blackwell.

Raub, Werner. 1988. "Problematic Social Situations and the 'Large-Number Dilemma.' A Game-Theoretical Analysis." *Journal of Mathematical Sociology* 13: 311–57.

Raub, Werner, and Thomas Voss. 1986. "Conditions for Cooperation in Problematic Social Situations." In *Paradoxical Effects of Social Behavior*, edited by Andreas Diekmann and Peter Mitter. Heidelberg: Physica.

———. 1990. "Individual Interests and Moral Institutions." In *Social Institutions*, edited by Michael Hechter, Karl-Dieter Opp, and Reinhard Wippler. New York: Aldine.

Raub, Werner, and Jeroen Weesie. 1990. "Reputation and Efficiency in Social Interactions: An Example of Network Effects." *American Journal of Sociology* 96: 626–54.

Samuelson, Larry. 1997. *Evolutionary Games and Equilibrium Selection*. Cambridge, Mass.: MIT Press.

Schelling, Thomas C. 1960. *The Strategy of Conflict*. New York: Oxford University Press.

Schotter, Andrew. 1981. *The Economic Theory of Social Institutions*. Cambridge: Cambridge University Press.

Schüssler, Rudolf. 1989. "Exit Threats and Cooperation under Anonymity." *Journal of Conflict Resolution* 33: 729–49.

Selten, Reinhard. 1965. "Spieltheoretische Behandlung eines Oligopolmodells mit

Nachfrageträgheit." *Zeitschrift für die gesamte Staatswissenschaft* 121: 301–24, 667–89.

Sen, Amartya. 1974. "Choice, Orderings, and Morality." Reprint in: *Choice, Welfare and Measurement.* Oxford: Basil Blackwell.

Sugden, Robert. 1986. *The Economics of Rights, Co-operation and Welfare.* Oxford: Basil Blackwell.

Taylor, Michael. 1976. *Anarchy and Cooperation.* Chichester: Wiley.

———. 1982. *Community, Anarchy, and Liberty.* Cambridge: Cambridge University Press.

———. 1987. *The Possibility of Cooperation.* Cambridge: Cambridge University Press.

Thaler, Richard H. 1992. *The Winner's Curse.* New York: Free Press.

Tullock, Gordon. 1985. "Adam Smith and the Prisoner's Dilemma." *Journal of Political Economy* 100: 1073–81.

Ullmann-Margalit, Edna. 1977. *The Emergence of Norms.* Oxford: Clarendon.

Vanberg, Viktor, and Roger Congleton. 1992. "Rationality, Morality and Exit." *American Political Science Review* 86: 418–31.

Voss, Thomas. 1985. *Rationale Akteure und soziale Institutionen.* Munich: Oldenbourg.

———. 1998a. "Strategische Rationalität und die Realisierung sozialer Normen." In *Norm, Herrschaft und Vertrauen,* edited by Hans-Peter Müller and Michael Schmid. Opladen: Westdeutscher Verlag.

———. 1998b. "Vertrauen in modernen Gesellschaften. Eine spieltheoretische Analyse." In *Der Transformationsprozess,* edited by Regina Metze, Kurt Mühler, and Karl-Dieter Opp. Leipzig: Universitätsverlag.

Weber, Max. [1922] 1976. *Wirtschaft und Gesellschaft. Studienausgabe 3. Aufl.,* Tübingen, Germany: Mohr.

Young, H. Peyton. 1996. "The Economics of Convention." *Journal of Economic Perspectives* 10: 105–22.

———. 1998. *Individual Strategy and Social Structure.* Princeton, N.J.: Princeton University Press.

Young, H. Peyton, and Dean Foster. 1991. "Cooperation in the Short and in the Long Run." *Games and Economic Behavior* 3: 145–56.

Ziegler, Rolf. 1984. "Norm, Sanktion, Rolle. Eine strukturelle Rekonstruktion soziologischer Begriffe." *Kölner Zeitschrift für Soziologie und Sozialpsychologie* 36: 433–63.

# Part II

Norms in Social Context

# 5

# ENACTING NORMS: MUSHROOMING AND THE CULTURE OF EXPECTATIONS AND EXPLANATIONS

*Gary Alan Fine*

I F GROUPS are to maintain a stable social order—an order that supports social psychological needs for predictability—members must develop a robust and complex system of expectations of behavior that allows for the actions of others within their perceptual fields to be treated as routine. These anticipations and their associated meanings constitute a group's culture. Despite the assumption of creativity in cultural production, it is the mundane, the ritual, and the foreseen that make a culture the collective property of individuals. The creation of a fine-graded, shared understanding leads to the Hobbesian conundrum, the defining ur-question of sociology: How is social order possible in the face of individual interpretations and interests?

Answers to the Hobbesian normative question have been plentiful on both the micro and the macro level of analysis. Micro-level theorists emphasize the meshing of individual actions through the coordination of rational decision making, weighing costs and benefits in light of the expected choices of others. On the macro level, theorists have stressed the power of societal standards (or values), arrived at by consensus, to which individuals are socialized. Proponents of each perspective have contributed to the debate on norms in organizing social life. The approach I propose here, emphasizing the centrality of the enactment of negotiated meanings, is situated in what has been labeled the "meso level" of analysis (Maines 1982) and examines individual action within an institutional world.

The term "norm" is one of the few sociological constructs that has seeped into popular discourse, and it is a feature that provokes confusion. A norm, as I use the term, extends beyond a statistical regularity of behavior. Associated with any action is the expectation that a particular behavior is right and appropriate; thus, norms can be linked to a cultural perspective. Norms have a rulelike quality, tied to widely held values, but go beyond cognition to incorporate behavior. Norms are ultimately performed by individuals within a social system. In practice, the likelihood of any normative behavior varies, although these behaviors are often predictable. Furthermore, because of their "ought" quality, normative behaviors do not just occur, they are taught. They emerge through socialization, even though different standards exist in subsocieties, given the variability in backgrounds, interests, and behavioral contexts. Socialization does not just "happen": it is enacted within a locally constituted environment, a reality that permits microscopic variations in the moral order to be finely tuned to the ongoing situation.

In this analysis I draw on two distinct, but related, bodies of literature: the sociology of culture and the symbolic interactionist perspective. These approaches emphasize the centrality of a pair of connected issues, the construction of meaning and the creation and negotiation of order through interaction. Meanings derive initially from interaction and then come to constitute and direct that interaction. Norms constitute a "frame" within which individuals interpret a given situation and from which they then take direction for their responsibilities as actors in that domain.

This chapter draws on my previous research on mushroom collectors (Fine 1998) to explore the question of how norms are negotiated. In this research I explored how individuals thought about and acted toward the natural environment by focusing on one voluntary group that spends its leisure time in the wild. I sought to explore how norms dealing with our relations with nature are enacted and how they are discussed. In this way I was able to avoid a strictly theoretical analysis, grounding my claims, instead, in the empirical world.

## Norms and the Sociology of Culture

Over the past two decades, the analysis of culture has developed from a minor concern into a central element of the sociological enterprise. Unlike symbolic interactionism, which is a distinct theoretical perspective with its own orienting statements, the sociology of culture is a substantive arena in which the contributions of scholars from various theoretical perspectives meet. Although we can readily point to common concerns, it is more difficult to suggest a set of theoretical claims upon which all practitioners agree.

The growth and increasing importance of this specialty area is exemplified by the founding of the sociology of culture section of the American Sociological Association in 1986 and its subsequent growth into one of the association's largest sections, with approximately eight hundred members. The explicit treatment of culture and its particular forms was once linked to anthropology, with sociologists occasionally referring to leading cultural anthropologists such as Ralph Linton and Alfred Kroeber. "Culture," of course, was never wholly absent from sociological analysis—how could it be?—but many sociologists, particularly those scholars labeled structural functionalists, discussed culture in light of norms and values, playing down public representations of culture (expressed claims, public behavior, and material artifacts) (Peterson 1979).

Norms and values as central organizing concepts have been underestimated for several reasons: they appear to relegate personal agency to the margins, suggesting an oversocialized concept of social actors without agency; they seem to lack a clear empirical referent; and they tend to justify functional analyses that emphasize the stability and consensus of social order and thereby marginalize conflict. Despite this preference, in practice the term "culture" incorporates the concept of norms, in that any examination of culture must recognize the existence of behavioral regularities. Although the term "norms" is less often mentioned today than it was in the heyday of structural fuctionalism, the concept is still very much present in the sociology of culture. The concept of "culture" provides a framework for behavior and can be seen as another way of referring to norms without denying the importance of human agency.

Cognitive choices (and the regularities of these choices) can coexist with structure. Such an approach is implicit in the attempts to develop a what is now called a cognitive sociology. Eviatar Zerubavel (1997) argues that the way we perceive the world is shaped by our social environment. Our categorization of objects (for example, what is considered food) may seem natural but, in fact, depends upon collective choices. More edible objects exist than those that the members of any society will eat. Edibility is an objective, consequential reality, but food acceptability depends upon the boundaries of the concept of food, based upon a cognitive sociology. Even those aspects of our existence that we think of as being most "natural" are, in fact, normative constructions to which we have been socialized. In this, a connection is evident between a cognitive sociology and Christine Horne's (chapters 1 and 10, this volume) discussion of individualist explanations based on the choices of actors and their association of behaviors with a sense of "oughtness."

Furthermore, the perspective of the sociology of culture emphasizes that behavior is meaningful. Even habitual or ritualistic behavior, "thoughtlessly" enacted, can be explained, although the explanations do not, in fact, describe how the behaviors originated or what purposes they serve. Still, the explanations suggest that we belong to a community and share standards. These explanations are central to an understanding of the discursive features of norms, and instances in which expected behaviors are absent may be seen as notable events that are the subjects for narratives. One can see society metaphorically as consisting of a bundle of stories—stories that gain power from the implications of violations of the moral order. Similarly, jokes centered on an actor who violates what is "normative" are salient in presenting a violation and its resolution (usually, in the case of a joke, shame). Expectations and violations of normative behavior become a theme of cultural productions. Such an approach is consistent with Ann Swidler's (1986) provocative metaphor of culture as a "tool kit," a set of meanings that can be referred to or enacted by participants to make a claim about the social order. A norm presents a socially preferred behavioral option, one that avoids the sanctions that come with other choices. Society cannot be dissolved into culture; it has structures, resources, and relations, as well. Yet the image of society as cultural text directs our attention to what individuals and groups choose to do and why.

Perhaps the central conceptual model within the sociology of culture approach is the cultural diamond described by Wendy Griswold (1994, 14–16). Griswold argues that four interconnected elements are necessary for understanding cultural dynamics: (1) cultural objects, including symbols, beliefs, values, and practices; (2) cultural creators, the organizations and systems that produce and distribute cultural objects; (3) cultural receivers; and (4) the social world, the context in which culture is created and experienced. Perhaps more significant than describing the concepts themselves is understanding their relations, both as existing simultaneously and as they change over time. Some see this structure as excessively general, but it has the virtue of providing a grounding by which the linkages among theoretical domains can be understood. The student of social norms, for instance, begins with the relation between the social world and the cultural object, recognizing that norms exist in social space. To understand how norms emerge requires the incorporation of the cultural creator as a normative entrepreneur. The role of receivers and their links with creators and to the social world is the focus of this chapter, as I examine the process by which norms become framed, negotiated, and narrated.

## Norms and Symbolic Interactionism

Whereas the sociology of culture emphasizes the importance of meaning, symbolic interactionism attempts to link the production of meaning with the demands of interaction—analyzing how meanings are negotiated in context. The symbolic interactionist perspective developed from the concerns of University of Chicago sociologists in the first half of the twentieth century—concerns linked to pragmatist philosophy (Rochberg-Halton 1987; Shalin 1986; Lewis and Smith 1980), notably the writings of Charles S. Peirce, William James, and John Dewey. Pragmatism argues that the value of an act is created through interaction and is judged by its outcome. Acts are not inherently good or evil, other than how groups define them, particularly in light of their consequences. This philosophical approach entered sociology through the writings and teachings of George Herbert Mead (1863–1931), a philosopher at the University of Chicago. *Mind, Self, and Society,* published in 1934, was a transcription of Mead's lecture notes and proved seminal in the development of symbolic interaction. Mead's theories were subsequently disseminated by his student Herbert Blumer, whose compilation of writings, *Symbolic Interactionism* (1969), is the major explication of the symbolic interactionist perspective.

The label "symbolic interactionism" was coined by Blumer in 1937 in a review essay on social psychology. Symbolic interactionism was further developed by a cohort of students trained by Blumer and Everett Hughes at the University of Chicago in the 1940s and early 1950s, known as the Second Chicago School. Members included Erving Goffman, whose book, *Presentation of Self in Everyday Life,* published in the United States in 1959, uses the metaphor of the theater to present a dramaturgical model of social life. Although Goffman's work, emphasizing the creation of social order, borrowed from other theoretical traditions, including that of Émile Durkheim, his writings have also had an enormous impact on symbolic interactionism.

Critics sometimes dismiss the symbolic interactionist perspective as being focused on a microsociological or social psychological view without a concern with structure, with no belief in the power of organizations and institutions and no constructs with which to examine such issues (Maines 1988; Strauss 1991; Hall 1987). Although this may be true of certain early interactionist writings, the criticism is misleading in that even such writers as Blumer (1969) regularly examine "acting units." In its concern with how interacting units, not individuals, create order and meaning, the interactionist perspective is properly tied to the meso-level of analysis, attempting to bridge individuals and organizations. Over the past two decades, scholars have incorporated the existence of social structure. Interactionist concepts such as negotiated order, constraint, network, collective activity, and symbolic meaning contribute to an emerging macrointeractionism.

Central to interactionism are Blumer's three premises of symbolic interaction: "The first premise is that human beings act towards things on the basis of the meanings that the things have for them. . . . The second premise is that the meaning of such things is derived from, or arises out of, the social interaction that one has with one's fellows. The third premise is that the meanings are handled in, and modified through, an interpretive process used by the person in dealing with the things he encounters" (Blumer 1969, 2). Blumer argues that although we routinely recognize objects, objects do not invariably carry these meanings. As they relate to behavioral expectations, our choices of how to act toward other people depends on how we identify them: as mugger, lover, teammate, opponent. Our identifications lead to "local" expectations of behaviors (local norms). How we identify others is learned through socialization—explicit and implicit—and can be changed only through a process of redefinition. Social actors master the meaning of objects collectively, and the meanings one person holds are likely to be acquired from and similar to the meanings of others. The power of our drive for collective meaning is such that, as Blumer recognizes, we modify meanings in interaction, negotiating a relatively stable set of meanings. Although interpretations are socially generated, they are not random or unpredictable, nor are they unchangeable. Whatever choices we make have consequences, shaping our own experiences and those of others. Thus, definitions of situations are real in their consequences (Thomas and Thomas 1928).

As a consequence of emphasizing the negotiation of meaning, interactionists tend to be deeply suspicious of claims of generalized societal norms and argue that broad claims about the power of norms ignore the alterations of meaning and local interpretations of social life. As do sociologists of culture, interactionists feel that human agency deserves great emphasis. Thus, interactionists speak of behavioral or social expectations, rather than norms, placing the locus of actions in the context of the person and the domain of interaction. A norm may exist as a statistical regularity or as part of a global ideology, but the choice of what behavior to enact is a consequence of the locally produced "microscopic" demands of a situation.

That behaviors often look as if they are normative—that is, demanded by the social order, even when strategically selected as part of the demands of impression management—is a central point emphasized by Erving Goffman (1959). Goffman asserts that patterns of behavior exist in public life because of the desires of individuals to look "good" in the eyes of others (for example, to be seen as morally responsible actors) and to have the interactional sequence flow smoothly, avoiding embarrassment. The wish of social actors to avoid "trouble" is crucial to dramaturgical theory (Emerson and Messinger 1977). The rewards—symbolic and material—that derive from situations are linked to fine-tuned evaluations of behavior. In later work, such as *Frame Analysis* (1974), Goffman suggests that the establishment of frames of meaning helps individuals determine what kinds of behavioral expectations are appropriate. Social situations have frames of meaning associated with them that direct action, a point emphasized in analyses of social movement activism (Snow et al. 1986).

Although Goffman never specifies the process by which actors acquire the skills to participate in social life and to define frameworks of interaction, the socialization of children is recognized as central to their learning to be respectable and responsible persons (Cahill 1987; Fine 1987; Thorne 1993): actors are taught, with a subtle dance of rewards and punishments, to be sensitive to what they subsequently recognize as the norms, or expectations, of particular settings. These rewards and punishments are typically similar across families and institutions. In this, one sees the connection between symbolic interactionism and rational choice theory, which, while they differ in their level of precision and validity, both argue that actors take into account the circumstances in which they reside and attempt to gain the best "deal" for themselves, either in terms of material resources or reputation (which brings rewards in its train). As Douglas Heckathorn notes, even those who might seem least interested in the acquisition of

goods attempt to maximize their inclinations in light of resource preferences and regulation by others. Presentation of self is crucial to realization
of this end.

Although many norms are widely accepted, in practice they are enacted in appropriate occasions as locally constituted phenomena. Norms
are not treated as objects that are given by society. Instead, they are understandings that are recognized in situ, tied to meaning systems. Norms refer
to a generalization of behavior; they are in this sense based on doing, not
on having—on action, not on broad ideology. In the words of constructionist sociologists, one does not "obey" norms, one "performs" them. Yet, although norms are enacted, they are also capable of being reported, incorporated into various discourses, and, as a result, they become general and
constraining. Especially in violations of behavior that is taken for granted,
reference to norms can become the basis for narratives or stories that are
used to make a moral argument about how social life should operate.
Given that individuals are similarly socialized, these understandings are
widely spread; as a consequence, norms are generalities, as well as being
locally enacted.

To explore how norms are organized, I analyze social order through
three broad social processes central to contemporary sociological analysis:
framing (the contextualization of meaning), negotiating (coordinating lines
of action), and narrating (making public claims about the nature of the
"ought"). To make the argument concrete, I focus on a particular social
scene: the world of mushroom gatherers. Although all groups and social
settings have local norms associated with them (and thus, I hope, this example permits generalization of the processes used),[1] the examination of
mushroom collectors is particularly propitious for this analysis in that the
issue of how nature should be treated is never far from the surface. Mushrooming may be a leisure activity, but it also has a moral dimension, as
does all environmental engagement.

## A Mushroomer's World

Those unfamiliar with mushrooming might be surprised to discover that
the North American Mycological Association (NAMA) is an active organization of some eighteen hundred members. In most major metropolitan
areas, amateur collectors have banded together for support and community
in learning about and gathering mushrooms. According to a 1993 list of
NAMA-affiliated state and local organizations, seventy-seven mycological
clubs operate in the United States and Canada. These groups have an estimated ten thousand members (Friedman 1986). The Minnesota Mycological
Society, the site for the bulk of my observations and interviews, was founded in 1898, making it the second oldest continuously active mushroom
society in the United States.[2] Mushroomers treasure the experience of hik-

ing through forest and fields, the thrill of danger in the wild, and the satisfactions inherent in hunting for valued objects. The discovery, identification, and (on occasion) consumption of natural objects of which others are unaware provides a powerful lure for participants.

As in many voluntary organizations, interest groups operate under the banner of the larger organization. Although virtually all members of the organization pick mushrooms, and some 95 percent eat the mushrooms they pick, their other mycological interests are more diverse. Some of the approximately two hundred members of the Minnesota society are primarily interested in examining mushrooms from a quasi-scientific perspective—part of a group sometimes labeled amateur mycologists; some enjoy compiling lists or collections of the mushrooms they find; and others have photography as their first love. Although relations in the organization are friendly, tension occasionally flares up over the division of resources.

The Minnesota Mycological Society meets one evening a week for approximately two hours during the prime mushroom-picking months, May, June, September, and October. At these meetings the president describes the mushrooms that members bring and that the Identification Committee has identified. Members describe their memorable mushroom finds, and, consistent with norms of secrecy (Fine and Holyfield 1996), where and how their caches were discovered. At some meetings, members give talks (on cultivating mushrooms, mushrooms in other nations, or foreign travel, for example) or show slides. In addition to these weekly meetings, the club annually organizes approximately half a dozen forays to state and county parks and to private properties. Two of these forays last a weekend. The club holds a banquet during January and organizes a mycology study group that meets monthly to examine mushrooms more closely, using microscopes and chemicals.

To investigate the norms of mushroom collectors I draw on participant observation, in-depth interviews, surveys, and document analysis (see Fine 1998). For three years I attended most meetings, forays, and banquets of the Minnesota Mycological Society, compiling detailed field notes. These notes were supplemented by a questionnaire sent to all members (with a 66 percent response rate) and by two dozen in-depth interviews, lasting approximately ninety minutes each. In the course of my research I also attended a national foray organized by the North American Mycological Association and two regional forays—one in the Midwest and one in the Northeast. I later mailed a survey to a 10 percent sample of the members of the North American Mycological Association (with a 60 percent response rate). These data are supplemented by newsletters published by some two dozen mycological societies, personal correspondence, and field guides and other publications (memoirs, cookbooks, and collections of essays). I also examined the first twelve years of *Mushroom: The Journal of Wild Mushrooming*, a quarterly periodical for amateur mushroomers with a national circulation of approximately two thousand.

# Framing Norms

Social life depends on the assumption that norms are meaningful. This suggests not that we necessarily enact "normative" behavior with full consciousness but rather that these behaviors are capable of being recognized and depend upon a set of cultural ideals or idioms that are, in themselves, capable of explication and justification. Furthermore, these behaviors are not enacted by rote but occur in those situations in which they are judged to be appropriate. Few behaviors are fully ritualized outside of ceremonial occasions. Enacting norms is part of impression management and depends on frame analysis (Goffman 1959, 1974).

Drawing on the anthropologist Gregory Bateson's construct of frame, Goffman suggests that principles of organization govern events and our subjective experience of these events. By framing, Goffman argues, individuals can rely on cultural templates to understand particular events and circumstances as exemplifying a meaningful category. This template provides a mechanism by which acts are linked to underlying assumptions about the motivations of their doers, answering the question of why individuals are acting as they are. As a consequence, framing presumes a set of values, recognizable motivations, and shared behavioral expectations.

The underlying principle that prevents this perspective from being purely individualistic and idiosyncratic is the claim that situated interpretations and subjective experiences are not random but, within limits, are routinized and knowable. People recognize types of situations, and from this understanding they draw upon socially acquired patterns of behavior, judging one context against others (Fine 1992). As Paul Rock (1979, 71) has argued, "Situations order and direct the process of knowing." People act in situations on the basis of the meanings provided by previous experiences and the contexts in which they occurred. Goffman (1974, 1–2) writes that:

> defining situations as real certainly has consequences, but these may contribute very marginally to the events in progress; in some cases only a slight embarrassment flits across the scene in mild concern for those who tried to define the situation wrongly. All the world is not a stage—certainly the theater isn't entirely. . . . Presumably, a "definition of the situation" is almost always to be found, but those who are in the situation ordinarily do not create this definition, even though their society often can be said to do so; ordinarily, all they do is to assess correctly what the situation ought to be for them and then act accordingly.

In other words, participants search for norms. Contexts that individuals rely upon to learn proper action include both scenes in which people have participated and those that they have learned about through secondary sources. Having directly or vicariously experienced action scenes, individuals evaluate them for their typicality and their relevance as a guide for current action. Contexts are stored and sorted through to find "frames" for judging appropriate responses.

In contrast to the view that individuals have the power to create their own "worlds," as the radical constructionists claim, or that individuals merely respond to the world as given to them, the claim of positivists or structuralists, I argue that contexts are made meaningful through a reconstruction by which frameworks of meaning are applied to present contingencies (Giddens 1984). This approach adds a temporal component to the interactionist perspective in that previous experiences reverberate through time. In Goffman's (1981) felicitous phrase, experience has a "referential afterlife." Our conceptions of structures are real and provide a foundation for understanding the social world. We do not judge acts or objects isolated from their surroundings; rather, we ask embedded questions: What is going on? What should I be doing? What is this thing here? We strive for a situated, contextual meaning. Past situations—and our interpretation of them—constitute the context by which we make sense of our present activities. Accepting the consequences of time and space means that structure is linked to interpretation, as regularities of things, acts, and settings are incorporated into information processing (Giddens 1984).

People comprehend things in context. Because agents alter or reshape the meanings of things in context through interpretive challenges, and perceive things from different perspectives, one person's understandings can differ from the understandings of others. Structures, being mediated, do not affect everyone identically, although the effects may be similar enough to allow for meaningful interaction and a perception of consensus.

One way to make contexts consistent is through definitional work, either reshaping the past or defining the present. If one concludes that a situation is discrepant from those of the past, one may retrospectively redefine the past situations, reconstructing them to serve as guides for action in the present. Alterations in historical memory are common—both for communities and for persons. For example, learning that a person engages in homosexual acts may not only redefine the actions of that person in past situations (that had previously not been defined as homosexual in character) but may also redefine retrospectively the character, or frame, of the shared situation.

The process by which individuals generalize or abstract and thereby achieve some measure of cognitive consistency (Abelson et al. 1968), an important theme of social psychology, is grounded in the belief that although contexts vary, the object that is their focus will have a nearly immutable meaning. This realization of the relation between contextual variation and the obdurate character of objects (and, hence, their generalizability) is central to the theoretical underpinning of both attribution theory and labeling theory. The claim that norms cause action serves as a means by which consistent behavior can be explained: norms, rather than common socialization or interpretations, serve as the engine that produces uniformity. Individuals frame situations based upon their assumption that social facts ("reality") matter in directing behavior—this, in essence, is the consequence of a norm.

Learning appropriate behaviors (for example, socialization) is based on determining the type of situation one confronts and what standards of action are appropriate, a problem of framing that is especially evident in children. With each new situation we build upon our experiences of being in situations and acquire one more instance by which to interpret future occasions. When a context differs from what we expect based on past contexts, we review previous relevant situations and revise our theory about them or make some additional differentiation of their meaning (perhaps specifying differences in time, place, personnel, or forms of social control).

Although situations are never identical, they can be abstracted and typified and used to make sense of new situations. Furthermore, they are perceived as being both controlled by and constitutive of organizations, groups, institutions, and societies. The ability to refer to norms constitutes an essential means by which framing occurs. As attribution theorists emphasize, although immediate behavior may be defined as a function of situated demands, the behaviors of others are connected to enduring traits of a group, organization, or culture.

Norms are an outcome of socialization that, in turn, is based on expectations held by most members of a community. The fundamental issue is the kind of situation an individual is facing and, given this interpretation, the range of appropriate behavioral options. In most situations no single behavior is demanded, but individuals have a range of options (a cultural tool kit) from which to choose. Here, personal preferences or immediate contingencies determine which option is selected.

Following Goffman, these understandings of appropriateness constitute the situational frame. Norms, thus, result from framing. Fortunately for the existence of smooth interaction and the maintenance of the "interaction order," these understandings are usually easily comprehensible, but there are notable and dramatic occasions in which ambiguities and misunderstandings occur, in which the smoothness of interaction is breached. Through these understandings, framing gives meaning to norms: behaviors that are not demanded by an overarching society but ones that make sense within an interaction domain.

# Framing Mushrooming

Consider how mushroomers attempt to use rhetorics of nature to justify the fact that their activities fly in the face of normative claims that the woods should be protected from human intrusion. By framing their activities in particular ways, they justify their leisure doings as normatively acceptable.

They have their behaviors "make sense" as moral actions—in accord with other moral claims and with expectations of symbolic rewards and punishments. They make choices as to how to typify their behavior in the wild, supporting principles of cognitive consistency.

Many mushroomers would object to this characterization, but in practice they are engaged in an extractive activity. Mushroomers affect the microecology of forests and fields, and most would not engage in their hobby if they were not allowed to do so. They borrow a term from agricultural cultivation in speaking of "harvesting" mushrooms. Even the common terms used to describe mushroomers pay heed to their effects: they are collectors, pickers, and hunters—not fungus watchers. In their talk, the tension between picking mushrooms and preserving the environment is evident: "Andy recounts how he found several Hen of the Woods in a local nature reserve. Molly notes that it is illegal to pick there, commenting, 'If they catch you, you'll be one sorry person.' Andy responds: 'I told them [the rangers] that there were kids picking flowers and when they went down there, I picked the mushrooms.' [Loud laughter.] Someone jokes: 'You're evil.' Molly adds: 'That's the height of ingenuity'" (field notes). Such "ingenious" mushroomers are esteemed, but with a certain normative ambivalence.

Mushroomers tell each other repeatedly and heatedly that they must treat the woods with respect. They are devoted to this normative belief. Any suggestion that this is not so is met with indignation. They are equally devoted, however, to gaining natural treasures. Humor reflects their attempts to frame their activities, as when we are foraging for highly esteemed morel mushrooms in a nature area where we should only be picking for study. One mushroomer jokes: "We might study them as they're cooking in the pan. We have to have a certain amount of respect for things" (field notes).

How can mushroomers frame their activities to justify what might seem to be behaviors that "serious" naturalists would oppose? As is typical, they provide excuses and justifications. First, they minimize the extent of the harm, and second, they differentiate themselves from and stigmatize those who do more damage, preserving their normative decency through boundary work—drawing distinctions between those who behave properly and those who do not.

## Minimization

Many mushroomers minimize potential damage. They frame their activity as food gathering, similar to the activities of animals. We must eat *something,* and so, one mushroomer claims, somewhat implausibly, there is "no difference between the man who buys the mushrooms at the store and the person who picks the mushrooms out of the woods" (interview). Mushroomers note that there are sufficiently few of them that damage is limited. Indeed, some collectors avoid picking all the mushrooms in an area, leaving some to produce spores for following years.

Furthermore, some mushroomers claim that because of fungal structure, picking fungi does not harm the environment. A mushroom, growing on the forest floor, appears to be a plant, rooted in the soil. However, a mushroom is, in fact, a fruiting body of a plant. Mushroomers use scientific discourse to define their activity as "mere" fruit picking. Done with care, mushrooming does not harm the environment. This comforts individuals doing what they would likely do in any case, suggesting to themselves that they are contributing to an ecological process: "Since the mushroom we eat is only the fruiting body of the hidden plant, I have no . . . qualms about my harvest interrupting a valuable natural process. . . . Anybody who likes oysters (and many who do not) will like oyster mushrooms. So will anyone who likes to contemplate the recycling of nutrients in a forest. When I began eating oyster mushrooms from wasted logs, I became a part of that useful cycle" (Kaufman 1983, 8–9). This claim is a bit of a fiction, in that the fruiting body contains the seeds (spores) that give birth to new mushrooms, but it is a fiction that preserves the normative legitimacy of mushrooming by suggesting that damage is not done and mushroomers are "environmentally aware."

## Differentiation

A second framing technique is to differentiate oneself from stigmatized others, drawing powerful normative boundaries. At one extreme are those who pick mushrooms only for investigation, avoiding picking "for the pot." John Schaaf (1983, 37), the former editor of the *Mycena News,* the newsletter of the San Francisco Mycological Society, expresses this position thus:

> Just as the joy of birdwatching is enhanced by investigating the subject while disturbing it the least, so the mycologist can derive pleasure from the study of any fungus, edible or not, by observing it in its habitat over a time, watching its growth and succession patterns, discovering its higher purpose. A few specimens are sometimes taken, any one of which may provide the makings of a hundred microscope slides. . . . Some of our Council members don't even eat mushrooms; but then you wouldn't expect the head of the local Audubon chapter to go around biting cassowaries.

Schaaf's position is not popular: approximately 95 percent of mushroomers eat wild mushrooms, and it is the main interest for many. More typically, mushroomers condemn "greedy" colleagues, who scour the woods for every mushroom: "[In *Boletus edulis* season] enthusiastic gatherers destroy every fruiting body to be found. Bushes are leveled, branches torn away, duff scattered. . . . Joan Plumb was collecting in the state of Washington and found hunted areas torn up as if furrowed by wild pigs" (Freedman and Freedman 1983, 21). "Joyce tells me that she is angered by how some people pick all the mushrooms they can, and then drop the ones that are inedible by the side of the road. She gives the example of 'Latvians' who go through the woods kicking and picking up those mushrooms that they can't dry for eating" (field notes).

An implicit belief exists as to what constitutes one's proper share: those individuals who mushroom without respect for limits violate justice norms, which are linked to assumptions about the carrying capacity of the natural environment. These examples emphasize the framing of the activity as moral action. It is bad enough to pick all the mushrooms, but to level bushes and leave broken mushrooms offends the mycological sensibility. There is an understanding that mushroomers must be socialized to the normative expectations of the activity to minimize the extent to which the human presence undermines the harm to the woods.

As these mycological examples suggest, the framing of social situations is critical to the performance of norms, just as the existence and knowledge of norms is crucial for framing. Frameworks of meaning allow us to perceive the class of situation that we are facing. With our skills in dealing with situations, we can key situations in particular ways so that others will recognize the meaning that we provide. Our behavior is always potentially meaningful to others, and it becomes incumbent on participants to provide these meanings. Socialization of new members and drawing boundaries between insiders and outsiders are two techniques by which communal norms are made real within a social setting.

## Negotiating Norms

Externalities constrain the possibilities of interpretation (Fine 1991, 1992): a macrofoundation provides a basis for microanalysis. Norms are not simply personal choices, nor are they created in an immediate situation; typically, their effects are consequential and lasting.

Yet, recognizing that stable structures exist "out there" and that individuals wish to incorporate consistency and continuity into their worlds, we also realize that social actors, because they have different experiences and interests, often differ on situational proprieties. Given this, how do situations operate smoothly? The answer is embedded in the interaction itself. Interactants engage in negotiation, by which individual perspectives are brought together to create a social world (Strauss 1978; Fine 1984).

Within the interactionist domain few images have had a more profound and enduring impact than negotiation, a metaphor derived from the research that Anselm Strauss and his colleagues (Strauss et al. 1963, 1964) conducted in two psychiatric hospitals, focusing on differences in psychiatric ideologies and norms of practice. Several aspects of negotiation are similar to normative analysis. First, Strauss suggests that all social order is negotiated order and that organization is impossible without some measure of negotiation. Second, negotiations are contingent upon the structural conditions of the organization. Negotiations follow lines of communication, being patterned, and not random, creations of meaning. Third, negotiations have temporal limits, and, like norms, they may be renewed, revised, and reconstituted over time. Fourth, structural changes in the organization require a revision of the negotiated order. External features of lifeworlds are closely linked to the micropolitics of negotiated order. Individuals and society, as reflected in the normative order, continually generate each other through negotiation.

Three assumptions are central to the negotiated order perspective. First, negotiated order is based upon how interactants perceive the rules of the structure in which they are embedded; thus, rules are contextual. Second, change is inevitable and continuous. Third, individuals and groups continually adjust the situations in which they are embedded, assuming that actors are conscious of their own positions and act in such a way as to control others' impressions of them and their communities, a point consistent with dramaturgical theory.

Face-to-face contact introduces diverse potential meanings. In situations in which the understanding of norms is perfect and agreement on the desirability of these rules is universal, negotiation will be unnecessary. Even when a legitimate authority sets the norms, however (as with legislation), this scenario is unrealistic: diversity is part of any community. Yet diversity must be contained for social order to be achieved. The belief in the reality of norms limits potential meanings by creating traditional, shared interpretations, modes of action that become ritualized and "thoughtless." Although an actor may attempt to maintain consistent meaning, this consistency is imperfect, given the need to deal with others. When coordinating behaviors to achieve their ends, individuals adjust their lines of action.

Negotiation takes several forms. The "what" of negotiation is not always simple. One element that becomes negotiated is whether a particular norm is desirable. Is it "good" to pick mushrooms from forest preserves? A second issue is whether a particular action constitutes an instance of a norm. If the norm is not to pick all the mushrooms in an area, what will constitute "all" or "an area"? Both the legitimacy (and scope) of the norm and its relevance are subject to negotiation. The ambiguity of normative relevance provides a cushion for the disagreement of individuals. However, once this disagreement has been recognized (and becomes notable), some response is necessary. As Goffman (1959) has observed, individuals are strongly motivated to permit interaction to proceed smoothly; thus, negotiations often prove successful, at least in the immediate circumstances or in small groups. In larger groups, in which negotiation is necessarily more formal and the consequences for violation of decisions more consequential, negotiation may break down. To the extent that individuals place priority on "getting along," negotiation (typically implicit, through mutual—and often unstated—adjustments) will be the preferred method of reaching agreement on behavioral proprieties, but when the establishment of formal and explicit rules becomes necessary, more formal mechanisms (for example, voting and explicit social control) will be invoked, less subject to negotiation within the setting itself.[3]

## Negotiating Mushrooming

Although much leisure is a solitary pursuit, participants often prefer the presence of others. Yet having others share one's space requires coordination. This is especially true when competition or a diversity of vision is present. People must ensure that their values and their behavioral norms are similar to those of others, and they must adjust their actions to ensure that their interaction is harmonious.

Sharing the woods may build community, but a danger also exists: searching for mushrooms may breed competition. In some sense finding mushrooms is a zero-sum game. The mushroom that I pick, you cannot. What are the rules by which these resources are to be allocated? In activities that involve shared space and limited resources, participants must understand the norms that smooth transactions.

Despite claims to the contrary, mushrooming is often competitive: the competition positions not only human against nature but also human against human. Demonstrating that one has found the largest pile of mushrooms carries status. This is particularly evident in morel hunting expeditions in which participants compare the number or weight of morels. Although this competition is friendly, it is nonetheless significant: one couple reported that seven years previously they had found more morels than anyone else in the club (170 pounds), a fact dutifully reported in the club newsletter (interview).

A joking culture legitimates bragging rights but simultaneously reveals norms of social control. Mushroomers wish to reveal their prowess, but to do so may cause resentment or jealousy. The author of a "mushroom etiquette" column, Ms. Mushroom (1984, 28), warns that "one should not overstate one's good fortune. No matter that one has an entire pickup load of Morels to process, one is permitted only to allude to having found a few, and to state that knowing one's friend might be wanting some, one would like to share. Not only does this induce in every acquaintance a warm feeling of friendship, but one appears beneficent while simultaneously retaining a goodly number of mushrooms for oneself."

Friends may have relations that permit these teasing competitions:

"Another friend [inquired] as to our success. I told him of the [one] *Verpa.*
He said that he didn't wish to offend, but I might be interested to know
that he, with a little help from a few of his friends, had picked three hundred and twenty-two (322) pounds of morels on Saturday and Sunday, and
had done so not more than 25 miles from where we had found our solitary
*Verpa.* 'That's obscene,' I said" (Wells 1986, 28). This friend, prefacing his
remarks with the wish not to offend, did indeed provide information in
which his friend was interested, so interested that he could include this fact
into a humorous narrative about his own skills and the variability of nature.

These bragging rights are legitimate, as people enjoy telling their stories, but there are limits. Needless to say, mushroomers are quick to point
out that they themselves do not engage in extreme forms of status display,
often emphasizing that they do not count or weigh their finds, defending
themselves against the accusation that they see the activity as more serious
than might be appropriate. The couple described above, with their 170
pounds of morels, emphasized that "we were counting for a while, then we
started weighing them. Last year, we didn't even do that. We were very
approximate" (interview). These accounts, if they are to be effective, require good listeners, a supportive community. Jealousy is a natural response but one that must be tamed in the name of good fellowship.

The need to tame competition is even more evident in the woods. Here
the zero-sum quality of the hunt is crystal clear. Either I pick the mushroom or someone else does. It goes into my basket or into someone else's.
An ethic of "finders keepers" operates: "Suddenly one person stopped,
exclaiming, and turned to collect two obscure brownish morels in the
shade of a rounded white granite rock. I stopped, too, and saw a morel
almost under one of her feet. . . . In mushrooming. . . . it was all right for
me to collect that morel, and so I did" (Geary 1982, 72). Despite this norm's
seemingly universal quality, in practice it is negotiated. That the author
was a novice and the other mushroomer had just found a pair of morels
surely bolstered this politemess. To take a mushroom from another's personal space is a matter of delicacy; to find too many when searching with
others is also questionable. One must balance one's own success with the
need for harmonious relations: "Should one encounter what is termed a
'mushroom garden' while at a fellow mushroomer's side, it is considered
ill form to sweep the entire contents of the garden into one's own basket.
However, should one be confronted by a garden of 100 or so Morels while
momentarily alone, one is permitted to gather the first 80 or so specimens
before alerting one's bosom companion to the situation. It is wise to leave
at least one or two fresh, non-rotten Morels among the remaining 20" (Ms.
Mushroom 1984, 28). The jocular tone of the advice only partially hides the
tension between the instrumental goals of the hunt and the expressive
needs of the community.

The importance of negotiating competition emerged when we found an oyster mushroom with a reddish stain. Jerry joked that it was blood from mushroomers fighting over it (field notes). More serious are instances in which collectors race through the woods gathering all that they can (either at competitive morel hunts, such as those at the Boyne City, Michigan, festival, or by commercial matsutake pickers in the Pacific Northwest) without regard for either aesthetic appreciation or sociability: norms of cooperation are ignored. As in any social world, negative examples warn against improper behavior:

> I'm thinking in particular of the morel pickers who are going out with the idea that it's not just a hunt, it's a race. Fill a basket as quickly as possible. . . . There's an awful lot of greed involved in this. . . . You've got grownups acting like children in the woods. . . . If you grab all the mushrooms[,] that is in many places considered good form. . . . Some people go out of their way to share; they find a patch of mushrooms, and they call their friends in; they share. And other people would never say a word; they would pick every bloody mushroom. And they'll come back with a basket full of mushrooms, and, if on the way back home, they got a full basket and everybody else has little bits, too bad for those people. (Interview)

Recalled another disgruntled mushroomer, "I took some people out to this area that I had picked earlier, and I had left some puffballs to grow. And I had found them, and since I was bringing them to my puffballs, I had expected them to share them. They grabbed them and put them in their bags. And I thought, 'I'm never taking you out again!' So, one of the etiquette things is to determine in advance how you are going to divide up the spoils" (interview).

These instances of greed are, in my experience, rare and perhaps were exaggerated in the telling. Yet there is evident strain over the degree to which one should be willing to trade off personal rewards in order to build relations. Needless to say, this strain is not a characteristic only of mushrooming but can be expected in any situation (business, sexual intimacy, parenting) in which the maximization of one's own desires conflicts with other values—values that may be linked to other rewards.

Negotiation ultimately depends on identification, imagining the perspective of the other and adjusting to it (Couch 1989; Mead 1934). Society depends on the mutual adoption of roles. Identification and role taking require comprehension of the perspective of the other, a skill that is grounded in knowledge of a particular other. Norms—with their behavioral patterns—can become an easy way out in otherwise ambiguous circumstances, serving, in effect, as "interaction rituals" (Goffman 1967; Collins 1981). Whether or not norms do, in fact, maximize potential rewards for individuals, the recognition of their presence provides for outcomes that maximize the smoothness of interaction. If norms are not real, they are as good as real in providing the groundwork for mutual identification.

## Narrating Norms

Although I treat norms as actions that are performed, as behaviors or doings, they are also things that can be narrated. Just as norms can be performed, so too can they be told. Norms are implicated in the rhetorical construction of society. The telling of society permits participants to have their perspective ratified by an audience, and, of course, telling itself is a behavior—the action of talk (Austin 1975).

To speak of norms as narrated can be understood in at least three distinct ways. First, socialization is often achieved through talk. Individuals are not merely shown what they should and should not do, but frequently they are exhorted to choose certain behaviors at the expense of others. The exhortation to "do as I say, whatever I may do" is an efficient, if not always fully effective, technique of education. Surely the novice mushroomer must be trained verbally (and through images) as to those objects that they should consume and how to differentiate different species. Individuals enter the leisure world without a firm sense of proprieties, and talk presents models of appropriate behavior.

Linked to teaching is a second form of normative narrative: those warnings in which individuals are hectored (even after the original learning has ostensibly occurred) to behave in a socially ratified way, in conformance with group expectations. Often these warnings are backed by threats as to what may happen if one violates behavioral prescriptions—including the possibility of invoking institutional punishments, as when mushroomers violate the demands of wildlife. Officials may remind actors of the potency of organized social control. Because collecting edible mushrooms is so desirable an activity, these demands may have little effect unless consequences are obvious. Just because a claim is made for a formal norm does not mean that actors will relinquish their usual practices.

The third, and most interesting, example of talking about norms is the process by which norms are transformed into stories, moral messages within a narrative. Social actors are continually presenting narratives about the world that surrounds them, stories that encourage or discourage forms of action—an issue to which I now turn.

## Narrating Mushrooming

The narration of norms is evident among mushroomers. Although various forms of discourse could be selected for analysis, I choose humor, because jokes emphasize the moral boundaries of a community; boundary work, separating proper and improper behavior, is central to amusement. Both teller and audience know the point of the remark, even when the talk is only for amusement. The reality of a normative order within a community imbues talk with power. The "bundle of stories" (Fine 1995, 128) participants tell transforms a collection of individuals into a community.

A central issue for mushroomers is the control of risk. Despite the fact that mushrooms are potentially deadly, some venture into the woods expressly to consume these objects. By what rules do they choose their level of danger and risk? Humor is one way that people collectively transform the dangerous into the manageable (Freud [1905] 1960; Fry 1963). The use of humor to deflect unpleasant thoughts is not merely a technique of individual psychology but a property of self-conscious groups, organizations, and communities, requiring a social connection between performer and audience. Humor is a form of social control (Coser 1960).

In the case of mushroomers, concern over the expertise and competence of group members is central. The humor of competence is in reality humor that centers on norms for dealing with risk—coping with potential personal and communal danger. As many scholars have noted, although external dangers can have real consequences, our estimates of risk are not objective (Short 1984; Clarke 1989); rather, these assessments are collective constructs (Douglas and Wildavsky 1982, 186–98). Furthermore, risk is not considered undesirable when we are confident that we can manage it (Csikszentmihalyi 1975). Individuals and groups control risk by processing it through talk. Humor provides a means by which actors address their fears while convincing themselves that the risk they are taking is manageable: if they can laugh about it, how can the risk be serious?

Central to understanding humor about poisoning is the reality that individuals differ in how much risk they define as appropriate. Through humor, mushroomers confront different normative standards. Some collectors are conservative in deciding which mushrooms to eat; others are more liberal, enduring diarrhea in return for a new experience. For both the cautious and the daring the possibility of poisoning is real, however close to the boundary of toxicity they are willing to explore.[4]

## Conservative Humor

Mushroomers who express fear of poisonous mushrooms reveal what others consider excessive concern. Some collectors prefer not even to touch lethal mushrooms for fear that contact alone might be toxic, because spores might seep through their skin or might be inadvertently transferred to their mouths. Although the amount of toxins consumed in this way is clinically insignificant, and fears about these dangers relate more to cultural traditions of mycophobia and beliefs in "sympathetic magic," they affect the norms of behavior: "Mark worries about touching *Amanitas* and *Galerinas* [both deadly poisonous]. He only touches an *Amanita* with the edge of his knife, and then wipes the knife carefully. He doesn't want physical contact with them. When I touched a *Galerina* on a foray, he told me: 'Now you can't pick any mushrooms for the table'" (field notes).

Given that these "conservative" mushroomers forgo one of the main pleasures of the activity—eating the mushrooms they gather—they feel the need to defend their position. They do this by battling "liberals" over appropriate norms of consumption through jocular "insults": "Beth says of cooking Honey Caps: 'Bring the water to a boil, then throw out the water' [because the poison found in the mushrooms might remain in the water]. Dave, more liberal, responds, 'I never did that, and I never got sick.' Beth retorts, rejecting his 'rashness,' 'You're crazy anyhow, Dave'" (field notes).

The problem for the conservatives is that if they are wrong, they have missed out on a treasure. The reality that others consume these mushrooms and survive is a challenge that humor must diffuse. As a result, conservatives present themselves as rational actors who, after weighing the dangers, have made a judgment, even though this rationality is contested by those who disagree. They reject trusting in luck and rely, instead, on certain knowledge. The presentation of their "rational" stance results not in measured discussion but in amusing banter. The issue is addressed, but the sense of community is not breached because the remarks are not taken seriously.

## Liberal Humor

Some mushroom "liberals" argue that as long as one avoids deadly mushrooms, the experience is worth the risk. Life is filled with difficulties, and one learns from adversity. An aesthetic experience need not necessarily be pleasant. For these individuals, mushrooming includes risk and discomfort. One mushroomer described his desire to try numerous species of mushrooms, even some that are allegedly dangerous:

> *Howard:* I eat mushrooms every year that I haven't eaten before, and the rule is that you don't eat a mushroom unless you are 100 percent sure. Yet, I question 100 percent.
>
> *GAF:* Why would you want to try a possibly dangerous mushroom?
>
> *Howard:* To see what it was like. To tell someone that this is what it was like, so they don't have to read it out of a book, because books aren't necessarily true. . . . I've put up with a lot of unpleasantness for the sake of the experience. (Interview)

To defend themselves against the suggestion that they are suicidal or "crazy," these mushroomers rely on humor directed toward those who self-consciously avoid any mushroom that might carry risk. Although most of these liberals are confident in their judgment, and most do not consume mushrooms of which they are not reasonably certain, this attitude involves a measure of bravado that conservatives reject.

Some liberals explicitly counter the belief that they should avoid anything potentially unpleasant or which they can not exactly identify by bravely claiming that the effects of mushroom "poisoning" are not so bad: "Don tells the club that eating *Verpa bohemica* makes some people temporarily lose coordination in their arms and legs. Kristi jokes, 'You just get a little spastic, so what?' [Laughter] Don jokes back, 'I was there before I started.' [Laughter]" (field notes).

The attitudes that attribute illness to the mere touch of mushrooms are scorned by those who feel that such fastidiousness is unnecessary or even a neurotic manifestation of mycophobia: "Sam jokes to Jerry, the club president, about showing mushrooms to the club: 'Be sure you can handle the *Amanitas* first. It sparks conversation.' This refers to the time the previous year when the then president was criticized by some for holding an *Amanita,* and then touching edible mushrooms" (field notes). This joker adopts a persona at the same time as he is altercasting others. It is recognized that, in a sense, Sam is not speaking in his own voice when making this remark. Yet his orientation toward mushrooming is reflected in the self that is portrayed in his humor. The selves that are projected or implied in humor are a joking transformation of real attitudes in the community, but because they do not reflect "real persons," the jokes do not undermine friendships. Speakers are "just" joking, while expressing their own normative standards.

Here we witness a normative battle, sheathed in humorous talk, which preserves community. Humor creates a sympathetic "animator" who can satirize those considered either too liberal and too conservative, revealing communal ambivalence over "proper" behavior. Because few participants define themselves as representing an extreme position, they can laugh at jokes that target extreme attitudes toward risk—both those whose desire for certainty is too great and those whose desire is not great enough. The humorist verbally satirizes normative extremes and inflexibility, and so the talk can be enjoyed by all.

Although these jokes provide a warning or lesson, they also make sense in the context of a smooth and enjoyable conversation. By virtue of the parties' sharing moral values (at least during the duration of the conversation), they reaffirm the existence of a set of normative perspectives underlying the reality of community. The talk may have the express purpose of entertainment, but it works because of its ability to bolster belief. Social order can, in this sense, be seen as consisting of a bundle of shared discourse. In other words, conversation involves social propriety made rhetorical.

# Norms as Cultural Productions

Norms and behavioral expectations should not be separated from the meaning systems of individuals who enact them or from interaction that occurs in local spaces in which they are enacted. The performance of norms involves a complex construction based on the framing of local context, negotiation of the interest of social actors, and the narrative depiction of behavioral rules. Although I emphasize the agency of social actors to producing and shaping meaning, I recognize that this process is based upon an obdurate material reality and a consequential structure. Like all social construction, this depends on social actors' adjusting their behavior in situ so that interaction flows smoothly. From an interactionist standpoint, this desire for social comity provides the core motivation for individuals to give up their own material interests for the sake of others. Actors share a powerful desire to allow interaction to proceed without strain, and they often make substantial adjustments in their behavior to ensure this result—choosing to satisfice outcomes for the sake of harmony. This suggests that significant interpretive leeway may exist in response to behaviors—especially on occasions in which one's expectations are upended but even when things go as expected.

In any social system, norms are linked to culture in that violations become markers for talking about social standards. The stories we tell are often taken as the reality that ostensibly stands behind the narrative. Symbols come to serve as symbolic rewards and punishments. Narratives provide accounts of what is and what should be. Postmodernists suggest that everything is a "text." Whatever this claim means in practice, it implies that stories are a means by which expectations are made concrete. Presenting a violation of social standards is the kind of notable event that individuals may reasonably share.

I have emphasized the existence of three processes, drawn from the sociology of culture and contemporary interactionist theory: framing norms, negotiating norms, and narrating norms. Each is an attempt to solve a core problem of the normative order—norm ambiguity, norm variability, and norm socialization, respectively (see table 5.1). Each concept addresses the way particular norms are developed within the social systems, and then, once recognized, the process by which they become shared and adjusted in response to the fine-grained aspects of situations. For each of these processes, I have presented an empirical case to serve as an example of the course of the process, drawing from my research with mushroom collectors—a case study that, I trust, stands for other domains.

Ultimately, the normative structure presumes interpretative options, linked to the existence of a cultural tool kit. In responding to a particular interactional context, individuals select from among a set of possibilities. It

TABLE 5.1    *The Emergence and Shaping of Norms Among Mushroomers*

| Empirical Case | Problem | Process |
|---|---|---|
| Protecting a shared value | Norm ambiguity | Framing |
| Allocation of resources | Norm variability | Negotiating |
| Rules of consumption | Norm socialization | Narrating |

*Source:* Author's compilation.

is rare that a single behavior is judged to be the only appropriate option. This is particularly true in those situations in which formal, established rules do not exist or are ambiguous.

Finally, as also noted by the authors of chapters 1 and 6 in this volume, norms are often sponsored by individuals who become, in effect, normative entrepreneurs, helping particular norms and expectations emerge or change. Social actors may endorse or oppose normative emergence, shaping the social order. Individuals take responsibility for encouraging a particular relationship to the interaction order and encouraging some frameworks of meaning at the expense of others. Thus, norms are always potentially "in play," in a state of dynamic tension, being created, altered, or negated.

Norms are not separate from interaction. In this, my chapter differs from several other chapters (especially those grounded in economic theory) that distance norms from their sponsors and de-emphasize the contexts in which they are enforced or violated. In contrast, I argue that by conceiving norms as a part of a locally constituted interaction order and as belonging to the cultural domain, the vibrancy and vitality of norms as they are lived can be appreciated.

## Notes

1.  In the case of students, for example, the normative system of grading and test scoring may be complex and seemingly symbolic, but the effects on behavior are real and powerful. Although each system has its own distinctive characteristics, the possibility of generalization is real.

2.  Only one mushroom club operates in the Twin Cities area. I felt that it would be disingenuous to create a pseudonym that would not shield the identity of the group as a whole. Following standard ethnographic practice, I do, however, use pseudonyms for individuals, except when quoting published materials.

3.  However, even here some negotiation is possible, as anyone who has been stopped for speeding can attest. The institution of plea bargaining suggests that negotiation is built into even the most formal arenas.

4.  Although attitudes fall in a continuum, I divide mushroomers into liberals and conservatives according to their consumption choices: these political terms, as used by mushroomers, do not necessarily correlate with national politics but are

linked to other social categories. In general, mushrooming liberals tend to be younger, entering the hobby through other environmental activities; conservatives tend to be older and often learned about mushrooms from relatives or within their ethnic groups. Many conservatives, at least in the Minnesota club, are women; men are more likely to be liberals and risk takers.

# References

Abelson, Robert, Eliot Aronson, William J. McGuire, Theodore M. Newcomb, M. J. Rosenberg, and Philip H. Tannenbaum, eds. 1968. *Theories of Cognitive Consistency: A Sourcebook*. Chicago: Rand McNally.

Austin, J. L. 1975. *How to Do Things With Words*. Cambridge, Mass.: Harvard University Press.

Bateson, Gregory. 1972. *Steps Toward an Ecology of Mind*. New York: Bantam.

Blumer, Herbert. 1937. "Social Psychology." In *Man and Society*, edited by Emerson Schmidt. New York: Prentice Hall.

———. 1969. *Symbolic Interactionism*. Englewood Cliffs, N.J.: Prentice-Hall.

Cahill, Spencer. 1987. "Children and Civility: Ceremonial Deviance and the Acquisition of Ritual Competence." *Social Psychology Quarterly* 50: 312–21.

Clarke, Lee. 1989. *Acceptable Risk? Making Decisions in a Toxic Environment*. Berkeley: University of California Press.

Collins, Randall. 1981. "On the Microfoundations of Macrosociology." *American Journal of Sociology* 86: 984–1014.

Coser, Rose L. 1960. "Laughter Among Colleagues." *Psychiatry* 23: 81–89.

Couch, Carl. 1989. *Social Processes and Relationships: A Formal Approach*. Dix Hills, N.Y.: General Hall.

Csikszentmihalyi, Mihalyi. 1975. *Beyond Boredom and Anxiety*. San Francisco: Jossey-Bass.

Douglas, Mary, and Aaron Wildavsky. 1982. *Risk and Culture*. Berkeley: University of California Press.

Emerson, Robert, and Sheldon Messinger. 1977. "The Micropolitics of Trouble." *Social Problems* 25: 121–34.

Fine, Gary Alan. 1984. "Negotiated Orders and Organizational Cultures." *Annual Review of Sociology* 10: 239–62.

———. 1987. *With the Boys: Little League Baseball and Preadolescent Culture*. Chicago: University of Chicago Press.

———. 1991. "On the Macrofoundations of Microsociology." *Sociological Quarterly* 32: 161–77.

———. 1992. "Agency, Structure, and Comparative Contexts: Toward a Synthetic Interactionism." *Symbolic Interaction* 15: 87–102.

———. 1995. "Public Narration and Group Culture: Discerning Discourse in Social Movements." In *Social Movements and Culture*, edited by Hank Johnston and Bert Klandermans. Minneapolis: University of Minnesota Press.

———. 1998. *Morel Tales: The Culture of Mushrooming*. Cambridge, Mass.: Harvard University Press.

Fine, Gary Alan, and Lori Holyfield. 1996. "Secrecy, Trust, and Dangerous Leisure: Generating Group Cohesion in Voluntary Organizations." *Social Psychology Quarterly* 59: 22–38.

Freedman, Bill, and Louise Freedman. 1983. "Letter to the Editor." *Mycena News* 32(April): 21.

Freud, Sigmund. [1905] 1960. *Jokes and Their Relationship to the Unconscious*. New York: Norton.

Friedman, Sara Ann. 1986. *Celebrating the Wild Mushroom*. New York: Dodd, Mead.

Fry, William F., Jr. 1963. *Sweet Madness*. Palo Alto, Calif.: Pacific.

Geary, Ida. 1982. "Hunting the Wild Morels." *California Magazine,* May, 72.

Giddens, Anthony. 1984. *The Constitution of Society*: Berkeley: University of California Press.

Goffman, Erving. 1959. *Presentation of Self in Everyday Life*. Garden City, N.Y.: Anchor.

———. 1967. *Interaction Ritual*. Garden City, N.Y.: Anchor.

———. 1974. *Frame Analysis*. Cambridge, Mass.: Harvard University Press.

———. 1981. *Forms of Talk*. Philadelphia: University of Pennsylvania Press.

Griswold, Wendy. 1994. *Cultures and Societies in a Changing World*. Thousand Oaks, Calif.: Pine Forge.

Hall, Peter. 1987. "Interactionism and the Study of Social Organization." *Sociological Quarterly* 28: 1–22.

Kaufman, Wallace. 1983. "Tree Oysters." *Coltsfoot* 4 (November–December): 7–9.

Lewis, J. David, and Richard Smith. 1980. *American Sociology and Pragmatism*. Chicago: University of Chicago Press.

Maines, David. 1982. "In Search of Mesostructure." *Urban Life* 11: 267–79.

———. 1988. "Myth, Text, and Interactionist Complicity in the Neglect of Blumer's Macrosociology." *Symbolic Interaction* 11: 43–58.

Mead, George Herbert. 1934. *Mind, Self, and Society*. Chicago: University of Chicago Press.

Ms. Mushroom. 1984. "Etiquette." *Mushroom* 2(3): 28–29.

Peterson, Richard. 1979. "Revitalizing the Culture Concept." *Annual Review of Sociology* 5: 137–66.

Rochberg-Halton, Eugene. 1987. *Meaning and Modernity*. Chicago: University of Chicago Press.

Rock, Paul. 1979. *The Making of Symbolic Interactionism*. Totowa, N.J.: Rowman and Littlefield.

Schaaf, John. 1983. "Biting Cassowaries." *Mycena News* 33(September): 37.

Shalin, Dmitri. 1986. "Pragmatism and Social Interactionism." *American Sociological Review* 51: 9–29.

Short, James F., Jr. 1984. "The Social Fabric at Risk: Toward the Social Transformation of Risk Analysis." *American Sociological Review* 49: 711–25.

Snow, David, E. Burke Rochford Jr., Steve K. Worden, and Robert D. Benford. 1986. "Frame Alignment Processes, Micromobilization, and Movement Participation." *American Sociological Review* 51: 464–81.

Strauss, Anselm. 1978. *Negotiation*s. San Francisco: Jossey-Bass.

———. 1991. *Creating Sociological Awareness*. New Brunswick, N.J.: Transaction.

Strauss, Anselm, Leonard Schatzman, Rue Bucher, Danuta Ehrlich, and Melvin Sabshin. 1964. *Psychiatric Ideologies and Institutions*. Glencoe, Ill.: Free Press.

Strauss, Anselm, Leonard Schatzman, Danuta Ehrlich, Rue Bucher, and Melvin Sabshin. 1963. "The Hospital and Its Negotiated Order." In *The Hospital in Modern Society*, edited by Eliot Freidson. New York: Free Press.

Swidler, Ann. 1986. "Culture in Action." *American Sociological Review* 51: 273–86.

Thomas, W. I., and Dorothy S. Thomas. 1928. *The Child in America: Behavior Problems and Programs*. New York: Knopf.

Thorne, Barrie. 1993. *Gender Play*. New Brunswick: Rutgers University Press.

Wells, Mike. 1986. "One Verpa." *Mushroom* 4(3): 28–29.

Zerubavel, Eviatar. 1997. *Social Mindscapes: Invitation to Cognitive Sociology*. Cambridge: Harvard University Press.

# 6

# THE EMERGENCE OF THE OBJECTIVITY NORM IN AMERICAN JOURNALISM

## Michael Schudson

O BJECTIVITY is the chief occupational value of American journalism and the norm that historically and still today distinguishes U.S. journalism from the dominant model of continental European journalism (Donsbach 1995, 17–30).[1] Objectivity is at once a moral ideal, a set of reporting and editing practices, and an observable pattern of news writing. Its presence can therefore be identified by several measures: (1) journalists' express allegiance to the norm—in speeches, conferences, formal codes of professional ethics, textbooks in journalism education, debates and discussions in professional journals, and scientific surveys of journalists' opinions; (2) ethnographers' observations of journalists at work and the occupational routines to which they adhere; (3) content analysis of the texts of newspapers and news broadcasts that measure the degree of impersonality and nonpartisanship in news stories; and (4) the resistance displayed by adherents to the norm when it is openly challenged or criticized (Tuchman 1972, 660–79).[2]

The objectivity norm directs journalists to separate facts from values and to report only the facts. Objective reporting is supposed to be cool, rather than emotional, in tone. Objective reporting takes pains to represent fairly each leading side in a political controversy. According to the objectivity norm, the job of the journalist consists of reporting something called "news" without commenting on it, slanting it, or shaping its formulation in any way. The value of objectivity is upheld specifically against partisan journalism, in which newspapers are the declared allies or agents of political parties and their reporting of news is an element of partisan struggle. Partisan journalists, like objective journalists, typically reject inaccuracy, lying, and misinformation, but partisan journalists do not hesitate to present information from the perspective of a particular party or faction.

Where did the objectivity norm come from? It was not always a norm in American journalism. It has a history and a point of origin. Specifying that point of origin, identifying its sources, and locating it in particular journalists or news organizations is not easy. Many matters are in dispute. Some authors would say that objectivity emerged at the point at which newspaper proprietors saw opportunities for commercial success and were therefore willing to bid farewell to political party underwriters. They stress that the increasingly lucrative market for newspapers in the late nineteenth century led publishers to seek out readers across political parties and so forced them to abandon strident political partisanship. Others have argued that technological change, specifically the invention of the telegraph, placed a premium on economy of style and inaugurated reporting habits that stressed bare-bones factuality rather than discursive commentary, thereby giving rise to an ethic of objectivity (Emery, Emery, and Roberts 1996, 185).[3]

However, the process by which a practice generates a norm is rarely explored. In my view, the position that the wide distribution of social behavior naturally and normally gives rise to a norm prescribing that behavior and attributing moral force to its observation skips over a necessary step. What causes the norm to be articulated? Explaining the articulation of a norm is part of explaining the norm itself. If, for example, incest is naturally repellent, and so the avoidance of incest is widely distributed, why would an incest taboo arise? If a behavior is already in place, what additional work does an articulated norm accomplish? If technology made objectivity an inevitable practice or if economic self-interest made objectivity the news industry's obvious best choice, what purpose was served by moralizing a practice that would have survived regardless?

I share with other authors in this volume an understanding of norms as moral prescriptions for social behavior. Norms are "obligations" rather than "regularities," to borrow Robert Cooter's distinction (Cooter 1988, 587).[4] The term "norm" can also refer to prevalent patterns of behavior (generally speaking, leading government officials in the United States, if married, do not have sexual relations with office interns), but the focus here is the emergence of morally potent prescriptions about what should be prevalent behavior (leading government officials, if married, should not have sexual relations with office interns). Could it be that a prevalent pattern of behavior gives rise to moral norms? Do widely distributed social practices for some reason ooze prescriptive rules that insist on the prevalent pattern? Perhaps the prevalence of certain behaviors contributes to their moral authority. Many habits, however, are widespread but have no prescriptive force. Most people like to eat ice cream, but no one insists that those who do not like it have failed to live up to a moral requirement. Most people watch several hours of television a day, but no one believes that they should; if anything, television viewing receives moral disapproval in general public discussion.

Different kinds of norms may have different kinds of explanations.

Some norms apply to all people or almost all people in a society; others are specific to people of a particular class, religious group, or occupation. Some norms are supported by the state, expressed in laws, and backed by threat of force if violated, but others do not have legal or political support. Some norms have intense moral urgency, and their violation is judged a crime or a sin; others are something more like rules of propriety, and their violation is taken merely as impoliteness or social gracelessness. One dimension on which norms vary is how formalized they are: is a particular norm widely understood but implicit, or is it spelled out and made visible in law, a code of ethics, a religious commandment, and folk counsel? These different kinds of norms may not all be explainable in the same manner, either in how they originate, how they are maintained, or how they influence individual behavior.

Any of the many factors that influence human behavior could influence the introduction of norms. Economic, technological, legal, political, social, cultural, and intellectual factors could all contribute to the emergence of prescriptive rules. One of the distinctive features of norms as prescriptive rules, rather than norms as prevalent practices, is that they are self-consciously articulated. What circumstances lead people or institutions to become self-conscious about their patterns of behavior and to articulate them in the form of moral norms?

At least four conditions encourage the articulation of norms. Two of these we might think of as Durkheimian, having to do with horizontal solidarity or group identity, and two are Weberian, concerning hierarchical social control across an organization at one point in time or across generations over time. The first Durkheimian condition is that the articulation of moral norms is encouraged by forms of ritual solidarity that call on a group or institution to celebrate itself, to honor its members, to recognize the introduction of new members of the group or the passing of old ones or the induction of fully adult or assimilated new members to higher status in the group. Thus births, confirmations, funerals, retirements, annual meetings, awards banquets, and other such events provide occasions in which speakers are often called upon to state explicitly, and as moral rules, the ways of the group.

A second Durkheimian condition is more outward than inward looking: cultural contact and conflict can provoke the articulation of norms inside the group. Here the prescription that "the way we do things" is "the way one should do things" is a function of a kind of group egoism, a way of defining the group in relation to other groups. This may lead groups to claim independence or separation from other groups, but equally it may prod them to claim affiliation with other groups.

A Weberian condition for the articulation of norms arises in any institutional setting so large that socialization or enculturation cannot take place informally. Wherever people must be handled in batches and trained in the ways of the group, there will be a kind of pedagogical economy in saying out loud what the prescribed rules of behavior are. Where the ways of the group must be handed down from one generation to the next—where, in other words, some form of schooling is necessary—the teaching generation will benefit from formulating rules of general applicability and rules with moral force. These rules will be of great use to the learning generation, too, in providing certainty about how to behave under inherently ambiguous conditions. The pedagogical imperative for the articulation of norms often leads to an overly rigid or absolute statement of norms and the overlearning of norms on the part of the students. Thus children overlearn gender-appropriate behaviors and are sometimes unwilling to tolerate variation in behaviors that to adults seem innocuous. Bureaucrats, likewise, overlearn rules and may take their own rules too seriously.

A second Weberian condition arises less from the need to pass on organizational culture in a large institution than from the need of superiors to control subordinates in a complex organization. Superiors may wish to be free from normative constraints on their liberty to act with their best discretion, but they would like their subordinates to be constrained by rules. Here political control encourages the emergence of formalized norms.

These four social conditions prompt the rhetorical formalization of norms. Each of them offers a set of reasons for speech or for the codification into speech or writing of implicit norms. Both needs for social cohesion (the Durkheimian conditions) and needs for social control (the Weberian conditions) can generate articulate moral norms.

## The Business Neutrality of Colonial Printers

In colonial American journalism, printers testified to a concern for fairness in order to shed responsibility for what appeared in their pages. Benjamin Franklin insisted in his "Apology for Printers" ([1731] 1989) that the printer was just that—one who prints, not one who edits, exercises judgment, or agrees with each opinion in his pages. "Printers are educated in the Belief that when Men differ in Opinion, both Sides ought equally to have the Advantage of being heard by the Publick; and that when Truth and Error have fair Play, the former is always an overmatch for the latter: Hence they chearfully serve all contending Writers that pay them well, without regarding on which side they are of the Question in Dispute." In the same passage, however, Franklin also declares that newspaper contributions must exhibit good taste and refrain from character assassination. Clearly, he exercised editorial judgments even as he denied doing so (Franklin [1731] 1989, 172–73).

Franklin's "Apology" is not only a mess of contradictions; it is also a rare effort on the part of a printer to defend his behavior at all. Colonial newspaper proprietors had little theory of the press and little occasion to articulate a rationale. Printers ran their newspapers with little consistent purpose or principle. They saw themselves as operators of a small trade, not learned professionals. At first, colonial printers did not imagine their newspapers to be either political instruments or professional agencies of news gathering. None of the early papers reached out to collect news; they simply printed what came to them. Colonial printers, more than their London brethren, were public figures—running the post office, serving as clerks for the government, and printing the laws. Their business concerns may have been small, but they were first of all businessmen.

In the first half century of American journalism, there was little indication that the newspaper would become a central forum for political discourse. Colonial printers avoided controversy when they could, preached the printer's neutrality when they had to, and printed primarily foreign news because it afforded local readers and local authorities no grounds for grumbling. Foreign news came primarily from the London press and looked out at the world from an English Protestant perspective; although there were American colonists from Sweden, the Netherlands, Germany, and elsewhere, the overwhelming majority were from England and no doubt found London-inflected news interesting, perhaps reassuring, but rarely controversial. The preponderance of foreign news was overwhelming. Out of a sample of nineteen hundred items that Franklin's *Pennsylvania Gazette* printed from 1728 to 1765, only thirty-four touched on politics in Philadelphia or Pennsylvania (Clark and Wetherell 1989, 292).

As conflict with England heated up after 1765, politics entered the press, and printerly "fairness" went by the board. It became more troublesome for printers to be neutral than to be partisan; nearly everyone felt compelled to take sides, and the newspaper began its long career as the mouthpiece of political parties and factions. Patriots had no tolerance for the pro-British press, and the new states passed and enforced treason and sedition statutes in the 1770s and 1780s. By the time of the state-by-state debates over ratification of the Constitution in 1787 and 1788, Federalists, those leaders who supported a strong national government, dominated the press and squeezed Anti-Federalists out of public debate. In Pennsylvania, leading papers tended not to report the speeches of Anti-Federalists at the ratification convention. When unusual newspapers in Philadelphia, New York, and Boston sought to report views on both sides, Federalists stopped their subscriptions and forced the papers to end their attempt at even-handedness (Main 1961).

Some of the nation's founders believed outspoken political criticism was well justified as long as they were fighting a monarchy for their independence but that open critique of a duly elected republican government could be legitimately curtailed. Samuel Adams, the famed Boston agitator in the struggle for independence, changed his views on political action once republican government had been established. This great advocate of open talk, committees of correspondence, an outspoken press, and voluntary associations of citizens now opposed all hint of public associations and public criticism that operated outside the regular channels of government (Maier 1980). As one contemporary observed, it did no harm for writers to mislead the people when the people were powerless, but "to mislead the judgement of the people, where they have *all* power, must produce the greatest possible mischief."[5] The Sedition Act of 1798 forbade criticism of the government, and as many as one in four editors of oppositional papers were brought up on charges under this law. This move went one step further than many Americans of the day were willing to go, however. Federalist propaganda notwithstanding, Thomas Jefferson won the presidency in 1800, the Sedition Act expired, and party opposition began to be grudgingly accepted.

In this era, no norm of objectivity appeared. The printer's neutrality was supported in a rhetorical setting in which an admission of partisanship or preferences would have opened a Pandora's box. Neutrality was perhaps prudential counsel, but it was not a moral norm. In any event, all of this referred only to what the printer would print; none of it touched on what a printer might write. What writing there was tended not to be reporting as we would think of it today but commentary. The occupational preconditions for a modern concept of objectivity simply did not exist. Thus, when political partisans made demands on printers, there was no defense against them, no ideological resources to counterpose the integrity of journalists against the corruption of party, even in a day when the legitimacy of parties was much in doubt. A language of occupational virtue for journalists had not yet developed.

## Partisan Predictability and Stenographic Fairness

In nineteenth-century American journalism, editors came to take great pride in the speed and accuracy of the news they provided. With the introduction in the 1830s of the rotary press and soon the steam-powered press, amid an expanding urban economy on the eastern seaboard, and in the rush of enthusiasm for Jacksonian democracy, commercial competition heated up among city newspapers. A new breed of "penny papers" hired newsboys to hawk copies on the street, and editors competed for a wider readership and increasingly sought out local news—of politics, crime, and high society. This newly aggressive commercialism in journalism was an important precondition for modern notions of objectivity or fairness, but, at first, it fostered only a narrow concept of stenographic fairness. The papers grew increasingly boastful about the speed and accuracy of their news gathering, but editors found this perfectly consistent with political partisanship and their choosing to cover the speeches or rallies only of the party they favored. It was equally consistent, in their eyes, for reporters to go over speeches with sympathetic politicians to improve, in printed form, on the oral presentation. Into the 1870s and 1880s, Washington correspondents routinely supplemented their newspaper income by clerking for the very congressional committees about which they wrote. They often lived at the same boarding houses as congressmen, and the boarding houses tended to divide along party lines (Ritchie 1991, 60–63).[6]

As late as the 1890s, a standard Republican paper covering a presidential election not only sometimes deplored and derided Democratic candidates in editorials but often neglected even to mention them in the news. In the days before public opinion polling, the size of partisan rallies was taken as a proxy for likely electoral results. Republican rallies would be described as "monster meetings," and Democratic rallies were often not covered at all. In the Democratic papers, of course, it was just the reverse.

## Journalism as an Occupational Culture

Partisanship ran deep in nineteenth-century American journalism. Popular historians of journalism like to quote the paragraph in Adolph Ochs's statement of purpose on taking over the *New York Times* in 1896, stating that the paper would give the news "impartially, without fear or favor, regardless of any party, sect or interest involved." They invariably fail to quote the next paragraph, which lays out Ochs's commitment to sound money, tariff reform, low taxes, and limited government. Ochs took these principles seriously enough to march, along with top editors of his paper, in the parade for the so-called Gold Democratic ticket in 1896 (Davis 1921, 218). Objectivity was far from an established practice or ideal in the 1890s.

Partisanship endured, but reporters came increasingly to enjoy a culture of their own independent of political parties. They developed their own mythologies (reveling in their intimacy with the urban underworld), their own clubs and watering holes, and their own professional practices. Interviewing, for instance, had become a common activity for reporters in the 1870s and 1880s. In the antebellum years, reporters had talked with public officials but did not refer to these conversations in print. Politicians and diplomats dropped by the newspaper offices but could feel secure, as one reporter recalled, that their confidences "were regarded as inviolate." President Abraham Lincoln often spoke with reporters informally, but no reporter ever quoted him directly. No president submitted to an interview before Andrew Johnson in 1868, but by the 1880s the interview was a well-accepted and institutionalized media event, an occasion created by journalists from which they could then craft a story. This new style of journalistic intervention did not erase partisanship, but it did presage reporters' new dedication to a sense of craft and their new location in an occupational culture with its own rules, its own rewards, and its own esprit (Schudson 1995, 72–93).[7]

Interviewing was a practice oriented more to pleasing an audience of news consumers than to parroting or promoting a party line. The newspaper industry had become big business by the 1880s, with towering downtown buildings, scores of reporters, splashy sponsorship of civic festivals, and pages of advertising from the newly burgeoning department stores. The papers vastly expanded their readership in this growing marketplace; increasing numbers of papers counted their circulation in the hundreds of thousands. Accordingly, reporters writing news came to focus more on making stories and less on promoting parties. Newspapers were becoming highly profitable businesses. Circulation leaped forward while the cost of production plummeted, with wood pulp as a new source of paper and mechanical typesetting a new labor-saving device. Advertising revenue surpassed subscription fees as the primary source of income as the papers courted new audiences (particularly women). The increasingly commercial orientation of the newspaper certainly helped sustain the innovation of interviewing.

The idea of interviewing "took like wildfire," wrote Atlanta reporter Henry Grady (1879). What one would like to know, of course, is just why. One would also like to know why it became immediately popular in the United States but not in Europe—a matter to which I shall return. It would be two more generations before European reporters began to adopt what was by then standard practice in the United States. In Britain, journalists began to accept the interview after 1900, often through American tutelage. Europeans learned from the American example that their own elites would also submit to interviews. This education accelerated during World War I. One American reporter recalled that his assignment to interview European heads of state in 1909 seemed "ridiculous and impossible" (and he failed at it); but twenty years later it was easy, the interview no longer "a shocking innovation to the rulers of Europe" (Abbott 1933, 270).

In the late nineteenth century and into the twentieth century, leading journalists counseled against note taking, and journalists were encouraged to rely upon their own memories. By the 1920s, however, journalism textbooks dared to recommend "the discriminate and intelligent use of notes" (Williams and Martin 1922, 170–71). The growing acceptance of note taking suggests the acceptance and naturalization of interviewing. This is not to say the interview was no longer controversial. The English writer G. K. Chesterton reported in 1922 that even before his ship touched land in New York, interviewers had "boarded the ship like pirates" (Chesterton 1922, 47). There was still a sense that the interview was a contrived event in which the journalist, in collusion with a person seeking publicity, invented rather than reported news. As late as 1926 the Associated Press prohibited its reporters from writing interviews. Generally, however, reporting in the United States by that time meant interviewing.

The rapid diffusion of this new practice among American journalists seems to have been unaccompanied by any ideological rationale. It fit effortlessly into a journalism already focused on facts and newsworthy events rather than devoted primarily to political commentary or preoccupied with literary aspirations. It did not give rise to the objectivity norm but was one of the growing number of practices that identified journalists as a distinct occupational group with distinct patterns of behavior. The growing corporate coherence of that occupational group, generating a demand both for social cohesion and occupational pride, on the one hand, and internal social control, on the other, would by the 1920s eventuate in a self-conscious ethic of objectivity.

## Alternative Perspectives on Late-Nineteenth-Century Journalism

One of the most stubborn beliefs in journalism history is that objectivity became the common practice in journalism in the late nineteenth century because (1) the telegraph put a premium on a terse, factual style, (2) the wire services required value-free reporting to serve clients of various political allegiances, and (3) newspapers in general found profit in winning over both Democratic and Republican readers. This perspective, however, is largely myth.

The case for the decisive role of the telegraph is made well by Donald L. Shaw in several key articles. His study of Wisconsin newspapers from 1852 to 1916 found a decline in news bias over the period, as general accounts would have led him to expect. Shaw finds a particularly sharp decline, however, between 1880 and 1884, a period in which there was a leap from 47 to 89 percent in the proportion of wire-based stories in Wisconsin newspapers' coverage of the presidential campaign. Later, and more slowly, nonwire news also showed declining bias, a fact that Shaw attributes to reporters' learning to imitate wire service style (Shaw 1971, 64–86; Shaw 1967, 3–12, 31; Shaw 1968, 326–29).

Shaw's quantitative study is reinforced, more allusively, by James Carey's "Technology and Ideology," a justly famous essay brimming with ideas. Carey argues that the telegraph required that colloquialisms and the regional twang be removed from a language that would now be available everywhere; that it turned the correspondent who analyzed news into a stringer who just relayed facts; and that the high cost of telegraphic transmission forced journalistic prose to become "lean and unadorned" (Carey 1989, 211).

The logic of Shaw's and Carey's arguments seems at first glance unassailable, and there is genuine satisfaction in finding so complex a social change as a shift in literary style and normative orientation to be so neatly explained. However, that is exactly the temptation of economic and technological reductionisms that must be resisted.

The beauty in these explanations may be only skin deep. In this case, there are three problems. First, the explanation is vague about just what it explains. At most, it explains new social practices (in this case, a new literary style), not new moral norms. In that sense, it does not explain enough. On the other hand, it may explain too much. If Shaw and Carey are correct, should we not expect newspapers by the 1890s or at least by 1900 or the first years of the twentieth century, a full generation after Shaw's critical period, to be decreasingly partisan or, at least, to be displaying their partisanship in increasingly subtle ways? Should we not expect newspaper prose to be "lean" and telegraphic? Should we not expect leading newspapers to be focusing increasingly on relaying only "facts"? In 1900, however, newspaper partisanship was still in most cases blatant, its prose, by modern standards, still long winded. In fact, the ideals of journalistic prose by 1900 seem to have been quite varied. Far from cohering around a telegraphic center, the language of dashing correspondents from Cuba just before and during the Spanish-American War was personal, colorful, and romantic. The human interest reporting of journalists enchanted with urban life was sentimental. Coverage of politics was often self-consciously sarcastic and humorous. This was not prose stripped bare.

This is my own observation, based on reading a fair number of newspapers of the turn of the century; it is not based on any systematic evaluation, and it would be flimsy ground for disputing Shaw and Carey if their own work were based on more systematic content analysis. This raises the second problem with the technological and economic explanation: it is based on limited data, including data not easily bent to the overall argument. Carey's work is apparently entirely impressionistic. As for Shaw's, it has some curious features if it is to be a basis for a technologically determinist argument. Between 1852, when Wisconsin newspapers used no wire service stories in campaign coverage, and 1880, when half of the stories originated with wire services, there was no decrease in measured bias (actually, there was a small increase) (Shaw 1967, 6). Why should this increase from zero to 47 percent wire stories have produced no decrease in bias, given that the increase from 47 to 89 percent in the next four years led to a dramatic drop in news bias? (Shaw also finds a fairly steep increase in news bias from 1888 to 1892; only after that is there is a steady decline. This is another anomaly that does not fit Shaw's explanation.) This makes no sense if the constraints of telegraphy necessarily force or at least have a very close affinity to a new prose style.

What is at issue is not only a new style of prose but the self-conscious articulation of rules with moral force that direct how that prose will be written and provide a standard of condemnation when the writing does not measure up. Here the technological and economic explanations by themselves help not at all.

Neither Carey nor Shaw gives close consideration to alternative hypotheses. One hypothesis I advance in *Discovering the News* (Schudson 1978) is that professional allegiance to a separation of facts and values awaited, first, the rising status and independence of reporters relative to their employees, a change in journalism that developed gradually between the 1870s and World War I, and second, the emergence of serious professional discussion about objectivity, which came only after World War I. Only with these developments did the social, organizational, and intellectual foundations arise for institutionalizing a set of journalistic practices to give force to objectivity (Schudson 1978). Subsequent work confirms my original point that a self-conscious, articulate ideology of objectivity can be dated to the 1920s (Streckfuss 1990, 973–83).

In addition, most newspapers remained deeply partisan until the end of the nineteenth century. In places like Wisconsin, the vast majority of these partisan papers were Republican. That might have made 1884 an unusual year, because many of the most prominent Republican papers in the country (including papers like the *New York Evening Post*, the *Boston Herald*, and the Massachusetts based *Springfield Republican*) abandoned Republican standard-bearer James G. Blaine. It is quite possible that the decline in news bias from 1880 to 1884, on which Shaw builds his argument, had more to do with the unusual nature of the 1884 campaign, when issues of the personal integrity or corruption of the candidates, rather than party loyalty, played an unusually important role (King 1992, 185–87).

The notion that the move from partisanship to objectivity was economically motivated is widely believed but nowhere justified. The leading textbook in the history of journalism puts it this way: "Offering the appearance of fairness was important to owners and editors trying to gain their share of a growing readership and the resulting advertising revenues" (Emery, Emery, and Roberts 1996, 181)—but was it? Readership was growing so rapidly in the late nineteenth century—from 3.5 million daily newspaper readers in 1880 to 33 million in 1920—that a great variety of journalistic styles were becoming economically rewarding. Very likely the most lucrative option was strident partisanship. Certainly this characterized circulation leaders of the day like William Randolph Hearst's *New York Journal* and Joseph Pulitzer's *New York World*. Heated political campaigns and the newspapers' ardent participation in them were circulation builders, not circulation losers (King 1992, 396–98, 467–68).

Another factor in the eventual triumph of a professional journalism is that the very concept of politics changed from 1880 to 1920 under the impact of mugwump and Progressive reforms. Liberal reformers began to criticize unquestioning party loyalty. They promoted new forms of electoral campaigning, urging an "educational" campaign with more pamphlets and fewer parades. Newspapers at the same time became more willing to take an independent stance. By 1890, a quarter of daily newspapers in the northern states, where the reform movement was most advanced, claimed independence of party.

By 1896, a reform known as the Australian ballot had swept the country, changing forever the way Americans went to the polls. Until the 1890s, American election days were organized to the last detail by the competing political parties. The state did not prepare a ballot; rather, the parties printed up their own tickets and distributed them to voters near the polls. The voter then did not need to mark the ballot in any way—the voter did not need, in fact, to be literate. He just took the ticket from the party worker and deposited it in the ballot box. The act of voting was thus an act of affiliation with a partisan cause (Schudson 1998a, 168–74).[8]

Introduction of the Australian ballot (the reform originated in Australia) symbolized a different understanding. The state now prepared a ballot that listed candidates of all contending parties. The voter received the ballot from an election clerk and, in the privacy of the voting booth, marked the ballot, choosing candidates from one or several parties, as he wished. Voting became a performance oriented to an ideal of objectivity, a model of rational choice, if you will. An increasingly strident rhetoric prevailed, condemning the corruption of parties and stressing the need for forms of governing that transcended party politics. Civil service reform, taking off in this same era, promoted this rhetoric powerfully in many nations around the world. In the American case, however, and in those other nations that adopted ballot reform, there was not only a verbal rhetoric but also a kind of performative rhetoric in which millions of people acted out a social practice that incorporated a new model of objectivity.

With the adoption of the Australian ballot, civil service reform, corrupt practices acts, voter registration laws, the ballot initiative and referendum, the popular primary, the direct election of senators, and nonpartisan municipal elections, politics began to be seen as an administrative science that required experts. Voting came to be seen as an activity in which voters make choices among programs and candidates, not one in which they loyally turn out in ritual solidarity to their party. This new understanding of politics helped transform a rabidly partisan press into an institution differentiated from the parties, with journalists more likely to see themselves as journalists, or as writers, rather than as political hangers-on (McGerr 1986).[9]

## Modern Objectivity

What we might call modern analytical and procedural fairness dates to the 1920s. Analytical fairness had no secure place until journalists as an occupational group developed loyalties to their audiences and to themselves as an occupational community rather than to their publishers or their pub-

lishers' favored political parties. At this point journalists also came to articulate rules of the journalistic road more often and more consistently. The
general manager of the Associated Press, Kent Cooper, announced his
creed in 1925: "The journalist who deals in facts diligently developed and
intelligently presented exalts his profession, and his stories need never be
colorless or dull" (Gramling 1940, 314). Newspaper editors formed their
first national professional association, the American Society of Newspaper
Editors, in 1922. At its opening convention, the organization adopted a
code of ethics, "Canons of Journalism," that prescribed principles of "sin-
cerity, truthfulness, accuracy, [and] impartiality," the latter including the
declaration that "news reports should be free from opinion or bias of any
kind" (Pratte 1995, 206).

   This newly articulate fairness doctrine was related to the sheer growth
in news gathering; rules of objectivity enabled editors to keep lowly reporters in check, although they had less control over high-flying foreign
correspondents. Objectivity as ideology was a kind of industrial discipline;
a Weberian condition was at work. At the same time, objectivity seemed a
natural and progressive ideology for an aspiring occupational group at a
moment when science was god, efficiency was cherished, and increasingly
prominent elites judged partisanship a vestige of the tribal nineteenth century (Purcell 1973).[10] Here Durkheimian affiliation was a factor promoting
the articulation of a norm of objectivity.

   Another Durkheimian condition was also at stake: journalists sought
not only to affiliate with the prestige of science, efficiency, and Progressive
reform but also to disaffiliate from the public relations specialists and pro-
pagandists who were suddenly all around them. Journalists had rejected
parties only to find their newfound independence besieged by a squadron
of information mercenaries available for hire by government, business, politicians, and others. Early in the twentieth century, efforts by businessmen
and government agencies to place favorable stories about themselves in the
press multiplied. A new "profession" of public relations emerged and got a
great boost from President Woodrow Wilson's attempt in World War I to
use public relations to sell the war to the American public. The war stimulated popular public relations campaigns for war bonds, the Red Cross, the
Salvation Army, and the Young Men's Christian Association (YMCA). By
1920, one journalism critic noted, there were nearly a thousand "bureaus of
propaganda" in Washington modeled on the war experience (Irwin 1923,
27). Rumors circulated among journalists that between 50 and 60 percent of
stories even in the *New York Times* were inspired by press agents. The publicity agent, wrote the philosopher John Dewey in 1929, "is perhaps the
most significant symbol of our present social life" (Dewey 1930, 43; Schudson 1978, 121–59).[11]

   Journalists grew self-conscious about the manipulability of information in the propaganda age. They felt a need to close ranks and assert their

collective integrity in the face of their close encounter with the publicity agents' unembarrassed effort to use information (or misinformation) to promote special interests. When Joseph Pulitzer endowed the School of Journalism at Columbia in 1904 (although classes did not begin until 1913), he declared that he wanted to "raise journalism to the rank of a learned profession" (Pulitzer 1984, 657). By the 1920s, it seemed to at least some of the more intellectual-minded advocates of journalistic professionalism that this meant a scrupulous adherence to scientific ideals. "There is but one kind of unity possible in a world as diverse as ours," Walter Lippmann wrote. "It is unity of method, rather than of aim; the unity of the disciplined experiment." He wanted to upgrade the professional dignity of journalists and provide a training for them "in which the ideal of objective testimony is cardinal" (Lippmann 1920, 67, 82).

Nothing was more threatening to this ideal than the work of public relations. "Many reporters today are little more than intellectual mendicants," complained the political scientist Peter Odegard in 1930, "who go from one publicity agent or press bureau to another seeking 'handouts'" (Odegard 1930, 132). Just before World War I, the New York newspaper editor Don Seitz assembled a list of fourteen hundred press agents for the American Newspaper Publishers Association, distributed the list to the association's members, and urged them not to accept material for publication from any of them. This was a losing battle, however, and by 1926 Seitz complained that the Pulitzer School of Journalism "turns out far more of these parasites than it does reporters" (Seitz 1926, 209–10, 210).[12] He may have been right. By the time the sociologist Leila Sussmann wrote her dissertation on public relations in 1947, her survey of some six hundred public relations agents found that three-quarters of them had worked as newspaper journalists before turning to public relations (Sussmann 1947, 87).

At this time—the 1920s—the objectivity norm had become a fully formulated occupational ideal, part of a professional project or mission. Far more than a set of craft rules to fend off libel suits or a set of constraints to help editors keep tabs on their underlings, objectivity was finally a moral code. It was asserted in journalism textbooks and in codes of ethics of professional associations. By the 1930s, publishers would use the objectivity norm as a weapon against unionization in the newsroom (on the grounds that a reporter who was also a member of the Newspaper Guild could not possibly be objective). The Weberian condition of social control inside the organization gave publishers reason to promote the objectivity norm to serve their own purposes even if they had done little or nothing to invent it (Schudson 1978, 156–57).[13]

The relevance of this Weberian condition may be better recognized by the observation that the farther a reporter is from the home office, the greater that reporter's freedom to violate objectivity norms. Foreign correspondents are treated more as independent experts, free to make judgments, and less as dependent employees who could be supervised. In truth, they cannot be supervised, nor do editors often have the knowledge to second-guess them. For that matter, readers do not normally have the background to fill in a context to make bare facts comprehensible.

Others—notably sports reporters—are exempt from rules of objectivity on different grounds. All journalism is ethnocentric, giving more attention to national news than foreign news. Where news organizations cater to local rather than national audiences, as is decidedly the case in the American press, they are ethnocentric with respect to their own city or region. In the rare cases in which an American news organization is designed with a national audience in mind—*USA Today*, for instance—sports reporting operates by an objectivity norm, but ordinarily sports reporters openly favor local teams. If a Chicago newspaper were to provide a visiting basketball team coverage as sympathetic as it provides the hometown Chicago Bulls, the act would be understood as treachery, as if the *Times* of London had treated press releases from Hitler's Germany with the same deference as those from 10 Downing Street.

From the perspective of the local news institution, the triumphs and defeats of the local team are examined from a stance that presumes enthusiastic backing of the team. The home team is within what Daniel Hallin has called the "sphere of consensus" in journalism, a domain in which the rules of objective reporting do not hold (Hallin 1986, 116–17). Journalism is a complex social and discursive domain. American newspapers not only report conflicts and competitions with professional detachment but also contribute to establishing a local community identity. Not infrequently, in the nineteenth century, newspapers were founded in order to draw attention to and increase the real estate values of frontier towns. This booster spirit survives and colors the American press. European newspapers, typically national in orientation, with close ties to national party organizations rather than to local business elites, are much less susceptible to boosterism. In the central arena of political news reporting, however, American journalism embraced the objectivity norm.

At the very moment that journalists claimed objectivity as their ideal, they also recognized its limits. In the 1930s there was a vogue for what contemporaries called "interpretive journalism." Leading journalists and journalism educators insisted that the world had grown increasingly complex and needed not only to be reported but to be explained. The political columnists, like Walter Lippmann, David Lawrence, Frank Kent, and Mark Sullivan, came into their own in this era. Journalists insisted that their task was to help readers not only know but understand. They took it for granted by that point that understanding had nothing to do with party or partisan sentiment. In this respect, even interpretive forms of journalism paid homage to nonpartisanship.

Was this progress—a professional press taking over from party hacks?

Not everyone was so sure. If the change brought a new dispassion to news coverage, it also opened the way to making entertainment rather than political coherence a chief criterion of journalism. The Speaker of the House "Uncle" Joe Cannon objected:

> I believe we had better publicity when the party press was the rule and the so-called independent press the exception, than we have now. The correspondents in the press gallery then felt their responsibility for reporting the proceedings of Congress. Then men representing papers in sympathy with the party in power were alert to present the record their party was making so that the people would know its accomplishments, and those representing the opposition party were eager to expose any failures on the part of the Administration. (Cannon and Busbey 1927, 295)

In the independent press, in contrast, serious discussion of legislation gave way to entertainment: "The cut of a Congressman's whiskers or his clothes is a better subject for a human interest story than what he says in debate" (Cannon and Busbey 1927, 295). News, Joseph Cannon mourned in 1927, had replaced legislative publicity. What had really happened is that journalists had become their own interpretive community, writing to one another and not to parties or partisans, determined to distinguish their work from that of press agents, eager to pass on to younger journalists and to celebrate in themselves an ethic and an integrity in keeping with the broader culture's acclaim for science and nonpartisanship.

## Conclusion

Journalists live in the public eye. They are uninsulated from public scrutiny—they have no recondite language, little fancy technology, no mirrors and mysteries to shield them from the public. There are strong reasons for journalists to seek moral norms that appeal to the public in order to protect themselves from criticism, embarrassment, or lawsuits to give them guidance in their work in preventing practices that would provoke criticism or even lawsuits, and to endow their occupation with an identity they can count as worthy. This instrumentality, however—the practical utility of having some norm—does not explain why this particular norm, the objectivity norm, came to dominate.

A variety of moral norms are capable of achieving the ends of providing public support and insulation from criticism. Journalists in Germany or China or Cuba or Argentina work with norms that differ from the objectivity norm. To understand the emergence of a norm historically, it is necessary to understand not only the general social conditions that provide incentives for groups to adopt "some" norm but the specific cultural circumstances that lead them to adopt a specific norm. Strategic uses for normativity help explain why journalists have norms at all, and I have spoken of the Durkheimian and Weberian conditions that promoted the generation of a new norm in American journalism; but these components do not explain why a group selects the particular norm it does. The latter problem requires an understanding of the cultural environment the group draws on, the set of ideas, concepts, and values they have access to, find attractive, and can convey convincingly to themselves and others.

At this point, I return to the question of why European journalism did not initially develop the norm of objectivity and, when later they came to accept it, did so with less fervor than Americans. Some of the sociological conditions that affected journalistic norms in America were absent or less pronounced in Europe. Public relations developed more extensively and influentially in the United States than in Europe, and thus journalists' desire to distinguish themselves from public relations practitioners was absent in Europe. Moreover, the growing antipartisan nature of American political life, intensified in the Progressive years, went much further than efforts to contain party corruption in Europe. In America, a civil service tradition had to be invented, and it emerged as the result of a political movement; in Europe, a degree of bureaucratic autonomy, legitimacy, and professionalism could be taken for granted, so there was less reason for European civil servants to ideologize themselves the way American reformers did. The ideological virtues of a journalistic divorce from party, so readily portrayed in America against this reform background, had no comparable political ballast in European journalism.

Approaching the comparative question from a different angle, it may also be that the space that could be occupied by objectivity as a professional value in American journalism was already occupied in European journalism. It was occupied by a reasonably successful journalistic self-understanding that journalists were high literary creators and cosmopolitan political thinkers. European journalists did not have the down-and-dirty sense of themselves as laborers whose standing in the world required upgrading, as American journalists did. If there was to be upgrading, in any event, it was to a literary rather than professional ideal.

Jean Chalaby goes so far as to observe that journalism is an "Anglo-American invention" (Chalaby 1996, 303–26). British and American journalism became focused on information and facts in the mid-nineteenth century, but French journalism did not. Until late in the century, when leading British and American newspapers employed numerous foreign correspondents, the French press drew most of its foreign news straight from the London papers. The French were much less concerned than the British and Americans to draw a line between facts and commentary in the news. French journalism, and other Continental journalisms, did not participate in the "unique discursive revolution" that characterized British and American journalism—and so would not come around to an objectivity-oriented journalism until many decades after the Americans and, even then, less fully (Chalaby 1996, 313).

Chalaby treats the American and British cases as more similar than I think is warranted. The British case may be a kind of halfway house between American professionalism and Continental traditions of party-governed journalism with high literary aspirations. Even so, Chalaby's explanation that French journalism could not partake of the Anglo-American discursive revolution because it was dominated by literary figures and literary aspirations is a point well taken.

It would be wonderful to find a person, a moment, an incident that gave birth to the objectivity norm in American journalism and then to simply trace the mechanisms of diffusion from newspaper to newspaper, and from American newspapers to world journalism; but there is no magic moment. The social conditions that made possible, desirable, and convenient the occupational practices that are now understood as objective reporting emerged during the late nineteenth century in ways that did not initially produce a strong, self-conscious articulation of the objectivity norm. At the point at which the norm became clearly articulated—in the 1920s—it was already operating in the daily activities of American journalists. It is easier to explain the articulation of the norm, arising from the Durkheimian and Weberian conditions I have sketched, than to establish exactly which features of the American cultural landscape and the changing social conditions of the late nineteenth century were most vital in preparing the soil for it. What is clear is that the moral norm American journalists live by in their professional lives, use as a means of social control and social identity, and accept as the most legitimate grounds for attributing praise and blame is a norm that took root first, and most deeply, in this journalism and not in others across the Atlantic.

## Notes

1. Wolfgang Donsbach (1995) conducted a survey to compare German, Swedish, Italian, British, and American journalists. He found Americans "still uphold norms of objectivity, fairness and neutrality." They do so more than their European counterparts, who are much more likely to say that it is important for them to "champion particular values and ideas." Differences in norms seem also matched in differences in the social organization of work: only a sixth of American journalists who say their primary function is reporting or editing also acknowledge spending some time writing commentary, whereas for German journalists the figure is greater than 60 percent, and among Italians and British reporters and editors about half acknowledge spending time in commentary. See also Donsbach and Klett 1993 and Chalaby 1996.

2. On newsroom practices, the landmark work is Tuchman 1972. On journalistic defenses of objectivity against its critics, the two chief moments came in the

1960s in response to "new journalism" and New Left critiques of journalism and in the 1990s in response to the movement for "public" or "civic" journalism. The former is summarized in Schudson 1978, 160–94, and many of the latter defenses are cited and discussed in Schudson 1998b, 132–49.

3.  The eighth edition of the leading journalism history textbook emphasizes both explanations but also acknowledges growing uncertainty about their validity (Emery and Emery 1996, 185).

4.  Richard McAdams defines a norm as "a decentralized behavioral standard that individuals feel obligated to follow." This definition is meant to distinguish general social norms from law, the latter being a highly centralized and authoritative standard backed, at least in principle, by force. I think law is a particular kind of norm rather than something altogether different from a norm; see McAdams 1997, 381.

5.  Buel 1980, 86, quoting Pennsylvania jurist Alexander Addison. On Addison, see also Rosenberg 1984.

6.  For historical materials not otherwise footnoted, I draw primarily on Schudson 1978.

7.  I draw here on a much fuller account of the history of the newspaper interview in Schudson 1995, 72–93.

8.  The symbolic and substantive importance of ballot reform is emphasized in Schudson 1998a, 168–74.

9.  See especially McGerr 1986.

10.  Edward Purcell (1973) lucidly discusses the general prestige of objectivist or "scientific naturalist" understandings of science and social science in the 1920s.

11.  The history of public relations is not well developed. The material here comes from Schudson 1978, 121–59.

12.  See also Hanna 1920, 398–99; Michael 1935; Gruening 1931; Bent 1927; and Kelly 1935, 307–18, for other critiques of press agentry.

13.  The changing economics of newspaper publishing allowed publishers increasing independence from parties and made them more open to the "public service" talk of the Progressive Era. Richard Kaplan (1998) emphasizes this in his study of Detroit newspapers. He finds that at least one leading publisher, George G. Booth of the *Detroit Evening News,* adopted the language of "public service" and "impartiality" in the early 1900s. I do not myself see how the self-justifying talk of publishers creates a psychologically powerful sense of obligation to impartiality on the part of reporters—although certainly declining pressure from publishers for their journalists to toe a party line would have been conducive to journalists taking themselves as serious, independent professionals.

# References

Abbott, Willis J. 1933. *Watching the World Go By.* London: John Lowe.

Bent, Silas. 1927. *Ballyhoo.* New York: Boni and Liveright.

Buel, Richard, Jr. 1980. "Freedom of the Press in Revolutionary America: The Evolution of Libertarianism, 1760–1820." In *The Press and the American Revolution,* edited by Bernard Bailyn and John B. Hench. Worcester, Mass.: American Antiquarian Society.

Cannon, Joseph, and L. White Busbey. 1926. *Uncle Joe Cannon*. New York: Henry Holt.

Carey, James. 1989. "Technology and Ideology: The Case of the Telegraph." In *Communication and Culture*. Boston: Unwin Hyman.

Chalaby, Jean K. 1996. "Journalism as an Anglo-American Invention: A Comparison of the Development of French and Anglo-American Journalism, 1830s–1920s." *European Journal of Communication* 11(3): 303–26.

Chesterton, G.K. 1922. *What I Saw in America*. London: Hodder and Stoughton.

Clark, Charles, and Charles Wetherell. 1989. "The Meaning of Maturity: *The Pennsylvania Gazette*, 1728–1765." *William and Mary Quarterly* 46(2): 279–303.

Cooter, Robert. 1998. "Expressive Law and Economics." *Journal of Legal Studies* 27(2): 585–608.

Davis, Elmer. 1921. *History of the New York Times, 1851–1921*. New York: New York Times.

Dewey, John. 1930. *Individualism Old and New*. New York: Minton, Balch.

Donsbach, Wolfgang. 1995. "Lapdogs, Watchdogs, and Junkyard Dogs." *Media Studies Journal* 9(Fall): 17–30.

Donsbach, Wolfgang, and Bettina Klett. 1993. "Subjective Objectivity: How Journalists in Four Countries Define a Key Term of Their Profession." *Gazette* 51(1): 53–83.

Emery, Michael, and Edwin Emery, with Nancy Roberts. 1996. *The Press and America: An Interpretive History of the Mass Media*. Boston: Allyn and Bacon.

Franklin, Benjamin. [1731] 1989. "Apology for Printers." In *Benjamin Franklin: Writings*, edited by J. A. Leo LeMay. New York: Library of America.

Grady, Henry. 1879. "On Interviewing." *Atlanta Constitution*, August 16, 1879, p. 1.

Gramling, Oliver. 1940. *AP. The Story of News*. New York: Farrar and Rinehart.

Gruening, Ernest. 1931. *The Public Pays*. New York: Vanguard.

Hallin, Daniel C. 1986. *The "Uncensored War": The Media and Vietnam*. New York: Oxford University Press.

Hanna, Paul. 1920. "The State Department and the News." *Nation*, October 13, 1920, pp. 398–99.

Irwin, Will. 1923 "If You See It in the Paper, It's _____?" *Collier's* 72, August 18, 1923, p. 27.

Kaplan, Richard. 1998. "Power, Objectivity, and the Press: A Neo-Institutionalist Theory of the Origins of Contemporary Press Ethics." Paper presented to the Social Science History Association, annual meeting. Chicago (November 1998).

Kelly, Eugene A. 1935. "Distorting the News." *American Mercury* 34 (March): 307–18.

King, Elliot. 1992. "Ungagged Partisanship: The Political Values of the Public Press, 1835–1920." Ph.D. diss., University of California, San Diego.

Lippmann, Walter. 1920. *Liberty and the News*. New York: Harcourt, Brace, and Hone.

Maier, Pauline. 1980. *The Old Revolutionaries*. New York: Norton.

Main, T. Jackson. 1961. *The Antifederalists*. Chapel Hill: University of North Carolina Press.

McAdams, Richard H. 1997. "The Origin, Development, and Regulation of Norms." *Michigan Law Review* 96: 338–433.

McGerr, Michael. 1986. *The Decline of Popular Politics*. New York: Oxford University Press.

Michael, George. 1935. *Handout*. New York: Putnam's.

Odegard, Peter. 1930. *The American Public Mind*. New York: Columbia University Press.

Pratte, Paul A. 1995. *Gods Within the Machine: A History of the American Society of Newspaper Editors, 1923–1993*. Westport, Conn.: Praeger.

Pulitzer, Joseph. 1984. "The College of Journalism." *North American Review* 178, May 1984, p. 657.

Purcell, Edward. 1973. *The Crisis of Democratic Theory*. Lexington: University Press of Kentucky.

Ritchie, Donald. 1991. *The Press Gallery*. Cambridge: Harvard University Press.

Rosenberg, Norman. 1984. "Alexander Addison and the Pennsylvania Origins of Federalist First-Amendment Thought." *Pennsylvania Magazine of History and Biography* 108: 399–417.

Schudson, Michael. 1978. *Discovering the News*. New York: Basic Books.

———. 1995. *The Power of News*. Cambridge: Harvard University Press.

———. 1998a. *The Good Citizen: A History of American Public Life*. New York: Free Press.

———. 1998b. "The Public Journalism Movement and Its Problems." In *The Politics of News/The News of Politics*, edited by Doris Graber, Denis McQuail, and Pippa Norris. Washington, D.C.: Congressional Quarterly Press.

Seitz, Don C. 1926. "The American Press: Self-Surrender." *Outlook* 142 (February 10): 209–10.

Shaw, Donald L. 1967. "News Bias and the Telegraph: A Study of Historical Change." *Journalism Quarterly* 44(Spring): 3–12.

———. 1968. "The Nature of Campaign News in the Wisconsin Press, 1852–1916." *Journalism Quarterly* 45(Summer): 326–29.

———. 1971. "Technology: Freedom for What?" In *Mass Media and the National Experience*, edited by Ronald T. Farrar and John D. Stevens. New York: Harper and Row.

Streckfuss, Richard. 1990. "Objectivity in Journalism: A Search and a Reassessment." *Journalism Quarterly* 67(4): 973–83.

Sussmann, Leila A. 1947. "The Public Relations Movement in America." Master's thesis, University of Chicago.

Tuchman, Gaye. 1972. "Objectivity as Strategic Ritual: An Examination of Newsmen's Notions of Objectivity." *American Journal of Sociology* 77(4): 660–79.

Williams, Walter, and Frank I. Martin. 1922. *The Practice of Journalism*. Columbia, Mo.: E.W. Stephens.

# 7

# NATIONAL SELF-DETERMINATION:
# THE EMERGENCE OF
# AN INTERNATIONAL NORM

*Michael Hechter and Elizabeth Borland*

T HIS CHAPTER contrasts two leading views on the emergence of norms: an institutionalist view advocated by many sociologists (see chapters 1 and 10, this volume) and an individualist view, which underlies most economic, rational choice, and evolutionary analyses (see chapters 2, 3, 4, and 9, this volume). These two views are used as prisms through which to examine the emergence of the norm of national self-determination.

Self-determination can refer to individuals as well as to groups like nations. For individuals, self-determination is a synonym for the attainment of personal autonomy; it refers to "acting as a causal agent in one's life and making choices and decisions regarding one's quality of life free from . . . external influence or interference" (Wehmeyer 1992, 305). For nations, self-determination entails two distinct elements that are often conflated. The first is the belief that citizens should choose their own form of government. The second is the idea that citizens have both the right and the responsibility to determine their own collective identity—that is, "we decide who we are."

If, as James Coleman (1990, 243) argues, a norm concerning a specific action exists when the socially defined right to control the action is held not by the actor but by others, then national self-determination surely qualifies as a norm. Here, the act in question is the attainment of sovereignty or substantial autonomy within the framework of a state; and the actor affected by the norm is that collectivity known as the nation—that is, a culturally distinct, spatially concentrated group with a sense of its own history (Hechter 2000). The "others" controlling the action are the members of the community of sovereign states having the power to recognize the sovereignty of any given nation.[1]

# The Institutionalist View

Although individualists traditionally have paid scant attention to them, norms have always loomed large in the sociologist's lexicon (see chapters 1 and 10, this volume). For many sociologists, norms are quintessentially and irreducibly social; they represent that emergent je ne sais quoi that Émile Durkheim ([1893] 1933) once referred to as the noncontractual basis of contract. Durkheim's emphasis is placed not on the emergence of norms (for he presumed that this process lay beyond the reach of social science) but rather on the conditions promoting their maintenance and diffusion.

In one currently popular institutionalist view, norms are regarded as cognitive templates, or frames, that define and designate as appropriate given agendas for action, shaping social institutions and policies in their wake (Meyer et al. 1997; chapter 5, this volume). To the degree that norms are countenanced as part and parcel of people's cognitive apparatus rather than as externally imposed obligations, their enforcement is largely unnecessary. Many such norms are universalistic and diffuse inexorably outward from cultural centers to peripheries. The mechanisms responsible for their diffusion are identity formation and legitimation.[2]

On this view, the international environment is conceived as nothing less than a world society replete with shared values and norms. Hence, when the norm of national self-determination arises, it becomes a dominant cognitive frame. From this follows a number of empirical implications. Far from requiring enforcement, the norm operates more as an internal state than as a collective obligation. Thus, with respect to national self-determination, cultural groups learn to organize their claims for resources around a "national" identity that implies specific kinds of institutions, programs, and policies. To be regarded as a legitimate participant in the international community, actors (here, sovereign polities) must present a face (that is, an identity) that is readily recognizable to other members. Unless an actor sufficiently resembles other members, it cannot be countenanced as a community participant.

Because institutionalists believe that norms diffuse through mimicry, they expect norms to be adopted regardless of their instrumental appropriateness.[3] For example, a newly sovereign but utterly impoverished country with little in the way of paved roads is nonetheless likely to create a national airline—especially one with at least one Boeing 747. The reason is that having this kind of a national airline is part and parcel of what it means to be a sovereign state in the contemporary era. No state lacking such an airline could be considered legitimate. Even if the necessary resources could be more profitably invested elsewhere—in road construction, for instance—this normative pressure for a national airline is likely to win the day.[4]

## The Individualist View

While institutionalists often take norms—and compliance to them—for granted, individualists are more likely to be interested in the emergence and enforcement of norms (see chapters 2, 3, 4, and 8, this volume). In the individualist view, norms are collective goods whose production is inherently problematic. Writers like Harold Demsetz (1967), Robert Axelrod (1984), Robert Ellickson (1991), and Coleman (1990), among others, have suggested that norms emerge either to overcome negative externalities or to foster positive ones. What distinguishes their arguments from those of the functionalists of the 1950s is the newfound understanding that many socially beneficial norms are unlikely to emerge, because of free riding and other well-known obstacles to collective action (Olson 1965). These obstacles are likely to be overcome only in situations in which relatively small numbers of individuals having at least one common interest are locked into indefinitely repeated mutual interactions.[5] The resulting norms are not universal but are limited to members of the collectivity that produce them.

Whereas most individualist accounts provide post hoc explanations of existing norms, hardly any describe the process of norms in the making. Ethnographers, novelists, and journalists are more promising sources of evidence about the emergence of norms. Indeed, one of the most elegant descriptions of norm formation is by a novelist—John Steinbeck's *Grapes of Wrath* (1939, 264–67)—telling of the migration from the dust bowl to California during the Great Depression.

The westward trek described in *The Grapes of Wrath* produced something like conditions of repeated exchange among relatively small numbers of participants. The people with whom a given family shared a campground one day might well have reappeared on the next. They might have helped repair a flat tire or cool an overheated radiator. This individualist view tells of the emergence of a system of mutual obligation that arises to ensure migrants against breakdown, assault, illness, and other misfortunes.[6] The normative system of *Grapes of Wrath* is formed, as in the Hobbesian world, by families having one overriding interest in common—in this case, the desire to reach California's promised land—and possessed of roughly equal resources. People comply with these norms because others are willing to sanction deviants by fighting with them or ostracizing them. Whether these socially beneficial norms diffuse to other families in the same situation or whether, alternatively, they are established independently is not made clear.

Although both institutionalists and individualists agree that norms spread in the absence of a central authority, in other respects they provide contrasting images of norms (see table 7.1). The norms that institutionalists are concerned with emerge by diffusion, are universal, require little in the way of sanctions for their effectiveness, and are adopted regardless of their

TABLE 7.1    *Two Contrasting Views of Norms*

| Element | Institutionalist View | Individualist View |
|---|---|---|
| Essence of the norm | Cognitive template or frame | Collective obligation |
| Locus of the norm | Internal to the actors | External to the actors |
| Enforcement of the norm | Not problematic | Problematic |
| Emergence of the norm | Diffusion, through identification and legitimation mechanisms | Instrumental adoption, to address externalities in situations of repeated exchange |
| Extensiveness of the norm | Universal, spreading from centers to peripheries | Limited to the collectivities that produce them |
| Efficiency of the norm | Not necessarily welfare enhancing | Welfare enhancing |

*Source:* Authors' compilation.

consequences for collective welfare enhancement (Meyer et al. 1997; March and Olsen 1998). In contrast, the norms that individualists are concerned with emerge to overcome negative externalities or create positive ones, are limited to those groups that are affected by these externalities, are enforced by sanctions, and generally enhance collective welfare (that is, social efficiency). Which of these views best accounts for the emergence and spread of the norm of national self-determination?

## The Norm of National Self-Determination

Once merely an ideal proposed by intellectuals like Johann Herder, Giuseppe Mazzini, and John Stuart Mill, the principle of national self-determination became a rationale for nationalist collective action from the early nineteenth century onward and for the unification of Germany and Italy in 1870. Following actions taken by the United Nations, national self-determination attained a quasi-legal status. It became codified as a norm when the United Nations (UN) stated, in its initial charter, that any nationality subject to culturally alien rule had a legitimate right to self-determination (UN 1945, article 1).[7]

Because the UN General Assembly's *Declaration on Principles of International Law Concerning Friendly Relations and Co-operation Among States in Accordance with the Charter of the United Nations* (UN 1970) contains this body's most explicit definition of national self-determination, it is worth quoting at length:

- By virtue of the principle of equal rights and self-determination of peoples enshrined in the Charter of the United Nations, all peoples have the right freely to determine, without external interference, their political status and to pursue their economic social and cultural development, and every State has the duty to respect this right in accordance with the provisions of the Charter.

- Every State has the duty to promote, through joint and separate action, realization of the principle of equal rights and self-determination of peoples, in accordance with the provisions of the Charter, and to render assistance to the United Nations in carrying out the responsibilities entrusted to it by the Charter regarding the implementation of the principle in order:

  (a)  To promote friendly relations and co-operation among States; and

  (b)  To bring a speedy end to colonialism, having due regard to the freely expressed will of the peoples concerned; and bearing in mind that subjection of peoples to alien subjugation, domination and exploitation constitutes a violation of the principle, as well as a denial of fundamental rights, and is contrary to the Charter.

- Every State has the duty to promote through joint and separate action universal respect for and observance of human rights and fundamental freedoms in accordance with the Charter.

- The establishment of a sovereign and independent State, the free association or integration with an independent State or the emergence into any other political status freely determined by a people constitute modes of implementing the right of self-determination by that people.

- Every State has the duty to refrain from any forcible action which deprives people referred to above in the elaboration of the present principle of their right to self-determination and freedom and independence. In their actions against, and resistance to, such forcible action in pursuit of the exercise of their right to self-determination, such peoples are entitled to speak and to receive support in accordance with the purposes and principles of the Charter.

- The territory of a colony or other Non–Self Governing Territory has, under the Charter, a status separate and distinct from the territory of the State administering it; and such separate and distinct status under the Charter shall exist until the people of the colony or Non–Self Governing Territory have exercised their right of self-determination in accordance with the Charter, and particularly its purposes and principles.

- Nothing in the foregoing paragraphs shall be construed as authorizing or encouraging any action which would dismember or impair, totally or in part, the territorial integrity or political unity of sovereign and independent States conducting themselves in compliance with the principle of equal rights and self-determination of peoples as described above and thus possessed of a government representing the whole people belonging to the territory without distinction as to race, creed or colour.

- Every State shall refrain from any action aimed at the partial or total disruption of the national unity and territorial integrity of any other State or country.

Arguably, the norm of national self-determination has altered the political map of the modern world (Tilly 1993). It has been used as a justification for holding plebiscites, as a call to change national boundaries so as better to reflect the cultural differences of the population, as a demand for secession or decolonization, and as a rationale for nationalist violence. More than 130 colonial dependencies of Western governments have been recognized as independent states or have become incorporated into neighboring sovereign nations during the course of the twentieth century (Strang 1990, 846). Between 1945 and 1979 alone, 70 territories achieved independence, and in only a small number of cases was the right to self-determination claimed without the subsequent attainment of independence. (Because no such enumeration is currently available in the literature, we have provided a list of these self-determination claims in the appendix to this chapter.)

Given this record of success, it is no wonder that groups all over the world—from the Quebecois, Palestinians, Kurds, and Basques to indigenous groups in North, Central, and South America, Asia, and Australasia—currently seek self-determination. Although their demands are based on different arguments, all these groups view national self-determination as their right. Yet the assertion of this right is highly controversial: it always engenders some counterclaim involving the territorial integrity of an existing state (Knight 1984, 176).[8] Some claims for national self-determination, therefore, are regarded as more valid than others.

The United Nations declaration upholds "the principle of equal rights and self-determination of peoples," but interpreting this principle is problematic because there is an inherent ambiguity surrounding the referent of the word "self." The term can refer to groups defined on the basis of territory, nationality, or mere economic interest. A group can claim that it constitutes a separate people, but third parties can reject this claim (and often do, as in Kurdistan and Corsica). Hence, it is no surprise that the term "people" has also been applied variously (Hannum 1996) to

- groups living entirely within a state ruled by another, such as the Irish before 1920 (some of these groups qualify as internal colonies, see Hechter [1975] 1999)
- groups living as minorities in various countries without control of a state of their own, such as the Kurds, who are the fourth-most-numerous cultural group in the Middle East

- groups constituting majorities in a territory under foreign domination, such as the people of India before they gained independence from Britain

- groups living as minorities in a state but understanding themselves as forming part of the people of a neighboring state, such as Haitians in the Dominican Republic

- groups dispersed throughout many separate states, such as Bolivians who live in the Southern Cone nations.

Which of these "peoples" is qualified to pursue self-determination? Groups cannot be regarded as separate peoples if they are not spatially concentrated.[9] Beyond this, however, there are thousands of possible cultural groups to consider, and even the number of language groups is impressively large: an estimated 6,170 languages are currently spoken in the world (Moynihan 1993, 72). The most successful claims to self-determination have come from colonized populations, but at the present time most claims emanate from internal colonies and cultural minorities that are dispersed among several sovereign states.

# A Brief History of the Norm of National Self-Determination

The norm of national self-determination evolved in four distinct historical periods. It first made its appearance as an ideal in the era of democratic revolution, following the independence movement in the United States and the French Revolution. It then evolved into a rather shadowy principle that guided the formation of state boundaries in the aftermath of World War I. The period following World War II witnessed the birth of a full-fledged norm with accompanying sanctions that was pervasively applied to external colonies. In the current period, most claims for national self-determination emanate from indigenous peoples and cultural minorities.

## The Era of Democratic Revolutions

The concept of national self-determination dates back to independence movements in the United States and France. Before this era, most individuals were largely subject to the whims of their respective rulers.[10] By contrast, the American revolutionaries put forth the novel argument that just governments must rest on the authority of "the people" alone. The Declaration of Independence (1776) pledged that governments are properly created to secure the "inalienable rights" of humankind, that governments derive "their just powers from the consent of the governed," and that "it is the right of the people to alter or abolish" any form of government that "becomes restrictive of these ends." The victory of the United States over Britain gave legs to this conception of popular sovereignty.

The French Revolution promulgated similar ideals in support of national self-determination. For the French revolutionaries, "sovereignty is one, indivisible, inalienable and imprescriptable: it belongs to a nation" (Cobban [1945] 1969, 33–34). Following the Revolution, the French justified their military occupation of nearby territories by asserting that the inhabitants of these areas favored liberation by their armies. They argued that if the residents of lands like Sardinia, Austria, or the petty German states wished to have true national self-determination then they would have to be ruled by the French rather than by their traditional authorities.

To demonstrate its rectitude to other governments, France held plebiscites in Avignon and the Comtat Venaissin (in 1791), Savoy (in 1792), and in the Belgian communes, Nice, and the Rhine Valley (all in 1793). These plebiscites gave inhabitants the choice between French rule and a continuance of the previous regime. None of these plebiscites offered an option for outright independence.[11] In some territories, such as the papal enclaves of Avignon and the Comtat Venaissin, there was considerable sentiment for French rule. In others, such as Savoy, Nice, the Belgian Netherlands, and the Rhineland, however, the French "liberated" populations solely by dint of their military occupation (Johnson 1967, 72–73). Following French occupation, local authorities were replaced and new administrations were established, along with the Code of Napoleon. Whereas many French-sponsored plebiscites supported French rule, they cannot be regarded as impartial exercises. To the rest of Europe, France's actions appeared simply as conquest, if with a fairer face (Johnson 1967, 74).

After the Napoleonic era, plebiscites increasingly became a means of assessing the governance preferences of a people. The results of such plebiscites could be used to legitimate changes in regimes or in international boundaries. Like other electoral mechanisms, of course, the fairness of any given plebiscite could always be questioned because of threats of violence, economic pressures, or other forms of influence.

## The Aftermath of World War I

Although many colonial uprisings led to the establishment of new states between the French Revolution and World War I, there is little evidence that self-determination emerged as a norm during this period. True, there was ample sympathy in Western Europe for national self-determination in Greece, Serbia, and other largely Christian territories in the Ottoman Empire,[12] but this owed more to Western antipathy to the Ottomans than to any enthusiasm for the concept of national self-determination. Although many Latin American colonies gained independence from Spain in the early nineteenth century, arguments for independence were principally couched in terms of economic interest rather than national identity.[13] National self-determination was not a factor in Brazilian independence, which was won only after a failed attempt to set up a monarchy; the pretender, a Portuguese prince named Dom Pedro, declared Brazil's independence in 1822. The Haitian revolt of 1803, in which the slave population was inspired by the French revolutionary ideals of self-determination and equality, was exceptional in this respect. Yet, far from lauding Toussaint L'Ouverture as a national hero, most Western countries (especially those with legalized slavery) considered Haitian independence to be a scourge.

The nineteenth century saw an increasing use of plebiscites to test national self-determination. They were held in the transfer of control of Rome from the Papal State to Italy in 1870, in Denmark's sale of St. Thomas and St. John to the United States in 1868,[14] and in Sweden's cession of St. Bartholomew to France in 1877. Aside from the Ionian Islands, which passed from Great Britain to Greece after a plebiscite in 1863, all these plebiscites merely led to a change in colonial status rather than to decolonization.[15]

At the same time, peripheral nationalism was on the rise, particularly among national groups subject to Habsburg and Russian imperial rule (Hechter 2000). That this kind of nationalism could have a highly destabilizing effect on world politics was made crystal clear: the Habsburgs' attempt to crush Serbian nationalism effectively precipitated World War I. It was during this war that the right of national independence began to be called the principle of self-determination (Cobban [1945] 1969, 39).

The aftermath of World War I brought new attention to the principle of national self-determination: both Lenin and Woodrow Wilson saw it as a key to determining changes in governance. Lenin argued that self-determination should be a criterion for the liberation of oppressed peoples; hence, it would encourage socialist revolutions. Wilson's views on self-determination contrasted sharply with Lenin's. For him, self-determination was an ideal to promote democracy, "a corollary of democratic theory" (Cobban [1945] 1969, 63). Wilson argued that self-determination ought not to apply to colonies and that it should never be used to justify violence. Despite Wilson's interest in the principle of self-determination, the term did not appear in his Fourteen Points nor in any other principle of peace that he declared.[16] In the preamble to his speech presenting the Four Supplementary Points (on February 11, 1918)—not in the four points themselves—he called self-determination an "imperative principle of action," adding that "peoples are not to be handed about from one sovereignty to another by an international conference or an undertaking between rivals and antagonists. National aspirations must be respected; people may now be dominated and governed only by their own consent. 'Self-determination' is not a mere phrase. It is an imperative principle of action which statesmen will henceforth ignore at their peril" (Wilson, cited in Ofuatey-Kodjoe 1977, 75).

Wilson's notions about self-determination were controversial; many statesmen held that they would lead to chaos.[17] Accordingly, the Covenant of the League of Nations left the definition of self-determination to the discretion of member states. From other League of Nation declarations one can discern what self-determination did *not* imply, however. The Committee of Jurists declared that international law "does not recognize the right of national groups to separate themselves from a State" (Cobban [1945] 1969, 88). The member states were wary about their own interests in the colonies and feared that their full support of the principle would unravel their empires.

In the years following the Treaty of Versailles, both the Allies and the Axis powers adverted to the principle of national self-determination. Hitler used it to justify the German invasion of Sudetenland, ostensibly designed to "liberate" the German-speaking population of this Czech region.[18] In 1941, the United States and United Kingdom proclaimed self-determination as an objective in the Atlantic Charter.[19]

Because most of the victors of World War I were colonial powers concerned about maintaining their empires, however, world leaders limited the scope of the principle of self-determination: it was used to create boundaries for the new states carved from the former Austro-Hungarian empire. Britain and France proposed a series of plebiscites to allow the inhabitants to exercise their right to self-determination, but Italy and the United States opposed this plan. In the view of the American delegation, boundaries had to be determined on the basis of nationality, which could best be revealed by impartial censuses. The resulting policy outcome was to avoid plebiscites unless the nationality of border populations was unclear (owing to "an extreme mixture of national groups, or in cases where the allied powers were having difficulty deciding between the counter-claims of their own allies" [Ofuatey-Kodjoe 1977, 81]). Twelve plebiscites were held, including those in Allenstein and Marienwerder, the Klagenfurt Basin, Schleswig, Sopron, Upper Silesia, and the Saar. These effectively removed territory from Germany. Thus, the victors of World War I used self-determination to justify new political boundaries that were congruent with their own national interests.

Whereas the use of plebiscites can be seen as a step toward the institutionalization of the norm of national self-determination, the League of Nations did not regard it as anything approaching a universal norm. This can be appreciated by considering the experience of the Åland Islanders, a Swedish-speaking population that attempted to secede from Finland in 1920. The Åland Islanders pressed their claim to the League of Nations, which issued two reports on the matter. The first report upheld Finland's claim to the Ålands, saying that "it pertains exclusively to the sovereignty of any definitely constituted State to grant to, or withhold from, a fraction of its population the right of deciding its own political destiny by means of a plebiscite, or in any other way" (League of Nations, cited in Cassese 1995, 29). The second held that self-determination could be used to protect cultural minorities when such protection was the only sensible means of providing safeguards to ethnic and religious groups, preventing abuse of authority, or combating oppression of peoples. The league held that the Åland Islanders could not demonstrate that the Finns were violating their rights. The stipulation that self-determination could be used to "protect minorities" further extended the scope of the norm of national self-determination. The Åland Islands precedent also demonstrated that international bodies were hardly impartial in adjudicating claims about national self-determination. In this instance, Finland was probably rewarded for its successful resistance to communism during the 1918 Finnish War of Independence (Hannum 1996).

The principle of self-determination was used not only to create new states from the ruins of the defeated empires but also to redistribute some of the colonies previously held by the losers. In the postwar period, the League of Nations initiated the mandate system, which attempted to control and categorize demands for self-determination from colonies, now called mandates. It broke these mandates into three categories. Categorized as Class A were areas (such as Iraq, Syria-Lebanon, Palestine, and Transjordan) promised independence in the near future; Class B denoted areas (such as the Cameroons, Tanganyika, and Togoland) that had been given to European powers; and Class C areas (such as the Mariana and Marshall Islands, Western Samoa, and Eastern New Guinea) had been given to non-European powers (Chamberlain 1998). In Class B and Class C, the mandatory powers were not obliged to encourage future independence.

Britain divided white colonies in areas it had populated (for example, New Zealand and Australia) from nonwhite regions. The former achieved dominion status in 1907, whereas the number of nonwhite colonies expanded during the war. The zenith of colonialism occurred in 1919 with the completion of the Treaty of Versailles, because it brought new areas into the ambit of European rule (Holland 1985, 1). Thus, colonization actually spread after World War I, just as self-determination was being tested with plebiscites and being extolled by Wilson and the League of Nations. Although national self-determination may have been bruited about as an international norm, it had little if any impact on the behavior of colonial states at this time.

## The Aftermath of World War II

After World War II, the Allies fulfilled their wartime promises about national self-determination by creating the United Nations. National self-determination was stated as a major objective for the formation of the United Nations and is emphasized in its charter. The norm was linked to two other assumptions: First, once a state has joined the United Nations, its territorial integrity is established (Emerson 1971, 464); this has caused confusion in postcolonial states—including India, Ethiopia, Nigeria, and others—in which not all minorities agree with the new government or its territorial boundaries. Second, "since self-determination was not considered to have a value independent of its use as an instrument of peace, it could easily be set aside when its fulfillment raised the possibility of conflicts between states" (Cassese 1995, 43).

Like the League of Nations before it, the UN General Assembly initially refused to define self-determination. This allowed each member state to define it unilaterally and decide the conditions under which it would be honored. The term was not clarified by a General Assembly resolution until 1960 (Ofuatey-Kodjoe 1977, 114–15). To most of the founders of the United Nations, however, it is clear that self-determination did not imply the right of a minority to secede, the right of colonial people to achieve independence, or the right of two or more nations to join together as a larger state (Cassese 1995, 42). Although the Allies paid lip service to the establishment of national self-determination as an international norm, they did not want to encourage secession and the creation of "microstates." Nor did they intend to give up their colonies.

The strongest evidence for the normative status of national self-determination comes from the rapid increase in new states created out of former colonies that occurred from 1945 to 1967. During this period, the rate of decolonization was many times higher than in any comparable period in history (Strang 1990, 853). Some plebiscites were used to determine divisions of territory or the creation of new states, resulting in independence in Cameroon, Western Samoa, and Togo. Most colonies became independent without plebiscites, however. Arguments about decolonization were considered enough of a justification in most cases—especially after 1960, at which time newly independent countries were allowed to vote in the General Assembly.

Yet the scope of the norm was far from universal. Its limits can be discerned by considering examples in which claims for self-determination were denied or not even seriously considered. A majority of these were countries in which decolonization had occurred to the dissatisfaction of other groups desiring their own self-determination.[20] Postcolonization problems resulted in claims for self-determination in Bangladesh, Biafra, southern Sudan, and East Timor. Bangladesh claimed self-determination from Pakistan soon after it gained independence based on linguistic, racial, and economic differences as well as violent persecution. Biafrans and the southern Sudanese justified their claim for self-determination from Nigeria and northern Sudan, respectively, for similar reasons.

Save that for East Timor, none of these claims was supported by the United Nations. The governments of Pakistan, Nigeria, Indonesia, and northern Sudan found allies in the United States and other powerful Western countries. Existing regimes were able to make the argument that rebel groups claiming self-determination had leftist leanings and on that account should not be supported by the international community. Bangladesh did gain independence in 1971, but not because of efforts of the United Nations; rather, it profited mightily from India's antipathy toward Pakistan. In all these instances, demands for self-determination based on differences in language, culture or religion or on discrimination and even violent oppression of minorities failed to sway the United Nations.[21] The powers that be did not want to contribute to the proliferation of "microstates" in the United Nations:

> At least half of the world's 156 independent countries have a population of under 5 million, nearly 35 have less than one million, 17 micro-states—such as the Bahamas, Grenada, the Maldives, and Qatar—have fewer than 300,000 people, while one, Nauru, has a population of fewer than 7,000. Projections by the Department of State reportedly raise the possibility of 50 additional micro-states—such as Antigua, Ifni, and Tahiti, each under 100,000 people— in the foreseeable future. This would expand the community of nations to more than 200, tripling the number since World War II. For a time, the United States led an effort in the United Nations to establish procedures to prevent a worsening of the current situation in which the United States pays 25 per cent of the organization's budget while eighty member countries—contributing at a rate of .02 per cent—jointly pay only 1.6 per cent but wield eighty times the voting power of the United States (Murphy 1980, 47).

Owing to ambiguities and outright contradictions within international documents regarding under what circumstances, and by whom, claims to national self-determination can be made, the norm can be readily ignored. The very ambiguity of the norm ensures that its instantiation is always a social construction (chapter 5, this volume, also highlights the ambiguity of many norms).[22] Enforcement of this norm is a quintessentially political decision.

Of course, this does not prevent many national minorities from pursuing self-determination. Walker Connor (1985) has estimated that less than 4 percent of the world's population lives in seven countries that have had no recent border disputes: Denmark, Iceland, Japan, Luxembourg, the Netherlands, Norway, and Portugal.

## The Present Situation

Currently unresolved claims of self-determination fall into two categories. The first involves settler populations. For example, claims to the territories of the Islas Malvinas (the Falkland Islands) (by Argentina) and Gibraltar (by Spain) are based on the principle of contiguity, but the colonial power still holds the land. In both of these cases, the United Nations urges negotiations and leans toward the side of the contiguous nation.

Claims for national self-determination by cultural minorities in sovereign states have received the coldest of shoulders from the United Nations, however. The United Nations has not supported self-determination in the Basque Region and Catalonia in Spain, in Scotland, in Quebec, in the Kurdish territories of Turkey or Iraq, nor in Chechnya. Such claims tend to be countenanced only to the degree that ignoring them might pave the way to geopolitical instability.[23] Thus, as of this writing, peacekeeping troops have been installed by third parties in Bosnia and in Kosovo. The historical record, therefore, reveals that the United Nations regards colonized populations as having the greatest right to self-determination (see table 7.2).[24]

If decolonization was out of the question after World War I, why then has it won the day since the end of World War II? Whereas the victors of the former war were colonial powers, this was most decidedly not the case for the latter. The Soviet Union, of course, was militantly anti-imperialist, and many leaders of the colonial national liberation movements (like Ho Chi Minh) received their training in Moscow. The United States had few colonies of its own; because it had no particular interest in the preservation of the European colonial empires, it was less reluctant to countenance application of the norm of national self-determination to colonial territories throughout the world. American support for decolonization also grew apace with the Cold War, which pitted the two hegemonic powers against each other for global dominance. The Americans would have had little hope of gaining influence in the developing world had they attempted to thwart its increasingly popular anticolonial movements. Once former colonies began to attain membership—and attendant voting rights—in the United Nations, this process could only accelerate.[25]

That culturally alien rule is deemed illegitimate in colonies but legitimate when it occurs within sovereign states (as in internal colonies) seems both logically and ethically inconsistent; but this is not necessarily so. Because decolonization does not tend to alter international boundaries, it does not directly threaten existing sovereign states. The secession of a region does cause a shift in international boundaries, however, and thus it represents a potential threat to the territorial integrity of many, if not most, extant states. This fact provides a political rationale for what otherwise appears to be a glaring inconsistency. Although few sovereign states, if any, might be prepared to endorse a principle that could threaten their own territorial integrity, a majority could (and did) vote for this much more restrictive conception of self-determination. This also explains why the norm is more likely to be applied in the case of indigenous than settler majorities. Thus, the United Nations has been sympathetic to claims coming from Argentina and Spain in disputes about the Malvinas and Gibraltar. It also recognized the claims of black South Africans during the apartheid regime.

Although national minorities in decolonized territories may claim autonomy—as in Eritrea, Bangladesh, and Aceh—international organizations have usually failed to support these claims initially (save in rare cases, like

TABLE 7.2    *Outcomes of Claims for National Self-Determination*

| Outcome | External Colony | Fragment of a Decayed or Decaying Empire | Internal Colony or Minority Nation Within an Already Sovereign State |
|---|---|---|---|
| Sovereignty Recognized | United States (1783) | Avignon and the Comtat | Norway (1905) |
| | Ionian Islands (1883) | Venaissin (1791) | Eire (1924) |
| | Haiti (1825) | Savoy (1792) | Bangladesh (1971–) |
| | Brazil (1815) | Nice (1793) | East Timor (2000) |
| | St. Thomas and St. John (1817) | Belgian Communes (1793) | |
| | St. Bartholomew (1877) | Rhine Valley (1793) | |
| | Norway (1905) | Greece (1831) | |
| | Cuba (1934) | Serbia (1878) | |
| | Weihaiwei (1930) | Bulgaria (1908) | |
| | Canada (1931) | Albania (1920) | |
| | Iraq (1932) | Allenstein and Marienwerder (1920) | |
| | Nicaragua (1933) | Klagenfurt Basin (1920) | |
| | South Africa (1934) | Schleswig (1920) | |
| | Haiti (1934) | Sopron (1921) | |
| | Levant States (1941) | Upper Silesia (1921) | |
| | Australia (1942) | The Saar (1935) | |
| | Great Lebanon (1943) | Iceland (1944) | |
| | Philippines (1946) | Levant States (1946) | |
| | Transjordan (1946) | Italian East Africa (1947) | |
| | India (1947) | The Saar (1955) | |
| | New Zealand (1947) | Italian Somaliland (1960) | |
| | Ceylon (1947) | Slovenia (1991) | |
| | Hyderabad (1948) | Croatia (1991) | |
| | Palestine (1948) | Macedonia (1991) | |
| | Burma (1948) | Azerbaijan (1991) | |
| | Dutch East Indies (1949) | Belarus (1991) | |
| | Newfoundland (1949) | Georgia (1991) | |
| | Bhutan (1949) | Kazakhstan (1991) | |
| | Oman (1951) | Kyrgyzstan (1991) | |
| | Libya (1951) | Moldova (1991) | |
| | Egypt (1953) | Tajikistan (1991) | |
| | Laos (1954) | Ukraine (1991) | |
| | Cochin China (1954) | Uzbekistan (1991) | |
| | Cambodia (1954) | Armenia (1991) | |
| | Annam (1954) | Slovakia (1993) | |
| | Tonkin (1954) | | |
| | Togoland (1955) | | |
| | French Morocco (1956) | | |
| | Spanish Morocco (1956) | | |
| | Tunisia (1957) | | |
| | Gold Coast (1957) | | |
| | French Guinea (1958) | | |
| | Singapore (1959) | | |
| | Gabon (1960) | | |
| | Cyprus (1960) | | |
| | British Somaliland (1960) | | |
| | Madagascar (1960) | | |
| | Togo (1960) | | |
| | Belgian Congo (1960) | | |
| | Ivory Coast (1960) | | |

TABLE 7.2   *Continued*

| Outcome | External Colony | Fragment of a Decayed or Decaying Empire | Internal Colony or Minority Nation Within an Already Sovereign State |
|---|---|---|---|
| | Dahomey (1960) | | |
| | Ubangi Shari (1960) | | |
| | Mauritania (1960) | | |
| | Federation of Nigeria (1960) | | |
| | Niger (1960) | | |
| | French Cameroon (1960) | | |
| | Middle Congo (1960) | | |
| | Upper Volta (1960) | | |
| | Federation of Mali (1960) | | |
| | British Cameroon (1961) | | |
| | Sierra Leone (1961) | | |
| | Kuwait (1961) | | |
| | Tanganyika (1961) | | |
| | Zanzibar (1961) | | |
| | Western Samoa (1962) | | |
| | French India (1962) | | |
| | Algeria (1962) | | |
| | Uganda (1962) | | |
| | Rwandi-Burundi (1962) | | |
| | Jamaica (1962) | | |
| | Trinidad and Tobago (1962) | | |
| | British North Borneo (1962) | | |
| | Kenya (1963) | | |
| | Sarawak (1963) | | |
| | Malaya (1963) | | |
| | Malta (1964) | | |
| | Nyasaland (1964) | | |
| | North Rhodesia (1964) | | |
| | Maldives (1965) | | |
| | The Gambia (1965) | | |
| | British Guiana (1966) | | |
| | Barbados (1966) | | |
| | Basutoland (1966) | | |
| | Bechuanaland (1966) | | |
| | Federation of South Arabia (1967) | | |
| | Mauritius (1968) | | |
| | Equatorial Guinea (1968) | | |
| | Swaziland (1968) | | |
| | Nauru (1968) | | |
| | Ifni (1969) | | |
| | Fiji (1970) | | |
| | Tongo (1970) | | |
| | Bahrain (1971) | | |
| | Trucial States (1971) | | |
| | Quatar (1971) | | |
| | Bahamas (1973) | | |

*(Table continues on p. 202.)*

TABLE 7.2    *Continued*

| Outcome | External Colony | Fragment of a Decayed or Decaying Empire | Internal Colony or Minority Nation Within an Already Sovereign State |
|---|---|---|---|
| | Portuguese Guinea (1974) Grenada (1974) Cape Verde Islands (1975) Mozambique (1975) Saõ Tome and Principe (1975) Angola (1975) Surinam (1975) Papua and New Guinea (1975) Seychelles (1976) Belize (1977) Djibouti (1977) Solomon Islands (1978) Ellice (1978) Saint Lucia (1979) St. Vincent (1979) Gilbert (1979) Saint Kitts–Nevis (1983) Brunei (1984) Southern Rhodesia (1984) Eritrea (1993) | | |
| Sovereigny Not Recognized (select list) | Åland Islands (1920) Gibraltar (1957–) West Irian (1975) Hong Kong (1997) Puerto Rico | Bosnia-Herzegovina (1991) | Biafra (1967–) Moro (1972–) Aceh North Ireland Scotland Wales Brittany Kurdistan (Turkey, Iraq, Iran) Palestine (1948–) Catalonia Basque Provinces Padania (Italy) Quebec Corsica (France) Tibet Xinjiang Taiwan Kosovo Kashmir (India) Punjab (India) Southern Sudan Puerto Rico Chechnya Ingushetya Dagestan |

*Source:* Authors' compilation.

certain territories of the former Yugoslavia, in which the political stability of an entire region is perceived to be threatened). It is hard to avoid concluding that benevolent motivations play an insignificant role in applying the norm; thus, the United Nations failed to recognize the right of self-determination for the minorities who were victims of genocide in Rwanda and Burundi.[26]

In sum, national self-determination is a norm that is presently invoked by groups all over the world. It emerged following the American and French Revolutions and became gradually institutionalized by the use of plebiscites and, later, by its inclusion in the United Nations charter. Although the norm is not always recognized or sanctioned by international bodies, the assertion of national self-determination is increasingly common. Because the norm is both ambiguous and controversial, decisions about countenancing the norm are highly discretionary.

## Theoretical Implications

Even in this highly truncated form, the history of the norm of national self-determination is complex. As such, it raises many difficult challenges for theorists of norms. Here, we merely focus on several of the dimensions that are outlined in table 7.1.

Institutionalists regard national self-determination as a universalistic norm that emerges through diffusion and is adopted for reasons of identity and legitimation (Meyer et al. 1997; March and Olsen 1998). The evidence presented in this chapter resonates with some parts of the institutionalist account. Legitimation mechanisms might well be responsible for the timing of decolonization, which began to escalate in the mid-1950s (Strang 1990). From this point onward, it was no longer seemly to maintain, let alone initiate, a colonial empire, regardless of its welfare consequences. Although sovereignty offers no guarantee of increased development (a fact that too many former colonies have discovered through bitter experience), native politicians were unable to argue against self-determination in colonial territories even if they were inclined to do so. Whether national self-determination is, on balance, welfare enhancing is also questionable, for the claims and counterclaims generated in its name are responsible for the bulk of political violence in the world today.

Many other characteristics of the norm seem more consistent with an individualist account, however. The norm emerged only because the United Nations (and its various predecessors, such as the League of Nations) is composed of a relatively small number of individual states, each of which is locked into repeated interactions for an indefinite future. The norm is generally adverted to by groups for whom sovereignty is a collective good. In addition, third parties enforce the norm in a highly discriminating fashion.

One of the most striking features of the norm of national self-determination is its selective rather than universal application (chapter 8, this volume, refers to this as the conditionality of the norm). The norm was forged in political conflict and has been applied instrumentally by third parties for *raisons d'état*.[27] Decolonization accelerated after World War II, owing, in part, to the fact that the colonies were no longer as lucrative, as in the case of India (see Holland 1985). More recently, international organizations have seldom supported the claims of national minorities in decolonized or noncolonized countries to self-determination. Evidently, benevolent motivations count for little in the norm's application. As already noted, the United Nations failed to recognize the right of self-determination for the minorities who were victims of genocide in Rwanda and Burundi; it has remained mute about the fate of the Kurdish people and it has refused to endorse national self-determination in Kosovo following the air war of May and June 1999.

That the norm holds for external colonies but not for internal ones derives from a very important cause. Norms do not inhabit a vacuum; they coexist with other norms in what might be loosely termed normative systems. National self-determination is but one norm; the Westphalian notion of state sovereignty is another. It so happens that these two particular norms are in almost perpetual contradiction (Krasner and Froats 1998). Their relative salience is determined not by some overarching metanorm but by the sanctions of powerful participants in the international system.[28]

Because the norm of national self-determination depends on the willingness of third parties to countenance it—by supporting given nationalist movements and ultimately extending diplomatic recognition—its emergence is inextricably linked to issues of enforcement. Nevertheless, national self-determination differs in kind from most of the norms that have been highlighted in individualist accounts, such as those prescribing hay sharing in Iceland (chapter 3, this volume) and proscribing smoking in public places (chapter 2, this volume). The individualist literature on the emergence of norms typically paints a rosy portrait. Time and again, it tells how previously unrelated individuals facing common problems or opportunities (or both) converge—under specific conditions, to be sure—to create norms that facilitate cooperative behavior. Social institutions and social order writ large are then built as if on the shoulders of these norms. From the perspective of the individuals who construct them, therefore, these norms are welfare enhancing.[29]

This picture contains some truth, but it is far from the whole story. It overlooks the possibility (often stressed by institutionalists) that some norms may not remotely enhance the welfare of the people who are subjected to them.[30] This is because the typical individualist account ignores an important class of norms that tends to arise in social hierarchies. Coleman refers to such norms as "disjoint," in contrast with the conjoint norms that are the staple of most individualist analyses. Conjoint norms emerge from a given set of actors and apply to the actions of this selfsame set. However, norms that benefit one set of actors and are directed toward the actions of another set are disjoint because there exists "a physical separation of opposing interest. The beneficiaries have an interest in the norm being observed, and the targets have an interest in the focal action being unmodified by the norm" (Coleman 1990, 247).

Most disjoint norms are exploitative: they enhance the welfare of powerful members of the group at the expense of weaker ones (Coleman 1990, 243–63). Examples run the gamut from relatively benign exploitative norms, such as those concerning etiquette (Elias 1982) and marriage (Ermakoff 1997), to extremely serious ones, such as those mandating conscription in time of war (Levi 1997), the binding of Chinese women's feet, the genital mutilation of African females (both discussed in Mackie 1996), and the honor killings of unmarried Islamic women accused of having lost their virginity (Douglas Jehl, "Arab Honor's Price: A Woman's Blood," *New York Times,* June 20, 1999).

At first glance, exploitative norms may not seem to be difficult to account for theoretically. After all, it is clearly in the interest of the powerful to maintain their privileges, if not extend them, by all available means—including force and fraud. Yet exploitative norms are far more than mere directives of the powerful. What is interesting about them is that once institutionalized, they become largely self-enforcing. Members of the weaker group (the lower classes, in the case of etiquette; women, in the other cases) tend to impose these obligations on themselves so as to reap maximum individual benefit in their social system. Because Chinese women with unbound feet were regarded as unmarriageable, foot binding was acceded to as the lesser of two evils.

Benevolent disjoint norms are even more challenging to account for on individualistic grounds. These provide benefit to the less powerful or disadvantaged members of hierarchical groups. For example, some norms encourage people in developed countries to contribute aid to those living in poor countries. Others protect children from the predation of adults and women from the physical abuse of men. The altruistic effects embodied in benevolent norms pose a thorny theoretical challenge to individualists, for although such norms enhance the welfare of their beneficiaries, it is difficult to understand why individuals would ever bear the cost of establishing them.[31]

National self-determination is an example of a benevolent norm, for it obliges powerful states to divest themselves of political control over weaker national minorities or colonies. Because individualists have difficulty explaining them, the diffusion of benevolent norms would seem to provide grist for the institutionalist mill. On institutionalist grounds, benevolent norms are at least as probable as exploitative ones, for legitimation is the mechanism responsible for their spread. Indeed, legitimation ought to favor the spread of benevolent norms, for they are easier to justify than exploitative ones.

The evidence presented here, however—that national self-determination applies principally to external rather than internal colonies—suggests that legitimation is probably not the mechanism responsible for the emergence of this norm. From the standpoint of legitimation, the distinct treatment of external and internal colonies is a glaring logical and ethical inconsistency.

This apparent inconsistency is resolved if we regard the emergence of norms more instrumentally. The force of national self-determination is attenuated by other norms that are more salient to powerful third parties. Whereas decolonization does not directly threaten existing state boundaries, secession does do so. This provides the rationale for an outcome that otherwise makes little sense. Although few, if any, sovereign states might be prepared to endorse a principle that could threaten their own territorial integrity, a majority could (and did) vote for this much more restrictive conception of self-determination. This chapter therefore raises doubts about the motivations underlying the emergence of the norm of national self-determination.[32]

Similar doubts have been raised in studies of other kinds of benevolent norms. What could be more benevolent than the foreign aid extended from rich countries to poor ones in the wake of natural disasters? Yet Alex de Waal (1999) shows that most Western aid for famine relief in Africa serves political rather than humanitarian ends. Although norms protecting children usually are attributed to benevolent motivations, Neil Smelser (1959) explains prohibitions against child labor in British factories during the Industrial Revolution in terms of the benefits these laws provided to their fathers (principally, by restricting lower-cost labor on the factory floor). In much the same vein, Debra Friedman (1994) suggests that shifts in the award of child custody from fathers to mothers occurred not out of concern for the welfare of children but from a desire to shift the burden of supporting these mothers from the state to (morally culpable) divorced fathers. Together with the evidence in this chapter, these studies suggest that benevolent norms emerge in much the same fashion as their exploitative counterparts—largely when they are in the interest of powerful social actors.

On balance, neither of the two stock approaches presented in table 7.1 fare particularly well in explaining the emergence of the norm of national self-determination. Because each is to some degree a caricature, this conclusion is hardly startling. Even so, some important general lessons can be gleaned from this case study. Institutionalists would be wise to pay greater heed to the mechanisms responsible for the diffusion of norms. It matters a great deal whether norms diffuse from cultural centers to cultural peripheries or whether they are adopted by the most powerful actors in a social system for their own instrumental reasons. In the first case, norms tend to sweep across the globe indiscriminately; in the second, they are adopted selectively. Evidently, national self-determination is the kind of norm that falls into the second category.

The standard individualist account tackles the emergence of norms as a contract between individuals who share an interest in some collective good. The resulting conjoint norms are welfare enhancing. Although this account has ample real-world relevance, a great deal of interaction also occurs between individuals who vary widely in power and other resources. The norms that emerge in such hierarchical groups tend to be disjoint rather than conjoint. Because these norms are likely to enhance the welfare of the powerful at the expense of the powerless, they cannot be said to maximize collective welfare. Those individualists who ignore the emergence of disjoint norms are telling only one side of a more complex—and far more pessimistic—story.

# APPENDIX

TABLE 7.A1    *The Use of the Norm of Self-Determination in World History*

| Country or Group Location | Country from Which Self-Determination Was Claimed | Year of Claim | Reason Given for Self-Determination | International Response and Result |
|---|---|---|---|---|
| | | | Resolved (or Resolvable) Claims of Self-Determination | |
| United States | Britain | 1783 | Decolonization | Independence |
| Avignon and the Comtat Venaissin[a] | Papal Enclave | 1791 | • Plebiscite after the French Revolution • Issue: annexation | Resulting status: French |
| Savoy[a] | Sardinia | 1792 | • Plebiscite (corrupt) after the French Revolution • Issue: Annexation | Resulting status: French |
| Nice[a] | Sardinia | 1793 | See Savoy | |
| Belgian communes[a] | Austria | 1793 | See Savoy | |
| Rhine Valley[a] | German princes | 1793 | See Savoy | |
| Ionian Islands[a] | United Kingdom | 1856 to 1883 | • Decolonization • In a treaty between Great Britain, France, Russia, and Denmark establishing Danish king as ruler of Greece, Great Britain pledged to turn over the islands if the inhabitants voted in favor | • Plebiscite (1863) resulting in Greek control • British surrender and leave islands |
| Haiti | France | 1803 to 1825 | • Revolt (mostly by slaves) inspired by American and French independence | Independence |
| Brazil | Portugal | 1775 to 1815 | No claim of self-determination | • Incorporated by Portugal • Independence claimed by Portuguese prince (Dom Pedro) in 1822 |

| Entity | Former sovereign | Year | Method | Outcome |
|---|---|---|---|---|
| Greece | Ottoman Empire | 1831 | War of Independence (1821 to 1831) | Independence |
| Moldavia, Wallachia | Austro-Hungarian Empire | 1858 | Cession | Fused to Rumania |
| Rome[a] | Papal State | 1870 | • Occupied • Issue: annexation • Plebiscite | Popular sovereignty under Italy |
| St. Bartholomew[a] | Sweden | 1877 | Cession | Vote in favor of French control |
| Serbia | Ottoman Empire | 1878 | Serbo-Turkish War | Independence |
| Montenegro | Ottoman Empire | 1878 | Cession | Independence |
| Rumelia | Ottoman Empire | 1878 | Cession | Independence (joined Bulgaria 1885) |
| Crete | Ottoman Empire | 1898 | Cession | Independence |
| Norway | Sweden | 1905 | Cession | Independence |
| Bulgaria | Ottoman Empire | 1908 | Cession | Independence |
| Macedonia | Ottoman Empire | 1913 | Cession | Divided between Greece and Serbia |
| Drobrudja | Ottoman Empire | 1913 | Cession | Joined Rumania |
| St. Thomas and St. John[a] | Denmark | 1868 to 1917 | • Danish refuse to cede islands to the United States as coaling stations without the approval of the inhabitants | • Vote in favor of the United States • Finally ceded in 1917, after years of tabling by the U.S. Senate (no second vote) |
| Bohemia | Austro-Hungarian Empire | 1919 | Cession | Formed Czechoslovakia |
| Moravia |  |  |  |  |
| Slovakia |  |  |  |  |
| Albania | Ottoman Empire | 1920 | • Albania declared independence in 1912 • Occupied by Allies during World War I | Provisional government until 1925 |
| Ireland[b] | United Kingdom | 1922 | Cession after civil war | Dominion status |
| Austria | Austro-Hungarian Empire | 1920 | Post-World War I | Independence |
| Hungary | see Austria |  |  |  |

(Table continues on p. 210.)

TABLE 7.A1    Continued

| Country or Group Location | Country from Which Self-Determination Was Claimed | Year of Claim | Reason Given for Self-Determination | International Response and Result |
|---|---|---|---|---|
| | | | Resolved (or Resolvable) Claims of Self-Determination | |
| Transylvania | Austro-Hungarian Empire | 1920 | Seized by Rumania 1918 | Cession to Rumania by Hungary, 1920 |
| Tacna-Arica[a] | Peru | 1883 to 1926 | Chilean occupation: Chile or Peru | • Plebiscite attempted: authority for treaty after Nitrate War |
| Åland Islands[c] | Finland | 1920 | • Regarding whether the inhabitants were free to secede from Finland to join Sweden (people there spoke Swedish), they applied to the League of Nations. | • League of Nations upheld Finland's claim to the Ålands, saying "it pertains exclusively to the sovereignty of any definitely constituted State to grant to, or withhold from, a fraction of its population the right of deciding its own political destiny by means of a plebiscite, or any other way" (Cassese 1955, 29). |
| | | | | • The second report suggested policy lines, saying that self-determination could be used in the case of protection of minorities, when the protection of these minorities was the only sensible solution for providing safeguards to ethnic and religious groups, abuse of authority, oppression and persecution of people. The Åland islanders could not claim this, because they wanted to secede because of language difference and xenophobia of mainland Finnish. |

| Location | Colonial power | Dates | Circumstances | Outcome |
|---|---|---|---|---|
| Allenstein and Marienwerder | Germany | 1920 | • Post-World War I: Germany or Poland? | Plebiscite for Germany |
| Klagenfurt Basin | Austria | 1920 | • Post-World War I: Austria or Yugoslavia? | Plebiscite for Austria (no change) |
| Schleswig | Germany | 1920 | • Post-World War I: Denmark or Germany? | Plebiscite: partition |
| Sopron | Austro-Hungary | 1921 | • Post-World War I: Hungary or Austria? | Plebiscite: control by Hungary |
| Slovenia Dalmatia Croatia Bosnia | Austro-Hungarian Empire | 1921 | Post-World War cession | Combined with Serbia to form Yugoslavia |
| Turkey | Ottoman Empire | 1922 | • Nationalists overthrow Muhammad VI | Independence |
| Cuba | United States | 1901 to 1934 | • After three years of independence from Spain (1898 to 1901), the United States occupied Cuba. • Decolonization | • Independence, establishment of government friendly to U.S. interests. |
| Upper Silesia | Germany | 1921 | Post-World War I: Germany or Poland? | Plebiscite resulting in partition |
| The Saar | Germany | 1935 | • Post-World War I: Germany, France, or the League of Nations? | Both plebiscites in Germany |
| Weihaiwei (now Weihai, China)[d] | United Kingdom | 1898 to 1930 | Decolonization | Became part of China |
| Canada | United Kingdom | 1867 to 1931 | Decolonization | Commonwealth status |
| Iraq | United Kingdom | 1920 to 1932 | • Became a mandate of the United Kingdom in 1920 • Decolonization | Accepted into League of Nations in 1932 |
| Nicaragua | United States | 1912 to 1933 | • Occupied by the United States • Decolonization | • Independence, a new constitution, and the establishment of government friendly to U.S. interests under Somoza |

(Table continues on p. 212.)

TABLE 7.A1    Continued

| Country or Group Location | Country from Which Self-Determination Was Claimed | Year of Claim | Reason Given for Self-Determination | International Response and Result |
|---|---|---|---|---|
| | | | Resolved (or Resolvable) Claims of Self-Determination | |
| South Africa | United Kingdom | 1910 to 1934 | Decolonization | • Commonwealth status until 1960, when it became a republic |
| Haiti | United States | 1915 to 1934 | • Occupied by U.S. Marine Force<br>• Decolonization | • Independence and the establishment of government friendly to U.S. interests |
| Levant States (Syria and Lebanon) | France | 1919 to 1941 | • Became a mandate of France after World War I<br>• Decolonization | • Free French declared independence, but troops stayed until 1946 |
| Australia | United Kingdom | 1901 to 1942 | Decolonization | Commonwealth status |
| Great Lebanon | France | 1943 | Decolonization | Independence |
| Iceland | Denmark | 1523 to 1944 | Dissolution of union | • Collapse of Denmark during World War II brought occupation by the United States and Britain |
| Philippines | United States | 1899 to 1946 | • Spanish colony until Spanish-American war, then U.S. protectorate<br>• Japanese occupation, 1942 to 1945<br>• Decolonization | Independence |
| Transjordan (now Jordan) | United Kingdom | 1920 to 1946 | • Mandate territory after World War I<br>• Decolonization | Granted independence |
| India[b] | United Kingdom | 1765 to 1947 | • Decolonization<br>• After India helped in World War I, British promised gradual self-determination. | Indian independence, August 1947 |

| Territory | Colonial power | Dates | Description | Result |
|---|---|---|---|---|
| Hyderabad[e] | India | 1947 to 1948 | • When World War II left Britain dependent on the United States, the United States was not interested in actively preserving India<br>• Demands on British military resources<br>• Labor party gains control in 1945 in Britain, pushing decolonization<br>• Large and wealthy state that maintained sovereignty and was sovereign until independence in 1947<br>• Placed case before U.N. Security Council in 1948<br>• While the United Nations was considering the matter, India invaded, and the complaint was withdrawn in favor of a negotiated compromise with the Indian government | Became part of India |
| New Zealand | United Kingdom | 1841 to 1947 | Decolonization | Commonwealth status |
| Italian East Africa (Eritrea, Ethiopia and Italian Somaliland) | Italy | 1935 to 1947 | • 1934 to 1935 Italy invaded Ethiopia in Italo-Ethiopian War<br>• Lost in World War II<br>• Decolonization | Independence |
| Ceylon (now Sri Lanka) | United Kingdom | 1803 to 1947 | Decolonization | Joined the Commonwealth |
| Palestine | United Kingdom | 1920 to 1948 | • Mandate territory in League of Nations with plan for Jewish state<br>• Decolonization | • Israel created in 1948<br>• Current uncertainty regarding territory |
| Burma (now Mynamar) | United Kingdom | 1937 to 1948 | • Separated from India in 1937<br>• Decolonization | Independence |

(Table continues on p. 214.)

TABLE 7.A1    *Continued*

| Country or Group Location | Country from Which Self-Determination Was Claimed | Year of Claim | Reason Given for Self-Determination | International Response and Result |
|---|---|---|---|---|
| | Resolved (or Resolvable) Claims of Self-Determination | | | |
| Dutch East Indies | The Netherlands | 1609 to 1949 | • Nationalist movement started in 1927<br>• Japanese invade 1942 to 1945<br>• Proclaimed independence, 1945<br>• Decolonization | 1949 Indonesia granted independence after four year war with the Netherlands |
| Newfoundland | United Kingdom | 1729 to 1949 | Decolonization | Became province of Canada |
| Bhutan | United Kingdom | 1910 to 1949 | Decolonization | • Admitted to the United Nations, 1971<br>• India guides foreign affairs<br>• Claimed independence from India in 1949 |
| Oman | United Kingdom | 1798 to 1951 | Decolonization | Independent sultanate |
| Libya | Italy | 1928 to 1951 | • United Nations gained control after World War II<br>• Decolonization | Independence |
| Egypt | United Kingdom | 1883 to 1953 | • Declared independent by Britain in 1922, but British troops remain until 1936<br>• Neutral in World War II, some occupation<br>• 1950 to 1952, nationalists call to withdraw troops | Independent republic |
| Laos | France | 1893 to 1954 | • 1942 to 1945, occupied by Japan<br>• 1946, French reestablish control<br>• Decolonization | Independence |

| Colony | Colonial Power | Dates | Issues | Outcome |
|---|---|---|---|---|
| Cochin China (joined with other territory to form Vietnam) | France | 1862 to 1954 | • French-Indochine war of 1946 • 1949, state of Vietnam founded • Demand withdrawal of French troops • French leave in 1954, Cochin China joins Vietnam | 1954, invaded by Vietminh, French leave |
| Cambodia | France | 1863 to 1954 | • 1940 to 1945, Japanese control • 1945, French regain control | |
| Annam (central Vietnam) | France | 1883 to 1954 | See Cochin China | |
| Tonkin (joined with other territory to form Vietnam) | France | 1888 to 1954 | See Cochin China | |
| The Saar[a] | Germany | 1955 | • Post World War II: autonomy or Germany? | • Both plebiscites result in German rule |
| Togoland[a] | United Kingdom | 1955 | • Decolonization • Issue: upon independence from Britain, should Togoland join the Gold Coast or continue as a trust area of Britain? | • U.N.-sponsored plebiscite, resulting in Ghanaian authority |
| French Morocco | France | 1912 to 1956 | Decolonization | • Joined with Spanish Morocco to form Morocco |
| Spanish Morocco | Spain | 1912 to 1956 | Decolonization | See French Morocco |
| Tunisia | France | 1881 to 1957 | • Occupied during World War II • French reenter after the war • Nationalist guerilla war for decolonization | French withdraw |
| Gold Coast (now Ghana) | United Kingdom | 1874 to 1957 | Decolonization | • Became part of the British Commonwealth in 1957 • Independence as a republic in 1960 |

*(Table continues on p. 216.)*

TABLE 7.A1   *Continued*

| Country or Group Location | Country from Which Self-Determination Was Claimed | Year of Claim | Reason Given for Self-Determination | International Response and Result |
|---|---|---|---|---|
| | | Resolved (or Resolvable) Claims of Self-Determination | | |
| French Guinea[f] | France | 1893 to 1958 | Decolonization | • Voted for independence in French-held referendum in 1958 |
| Singapore | United Kingdom | 1942 to 1959 | • Surrendered to the Japanese during World War II • Reoccupied in 1945 • Decolonization | Independence |
| Gabon | France | 1845 to 1960 | Decolonization | • 1958, vote to be part of French Community • 1960, independence |
| Cyprus | United Kingdom | 1878 to 1960 | Decolonization | Independence |
| British Somaliland | United Kingdom | 1884 to 1960 | Decolonization | • Joined with Italian Somaliland to form Somalia |
| Madagascar | France | 1885 to 1960 | Decolonization | • 1958, vote to be part of French Community • 1960, independence |
| Togo[a] | France | 1922 to 1960 | Decolonization | • 1958, vote to be part of French Community • 1960, independence |
| Belgian Congo | Belgium | 1887 to 1960 | Decolonization | Independence |
| Italian Somaliland | Italy | 1889 to 1960 | • Surrendered in World War II to the British • Decolonization | • Joined with British Somaliland to form Somalia |
| Ivory Coast | France | 1893 to 1960 | Decolonization | • 1958, vote to be part of French Community • 1960, independence |

| Country | Colonial power | Date | Process | Notes |
|---|---|---|---|---|
| Dahomey (now Benin) | France | 1894 to 1960 | Decolonization | • 1960, independence |
| Ubangi Shari (now Central African Republic) | France | 1894 to 1960 | Decolonization | • 1958, vote to be part of French Community, became the Central African Republic<br>• 1960, independence |
| Mauritania | France | 1902 to 1960 | Decolonization | • 1958, vote to be part of French Community<br>• 1960, Independence |
| Federation of Nigeria | United Kingdom | 1906 to 1960 | Decolonization | Independence |
| Niger | France | 1911 to 1960 | Decolonization | • 1958, vote to be part of French Community<br>• 1960, independence |
| French Cameroon | France | 1922 to 1960 | Decolonization | • 1958, vote to be part of French Community<br>• 1960, independence<br>• Joined with Cameroon in 1961 |
| Middle Congo | France | 1941 to 1960 | Decolonization | • 1958, vote to be part of French Community<br>• 1960, independence |
| Upper Volta (Burkina Faso) | France | 1947 to 1960 | Decolonization | • 1958, vote to be part of French Community<br>• 1960, independence |
| Federation of Mali | France | 1881 to 1960 | Decolonization | • 1958, vote to be part of French Community<br>• 1960, independence |
| British Cameroon | United Kingdom | 1961 | United Nations trust territory | • Upon independence, joined with French Cameroon to form Cameroon |
| Sierra Leone | United Kingdom | 1792 to 1961 | Decolonization | Independence |
| Kuwait | United Kingdom | 1899 to 1961 | Decolonization | Independence |

(Table continues on p. 218.)

TABLE 7.A1 *Continued*

| Country or Group Location | Country from Which Self-Determination Was Claimed | Year of Claim | Reason Given for Self-Determination | International Response and Result |
|---|---|---|---|---|
| Resolved (or Resolvable) Claims of Self-Determination | | | | |
| Tanganyika | United Kingdom | 1920 to 1961 | • Before World War I, German colony<br>• Became a mandate in 1920<br>• 1946, trust territory<br>• Decolonization | • Joined with Zanzibar to form Tanzania in 1964 |
| Zanzibar | United Kingdom | 1894 to 1963 | Decolonization | See Tanganyika |
| Goa | Portugal | 1961 | Annexed by India | |
| Western Samoa[a] | United Kingdom: New Zealand | 1946 to 1962 | Decolonization | • Plebiscite resulting in independence |
| French India[d] | France | 1668 to 1962 | Decolonization | Joined India |
| Algeria | France | 1830 to 1962 | Decolonization after a brutal civil war | Independence |
| Uganda | United Kingdom | 1894 to 1962 | Decolonization | Independence |
| Rwanda-Urundi | Belgium | 1920 to 1962 | Decolonization | Divided in 1962 |
| Jamaica | United Kingdom | 1655 to 1962 | Decolonization | Independence |
| Trinidad and Tobago | United Kingdom | 1721 to 1962 | Decolonization | Independence |
| British North Borneo[b] | United Kingdom | 1877 to 1962 | • Administered by a chartered company until 1946 | Joined Malaysian Federation |
| Kenya | United Kingdom | 1887 to 1963 | Decolonization | Independence |
| Sarawak[b] | United Kingdom | 1888 to 1963 | Became a Crown Colony in 1946 | See British North Borneo |

| Territory | Colonial power | Dates | Process | Outcome |
|---|---|---|---|---|
| Malaya | United Kingdom | 1946 to 1963 | Decolonization | • Divided between Malaysia and Singapore<br>• Joined the British Commonwealth in 1974 |
| Malta | United Kingdom | 1799 to 1964 | Decolonization | • Split for independence in 1963 |
| Nyasaland (now Malawi) | United Kingdom | 1889 to 1964 | • Became part of the federation of Rhodesia and Nayasaland | |
| North Rhodesia | United Kingdom | 1911 to 1964 | • Became part of the federation of Rhodesia and Nayasaland<br>• Black nationalist movement protests in 1962 | • 1964, independence, with black vote |
| Maldives | United Kingdom | 1887 to 1965 | Decolonization | • Independence, joined the Commonwealth in 1985 |
| Gambia | United Kingdom | 1888 to 1965 | Decolonization | Independence |
| British Guiana (Guyana) | United Kingdom | 1831 to 1966 | • Decolonization<br>• Movement began in 1952 | Independence |
| Barbados | United Kingdom | 1855 to 1966 | Decolonization | Independence |
| Basutoland (Lesotho) | United Kingdom | 1883 to 1966 | Decolonization | Independence |
| Bechuanaland (Botswana) | United Kingdom | 1895 to 1966 | Decolonization | Independence |
| Federation of South Arabia | United Kingdom | 1959 to 1967 | Decolonization | Independence |
| Biafra, eastern Nigeria[g] | Nigeria | May 1967 to January 1970 | • Mostly Ibo, better educated, not satisfied with less than control of Nigeria<br>• Physical violence and massacre; "cultural as well as physical extermination"<br>• Claimed support of all eastern ethnic groups and that "Ibos and Non-Ibos in the region were culturally, socially, and economically interwoven for decades" | • Critics deny support by minorities for Biafra<br>• Recognized by four African states and France<br>• United Nations does not respond, except to send UNICEF aid |

(Table continues on p. 220.)

TABLE 7.A1   *Continued*

| Country or Group Location | Country from Which Self-Determination Was Claimed | Year of Claim | Reason Given for Self-Determination | International Response and Result |
|---|---|---|---|---|
| | | | Resolved (or Resolvable) Claims of Self-Determination | |
| Mauritius | United Kingdom | 1814 to 1968 | Decolonization | • Became part of the Commonwealth in 1992 |
| Equatorial Guinea[b] | Spain | 1855 to 1968 | Became autonomous in 1963 | • Joined with Rio Muni, Fernando Po, and other small islands to form Equatorial Guinea in 1968 Independence |
| Swaziland | United Kingdom | 1903 to 1968 | Decolonization | Independence |
| Nauru[b] | Australia | 1945 to 1968 | • Colonized by Germany in 1888 • Passed to Australia in 1920 • Occupied by Japanese in 1942 • Became trusteeship in 1947 | • Independence, with associate membership in the Commonwealth |
| Ifni[b] | Spain | 1958 to 1969 | Spain versus Morocco | Transferred to Morocco |
| Fiji[b] | United Kingdom | 1874 to 1970 | Decolonization | Joined the Commonwealth |
| Tonga[b] | United Kingdom | 1900 to 1970 | • Protected state, retained its own monarchy and control of internal affairs | Joined the Commonwealth |
| Bahrain | United Kingdom | 1861 to 1971 | Decolonization | Independence |
| Trucial States (United Arab Emirates) | United Kingdom | 1891 to 1971 | Decolonization | • British withdrawal • Independence |
| Quatar | United Kingdom | 1916 to 1971 | Decolonization | Independence |

| | | | | |
|---|---|---|---|---|
| Bangladesh (East Pakistan)ᵍ | Pakistan | 1971 | • Language: Bengalis do not speak Urdu<br>• Economic discrimination<br>• Racism from Punjabi, who came to dominate Pakistan<br>• 3 million Bengalis killed from March to December 1971<br>• 8 million to 9 million refugees | • India's support in war that made Bangladesh independent, and diplomacy<br>• The majority of states in the United Nations supported Pakistan<br>• Soviet bloc supports Bengalis<br>• First successful secession after World War II |
| Bahamas | United Kingdom | 1670 to 1973 | Decolonization | Joined the Commonwealth |
| Portuguese Guinea (Guinea-Bissau) | Portugal | 1875 to 1974 | • Decolonization<br>• Independence movement in the 1960s | • Declared independence in 1973<br>• Granted independence in 1974 |
| Moro (Southern Philippinesᵍ) | Philippines | 1972 to 1974 | • Moslem group of 2 million to 3 million in 1970, about 6 percent of total population on 34 percent of land<br>• Claims: Filipino "colonial domination," land grabbing, "Christianization," napalm bombing in the early 1970s | • Support from Malaysia, Libya, Egypt, Kuwait, Senegal<br>• No resolution of conflict |
| Grenada | United Kingdom | 1792 to 1974 | Decolonization | Joined the Commonwealth in 1974 |
| Cape Verde Islands | Portugal | 1462 to 1975 | Became overseas province, 1951 | Independence |
| Mozambique | Portugal | 1752 to 1975 | • Decolonization<br>• War for independence, 1964 to 1974 | Independence |
| Saõ Tome and Principe | Portugal | 1485 to 1975 | Decolonization | Independence |
| Angola | Portugal | 1575 to 1975 | • Decolonization<br>• 1961, nationalist resistance movement began | |

(Table continues on p. 222.)

TABLE 7.A1    *Continued*

Resolved (or Resolvable) Claims of Self-Determination

| Country or Group Location | Country from Which Self-Determination Was Claimed | Year of Claim | Reason Given for Self-Determination | International Response and Result |
|---|---|---|---|---|
| Surinam (now Suriname) | Holland | 1667 to 1975 | • Guerrilla warfare, establishment of competing governments in exile<br>• Decolonization<br>• Autonomous state in 1954 | • Portuguese stop fighting 1974<br>• Independence |
| Papau and New Guinea (joined to form Papua New Guinea) | Australia | 1905 to 1975 | • Decolonization<br>• Mandate territory after 1945 | Independence<br><br>Merged upon independence |
| West Irian | Indonesia | 1975 | • Decolonization<br>• Military occupation | • Agreement had been reached whereby the Netherlands would transfer administration of West Irian to the U.N. Temporary Executive Authority and they would administer a vote<br>• After corrupt elections, passed to Indonesia |
| Seychelles | United Kingdom | 1903 to 1976 | Decolonization | • Joined the Commonwealth in 1976 |
| Belize (British Honduras)[h] | United Kingdom (1862 to 1976); Guatemala | 1977 | Decolonization | • United Nations affirmed right of the people to self-determination<br>• Independence |
| Djibouti | France | 1862 to 1977 | Decolonization | • 1958, vote to be part of French Community<br>• 1977, independence |

| Country | Colonial power | Years | | |
|---|---|---|---|---|
| Solomon Islands[b] | United Kingdom | 1893 to 1978 | • British protectorate • Japanese occupation in 1942 • Independence movement | • Independence, joined the Commonwealth |
| Ellice (now Tuvalu)[b] | United Kingdom | 1976 to 1978 | • Decolonization | • Independence, joined the Commonwealth in 1978 |
| Saint Lucia[b] | United Kingdom | 1960 to 1979 | • Became an associated state with Britain in 1966 See Saint Lucia | |
| Saint Vincent[b] | United Kingdom | 1960 to 1979 | | |
| Gilbert (now Kinbati)[b] | United Kingdom | 1892 to 1979 | • British protectorate in 1892 • Annexed and became colony in 1916, administered with Ellice Islands • Occupied by the Japanese in 1942 1966, associated State | • Referendum • Independence, joined the Commonwealth in 1978 |
| Saint Kitts-Nevis[b] | United Kingdom | 1969 to 1983 | | |
| Brunei[b] | United Kingdom | 1888 to 1984 | 1906, British protectorate | Independence, joined the Commonwealth |
| Southern Rhodesia (now Zimbabwe) | United Kingdom | 1893 to 1984 | • Decolonization • 1960s and 1970s, white minority government seizes power | • First declared a republic in 1980, when blacks take control • Independence |
| Estonia Latvia Lithuania Armenia Azerbaijan Georgia Kazakhstan Kyrgyzstan Moldova Tajikistan Turkmenistan Ukraine Uzbekistan | Soviet Union | 1991 to 1992 | • Fragmentation from the demise of the Soviet Union | • All gained membership in the United Nations |

(Table continues on p. 224.)

TABLE 7.A1    *Continued*

| Country or Group Location | Country from Which Self-Determination Was Claimed | Year of Claim | Reason Given for Self-Determination | International Response and Result |
|---|---|---|---|---|
| Resolved (or Resolvable) Claims of Self-Determination | | | | |
| Slovenia Croatia Macedonia Bosnia-Herzegovina[c] | Yugoslavia | 1991 to the present | • Fragmentation from the demise of the Yugoslav federation | • All but Bosnia-Herzegovina completed all requirements of the European Community for independence and gained independence<br>• In Bosnia, there was no referendum for the whole population until 1992; this referendum was boycotted by the Serbs, so they could not claim self-determination |
| Eritrea[c] | Ethiopia | 1960 to 1993 | • After World War II, the United Nations got control from Italy, but failed to reach an agreement based on wishes of inhabitants<br>• The United Nations recognized claims of Ethiopia (wanted access to the sea), as well as the interest "of peace and security in East Africa" and a 1952 Eritrean Assembly vote, but no action was taken<br>• 1962, Ethiopia forcibly annexes Eritrea | 1993 referendum; independence |
| Hong Kong | United Kingdom; China | 1997 | Transfer of power | Did not claim self-determination |
| Macao | Portugal; China | 1999 | Transfer of power | Did not claim self-determination |

| Region | Country | Dates | Basis | Response |
|---|---|---|---|---|
| Basque Region | Spain | 1975 to present | Cultural, language differences | • Spanish constitution (1978) grants regional devolution |
| Catalonia | Spain | 1975 to present | Language, cultural | • Spanish constitution (1978) grants regional devolution |
| Chechnya | Russia | 1989 to present | Cultural, religious differences | • Russian army crushes Chechen government in a territory that claims sovereignty; no international response |
| Corsica | France | 1976 to present | Cultural differences | • Formation of Front of National Liberation of Corsica (FLNC); no international response |
| Faeroe Islands | Denmark | 2000 | • Government of the Faeroes presented Danish officials with a plan to grant independence but keep Queen Margrethe of Denmark as their head of state | • Government says that the price of independence for the Faeroes will be loss of Danish subsidies within four years |
| Gibraltar | United Kingdom versus Spain | 1957 to present | • Spain disputed right of United Kingdom to get "non-self-governing status" for Gibraltar (attempted in 1946) | • 1963, United Nations urges negotiation • 1964, United Nations sides with Spain • 1968, United Nations urges United Kingdom to decolonize • 1967, plebiscite held in favor of United Kingdom • Unresolved |
| Hawaii | United States | 1893 to present | Decolonization | • Statehood (1959), but no response to subsequent demands for self-determination |
| Karen region | Myanmar | 1949 to present | • Karen National Union seeks regional autonomy to reduce discrimination against Karens; advocates a Federal Union | • Government responds with military force; at present there is a civil war |

(Table continues on p. 226.)

TABLE 7.A1  *Continued*

| Country or Group Location | Country from Which Self-Determination Was Claimed | Year of Claim | Reason Given for Self-Determination | International Response and Result |
|---|---|---|---|---|
| Unresolved Claims of Self-Determination | | | | |
| Kashmir and Punjab | India | 1949 to present | • Strong separatist movements based on religious minorities in these Indian states resort to violent tactics | • Government refuses to devolve political authority to religious minorities |
| Kurdistan | Mountains of Iraq, Turkey, and Iran | 1920 to present | Independence movements | • No territorial integrity, no single ethnic group<br>• Divisions between mountain and valley populations, languages<br>• Geopolitics |
| Mindanao; Cordillera Mountains | Philippines | 1971 to present | • Religion: Muslims seek redress from Christian majority in the country | • No international response; armed movement for autonomy and independence |
| Malvinas-Falkland Islands[c] | United Kingdom, on the part of Argentina | 1982 to present | • Argentina: territorial integrity, decolonization<br>• United Kingdom: self-determination of the settler population | • United Nations pushed for negotiations<br>• Unresolved |
| Northern Ireland | United Kingdom | 1916 to present | Religious division | • Peace agreement being implemented, providing the region with self-determination |
| Palestine[c] | Israel | 1948 to present | Military occupation by Israel after 1967 | • Almost all states take view that Palestinians are entitled to self-determination based on military occupation, but also want to secure existence of Israel<br>• Favor negotiation<br>• Unresolved |
| Puerto Rico | United States | 1898 to present | • Decolonization: annexation? independence? autonomy? associate status? | • 1980, plebiscite: for Commonwealth status<br>• 1993, plebiscite: for Commonwealth status |

| | | | | |
|---|---|---|---|---|
| Quebec[c] | Canada | 1976 to present | • Those favoring independence are a small minority<br>Language, culture | • 1998, plebiscite: for Commonwealth status<br>• Opposed by native Canadians<br>• Public referendum, 1980: against separatism<br>• Public referendum, 1992: 54 percent no<br>• Public referendum, 1995: 50.6 percent no |
| Scotland, Wales[i] | United Kingdom | 1960 to present | Cultural, language differences | • British government grants Scottish and Welsh parliaments, 1999, after public referenda in 1997 |
| Southern Sudan | Northern Sudan | 1961 to 1972 | • South underdeveloped, and when Sudan gained independence in 1956, no attempt to address inequality<br>• Physical violence and slavery<br>• Racial to cultural domination and assimilation by the "Arabs" in northern Sudan | No response |
| Southern Senegal | Senegal | 2000 | • Separatist movement of the Democratic Forces of Casamance involved in violence as presidential election nears | No response |
| Tamil region | Sri Lanka | 1948 to present | • Tamils seek to secede from a Sinhalese-dominated state. | Government responds with military force |

*Source:* Authors' compilation.

[a]Johnson 1967.
[b]Chamberlain 1998.
[c]Cassese 1995.
[d]Strang 1991.
[e]Hannum 1996.
[f]Holland 1985.
[g]Heraclides 1991.
[h]Lerner 1980.
[i]Ronen 1979.

# Notes

1.  The international relations literature has long treated nation-states as actors on a world stage, examining norms and decision-making processes (see Jackson 1996 and Haufler 1993 for recent statements).

2.  Lest there be any doubt on this score, this view of norms falls far short of a theory that is adequate to explain when and where a given norm spreads.

3.  In an excellent essay, Stephen Krasner (1999) characterizes this approach as implying a logic of appropriateness, in contrast to a logic of consequences, and then discusses each with reference to the literature in international relations.

4.  This is also true with respect to educational investment: "The implementation of standard scripts for educational development in countries of all sorts, without regard to their particular circumstances, produces results that often seem quite bizarre, especially when viewed through the rationalized lenses of the functional theories that justify these scripts. Children who will become agricultural laborers study fractions; villagers in remote regions learn about chemical reactions; members of marginalized groups who will never see a ballot box study their national constitutions. Deeming such practices rationally functional requires a breathtaking leap of faith" (Meyer et al. 1997, 149–50). Although institutionalists sometimes claim that institutional mimicry is an irrational outcome, any such conclusion is, at best, overstated. The rulers of a regime may be less interested in making sound investments than in endowing themselves with greater prestige and perquisites. Moreover, to the degree that institutional mimicry is the price of admission to the international community, its short-term instrumental payoffs may dwarf its long-term costs.

5.  This is also the thrust of the burgeoning literatures on social capital and trust. Many other conditions facilitating collective action have been proposed, but they are tangential to the purposes of this chapter.

6.  Compare this account with descriptions of the emergence of friendly societies, insurance groups, and rotating credit associations in Hechter 1987, chapter 5.

7.  Because the United Nations resembles a legislative body, we regard the content of its charter as the outcome of a constitutional decision-making process. In this respect, its promulgation of the norm of national self-determination reflects an existing consensus among member states.

8.  Here, too, there are important exceptions. Thus, a woman's right to control her body is fiercely debated in the current abortion wars. Although there are limits to self-determination for the mentally ill and for persons who have been convicted of criminal activity, most of these limits are not controversial.

9.  One example is the case of Burundi and Rwanda.

10. The degree to which central rulers took the interests of key nobles and merchants into account, of course, varied across polities.

11. Similarly, many subsequent plebiscites, such as in those held in the aftermath of World War I, also failed to offer voters an option for outright independence.

12. For example, both Lord Byron and Eugène Delacroix were enthusiastic supporters of the Greek nationalists.

13. This later contributed to a series of regional squabbles and a tendency toward secession in the nineteenth century, which abated only when the fledgling

Latin American countries gained entry into the world capitalist market and required strong central governments to protect local interests and build infrastructure (Oszlak 1981).

14. The Danish refused to cede the islands to the United States for use as coaling stations without the approval of the inhabitants. The vote was in favor of the United States (there was no option for independence). The islands were not finally ceded until 1917; there was no second plebiscite, despite the forty-nine years that had passed since the first election (ample time for the residents' governance preferences to have changed).

15. This period also witnessed the beginning of U.S. imperialism. At the end of the Spanish-American War (in 1898), the United States acquired the Philippines (in 1899). America's first taste of empire led to a distinctly American kind of colonization in Cuba (in 1901), Nicaragua (in 1912) and Haiti (in 1915). Whereas the impetus for European colonies was the extraction of primary products and the creation of new markets, American colonization largely aimed to protect U.S. investments that were already in place. The relatively short duration of American colonies suggests that the Americans entered, arranged things to their liking, and soon departed. By contrast, the British held on to their colonies for a century or more. American decolonization in this period had delayed effects on British and French decolonization following World War II.

16. "The Fourteen Points were anything but a wholehearted exposition of the principle of national self-determination. . . . Apart from the loose phraseology about 'every peace-loving nation' wishing 'to live its own life' and 'the principle of justice to all peoples and nationalities,' there is no general pronouncement stating adherence to national self-determination. . . . [Wilson's] problem was that he recognised the need to take other considerations, mainly economic and strategic, into account, and immediately before his speech Secretary of State Lansing had warned of the impracticability of the principle" (Heater 1994, 43–44).

17. Wilson's own secretary of state, Robert Lansing, argued that "self-determination should be forgotten. It has no place in the practical scheme of world affairs. It has already caused enough despair, enough suffering and enough anarchy" (Ofuatey-Kodjoe 1977, 3). Georges Clemenceau told Lloyd George "that he did not believe in the principle of self-determination, which allowed a man to clutch at your throat the first time it was convenient for him" (Knight 1984, 72). In fact, the fifth of Wilson's Fourteen Points stated that all claims of sovereignty from colonies must be evenly balanced with the interests of the mother country.

18. This subsequently led to passages in United Nations documents stating that self-determination requires the free will of the people, to forestall populist authoritarian regimes from using it as an excuse to annex territory (Cassese 1995, 40; Cobban [1945] 1969, 94).

19. The signing of the Atlantic Charter stimulated later nationalism in the colonies by giving them the idea that the United States sided with the colonies against colonialism, an impression strengthened by the fact that it had already decolonized Cuba (in 1934), Nicaragua (in 1933), and Haiti (in 1934). Churchill attempted to counteract this impression when he proclaimed that self-determination did not apply to colonies but was for "restoring the sovereignty, self-government to nations of Europe under the Nazi yoke," besides providing for

"any alterations in the territorial boundaries which may have to be made" (Churchill, quoted in Cassese 1995, 37).

20.   John A. Hall (1993) colorfully refers to such situations as examples of "matrioshka nationalism."

21.   Only in the case of East Timor did the United Nations take some action. Note, however, that its intervention came at a time when the Indonesian central state was extremely weak—racked by a currency crisis and subject to enormous protest in its Javanese homeland. Even so, UN intervention on behalf of East Timor cannot be said to have set a new precedent. Shortly thereafter, Russia's violent repression of the Chechnyan separatists occasioned no response at all from the international community.

22.   Of course, many other socially relevant distinctions are also social constructions, as well; see Wildavsky 1993.

23.   However, another third party, the European Community (at the instigation of Germany), did play an active role in the dissolution of Yugoslavia by effectively recognizing the right to self-determination of Slovenia and Croatia in 1991 (Woodward 1995, chapter 7). This rare application of the norm of national self-determination unleashed horrendous violence in the former Yugoslavia and served as a cautionary tale for future policy makers. The North Atlantic Treaty Organization's air war to rid Kosovo of its Serbian military occupation in the spring of 1999 pointedly did not offer the Kosovars the prospect of sovereignty.

24.   Although the evidence presented here strongly suggests that the norm of self-determination is not generally honored for national minorities located within sovereign states, the norm is sometimes, perhaps increasingly, applied by the central governments of a number of states. The British government's decision to extend political devolution in Scotland and Wales, the Canadian government's recognition of the new state of Nunavut, and Indonesia's new agreement to consider self-determination for East Timor are all cases in point.

25.   For an alternative institutionalist account of decolonization placing greater emphasis on the causal role of the international norm of national self-determination, see Strang 1991, 1992. Strang argues that differences in the timing of British and French decolonization are the result of normative differences between Britain and France.

26.   "Rwanda offers us not one but several lessons. The U.N. did not just withdraw; it also authorized a humanitarian intervention by the French, code-named Operation Turquoise. That intervention did save many Tutsi, but it also saved the political and military leadership that carried out the genocide. . . . Neither the U.N. nor any other international forum has held the French accountable for this intervention" (Mamdani 2000, 22). Although Ted Gurr (2000) argues that international intervention on behalf of cultural minorities increased in the 1990s, the evidence is ambiguous, as the above quote suggests.

27.   One Kenyan delegate to the conference of the Organization for African Unity argued that the United Nations' definition of self-determination "has no relevance where the issue is territorial disintegration by dissident citizens" (Knight 1984, 173–75). As an attempt to clarify some of the terminological confusion, self-determination has been divided into two categories: external and internal. External self-determination is the ability of a group to choose its actions freely in international relations, whether opting for independence or union with

other states (Cassese 1995). It is a collective claim for national government (Johnson 1967, 28). Thus, the United Nations charter refers to external self-determination alone. By contrast, internal self-determination is either the freedom enjoyed by a people in a sovereign state to elect and maintain the government of its choice or an ethnic, racial, religious, or other minority's right within a sovereign state to freedom from oppression at the hands of the central government (Cassese 1995). Internal self-determination is demanded today by groups who want more autonomy but do not seek secession, such as the indigenous groups in Chiapas, Mexico.

28. Much the same can be said about other ostensibly universalistic norms involving human rights and environmental protection. In both cases, arguments about policy implementation revolve around trade-offs between commitment to the ethical norm and competing interests in maintaining jobs (in industries like timber) or creating economic growth (by encouraging urban development).

29. The cooperative norms that emerge in the wake of community disaster are often cited in the sociological literature (Quarantelli and Dynes 1977; Erikson 1976).

30. Thus, institutionalists argue that ostensibly welfare-enhancing norms, such as those dictating educational policy in developing countries, are not welfare enhancing at all. (See note 4, which discusses educational policy.) In challenging the view that all norms are outcome oriented, Jon Elster (1990) in effect denies that all norms are collective goods. In his view, norms such as feuding and dueling are closer to collective bads (but see Hardin 1995 for an opposing argument). Furthermore, norms of honor may be a collective good for thieves, but they are a collective bad for the rest of society.

31. Although benevolent norms may be beneficial for the groups adopting them, this alone cannot explain their emergence. Group selection arguments of this sort have been the targets of withering criticism (see, however, Sober and Wilson 1998).

32. Krasner (1999) raises similar doubts. He shows that the United States has supported the norm of national self-determination only in countries in which it has little interest, such as Rwanda and Tibet. In Grenada, Cuba, Panama, and Haiti, however, where the United States has strong interests, it has not hesitated to intervene in the internal affairs of sovereign states.

# References

Axelrod, Robert. 1984. *The Evolution of Cooperation*. New York: Basic Books.

Cassese, Antonio. 1995. *Self-determination of Peoples: A Legal Reappraisal*. New York: Cambridge University Press.

Chamberlain, Muriel E. 1998. *The Longman Companion to European Decolonisation in the Twentieth Century*. London: Longman.

Cobban, Alfred. [1945] 1969. *The Nation State and National Self-determination*. London: Collins.

Coleman, James S. 1990. *Foundations of Social Theory*. Cambridge: Harvard University Press.

Connor, Walker. 1985. *Mexican Americans in Contemporary Perspective*. Washington D.C.: Urban Institute Press.

Demsetz, Harold. 1967. "Toward a Theory of Property Rights." *American Economic Review* 57(2): 347–59.

Durkheim, Émile. [1893] 1933. *The Division of Labor in Society.* Glencoe, Ill.: Free Press.

Elias, Norbert. 1982. *The Evolution of Manners.* New York: Pantheon.

Ellickson, Robert. 1991. *Order Without Law: How Neighbors Settle Disputes.* Cambridge, Mass.: Harvard University Press.

Elster, Jon. 1990. "Norms of Revenge." *Ethics* 100(4): 862–85.

Emerson, Rupert. 1971. "Self Determinism." *American Journal of International Law* 65(3): 459–76.

Erikson, Kai T. 1976. *Everything in Its Path.* New York: Simon & Schuster.

Ermakoff, Ivan. 1997. "Prelates and Princes: Aristocratic Marriages, Canon Law Prohibitions, and Shifts in Norms and Patterns of Domination in the Central Middle Ages." *American Sociological Review* 62(3): 405–22.

Friedman, Debra. 1994. *Towards a Structure of Indifference: The Social Origins of Maternal Custody.* New York: Aldine de Gruyter.

Gurr, Ted Robert. 2000. "Ethnic Warfare on the Wane." *Foreign Affairs* 79(3): 52–64.

Hall, John A. 1993. "Nationalisms: Classified and Explained." *Daedalus* 122(3): 1–28.

Hannum, Hurst. 1996. *Autonomy, Sovereignty, and Self-Determination.* Philadelphia: University of Pennsylvania Press.

Hardin, Russell. 1995. *One for All: The Logic of Group Conflict.* Princeton: Princeton University Press.

Haufler, Virginia. 1993. "Crossing the Boundary Between Public and Private: International Regimes and Non-State Actors." In *Regime Theory and International Relations,* edited by Volker Rittberger. Oxford: Clarendon.

Heater, Derek. 1994. *National Self-Determination: Woodrow Wilson and His Legacy.* New York: St. Martin's.

Hechter, Michael. 1987. *Principles of Group Solidarity.* Berkeley: University of California Press.

———. [1975] 1999. *Internal Colonialism: The Celtic Fringe in British National Development.* New Brunswick, N.J.: Transaction.

———. 2000. *Containing Nationalism.* Oxford: Oxford University Press.

Holland, R. F. 1985. *European Decolonization, 1918–1981: An Introductory Survey.* London: Macmillan.

Jackson, Robert. 1996. "Is There a Classical International Theory?" In *International Theory: Positivism and Beyond,* edited by Steve Smith, Ken Booth, and Marysia Zalewski. Cambridge: Cambridge University Press.

Johnson, Harold S. 1967. *Self-Determination Within the Community of Nations.* Leiden, Netherlands: A. W. Sijthoff.

Knight, David B. 1984. "Geographical Perspectives on Self-Determination." In *Political Geography: Recent Advances and Future Directions,* edited by Peter Taylor and John House. London: Croom Holm.

Krasner, Stephen D. 1999. "Logics of Consequences and Appropriateness in the International System." In *Organizing Political Institutions,* edited by Morten Egeberg and Per Laegreid. Oslo: Scandinavian University Press.

Krasner, Stephen D., and David T. Froats. 1998. "Minority Rights and the Westphalian Model." In *The International Spread of Ethnic Conflict: Fear, Diffusion, and Escalation,* edited by David A. Lake, and Donald S. Rothchild. Princeton, N.J.: Princeton University Press.

Levi, Margaret. 1997. *Consent, Dissent, and Patriotism.* Cambridge: Cambridge University Press.

Mackie, Gerald. 1996. "Ending Footbinding and Infibulation: A Convention Account." *American Sociological Review* 61(6): 999–1017.

Mamdani, Mahmood. 2000. "Humanitarian Intervention: A Forum." *Nation,* May 8, 2000, 22–24.

March, James G., and Johan P. Olsen. 1998. "The Institutional Dynamics of International Political Orders." *International Organization* 52(4): 943–69.

Meyer, John W., John Boli, George M. Thomas, and Francisco M. Ramirez. 1997. "World Society and the Nation-State." *American Journal of Sociology* 103(1): 144–81.

Moynihan, Daniel P. 1993. *Pandaemonium.* Oxford: Oxford University Press.

Murphy, John F. 1980. "Self-Determination: A United States Perspective." In *Self-Determination: National, Regional, and Global Dimensions,* edited by Jonah Alexander and Robert Friedlander. Boulder, Colo.: Westview.

Ofuatey-Kodjoe, Wentworth. 1977. *The Principle of Self-Determination in International Law.* New York: Nellon Publishing.

Olson, Mancur. 1965. *The Logic of Collective Action.* Cambridge: Harvard University Press.

Oszlak, Oscar. 1981. "The Historical Formation of the State in Latin America: Some Theoretical and Methodological Guidelines for Its Study." *Latin American Research Review* 16(2): 3–32.

Quarantelli, Eugene L., and Russell R. Dynes. 1977. "Response to Social Crisis and Disaster." *Annual Review of Sociology* 3: 23–49.

Smelser, Neil J. 1959. *Social Change in the Industrial Revolution: An Application of Theory to the British Cotton Industry.* Chicago: University of Chicago Press.

Sober, Elliott, and David Sloan Wilson. 1998. *Unto Others: The Evolution and Psychology of Unselfish Behavior.* Cambridge: Harvard University Press.

Steinbeck, John. 1939. *The Grapes of Wrath.* New York: Viking.

Strang, David. 1990. "From Dependency to Sovereignty: An Event History Analysis of Decolonization, 1870–1987." *American Sociological Review* 55(6): 846–60.

———. 1991. "Global Patterns of Decolonization." *International Studies Quarterly* 35(4): 429–54.

———. 1992. "The Inner Incompatibility of Empire and Nation: Popular Sovereignty and Decolonization." *Sociological Perspectives* 35(2): 367–84.

Tilly, Charles. 1993. "National Self-Determination as a Problem for All of Us." *Daedalus* 122(3): 122–36.

United Nations (UN). 1945. *The Charter of the United Nations: With Addresses Selected from the Proceedings of the United Nations Conference, San Francisco (April-June 1945).* Scranton, Pa.: Haddon Craftsmen.

———. General Assembly. 1970. Twenty-fifth Session. *Declaration on Principles of International Law Concerning Friendly Relations and Co-operation Among States in Accordance with the Charter of the United Nations.* General Assembly Resolution 2625. Geneva, October 24.

de Waal, Alex. 1999. *Famine Crimes: Politics and the Disaster Relief Industry in Africa.* Oxford: Currey.

Wehmeyer, M. L. 1992. "Self-determination and the Education of Students with Mental Retardation." *Education and Training in Mental Retardation* 27: 302–14.

Wildavsky, Aaron. 1993. "On the Social Construction of Distinctions: Risk, Rape, Public Goods, and Altruism." In *The Origin of Values,* edited by Michael Hechter, Lynn Nadel, and Richard E. Michod. New York: Aldine de Gruyter.

Woodward, Susan L. 1995. *Balkan Tragedy: Chaos and Dissolution After the Cold War.* Washington, D.C.: Brookings.

# 8

# SOCIAL NETWORKS AND THE EMERGENCE OF PROTEST NORMS

*Karl-Dieter Opp*

MANY citizens feel an obligation to participate in politics. For example, empirical studies have shown that a duty to participate in protests is accepted not only by activists in protest groups but by a great number of ordinary citizens, as well. This chapter explores the emergence of protest norms. Because there is no standard theory in the social sciences that can explain the rise of protest norms, it is first necessary to specify the relevant general propositions. Although there is much theoretical speculation on the importance of social networks for the emergence of norms, the precise role of social networks is unclear. The assumption seems to be that the effects of networks depend on the kinds of incentives that are provided in those networks. What exactly are those incentives, and how are they related to social networks? This chapter offers some propositions that explain the role of social networks for the emergence of protest norms.

A satisfactory explanation of norms should also address the mechanism—that is, the process—that leads to the emergence of a norm. At the present time, little in the way of a theory of these mechanisms exists. This chapter explores one particular mechanism that may occur when people organize to provide a public good. The emergence of protest norms is a low-cost by-product when people organize for collective action.

The empirical evidence for the propositions to be tested comes from a panel study conducted in East Germany in 1993 and 1996. This study enables us to distinguish several dimensions of norms that have not been explained in previous research and to provide a more rigorous test of the causal structure of the propositions than a cross-sectional study allows.

The propositions that follow draw on a broad or "thick" version of rational choice theory, one that admits a wide range of preferences and constraints.[1] On this view, people derive utility from conforming to norms and from gaining the approval of reference persons. This approach is consistent with that taken in part one of this volume. However, the present chapter differs from other contributions to this volume in three significant respects: First, it explicitly discusses the conditionality of norms. Because norms hold under certain conditions, and not in others, accounting for the emergence of norms is equivalent to explaining their conditionality. Second, it presents a two-step explanation of norms, stipulating first the general conditions that increase the likelihood that norms will emerge and then explaining what mechanisms are responsible for their emergence. Third, it provides survey data to test predictions derived from the general propositions.

## Theory

Norms are statements about what is allowed, what ought or ought not to be done.[2] Most scholars give similar definitions of norms but include reference to other aspects, such as sanctions (Rossi and Berk 1985, 333). I prefer to address these other aspects as separate factors whose empirical interrelationships may be explored.

I discern several other aspects of norms (Jasso and Opp 1997). One aspect of norms is their polarity, which can have two values. A norm is bipolar if it holds that a behavior is to be performed under certain conditions and not under others. Norms that are not bipolar may be either prescriptive (meaning that a behavior ought to be performed under all conditions) or proscriptive (meaning that a behavior ought not to be performed under any conditions). Norms may be further classified according to their conditionality. A given norm is conditional if it holds under certain conditions; if it holds or does not hold under all circumstances, it is unconditional. These last two dimensions are not identical: a bipolar norm is always conditional, but a conditional norm need not be bipolar.

To illustrate, the norm stating that "promises must be kept" is prescriptive, unconditional, and not bipolar. Imagine a medical doctor who has promised to attend a party and allows a patient to die so as to keep this promise. The doctor evidently feels that in this particular situation he must break his promise, but in other situations, he agrees, promises must be kept. Hence, this norm is bipolar and conditional. Now assume that there are some situations in which one is allowed to break promises, but that there is no situation in which promises must be broken. Such a norm would be conditional, because the strength of the obligation is different in different situations, but not bipolar. For example, a doctor promises to inform his patient if he finds that she has cancer. If a medical test indicates that this is so, and if the doctor thinks that keeping the promise would prompt the patient to commit suicide, he is justified in breaking the promise. So far the norm is conditional but not bipolar. However, if the doctor were obliged not to tell the patient the truth, the norm would be bipolar and conditional. Unconditional norms tend to be general ethical principles, such as the Kantian categorical imperative to "act as if your action were to become a general law" (see Raphael 1994, 56).

The polarity and conditionality of norms deserve to be explained if we want to capture the full complexity of normative phenomena in the real world. The data that will be analyzed show that individuals and groups differ with regard to those aspects, and it is therefore important to explain this. Propositions about the emergence of norms in the literature usually focus on prescription or proscription. In the first part of the chapter, I will follow this practice and focus on explaining the prescriptiveness (or pro-scriptiveness) of norms. I will then apply the propositions to explain the polarity and conditionality of norms.

## The Instrumentality of Norms

I begin with a widely shared proposition in the social sciences that I call the instrumentality proposition. It states that norms "are purposively gen-erated" (Coleman 1990, 242) to achieve the goals of a collectivity of actors, more precisely:

> Instrumentality Proposition: If members of a group have a goal and if they believe that a norm is instrumental for the attainment of their goal, it is likely that the norm emerges.

Many hypotheses advanced in the literature are variants of this proposi-tion. A widely shared version holds that the emergence of norms is likely if there are externalities—actions of individual or collective actors that im-pose costs (negative externalities) or benefits (positive externalities) on others.[3] People affected by negative externalities have an interest in estab-lishing norms that eliminate or reduce the costs, and people who produce positive externalities have an interest in establishing a norm by which they be compensated for providing them. Michael Hechter (1987, 41) argues that "groups exist in order to supply their members with some desired joint good. This good can be attained only if members comply with rules that are designed to assure its production." Thus, norms help groups to achieve their goals: norms are (second-order) public goods that are instrumental in providing (first-order) public goods (see, for example, Heckathorn 1989, 1990; Coleman 1990). It is not possible to discuss other possible variants in this chapter—the reader is referred to the chapter 13 of this volume. I men-tion here only a few of the implications of this version, in order to avoid misunderstandings.

1. The instrumentality of norms is only one condition that is relevant for the emergence of norms. Other conditions are addressed later in the chapter.

2.  The instrumentality proposition is not functionalist because it does not argue that norms emerge if they have positive consequences for the group. The proposition refers to individual goals and beliefs: it implies that situations or events that jeopardize the realization of group goals provide incentives to set up rules that are designed to make the group better off.

3.  It is consistent with the instrumentality proposition that a norm has disadvantages for some members of a group. For example, the academic "publish-or-perish" system may have been introduced by general consent, but many professors would be happy to be freed of the pressure the norm entails.

4.  The proposition does not imply that norms are efficient or welfare enhancing. The instrumentality proposition is subjectivist positing that groups create those norms that group members believe are effective. If information is imperfect, these beliefs may be at odds with reality. Although the subjectivist version of the proposition is plausible, it is also likely that groups (especially small ones) have largely valid beliefs that enable them to handle their everyday affairs efficiently.

5.  Many norms emerge not by human design but through the aggregate results of human action with no thought or no intention of bringing about a norm. Nonsmokers, for example, may punish smokers not to create an antismoking norm but only because they have been exposed to secondhand smoke. Collective punishments may, nonetheless, contribute to the emergence of an antismoking norm. The instrumentality proposition states that a norm is likely to emerge if a group goal will be furthered by its existence. This version of the proposition thus does not imply anything about the process of norm emergence.

The previously noted version of the instrumentality proposition assumes instrumental rationality: a group of individuals perceives that a particular norm will generate outcomes that work toward achievement of a group goal. Raymond Boudon (1997, 20) argues that "many moral feelings are not the product of instrumental rationality." For example, the act of stealing cannot be shown to have negative consequences. According to Boudon, stealing is "bad" because it contradicts basic moral principles. However, the instrumentality proposition does not rule out the possibility that the goal of a group may be to preserve general social principles (or values).[4]

## The Influence and Selective Incentives Proposition

The likelihood that a norm will emerge increases when members of a group think they can influence the provision of that norm is called here the influence proposition:[5]

> The Influence Proposition: The more strongly the members of a group of ac-
> tors believe they can influence the provision of norms by their contribution,
> the more likely they are to contribute, and the more likely it is that the norm
> will originate.

Individuals can contribute to the establishment of a norm in several ways. Often they believe that enunciating normative statements or behaving according to a norm that they would like to establish increases the likelihood that a norm will emerge because others may imitate the behavior or find it rewarding. Another contribution is direct punishment (or reward) of those who do not or who do perform the desired behavior. Individuals will choose the kind of contribution that they perceive as most effective—given legal or other constraints.

The theory of collective action (Olson 1965) holds that public goods are more likely to be provided in the presence of selective incentives. Because norms are second-order public goods, the existence of selective incentives makes their emergence more likely. Transaction costs—"costs incurred by individuals in defining, policing, negotiating, and enforcing resource rights and contractual agreements" (Furubotn and Pejovich 1974, 2)—are among the major negative selective incentives that jeopardize the emergence of norms (Taylor and Singleton 1993). Actors consider not only the costs associated with the establishment of a norm but also the costs of its maintenance in the future.

Positive selective incentives for establishing norms constitute social rewards by the members of a group when other members perform the desired behavior or when others reward those who reward conformity. One such reward is enhanced reputation within the group, which may be a consequence of heroic sanctioning (that is, sanctioning that is very costly and highly effective) (Coleman 1990, 278–82). Thus:

> The Selective Incentives Proposition: If positive selective incentives (benefits)
> for contributing to the establishment of a norm are high and negative selec-
> tive incentives (costs) are low, individuals are likely to contribute to the emer-
> gence of the norm.

This proposition raises several questions. One is what are the selective incentives in a group? They depend on the individual utility functions and may thus differ among groups. A rigorous test has to determine empirically what the selective incentives in the group are. Another question is when are sufficient selective incentives for the emergence of a norm provided? It seems that one condition is that there are strong ties among individuals. This proposition is discussed in more detail later in the chapter. It is beyond the scope of this chapter to explain in detail the provision of selective incentives. Instead, the reader may be referred to the discussion in the chapters by Ellickson and Voss in this volume.

The extent to which group members' contributions to norm establishment are costly or beneficial determines the kind of mechanism that is
chosen. For example, if individuals expect that normative statements, along
with approval or other positive direct informal rewards of the desired behavior, will lead to the establishment of a norm, contracting and collective
action will not occur, because such actions would be unnecessarily costly.
The mechanism in this case would be spontaneous norm emergence.

## The Polarity and Conditionality of Norms

The previous propositions explain the contributions actors make toward
establishing a norm. I assume that contributing to a norm implies acceptance of the norm. Furthermore, the previous propositions address prescriptive norms. Thus, if there are strong incentives (instrumentality, influence, selective incentives) for a given norm, it is likely that people will
contribute to its emergence and that the respective norm will be accepted.
How can polarity and conditionality be explained? If a norm is instrumental under condition C and not under other conditions, a norm will emerge
that is accepted under condition C and not under other conditions. In other
words, the norm will be bipolar. For example, there may be situations in
which breaking a promise is beneficial for a group and others in which
breaking a promise is very costly—such as the example of the medical
doctor who lets a patient die because he keeps his promise to go to a party.
In a case such as this, a norm will hold in one situation and not in the
other. A norm is likely to be unconditional if it is instrumental in all situations.[6]

It might be in the interest of all members of a group to establish a
norm that is largely unconditional and not bipolar, one in which a particular behavior is clearly prescribed (or proscribed) and there are no circumstances under which "exceptions" can be made. Nevertheless, members
might individually prefer norms that impose few constraints on them. The
requirement to conform to a norm in most or all situations is certainly often
a cost to an individual, and most members would probably prefer to be
exempt from the requirement to conform. This situation resembles a prisoner's dilemma (see table 8.1). It may be in the best interest of all members
of a group collectively that a given norm is neither bipolar nor conditional;
but the interest of a single member will be best served if the other members
accept the unconditional and nonbipolar norm and he or she accepts the
bipolar and conditional norm.

## Mechanisms of Norm Emergence

When the conditions conducive to emergence of a particular norm—instrumentality, influence, and selective incentives—are sufficiently present, it is
likely that certain social processes are set into motion that will lead to the

TABLE 8.1    *Acceptance of Conditional and Nonbipolar Norms as a*
             *Prisoner's Dilemma Situation*

| Group member A accepts a norm that is . . . | Other group members accept a norm that is . . . | |
| --- | --- | --- |
| | unconditional and not bipolar | conditional and bipolar |
| unconditional and not bipolar | 3,3 | 1,4 |
| conditional and bipolar | 4,1 | 2,2 |

*Source:* Author's compilation.

emergence of the norm. Thus, I suggest an explanation of norms in two steps. First, one determines the extent to which conditions exist so that the emergence of norms becomes likely. Second, the process of norm emergence is explained. Norms emerge through three basic processes: norm setting by collective actors (such as lawmaking), contractual norm setting (negotiation), and spontaneous norm emergence.[7] The new institutional economics and public choice theory in particular have provided extensive theory and research on these processes.

## Social Networks and the Emergence of Norms

I define "groups" as a collectivity in which there is leadership or role differentiation; in contrast, a "personal" network is given if the actors interact relatively frequently, that is, there is no leadership or role differentiation among the members. A tennis club is a group, whereas friends or colleagues from the workplace form a personal network. The term social networks—or simply networks—encompasses groups as well as personal networks. It is widely accepted that the emergence of norms is particularly likely in social networks in which members are closely connected. Michael Taylor (1996) argues, for example, that "a community provides the conditions in which normative motivation . . . [is] mobilized" (232).[8] What Taylor calls "community" is characterized by Robert Ellickson (1991, 177) as a "close-knit" group.[9] James Coleman (1990, chapter 11) also suggests that social networks facilitate the emergence of norms.[10]

This proposition raises several questions. What is meant by close relationships? Are repeated interactions sufficient to establish a close relationship, or is sympathy between the members important? I submit that both factors have effects on the emergence of norms. Why are groups and personal networks fertile grounds for the emergence of norms? The previous propositions do not include networks as relevant variables for the emergence of norms. Does this imply that networks are irrelevant for the emergence of norms? If the previous propositions are correct, networks are conducive to the emergence of norms if they provide positive incentives to a particularly high extent.

The existence of networks is not a separate variable affecting norm emergence. Whether networks further or impede the emergence of norms depends on the extent to which the conditions of instrumentality, influence, and selective incentive are present. Social networks may also be important in the actors' choice of mechanism. For example, in a close-knit group with homogeneous goals and beliefs, it is likely that many norms emerge spontaneously. Actors will choose the cheapest and—from their point of view—most effective actions, such as enunciating normative statements, and thus need not resort to costly actions such as bargaining or establishing a formal sanctioning staff.[11]

## Explaining Protest Norms: An Application of the Propositions

The foregoing propositions can be applied to a specific kind of norm: the felt obligation to protest. Predictions will be derived for the aspects of norms mentioned above that will be tested in a later section. The focus of these predictions is the effect of membership in groups and personal networks on norm emergence.

### Kinds of Groups and the Instrumentality of Protest Norms

The first prediction concerns the acceptance of prescriptive norms in different kinds of groups. If norms are instrumental—that is, if they further the attainment of group goals—a felt obligation to protest will be strong in alternative groups such as peace groups or environmental groups. These groups are defined by two characteristics: their major goal is to effect social change, and their major strategy is protest action—unconventional political action such as staging or participating in demonstrations. It would serve the interests of such a group if members were to accept a norm that everybody should participate in protest action; consequently, members of these groups are expected to accept a norm directing them to protest—in contrast with nonmembers.[12]

Protest norms are also instrumental for unions, although to a lesser extent than for alternative groups. In contrast with protest groups, unions' major strategy is to bargain with employers and, as a last resort, to strike. Protests are often a part of strikes or a supplementary strategy, and so the acceptance of protest norms is in the best interest of these groups, also. This holds for political parties as well. Protests contribute to the realization of party programs, and they are often organized by political parties.[13] Protest is not a basic strategy for political parties, however, as it is for alternative groups. There may be other interest groups for whom protest is equally instrumental, but this does not hold for the German context and for the group memberships there that have been ascertained in the study that is used to test the following predictions. If protest norms are instrumental for members of protest groups, unions, and political parties, members of these groups are likely to accept prescriptive protest norms to a high extent. This means that they subscribe to a norm of protest as a political duty.

I argued earlier that it is in the interest of the single group members to accept conditional and bipolar norms so that they can defect with a good conscience. Is this plausible?[14] The existence of an unconditional norm in a group would require extensive sanctioning and, in the extreme, exclusion of members. That would be a high cost to all other members. It would thus be instrumental to tolerate excuses and justifications for nonconformity—that is, for not performing the desired behavior—in certain situations. The prediction thus is that there will be high conditionality for instrumental norms. However, high bipolarity—which means that there is no obligation not to follow the rule in certain situations (as in the example of the medical doctor)—is implausible. Bipolarity is so clearly against the interest of a group for which a norm is instrumental that enunciation of such a norm or acting according to such a norm would be punished by other members and would probably cause strong cognitive dissonance for the single member. There will thus be low bipolarity for a norm that is instrumental in a group. Therefore,

> Prediction 1: Members of groups in which protest norms are particularly instrumental (protest groups and, to a lesser extent, unions and political parties) have prescriptive protest norms, show low bipolarity, and show high conditionality. Membership in other groups has no effect, or a lower effect, on these norm dimensions.

It could be argued that protest norms are learned in an early phase of the socialization process. They are learned together with other norms referring to civic duty, including norms directing citizens to participate in elections, to pay taxes, and to participate in peaceful nonconventional action if the government fails to act in the interest of the citizens. These norms may then be stable and are not influenced by group processes. In contrast to prediction 1, therefore, membership in groups should, in general, not affect the acceptance of such norms.

## The Mechanism of Norm Emergence

I have argued that obligations to protest will emerge if protest norms are instrumental, if group members feel they have sufficient influence to provide the norm, and if there are strong positive or weak negative selective incentives. In addressing the mechanism that leads to the emergence of protest norms, I make the following assumption: If individuals think that their efforts can make a difference in regard to the first-order public good, they also think that their efforts can bring about a norm (that is, a second-order public good).

The data of the East German panel study used to test the predictions, and other research as well, show that perceived influence to bring about a first-order public good by participating in protest action is in general not zero and is variant.[15] Furthermore, protest groups are often small, and members of parties or unions are organized in relatively small subgroups. This enhances the feeling that participation will have an impact.

The presumption is that if group members think their actions make a difference in the provision of the first-order public good, then they will also feel that they are able to contribute to the provision of the second-order public good. Thus, members of a protest group who are convinced that the planned protest actions are apt to provide the first-order public good will reason that they also have a chance to contribute to establishing a norm.

If individuals feel that they can bring about a norm, they will act only if the costs of doing so are not too high. The least costly way to bring about protest norms in a group is to enunciate statements that certain actions should or must be performed, that is that people have a duty to participate. A further low-cost strategy, also common in everyday life, is to reward participants and punish nonparticipants and also to reward those who reward participants and punish those who do not punish nonparticipants. It is likely that this mechanism is successful because the norm to protest is a conjoint norm. When a norm is conjoint, "each actor is simultaneously beneficiary and target of the norm" (Coleman 1990, 247). Under conjoint norms, those who punish or reward a behavior do not face costs as a result of the negative reactions of those who are punished or rewarded. The costs of monitoring are also low because participation is observable. Because they serve the group interest, enunciating normative statements and sanctioning offenders also provide status in the group. Another incentive to invest in the establishment of norms is the existence of sanctioning norms demanding that behavior that is detrimental to the goals of a group is bad and must be sanctioned. Thus, *the norm to protest will emerge spontaneously as a by-product of organizing collective action to provide some (first-order) public good.*

Are there other mechanisms that could have emerged? One such mechanism might be that a committee or the board of a group sets the norm. These group representatives could pass rules stating under what conditions participating is a duty and what happens if members defect. Setting up a committee or board and passing a statute requires negotiations, however, and thus is more costly, and certainly not more successful, than the process of decentralized norm emergence. The same can be said for the mechanism by which members make contracts with one another about norms of participating. The mechanism of spontaneous norm emergence is the least costly and most effective process for norms to become established in groups in which a norm to protest is instrumental. If this reasoning is correct, positive selective incentives to contribute to the establishment of norms can be expected to a large extent in the three kinds of groups. Thus,

> Prediction 2: If protest norms are highly instrumental for a group, members are faced with relatively strong positive external selective incentives for accepting protest norms.

These incentives were measured by ascertaining the extent to which members of a group feel encouraged by other members to participate in protests. A member who reports high protest encouragement indicates that social rewards for participating in protests have been expected and received. It is assumed that if protest is rewarded in a group, then accepting an obligation to protest is rewarded, as well. That is to say, if the members of a group indicate that they feel highly encouraged by other members to protest, it is assumed that the former also receive rewards for accepting a duty to protest. Therefore, encouragement is used as an indicator for positive selective incentives for accepting protest norms.

## Group Integration as a Selective Incentive

Not only repeated interaction (membership in a group) but also closeness of the members promotes the emergence of norms. This may be what authors mean when they refer to "community" or "close-knit groups" as important for the emergence of norms. Relationships of this kind provide internal selective incentives to contribute to the emergence of norms: people who feel close to others may be particularly inclined to do what is in the interest of those others. Thus,

> Prediction 3: If members of a group are exposed to external selective incentives for accepting protest norms (that is, if members of a group feel highly encouraged to protest) and also face internal selective incentives (that is, feel close to a group or, equivalently, are integrated in a group), the members' norms will be strongly prescriptive, show low bipolarity, and show high conditionality.

This prediction does not rule out the possibility that protest norms may already exist if a group originates. The prediction posits merely that the extent to which norms are accepted increases if external or internal selective incentives are provided.

We expect that conditionality will be particularly high and polarity low for highly cohesive groups (that is, if members feel close to a group). In this situation, sanctioning of nonconformity, including exclusion of members, is a particularly high emotional cost to pay so that conditionality may be tolerated. Because nonconformity is costly in a highly cohesive group and will thus happen rarely, it is not too risky to allow for conditionality to some extent. Bipolarity, on the other hand, would incur high costs to the members.

Although prediction 3 is plausible, it may hold true only under certain conditions. Some norms may be so easy to establish that close relationships between members of a network are not necessary. For example, in the process of organizing collective action, the idea that participation is a duty can be easily communicated, and a norm may emerge even if the members have no close ties. This situation may hold for the groups reported on in this chapter.

## Personal Networks

The instrumentality proposition is formulated for groups, but it can also be applied to personal networks. For example, friends may develop norms that are instrumental for shared goals as well. To illustrate, when friends are invited for dinner the group members expect a smooth and interesting conversation and a good meal. These are their joint goals. The instrumentality proposition predicts for such networks that in ongoing interactions norms will develop about the topics to be addressed in conversation (such as current political issues) or about the kind of food that is to be served.

In this research, networks of friends or work colleagues are addressed who are critical of the political situation or are involved in protest action and who share the goal that some political change should be effected. The predictions about the emergence of norms in these networks are similar to those for groups in which protest norms are instrumental. Thus:

> Prediction 4: The norms accepted by members of critical personal networks will be strongly prescriptive, demonstrate low bipolarity, and demonstrate high conditionality.

The following prediction is similar to prediction 3.

> Prediction 5: If members of critical personal networks are exposed to external selective incentives for accepting protest norms and face internal selective incentives, their norms will also be strongly prescriptive, show low bipolarity, and show high conditionality.

## Research Design and Measurement

The prescriptiveness, polarity, and conditionality of norms were measured by Peter H. Rossi's factorial survey method.[16] In brief, respondents are presented with hypothetical protest situations consisting of the factors identified as potential norm-relevant conditions. The respondents are asked to judge to what extent the protagonist in each situation has an obligation to participate in protest activities. This method allows us to measure the level of acceptance, the polarity, and the conditionality of the norm.

## The Vignettes

The design of a factorial survey (also called "vignette analysis") has three main ingredients: a population of hypothetical situations (the vignettes), a rating task, and a sample of respondents. The construction of the vignettes first requires a decision about what dimensions are to be selected. A second decision is what values these dimensions should have. Furthermore, the population of the vignettes has to be constructed and the vignettes have to be distributed among the respondents.

*Vignette Characteristics*   The literature on collective action and the results of a survey I carried out in 1990 (Opp 1994; Opp and Gern 1993; Opp, Voss, and Gern 1995) served as guidelines in the selection of vignette characteristics. This earlier survey reflected the situation in East Germany under Communist rule in 1989. In exploratory conversations, respondents indicated that they felt an obligation to protest only under specific conditions that were in existence in the fall of 1989 and not before.

Table 8.2 lists these conditions under which an obligation to protest might hold. High discontent appeared to be a universal and necessary condition for protest to be perceived as a duty. Expected personal risk from participating in protests against the regime seemed to be another factor affecting the felt obligation to protest. A citizen of the German Democratic Republic (GDR) who thought that few others would protest, and consequently that she or he would bear much of the cost of protesting, was considerably less likely to regard protest participation as obligatory. In other words, the higher the expected number of participants in a protest, the more the citizens felt an obligation to participate. Perceived personal influence also seemed to be an important dimension, as was the kind of protest planned. In Western societies participation in illegal protest action seems to be regarded as immoral (Wolfsfeld et al. 1994). This holds for violent forms of protest (for example, seizing construction sites) as a subset of illegal protest actions. The Leipzig study indicates that under Communist rule, violent protest was also regarded as morally questionable. The final dimension included in the vignette is the gender of the prospective protest participant as a control variable.

*Values of Vignette Characteristics*   Having selected the conditions that are presumed to be relevant for the perceived obligation to protest, the next step was to choose the values for each vignette characteristic. In order to ease statistical analyses, the categories of the qualitative dimensions were designed so that their number was small yet captured potentially normatively relevant situations.

Regarding discontent, a distinction was made between economic discontent ("30 percent increase in rents") and political discontent ("persons can be arrested and held for two weeks for unstated cause") because the

TABLE 8.2    *Vignette Control Variables*

| Characteristic | Value | Meaning |
|---|---|---|
| Discontent | | |
| economic | 1 | There will be an increase in rents of about 30 percent |
| political | 2 | There is a new law stating that persons can be arrested and held for two weeks for unstated cause |
| Kind of protest | | |
| legal | 1 | To protest against this, protagonist could participate in a legal demonstration in the city (legal) |
| illegal | 2 | To protest against this, protagonist could participate in a traffic blockade in the city (illegal) |
| Perception of personal influence | | |
| low | 1 | Protagonist believes that his or her protest would make a difference |
| high | 2 | Protagonist believes that his or her protest would hardly make a difference |
| | 3 | This dimension is not mentioned in a vignette |
| Anticipated risk | | |
| police action | 1 | A violent police action is expected, in which many participants might be injured |
| no problem | 2 | No problems are expected |
| — | 3 | This dimension is not mentioned in a vignette |
| Expected number of participants | | |
| — | 1 | About 100,000 participants are expected |
| — | 2 | About 10,000 participants are expected |
| — | 3 | About 1,000 participants are expected |
| — | 4 | About 100 participants are expected |
| — | 5 | About 20 participants are expected |
| — | 6 | It is unknown how many people will participate |
| — | 7 | This dimension is not mentioned in a vignette |
| Gender of protagonist | | |
| male | 1 | Mr. Müller (male) |
| female | 2 | Mrs. Meier (female) |

*Source:* Author's compilation.

two kinds of discontent had different effects on participation in the GDR protests in 1989 (Opp, Voss, and Gern 1995). Both categories described situations of relatively high discontent.

The kind of protest included examples of a legal form of protest (demonstration) and an illegal form of protest (traffic blockade). "Demonstration" and "traffic blockade" were chosen because among legal and illegal actions, they are relatively frequent forms of political protests.

The perception of personal influence was also dichotomized (protest of the respondent would "make a difference" or would "hardly make a difference"). In this and the two following dimensions the category "not mentioned in the vignette" is included. The reason for omitting these dimensions from the vignette is to examine whether they enter in to a respondent's consideration of his or her duty to protest.[17] Among the expected personal risks of protesting in Western societies, the major one is becoming involved in violence generated by the police or by other participants. The normal case, however, is political action without any violence and, thus, without any personal risk arising during the protest. Therefore, two categories ("violent police action with many participants injured" and "no problems") seem adequate.

The categories of the quantitative dimension, "expected number of participants," refer to relatively large (100,000), medium-size (10,000), and relatively small numbers of participants (1,000, 100, or 20). Numbers with large differences in size were chosen in order to be able to detect the effects of size, if any.[18]

*The Population of Vignettes*   Having selected the vignette dimensions and their values, the population of all possible vignettes, that is, all possible combinations of the values of the dimensions, was constructed next. The number of possible vignettes (Cartesian product) is $2 \times 2 \times 3 \times 3 \times 7 \times 2 = 504$. To illustrate, one of the vignettes states: "There is a new law stating that *persons can be arrested and held for two weeks without being given any reasons for this*. To protest against this, *Mrs. Meier* could participate in a *traffic blockade* in the city. This is illegal. Mrs. Meier believes that her protest *would hardly make a difference*. A *violent police action* is expected where many participants might be injured. About *100 participants* are expected."

Not all the possible vignettes were meaningful. One combination of values of "kind of protest" and "expected number of participants" was excluded: vignettes saying that there is a traffic blockade and that 100,000 participants are expected were not presented, because no illegal action in Western countries involves such a large number of participants. Excluding this combination resulted in the elimination of 36 vignettes, leaving an effective modified population of 468 meaningful vignettes.

*Drawing Vignette Samples*    The last two decisions to be made were: how many vignettes to present to each respondent, and how many ratings to obtain for each distinctly different vignette. With respect to the first decision, each respondent was asked to rate ten vignettes, a small number relative to the usual number of vignettes rated by each respondent (for example, sixty in Jasso and Rossi 1977 and forty in Jasso 1988).[19] With respect to the second, in order to maximize the richness of the study, a large set of the vignettes are presented to respondents. In the present case, forty-seven samples from the vignette population were drawn, and replicates of each of the samples to randomly selected subsets of respondents were presented.

## The Rating Task

The vignette module was presented to each respondent following an oral interview with a standardized questionnaire. It was first explained that the task is to judge to what extent a person—specifically, the protagonist in the vignette—might feel obligated to protest (or not to protest) in certain situations or, alternatively, feel no obligation either way. One of the vignettes was then presented as an example. The respondent was asked to rate the sample vignette on a scale consisting of 11 possible values, ranging from −5 to +5, including the value 0. Positive numbers represent an obligation to protest, negative numbers represent an obligation not to protest, and zero represents the absence of any obligation at all. The absolute value of the number indicates the strength of the judged obligation. The meaning of the extreme points and of the value 0 are illustrated in a figure presented to the respondent (figure 8.1) and, in the questionnaire, by detailed comments on the figure. As shown, a rating of −5 corresponds to the judgment that the vignette's protagonist "should by no means participate" in the protest, and a rating of +5 corresponds to the judgment that the protagonist "should by all means participate" in the protest. The respondent was then asked to rate the ten vignettes in the randomly drawn vignette sample, using the 11-point scale.

## The Respondent Sample

The hypotheses are tested with a two-wave panel study of 438 respondents in which the same respondents were interviewed with a structured questionnaire in 1993 and once again in 1995 and 1996—I refer to the latter sample as the 1996 wave. The panel is used to provide a more severe test of the causal order of the variables than is possible with a cross-sectional design. As is shown in detail later, I examine the effects of the independent variables, measured in 1993, on the dependent variables, measured in 1996. The data was collected by a professional survey institute.

Table 8.3 gives an overview of the samples. The data consists of three

FIGURE 8.1    *The Rating Scale Presented with Each Vignette*

| Protagonist should by no means participate | | | | | No obligation | | | Protagonist should by all means participate | | |
|---|---|---|---|---|---|---|---|---|---|---|
| −5 | −4 | −3 | −2 | −1 | 0 | +1 | +2 | +3 | +4 | +5 |

...should not participate        ...should participate

*Source:* Author's compilation.

subsamples. A representative sample of the population of Leipzig that was first administered in 1990 ($N = 1,300$) referring to the situation in 1989, that is, before the collapse of the East German Communist regime.[20] In 1993, 513 of these original respondents were available to be interviewed again. I refer to this (1993) sample as the wave 1 sample. In wave 2, a total of 323 of these respondents were available to be interviewed again in 1996. I use this sample of 323 original (1989) respondents who were reinterviewed in 1993 and again in 1996. I further analyze a nonrepresentative sample of 209 Leipzig citizens who had been members of, or at least close to, opposition groups under communist rule (for details, see Opp et al. 1995). This sample—called the opposition sample—was first administered in 1990 ($N = 209$); a total of 34 respondents were reinterviewed in 1993 and again in 1996. The third sample used is an additional representative study of Leipzig, with 212 respondents who were first interviewed in 1993; of those 212 respondents, 81 were interviewed again in 1996.

To dispose of a larger data set of cases, the samples from 1993 and 1996 were combined, resulting in 438 cases (323 of the first, 81 of the second representative sample, and 34 of the opposition sample). A large number of cases is particularly important for the analysis of the effects of group memberships.

The high rate of attrition of respondents is not uncommon in panel studies conducted in East Germany, which has experienced substantial out-migration to West Germany since the fall of Communism. For the test of the propositions, two questions are of importance. To what extent are the respondents who participated in the last wave of the panel different from the respondents who did not participate in wave 2? Whatever the bias in the samples is, is the pooled data set appropriate for a test of the propositions?

To answer the first question I first analyzed the data of the first representative study. I computed bivariate Pearson coefficients between participation in 1996 (yes: $N = 323$; no: $N = 977$; total 1,300) and various demographic variables. The correlations were rather low: participants in 1996 were more educated ($r = .10$), more likely to be married or living with a partner ($r = .12$), and had a higher household income ($r = .11$). Each of

TABLE 8.3    *Samples of the Leipzig Panel Study*

| Data Not Used | Data Used | |
|---|---|---|
| First data collection: November and December 1990 | Wave 1: June to August 1993 | Wave 2: November 1995 to January 1996 |
| Representative sample: N = 1,300 | ← Same population: N = 513 | ← Same population: N = 323 |
| Opposition sample: N = 209 | ← Same population: N = 58 | ← Same population: N = 34 |
| | Representative sample: N = 212 | ← Same population: N = 81 |
| | Pooled sample for wave 1 and wave 2: N = 438 | |

*Source:* Author's compilation.

these coefficients is significant at the .01 level. For the second representative sample, most of the coefficients are lower, and no coefficient is higher. The differences for participants and nonparticipants in the opposition sample are somewhat larger: the highest coefficient is .22 (for years of schooling and being married or living with a partner). Because of these small differences between participants and nonparticipants in the panels, the bias owing to attrition is low and it does not invalidate the data. Nonetheless, it might be argued that the statistical analysis does not establish that the data are representative. Even if this is granted, for the purpose of testing the theoretical propositions representative data are not required because the analysis is not intended to make any descriptive statements about a population such as the inhabitants of Leipzig in 1993 or 1996. The purpose is to test general propositions. If the propositions are correct, they should be confirmed by the data.

## Measuring Prescriptiveness, Bipolarity, and Conditionality of Protest Norms

As I have already noted, each respondent was asked to rate ten vignettes, and each vignette could receive a rating from −5 to +5. I will now show how the norm dimensions discussed previously can be operationalized from those patterns of ratings. An illustration of these measures with the data of three respondents is given in the appendix.

The prescriptiveness of a norm is measured as the percentage or proportion of the ten ratings of a given respondent that exceed 0. For example, a respondent who gives a positive rating (that is, greater than 0) to six of the ten vignettes receives a value of .60. The highest possible value, 100, is given if a respondent's normative judgment is greater than 0 for each of the ten vignettes, representing the respondent's acceptance of an obligation to protest for each of the ten vignettes. The lowest value, 0, means that no vignette has been judged greater than 0. Thus, high values indicate a high percentage of judgments greater than 0 and, thus, a strong perceived obligation to protest.[21]

Bipolarity has code 1 for a respondent (that is, the norm is bipolar) if there are positive as well as negative ratings. Otherwise, code 0 is assigned (indicating that the norm is not bipolar).

If all judgments are equal and not 0, the norm is unconditional, and code 0 is assigned. This means that a respondent assigns the same (positive or negative) obligation to protest to all vignettes. If at least one rating is different from 0 and not equal to the other ratings, the norm is conditional, and code 1 is assigned.

Of the 438 respondents in the first wave (the 1993 Leipzig sample), 418 (95 percent of the original 438 respondents) rated all ten vignettes presented to them, whereas in the second wave, in 1996, 429 (98 percent) did so. The analyses are based on those respondents who rated all ten vignettes. The value of $N$ is 409 if both waves are analyzed simultaneously.

## Measuring Involvement in Groups and Personal Networks

In order to measure membership in groups, the respondents were asked to indicate whether they are members ("no," with code 0, and "yes," with code 1) in the following groups or organizations: alternative groups (peace groups, environmental groups, or other alternative political groups), political parties, unions, professional interest groups (such as occupational organizations), charity organizations, hobby groups (including choirs and other social clubs), and sports groups. Respondents who were members of one of these groups were asked to what extent (legal) political actions were encouraged or discouraged in the group or whether group members were indifferent to their participation. Because there was almost no discouragement, I constructed the encouragement variable for a group as a dichotomy ("not encouraged," with code 0, and "encouraged," with code 1). People who belonged to one of these groups were further asked whether they felt very close, rather close, or not so close to other members of the group. I combined categories: "not so close" was coded as 0 and "very close or rather close" as 1.

Two kinds of personal networks are distinguished: networks of friends and networks of colleagues at the workplace. Involvement in networks of friends was measured by the respondents' estimate of how many friends are critical of the situation in East Germany (the former Communist part of Germany) or have ever participated in protest actions. Each item had four possible responses: none, some, many, almost all (coded 1 to 4, respectively). The scale number of critical and politically active friends consists of the average of the codes of those two items.[22]

Respondents' involvement in networks of work colleagues was measured by the respondents' estimate of how many colleagues are critical of the situation in the new states or have participated in protest actions—and the same responses were allowed (none, some, many, almost all, coded 1 to 4, respectively). The scale number of critical and politically active colleagues consists of the average of the codes of those items.[23] I assume that in these personal networks protest norms are instrumental and that the process of establishing protest norms resembles that in groups, as described before.

We did not measure the intensity of friendship. "Closeness" was ascertained only for colleagues. Respondents were asked to what extent they feel, on average, more or less close to their colleagues (from "very loose," with code 1, to "very close," with code 4). In order to test for an interaction effect of being a member of networks of critical and active colleagues, on the one hand, and of feeling close, on the other, I multiplied the preceding scale by the closeness item. The multiplicative scale is identified as the number of critical, politically active, and close colleagues. I further include the item referring to the closeness to colleagues ("closeness to colleagues") as a separate variable.

# Results

To what extent are the previous hypotheses confirmed by the data? To answer this question, I will first address the effects of group membership and then the effects of membership in personal networks on the norms dimensions.

## Do Groups Differ in Regard to Protest Norms?

If prediction 1 is correct, the following bivariate correlations are to be expected: Membership in alternative groups, unions, and political parties correlates positively with prescriptiveness, negatively with bipolarity, and positively with conditionality. For the other groups there should be no correlation between membership and the norms dimensions.

The first column of table 8.4 lists the kinds of groups of which respondents could be members. It is important to note that group memberships—the independent variables—are measured in the first wave (1993), whereas the dependent variables—the norms dimensions—are measured in the second wave (1996). The norms dimensions are listed in the second, third, and fourth columns. The table reveals that prediction 1 is only partially confirmed. As expected, membership in alternative groups and political parties demonstrates a positive correlation with prescriptiveness. Thus, members of alternative groups and political parties accept, in general, the norm that protest is a duty. The table further reveals negative correlations between membership in these two kinds of groups and bipolarity, although

TABLE 8.4    *The Effects of Group Membership in 1993 on the Norms Dimensions in 1996 (Bivariate Pearson Correlations and Standardized Regression Coefficient, N ≥ 428)*

| Membership, 1993 | Prescriptiveness, 1996 | Bipolarity, 1996 | Conditionality, 1996 |
|---|---|---|---|
| Bivariate correlations | | | |
| Alternative group | .13** | −.10* | .05 |
| Political party | .11* | −.08 | −.009 |
| Union | −.02 | .06 | −.007 |
| Alternative group or political party | .15** | −.11* | .02 |
| Alternative group, political party, or union | .08 | −.01 | .007 |
| Professional interest group | .04 | .03 | .03 |
| Charity group | .09* | −.01 | .04 |
| Hobby group | .009 | .13** | .03 |
| Sports group | .04 | −.02 | −.03 |
| Hobby or sports group | .03 | .07 | .002 |
| Standardized regression coefficients | | | |
| Alternative group or political party | .09* | −.11* | .01 |
| Number of memberships in other groups | .03 | .10* | .02 |
| Lagged norms dimension | .24** | .02 | .01 |
| Adjusted $R^2$ | .07** | .01* | −.007 |

*Source:* Author's compilation.
*Significant at the .05 level; **significant at the .01 level; one-tailed tests.

the correlations are weak. There appears to be no relation between membership in these groups and conditionality. This is not in line with the prediction.

Thus far I have dealt with each group separately. This is problematic because only a few respondents are members of alternative groups (sixteen members in 1993, see table 8.5). I therefore collapsed membership in alternative groups and political parties: a new measure was constructed with value 0 if a respondent was not member of one of the two groups, value 1 for membership in one of the two groups, and value 2 if a respondent was a member in both groups. Table 8.4 shows that in general the correlations of the composite measure with the norms dimensions are a little stronger than correlations of the single measures. Again, however, there is no correlation between membership and conditionality. If a similar composite measure is constructed for number of memberships in the three groups for which protest norms are most instrumental (alternative groups, political parties, unions), all correlations are close to zero.

Prediction 1 further posits that there are no correlations between membership in all other groups and the norms dimensions. This is, in general, confirmed, with two exceptions: there is a statistically significant correlation of .09 between membership in charity groups and prescriptiveness and a correlation of .13 between membership in hobby groups and bipolarity. I comment on this result later.

Are the relationships of group membership and the norms dimensions causal effects? Membership in groups was ascertained more than two years before the norms dimensions were measured. A necessary condition for causality is thus met—namely, that an event that may be a cause must occur before the event that may be an effect. This condition is not yet conclusive evidence, however, for a causal effect. It is possible that membership at time 1 correlates with protest norms at time 2 but that the effect is one of recruitment, not membership. This means that before 1993, alternative groups and political parties may have been joined by those citizens who were disposed toward strong protest norms. If this holds and if the norms remained stable until 1996, one would find significant correlations between group membership and the norms dimensions, but there would not be a causal effect of group membership. Stronger evidence about the causality of group membership on the norms dimensions can be obtained when the effects of membership in 1993 on norms in 1996 are analyzed, holding norms in 1993 (the lagged dependent variable) constant.[24] To illustrate, the equation for acceptance of a prescriptive protest norm in 1996 (Prescr_96) as a dependent variable and membership in a group in 1993 (GrMem_93) as an independent variable and, in addition, with norm acceptance in 1993 (Prescr_93) as the control variable (that is, as the lagged dependent variable) reads as follows:

$$\text{Prescr\_96} = a + b_1 \, \text{GrMem\_93} + b_2 \, \text{Prescr\_93}$$

If $b_1$ is positive, then membership raises acceptance of prescriptive protest norms in 1996—given the respondent's norm acceptance in 1993. The $b_1$ coefficient thus measures the extent to which membership in a group raises norm acceptance in 1996 beyond norm acceptance in 1993. Including the lagged dependent variable thus provides stronger evidence for causality than just computing correlations.

The respective regressions are shown in the lower panel of table 8.4. The norms dimensions are again the dependent variables. I include the following independent variables, all measured in 1993: membership in an alternative group or a political party, because these are the only memberships that had effects on norm dimensions; a composite measure, "number of memberships in other groups" (with value 0 for not being a member in any of the other kinds of groups listed in the table—the highest value is 5, for being a member in five other groups); and the lagged norm dimension (measured in 1993), corresponding to the dependent variable. The results indicate that the statistically significant correlations that were found for membership in alternative groups and political parties reflect causal effects: membership in these groups leads to acceptance of prescriptive protest norms and to low polarity. Membership in other groups has a significant effect only on bipolarity. This is owing to the bivariate correlation of membership in hobby groups and bipolarity. I did not find any explanation for this result. The results of the regression analyses thus resemble the results of the correlations.[25]

## Instrumentality and External Selective Incentives

Prediction 2 asserts that members of groups with instrumental protest norms are faced with strong external positive selective incentives. As has been noted, external incentives were measured by perceived encouragement of protest of group members. Table 8.5 shows the data of the first wave. The kinds of groups are listed in the first column. The second column shows the number of respondents who reported that they were members of these groups in 1993. The third column shows the number of these members who reported encouragement, and the fourth the respective percentages. There is great variability: about 69 percent of the members of alternative groups and 86 percent of members of political parties say they felt encouraged, whereas 56 percent of members of unions reported encouragement. Members of all other groups reported much less encouragement. As the table shows, the two groups with the least protest encouragement are hobby and sports clubs. These findings confirm prediction 2. As expected, encouragement is highest in those groups for which protest norms are most instrumental; these are alternative groups, political parties, and, at the third place, unions. As can be seen from table 8.6, the results for the second wave are similar to those for the first wave.

## The Effects of Selective Incentives on Norms

Prediction 3 addresses the effects of external and internal incentives (that is, of encouragement and closeness) on the norms dimensions for groups with instrumental protest norms. The prediction should thus hold for alternative groups, political parties, and unions. Membership in alternative groups or political parties had effects on the norms dimensions (see table 8.4). Let us therefore first test prediction 3 for these two groups. In order to understand the results presented in table 8.7, it is important to note that encouragement and closeness can be ascertained only for members of groups, not for nonmembers. Consequently, the $N$ of these analyses is much smaller than the $N$ of previous analyses. The first panel of table 8.7

TABLE 8.5    *Membership and Encouragement of Protest in Groups, Leipzig Panel, 1993 (N = 438)*

| Kind of Group | Number of Members | Members Indicating That Protest Is Encouraged | |
|---|---|---|---|
| | | N | % of Members |
| Alternative group | 16 | 11 | 68.8 |
| Political party | 28 | 24 | 85.7 |
| Union | 133 | 75 | 56.4 |
| Professional interest group | 63 | 18 | 28.6 |
| Charity group | 30 | 6 | 20.0 |
| Hobby group | 82 | 11 | 13.4 |
| Sports group | 73 | 6 | 8.2 |

*Source:* Author's compilation.

shows that only thirty-four respondents were members of at least one of the two kinds of groups in 1993.[26] Those members who feel encouraged to protest in the two groups accept a prescriptive protest norm to a high extent ($r = .20$). The effect on bipolarity is negative ($r = -.17$), whereas the effect on conditionality is positive ($r = .23$). Prediction 3 thus accords with the data. The results for closeness are similar: those who are close to a group accept prescriptive protest norms, and their norms are not bipolar but are conditional.

It is not implausible that encouragement and closeness interact. In

TABLE 8.6    *Membership and Encouragement of Protest in Groups, Leipzig Panel, 1996 (N = 438)*

| Kind of Group | Number of Members | Members Indicating That Protest Is Encouraged | |
|---|---|---|---|
| | | N | % of Members |
| Alternative group | 11 | 10 | 90.9 |
| Political party | 24 | 18 | 75.0 |
| Union | 112 | 62 | 55.4 |
| Professional interest group | 50 | 15 | 30.0 |
| Charity group | 40 | 11 | 27.5 |
| Hobby group | 73 | 8 | 11.0 |
| Sports group | 81 | 4 | 4.9 |

*Source:* Author's compilation.

TABLE 8.7    *Bivariate Correlations Between Selective Incentives in 1993 and the Norms Dimensions in 1996*

| Group Properties and Personal Networks, 1993 | Prescriptiveness, 1996 | Bipolarity, 1996 | Conditionality, 1996 | N |
|---|---|---|---|---|
| Alternative groups and Political Parties (high instrumentality) | | | | |
| Encouragement[a] | .20 | −.17 | .23 | 34 |
| Closeness[b] | .30* | −.15 | .20 | 34 |
| Encouragement and closeness | .26 | −.28 | .12 | 34 |
| Alternative Groups, Political Parties, and Unions (high instrumentality) | | | | |
| Encouragement[a] | .13 | −.23** | .02 | 146 |
| Closeness[b] | .16* | −.21** | .05 | 145 |
| Encouragement and closeness | .18* | −.24** | .01 | 146 |
| Hobby and Sports Groups (low instrumentality) | | | | |
| Encouragement[a] | −.003 | .11 | .03 | 125 |
| Closeness[b] | −.02 | .05 | .10 | 125 |
| Encouragement and closeness | .03 | .09 | .02 | 125 |

*Source:* Author's compilation.
[a]"Encouragement" is an indicator for exposure to positive external selective incentives to protest.
[b]"Closeness" to the respective group is an indicator for internal selective incentives.
*Significant at the .05 level; **significant at the .01 level; one-tailed tests.

other words, the effect of external incentives (encouragement) depends on the existence of internal incentives (closeness), and the converse is also true. To examine this effect, both variables were multiplied, and correlations of the resulting composite interaction term with the norms dimensions were computed. A clear interaction effect would yield higher correlations of the interaction term with the norms dimension than of the terms that make up the interaction term with the norms dimensions. This is only the case for bipolarity: those who feel encouraged and feel close to a group (that is, are exposed to both external and internal selective incentives) think to a particularly low extent that protest is a duty in some and not in other situations.

The correlations for the three groups with highly instrumental protest norms are, by and large, similar to those for the two groups but are most of the time lower (see the second panel of table 8.7). Encouragement and closeness lead to prescriptive protest norms and to low bipolarity, but there is no effect on conditionality. The table also shows that there are no interaction effects.

Protest norms are not instrumental for hobby and sports clubs. As tables 8.5 and 8.6 indicate, however, there is some encouragement of protest. However, for these groups correlations of encouragement and closeness with the norms dimensions are very low (table 8.7, third panel). There are no interaction effects, either. In general, these results are consistent with prediction 3.

As was noted earlier, regression analyses provide stronger evidence for causal effects. Table 8.8 demonstrates that for the alternative groups and political parties, encouragement as well as closeness lead to acceptance of norms. The effects of closeness on acceptance of prescriptive norms are stronger than those of encouragement. It thus seems that internal selective incentives are more important than external selective incentives. For conditionality, the effects are .20 (encouragement) and .11 (closeness). Encouragement thus leads to higher conditionality than does closeness. For the three groups with instrumental protest norms, the results confirm the prediction only in part: there are effects of encouragement and closeness only on bipolarity ($-.16$ and $-.12$).

## The Effects of Personal Networks on Norms

Table 8.9 shows the effects of involvement in personal networks on prescriptiveness, bipolarity, and conditionality. The upper panel of table 8.9 indicates that there are positive effects on the acceptance of prescriptive protest norms, whereas the effects on bipolarity and conditionality are close to zero. The table further shows that the number of critical, politically active colleagues and the respondent's closeness to colleagues do not have interaction effects. The multiplicative term, consisting of both of these variables, does not correlate higher with the norms dimensions than each of the additive variables. For example, the correlation of "number of critical and politically active colleagues" with prescriptiveness is .21; if this scale is multiplied by the closeness item, the correlation is only .18.[27] The correlation of closeness to colleagues and the norms dimensions is in general close to zero.

We tested the joint effects of membership in networks of critical and politically active friends or colleagues on the norms dimensions by including both variables simultaneously in the regression analyses as well as the lagged dependent variables. The results, exhibited in the lower panel of table 8.9, are similar to those of the bivariate correlations: only the coefficients for prescriptiveness are positive and significant, and all other coefficients are close to zero.

TABLE 8.8    *The Effects of Selective Incentives in 1993 on the Norms Dimensions in 1996 (Regression Analysis, Standardized Coefficients)*

| Group Property and Personal Networks, 1993 | Prescriptiveness, 1996 | Bipolarity, 1996 | Conditionality, 1996 | N |
|---|---|---|---|---|
| Alternative groups and political parties (high instrumentality) | | | | |
| Encouragement[a] | .10 | −.07 | .20 | 30 |
| Closeness[b] | .25 | −.09 | .11 | 30 |
| Lagged dependent variable | .25 | −.05 | −.12 | 30 |
| Adjusted $R^2$ | .09 | −.09 | −.02 | 30 |
| Alternative groups, political parties, and unions (high instrumentality) | | | | |
| Encouragement[a] | .02 | −.16 | −.02 | 137 |
| Closeness[b] | .09 | −.12 | .07 | 137 |
| Lagged dependent variable | .30** | −.03 | .06 | 137 |
| Adjusted $R^2$ | .09 | .04 | −.02 | 137 |

*Source:* Author's compilation.
[a]"Encouragement" is an indicator for exposure to positive external selective incentives to protest.
[b]"Closeness" to the respective group is an indicator for internal selective incentives.
*Significant at the .05 level; **significant at the .01 level; one-tailed tests.

## Is Membership in Groups or in Personal Networks More Important?

Respondents may be involved in groups as well as in personal networks. For example, a respondent may be a member of a protest group and may also have critical and politically active friends. Are the effects of involvement in groups and personal networks different? The general propositions in the first part of this chapter suggest that the answer to this question depends on the instrumentality of protest norms, on perceived influence, and on selective incentives. Although the extent to which these factors differ in groups and personal networks was not measured, it is instructive to examine empirically the relative effects of involvement in groups or social networks on the norms dimensions. Table 8.10 shows the results of regression analyses that include both kinds of network variable simultaneously. It is striking that the relatively strong effects of membership in alternative groups or political parties that was found earlier (see table 8.4) are close to zero when personal networks are controlled for (see the upper panel of

TABLE 8.9    *The Effects of Involvement in Personal Networks in 1993 on the Norms Dimensions in 1996*

| Membership in Personal Networks, 1993 | Prescriptiveness, 1996 | Bipolarity, 1996 | Conditionality, 1996 | N |
|---|---|---|---|---|
| Bivariate correlations | | | | |
| Number of critical and politically active friends | .22** | .06 | .009 | 429 |
| Number of critical and politically active colleagues | .21** | −.03 | .07 | 429 |
| Number of critical and politically active and close colleagues | .18** | −.002 | .07 | 429 |
| Closeness to colleagues | .07 | .05 | .04 | 429 |
| Regression analyses (standardized regression coefficients) | | | | |
| Number of critical and politically active friends | .12* | −.05 | −.01 | 409 |
| Number of critical and politically active colleagues | .15** | −.04 | .07 | 409 |
| Lagged dependent variable | .20** | .04 | .007 | 409 |
| Adjusted $R^2$ | .10** | −.001 | −.002 | |

*Source:* Author's compilation.
*Significant at the .05 level; **significant at the .01 level; one-tailed tests.

table 8.10). Only the effects of personal networks are preserved. This indicates that the effects of membership in the two groups on the norms dimensions that were found before is explained by the fact that members of those groups were members of personal networks and that membership in these networks affects the acceptance of protest norms. The bivariate correlations of membership in the two groups with the personal network variables are .25 (for critical and active friends) and .15 (for critical and active colleagues).

What about the simultaneous effects of encouragement in and closeness to the two groups, on the one hand, and involvement in personal networks, on the other? To compare these effects, two scales were constructed. For each respondent, the values of encouragement and closeness, on the one hand, and having critical and active friends and colleagues, on the other, were added. It is thus possible to compare the two types of effects. The lower panel of table 8.10 shows that members of the two groups

TABLE 8.10    *Joint Effects of Group Membership and Personal Networks in 1993 on Norms in 1996 (Regression Analysis, Standardized Regression Coefficient)*

| Membership in Kinds of Networks, 1993 | Prescriptiveness, 1996 | Bipolarity, 1996 | Conditionality, 1996 | N |
|---|---|---|---|---|
| Group membership and personal networks | | | | |
| Membership in alternative groups or political parties | .04 | −.08 | .005 | 408 |
| Number of critical and politically active friends | .11* | −.03 | −.01 | 408 |
| Number of critical and politically active colleagues | .14** | −.03 | .07 | 408 |
| Lagged dependent variable | .20** | .03 | .007 | 408 |
| Adjusted $R^2$ | .10** | .003 | −.05 | |
| Group encouragement, closeness, and personal networks | | | | |
| Encouragement in and closeness to alternative groups or political parties | .21 | −.09 | .26 | 30 |
| Number of critical and politically active friends and colleagues | .32* | −.18 | .007 | 30 |
| Lagged dependent variable | .30* | −.03 | −.11 | 30 |
| Adjusted $R^2$ | .19* | −.06 | −.03 | |

*Source:* Author's compilation.
*Significant at the .05 level; **significant at the .01 level; one-tailed tests.

who feel encouraged and are close to the groups subscribe to protest norms: the standardized regression coefficient for prescriptiveness is .21. The effects of involvement in personal networks is stronger (.32). For both independent variables there is a negative effect on bipolarity. Conditionality is high only for members of the two groups who are strongly encouraged and feel close to their groups.

## Summary and Discussion of the Results

The results of this study confirm the widely held proposition that social networks are important for the emergence of norms. This is no surprise, because networks are important for everything. However, this research shows that the role of networks in the emergence of norms is much more complicated than existing theory and research suggest. I have addressed one specific kind of norm, the felt obligation to protest. I have sought to explain three dimensions of this norm: acceptance (how morally compelling is the norm?), bipolarity (is there a duty to protest in certain situations and not in others?), and conditionality (does the strength of the obligation depend on the situation?). Based on some general propositions, the first prediction was that members (in contrast with nonmembers) of three groups for whom a norm to protest is instrumental will show high acceptance, low bipolarity, and high conditionality. These groups were alternative political groups, political parties, and unions. The data analyses (see table 8.4) indicate that only members of alternative groups and political parties accept protest norms to a high extent and that for them, bipolarity is low. There is no difference between members and nonmembers of unions; union membership does not have the expected effect on conditionality. Thus, there is some evidence that it is likely that if in groups instrumental norms are accepted to a high extent, the bipolarity of the norms is low.

This prediction compares members and nonmembers of groups, such as union members and nonmembers. It is likely that membership matters more if a member is involved in the daily affairs of a group. Therefore, the second and third predictions address only members of groups. The second prediction, which is confirmed, holds that in groups in which protest norms are instrumental, members are exposed to external incentives for accepting protest norms to a high extent (see tables 8.5 and 8.6).[28]

The third prediction addresses the effects of these external incentives on norms. It further assumes that feeling close to members of a group engenders internal incentives for accepting instrumental norms: if a person feels close to a group, nonconformance to a norm that is instrumental for the group is likely to make her or him have a bad conscience or experience feelings of guilt. For protest groups and political parties, the data indicate that members who are exposed to external as well as internal incentives to a high extent accept protest norms, low bipolarity, and high conditionality (tables 8.7 and 8.8).

The literature about the effects of networks on the emergence of norms does not distinguish between different kinds of networks. The preceding predictions should thus also hold for personal networks, that is, for networks of friends or colleagues at the workplace who are critical of the political situation and for whom protest norms are instrumental. It was found that those who have many friends or colleagues who are critical of the present political situation or are politically active accept protest norms to a high extent. This is consistent with the finding that membership in alternative groups and political parties leads to the acceptance of protest norms. However, involvement in personal networks did not have any effect on bipolarity and conditionality (see table 8.9).

Membership in groups overlaps with membership in personal networks—that is, some people are members both of groups and of personal networks. It can thus be examined how important membership in the two groups (alternative groups and political parties) or in the two kinds of personal networks (friends and colleagues) is for the emergence of norms. Regression analyses in which these factors were included simultaneously indicate that the effects of membership in groups on the norms dimensions mentioned earlier can be explained by the fact that members in those groups are often involved in personal networks in which protest norms are instrumental (see table 8.10, upper panel). These findings indicate that personal networks are particularly important for the emergence of protest norms.

The third prediction referred only to members of the two groups. Are the effects of external and internal incentives preserved if involvement in personal networks is included in the analyses?[29] This time, being exposed to external or internal incentives in the two groups and being a member of critical and active personal networks both increase acceptance of norms; in both cases, bipolarity is low; in regard to the conditionality of norms, only exposure to external and internal incentives of groups demonstrates a clear-cut effect (see table 8.10, lower panel).

The findings suggest that personal networks are more effective than groups in bringing about norms. A possible explanation is that in a personal network ties between members are more intimate than in a group and that intimate personal ties (including frequent interaction) matter for the acceptance, bipolarity, and conditionality of norms. In order to test this hypothesis, identical measurements of the kind of relationship between members in personal networks and members in groups are required; such data were not available for use in the present research.

Feeling close to colleagues at the workplace did not have any additional effect on norms—beyond the effect of membership in these networks. This suggests that sometimes membership in personal networks is sufficient to bring about norms, whereas additional internal incentives increase the likelihood of norm emergence in groups. There might thus be a threshold beyond which additional integration or "intimacy" does not make a difference for the emergence of norms.

It is surprising that the effects of the network variables on bipolarity and conditionality are so different. The analyses suggest that if network involvement has a relatively strong effect on norm acceptance, then, most of the time either bipolarity is low or conditionality is high (see tables 8.7, 8.8, and 8.10). In the analyses that include only members of the two groups (table 8.10, lower panel), bipolarity is generally low. The effect is stronger for strong involvement in personal networks. It thus seems that strong identification with the members of a network reduces bipolarity. If network involvement is less intense, however, only conditionality increases.

It is difficult to explain why the propositions do not hold for unions. It might be that protest norms are less instrumental for these groups. This is a possibility, but as long as data do not support the claim, this explanation is at best ad hoc.

Methodological purists might dismiss some results of this research as irrelevant because the coefficients of the analyses referring to the members of the groups ($N$ is 30 or 34) are most of the time not statistically significant. I have examined whether the sign of the coefficients is in line with the predictions and whether the coefficients exceed an absolute value of .10, which is often regarded as the minimal size for a "significant" relationship. If this is rejected the data might still be regarded as an exploratory study that needs to be supplemented by further research.

## Further Research

Two things need further attention: one is the suggestion that norm emergence is more likely in personal networks than in groups; the other is that the intensity of the relationships between members matters. It is thus necessary to specify the kinds of rewards that operate in different networks and test their effects. "Integration" encompasses, besides frequent interactions, closeness of the members or mutual identification. Is friendship (or an intimate relation) of importance (see Homans 1974, chapter 7), or is sympathy enough, or does mere interaction suffice? There are further derivative or second-order rewards. As George C. Homans (1974, 150) notes, "If a group can offer much in the way of friendships to its members, it can exert much control over them, since it can deprive them of much if they don't conform." Is this perceived by the members of a network? To what extent is the value of the public good the group tries to produce relevant for norm acceptance? Case studies of different kinds of networks (including the kind of relationship between the members) that ascertain the extent of prescriptiveness, bipolarity, and conditionality could contribute to answers to these questions.

Norms are phrased in different ways. A norm sometimes refers to desirable and sometimes to undesirable behavior. For example, the statement "Thou shalt not kill" highlights the undesirable behavior, in contrast with the statement "You should save lives." In regard to promise keeping, the rule is formulated as "You should keep promises" as well as "You should not break promises." It is not clear under what conditions a proscriptive or prescriptive formulation of a norm is more common. It may be an interesting question for further research to investigate why some of several equivalent formulations of norms are preferred in everyday discourse.

The factorial survey design is a useful instrument to measure the norms dimensions outlined in this chapter. With the development of some general measurement devices, this instrument could also be applied to various other kinds of norms. It would be worthwhile, as well, to examine to what extent such measures yield similar results as other measures for norms that are used in empirical research.

This research uses a panel design to get some indication of the causal order of the variables. Although a panel design is superior to cross-sectional analyses, it is not without problems, either. A panel design looks at the effects of variables measured at time 1 on variables measured at time 2. The problem is the time interval between time 1 and time 2. Assume that an independent variable is measured at time 1, and that the values of this variable affect protest at time 2; assume further that after time 2 the values of the independent variable change dramatically; and lead to a change of the dependent variable at time 3. If the dependent variable is measured at time 3, any causal effects that may exist may not be discovered, because the time interval was badly chosen: the values of the independent variable that were measured at time 1 did not cause the protest that was measured at time 3. As long as nothing is known about the amount of time required for an effect to appear, we must have some luck in regard to the choice of the time intervals. It is not clear whether we had this luck in our research design. The time between the two measurements in this study is more than two years. It is not implausible that the independent variables changed during that time to such an extent that effects on the dependent variables were rather weak. It would be interesting to conduct a new panel study with a shorter time period between the two waves.

Norms are second-order public goods. Therefore, hypotheses from the theory of public goods can be applied to generate propositions about the emergence of norms. Norms are a special kind of public good, however. Other public goods are not prescriptive or proscriptive, bipolar, and conditional; and, unlike most other public goods, norms can be internalized. Furthermore, public goods are, by definition, goods that, once provided, can be consumed by all members of a group, whereas it is easy to exclude people from "consuming" a norm. For example, it takes a simple decision by a parliament to determine that the penal law must not be applied to youths below the age of fourteen years or to foreigners. Further discussion is needed to explore the extent to which public goods theory can be applied or must be extended to explain the emergence of norms. The reader is also referred to the discussion in chapter 13 of this volume.

The variables that explain the emergence of protest norms are similar to those used in a rational actor model explaining the emergence of political protest.[30] This is plausible: if protest norms are a by-product of the organization of collective action, then the conditions that lead to protest should also bring about protest norms. It would be an interesting task for future research to explore more systematically the extent to which the same variables explain political protest and the norms that encourage it.

# Appendix

Table 8.A1 shows for three respondents—numbers 801001, 801004, and 801017—the values of the six vignette characteristics given in table 8.1. The characteristics in the table are gender, discontent, kind of protest, perception of personal influence, risk, and expected number of participants. The definitions of prescriptiveness, bipolarity, and conditionality, which are provided in the text, are repeated in a footnote to the table. The table also gives the values of these variables for each respondent.

In the data analyses, the data matrix is aggregated, that is, prescriptiveness, bipolarity, and conditionality each have one value for each respondent.

TABLE 8.A1    *Data Matrix for Three Respondents with Vignette Characteristics and Judgments*

| Respondent | Gender | Discontent | Protest | Influence | Risk | Number of Participants | Judgment |
|---|---|---|---|---|---|---|---|
| 801001 | 2.00 | 2.00 | 2.00 | 2.00 | 3.00 | 4.00 | −5.00 |
|  | 2.00 | 1.00 | 1.00 | 1.00 | 2.00 | 1.00 | 5.00 |
|  | 1.00 | 1.00 | 1.00 | 2.00 | 1.00 | 4.00 | −5.00 |
|  | 2.00 | 1.00 | 2.00 | 2.00 | 2.00 | 6.00 | 5.00 |
|  | 1.00 | 2.00 | 1.00 | 2.00 | 1.00 | 6.00 | 1.00 |
|  | 2.00 | 1.00 | 1.00 | 3.00 | 2.00 | 3.00 | 5.00 |
|  | 2.00 | 2.00 | 2.00 | 3.00 | 3.00 | 3.00 | 5.00 |
|  | 2.00 | 2.00 | 2.00 | 2.00 | 1.00 | 4.00 | −5.00 |
|  | 1.00 | 1.00 | 1.00 | 3.00 | 1.00 | 4.00 | −5.00 |
|  | 1.00 | 1.00 | 2.00 | 2.00 | 1.00 | 6.00 | 1.00 |
| 801004 | 1.00 | 2.00 | 1.00 | 1.00 | 2.00 | 1.00 | 5.00 |
|  | 1.00 | 2.00 | 1.00 | 1.00 | 2.00 | 3.00 | 5.00 |
|  | 2.00 | 1.00 | 2.00 | 1.00 | 3.00 | 6.00 | 5.00 |
|  | 2.00 | 2.00 | 2.00 | 2.00 | 1.00 | 2.00 | .00 |
|  | 1.00 | 1.00 | 2.00 | 3.00 | 3.00 | 6.00 | .00 |
|  | 2.00 | 2.00 | 1.00 | 3.00 | 1.00 | 6.00 | 5.00 |
|  | 2.00 | 2.00 | 2.00 | 1.00 | 3.00 | 7.00 | 5.00 |
|  | 2.00 | 2.00 | 1.00 | 1.00 | 1.00 | 2.00 | 5.00 |
|  | 2.00 | 2.00 | 1.00 | 3.00 | 3.00 | 6.00 | 5.00 |
|  | 1.00 | 2.00 | 1.00 | 2.00 | 1.00 | 5.00 | .00 |

*Source:* Author's compilation.
*Notes:*
**Prescriptiveness** (percentage of judgments per respondent greater than 0); respondent 1: 60; respondent 2: 70; respondent 3: 50.
**Bipolarity** (is given, that is 1, if there is at least one negative value per respondent, otherwise bipolarity is 0); respondent 1: 1; respondent 2: 0; respondent 3: 1.
**Conditionality** (is not given or 0, that is a norm is unconditional, if all judgments are equal and not 0; otherwise a norm is conditional, that is conditionality has value 1). All respondents have value 1, that is for each respondent, the norm is conditional.

# Notes

1. It is not possible to provide a discussion about the usefulness of such a model in this chapter. Various arguments for and against using such a model are analyzed in Opp 1999.

2. See, for example, Homans 1950, 123, and Homans 1974, 96, for a similar definition. My definition draws on deontic logic, in which prescriptive or proscriptive statements are characterized by the deontic operators "permitted," "obliged," or "forbidden"; for details, see Crawford and Ostrom 1995.

3. The basic reference for this theory is Demsetz 1967. For a discussion, see Barzel 1989; Eggertsson 1990; Opp 1990. This theory underlies Coleman's explanation of the emergence of norms (Coleman 1990, chapters 10 and 11), but he does not cite Demsetz.

4. The often heard claim that the instrumentality proposition (and rational choice theory in general) assumes "instrumental rationality" or is "consequentialist" has different meanings. First, a behavior (or a norm) may be "instrumental" in the sense that it has causal effects that are intended. Thus, a norm may be instrumental in the sense that it leads to the reduction of negative externalities, which is the goal of the actors. Second, a behavior (or a norm) may be instrumental in the sense that it is related to events or phenomena in a noncausal manner. For example, assume a person performs action A and knows that this is in accordance with a norm N. The fact that A corresponds to N certainly cannot be construed as a causal effect of this behavior. It is, however, a behavioral "consequence" that may be an incentive for an individual actor to perform the given behavior. As this example shows, the instrumentality proposition as well as rational choice theory use terms such as "outcomes," "behavioral consequences," and "instrumentality" in a broad sense that does not include only (actual or perceived) causal effects of actions or norms (a disctinction that is confused by Elster 1989, chapter 3; for a critique, see Opp 1997). Incidentally, if "instrumental rationality" is used in this broad sense, values are legitimate explanatory factors for norms in a rational choice framework (Opp 1983). The reason is that actors may realize that certain norms contradict their values, and this may be a cost that discourages the acceptance of a norm (and, thus, the performance of certain behaviors).

5. It might be argued that it is the perceived efficacy of the group, not that of the individual, that is relevant for contributing to the provision of a norm. However, if the group is regarded as efficacious, why should an individual contribute if she or he can get the norm without any effort? On the other hand, if group action is regarded as completely inefficacious the individual's action will not be effective either. Thus, individual and group influence have an interaction effect. For the theoretical discussion and the empirical test of this effect, see Finkel, Muller, and Opp 1989; Finkel and Muller 1998. Research (Opp, Voss, and Gern 1995, chapter 4) has shown, however, that individual efficacy seems to be more important than group efficacy. This chapter therefore focuses on individual efficacy.

6. It is often difficult for members of a group to state exactly the conditions under which a norm holds. This happens if it is not clear under which conditions a behavior serves the group interest. Thus, the previous propositions are also capable of yielding predictions in regard to the clarity of a norm.

7. Spontaneous norm emergence is of particular importance for the norm of protest, which is the subject of this chapter. This process was especially emphasized by Friedrich A. Hayek (see Vanberg 1994). Possible processes of the evolutionary emergence or attenuation of norms are suggested in Axelrod 1986; Knight 1992; Nee and Ingram 1998; Oberschall 1986; Opp 1982, 1983, 1990. See also chapters 1 through 4, this volume.

8. In an earlier work, Taylor notes that "the set of persons who compose a community have beliefs and values in common" (Taylor 1982, 26). In this respect, values can no longer be explained by "community." See also Taylor and Singleton 1993 in which his definition of "community" includes "shared beliefs and preferences" (199) and thus, norms.

9. For a more extensive summary, see Ellickson 1991, chapter 9.

10. For a summary of the effects of networks on cooperation and on the emergence of norms, see Putnam 1993, 172–76, and the discussion in Voss 1998.

11. It may be argued that social networks originate only if the members share some norms and that therefore networks cannot be used as explanatory variables. There may be social networks whose members share norms when the network originates, but after the emergence of networks those norms may be modified and new norms may emerge in the course of interactions. In regard to protest norms, I test empirically the extent to which networks are causal factors for the emergence of protest norms or whether people join who share already protest norms.

12. These statements are in no way tautological. If alternative groups would be defined as those groups that protest frequently, and if it would then be predicted that protest groups protest rather frequently, that would indeed be a tautology. The argument in this section is, however, that alternative groups, as defined above, develop a certain kind of norm. This is not part of the definition of a protest group and, therefore, no tautology is involved.

13. In her research about the development of protest in East Germany from 1989 to 1994, Christiane Lemke (1997) found that political parties and unions are— besides social movements—among the political actors who most frequently organize protests.

14. The following argument was suggested to me by Heike Diefenbach.

15. See Finkel, Muller, and Opp 1989; Finkel and Muller 1998; Gibson 1991; Moe 1980; Muller and Opp 1986; Opp 1988, 1989.

16. See Rossi 1951, 1979; Rossi et al. 1974; Rossi and Anderson 1982; Rossi and Berk 1985. For other applications of Rossi's method, see, for example, papers collected in Rossi and Nock 1982 and Jasso 1988. This section draws on Jasso and Opp 1997. In contrast to this earlier article, the present chapter provides a more detailed account of the measurement, applies the factorial survey design to test new hypotheses, uses a pooled data set and a panel, and defines a quantitative measure of prescriptiveness.

17. I do not use these categories in the present analysis; for details, see Jasso and Opp 1997.

18. In addition to the numerical categories, one category reads that it is unknown how many people will participate, and another does not mention the number of expected participants. Again, I do not analyze these categories in the present chapter; for details, see Jasso and Opp 1997.

19. There is a trade-off. On the one hand, it is desirable to obtain as many ratings as possible from each respondent in order to maximize the precision of the estimates. On the other hand, the number of ratings requested must not be so large that the respondent refuses to carry out the rating task or that fatigue interferes with the quality of the ratings. Because this research was the first factorial survey in a formerly socialist country, the conservative course was followed, and relatively few vignettes were presented.

20. For details, see Opp and Gern 1993; Opp 1994; Opp, Voss, and Gern 1995.

21. In Jasso and Opp 1997 this dimension is called "strong" prescriptiveness. This article further defines weak prescriptiveness as the percentage of ratings of a respondent that is greater than or equal to zero. I concentrate here on strong prescriptiveness because I am interested in explaining when a norm exists in the strict sense, and this means, in terms of the vignettes, that ratings are greater than zero.

22. A total of 19 among the 438 respondents indicated that they did not know how many of their friends were critical of the current situation, and 115 said they did not know how many of their friends were politically active. I assigned code 1 to these respondents because not knowing anything about friends is equivalent to having no friends who are critical or politically active.

23. A total of 114 respondents did not answer the question because of unemployment (because of which they had no colleagues); 25 and 110, respectively, did not know how many of their colleagues were critical or politically active. Again, I assigned a value of 1 to these respondents because having no colleagues is equivalent to having no colleagues who are critical or politically active.

24. This is part of the Granger test of causality; for details, see Gujarati 1995, 620–24, Finkel 1995.

25. Because each of the dependent variables "bipolarity" and "conditionality" is dichotomous, logistic regressions were performed. The results in terms of the signs of the coefficients and the statistical significance are the same. This holds for all the following analyses as well.

26. Owing to the small number of cases for the two most protest-encouraging groups, only coefficients of about .30 become statistically significant at the .05 level (one-tailed tests). In survey research, coefficients of this size are rather rare. In testing the predictions I examine in particular whether the sign of the coefficients is in line with the predictions and whether the coefficients exceed an absolute value of .10, which is regarded as the minimal level for a relationship of sufficient size.

27. To test for an interaction effect, the dependent norm dimensions were further regressed on "number of critical and politically active colleagues" for those who do not feel close (categories 1 and 2) and for those who feel close (categories 3 and 4) to colleagues. There are no clear-cut differences between the regression coefficients.

28. Exposure to external incentives was measured by the extent to which respondents reported encouragement of protest and, so it was assumed, encouragement for accepting an obligation to protest.

29. Again, regression analyses were performed in which exposure to external and internal incentives (which can only be ascertained for members of groups) and membership in personal networks were included simultaneously.

30.  For a recent summary of such a model, see Opp 1998. Good reviews of the literature are provided by Leighley 1995, Lofland 1996 (chapter 8), Moore 1995, and Whitely 1995.

# References

Axelrod, Robert. 1986. "An Evolutionary Approach to Norms." *American Political Science Review* 80(4): 1095–1111.

Barzel, Yoram. 1989. *Economic Analysis of Property Rights.* Cambridge: Cambridge University Press.

Boudon, Raymond. 1997. "The Present Relevance of Max Weber's Wertrationalität." In *Methodology of the Social Sciences, Ethics, and Economics in the Newer Historical School: From Max Weber and Rickert to Sombart and Rothacker,* edited by Peter Koslowski. Berlin: Springer.

Coleman, James S. 1990. *Foundations of Social Theory.* Cambridge, Mass.: Harvard University Press, Belknap Press.

Crawford, Sue E. S., and Elinor Ostrom. 1995. "A Grammar of Institutions." *American Political Science Review* 89(3): 582–600.

Demsetz, Harold. 1967. "Toward a Theory of Property Rights." *American Economic Review* 57(2): 347–59.

Eggertsson, Thráinn. 1990. *Economic Behavior and Institutions.* Cambridge: Cambridge University Press.

Ellickson, Robert C. 1991. *Order Without Law: How Neighbors Settle Disputes.* Cambridge, Mass: Harvard University Press.

Elster, Jon. 1989. *The Cement of Society: A Study of Social Order.* Cambridge: Cambridge University Press.

Finkel, Steven E. 1995. *Causal Analysis with Panel Data.* Thousand Oaks, Calif.: Sage.

Finkel, Steven E., and Edward N. Muller. 1998. "Rational Choice and the Dynamics of Collective Political Action." *American Political Science Review* 92: 37–49.

Finkel, Steven E., Edward N. Muller, and Karl-Dieter Opp. 1989. "Personal Influence, Collective Rationality, and Mass Political Action." *American Political Science Review* 83(3): 885–903.

Furubotn, Eirik G., and Svetozar Pejovich. 1974. *The Economics of Property Rights.* Cambridge, Mass.: Ballinger.

Gibson, Martha Liebler. 1991. "Public Goods, Alienation, and Political Protest: The Sanctuary Movement as a Test of the Public Goods Model of Collective Rebellious Behavior." *Political Psychology* 12(4): 623–51.

Gujarati, Damodar N. 1995. *Basic Econometrics.* New York: McGraw-Hill.

Hechter, Michael. 1987. *Principles of Group Solidarity.* Berkeley: University of California Press.

Heckathorn, Douglas. 1989. "Collective Action and the Second-Order Free-Rider Problem." *Rationality and Society* 1(1): 78–100.

———. 1990. "Collective Sanctions and Compliance Norms: A Formal Theory of Group-Mediated Social Control." *American Sociological Review* 55(3): 366–84.

Homans, George C. 1950. *The Human Group.* New York: Harcourt, Brace.

———. 1974. *Social Behavior: Its Elementary Forms.* New York: Harcourt.

Jasso, Guillermina. 1988. "Whom Shall We Welcome? Elite Judgments of the Criteria for the Selection of Immigrants." *American Sociological Review* 53(6): 919–32.

Jasso, Guillermina, and Karl-Dieter Opp. 1997. "Probing the Character of Norms: A Factorial Survey Analysis of the Norms of Political Action." *American Sociological Review* 62(6): 947–64.

Jasso, Guillermina, and Peter H. Rossi. 1977. "Distributive Justice and Earned Income." *American Sociological Review* 42(4): 639–51.

Knight, Jack. 1992. *Institutions and Social Conflict.* Cambridge: Cambridge University Press.

Leighley, Jan E. 1995. "Attitudes, Opportunities, and Incentives: A Field Essay on Political Participation." *Political Research Quarterly* 48(1): 181–209.

Lemke, Christiane. 1997. "Protest und Gewaltbereitschaft in Ostdeutschland." *Politische Vierteljahresschrift* 38: 79–113.

Lofland, John. 1996. *Social Movement Organizations: Guide to Research on Insurgent Realities.* New York: Aldine de Gruyter.

Moe, Terry M. 1980. *The Organization of Interests: Incentives and the Internal Dynamics of Political Interest Groups.* Chicago: University of Chicago Press.

Moore, Will H. 1995. "Rational Rebels: Overcoming the Free-Rider Problem." *Political Research Quarterly* 48(2): 417–54.

Muller, Edward N., and Karl-Dieter Opp. 1986. "Rational Choice and Rebellious Collective Action." *American Political Science Review* 80(2): 471–89.

Nee, Victor, and Paul Ingram. 1998. "Embeddedness and Beyond: Institutions, Exchange, and Social Structure." In *The New Institutionalism in Economic Sociology,* edited by Mary Brinton and Victor Nee. New York: Russell Sage Foundation.

Oberschall, Anthony. 1986. "The California Gold Rush: Social Structure and Transaction Costs." In *Approaches to Social Theory,* edited by Siegwart Lindenberg, James S. Coleman, and Stefan Nowak. New York: Russell Sage Foundation.

Olson, Mancur. 1965. *The Logic of Collective Action.* Cambridge, Mass.: Harvard University Press.

Opp, Karl-Dieter. 1982. "The Evolutionary Emergence of Norms." *British Journal of Social Psychology* 21: 139–49.

———. 1983. *Die Entstehung sozialer Normen: Ein Integrationsversuch soziologischer, sozialpsychologischer und ökonomischer Erklärungen.* Tübingen, Ger.: Mohr Siebeck.

———. 1988. "Grievances and Participation in Social Movements." *American Sociological Review* 53(6): 853–64.

———. 1990. "The Attenuation of Customs." In *Social Institutions: Their Emergence, Maintenance, and Effects,* edited by Michael Hechter, Karl-Dieter Opp, and Reinhard Wippler. New York: Aldine de Gruyter.

———. 1994. "Repression and Revolutionary Action: East Germany in 1989." *Rationality and Society* 6(1): 101–38.

———. 1997. "Norms, Rationalizations, and Collective Political Action: A Rational Choice Perspective." *Swiss Journal of Economics and Statistics* 133: 241–74.

———. 1998. "Does Antiregime Action Under Communist Rule Affect Political Protest After the Fall? Results of a Panel Study in East Germany." *Sociological Quarterly* 39(2): 189–214.

———. 1999. "Contending Conceptions of the Theory of Rational Action." *Journal of Theoretical Politics* 11(2): 171–202.

Opp, Karl-Dieter, in collaboration with Peter Hartmann and Petra Hartmann. 1989. *The Rationality of Political Protest: A Comparative Analysis of Rational Choice Theory.* Boulder, Colo.: Westview.

Opp, Karl-Dieter, and Christiane Gern. 1993. "Dissident Groups, Personal Networks, and Spontaneous Cooperation: The East German Revolution of 1989." *American Sociological Review* 58(5): 659–80.

Opp, Karl-Dieter, Peter Voss, and Christiane Gern. 1995. *The Origins of a Spontaneous Revolution: East Germany, 1989.* Ann Arbor: University of Michigan Press.

Putnam, Robert D. 1993. *Making Democracy Work: Civic Traditions in Modern Italy.* Princeton, N.J.: Princeton University Press.

Raphael, D. D. 1994. *Moral Philosophy.* Oxford: Oxford University Press.

Rossi, Peter H. 1951. *The Application of Latent Structure Analysis to the Study of Social Stratification.* Ph.D. diss., Columbia University.

———. 1979. "Vignette Analysis: Uncovering the Normative Structure of Complex Judgments." In *Qualitative and Quantitative Social Research: Papers in Honor of Paul F. Lazarsfeld,* edited by Robert K. Merton, James S. Coleman, and Peter H. Rossi. New York: Free Press.

Rossi, Peter H., and Andy B. Anderson. 1982. "The Factorial Survey Design: An Introduction." In *Measuring Social Judgments: The Factorial Survey Approach,* edited by Peter H. Rossi and Steven L. Nock. Beverly Hills, Calif.: Sage.

Rossi, Peter H., and Richard A. Berk. 1985. "Varieties of Normative Consensus." *American Sociological Review* 50(3): 333–47.

Rossi, Peter H., and Steven L. Nock, eds. 1982. *Measuring Social Judgements: The Factorial Survey Approach.* Beverly Hills, Calif.: Sage.

Rossi, Peter H., William A. Sampson, Christine E. Bose, Guillermina Jasso, and Jeffrey Passel. 1974. "Measuring Household Social Standing." *Social Science Research* 3: 169–90.

Taylor, Michael. 1982. *Community, Anarchy, and Liberty.* Cambridge: Cambridge University Press.

———. 1996. "When Rationality Fails." In *Pathologies of Rational Choice Theory: Economic Models of Politics Reconsidered,* edited by Jeffrey Friedman. New Haven, Conn.: Yale University Press.

Taylor, Michael, and Sara Singleton. 1993. "The Communal Resource: Transaction Costs and the Solution of Collective Action Problems." *Politics and Society* 21: 194–214.

Vanberg, Viktor J. 1994. *Rules and Choice in Economics.* London: Routledge.

Voss, Thomas. 1998. "Strategische Rationalität und die Realisierung sozialer Normen." In *Norm, Herrschaft, und Vertrauen: Beiträge zu James S. Colemans Grundlagen der Sozialtheorie,* edited by Hans-Peter Müller and Michael Schmid. Opladen, Ger.: Westdeutscher Verlag.

Whitely, Paul F. 1995. "Rational Choice and Political Participation: Evaluating the Debate." *Political Research Quarterly* 48(1): 211–33.

Wolfsfeld, Gadi, Karl-Dieter Opp, Henry Dietz, and Jerrold D. Green. 1994. "Dimensions of Political Action: A Cross-Cultural Analysis." *Social Science Quarterly* 75(1): 98–114.

# 9

# THE EMERGENCE OF MARRIAGE NORMS: AN EVOLUTIONARY PSYCHOLOGICAL PERSPECTIVE

*Satoshi Kanazawa and Mary C. Still*

EVOLUTIONARY psychology is an application of evolutionary biology to human behavior. It is an emerging perspective that is sweeping psychology and anthropology, one that promises to provide a universal microfoundation to all social and behavioral sciences. Although evolutionary psychology proper is a micro theory of human cognition and behavior, we believe that, coupled with reasonable assumptions, we can extend it to explain emergent properties, such as norms. It is our contention in this chapter that the evolutionary psychological perspective can explain the emergence of a large number of norms, particularly those that are considered to be morally significant.

## Principles of Evolutionary Psychology

Evolutionary psychology seeks to discover universal human nature, which is a collection of domain-specific psychological mechanisms.[1] A psychological mechanism is an information-processing procedure or decision rule, acquired through natural and sexual selection, that allows human beings to solve a particular adaptive problem (a problem of survival or reproduction). Unlike decision rules in game theory or the microeconomic subjective expected utility maximization theory, however, psychological mechanisms mostly operate *behind our conscious thinking*.

Male sexual jealousy is one example of a psychological mechanism (Daly, Wilson, and Weghorst 1982). Because gestation in humans and most other mammalian species occurs inside the female body, males of these species can never be certain of the paternity of their mates' offspring, whereas females are always certain of their maternity. In other words, the possibility of cuckoldry exists only for males. Men who are cuckolded and invest their resources in the offspring of other men end up wasting these resources, for their genes will not be represented in the next generation. Men therefore have a strong reproductive interest in making sure that they will not be cuckolded, whereas women do not share this interest. Accordingly, men have developed a psychological mechanism that engenders jealousy at even the most remote possibility of their mates' sexual infidelity. The psychological mechanism of sexual jealousy helps to attenuate men's adaptive problem of paternal uncertainty. The same psychological mechanism often leads to men's attempt at mate guarding, to minimize the possibility of their mates' sexual contact with other men, sometimes with tragic consequences (Buss 1988; Buss and Shackelford 1997).

Although men and women are the same in the frequency and intensity of their jealousy in romantic relationships (White 1981; Buunk and Hupka 1987), there are clear sex differences in the triggers for jealousy. Both survey and physiological evidence from different cultures show that men get jealous of their mates' sexual infidelity with other men, belying their reproductive concern for cuckoldry. In contrast, women get jealous of their mates' emotional involvement with other women, because emotional involvement elsewhere often leads to diversion of their mates' resources from them and their children to their romantic rivals (Buss, Larsen, and Westen 1992; Buss et al. 1999).

This does not mean that we consciously *choose* or *decide* to get jealous. We just get jealous under some circumstances, in response to certain predictable triggers, but otherwise do not know why. These triggers are always understandable to others, and they are cross-culturally constant (Thiessen and Umezawa 1998). (Otherwise, no romance novels or romantic comedies would ever become an international hit.) Evolutionary psychology contends that evolved psychological mechanisms are responsible for most of our emotions, and they are also behind most of our preferences and desires (Kanazawa, forthcoming). Evolutionary psychology accounts for human behavior in terms of these evolved psychological mechanisms (and the preferences, desires, and emotions that they produce in us), and it can also account for emergent properties like norms. By providing endogenous explanations of actors' values and preferences, evolutionary psychology goes a long way toward what Thráinn Eggertsson (chapter 3, this volume) calls dynamic institutional theory.

Evolutionary psychology is premised on two broad generalizations. The first generalization, put bluntly, is there is nothing special about Homo sapiens. To put this more precisely, "Certainly we are unique, but we are not unique in being unique. Every species is unique and *evolved* its uniqueness in adaptation to its environment. Culture is the uniquely human way of adapting, but culture, too, evolved biologically" (van den Berghe 1990, 428). Human beings are just like other animal species (Betzig 1997; De Waal 1996); all the laws of nature, in particular, the laws of evolution by natural and sexual selection, apply equally to humans as they do to other species.

The second broad generalization is that there is nothing special about the brain as a human body part; it is just like the hand or the pancreas or any other body part. Just as a long history of human evolution has shaped the hand or the pancreas to perform specific functions, so has evolution shaped the human brain to perform certain tasks (solving adaptive problems).

The second generalization leads to an important implication of evolutionary psychology. Just as the basic shape and functions of the hand and the pancreas have not changed since the end of the Pleistocene epoch about ten thousand years ago, the basic functioning of the brain has not changed in the past ten thousand years. The human body (including the brain) evolved, over the course of millions of years, in the African savanna, where humans lived as hunter-gatherers in small bands of fifty or so related individuals during most of the Pleistocene epoch (Maryanski and Turner 1992, 69–90). This environment is known as the environment of evolutionary adaptedness (EEA) (Bowlby 1969), and it is to this ancestral environment that the human body (including the brain) is adapted.[2]

Figure 9.1 presents the basic theoretical structure of evolutionary psychology. It argues that an adaptive problem leads to an evolved psychological mechanism, which then produces adaptive (fitness maximizing) behavior in the EEA. Evolutionary psychology assumes that behavior in the EEA is fitness maximizing—that is, it enables individuals to transmit their genes into the next generation, not only through their own descendants but also through their genetic relatives. However, evolutionary psychology recognizes that our current environment may be radically different from the EEA, yet our psychological mechanisms (just like our hands and our pancreas) are still the same as they were in the EEA and produce the same behavior as they did in the EEA. "The adaptive correspondence between present conditions and present behavior, to the extent that it exists, is contingent, derived and incidental to Darwinian explanation. It depends solely on how much the present ontogenetic environment of an individual happens to reflect the summed features of the environment during recent evolutionary history, that is, on how different the present environment is from ancestral conditions" (Tooby and Cosmides 1990, 378). "There is no *a priori* reason to suppose that any specific modern cultural practice is adaptive" (Tooby and Cosmides 1989, 35), and, to the extent that our current environment is different from the EEA (to which all psychological mechanisms are adapted), evolutionary psychology predicts that our current behavior is maladaptive.

Recall the example of male sexual jealousy as an evolved psychological mechanism. This psychological mechanism solved the adaptive problem of successful reproduction in the EEA by allowing those men who possessed it to maximize paternal certainty and minimize the possibility of cuckoldry. Their sexual jealousy was therefore fitness maximizing in the

FIGURE 9.1    *The Basic Theoretical Structure of Evolutionary Psychology*

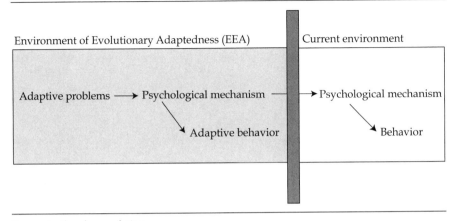

*Source:* Authors' compilation.

EEA. However, we now live in an environment in which sex and reproduction are often separated (in that many episodes of copulation do not lead to reproduction). Many women in romantic relationships in industrial societies use birth control. For these women, sexual infidelity does not lead to childbirth, and their mates do not face the possibility of wasting resources on the offspring of someone else. The original adaptive problem no longer exists. Yet men still possess the psychological mechanism that makes them jealous at the possibility of their mates' sexual infidelity and to compel them to guard their mates to minimize the possibility of cuckoldry. No man is likely to be comforted by the knowledge that his adulterous wife was on the pill at the time of her infidelity.

Furthermore, because our present environment is vastly different from the EEA, we now face a curious situation in which those who behave according to the dictates of the evolved psychological mechanism are often worse off in terms of survival and reproduction: Extreme forms of mate guarding, such as violence against mates or romantic rivals, are felonies in most industrialized nations. Incarceration, and consequent physical separation from their mates, reduces the reproductive success of the men. Just as the intense use of our hands (which were designed for primitive activities in the EEA) for typing on a QWERTY keyboard leads to carpal tunnel syndrome, and just as our taste for fats and sweets (which increased our chances of survival and reproductive success in the EEA) now leads to obesity and thus reduces our chances of survival and reproductive success today, uncritically following the emotions and desires created in us by our evolved psychological mechanisms often leads to maladaptive behavior.

# How Evolutionary Psychology Can Explain the Emergence of Norms

Evolutionary psychology explains phenomena at the individual level, in terms of psychological mechanisms in the brain and the behavior that results from them. How then can it explain the emergence of norms, which are macrosocial phenomena?

We define norms as socially shared prescriptions or proscriptions for behavior. Norms tell people what to do or what not to do. Norms are usually accompanied by sanctions, which serve as reinforcers and punishers designed to ensure compliance with norms. Although norms and sanctions are empirically connected, we believe they are conceptually and causally distinct. Norms emerge from behavioral regularity and expectation, whereas sanctions emerge from negative externalities. In other words, norms exist when many or most people behave in certain ways, and they become statistically expected and socially prescribed, whereas sanctions exist when many people are negatively affected by others' noncompliance with the norms.

Our definition of norms is consistent with those of Christine Horne and Robert Ellickson (chapters 1 and 2, this volume, respectively); unlike Ellickson, however, we do not exclude laws from our definition of norms. Whereas Thomas Voss (chapter 4, this volume) and game theory in general *define* norms in terms of behavioral regularity, we *explain* them in those terms. We contend that behavioral regularity in itself is not a norm but rather a cause of a norm. It is no coincidence that the word "norm" means both a rule and a statistical expectation: we believe this is because the statistical expectation becomes the rule. Similarly, it is no coincidence that the words "regular" (as in behavioral regularity) and "regulation" (rule) both stem from the same Latin root, regula: we believe this is because what is regular becomes a regulation. Contrary to Horne, we assert that the sense of oughtness derives from statistical expectation.

To explain the spontaneous emergence of norms, one must begin with the state of nature, the state that assumes the prior existence only of self-interested individuals. There are no norms in the state of nature; the behavior of individuals follows their inclinations. They are unconstrained by norms, and thus individual behavior varies: some people do X, and others do Y. In the state of nature, neither behavior is prescribed or proscribed; neither carries any normative significance. Under such conditions, it is reasonable to assume that a norm prescribing the more common behavior might emerge, purely as a matter of statistical expectation (Knight 1992). We therefore make a critical assumption that norms prescribing X will emerge when many or most people already do X, in the absence of any rules regarding such behavior (Homans 1950, 265–68; Knight 1992). If most people do Y, then the emergent norms will prescribe Y.

Once norms are in place, however, they will have further effects on individual behavior. If the emergent norms dictate behavior X, then those who were inclined to do behavior Y are now forced to do X (in order to avoid negative sanctions), and those who mostly but not always did X are now required to do X all the time (for the same reason).

A microscopic evolutionary psychological theory explains behavior at the individual level as a function of evolved psychological mechanisms. A macroscopic evolutionary psychological theory of the emergence of norms, then, would predict that norms will emerge at the macro level prescribing the behavior that evolutionary psychology predicts at the micro level.

Alan S. Miller and Satoshi Kanazawa (2000, chapter 10) rely on the evolutionary psychological perspective to explain the emergence of cooperative norms in Japan. The authors use Elliott Sober and David Sloan Wilson's (1998) multilevel selection theory, a sophisticated version of group selection theory, to explain how cooperation evolves over time.[3] In essence, they explain, cooperation can overcome defection, even though defection is more advantageous to the individual than cooperation, because groups that contain more cooperators do better and thus grow faster than groups that contain fewer cooperators. Cooperation (and any psychological mechanisms that promote it) are therefore selected for at the group level, even though they are selected against at the individual level.

The evolution of cooperation by multilevel selection, however, is a gradual process. Miller and Kanazawa begin by pointing out that China is the only ancient civilization that has not been invaded by a younger Western civilization. Because occupying powers, upon invasion, usually supplant native norms with their own, and because the evolution of cooperative norms through multilevel selection takes a long time, there is reason to expect that Chinese norms are more cooperative than norms in other societies. Many cultural practices (including norms) in eastern Asia historically originated in China and were then exported to Korea and, finally, to Japan. Because it is usually the socially ascendant groups in a country that influence foreign cultures, and because the more cooperative groups within a country are more ascendant (because they have greater solidarity and thus overtake other, less cooperative groups), there is good reason to believe that the norms Korea inherited from China are more cooperative than the average norms in China and, furthermore, that the norms Japan inherited from Korea are more cooperative than the average norms in Korea. Miller and Kanazawa suggest that this might be why contemporary Japan seems to have more cooperative norms, which increase the solidarity of Japanese groups, than other societies (Hechter and Kanazawa 1993). In Miller and Kanazawa's macroscopic evolutionary psychological theory, more cooperative norms emerge in societies in which there are more cooperators (as a result of multilevel selection).

Leda Cosmides and John Tooby's (1992) work on cooperative food sharing, and their notion of evoked culture provides another example of an evolutionary psychological theory of the emergence of norms. Evoked culture refers to differences between groups that are triggered by differential local circumstances. They are varied manifestations of universal psychological mechanisms that arise in response to varied environmental conditions. They result from the interaction of universal human nature and local environments.

One of the psychological mechanisms that humans (and other species) possess is reciprocal altruism (Trivers 1971). This psychological mechanism compels us to help one another in times of need. It also makes us expect reciprocity in exchange. When we help our neighbors in their times of need, we expect them to help us in our times of need. This psychological mechanism is the reason why simultaneously we get angry at those who do not reciprocate our favors and why we feel guilty when we fail to reciprocate the favors of others. Human beings have developed this psychological mechanism because, given the level of uncertainty in the EEA, those who possess it were more likely to survive and prosper than those who did not. It is interesting to note that species as primitive as vampire bats also engage in reciprocal altruism (Wilkinson 1984).

Cosmides and Tooby (1992, 206–20) note that the condition in the local environment that triggers the norm of cooperative food sharing is the high variance in food resources and availability. When the variance is high (as it is for large game hunting), on any given day some individuals will procure more food than they can consume, and others will procure nothing. High variance also creates uncertainty because whether or not one can procure food on any given day largely depends on luck. Under such conditions, the universal psychological mechanism of reciprocal altruism is triggered, and the norms of cooperative food sharing emerge at the macro level. In these cultures, there are strong negative sanctions against those who do not share their food with the less fortunate. When the variance is low (as it is in food gathering), the norms of cooperative food sharing do not develop because the amount of food one procures in these situations is largely proportional to one's effort.

As within-group evidence of this mechanism, Cosmides and Tooby (1992, 213–14) note that the Ache of Paraguay have the norm of sharing meat communally (because meat is a high-variance food). However, within the same tribe, gathered plant food is not shared outside the nuclear family (nuts and berries being low-variance food). As between-group evidence of the same mechanism, Cosmides and Tooby (214–15) cite Elizabeth Cashdan's (1989) work on the Kalahari San. Cashdan notes that the !Kung San face extreme variability in the availability of food and water, whereas the //Gana San manage to keep the variance low through horticulture and goat husbandry. As predicted by Cosmides and Tooby's theory, the !Kung San have developed norms of cooperative food sharing, whereas the //Gana San have not.

Cosmides and Tooby's work on evoked culture illuminates one crucial characteristic of the evolutionary psychological perspective on the emergence of norms. The perspective, relying as it does on the evolved psychological mechanisms and universal human nature, can effectively explain the cross-cultural universality of norms. It addresses the question of why all societies have certain important norms in common (such as norms prescribing cooperation or proscribing incest). However, by taking the local environment into consideration, it can also explain why certain norms emerge in some societies but not in others. Evolutionary psychology's reliance on universal human nature and evolved psychological mechanisms decidedly does not mean that it predicts the emergence of the same norms everywhere. The following analysis of the emergence of the marriage norms provides another example of how the interaction between universal human nature and the differential structural conditions lead to the emergence of divergent norms in different societies.

Although the evolutionary psychological theory of norms can explain both culturally universal and culturally variant norms, it has a significant scope condition. There are two distinct types of norms. The first type, which we call *moral norms*, prescribes behavior that most people would do anyway or proscribes behavior that most people would not do anyway, even in the absence of such norms and the accompanying threat of sanctions. The second type of norms, which we call *coercive norms*, prescribes behavior that most people would not otherwise do or proscribes behavior that most people would otherwise do, in the absence of such norms. Norms against murder, rape, incest, and those for reciprocal cooperation are examples of moral norms, and those against speeding and tax evasion are examples of coercive norms.

Paradoxically, sanctions against violations of moral norms are not as efficient as sanctions against violations of coercive norms, in the sense that most people are already inclined not to violate moral norms. For instance, even though norms prescribing reciprocal altruism or proscribing incest are culturally universal, we already possess psychological mechanisms to compel us to engage in reciprocal altruism (Trivers 1971) or to avoid incest (Westermarck 1891). Thus, people will engage in reciprocity and avoid incest even if there are no norms about them. In fact, as we argue elsewhere (Kanazawa and Still 2000), those who would violate moral norms (for instance, young men who commit murder and rape) would violate them even in the face of significant sanctions, because the potential individual benefit of such violations (or the opportunity cost of forgoing such violations) in terms of reproductive success are far greater than the losses they would incur as a result of any sanctions imposed on them (Daly and Wilson 1988).

Relying as it does on the evolved psychological mechanisms that constitute universal human nature, the evolutionary psychological theory of the emergence of norms can explain the emergence of moral norms but not of coercive norms. It is our contention that the psychological mechanisms that motivate human behavior at the micro level are also the cause of the emergence of moral norms prescribing the same behavior at the macro level. A long history of evolution by natural and sexual selection has equipped humans with psychological mechanisms that compel them to engage in, for instance, reciprocal altruism. This is why most of us are naturally inclined to engage in such behavior (even in the absence of any norms prescribing it) and also why we feel guilty when we fail to do so. (Guilt and other emotions are internal to us, and thus norms cannot prescribe them.) More important, the same psychological mechanisms that compel us to engage in reciprocal altruism are responsible for the emergence of the norm prescribing that behavior at the macro level.

Although the evolutionary psychological theory of norms can only explain the emergence of moral norms, not coercive norms, moral norms are more important in their consequences than coercive norms. Violations of moral norms are more likely to elicit moral outrage and other forms of strong visceral reactions. (We are far more likely morally to condemn rapists than speeders.)[4] The violations of moral norms are considered to be more significant because such norms spring directly from universal human nature rather than being externally imposed on us.

## An Illustration: The Emergence of Marriage Norms

Why are marriages in some societies monogamous while those in others are polygynous?[5] What accounts for the gradual historical shift from polygyny to monogamy in the course of human civilization? What explains the particular form marriage norms take in a given society or at a given time in history?[6]

Despite the central importance of marriage and the family in sociology, there has been no sociological theory of the marriage norms that addresses these questions. Marvin Sussman and Suzanne Steinmetz's sizable volume, *Handbook of Marriage and the Family* (1987), contains very little discussion of monogamy versus polygyny, and none of its thirty chapters (or any of their sections) is devoted to the cross-cultural or historical variations in the mating system. One must therefore look to neighboring disciplines for a theory of marriage norms.

### The Male Compromise Theory of Monogamy

In evolutionary biology and anthropology, Richard Alexander (1987; Alexander et al. 1979), Laura Betzig (1986, 103–6), and Kevin MacDonald (1990) all argue that monogamy is a compromise or concession that upper-class men make to lower-class men in exchange for their political support under democracy (Ridley 1993, 206–7; Wright 1994, 96–99). For purposes of illustration, we borrow a scenario presented by Robert Wright (1994, 96–99). Wright asks us to imagine a society composed of a thousand men and a thousand women, ranked in terms of their desirability as potential mates. There is by now considerable evidence that men value youth and physical attractiveness in women and women value wealth and status in men and that this is largely invariant both historically (Hill 1945; McGinnis 1958; Hudson and Henze 1969; Buss and Barnes 1986) and cross-culturally (Buss 1989; 1994, 19–72).[7] However, Wright's illustration works regardless of the nature of the underlying dimension as long as the men and women are uniquely and unambiguously ranked.

If the marriage market functions efficiently, then Man 1 (the most desirable man in this society) marries Woman 1 (the most desirable woman in this society), Man 2 marries Woman 2, and so on down the line, with Man 1,000 (the least desirable man) marrying Woman 1,000 (the least desirable woman). Even if there are minor glitches in the marriage market and the matching is not perfect, as long as the norms prescribe monogamy, each man (even the least desirable) is guaranteed a wife.

Now introduce polygyny. Assume Woman 400 decides to leave Man 400 and chooses to become the second wife of Man 40. If one-half share of Man 40 is better than all of Man 400 (for instance, if Man 40 is more than twice as wealthy as Man 400), then Woman 400 will be materially better off as the second wife of Man 40 than as the first and sole wife of Man 400. There is now, however, a vacancy in the wife market, and Women 400 to 1,000 each move up one place: Woman 401 marries Man 400, Woman 402 marries Man 401, and Woman 1,000 marries Man 999. Man 1,000 now is left wifeless. Thus after the introduction of polygyny,

- one woman (Woman 400) is greatly better off
- six hundred women (Women 400 through 1,000) are slightly better off
- one woman (Woman 40) is greatly worse off, because she now has to share her husband with Woman 400
- one man (Man 40) is somewhat better off, for having an additional wife
- six hundred men (Men 400 through 999) are slightly worse off
- one man (Man 1,000) is greatly worse off

Wright (1994, 97) therefore reaches a somewhat counterintuitive conclusion: most women are reproductively better off, and most men are similarly worse off, under polygyny. Some economists (Becker 1974, S17–S20; Grossbard 1978, 1980, proposition 1, 324–26) have reached the same conclusion. The value of any commodity in microeconomics is a function of supply and demand. Polygyny allows some men to monopolize the supply of women, decreasing the supply relative to the demand and thereby increasing the value of women. The reverse holds true for men.

What explains the gradual historical shift from polygyny to monogamy? Alexander (1987; Alexander et al. 1979), Betzig (1986, 103–6), and MacDonald (1990) variously argue that wealthy men have abolished polygyny and instituted monogamy in order to placate poor men, who would be wifeless under polygyny. Although they posit different mechanisms for the emergence and the maintenance of monogamy, they all argue that democracy plays a crucial role. Under democracy, and with male universal suffrage, the wealthy political leaders (who are most likely to be polygynous) had to give up their privilege of having multiple wives in exchange for the votes of poor men, who would not vote for the wealthy polygynists if they themselves were left wifeless (Ridley 1993, 206–7). Thus, in this theory, monogamy is the compromise struck (if implicitly) between wealthy (more desirable) and poor (less desirable) men in the face of democracy and male universal suffrage. However, the male compromise theory "remains only a thesis" (Wright 1994, 98) and has not been tested empirically.

If monogamy replaces polygyny as a compromise among men in the face of democracy, then one can deduce the following hypothesis from the male compromise theory:

> *democracy hypothesis*: The level of democracy has a negative effect on the level of polygyny in society.

Interestingly, in 1903, decades before the birth of modern evolutionary biology, George Bernard Shaw succinctly captured its essence in his "Maxims for Revolutionists": "Any marriage system which condemns a majority of the population to celibacy will be violently wrecked on the pretext that it outrages morality. Polygamy, when tried under modern democratic conditions, as by the Mormons, is wrecked by the revolt of the mass of inferior men who are condemned to celibacy by it; for the maternal instinct leads a woman to prefer a tenth share in a first rate man to the exclusive possession of a third rate one" (Shaw 1957, 254).

The male compromise theory, however, encounters a minor logical problem: What about women? Mating is an instance of intersexual selection, in which a male and a female choose each other. In every species in which the female makes greater parental investment in the offspring than the male (such as human beings), however, the female is more choosy about mating (because she has more to lose by making a mistake), and therefore all mating decisions are essentially left up to the female (Trivers 1972). Mating becomes a female choice among these species. It therefore stands to reason that, among humans, women (or their families and clans) would exercise greater control than men over whether or not a given marriage takes place. In her analysis of 133 societies from the Human Relations Area File, Meredith Small (1992, 146, 148) notes that "often marriages are arranged, but there is no reason to assume that the interests of the females in an arranged marriage are necessarily different from the interests of the families involved. . . . Thus, 'arranged' does not necessarily mean the woman is forced or coerced." In his comparative study of human mating, David Buss (1994, 91) maintains that "even where matings are arranged by parents and kin, . . . women often exert considerable influence over their sexual and marital decisions by manipulating their parents, carrying on clandestine affairs, defying their parents' wishes, and sometimes eloping." Furthermore, the genetic interest of the woman's male kin (her father and brothers) is largely (although not entirely) coincident with the woman's own genetic interest.

There is another problem with the male compromise theory. Although in general polygyny favors women and hurts men, the sons of wealthy political leaders are the few men who would benefit from polygyny (because they would inherit their fathers' wealth and power and be more likely to be polygynous). It therefore seems unlikely, given the principles of evolutionary biology, that the wealthy political leaders would diminish their own and their sons' evolutionary prospects by substituting monogamy for polygyny, especially given that wealthy political leaders are likely to have more sons than daughters (Betzig and Weber 1995).[8]

## An Alternative Theory: Monogamy As a Female Choice

In response to the male compromise theory, we present a theory of marriage norms as the outcome of choices made by women in the face of varying degrees of resource inequality among men.[9] We concur with Gary Becker (1974), Amyra Grossbard (1978), Matt Ridley (1993), and Wright (1994) that most women are materially better off under polygyny than under monogamy. However, there is one important scope condition for this statement, which remains implicit in the male compromise theory, and that is resource inequality among men. Women benefit from polygyny only when there is extreme resource inequality among men. To use Shaw's colorful language, women should prefer to marry polygynously only if "a tenth share in a first rate man" is greater than "the exclusive possession of the third rate one"—in other words, only if the first-rate man is more than ten times as desirable or wealthy as the third-rate one. If not, then a woman is better off marrying the third-rate man monogamously than marrying the first-rate one polygynously.

Assume that there are no norms concerning marriage in the form of a socially prescribed system of mating and that a woman who is contemplating marriage can choose to marry polygynously and become the second or third wife of a wealthy man or marry monogamously and become the first and sole wife of a less wealthy man. Most women will choose to marry polygynously if there is great resource inequality among men, and they will choose to marry monogamously if there is less resource inequality among men. If most women in society choose to marry polygynously, then the society will have de facto polygyny as the statistical, and hence social, norm. If most women in society choose to marry monogamously, then the society will have de facto monogamy. We therefore propose our first hypothesis, the inequality hypothesis.

> *inequality hypothesis*: The extent of resource inequality among men has a positive effect on the level of polygyny in society (Grossbard 1980, proposition 5, 329–30).

In essence, our inequality hypothesis is an extension to human society of the polygyny threshold model in biology, originally formulated to explain the breeding systems of avian species (Davies 1989; Orians 1969; Searcy and Yasukawa 1989; Verner 1964; Verner and Willson 1966). The polygyny threshold model (PTM) predicts that polygynous breeding systems are more likely to occur when males are heterogeneous in the quality of their territories. The difference between the territorial quality of a polygynous male and that of a monogamous male—a "premium" that allows a male bird to become polygynous—is called the polygyny threshold. The PTM has previously been applied to a human society (Borgerhoff Mulder 1990).

Furthermore, if a society's level of polygyny is the outcome of a large number of women having made their own marriage decisions, then it will also be a function of how much power women have over their own marriages. Specifically, increasing women's power will result in more polygynous marriages if men's resource inequality is great, but it will result in more monogamous marriages if men's resource inequality is small. In the face of extreme resource inequality among men, more powerful women will choose to marry polygynously; in the face of less resource inequality among men, the same women will choose to marry monogamously. We thus propose our second hypothesis, the female power hypothesis.

> *female power hypothesis*: The extent of resource inequality among men and the level of women's power have a positive interaction effect on the level of polygyny in society.

Unlike the proponents of the male compromise theory, who believe that norms are imposed on society from the top down by its political leaders, we believe that norms emerge spontaneously, from the bottom up, as an aggregation of individual choices among a large number of people in society. Figure 9.2 represents our theory of the marriage norms in a micro-

FIGURE 9.2    *Micro-Macro Model of the Emergence of Marriage Norms*

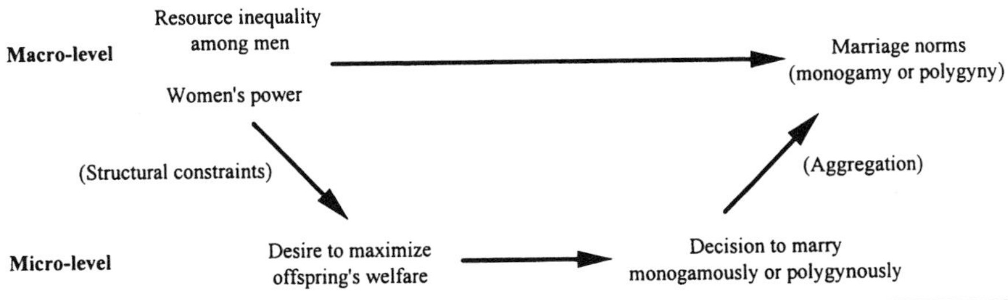

*Source:* Authors' compilation.

macro model ("the Coleman boat") (Coleman 1990, 1–23; Hechter and Kanazawa 1997). At the macro level, the society has given levels of resource inequality among men and of women's power, both of which are exogenous to the model. These macrostructural factors set constraints within which women must make their decisions. At the micro level, women, having the evolved psychological mechanism that compels them to maximize the welfare of their offspring, choose to marry either monogamously or polygynously, depending upon the societal conditions (set by the two macro exogenous factors). Separate and independent individual decisions of thousands or millions of women to marry either monogamously or polygynously will aggregate at the societal level to a particular type of marriage norm (prescribing either monogamy or polygyny). Of course, once the norm is in place, it will independently affect the future marriage choices of women. Our theory explains only the original emergence of the marriage norm and its subsequent gradual change.

Our theory therefore explains the historical shift from polygyny to monogamy as a function of resource inequality among men (which remains exogenous to our theory). As men have become more equal in their wealth and status over time, more women have chosen to marry monogamously because it was more beneficial for them to do so. The separate and independent decisions of a large number of women to marry monogamously rather than polygynously have brought about the change in the marriage norm from polygyny to monogamy.

## Computer Simulations

We conducted computer simulations to test the logical consistency of our theory of marriage norms, to ascertain whether the assumptions of our theory logically imply our hypotheses. The initial assumptions for the simulations are as follows:

1.  The society consists of $m$ men and $f$ women. (always $m = f$)

2.  There are $r$ resources distributed among $m$ men. The society has a level of resource inequality measured by the Gini coefficient $G = \frac{1}{2 \times m \times (m-1) \times \bar{x}} \sum_{i=1}^{m} \sum_{j=1}^{m} |x_i - x_j|$, where $x_i$ is the number of resources $i$ possesses ($\sum x_i = r$) (Foster 1985, 61–65). $G = 0.0$ indicates perfect equality (each man possesses the same amount of resources $r/m$), and $G = 1.0$ indicates maximum inequality (one man possesses all resources, $r$, in society).

3.  A woman randomly meets $k$ men and marries the one who has the greatest amount of resources. The resources of man $i$ is $x_i$ if he is not already married and $x_j/(w + 1)$ if he is already married and has $w$ wives. (In other words, a woman decides whom to marry regardless of whether the man is already married; she does so strictly on the basis of how many resources he will have available to her subsequent to her marriage to him.)

4.  The simulation ends when all women are married.

Figures 9.3 through 9.7 show the relation between resource inequality (measured by the Gini coefficient) and the proportion of all marriages that are polygynous. (The simulation results presented here assume that $m = f = 500$ and $r = 10,000$, but the basic results are robust across all levels of $m = f$ and $r$.) As the first four figures show, there is a clear positive relation between resource inequality and the extent of polygyny in society. The greater the resource inequality among men, the more polygynous the society. This relation confirms the internal logical consistency of our inequality hypothesis.

Figure 9.7 shows what happens when women do not make their marriage decisions on the basis of how many resources men have. As might be expected, the proportion of marriages that are polygynous remains around 37 percent regardless of the extent of resource inequality among men if women choose men randomly with respect to their resources. The figure indicates that the behavioral assumption of resource maximization that we posit for women in our computer simulations is integral to the relation between resource inequality and polygyny.[10]

Furthermore, the positive relation between inequality and polygyny is stronger as $k$ (the number of men a woman meets) becomes larger. When $k = 2$ (women randomly meet two men who are potential mates), the proportion of marriages that are polygynous ranges roughly from 24 percent (when $G = 0.0$) to 42 percent (when $G = 1.0$). However, when $k = 25$ (women randomly meet twenty-five men who are potential mates), the same proportion increases roughly from 3 percent (when $G = 0.0$) to 85

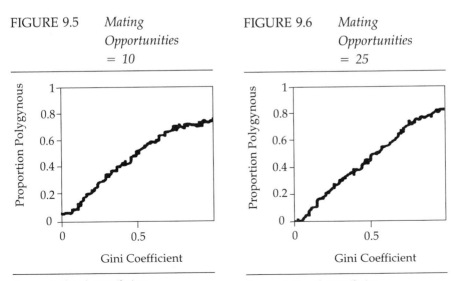

FIGURE 9.3    *Mating Opportunities = 2*

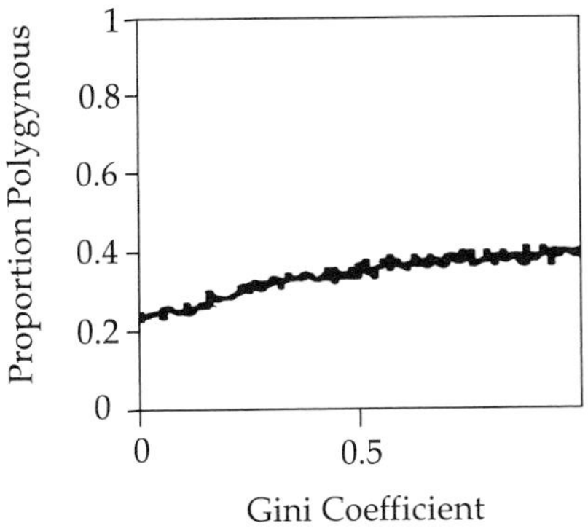

FIGURE 9.4    *Mating Opportunities = 4*

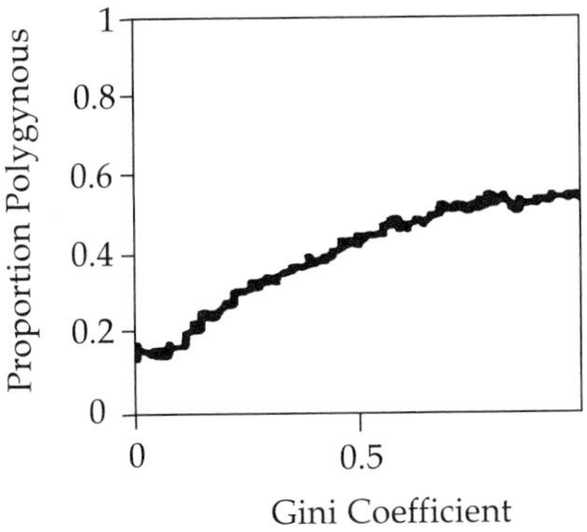

*Source:* Authors' compilation.

*Source:* Authors' compilation.

percent (when $G = 1.0$). There is, therefore, a clear positive interaction effect between $G$ and $k$ on polygyny. If we assume that the number of marriage opportunities a woman has generally increases with women's power in society, then our simulations also confirm the logical consistency of our female power hypothesis.

Our computer simulations therefore demonstrate that our alternative theory of marriage norms has internal logical consistency in that our as

FIGURE 9.5    *Mating Opportunities = 10*

FIGURE 9.6    *Mating Opportunities = 25*

*Source:* Authors' compilation.

*Source:* Authors' compilation.

FIGURE 9.7     *Random Mating*

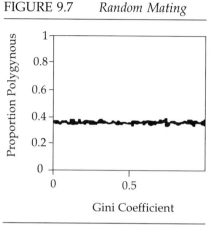

*Source:* Authors' compilation.

sumptions logically imply our hypotheses. We have yet to see, however, whether the empirical data actually support our theory.

## Empirical Tests

We test the two competing theories of marriage norms (the male compromise theory and our alternative female choice theory) with international data. Because species-typical evolved psychological mechanisms form the microfoundations of all evolutionary psychological theories of norm emergence, they are best tested with cross-cultural data to see whether the hypotheses hold in all human societies. We have compiled the data from various published sources, and they cover 127 countries (although because of missing data and listwise deletion, all hypotheses are tested with smaller samples).

### Dependent Variable

To measure the level of polygyny for each *country*, we first determine the level of polygyny for each *ethnic and cultural group* within the country. The *Encyclopedia of World Cultures* (Levinson 1991–1995) contains detailed descriptions of social and cultural practices of all known cultural groups in the world. Their marriage systems are coded on the following four-point scale.

   0: Monogamy is the rule and is widespread

   1: Monogamy is the rule but some polygyny occurs

   2: Polygyny is the rule or cultural ideal but is limited in practice

   3: Polygyny is the rule and is widespread

This scale is similar to the five-point scale that was proposed by Douglas White (1988) and is commonly used in cultural anthropology (White and Burton 1988). Unlike Betzig's (1982) four-point scale, which measures the extent of polygyny among political leaders, our scale (like White's) measures the practice of polygyny among the general populace.

We then multiply the score for each cultural group by its relative size within the population of the country. The weighted sum of such scores is the polygyny score for that country. For instance, in Turkey, there are two ethnic groups: the Turks and the Kurds. According to the *Encyclopedia of World Cultures,* the Turks are strictly monogamous (polygyny score of 0), whereas among the Kurds polygyny is the rule, even though its practice is limited (polygyny score of 2) (9: 375, 176). The Turks represent 80 percent of the population in Turkey, and the Kurds the remaining 20 percent (World Almanac 1996). Thus we compute the polygyny score for the country of Turkey: $0 \times .80 + 2 \times .20 = .40$ (on the scale of 0 to 3.00).

We fully realize that this weighting procedure inadvertently transforms the original four-point ordinal scale into an interval scale. However, given that all of our independent variables are available only for countries, not for ethnic or cultural groups, we have to use countries, not ethnic or cultural groups, as statistical cases and therefore need a means to compute the polygyny score for each country. We believe our weighting procedure represents the best compromise, because using the unweighted scores for the ethnic and cultural groups is not an option.

## Independent Variables

*Democracy*   We use Kenneth Bollen's (1980, 1993) index of political democracy as the measure of the level of democracy in a country. Bollen performs a confirmatory factor analysis to derive the index from many empirical indicators for a large number of countries at three points in time: 1960, 1965, 1980. We use all three indices to test the democracy hypothesis from the male compromise theory. Bollen's index of political democracy is widely used in political science and sociology as a valid and reliable measure of democracy (Simpson 1990; Muller 1995). The index varies from 0 (complete authoritarianism) to 100 (complete democracy).

*Resource Inequality*   We use four different measures of resource inequality: personal Gini, the Gini coefficient of income inequality among individuals or households (World Bank 1997b, table 2.6); sectoral Gini, the Gini coefficient that measures the inequality of economic productivity across three large economic sectors (agricultural, industrial, and service) (Taylor and Jodice 1983, table 4.2);[11] the percentage share of income or consumption of the top 10 percent (World Bank 1997a, table 5); and the percentage share of income or consumption of the top 20 percent (World Bank 1997a, table 5).

*Women's Power*   We use two disparate indicators of women's power in society: the percentage of female pupils in secondary schools (World Bank 1997b, table 2.10); and the percentage of women who marry after the age of twenty (United Nations 1997, table 26). Education, especially in less developed countries, enhances women's ability to exercise their rights and responsibilities (King and Hill 1993, 27–29) and thereby increases their power. Abdelrahman Ibrahim Abdelrahman's (1991) study suggests that more-educated women in Sudan exert greater control over the timing of their marriages, their choice of spouse, and the locations of postnuptial residence. Bhanu Niraula and Philip Morgan (1994) demonstrate that women's education increases their autonomy in one village in Nepal. As for the second indicator, we assume that women who marry at an older age exercise greater control over their marriage decisions than child or teenage brides. Thus the proportion of women in society who postpone marriage until they reach adulthood measures women's power over their decisions regarding choice of spouse, the timing of marriage, and other circumstances surrounding their marriage.

## Control Variables

*Economic Development*   It is well known that the level of economic development has a curvilinear (inverted-U) relations with the extent of income inequality (Kuznets 1955). We therefore control for the level of economic development (measured by gross domestic product [GDP] per capita [World Almanac 1996]) in our equations to control for the effect of this confound. To capture the curvilinear relation between economic development and income inequality, we enter both GDP per capita and GDP per capita squared.

*Sex Ratio*   Marcia Guttentag and Paul Secord (1983) observe that the society's sex ratio has profound effects on numerous aspects of interaction between men and women, and Scott South and Katherine Trent's (1988) empirical test in a cross-national analysis confirms the Guttentag-Secord theory. We therefore include a measure of a country's sex ratio in the equations as well. Following South and Trent, we use the ratio of men between the ages of fifteen and forty-nine to women of the same cohort for the measure of sex ratio.

## Results

Table 9.1 presents the results of regression analysis to determine the relative effects of democracy and resource inequality on polygyny. Because there are three measures of democracy and four measures of resource in-

TABLE 9.1    *The Effects of Democracy and Inequality on Polygyny*

| | Measures of Inequality | | | |
|---|---|---|---|---|
| | Personal Gini (1) | Sectoral Gini (2) | Top 10 Percent (3) | Top 20 Percent (4) |
| **Democracy 1960** | | | | |
| Constant | 9.2404 | 3.4334 | 7.5806 | 7.2214 |
| Democracy | .0021 | $4.6360^{-4}$ | .0023 | .0022 |
| | (.0048) | (.0036) | (.0031) | (.0031) |
| Inequality | .0210† | .0211*** | .0372*** | .0353*** |
| | (.0116) | (.0060) | (.0100) | (.0098) |
| Economic Development | $-4.6283^{-4}$* | $-4.4274^{-5}$ | $-1.4793^{-4}$*** | $-1.4729^{-4}$*** |
| | $(1.9693^{-4})$ | $(4.4500^{-5})$ | $(4.4222^{-5})$ | $(4.5551^{-5})$ |
| (Economic Development)$^2$ | $4.4931^{-8}$† | $3.6591^{-10}$ | $4.9871^{-9}$* | $4.8969^{-9}$* |
| | $(2.4767^{-8})$ | $(2.0222^{-9})$ | $(2.0891^{-9})$ | $(2.0975^{-9})$ |
| Sex Ratio | $-8.3888$* | $-2.7968$ | $-7.4828$** | $-7.5935$** |
| | (3.1623) | (1.9407) | (2.6540) | (2.6647) |
| $R^2$ | .4143 | .3871 | .5021 | .4971 |
| N | 54 | 84 | 81 | 81 |
| **Democracy 1965** | | | | |
| Constant | 9.1862 | 3.7054 | 7.0836 | 6.7060 |
| Democracy | $-.0028$ | $-.0022$ | .0019 | .0017 |
| | (.0047) | (.0036) | (.0033) | (.0033) |
| Inequality | .0252* | .0169** | .0354** | .0333** |
| | (.0109) | (.0060) | (.0109) | (.0107) |
| Economic Development | $-5.4182^{-4}$*** | $-3.2313^{-5}$ | $-1.2248^{-4}$* | $-1.2034^{-4}$* |
| | $(1.8525^{-4})$ | $(4.6992^{-5})$ | $(4.7431^{-5})$ | $(4.7704^{-5})$ |
| (Economic Development)$^2$ | $5.3895^{-8}$* | $-2.7632^{-10}$ | $3.7395^{-9}$† | $3.5926^{-9}$ |
| | $(2.3855^{-8})$ | $(2.1237^{-9})$ | $(2.2252^{-9})$ | $(2.2325^{-9})$ |
| Sex Ratio | $-8.1495$* | $-2.7540$ | $-6.9108$* | $-6.9712$* |
| | (3.0796) | (2.0093) | (2.8524) | (2.8656) |
| $R^2$ | .4150 | .3539 | .4151 | .4094 |
| N | 58 | 91 | 87 | 87 |
| **Democracy 1980** | | | | |
| Constant | 9.5525 | 2.5713 | 7.9681 | 7.5315 |
| Democracy | $-5.8191^{-4}$ | .0014 | .0057† | .0055† |
| | (.0035) | (.0029) | (.0029) | (.0029) |
| Inequality | .0145 | .0214*** | .0316** | .0299** |
| | (.0095) | (.0057) | (.0107) | (.0104) |
| Economic Development | $-5.6017^{-4}$*** | $-5.7035^{-5}$ | $-1.1645^{-4}$* | $-1.1578^{-4}$* |
| | $(1.6389^{-4})$ | $(4.4588^{-5})$ | $(4.6925^{-5})$ | $(4.7050^{-5})$ |
| (Economic Development)$^2$ | $5.4908^{-8}$* | $4.7286^{-10}$ | $2.5943^{-9}$ | $2.5313^{-9}$ |
| | $(2.1582^{-8})$ | $(2.0249^{-9})$ | $(2.2047^{-9})$ | $(2.2086^{-9})$ |
| Sex Ratio | $-8.1207$** | $-1.8199$ | $-7.7169$** | $-7.6775$** |
| | (3.0247) | (1.6861) | (2.8536) | (2.8665) |
| $R^2$ | .4247 | .3848 | .4153 | .4128 |
| N | 62 | 102 | 93 | 93 |

*Source:* Authors' compilation.
*Note:* Standard errors are in parentheses.
†$p < .10$  *$p < .05$  **$p < .01$  ***$p < .001$  ****$p < .0001$

equality, we estimate twelve separate equations to test the democracy and inequality hypotheses.

In none of the equations is the effect of democracy on polygyny significantly negative (as predicted by the male compromise theory)—that is, the democracy hypothesis is supported by none of the twelve tests. Interestingly, in two of the twelve tests, the effect of democracy is significantly positive, contrary to the prediction of the male compromise theory (1980, "top 10 percent" and "top 20 percent").

In contrast, the inequality hypothesis is supported in eleven of the twelve tests. When the measure of democracy is taken in 1980 and the measure of inequality is personal Gini, the effect of inequality has the right sign but is nonsignificant ($p = .1334$) (1980, personal Gini). In all other cases, however, the level of resource inequality significantly (often at the level of $p < .001$) increases the level of polygyny, even when we control for economic development and sex ratio. As our female choice theory predicts, the greater the resource inequality among men, the more polygynous the society.

Table 9.2 presents the results of our test of the female power hypothesis. Although both inequality and women's power appear in the equations as main terms (along with controls for economic development and sex ratio), the crucial test of the hypothesis is in the coefficient for the interaction term; the hypothesis predicts a significantly positive interaction effect of inequality and women's power on polygyny. The results indicate that the female power hypothesis is supported in seven of the eight tests. When the measure of women's power is the proportion of women who marry after the age of twenty and the measure of inequality is personal Gini, the coefficient for the interaction term is positive but nonsignificant ($p = .1045$). However, in all other cases, the interaction effects are significantly positive, as predicted by our female power hypothesis. It appears that, regardless of the measures of female power and resource inequality among men, increasing women's power increases polygyny in the face of greater resource inequality (when it benefits women to marry polygynously). However, increasing women's power decreases polygyny (and increases monogamy) in the face of relative resource equality (when it benefits women to marry monogamously). These findings are consistent with our prediction that women choose to marry polygynously or monogamously depending upon which choice most benefits them and their offspring.

## Summary

Why do some societies practice monogamy while others practice polygyny? Various scholars argue that monogamy emerges as a compromise between powerful, wealthy men and powerless, poor men whereby the former give up their multiple wives in exchange for the votes of the latter,

TABLE 9.2    *The Interactive Effect of Women's Power and Inequality on Polygyny*

| | Measures of Inequality | | | |
|---|---|---|---|---|
| | Personal Gini (1) | Sectoral Gini (2) | Top 10 Percent (3) | Top 20 Percent (4) |
| **Percentage female among secondary school pupils** | | | | |
| Constant | 11.0792 | 3.2743 | 8.1607 | 8.8873 |
| Inequality | $-.0796^{\dagger}$ | $-.0539^{*}$ | $-.0484$ | $-.0473$ |
| | (.0455) | (.0268) | (.0524) | (.0497) |
| Women's power | $-.0782^{\dagger}$ | $-.0466^{*}$ | $-.0691^{\dagger}$ | $-.0930^{\dagger}$ |
| | (.0390) | (.0225) | (.0361) | (.0493) |
| Interaction | $.0021^{*}$ | $.0018^{**}$ | $.0018^{\dagger}$ | $.0017^{\dagger}$ |
| | $(9.1162^{-4})$ | $(5.9518^{-4})$ | (.0011) | (.0010) |
| Economic development | $-5.2429^{-4**}$ | $-6.2755^{-5}$ | $-1.3216^{-4*}$ | $-1.3185^{-4*}$ |
| | $(1.8114^{-4})$ | $(4.7623^{-5})$ | $(5.0193^{-5})$ | $(5.0330^{-5})$ |
| (Economic development)$^2$ | $5.0464^{-8*}$ | $1.5645^{-9}$ | $4.6587^{-9*}$ | $4.5391^{-9*}$ |
| | $(2.2683^{-8})$ | $(2.1724^{-9})$ | $(2.2612^{-9})$ | $(2.2667^{-9})$ |
| Sex ratio | $-6.1628^{*}$ | $-.4985$ | $-4.7231^{*}$ | $-4.7631^{*}$ |
| | (2.3326) | (.8522) | (1.9263) | (1.9353) |
| $R^2$ | .4577 | .4603 | .5003 | .4973 |
| N | 60 | 91 | 88 | 88 |
| **Percentage female who marry after age twenty** | | | | |
| Constant | 7.0393 | 5.1586 | 4.3293 | 5.2825 |
| Inequality | $-.1078$ | $-.1103^{*}$ | $-.1000$ | $-.0930$ |
| | (.0802) | (.0461) | (.0803) | (.0762) |
| Women's Power | $-.0632$ | $-.0642^{*}$ | $-.0605^{\dagger}$ | $-.0802^{\dagger}$ |
| | (.0371) | (.0256) | (.0311) | (.0424) |
| Interaction | $.0016$ | $.0015^{**}$ | $.0016^{\dagger}$ | $.0015^{\dagger}$ |
| | $(9.2928^{-4})$ | $(5.3219^{-4})$ | $(9.2655^{-4})$ | $(8.7794^{-4})$ |
| Economic Development | $-6.2661^{-4***}$ | $-6.7296^{-5}$ | $-1.6172^{-4***}$ | $-1.6354^{-4***}$ |
| | $(2.0255^{-4})$ | $(5.9123^{-5})$ | $(5.3749^{-5})$ | $(5.3440^{-5})$ |
| (Economic development)$^2$ | $5.7774^{-8*}$ | $2.6694^{-9}$ | $6.1065^{-9**}$ | $6.0657^{-9**}$ |
| | $(2.4974^{-8})$ | $(2.2434^{-9})$ | $(2.2370^{-9})$ | $(2.2290^{-9})$ |
| Sex Ratio | $-.5273$ | $1.1206$ | $1.0302$ | $1.2759$ |
| | (2.9215) | (1.1614) | (2.2859) | (2.2775) |
| $R^2$ | .6823 | .5743 | .6045 | .6078 |
| N | 31 | 56 | 55 | 55 |

*Source:* Authors' compilation.
*Note:* Standard errors are in parentheses.
$^{\dagger}p < .10$ $^{*}p < .05$ $^{**}p < .01$ $^{***}p < .001$ $^{****}p < .0001$

and the latter give political support for the former in exchange for the guarantee of the opportunity to marry (Alexander 1987; Alexander et al. 1979; Betzig 1986; MacDonald 1990). Our analysis of cross-cultural data from 127 countries contradicts their theory, indicating that the level of democracy has no effect at all on the level of polygyny in society.

Although we concur with the proponents of the male compromise theory that polygyny is materially beneficial to most women, we point out that this is true only if there is extreme resource inequality among men. We posit that, consistent with the pattern observed among other species in which the female makes a greater parental investment in the offspring than the male, women should be able to choose how they marry, whether polygynously or monogamously. Furthermore, given their interest in their children's welfare, our model predicts that women will choose to marry polygynously if there is extreme resource inequality among men but will choose to marry monogamously if men's resources are distributed more or less equally. Marriage norms at the societal level should be allowed to emerge spontaneously as the aggregate phenomenon resulting from the millions of individual decisions that women make at the individual level (following the course presented in figure 9.2). Our theory explains the historical change in marriage norms from polygyny to monogamy as a function of resource inequality among men. As men became more equal over the course of history, more women chose to marry monogamously, and monogamy emerged as the predominant norm. Our analysis supports the two hypotheses from our female choice theory of the emergence of marriage norms.

Our computer simulations provide strong support for the logical consistency of the theory, though our empirical tests of the hypotheses are at best approximate, in that the hypothesized mechanism behind the emergence of the norm is at the micro level, whereas the data we use to test the hypotheses are at the macro level. Our data analysis merely shows that more women marry polygynously when there is more resource inequality among men, but it does not conclusively demonstrate that, consistent with the behavioral assumptions, it is indeed the resourceful men who take multiple wives in societies characterized by greater inequality. However, Grossbard's (1976) study of marriage in Nigeria, which shows wealthier men of higher status having more wives than less wealthy men of lower status, and Monique Borgerhoff Mulder's (1990) similar study of Kipsigis women in Kenya provide empirical support for the microfoundation of our theory. Our aggregate data are consistent with the macro-level implications of our micro-level mechanism. Nevertheless, an empirical test of our theory at the micro level in cross-cultural settings, with data that are presently nonexistent, is certainly necessary.

Our female choice theory can potentially solve one empirical puzzle:

Why is it that there appears to be a negative correlation between polygyny and women's status across societies? Why is it that polygyny seems to occur in societies (mostly in Africa and the Middle East) in which the status of women is low? We speculate that the negative correlation between polygyny and women's status might be spurious, created by an antecedent variable that might be called Western egalitarianism (see figure 9.8). Western egalitarianism simultaneously posits that all men are and ought to be equal and that men and women are and ought to be equal. The former tenent, equity among men, should function to reduce extreme resource inequalities among men, and the latter tenent, equality between men and women, should function to elevate the status of women in society. If our female choice theory of marriage norms is correct, as our initial data analyses seem to indicate, then the former should reduce the extent of polygyny among societies that exhibit such Western egalitarianism and therefore create a spurious negative correlation between polygyny and women's status in society.

## Conclusion

Although we contend that norms emerge from universal human nature, the evolutionary psychological theory of norms does not predict that the same norms will emerge in every society. As Cosmides and Tooby's (1992) work on cooperative food sharing and our analysis of marriage norms (Kanazawa and Still 1999) illustrate, the universal human nature and psychological mechanisms are differentially triggered to form evoked cultures. The psychological mechanisms at the individual level interact with the local environments and structures to produce different norms in different societies.

We have introduced in this chapter a distinction between moral norms and coercive norms. By its very nature, the evolutionary psychological theory can only explain the emergence of moral norms but not of coercive norms. However, we contend that moral norms are more significant in their consequences and are therefore important to explain. Furthermore, as the examples of speeding and tax evasion demonstrate, all norms might ultimately be moral norms. What necessitates the coercive norms of speed limits or tax contribution is fairness. There is little damage done to society if only a few people are allowed to drive as fast as they want (while everyone else obeys the posted speed limits) or if only a few people are absolved from their duty to pay taxes (while all others pay their share). These specific coercive norms therefore ultimately derive from the moral metanorm of fairness, and it is our contention that evolutionary psychology provides a useful means of explaining the emergence of moral norms.

FIGURE 9.8   *How There Might Be a Spurious Negative Relationship Between Polygyny and Women's Status*

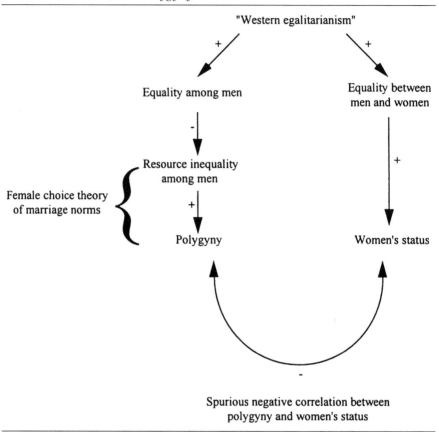

Spurious negative correlation between
polygyny and women's status

*Source:* Authors' compilation.

# Notes

1. Excellent introductions to evolutionary psychology include Barkow, Cosmides, and Tooby 1992; Buss 1994, 1995, 1999; Ridley 1993; and Wright 1994.

2. As a first approximation, it might be useful to think of the EEA as the African savanna during the Pleistocene epoch, because this is indeed where many psychological mechanisms evolved. Technically, however, the EEA "is not a place or a habitat, or even a time period. Rather, it is a statistical composite of the adaptation-relevant properties of the ancestral environments encountered by members of ancestral populations, weighted by their frequency and fitness-consequences" (Tooby and Cosmides 1990, 386–87). In other words, the EEA might be different for different adaptations.

For instance, to pinpoint the EEA for male sexual jealousy as an adaptation, we need to consider the entire period of evolution from the time when males did not have sexual jealousy (this is likely to be long before they were human) until the time when all human males had the psychological mechanism of sexual jealousy that they currently possess. This is likely the period during which cuckoldry was a problem for paternal certainty. Furthermore, we must emphasize the period during which cuckoldry was more prevalent (weight by frequency) and during which males with sexual jealousy had particularly greater reproductive success than those without it (weight by fitness consequences).

3. Although the naïve version of group selection theory (Wynne-Edwards 1962) has been thoroughly discredited within evolutionary biology (Williams 1966), the sophisticated version of group selection theory known as the multilevel selection theory (Sober and Wilson 1998; Wilson and Sober 1994) solves all of the logical problems of the earlier version and demonstrates that altruistic traits can evolve because they benefit the group even at the cost to individuals. A recent special issue of *Human Nature* (Boehm 1999) is devoted to the multilevel selection theory, and so far the reaction of the evolutionary biologists in general to the multilevel selection theory has been mostly positive. Even a critic of Sober and Wilson (1998) had to admit that the theory is "coherent and powerful" and "has the potential to unify all of evolutionary biology under a single conceptual framework" (Smuts 1999, 324).

4. While speeding and tax evasion are examples of violations of coercive norms, selective enforcement of these norms (whereby some people are caught speeding or evading taxes while others get away with it) violates a moral metanorm of fairness. Because fairness is a moral norm, its violation can elicit moral outrage. Note, however, that it is not speeding or tax evasion per se that elicits outrage but the selective enforcement or unfairness.

5. This section draws on Kanazawa and Still 1999.

6. Monogamy is the marriage of one man to one woman. Polygyny is the marriage of one man to more than one woman, while polyandry is the marriage of one woman to more than one man. Polygamy (although it is often used synonymously with polygyny) refers to both polygyny and polyandry. Evolutionary hypotheses predict that polyandry will be rare unless the cohusbands are brothers (because men would not invest in children when paternal uncertainty is very high as in the case of polyandry), and cross-cultural evidence indeed shows that nonfraternal polyandry is virtually nonexistent. We therefore treat monogamy and polygyny as the two possible marriage norms.

7. Evolutionary considerations (such as resources and physical attractiveness) serve as the ultimate causes, whose effects on behavior (mate selection) are mediated by proximate causes (love, desire, and other emotions). Human actors believe that they are choosing to mate with the ones they love and desire, not the ones with characteristics that increase their reproductive success (measured by the number of grandchildren). Human actors are not usually conscious of the evolutionary logic behind their emotions. The strength of evolutionary psychology is that it can predict from the ultimate causes those whom human actors are likely to love and find desirable.

8. Robert Trivers and Dan Willard (1973) were the first to propose that wealthy families prefer sons over daughters and poor families prefer daughters over sons in their parental investment. This is because sons from wealthy families

are expected to have greater reproductive success than their sisters (because the sons' reproductive success is largely determined by their wealth and status, which they normally inherit from their families) and because daughters from poor families are similarly expected to have greater reproductive success than their brothers (because the daughters' reproductive success is largely determined by their youth and physical attractiveness, which are distributed more or less orthogonally to class). The Trivers-Willard hypothesis has been supported by a large number of empirical studies on societies across history and throughout the world, including the contemporary United States (Gaulin and Robbins 1991; Betzig and Weber 1995). See Cronk 1991, table 9, for a comprehensive review of the empirical support for the Trivers-Willard hypothesis.

9. Although our theory seeks to explain the emergence of marriage norms, there is some question as to whether individuals in modern society with the norm of monogamy are truly monogamous in their individual mating behavior. Liberal divorce laws allow wealthy men to practice serial polygyny, in which a man leaves his wife when she passes her reproductive prime and marries a younger woman who is in her reproductive prime. By allowing the same men to monopolize the supply of women (not simultaneously but sequentially), liberal divorce laws hurt the reproductive interests of both poor men (whose marital options within their own age cohort are thus limited) and older women (who must often raise their children alone after the divorce).

   Further complicating the matter, monogamous *marriage* can coexist with polygynous *mating* through adultery, concubinage, and other extrainstitutional forms of mating. For instance, Betzig (1986) notes that even despotic rulers with hundreds of concubines in their harems often had only one legitimate wife and were therefore married monogamously. However, it is the contention of our bottom-up theory of norm emergence and change that, if a sufficient number of women choose to mate polygynously within the monogamous society, then the marriage norm will gradually shift to reflect and accommodate the individual behavior.

10. The condition of random mating on the part of women with $k > 2$ (that is, they have multiple choices of mates) is logically equivalent to the condition of women pursuing men with the largest number of resources when $k = 1$ (that is, they have only one man to "choose" from; in other words, when women have no choice). Thus we might alternatively argue that the assumption of female choice is integral to the relation between resource inequality and polygyny.

11. The sectoral Gini is a far cruder measure of resource inequality among men than the personal Gini, but it has the advantage of being available for a larger number of countries. Its use therefore allows us to include many more countries in our analysis.

# References

Abdelrahman, Abdelrahman Ibrahim. 1991. "Marriage Patterns, Trends, and Timing in Urban Khartoum, 1940–1975: Theory and Evidence." *Journal of Family History* 16(2): 177–90.

Alexander, Richard D. 1987. *The Biology of Moral Systems.* New York: Aldine de Gruyter.

Alexander, Richard D., John L. Hoogland, Richard D. Howard, Katharine M. Noonan, and Paul W. Sherman. 1979. "Sexual Dimorphisms and Breeding Systems in Pinnipeds, Ungulates, Primates, and Humans." In *Evolutionary Biology and Human Social Behavior: An Anthropological Perspective*, edited by Napoleon A. Chagnon and William Irons. North Scituate, Mass.: Duxbury Press.

Barkow, Jerome H., Leda Cosmides, and John Tooby, eds. 1992. *The Adapted Mind: Evolutionary Psychology and the Generation of Culture.* New York: Oxford University Press.

Becker, Gary S. 1974. "A Theory of Marriage: Part 2." *Journal of Political Economy* 82(2): S11–S26.

Betzig, Laura. 1982. "Despotism and Differential Reproduction: A Cross-Cultural Correlation of Conflict Asymmetry, Hierarchy, and Degree of Polygyny." *Ethology and Sociobiology* 3: 209–21.

———. 1986. *Despotism and Differential Reproduction: A Darwinian View of History.* New York: Aldine de Gruyter.

———. 1997. "People Are Animals." Introduction to *Human Nature: A Critical Reader*, edited by Laura Betzig. New York: Oxford University Press.

Betzig, Laura, and Samantha Weber. 1995. "Presidents Preferred Sons." *Politics and the Life Sciences* 14(1): 61–64.

Boehm, Christopher, ed. 1999. "Group Selection." Special Issue of *Human Nature* 10(3).

Bollen, Kenneth. 1980. "Issues in the Comparative Measurement of Political Democracy." *American Sociological Review* 45(3): 370–90.

———. 1993. "Liberal Democracy: Validity and Method Factors in Cross-National Measures." *American Journal of Political Science* 37(4): 1207–30.

Borgerhoff Mulder, Monique. 1990. "Kipsigis Women's Preference for Wealthy Men: Evidence for Female Choice in Mammals." *Behavioral Ecology and Sociobiology* 27(4): 255–64.

Bowlby, John. 1969. *Attachment and Loss.* Vol. 1, *Attachment.* New York: Basic Books.

Buss, David M. 1988. "From Vigilance to Violence: Tactics of Mate Retention." *Ethology and Sociobiology* 9(5): 291–317.

———. 1989. "Sex Differences in Human Mate Preferences: Evolutionary Hypotheses Tested in Thirty-seven Cultures." *Behavioral and Brain Sciences* 12(1): 1–49.

———. 1994. *The Evolution of Desire: Strategies of Human Mating.* New York: Basic Books.

———. 1995. "Evolutionary Psychology: A New Paradigm for Psychological Science." *Psychological Inquiry* 6(1): 1–30.

———. 1999. *Evolutionary Psychology: The New Science of the Mind.* Boston: Allyn and Bacon.

Buss, David M., and Michael Barnes. 1986. "Preferences in Human Mate Selection." *Journal of Personality and Social Psychology* 50(3): 559–70.

Buss, David M., Randy J. Larsen, and Drew Westen. 1992. "Sex Differences in Jealousy: Evolution, Physiology, and Psychology." *Psychological Science* 3(4): 251–55.

Buss, David M., and Todd K. Shackelford. 1997. "From Vigilance to Violence: Mate Retention Tactics in Married Couples." *Journal of Personality and Social Psychology* 72(2): 346–61.

Buss, David M., Todd K. Shackelford, Lee A. Kirkpatrick, Jae C. Choe, Mariko Hasegawa, Toshikazu Hasegawa, and Kevin Bennett. 1999. "Jealousy and the Nature of Beliefs About Infidelity: Tests of Competing Hypotheses About Sex Differences in the United States, Korea, and Japan." *Personal Relationships* 6(1): 125–50.

Buunk, Bram, and Ralph B. Hupka. 1987. "Cross-Cultural Differences in the Elicitation of Sexual Jealousy." *Journal of Sex Research* 23(1): 12–22.

Cashdan, Elizabeth. 1989. "Hunters and Gatherers: Economic Behavior in Bands." In *Economic Anthropology*, edited by Stuart Plattner. Stanford, Calif.: Stanford University Press.

Coleman, James S. 1990. *Foundations of Social Theory.* Cambridge, Mass.: Harvard University Press.

Cosmides, Leda, and John Tooby. 1992. "Cognitive Adaptations for Social Exchange." In *The Adapted Mind: Evolutionary Psychology and the Generation of Culture*, edited by Jerome H. Barkow, Leda Cosmides, and John Tooby. New York: Oxford University Press.

Cronk, Lee. 1991. "Preferential Parental Investment in Daughters over Sons." *Human Nature* 2(4): 387–417.

Daly, Martin, and Margo Wilson. 1988. *Homicide.* New York: Aldine de Gruyter.

Daly, Martin, Margo Wilson, and Suzanne J. Weghorst. 1982. "Male Sexual Jealousy." *Ethology and Sociobiology* 3(1): 11–27.

Davies, N. B. 1989. "Sexual Conflict and the Polygamy Threshold." *Animal Behaviour* 38(August): 226–34.

De Waal, Frans. 1996. *Good Natured: The Origins of Right and Wrong in Humans and Other Animals.* Cambridge, Mass.: Harvard University Press.

Foster, James E. 1985. "Inequality Measurement." In vol. 33 of *Fair Allocation*, edited by H. Peyton Young. Providence, R.I.: American Mathematical Society.

Gaulin, Steven J. C., and Carole J. Robbins. 1991. "Trivers-Willard Effect in Contemporary North American Society." *American Journal of Physical Anthropology* 85(1): 61–69.

Grossbard, Amyra. 1976. "An Economic Analysis of Polygyny: The Case of Maiduguri." *Current Anthropology* 17: 701–7.

———. 1978. "Towards a Marriage Between Economics and Anthropology and a General Theory of Marriage." *American Economic Review* 68 (May): 33–37.

———. 1980. "The Economics of Polygamy." *Research in Population Economics* 2: 321–50.

Guttentag, Marcia, and Paul F. Secord. 1983. *Too Many Women? The Sex Ratio Question.* Beverly Hills, Calif.: Sage.

Hechter, Michael, and Satoshi Kanazawa. 1993. "Group Solidarity and Social Order in Japan." *Journal of Theoretical Politics* 5(4): 455–93.

———. 1997. "Sociological Rational Choice Theory." In vol. 23 of *Annual Review of Sociology*, edited by John Hagan. Palo Alto, Calif.: Annual Reviews.

Hill, Reuben. 1945. "Campus Values in Mate Selection." *Journal of Home Economics* 37(November): 554–58.

Homans, George C. 1950. *The Human Group.* New York: Harcourt, Brace & World.

Hudson, John W., and Lura F. Henze. 1969. "Campus Values in Mate Selection: A Replication." *Journal of Marriage and the Family* 31: 772–75.

Kanazawa, Satoshi. Forthcoming. "De Gustibus *Est* Disputandum." *Social Forces.*

Kanazawa, Satoshi, and Mary C. Still. 1999. "Why Monogamy?" *Social Forces* 78(1): 25–50.

———. 2000. "Why Men Commit Crimes (and Why They Desist)." *Sociological Theory* 18: 434–47.

King, Elizabeth M., and M. Anne Hill. 1993. *Women's Education in Developing Countries: Barriers, Benefits, and Policies.* Baltimore: Johns Hopkins University Press.

Knight, Jack. 1992. *Institutions and Social Conflict.* Cambridge: Cambridge University Press.

Kuznets, Simon. 1955. "Economic Growth and Income Inequality." *American Economic Review* 45(1): 1–28.

Levinson, David, ed. 1991–1995. *Encyclopedia of World Cultures.* 10 vols. Boston: G. K. Hall.

MacDonald, Kevin. 1990. "Mechanisms of Sexual Egalitarianism in Western Europe." *Ethology and Sociobiology* 11(3): 195–238.

Maryanski, Alexandra, and Jonathan H. Turner. 1992. *The Social Cage: Human Nature and the Evolution of Society.* Stanford, Calif.: Stanford University Press.

McGinnis, Robert. 1958. "Campus Values in Mate Selection: A Repeat Study." *Social Forces* 36: 368–73.

Miller, Alan S., and Satoshi Kanazawa. 2000. *Order by Accident: The Origins and Consequence of Conformity in Contemporary Japan.* Boulder, Colo.: Westview.

Muller, Edward N. 1995. "Economic Determinants of Democracy." *American Sociological Review* 60(6): 966–82.

Niraula, Bhanu B., and S. Philip Morgan. 1994. "Gender Inequality in Two Nepali Settings." Paper Presented to the International Union for the Scientific Study of Population(IUSSP), Seminar on Women, Poverty, and Demographic Change. Oaxaca, Mexico (October 25–28, 1994).

Orians, Gordon H. 1969. "On the Evolution of Mating Systems in Birds and Mammals." *American Naturalist* 103(934): 589–603.

Ridley, Matt. 1993. *The Red Queen: Sex and the Evolution of Human Nature.* New York: Penguin.

Searcy, William A., and Ken Yasukawa. 1989. "Alternative Models of Territorial Polygyny in Birds." *American Naturalist* 134(3): 323–43.

Shaw, Bernard. 1957. *Man and Superman.* New York: Penguin.

Simpson, Miles. 1990. "Political Rights and Income Inequality: A Cross-National Test." *American Sociological Review* 55(5): 682–93.

Small, Meredith F. 1992. "The Evolution of Female Sexuality and Mate Selection in Humans." *Human Nature* 3(2): 133–56.

Smuts, Barbara. 1999. "Multilevel Selection, Cooperation, and Altruism: Reflections on *Unto Others: The Evolution and Psychology of Unselfish Behavior.*" *Human Nature* 10(3): 311–27.

Sober, Elliott, and David Sloan Wilson. 1998. *Unto Others: The Evolution and Psychology of Unselfish Behavior.* Cambridge, U.K.: Cambridge University Press.

South, Scott J., and Katherine Trent. 1988. "Sex Ratios and Women's Roles: A Cross-National Analysis." *American Journal of Sociology* 93(5): 1096–115.

Sussman, Marvin B., and Suzanne K. Steinmetz, eds. 1987. *Handbook of Marriage and the Family.* New York: Plenum.

Taylor, Charles Lewis, and David A. Jodice. 1983. *World Handbook of Political and Social Indicators.* 3d ed. New Haven, Conn.: Yale University Press.

Thiessen, Del, and Yoko Umezawa. 1998. "The Sociobiology of Everyday Life: A New Look at a Very Old Novel." *Human Nature* 9(2): 293–320.

Tooby, John, and Leda Cosmides. 1989. "Evolutionary Psychology and the Generation of Culture." Pt. 1, "Theoretical Considerations." *Ethology and Sociobiology* 10(1–3): 29–49.

———. 1990. "The Past Explains the Present: Emotional Adaptations and the Structure of Ancestral Environments." *Ethology and Sociobiology* 11(4–5): 375–424.

Trivers, Robert L. 1971. "The Evolution of Reciprocal Altruism." *Quarterly Review of Biology* 46(March): 35–57.

———. 1972. "Parental Investment and Sexual Selection." In *Sexual Selection and the Descent of Man, 1871–1971,* edited by Bernard Campbell. Chicago: Aldine.

Trivers, Robert L., and Dan E. Willard. 1973. "Natural Selection of Parental Ability to Vary the Sex Ratio of Offspring." *Science* 179(January 5): 90–92.

United Nations. 1997. *Demographic Yearbook: 1995.* New York: United Nations.

van den Berghe, Pierre L. 1990. "From the Popocatepetl to the Limpopo." In *Authors of Their Own Lives: Intellectual Autobiographies by Twenty American Sociologists,* edited by Bennett M. Berger. Berkeley: University of California Press.

Verner, Jared. 1964. "Evolution of Polygamy in the Long-Billed Marsh Wren." *Evolution* 18(June): 252–61.

Verner, Jared, and Mary F. Willson. 1966. "The Influence of Habitats on Mating Systems of North American Passerine Birds." *Ecology* 47(1): 143–47.

Westermarck, Edward A. 1891. *The History of Human Marriage.* New York: Macmillan.

White, Douglas R. 1988. "Rethinking Polygyny: Co-Wives, Codes, and Cultural Systems." *Current Anthropology* 29(4): 529–58.

White, Douglas R., and Michael L. Burton. 1988. "Causes of Polygyny: Ecology, Economy, Kinship, and Warfare." *American Anthropologist* 90(4): 871–87.

White, Gregory L. 1981. "Some Correlates of Romantic Jealousy." *Journal of Personality* 49: 129–47.

Wilkinson, Gerald S. 1984. "Reciprocal Food Sharing in the Vampire Bats." *Nature* 308: 181–84.

Williams, George C. 1966. *Adaptation and Natural Selection: A Critique of Some Current Evolutionary Thought.* Princeton, N.J.: Princeton University Press.

Wilson, David Sloan, and Elliott Sober. 1994. "Reintroducing Group Selection to the Human Behavioral Sciences." *Behavioral and Brain Sciences* 17: 585–654.

World Almanac. 1996. *The World Almanac and Book of Facts: 1997.* Mahwah, N.J.: World Almanac.

World Bank. 1997a. *The State in a Changing World: World Development Report, 1997.* Oxford: Oxford University Press.

———. 1997b. *World Development Indicators.* Washington, D.C.: World Bank.

Wright, Robert. 1994. *The Moral Animal: The New Science of Evolutionary Psychology.* New York: Vintage.

Wynne-Edwards, Vero C. 1962. *Animal Dispersion in Relation to Social Behaviour.* Edinburgh: Oliver and Boyd.

# 10

# SEX AND SANCTIONING: EVALUATING TWO THEORIES OF NORM EMERGENCE

*Christine Horne*

NORMS are most often seen as behavioral rules, about which there is some degree of consensus, that are enforced through social sanctions. Although much sociological research is relevant to the issues of norm distribution and effectiveness, there is little explicit focus on the content of normative rules. Two general approaches to the issue can be identified: for some scholars, norms reflect existing behaviors; for others, they constrain self-interested action that has negative consequences for the group. Examples that appear to support and to contradict both perspectives come readily to mind, but little empirical evidence exists that allows rigorous evaluation of the two possibilities.

## Two Views of Norm Emergence

The arguments outlined in this chapter describe two approaches to explaining norm emergence.[1] Understanding of these processes is necessary in order to make predictions about the content of rules that will be observed under different conditions.

One type of explanation, called here the behavior-based approach, suggests that norms reflect and reinforce existing behavior (Homans 1950; Opp 1982; Sumner 1979). Individuals seek to do those things that bring them pleasure and spare them pain (Sumner 1979; Weber 1978, 755). In this quest, they may calculate the best course of action, imitate others (Bandura and Walters 1963; Miller and Dollard 1941), or engage in trial and error (Macy 1993; Schwartz and Reisberg 1991).

As a behavior becomes common, group members begin to expect it. In turn, a sense of "oughtness" attaches to that behavior. This may occur because individuals value consistency and prefer that others behave in predictable ways; or it may be that, simply as a matter of chance, people are more likely to associate oughtness with behavior that is frequently observed than with that which is uncommon (chapter 9, this volume). Whatever the reason, those who make atypical decisions are subject to social sanction. Presumably, the more common a behavior, the greater the sense of oughtness and the stronger the negative reaction to deviance. On this view, group members do what is good for them individually, whatever that "good" might entail. Actions that are frequent and widespread come to be expected (Homans 1950, 266; Sumner 1979), and deviations, in turn, are sanctioned. Thus actions that are common become normative. Norms therefore reflect existing behavior.

A second kind of argument, called here the externality-based approach, holds that norms constrain self-interested action (Coleman 1990; Ellickson 1991).[2] Individuals prefer that others not engage in behaviors that have harmful externalities and instead do things that produce benefits for the group (or at least for them).[3] For example, to the extent that non-smokers do not enjoy or benefit from secondhand smoke, we would expect a normative rule against smoking to emerge. Norms are enforced when those who are affected by the externality-producing behavior either reward those who are cooperative or punish those whose actions are deemed antisocial (Coleman 1990; Ellickson 1991). On this view, behaviors that cause harm to group members are discouraged.

The distinction between these two perspectives is sometimes stated as one of causal order. Behavior-based approaches suggest that existing patterns of action lead to the emergence of normative rules. Externality-based approaches, by contrast, imply that rules emerge that then, in turn, as they are enforced, affect behavior. The two kinds of arguments also have implications for predicting norm content. Behavior-based theories often are associated with the view that norms enhance individual welfare, whereas externality-based explanations appear more compatible with the suggestion that they contribute to the well-being of the group.

## An Illustration: Norms Regulating Female Sexual Activity

On their face, many norms appear to be consistent with behavior-based approaches, and others seem to support externality-based arguments. Are alternative explanations necessary for explaining different types of norms? Is one approach more useful than the other in accounting for the variety of rules we observe?

Consider norms regarding sexual behavior. In a range of northern African countries, including Egypt, Kenya, the Sudan, and other parts of Islamic northeast Africa, circumcision, or female genital mutilation, is required for young females. Female genital mutilation has serious negative consequences for the girls subjected to it (as well as some disadvantages for their male partners). Immediate effects include "pain, hemorrhage, shock, acute urinary retention, urinary infection, blood poisoning (septicemia), fever, tetanus, and death" (Mackie 1996, 1003). Some of the more long-term effects are scars, painful intercourse, vaginal closure, anal incontinence, and brain damaged infants (Mackie 1996, 1003). The practice also reportedly contributes to sexual problems such as inability to achieve orgasm, anxiety, and depression (Koso-Thomas 1987, 25–28). Countering these negative effects, however, is a social benefit: having undergone the procedure enhances a girl's reputation in the community. It is believed that "if a girl is circumcised, . . . she won't be wild. She will also keep her virginity so she will get a husband" (Alemeneh 1999). The requirement of female genital mutilation appears to be an example of a norm that discourages women from engaging in sexual activity—behavior that in the absence of such a norm would be considered desirable. Although the norm constrains self-interested action, those who comply receive social rewards.

By contrast, norms in other parts of Africa, most notably among the Yao in Malawi, encourage female sexual activity. Young girls undergo initiation rites—called "chiputu" or "chinamwali choyamba"—in which they are taught about sex and encouraged to engage in it. Over a period of several days, girls learn about sexual behavior, their responsibilities as females, and the customs of the clan (Davison 1997, 45). "For those who attend the initiation, it is a celebration of the particular gender values that make them female" (Davison 1997, 45). The initiation involves "the passing on of a great deal of sexual knowledge that arouses the curiosity of girls who are then encouraged to experiment and then either become pregnant or form liaisons that lead to marriage" (Hyde and Kadzamira 1994, 29). In addition, the ritual itself may "include initiation in sexual intercourse and [may] result in pregnancy" (Hyde and Kadzamira 1994; see also Kornfield and Namate 1997). Norms in Yao communities encourage female sexual activity. They appear to reflect rather than constrain behavior in that they encourage actions in which women are likely to want to engage even in the absence of social reinforcement.

At least on their face, these two illustrations support different arguments regarding norm emergence. Are two explanations necessary to account for these contradictory norms? Can one approach suffice to explain the existence of these rules?

Consider first the emergence of the requirement of female genital mutilation. Gerry Mackie (1996) suggests an explanation that uses an externality-based approach. He begins with the assumption that people (both men and women) are interested in seeing their children successfully reach adulthood (Mackie 1996). Men, therefore, care about raising their own offspring. On the other hand, they do not want to pay the expenses of supporting the children of another man. Therefore, in order to ensure the identity of their offspring, men monitor and attempt to control women's sexual behavior. In polygynous societies in which great wealth disparities exist, it is more difficult for men to do this because of the large number of women they have to keep track of. In such communities, female genital mutilation acts as a signal of women's fidelity and discourages their sexual activity, thus lowering men's monitoring costs. In these societies, norms arguably constrain female behavior (sexual promiscuity) that produces negative externalities (uncertainty as to paternity) for males.

It is difficult to imagine, on the other hand, that norms requiring the practice emerged to reflect existing behavior—particularly considering the harmful and painful effects of the procedure. Given these consequences, it seems unlikely that female genital mutilation became widespread because of its inherent attractiveness. A more plausible explanation suggests that girls were subjected to the procedure as a response to, rather than an initiation of, social opinion. In this instance, behavior-based arguments are not satisfying.

By contrast, norms allowing, or even encouraging, sexual activity are easily explained by behavior-based theories because they are consistent with an activity in which women are likely to engage even in the absence of the norm. Can they also be explained by externality-based arguments? One way to address this question is to compare those societies that practice female genital mutilation with those, such as the Yao, that have more permissive norms.

One notable difference is that whereas those groups practicing female genital mutilation are patrilineal and patrilocal, the Yao are matrilineal and matrilocal (Davison 1997; Mitchell 1956).[4] In patrilineal societies, property is passed down through the male line. In the less common matrilineal societies, by contrast, property passes through females. In addition, whereas in patrilocal groups a woman leaves her home of origin to move to the man's village, in matrilocal societies, the man accompanies the woman. In these groups brothers, rather than husbands, have more responsibility for the woman and her offspring.

Does this difference in social structure suggest an explanation for the contrast in norms between the two groups? Can lineage and residence patterns account for the permissive norms found among the Yao? To answer this question I begin by making the same assumption that Mackie (1996) makes to explain the emergence of female genital mutilation, namely, that both men and women have an interest in seeing their children successfully reach adulthood, and argue that this assumption leads to contrasting outcomes under different structural conditions. In polygynous patrilineal societies, Mackie (1996) suggests, men's interest in the survival of their children results in a desire to monitor and control their wives' behavior. In societies that are matrilineal and matrilocal, this concern with the wellbeing of offspring arguably has different effects.

One consequence of the matrilineal and matrilocal social structure is that a woman is not as dependent on her husband for economic support. Because the wife remains in the village in which her family lives, she is more capable of providing for her children's needs without the help of the father than is a woman who lives with her husband's family. Rather than exerting control over resources, a husband "is economically dependent on his wife's people and working under their orders" (Richards [1957] 1982, 41). In addition, the woman, rather than her husband, has rights in the offspring. Thus any children born to a woman belong "to her matrilineage. Should she produce no offspring, her husband would be asked to leave her household and another man . . . would be solicited to assist in the production of children for the matrilineage" (Davison 1997, 82). Men are essential for their reproductive labor but not, at least in comparison with societies that are patrilineal and patrilocal, necessary for the material support of their children.

One implication of women's relative independence is that men can be more confident that their children will be raised to adulthood, even if they do not themselves contribute resources to the task. In other words, to the extent that fathers are satisfied that their children are being taken care of, they need not provide support. Thus the costs to men of seeing their offspring reach adulthood are lower in groups that are matrilineal and matrilocal.

This means that husbands can afford to be less concerned with ensuring the paternity of their wives' children.[5] In turn, they have less interest in monitoring and controlling women's behavior. Observations of European district officers in the early twentieth century are consistent with this view. They note that local marriage practices were different from those in societies that were patrilineal and patrilocal. "There was a valid kind of marriage . . . in which the husband's control over the woman and children was not so great" (Davison 1997, 120).[6]

The argument suggests that women's dependence on men's resources increases men's motivation to control their activity. Female independence limits not only men's ability to control women but also their desire to do so. Thus wives' dependence affects enforcement but also the content of norms regulating female sexual activity. We would expect such norms to be more permissive in a matrilineal and matrilocal society such as the Yao and more constraining in communities that are patrilineal and patrilocal such as those in Islamic northeast Africa.

On their face, the contrasting norms in these groups support different theories of emergence. The permissive norms found in parts of Malawi seem consistent with behavior-based approaches, and the requirement of female genital mutilation with externality-based explanations. However, although they appear to be consistent with different theories, in actuality, both can be explained using externality-based arguments.

# An Experimental Test: Norms Regulating Controller Selection Choices

The above application of the two general theoretical approaches to the explanation of norms regulating female sexual activity is merely illustrative. I now evaluate the two norm emergence arguments by turning to quantitative evidence produced using experimental methods. Here, rather than looking at substantive rules, I focus on controller selection norms (Ellickson 1991, 123–36). Instead of identifying specific rules in a particular context, I describe them in more general, abstract terms.[7]

Controller selection norms are rules regarding the institution upon which individuals rely in addressing deviant behavior. In other words, they dictate the choice between various solutions to the problem of order. Although there are many ways of organizing control efforts, I consider only two.[8] One approach is to rely on a third-party control agent, a Leviathan that promotes order and helps to avoid a "war of all against all" (Hobbes [1651] 1958). In the present study, a control agent is seen as punishing deviance in response to requests by group members.[9] Its expenses are paid to some extent by taxes imposed on all. As individuals make demands on this centralized control, it responds by engaging in sanctioning. The more the agent sanctions, the higher its expenses become. It therefore raises taxes to cover those costs. In turn, to the extent that the agent's sanctioning expenses are offset by tax resources, it is able to impose lower costs on the individuals who call upon it.[10] Turning to the agent is one option available to group members concerned with deviant behavior.[11]

A second approach to producing order holds that informal social controls exercised within groups are essential.[12] Groups are made up of people who are able to interact with one another over time. When individuals personally punish deviant behavior they bear the full burden of doing so, though they hope for the support of other group members. Thus, control is exercised as individuals personally impose sanctions.[13]

The essence of the distinction between these control structures, as defined here, lies in the way in which they allocate the costs of sanctioning.[14] Use of the agent is less personally costly but creates negative externalities, whereas informal sanctioning is more costly to the individual but does not increase expenses for the group as a whole. What do behavior- and externality-based arguments predict about the norms that will emerge regarding the choice between these two sanctioning options?

## Theoretical Predictions

The behavior-based and externality-based approaches yield a number of contrasting theoretical predictions.[15] They result in hypotheses regarding the content of norms that regulate sanctions. In addition, they predict different effects of varying the agent's resources, the cohesion of the community, and the length of time during which group members are able to interact. Changes in these variables are hypothesized to affect the strength of controller selection norms.

*Predictions Regarding the Content of Controller Selection Norms*   Behavior-based explanations of norm emergence hold that those actions that are common come to be accepted. Deviations from the expected pattern are subject to social sanction. On this view, those control choices that are observed most often will become normative. This approach yields the first prediction, hypothesis 1a: Norms will favor the sanctioning choice that is the most common.

Externality-based explanations focus on the fact that use of the central control contributes to increased costs for all group members. As people rely on the agent, it must raise taxes to cover its expenses. By contrast, the burdens of sanctioning personally are born by the individual and impose no costs on the collective. Therefore, if norms emerge in response to negative externalities, we would expect individuals to disapprove of people's turning to the agent and thereby potentially increasing everyone's taxes. Instead, individuals will encourage others to personally sanction deviant behavior. Thus, hypothesis 1b, the externality-based prediction regarding the form of sanction selected: Norms will favor personal sanctioning over use of the agent.

*Predictions Regarding the Effect of Agent Resources*   The extent to which an individual prefers either that others personally sanction or that they rely on the agent may be affected by the amount of the agent's resources. As defined here, when the resources of the central control agent increase, the personal costs of using it decline. Therefore, the temptation for individuals to turn to the agent is higher, and they are more likely to rely on it.

Behavior-based theories suggest that behaviors become normative when they are widespread. The precise mechanisms responsible for this correlation are unclear. Nevertheless, to the extent that oughtness emerges in response to the commonality of an action, we would expect that frequency of a behavior will affect the strength of norms regarding it: If a behavior is less frequent, it is less likely to be associated with a sense of oughtness. Conversely, the more widespread the behavior, the stronger the norms favoring it will be. On this view, the amount of the agent's resources affects the extent to which individuals make demands on the agent. In turn, this leads to greater disapproval directed towards those who do not make the same decision, but instead individually sanction proscribed behavior. Hypothesis 2a presents the behavior-based approach toward agent resources: Agent resources will have a positive effect on norms encouraging use of the agent.

Externality-based theories, instead of focusing on frequency of behavior, emphasize its consequences. As has been suggested, the greater an agent's resources, the greater is the temptation for individuals to rely on it. As people make demands on it, it will impose sanctions and increase taxes to cover its costs. Thus greater resources encourage use of the agent, which leads, in turn, to larger negative externalities.

According to externality-based theories, norms emerge when individual behaviors produce consequences for other group members. The more severe the consequences for the community, the greater the interest group members will have in controlling the behavior. Similarly, the more likely people are to engage in such behavior, the stronger the norms against it will be. After all, if people are unlikely to engage in a particular antisocial behavior, there is little need for sanctioning to control it. If a damaging behavior is likely to be frequent, however, the costs to group members will be high, and the interest in controlling it will be greater.

On this view, when the cost of turning to the agent is low and the likelihood of externalities is high, disapproval for using the agent will be stronger. Hypothesis 2b reflects the externality-based view of the effect of agent resources: Agent resources will have a positive effect on norms that encourage personal sanctioning.

*Predictions Regarding the Effect of Group Cohesion*    What about the cohesion of the group? Cohesion is defined here as the interdependence of group members (Emerson 1962).[16] The greater the value that group members place on their relationships and the goods they can receive from those relationships, the more cohesive the group. It is widely accepted that highly cohesive communities are able to exercise greater control. Behavior-based explanations of norms, however, provide no reason to think that cohesion affects people's control selection choices. Therefore, they predict no effect of group cohesion on the strength of normative rules.

By contrast, externality-based theories do predict such an effect. In communities that are more cohesive, individuals are highly dependent on one another. In turn, the outcomes and well-being of each person will affect the outcomes and well-being of all others in the group. A person with few resources will not have much to give; a person who has many resources will be more likely to engage in large-scale exchange and will therefore be a more profitable interaction partner. Thus, in cohesive groups we would expect people to be more concerned about antisocial behaviors that impose costs on group members. Norms against use of the agent (an action that creates costs for all) will be stronger. This is the essence of hypothesis 3: Group cohesion will have a positive effect on the strength of norms favoring personal sanctioning.

*Predictions Regarding the Effect of Time*    In addition to institutional characteristics—agent strength and group cohesion—time also may affect norms. As people interact with one another they have opportunities to observe control choices. According to behavior-based explanations, their expectations regarding those decisions will become entrenched as they see more and more of the same behavior. Thus, norms favoring that behavior should grow stronger. The behavior-based prediction concerning the effect of time on sanctioning choice is expressed in hypothesis 4: The length of time during which people are able to interact will have a positive effect on the strength of norms. By contrast, externality-based theories do not predict such effects. Assuming that individuals are aware that use of the agent results in increased taxes, their exposure to these increases over time should not exacerbate their disapproval of it.

## The Experiment

The hypotheses were tested using experimental methods.[17] I designed a setting in which participants were able to respond to deviance, and, in addition, to react to the sanctioning decisions of others.

*Design*    The experiment had a two-by-two, between-subjects factorial design, crossing resources of the agent (high versus low) by cohesion of the community (high versus low) to produce four conditions: high resources and high cohesion, high resources and low cohesion, low resources and high cohesion, and low resources and low cohesion. In each of these conditions subjects were able to make decisions about how to respond to deviant behavior—whether to call upon the agent, to personally impose a sanction, or to do nothing. They also could react to the control choices of others. These reactions were used as a measure of the controller selection norms that emerged.

*Subjects and Procedure*    The 160 participants in the study were recruited from undergraduate classes at the University of Arizona by offering students the opportunity to earn money. They were individually contacted by telephone to schedule their participation and were told to come to the Economic Science Teaching Laboratory on the University of Arizona campus. The lab had twenty computer terminals separated by partitions, which limited the subjects' ability to see one another. In addition, because more than one experimental session was scheduled for the same time, participants did not know with whom they were interacting. Each experimental group required four subjects. Ten experimental groups were run in each of the four conditions for a total of forty groups.

After being randomly assigned to an experimental condition and a subject number, participants read instructions on their computer screens.

They were told that the study was designed to examine social interaction processes. During the experiment they would be participating in a game in which they were vulnerable to theft, could punish the thief if they were stolen from, and could engage in exchange. Their decisions and those of others (as well as the experimental condition to which they were randomly assigned) would determine the number of points they made. Their monetary earnings would be based on the number of points they had accumulated by the end of the experiment.

After everyone finished reading the instructions, subjects engaged in practice trials to ensure their understanding. The experimenter answered questions individually so that other subjects would not be able to hear the question or the answer. There were five practice and fifty actual trials, though subjects were not told beforehand the exact number.

*Overview and Operationalization of the Variables*  The following is an overview of the experiment that describes chronologically what subjects experienced on each round, as well as how the theoretical concepts were operationalized.

INITIAL CONDITIONS  Initially, subjects were randomly assigned to one of four conditions in which the cohesion of the group and the resources of the agent varied. The agent was operationalized by creating a sanctioning option that was paid for through taxes imposed upon all group members. Its resources were manipulated by varying the amount of tax that was collected to support it, as well as the related cost of asking the agent to impose a sanction. In high-resource conditions, taxes were initially twenty points. Here taxes paid all of the expenses of using the central control—there was no personal cost associated with doing so. In the low-resource conditions, taxes were five points. Because taxes paid less of the agent's expenses, participants incurred a personal cost if they asked the agent to impose a sanction.

Group cohesion was manipulated by changing the value of points individuals kept for themselves relative to the value of those they received from others. The higher the value of the points received from others, the more valuable the subjects' relationships and the more cohesive the group. In high-cohesion conditions, points received from others were worth three times the amount of points that one kept for oneself. In other words, if subject W gave subject Z ten points, Z actually would receive thirty points. In these conditions, subjects were very dependent on others for making a profit. By contrast, in the low-cohesion conditions, points received from others were worth the same amount as points kept for oneself. Thus, if W gave Z ten points, Z would receive only ten points. Here, individuals could do just as well alone as they could by interacting. This operationalization reflects the conceptualization of cohesion as the interdependence of group members.

BEGINNING EACH TRIAL   At the beginning of each trial, subjects were given a personal income of fifty points, and they knew that others were given the same sum. A certain number of points (varying across conditions as described above) was deducted as a tax that was used to support the central agent. The size of the tax varied throughout the experiment, depending on subjects' sanctioning choices—that is, the more that people in the group called upon the agent, the higher everyone's taxes became. On each round, subjects saw the income that they had received minus the tax taken away in their "income window" on the computer screen.

THEFT   A computer-simulated actor then stole ten points from one randomly chosen subject. These points were subtracted from the victim's income. On any particular trial there could be one victim or none.[18]

SANCTIONING   The victim was then given the opportunity to respond to the deviant behavior. Victims could choose to do nothing, they could call upon the agent, or they could personally impose a sanction. These options were listed on the screen along with their associated costs and benefits.

The benefits of sanctioning were constant across all conditions. Choosing either sanctioning option resulted in each subject being given three points. The decision not to punish produced no benefit. By contrast, costs varied across options and conditions. The costs of sanctioning personally were completely born by the individual—the victim of the theft. In all conditions, this cost was ten points. The cost of sanctioning using the agent varied. In high-resource conditions, the cost to the victim was zero. In low-resource conditions, the cost was ten points. In both instances, making demands on the agent contributed to possible future tax increases. This operationalization reflects the theoretical notion that strong agents have more resources and, therefore, impose lower costs on users.

REWARDING   After the victim had made his or her sanctioning choice, everyone was told what that person decided. Then all subjects were able to exchange points. Decisions to give points to others were made simultaneously. Exchanges were not negotiated and were subject to no time limit. Subjects could give any number of points to anyone they wished, and they could keep points for themselves. They could use their experience from earlier trials in making their decisions. Of particular interest here, they could use information about the victim's sanctioning choice in making their rewarding decisions.

Controller selection norms were operationalized in terms of the approval—that is, the number of points—that subjects gave to victims who had made a sanctioning decision. This was a group-level measure reflecting the average size of rewards given across the group. Thus the rewards given to sanctioners by others provided a measure of the controller selection norm of the group. Larger rewards indicated stronger norms.

ENDING EACH TRIAL   After all exchanges were completed, subjects' personal incomes were transferred into their savings windows. Points in savings accumulated during the experiment and could not be used in any future trials. The transfer of points marked the end of a trial. A new trial then began, and subjects again were given an income of fifty points minus the tax.

## Results

All of the sanctioning and rewarding decisions made by each subject during each trial of the experiment were recorded. For each group, the fifty trials were divided into five time periods of ten trials each. The mean sanctioning and rewarding decisions during these time periods were calculated. This resulting group-level data set was used for all analyses.[19]

*The Content of Controller Selection Norms*   Do controller selection norms favor those sanctioning choices that are most common or, rather, those that create lower costs for the group? Focusing only on the conditions in which agent resources are high, the mean level of demands on the agent is .69 (sd = .24) and that of individual sanctions is .19 (sd = .20).[20] Thus, in these conditions, subjects are more likely to call upon the agent than to punish the thief themselves. Given this pattern, behavioral explanations would predict that subjects will give greater approval to those who use the agent, the more common response (consistent with hypothesis 1a). Externality-based explanations, by contrast, predict that group members will prefer that others engage in personal sanctioning (hypothesis 1b).

A look at the mean rewards suggests support for the externality-based hypothesis. The mean reward given to those who sanction personally is 5.3 (sd = 3.5), and the reward to those who call upon the agent, 4.3 (sd = 2.8). Thus group members apparently prefer that others sanction informally rather than by using the agent.

Statistical analyses support this conclusion. I calculate the ratio of the number of personal sanctions relative to the total number of sanctions imposed by group members. I then use ordinary least squares (OLS) regression to see whether this ratio is correlated with total reward levels. Hypothesis 1a predicts that the sanctioning ratio will have a significant negative effect on rewarding: that is, the less frequently people personally punish and instead rely upon the agent, the larger the rewards should be. In contrast, hypothesis 1b predicts that the more frequently people punish personally rather than using the agent, the larger the rewards will be. Thus the more often people sanction informally, the greater the mean rewards given. The results are consistent with hypothesis 1b (see table 10.1). The ratio of personal to total sanctions has a statistically significant, positive effect on overall reward levels. Norms do not favor the behavior that is most common (relying on the agent) but rather, the behavior that results in fewer negative externalities (sanctioning personally).

What effects do agent resources, community cohesion, and time have on the strength of the norm favoring individual sanctioning as opposed to reliance on the agent? To answer this question, I look at the effects of these variables on the size of the rewards given for using the agent and for personally sanctioning as well as on the difference between the size of rewards given in reaction to these two choices.

*The Effect of Agent Resources*    Behavior-based theories predict that the rewards given to those who use the agent will be higher when the agent has more resources and that such sanctioning therefore will be more frequent. Externality-based theories predict that the preference for personal sanctioning will be greater when the agent is less costly to use and the possibility of tax increases more real. OLS regression shows no correlation between the strength of the agent and the support given to those who use it (see table 10.2 for a description of means and table 10.3 for results of the analysis). If anything, increasing the resources of the agent in cohesive communities reduces rewards. The results, therefore, do not support the prediction that the agent's resources will positively affect the preference for reliance on the agent (hypothesis 2a). They also, however, fail to support the prediction that the agent's strength will positively affect the norm favoring individual sanctioning (hypothesis 2b). Agent resources have no effect on rewards given for personal sanctioning. Thus, central control strength appears to have no effect in either direction on controller selection norms. Neither behavior- nor externality-based predictions are confirmed.

*The Effect of Group Cohesion*    The results support the externality-based prediction that group cohesion will have a positive effect on the norm favoring individual sanctioning (hypothesis 3) (see tables 10.2 and 10.3). Strength of community has a statistically significant positive effect on the rewards given for personal sanctioning. This result is consistent with the externality-based hypothesis. Community cohesion also, however, has a positive effect on rewards given for using the agent. How can this result be explained? One possibility is that people prefer that others sanction rather than not because sanctioning produces benefits for all. Another possibility

TABLE 10.1   OLS Regression Coefficients for Sanctioning Decisions on Overall Reward Levels in High-Resource Conditions

| Variable | Overall Reward Levels |
|---|---|
| Intercept | 1.77**** |
| | (.692) |
| Group cohesion | 4.29**** |
| | (.346) |
| Ratio of personal to total sanctions | 2.41*** |
| | (.784) |
| $R^2$ | .65 |

Source: Author's compilation.
Note: Standard errors are in parentheses.
****$p < .0001$ ***$p < .005$

is that the increase in rewards for using the agent merely reflects an increased interest in exchange in general. A comparison of the difference in the rewards given for personal sanctioning and for using the agent clarifies the findings. Strength of community has a statistically significant, positive effect on this difference. Thus although rewards for both kinds of sanctioning increase, group strength has a greater positive effect on the norm favoring personal sanctioning than it does on that favoring reliance on the agent. This result is consistent with the externality-based hypothesis.

*The Effect of Time*   Finally, the results show no support for the behavior-based prediction that norms will grow stronger over time (hypothesis 4). There is little if any variation in the difference in the rewards given for the two sanctioning decisions across the five time periods. The difference ranges from .76 (sd = 1.4) in the first time period to .55 (sd = 3.8) in the last time period. Analyses show no statistically significant effect of time on

TABLE 10.2   Mean Sanctioning and Reward Levels

| | | High Resources | | | Low Resources | | |
|---|---|---|---|---|---|---|---|
| High Cohesion | Agent Sanctions | .687 | (.239) | Agent Sanctions | .269 | (.207) |
| | Individual Sanctions | .228 | (.213) | Individual Sanctions | .480 | (.293) |
| | Reward for Agent S | 6.41 | (2.03) | Reward for Agent S | 8.44 | (3.36) |
| | Reward for Individual S | 7.79 | (2.60) | Reward for Individual S | 9.90 | (4.16) |
| Low Cohesion | Agent Sanctions | .694 | (.235) | Agent Sanctions | .303 | (.235) |
| | Individual Sanctions | .153 | (.182) | Individual Sanctions | .342 | (.208) |
| | Reward for Agent S | 2.20 | (1.79) | Reward for Agent S | 2.22 | (2.38) |
| | Reward for Individual S | 2.25 | (1.49) | Reward for Individual S | 2.89 | (2.19) |

Source: Author's compilation.
Note: Standard deviations are in parentheses.

TABLE 10.3    *OLS Regression Coefficients for Various Factors on the Emergence of Controller Selection Norms*

| Variable | Rewards for Using the Agent | Rewards for Sanctioning Personally | Difference Between Rewards for Sanctioning Personally and Rewards for Using the Agent | Difference Between Rewards for Sanctioning Personally and Rewards for Using the Agent |
|---|---|---|---|---|
| Intercept | 2.22**** | 2.89**** | .353 | .0374 |
|  | (.374) | (.419) | (.459) | (.680) |
| Agent resources | −.0169 | −.642 | −.531 | −.559 |
|  | (.507) | (.682) | (.708) | (.711) |
| Group cohesion | 6.22**** | 7.01**** | 1.45* | 1.44* |
|  | (.528) | (.599) | (.657) | (.659) |
| Agent resources × group cohesion | −2.02** | −1.47 | −.431 | −.408 |
|  | (.718) | (.943) | (.985) | (.988) |
| Time | — | — | — | .112 |
|  |  |  |  | (.177) |
| $R^2$ | .56 | .56 | .06 | .06 |

*Source:* Author's compilation.
*Note:* Standard errors are in parentheses.
****$p < .0001$ **$p < .01$ *$p < .05$

rewarding (see table 10.2). Thus, overall, the results support externality-based rather than behavior-based explanations of norm emergence.

## Discussion and Conclusion

In this chapter I analyze norms regulating female sexual activity in parts of Africa and argue that externality-based approaches can account for the two very different substantive norms described. I also present the results of an experimental study that evaluates behavior- and externality-based approaches to explaining norm emergence. The findings suggest initial support for externality-based arguments and contradict behavior-based theories.

Additional research should be conducted, however, to more thoroughly evaluate the two theoretical approaches and the conditions under which they apply. For example, what factors contribute to group members' perceiving an action as having negative consequences? In the experiment, subjects recognized taxes as costly, and norms emerged accordingly. Similarly, sexual activity produces consequences for others, and therefore norms regulating it can be explained using externality-based theories. Such explanations, however, also would predict that these norms will change when the negative externalities produced by compliance increase.

In modern society, the disadvantages of female genital mutilation seem much greater than the benefits. Men no longer have large numbers of wives to monitor, and the costs of the practice are extreme. Similarly, in Malawi, as well as in Africa more generally, non-monogamous sexual activity has serious negative consequences. At a minimum, a person with no prior sexual partners may be exposed to the risk of disease if his or her current partner has had sexual contact with others. In addition, many children are born with the human immunodeficiency virus (HIV), and thousands are orphaned as their parents contract acquired immunodeficiency syndrome (AIDS). In this setting, norms that encourage early sexual experimentation seem problematic. Why have expectations not changed as externality-based arguments would seem to predict?

It may be that other positive values are associated with a normative rule that has become counterproductive in some ways. Costly initiation rituals may be viewed as part of a culture that people are reluctant to give up. They may symbolize adulthood and full-fledged membership in the community. They may provide information as to group members' trustworthiness. For example, Mackie (1996) argues that men who recognize that female genital mutilation identifies marriageable women (by providing a signal of women's fidelity) will be unwilling to take the risk of marrying someone who has not been subjected to the procedure, and girls' families will not want to doom their daughters to a life of singledom by failing to have them circumcised. As a result, although men, women, and their families may not like the practice, the costs of noncompliance are high. Thus female genital mutilation remains normative practice.

In addition to seeing positive aspects of a norm (aspects that outsiders may not always recognize), people may be unwilling to act on new information as to a rule's harmful effects. For example, information about AIDS may be viewed as Western propaganda that does not reflect the interests of Africans. Thus resistance to change is an assertion of independence against outside coercion. Factors such as these that may affect the perception of externalities should be specified theoretically and investigated empirically.

Under what conditions might existing behaviors come to be associated with a sense of oughtness and therefore be sanctioned? In the experiment, this association did not emerge. Arguably, it might under different circumstances. After all, it makes intuitive sense that what is familiar to people also will seem right to them. What conditions might foster such an outcome? Clearly, the identification of behavior to be sanctioned cannot be simply a matter of statistical regularity, given that, as the experimental results show, behavior and norms are not always consistent.

Further consideration also should be given to the issue of norm measurement. In the experiment, responses to deviance and compliance were used as an indicator that a norm existed. Deviance, however, was not affirmatively punished. Instead, levels of rewards varied. Sanctioners received more rewards when they obeyed the norm, but when they did not, they still received the same amount as did others who were not victims and made no sanctioning choices. Thus, for rewarders, there was little if any risk associated with reacting to others' sanctioning decisions because these reactions increased the size of the reward for compliance rather than impose damaging punishments for noncompliance. Under these circumstances, rewards provide useful information regarding the content and strength of normative rules.

In other situations, however, relying on reactions to deviance may be problematic. People who punish others who engage in deviant behavior bear the costs of doing so. These costs may be offset by other benefits, such as support from others. Thus sanctioning may indicate not only the existence of a rule but also other factors that affect the likelihood that people will punish, such as the cohesion of the group or the cost of imposing a particular sanction. Because normative rules may exist even if enforcement is weak, sanctioning may not always be a reliable indicator of the existence of a rule, though it may be highly relevant for determining a norm's effectiveness. Thus reliance on sanctioning as a measure may confound two separate aspects of norms, rule content and enforcement.

## Notes

1. The discussion of the two arguments is drawn, in part, from Horne forthcoming.

2. Game theoretic work on norms tends to be of this type. For the game theorist, norms, by definition, encourage cooperative behaviors that limit self-interested behaviors harmful to the group. Thus, on this view, existing work examining solutions to social dilemma problems, the resolution of coordination problems, and so forth are all relevant to understanding norm emergence. For a discussion of some of this literature, see chapter 4, this volume.

3. Norms may discourage behavior that has negative consequences or encourage actions that produce positive externalities.

4. Such female-centered structures may be observed in groups in which men travel away from home for long distances or for long periods of time (or both). In Yao society, the men were historically engaged in the slave trade, requiring their absence from home. More recently, Yao men (like other Malawians) travel to South Africa to work in the mines.

5. Note that brothers also have little interest in monitoring their sister's behavior, because any child born to her benefits the family regardless of the identity of the father.

6. In general, these observers thought that marriages in societies that were matrilocal and matrilineal were less stable (Trivedy 1987).

7. The discussion of controller selection norms is drawn from Horne forthcoming.

8. In addition, organizations may dictate the behavior of their members, and individuals may control their own actions (see Ellickson 1991, 132–36, for a taxonomy of types of norms).

9. Many scholars suggest that the legal system (one concrete example of an agent) acts primarily in response to demands by citizens (see Black 1973; Jones 1969; Pound 1917).

10. For example, in societies with a stronger legal system, people are more likely to take advantage of the services of state-provided judges and attorneys, whereas in communities with weak legal institutions, they may have to hire their own dispute adjudicators.

11. The central agent as described here has characteristics of a common pool resource—that is, it is likely to be used more than is optimal for the group. Much existing work focuses on the problem of the way groups limit excessive use of such resources. Elinor Ostrom, James Walker, and Roy Gardner (1992), for example, look at how opportunities for communication and repeated interaction affect the yields of common pool resources. Other scholars focus on the effects of experience (Allison and Messick 1985), trust (Brann and Foddy 1988), identity (Brewer and Kramer 1986; Kramer and Brewer 1984), group size (Brewer and Kramer 1986), and a variety of other factors.

12. See Hechter and Kanazawa 1993 for a discussion of informal social controls in Japan. For work by criminologists, see Sampson, Raudenbush, and Earls 1997 and Sampson and Groves 1989. See also Parsons 1937 and 1952.

13. This approach to organizing control efforts has characteristics of a public good in that informal sanctions are something that benefit the group, but no one individual is motivated to impose them. Many scholars examine the conditions under which public goods are likely to be provided, collective action to occur, and deviance to be punished. For examples of such research, see Flache and Macy 1996; Heckathorn 1988; Marwell and Ames 1979; Oliver 1980; Oliver and Marwell 1988; Yamagishi and Sato 1986.

14. For discussion of the distinction between legal and normative controls and the implications of this difference for understanding the relation between law and community, see Horne 2000.

15. The discussion of hypotheses 1a, 1b, and 3 is drawn from Horne forthcoming.

16. This argument sees cohesion as a function of the interdependence of group members. It may be that in close-knit groups people also have greater access to information regarding the behavior of others. This information, rather than simply the behavior itself, may affect the formation of norms. Here, however, I assume that information is the same across groups, in order to focus on the effects of varying dependence.

17. Discussion of the experiment is drawn from Horne 2000.

18. Theft occurred in seven out of eight trials. The trials in which theft occurred were randomly chosen by the computer.

19. Data regarding controller selection norms and the effect of cohesion on norm strength under high resource conditions only, without considering time, are analyzed in Horne forthcoming.

20. The remainder of the subjects chose not to sanction.

# References

Alemeneh, Abebech. 1999. "Circumcision: Is It Good for Our Daughters?" *Reporter*, Addis Ababa, Ethiopia, July 21, 1999.

Allison, Scott T., and David M. Messick. 1985. "Effects of Experience on Performance in a Replenishable Resource Trap." *Journal of Personality and Social Psychology* 49(1): 943–48.

Bandura, Albert, and Richard H. Walters. 1963. *Social Learning and Personality Development*. New York: Holt, Rinehart and Winston.

Black, Donald. 1973. "The Mobilization of Law." *Journal of Legal Studies* 2(2): 125–50.

Brann, Peter, and Margaret Foddy. 1988. "Trust and the Consumption of a Deteriorating Common Resource." *Journal of Conflict Resolution* 31(4): 615–30.

Brewer, Marilynn B., and Roderick M. Kramer. 1986. "Choice Behavior in Social Dilemmas: Effects of Social Identity, Group Size, and Decision Framing." *Journal of Personality and Social Psychology* 50(3): 543–49.

Coleman, James S. 1990. *Foundations of Social Theory*. Cambridge: Harvard University Press, Belknap Press.

Davison, Jean. 1997. *Gender, Lineage, and Ethnicity in Southern Africa*. Boulder, Colo.: Westview Press.

Ellickson, Robert C. 1991. *Order Without Law: How Neighbors Settle Disputes*. Cambridge, Mass.: Harvard University Press.

Emerson, Richard M. 1962. "Power-Dependence Relations." *American Sociological Review* 27(1): 31–41.

Flache, Andreas, and Michael W. Macy. 1996. "The Weakness of Strong Ties: Collective Action Failure in a Highly Cohesive Group." *Journal of Mathematical Sociology* 21(1): 3–28.

Hechter, Michael. 1987. *Principles of Group Solidarity*. Berkeley: University of California Press.

Hechter, Michael, and Satoshi Kanazawa. 1993. "Group Solidarity and Social Order in Japan." *Journal of Theoretical Politics* 5(4): 455–93.

Heckathorn, Douglas D. 1988. "Collective Sanctions and the Creation of Prisoner's Dilemma Norms." *American Journal of Sociology* 94(3): 535–62.

Hobbes, Thomas. [1651] 1958. *Leviathan*. Indianapolis, Ind.: Bobbs-Merrill.

Homans, George. 1950. *The Human Group*. New York: Harcourt Brace.

Horne, Christine. 2000. "Community and the State: The Relationship Between Normative and Legal Controls." *European Sociological Review* 16(3).

———. Forthcoming. "The Contribution of Norms to Social Welfare: Grounds for Hope or Pessimism?" *Legal Theory* 7(1).

Hyde, Karin A. L., and Esme C. Kadzamira. 1994. *Girls' Attainment in Basic Literacy and Education Project: Knowledge, Attitudes, and Practices—Pilot Survey, Final Report*. Malawi: University of Malawi Centre for Social Research.

Jones, Harry W. 1969. *The Efficacy of Law*. Evanston: Northwestern University Press.

Kornfield, Ruth, and Dorothy Namate. 1997. *Cultural Practices Related to HIV/AIDS Risk Behavior: Community Survey in Phalombe, Malawi*. Washington, D.C.: U.S. Agency for International Development, Support to AIDS and Family Health Project.

Koso-Thomas, Olayinka. 1987. *The Circumcision of Women: A Strategy for Eradication*. London: Zed Books.

Kramer, Roderick M., and Marilynn B. Brewer. 1984. "Effects of Group Identity on Resource Use in a Simulated Commons Dilemma." *Journal of Personality and Social Psychology* 46(5): 1044–56.

Mackie, Gerry. 1996. "Ending Footbinding and Infibulation: A Convention Account." *American Sociological Review* 61(6): 999–1017.

Macy, Michael W. 1993. "Backward-Looking Social Control." *American Sociological Review* 58(6): 819–36.

Marwell, Gerald, and Ruth E. Ames. 1979. "Experiments on the Provision of Public Goods." *American Journal of Sociology* 84(6): 1335–60.

Miller, Neal E., and John Dollard. 1941. *Social Learning and Imitation.* New Haven: Yale University Press.

Mitchell, J. Clyde. 1956. *The Yao Village.* Manchester: Manchester University Press.

Oliver, Pamela. 1980. "Rewards and Punishments as Selective Incentives for Collective Action: Theoretical Investigations." *American Journal of Sociology* 85(6): 1356–75.

Oliver, Pamela, and Gerald Marwell. 1988. "The Paradox of Group Size in Collective Action." *American Sociological Review* 53(1): 1–8.

Opp, Karl-Dieter. 1982. "The Evolutionary Emergence of Norms." *British Journal of Social Psychology* 21(2): 139–49.

Ostrom, Elinor, James Walker, and Roy Gardner. 1992. "Covenants With and Without a Sword: Self-Governance Is Possible." *American Political Science Review* 86(2): 404–17.

Parsons, Talcott. 1937. *The Structure of Social Action.* New York: McGraw-Hill.

———. 1952. *The Social System.* New York: Free Press.

Pound, Roscoe. 1917. "The Limits of Effective Legal Action." *International Journal of Ethics* 27(October 1916; January, April, July 1971): 150–67.

Richards, Audrey. [1957] 1982. *Chisungu: A Girls' Initiation Ceremony Among the Bemba of Zambia.* London: Tavistock.

Sampson, Robert J., and W. Byron Groves. 1989. "Community Structure and Crime: Testing Social Disorganization Theory." *American Journal of Sociology* 94(4): 774–802.

Sampson, Robert J., Stephen W. Raudenbush, and Felton Earls. 1997. "Neighborhoods and Violent Crime: A Multilevel Study of Collective Efficacy." *Science* 277(August 15): 918–24.

Schwartz, Barry, and Daniel Reisberg. 1991. *Learning and Memory.* New York: W. W. Norton.

Sumner, William Graham. 1979. *Folkways.* New York: Arno Press.

Trivedy, H. Roy. 1987. *Investigating Poverty: Action Research in Southern Malawi.* Balntyre, U.K.: Oxfam.

Weber, Max. 1978. *Economy and Society.* Edited by Guenther Roth and Claus Wittich. Berkeley: University of California Press.

Yamagishi, Toshio, and Kaori Sato. 1986. "Motivational Bases of the Public Goods Problem." *Journal of Personality and Social Psychology* 50(1): 67–73.

# Part III

Exploring the Emergence of Social Norms

# 11

# NORMS OF COOPERATIVENESS AND NETWORKS OF TRUST

## *Karen S. Cook and Russell Hardin*

W E MAY motivate cooperation either through norms of cooperativeness or through relationships of trust and trustworthiness. Although either device might work in any context, there appear to be distinctive realms in which these two devices work best. Norms work best for smaller groups or communities with long-standing relationships. Trust and trustworthiness play their role most clearly in more complex societies in which individuals establish or join multiple networks for achieving various purposes. Strong norms typically involve spontaneous within-group sanctioning of violators. The possible sanctions for violation of a group's norm are quite numerous and varied because there need be no strategic or logical connection between the form of the sanction and the nature of the norm that is violated. At an extreme, the sanction can entail shunning the violator altogether.[1] For someone whose life is lived more or less entirely within a close community, such a sanction could be devastating in its power.

Trust networks typically involve dyadic and reputational policing of failures of cooperation. The chief sanction is typically merely withdrawal from further interactions with the violator of a trust, or at least from further interactions of the kind in which trust has been violated. This sanction is strategically defined by the nature of the ongoing exchange relation, which will be focused on some limited range of matters in exchange. This is, de facto, the sanction of shunning, although it has far less force than shunning in a close community. This sanction excludes those who are shunned from interaction with only one of many networks in which they might be involved, whereas in the small community it can exclude the shunned from virtually all interactions. The sanctions for communal norm violation can therefore be substantially more severe than those for failure of trustworthiness in network interactions.

Although trust may take other forms, the modal trusting relationships at issue here grow out of ongoing interactions that give each party an incentive to be cooperative. The principal incentive is the desire to maintain the relationship itself for future activities. This incentive gives you an interest in doing what I trust you to do. In essence, my interest is encapsulated in yours to some extent, and therefore I can trust you. This is the encapsulated-interest view of trust.

## Norms

This chapter draws on Russell Hardin's account of norms (Hardin 1995, chapters 4 and 5). Norms can be exclusionary or universalistic. Norms of exclusion are specific to a group, community, or culture. In addition to defining a relevant behavior, they often define who is in and who is out of the group. Hence, if I violate my community's norms, my community might exclude me from active participation. If I value membership and participation in that community, I may see this exclusion as a severe sanction. Hence, I will have a strong interest in abiding by my community's norms in order to avoid exclusion. This interest might be trumped by other interests, such as the prospect of obtaining a good job that my community would frown on, such as a job outside the community.

Universalistic norms typically are thought to apply to everyone or to everyone in a particular kind of role. Some universalistic norms cover dyadic or small-group interactions, and others cover essentially collective interactions. For example, a more or less dyadic norm against lying typically covers interactions between two or very few people—although Presidents Richard Nixon and Bill Clinton apparently achieved the remarkable feat of lying to the entire American people and being subsequently formally chastised by only a few hundred of them. A collective norm against littering typically concerns not only my immediate associates but also people throughout the larger society, including many whom I do not and will not ever know.

A striking fact about these classes of norms is that some of them are far more likely to be congruent with interests than are others. It is prima facie in my interest to abide by my community's norms of exclusion. I would typically also find it in my interest not to violate the norm against lying, because such a violation is likely to make those to whom I lie reluctant to rely on me in the future, to both my disadvantage and theirs. Again, this interest might occasionally be trumped by other interests that would give me incentive to lie. I would not, however, so immediately see it as in my interest not to litter. Indeed, what makes it against my interest to litter is primarily, and maybe only, the possibility of being sanctioned in some way for doing so. I might personally prefer not to litter for my own moral or fastidious reasons, but it might often not narrowly be in my interest to avoid littering. In general, universalistic collective norms are less likely to be backed by interests independent of sanctions than are universalistic dyadic norms.

Although norms of exclusion are primarily backed by sanctions, many of which might entail costs to the sanctioner, one type of sanction is like that which is built into dyadic relationships in that delivering the sanction is immediately in the interest of the sanctioners. The members of a group whose norms I violate—even trivially by, say, dressing or speaking differently—might find it less comfortable to be around me therefore and would de facto shun me, not to punish me but merely to avoid the discomfort they find in being around me. They might be able to do this without making any effort contrary to their immediate interests. Members of the larger community might commonly have to make a special, perhaps unpleasant effort to rebuke me for my littering.

In all these cases, the sanctions against violating the norms typically come from within the relevant community, either the exclusionary or the universal community; and commonly they are spontaneously brought to bear. They are unlike the sanctions of the law in that they need not be formally decided and acted upon. No one need work out whether they are right or wrong.

Sanctioning by shunning can turn any norm into a norm of exclusion—if the shunning works more or less uniformly or at least broadly across some group. If virtually all of us shun you, you are excluded from our group. Small communities can achieve such shunning for whatever reason, including mere distaste, and they can do so with extraordinary viciousness, as in the instance of the French town that shuns the heroine of the novel (by Marguerite Duras) and movie, *Hiroshima, mon amour,* in retaliation for her having had an affair with a German officer at the end of World War II. In general, however, we are not here concerned with norms of exclusion per se but only with seemingly universalistic norms that, at the communal level, may have the enforcement system of norms of exclusion.

We are concerned with universalistic norms that work at the dyadic or small-group level, because that is the level at which trust and trustworthiness are commonly of interest, particularly in the encapsulated-interest view of trust. Indeed, it is our thesis that the typical strategic structure of relations of trust is in ongoing dyadic or small-group relations directed at specific matters or ranges of matters. Trust relations are governed by essentially dyadic sanctions—typically, of withdrawal from the relation. If there is a norm involved in trust relationships, it is a norm of trustworthiness. There need not be a norm, however, and, indeed, it is not part of the commonplace vernacular in English to say that people should be trustworthy in the way it is part of the vernacular to say that people should not lie.[2]

The structure of norms of cooperativeness is more likely to be that of the small collectivity using collective, not merely dyadic, sanctions against violators of their norms. Hence, the norm of cooperativeness may be reduced to a norm of exclusion in practice. This norm is essentially what Bronislaw Malinowski (1922) has called generalized reciprocity (see also Yamagishi and Cook 1993) in characterizing relations in small anthropological communities, in which the sanction of exclusion could be grim. The norm of cooperativeness is similarly generalized only in a specific context, particularly in a community. Note that, in both the case of a community governed in part by a norm of cooperativeness and the case of a network-based trust relationship, we may speak of the trustworthiness of people.

## A Network Conception of Trust

Our central assumption is that some of the most important conditions for trust are social, not psychological; they are outside the individual, they are not individual traits. In a Robert Weber cartoon, a kindergarten teacher tells a parent couple, "We teach them that the world can be an unpredictable, dangerous, and sometimes frightening place, while being careful not to spoil their lovely innocence. It's tricky" (*New Yorker*, November 18, 1991, 66). If the world were wholly unpredictable, dangerous, and frightening, we would have no grounds for trust. It is familial, communal, network, and other structured contexts that give us grounds for trust because they give grounds for being trustworthy to the people we might trust. Hence, grounded trust is inherently relational because it depends on this background of ordered incentives. If we are to discover under what circumstances people are likely to trust and to prosper as a result, we must be attentive to these background conditions. The commonplace discussion of trust between two individuals as though they were abstracted from their social context misses too much of what is at stake to make sense of social relations.

We concentrate here on a still more restricted view of trust as embedded in a network of relations. Consider a simple but important example. Elizabeth McIntosh explains the elitist character of the U.S. Office of Strategic Services, the World War II forerunner of the Central Intelligence Agency (CIA), as essentially a device for securing trustworthiness. The founder, William J. Donovan, "was forced to build his organization from scratch, with little time for tight security checks." He recruited people "whose loyalty was unquestionable: close friends, business clients, club members, professors from elite colleges, linguists, established writers" (McIntosh, quoted in Westlake 1998). In essence, he did what we commonly do when we need to find someone who is trustworthy or need to check on someone's trustworthiness. He relied heavily on network-based trust and trustworthiness. In addition, he depended on third parties to certify many of these people: clubs, elite colleges, friends. This latter device is itself a supreme instance of using networks. In this respect, Donovan relied on what James Coleman (1990, 185) calls "intermediaries in trust" or on third-party trust. This is analogous to the Chinese practice of using a "guanxi" contact as intermediary between two individuals who do not know each other well enough to have established any bond of trust. A guanxi is a social or economic matchmaker who can vouch for each of the two parties brought together, thus enabling them to enter a productive relationship with each other without preliminary trial-and-error testing. One can imagine such matchmakers would be especially valuable for making contacts between people in separate, relatively close, small communities or between families.

A model for a theory of trust as embedded in a richer network of social relationships is the work of Richard Emerson on power dependence relations (see Emerson 1962, 1964) and subsequent work by Karen Cook and others on power and exchange (Cook and Emerson 1978; Cook and Yamagishi 1992; Cook et al. 1983). Emerson's work on power dependence relations is an appropriate model because it does for the concept, power, what can be done for the concept, trust. It shifts the framework surrounding the study of power from that of an attribute of an individual (who governs or is perhaps more powerful in the community) to that of a property of a social relation. The unit of analysis in this work of Emerson and Cook is the exchange relation or network of exchange relations, not individuals or attributes of individuals. We view trust relations similarly and wish to ground the analysis of trust in social relations and networks.

In our actual experience, trusting is subject to quite specific constraints. It takes the restricted form, "A trusts B to do $x$" (Hardin 1992; see also Hardin 1991)—that is to say, a person (A) trusts another specific person (B) to do some limited range of things or perform some action with respect to some relatively defined matter $(x)$. For example, I trust you to repay minor debts, such as the debt incurred when you borrow money from me to buy lunch. I might not trust you to repay a large debt, and I might therefore not make a large loan to you, even if I had the resources to do so; or I might not trust you with confidential information. Hence, it is generally wrong to say, simply, I trust you, unless there is an implicit limitation on what I trust you to do. This means that many relational considerations come into play, that my trust is a property of our social relation. It depends, of course, on the nature of my interests, your interests, our knowledge of each other, and possibly other attributes (such as gender, occupation, or education level). It also depends, however, on the larger context of our social relations and the broader network of relations that surrounds us. In particular, in this account, the notion of trust is made relational, at least implicitly, by making it a function of iterated or ongoing interactions.

Note that thinking of trust as ground for cooperation in each instance of an iterated exchange immediately yields the result that distrust is easy to establish whereas trust is much harder to establish. Simply failing to fulfill an initial exchange makes for distrust, but it might take several successful fulfillments to induce us to trust someone. For example, suppose it takes the positive payoffs from five successful cooperations to outweigh the loss of one failed cooperation. Then it would take five first-time exchanges with optimistic cooperators to outweigh one failed first-time initiative with a pessimist. Hence, one will have incentive to avoid first-time interactions and to stick to interactions with those one already knows to be cooperative, that is, those already in one's network. As James Coleman notes, it takes time to develop trust (Coleman 1990, 104).

We start from the encapsulated-interest theory of trust: A trusts B with respect to matters $x$, and A trusts B for the reason that A thinks B has incentive grounded in A (typically, in A's interests) to be reliable to A. For example, A and B might be in an ongoing relationship that is of value to B, so that B will not wish to damage the prospects of continuing that relationship by defaulting on A's trust. The network conception of trust fits these characteristics with only a slight change: A trusts those in network B with respect to matters $x$. In this case, however, it is in B's interest to fulfill A's trust not merely because A may de facto sanction B by withdrawing from future exchanges with B but also because others in their network may also withdraw from future exchanges with untrustworthy B. Network trust brings in reputational effects, but specifically the reputational effects within the network itself, because it is within the network that they will have force (see also chapter 4, this volume). Trust that is based in a network can be backed by far greater sanctioning force than that which is based merely in a dyadic relationship—although for very important dyadic relationships, such as marriage, within-dyad sanctions may be most of the story. For matters $y$, A may trust those in network C but not many or even any of those in network B. A's trust is not general but is, rather, richly relational and embedded.

Other social theorists have implicitly assumed a relational context, as, for example, in Coleman's account of trust and trust-inducing social structures (Coleman 1990, especially chapter 5). It is hard to separate Coleman's relational conditions for trust from the background of normative social control and informal monitoring and sanctioning. If you have normative social control or informal monitoring and sanctioning, it is not at all clear that trust is "required" in any strong sense of the term. For example, the strategy of the Grameen (or village) Bank of Bangladesh is so-called peer lending. "To obtain a loan, an individual must band together with four neighbors. The group meets with a loan officer and then chooses one or two of the five to be eligible for an initial loan. Before another group member can receive a loan, the first borrowers must make regular repayments." This is clearly a device for small-group enforcement of the equivalent of a norm of responsibility to the group. The bank, therefore, need not trust the first loan recipient. It can merely rely on the peer sanctioning of that recipient by fellow villagers to secure repayment, which reputedly happens for an astonishing 98 percent of its loans (Holloway and Wallich 1992, 126).[3]

The Grameen Bank was created by an economist, Muhammad Yunus, who reports that 94 percent of its borrowers are landless, rural women (Yunus 1998, 1999).[4] It is instructive to note that the extraordinary achievement of the bank and its system is to create entrepreneurs in a village context in which norms commonly have been directed at keeping women in a secondary status with sometimes brutal sanctions, including the sexist sanctions of Islam. The women of Grameen have been empowered in ways that break those older norms, very much as Albert Hirschman (1977) argues that commercial society softened such stifling norms in the early days of capitalism. In effect, self-interest in commercial prospects and prosperity trumps norms backed by self-interest in not being sanctioned, because the former interest outweighs the latter. Some individuals are finally willing to flout communal norms and their sanctions in order to gain financially from exchange relations organized around interests—that is to say, from market relations—rather than around norms.

One of the bank's greatest benefits may prove to be that it has put many of its borrowers and communities into network that may be used for information sharing and coordination. These networks may develop relationships grounded in trust rather than in norms of exclusion, and they have the potential to enable people in them to develop their capacities and their economic opportunities more broadly.

## Small Towns, Urban Areas, and Trustworthiness

The central issue in understanding both communal norms and network trust is to understand how reliability or trustworthiness arises and is supported. The research of Paul Amato (1993) and others suggests that there are differences in the nature of helping and cooperative relations in small towns and large cities in the United States. Amato finds that helping behavior in small towns is a matter not of reciprocity norms but of helping or communal norms, whereas seemingly similar behavior in cities is typically a matter of reciprocity. Moreover, in small towns, such behavior is generalized to cover everyone in the community, whereas in cities the reciprocity governs behavior within particular networks. I reciprocate helping behavior toward those in my network who would help me in similar circumstances. An apparent implication of these differences is that trust and trustworthiness both grow out of reciprocal relations in cities and also ground or contribute to such relations.

Life in small towns, as in the villages that anthropologists and others have studied, typically generates reliability among its members because of the repeated nature of the interactions, the close-knit community, which fosters direct and indirect information sharing about the behavior of individuals, and the widespread opportunities for informal monitoring and sanctioning. Normative violations, such as the failure to keep an agreement or otherwise behave as expected, are the common currency of small-town talk. In such settings, social regulation is primarily accomplished through these normatively based mechanisms, that is, through the enforcement of norms. So effective are the practices of shunning and ostracism that more formal mechanisms of behavioral regulation in such tight-knit communities are commonly not required.

Francis Fukuyama idealizes small-town life in many respects, as he does family life, in noting that it is only in such contexts of shared values that moral communities form. He goes further to argue that "it is these moral communities alone that can generate the kind of social trust that is critical to organizational efficiency" (Fukuyama 1995, 309). He applies this basic thesis to the efficiency of national economies. The heart of his argument is that the balance between individualism and community has shifted recently in the United States (over the past five decades), and he surmises (as does Robert Putnam [1995a, 1995b]) that this is in part a result of the decline in general sociability in society. "The moral communities that made up American civil society at midcentury, from the family to neighborhoods to churches to workplaces, have been under assault," Fukuyama declares in support of Putnam's general thesis about the decline in membership in voluntary associations in the United States (Fukuyama 1995, 308).

Here, Fukuyama makes a causal claim that relations in the larger urban society depend on prior relations at a smaller scale. We do not make such a causal claim that trust or trustworthiness in general develops from small-community cooperativeness, and we do not claim that networks of dyadic interactions, in which trust and trustworthiness commonly do develop, generate a norm of cooperativeness. In fact, either or neither of these causal claims might be true sometimes and false at other times, but in any case we do not make them here. Our claims, as stated at the outset of the chapter, are merely that small communities and urban contexts are strategically different in ways that lead to different modal ways of resolving the problem of mutual assistance. The small community commonly works through norms that are quasi-universal for the community and that cover virtually all aspects of potential cooperativeness. The urban society works through networks of ongoing relationships that are embedded within the much larger context, and any one of these networks is partial in that it covers only a particular realm of potential cooperation, so that we are each involved in many quite different networks. The small-community norm is a collective norm, enforced through individual-level incentives of the threatened sanction of exclusion; the urban networks of trusting relations combine dyadic and reputational incentives that are enforced dyadically.

Moreover, it is difficult to accept the thesis that Fukuyama's moral communities are in fact what is causally required for the production of trustworthiness and thus trust in society. In a study comparing Swedish and German groups, Dietlind Stolle finds that the members of groups with weak bonds—that is, weak within-group trust—have higher levels of generalized trust than do members of groups with strong within-group trust (Stolle 1998, 515). Part of this difference may be explained by self-selection, but there is a significant additional effect of the kind of group membership on longer-run trustingness (518). Fukuyama's so-called moral communities are often models of exclusionary tactics that may foster within-group trustworthiness but almost as commonly foster distrust of outsiders. Hence, they can lower the possibility for intergroup trust within society (Hardin 1995, chapter 4). There is little or no effort to assess the balance in this trade-off.

Small communities with almost entirely overlapping networks for various purposes may have some of the characteristics of the political communities that have congruent cleavages and that therefore have weak or no ties with other communities. Arguments that prevailed in comparative politics three to four decades ago suggest that communities with congruent cleavages differ significantly in their politics from those with crosscutting cleavages. Those with congruent cleavages may be more inclined to extremist politics and separatism and less inclined to pluralist accommodation than are those with crosscutting cleavages. This claim seems to fit the patterns of support for the recent violence in Yugoslavia and separatism in Canada. Rural Serbs and rural French Canadians have been the chief backers of these movements (Hardin 1995, chapter 6). The joke in Canada, too true to be funny, is that those rural French Canadians who have never seen an anglophone Canadian are the ones most hostile to them. More generally, racism and other forms of often brutal ethnocentrism are commonly more evident in small, closed communities than in large, open communities. These conclusions cut strongly against some current paeans to the beauties of small communities, although the conclusion may be only that variance among such communities is likely to be greater than within urban communities with crosscutting cleavages.

In a comparative study of urban and small-town networks in two California communities, Claude Fischer (1982) analyzes in detail the network forms that emerge in urban settings to enable people to establish exchange relations and the social bases for collective action. These forms are different from those in small towns. Although subcommunities within urban settings may approximate small-town life (such as suburban enclaves or small ethnic neighborhoods), the modal form of interaction is more network based than group based. Individuals participate in modern life through many social networks (or social circles), which are usually overlapping. Such social networks have been mapped quite extensively by sociologists and anthropologists in various cultures (see Lin forthcoming; for example, on differences in social networks by gender).

In more urban settings the networks individuals form to establish relationships of social exchange and cooperation (or merely to coordinate joint activity) tend to be more specialized, less multiplex, more sparsely connected, and more numerous. They are multiple rather than multiplex. In addition, some of the networks are overlapping. For example, a friendship network may easily overlap with one's sport- or card-playing network but not at all with one's work network. Norms of reciprocity often develop within a network of relations defined on a particular domain of social activity (such as sport) but are less likely to be generalized across the members of one's various networks, in the same way that more generalized norms come to exist in small towns and closed communities in which membership is stable and the networks are multiplex with a high degree of overlap. By contrast, in a small town one's work, friendship, and recreation networks may all include most, if not all, of the same people.

The invention of the vocabulary of trust is relatively recent in the English language, and such vocabulary is still missing, nascent, or far more limited in many other languages. The fact that a vocabulary of trust is commonly absent surprises many writers on trust, who take it for granted that the notion has an almost Platonic reality and that it is fundamentally necessary for social relations. This fact fits well with the sense that trust is primarily at issue in contexts in which relationships and networks are multifaceted, if not so well in contexts in which a single communal network ties everyone together over virtually all issues, as in traditional small towns or villages. In the latter, norms of cooperativeness are often very strong, so that reciprocal trusting relationships have little additional role to play. Much of the current concern with declining generalized or social trust may therefore actually be misplaced. Such trust is supposedly trust in the generalized other whom one does not even know. "Trust" may not be the right term for what is at issue here—merely confident expectations might be all that is at stake, as in learning models of trust (Hardin 1992). What happens in the shift from small to large communities is a shift from reliance on normative regulation of behavior to the use of ongoing trust relationships. Trust and trustworthiness are more in need in larger communities with more diverse ties for varied activities than in smaller communities. That being the case, what people in smaller and larger communities mean when they say they trust most others probably differs. In smaller communities they mean that they can rely on almost everyone in the community, because the community will encourage everyone to be reliable and will sanction those who are not. In larger communities they cannot rely on everyone in this way because the close community sanctions are missing. Hence members of such communities can rely on those with whom they have trusting relationships but not so confidently on others. In both cases, it is not "most people" but only most people with whom they deal that they might actually trust.

The untrustworthy can often take advantage of the general level of trustworthiness of most people by, in essence, free riding on the expectations of others that they will fulfill trusts. (One who distrusts does not in any similar sense free ride on the trustingness of others.) Generalized or social trust therefore sets up individuals for being exploited. Such exploitation is relatively difficult in a small community in which reputational effects would enable an exploited person to bring broader sanctions to bear on the exploiter, but it would be hard to block in an urban setting. Hence, the setting in which we expect trust to play the larger necessary role is one in which generalized trust must fail fairly quickly, at least for matters in which risks from a failed trust might be substantial. Implicitly, therefore, the notion of generalized trust cannot apply.

Trustworthy behavior can be based on interest or normative commitments, and trust itself must be grounded in knowledge of either the interests or the normative commitments of the trusted. If helping behavior is based on norms, as in small communities, the relevant norms could have grown by a socioevolutionary process out of reciprocal exchange relations within groups. This could be a natural development for teaching children, to whom it might be much easier to teach a simple rule (as in a norm) than an understanding of the complexities of the interests of others. Indeed, many adults appear to be unable to grasp even the logic of the interests embedded in iterated-exchange interactions.

That a norm of trustworthiness might commonly be reinforced by interests might well help it to survive and to motivate people. The communal norms of helping and trustworthiness might arise out of reciprocal exchange relations and then be transformed into more generalized norms, albeit ones that are still reinforced most forcefully only as within-group norms, initiating a process characterized by the distressing tendency to develop exclusionary norms (Hardin 1995, chapter 4). The urban norms may be less normatively conceived and may more openly be grounded in reciprocal exchange relations within ongoing networks.

If reliability or trustworthiness is grounded in norms in the small-town context and in reciprocal networks in more complex contexts, we might expect to see consequential differences in behavior and judgment in the two contexts. In smaller communities, in which the prevailing reason for being cooperative is the strong group norm, one might expect to rely on people primarily according to their competence rather than according to their normative commitments, because the latter will be relatively similar from one individual to another, whereas competence with respect to any particular endeavor may vary considerably. Of course, some will be more fully motivated than others by local norms, but the direction of the motivation will be the same, whereas competence will vary greatly and will be noticed as a ground for selecting someone for cooperation in a relevant venture. In urban networks, however, there might be a marked tendency to rely on very particular people for their commitments, especially if each of one's various networks is based on different concerns often having to do with particular competencies. When disappointed by the failure of any of these network members, people may hold them morally responsible independently of whether the failure is one of commitment or of competence, because they will have been selected on their commitment, not their competence—that is, because it is their commitment that markedly distinguishes them from most other people.

Note a peculiar implication of strong communal or group norms. The imposition of such norms may make everyone or nearly everyone trustworthy over many important ranges of interaction. Yet one might expect cooperation from others not because they are competent but rather because they are subject to the sanctions of a relevant norm. Hence, in small communities, there might be general trustworthiness but almost no dependence on that fact and, hence, little trust. This is not to say that there would be distrust but merely to say that trust as encapsulated interest need not be a consideration in entering into cooperation with others. Alternatively, we might simply suppose that cooperativeness is overdetermined in such communities because it is backed both by norms enforced at the group level and by the sanctions of trust relationships at the dyadic level. It is plausibly for this reason that the vocabulary of trust apparently does not arise in societies until they cease to be essentially communal.

## Cross-Cultural Evidence on Networks, Norms, and Trust

In the study of organizations it is now commonplace to see references to the role of trust in facilitating social and economic transactions (Macaulay 1963). James Lincoln, Michael Gerlach, and Peggy Takahashi (1992), for example, indicate how important the keiretsu criteria of trust and long-term relationships are in the types of vertical and horizontal networks of interfirm linkages that occur in Japanese society and that have been argued to grant Japan an economic competitive advantage. The formation of networks of trusted contacts is viewed as essential in the context of highly uncertain and turbulent economic and political environments. As Lincoln and colleagues put it, "Economic actors appear to regard the market as too important to abandon to the free play of market forces alone" (561). The simple formation of fairly stable sets of regularized exchange relations reduces the market to a more structured set of exchange opportunities or trading partnerships (such as keiretsu networks). Networks of this type reduce transaction costs, and as Fritz Scharpf (1994, 27) argues, "when such ongoing relations do exist, the reliability of actors' expectations, and their trust in each other's commitments, may be raised far above the level that would be reasonable even among well-socialized strangers."

The widespread use of personal networks as the basis for business relations, which has been documented in many cultural contexts, is another example of the use of networks (and dyadic commitment mechanisms) to reduce uncertainty in trading relations. To avoid the uncertainty of the market (or political and social turmoil), business relations are often embedded within a broad network of long-standing social ties (frequently based on kinship). The Japanese keiretsu networks reduce risk, lower transaction costs, and make communication easier and interfirm relations more predictable (Lincoln, Gerlach, and Takahashi 1992). In addition, they generally provide "protection" against competition from firms outside the network. They may do this at considerable cost, however, because reliance on them may reduce the range of alternative partners one might use.

The use of personal ties as the basis for business relations is even more common in Chinese society, according to Gary Hamilton and Xiaotong Fei (1992), who characterize Chinese society as composed of overlapping networks of people linked through a variety of social relationships. Part of the importance of these networks is that they form the basis not only for social organization but also for social control. As they note, "the entire network of people joined through a set of relationships is implicated in any one person's failure to perform appropriately" (Hamilton and Fei 1992, 28). Hence, this system is similar in structure to the group responsibility for loans of the Grameen Bank of Bangladesh, which relies on the peer sanctioning of the recipient of a loan by fellow villagers to secure repayment. The Chinese system of overlapping networks of interconnected relationships allows for informal monitoring and sanctioning by third parties, also from within the group. Hence, the means of control in such a society is localized in the institutionalized network of relations (Hamilton and Fei 1992), as with the loans of the Grameen Bank. It is organized by norms, not by reciprocal relationships of trust.

In Chinese society these overlapping networks of personal relationships entail fairly explicit behavioral expectations. These expectations are embedded in what Hamilton and Fei call particular relational codes that are specific to the types of social relations represented in the network. Each network tie represents a dyadic link of social import and normative control, as in a guanxi relation, and these moral codes are highly differentiated according to type of tie (see also Lin 1982, forthcoming). These relational codes are deeply ingrained in the culture and are not easily picked up by "outsiders." Even if outsiders could learn these normative expectations, they cannot easily or soon enough develop the sets of relationships involved. As a result, the boundary between outsider and insider (or ingroup and out-group) is quite strong. (One implication of this feature of

Chinese society, as Hamilton and Fei [1992] suggest, is that the basis of social control in the society is the dyadic relationship, whereas in Western societies it is the individual that forms the basis of much law and social control.) These close relationships are the most predictable and reliable, in part, because "they are the most controlled, both internally and externally" (Hamilton and Fei 1992). In this way they provide a critical resource for economic enterprises. Typically, these kin-based networks are the main route of entrance into the economy for families. In the absence of kinship ties, relationships form on the basis of birthplace or a substitute that approximates kinship. For business purposes, at least, these people can be trusted as if they were kin (Hamilton and Fei 1992, 32).

Personal intermediaries are a central aspect of the Confucian vision of social interaction. When dealing with someone new, a Chinese might ask a guanxi contact for assurance that the new person is trustworthy. This is often equated with influence peddling in Western understandings—or misunderstandings—that presumably generalize from the use of a guanxi to break the ice with a new person or business associate. However, one might merely seek an intermediary's recommendations that another is competent, honest, knowledgeable, or trustworthy.[5] The use of a guanxi connection is an instance of Coleman's third-party or intermediary trust.

Commenting on the extensive use of personal networks in social and business relations in Japanese society, Toshio Yamagishi and Midori Yamagishi (1994) argue that what is commonly believed to characterize these relations in Japan is not mutual trust based on a general belief in human benevolence but rather the mutual insurance that comes from engagement in long-term personal relationships (that is, iterated interactions). Insurance against exploitation is built into the iterated nature of the interactions and the incentives they provide that inhibit opportunism and foster honesty, fidelity, and loyalty (Williamson 1975; Hardin 1991).

In his widely read study of differential success in the economic behavior of whole national economies, Fukuyama (1995) compares systems based on familial trust with those based on looser, more generalized trust. He argues that familial trust, which is based on thick, dependent, and long-term relationships, facilitates the creation of small-scale enterprises, even among immigrant families. However, familial trust is often exclusionary in the strong sense that it produces distrust of those who are not in the "family," and it therefore limits economic growth at some stages and sometimes generates severe ethnic conflict, as in mixed societies such as that of Malaysia and in immigrant communities such as those in American cities. He further contends that, for example, Taiwan, which depends on familial trust, has developed rapidly only because it has had a strongly interventionist state, despite the fact that its typical firm size remains very small. The creation of large firms, such as those in the United States, requires more generalized trust. Such trust has its disadvantages, too, however, because it is less effective for organizing the small, flexible, creative work environments that get economic development under way in a traditional society—as in China today, where the intensity of familial trust is especially useful in the transitional economy.

Fukuyama holds that Japan's economic success has depended on its use of generalized trust, which allows for large firms. This characterization is contested by many students of Japan, especially by social psychologists who have studied Japanese norms of group orientation and anti-individualism. What we need to explain in a society as advanced and economically dynamic and supple as Japan's is why and when individuals are or are not willing to give up committed, narrowly group-based relationships as the fundamental basis for their exchanges in favor of the riskier but higher return of transactions with those outside their groups. Recent experimental and survey research (Yamagishi and Yamagishi 1994, Yamagishi, Cook, and Watabe 1998) addresses the social psychological and social structural reasons why individuals may not be willing to give up committed relationships. Perhaps these studies especially tap issues that are organized by single, multiplex networks at the small-group level, whereas the economy is run by looser sets of multiple, overlapping networks, so that Fukuyama and the social psychologists might both be right but with respect to different matters.

Whether a society evolves a pattern of strong (Japanese-style) networks or one of loose, overlapping (U.S-style) networks might be a matter of coordination equilibria. The pattern of strong networks is similar to the pattern of a multiplicity of dimensions of group interests that is resolved into congruent cleavages. The pattern of loose networks is similar to overlapping cleavages of interests. We may instructively, if loosely, speak of autarkic and market organization of networks. With congruent cleavages, a community is organized autarkically without reliance on others outside their single group. As a rule, we can expect autarkic exchange relations in a small community to be very limited in what they can offer to us. They do not take advantage of the variety and richness of other offerings that might be available in much larger, more diverse communities. (This is, of course, merely an analogue to the standard claim for the benefits of free trade.) The risk averse might prefer the more limited, smaller setting even at the cost of reduced opportunities for richer outcomes.

To break the autarkic pattern of exclusive networks, it might be necessary first to go to a state of individualism from which a move to a quasi–market organization might then be possible. The prior move to individualism or even normlessness might be stimulated by the fact that the congruent cleavages of the closed autarkic system cease to map interests as a society changes in various ways—for example, as merit is increasingly a criterion for position and as entrepreneurialism spreads. The establishment of the market pattern in North America might have resulted from or have been reinforced by the multiethnic origins of Americans and by the unusually open opportunity structure that evolved as new lands opened over the course of the eighteenth and nineteenth centuries.

There might be alternative equilibria. For example, contemporary Parisian society almost rigidly separates professional from personal networks and in this respect seems nearly the opposite of Japanese society. Personal networks, however, follow the autarkic norm of exclusive groups without overlaps except as families intermarry, so that in this respect Parisian and Japanese societies seem similar. Parisian professional networks resemble the market norm of open, flexible, overlapping connections. Hence, social group autarky is coupled with market organization of professional life.

There may also be very destructive equilibria. For example, familial trust can turn exclusionary, so that outsiders may become actively distrusted. Various studies of peasant communities in southern Italy, Mexico, and Peru suggest that people in such communities sometimes develop what the political scientist Edward Banfield (1958) calls amoral familism (see Aguilar 1984; Westacott and Williams 1976; and, for a brief survey, Govier 1997, 135–46). Family members stick together and both lie to and distrust others. Rather than refer to peasant societies in general—many of which are very different from these—a better way to characterize the conditions of the societies in these studies is to say that they are subsistence societies, often at a level of poverty and hunger that is daunting.

People in these societies seem to see life as a zero-sum competition with others. There are at least four reasons for this. First, they are overwhelmingly dependent on land because theirs is an economy of agricultural subsistence. Land is essentially zero-sum: If my family has more land, some other family has less. Second, if we are all producing the same things (food for our families, for example), there are few opportunities for division of labor outside the family. Some of the opportunities for exchange or cooperative behavior in more complex societies are therefore not available in some subsistence societies, so that there are limited opportunities for learning the advantages of cooperation. Third, the form of agricultural production in these societies does not depend on joint efforts, so that there is no natural reason to have a system of broadly cooperative agricultural effort that might spill over into other realms. Finally, in a subsistence system it is natural, because sensible, to be highly risk averse and to develop practices that are sure to have the least likelihood of crop failure in especially bad years, when many would starve, rather than the greatest likelihood of producing a surplus in the average year. In the longer run, however, this risk aversion undercuts the possibility of escaping from the poverty of subsistence.

People in these societies therefore fail to cooperate—in part because it would do no good in many contexts and in part because they naturally focus on the competitive, zero-sum aspects of their lives. If there is no point in cooperation, there may even be advantage in deceit, secrecy, and cheating, as there typically is in a zero-sum conflict. Banfield's amoral society is metaphorically a poker game with life and death stakes. Of course, if everyone outside my family is likely to cheat me, I have good reason not to trust them.

We may sum up the distinctive quality of these societies by noting that they lack networks that go beyond the family. They have neither a multiplicity of networks nor a multiplex, all-inclusive network. They have only a collection of unrelated, mutually exclusive familial networks. Hence, they can achieve trustworthiness beyond the family neither through the imposition of group sanctions nor with the imposition of network or extended dyadic sanctions. John Locke supposed that no one could be trustworthy without the threat of punishment in the afterlife. In these societies it appears that one cannot be considered trustworthy without the threat of extrafamilial sanctions. For them, the world is sometimes a perverse variant on that of Weber's cartoon: it is a predictably dangerous and frightening place.

Such perverse equilibrium states might be extremely stable, unless there is finally intervention from outside. They are stable because anyone who tries to be cooperative is at risk of being exploited by others. To move away from pervasive distrust requires moves by several or many at once and cannot easily be initiated by a single member of the community. An endogenous change that might break the equilibrium would be a change in the relative wealth and prosperity of one family that made it willing to take the risk of relying on others for their services. Hence, initial inequality would plausibly be mutually beneficial (Hardin and Cook 1999).

Studies by Julian Rotter (1980) conclude that those who trust lead happier lives. Unfortunately, Rotter's conclusion is limited by the fact that his subjects were middle-class white American university students whose lives were relatively good and whose experiences with others were likely to have justified their trust in those others. People in such conditions might generally be expected to lead happier lives than those in environments in which people cannot be trusted. In other words, trust does not directly cause happiness; rather, trust and relative happiness are both likely to be the result of the benign conditions of Rotter's subjects—in particular, of the trustworthiness of those with whom these subjects generally interacted. Well-grounded trust—trust in others who are trustworthy—can indirectly contribute to happiness by spurring us to cooperate with those others (Hardin 1992). One would like to see what Rotter's studies would conclude if they were undertaken in zero-sum peasant societies based on familial, exclusionary norms. In such a society, it may be the most adamant distruster who prospers most and is happiest with life. Trudi Govier (1997, 134) remarks that "Rotter and Fukuyama seem willfully insensitive to the existence of cases in which distrust is warranted or people are greatly harmed because they have trusted." They are not alone among recent writers on the benignity and beauty of trust.

## Appendix: Some Related Accounts

Terminology about the issues of communal norms and network trust relations is quite varied in what is a growing and diverse literature. For the sake of conceptual clarification, we briefly canvass three closely related discussions that differ terminologically from one another and also differ strategically from the issues in our discussion.

The differences Amato notes between cooperative relations and helping behavior in small towns and large cities raise interesting issues concerning the nature of the groups and networks that produce trustworthiness in these settings. Yamagishi and Cook (1993) distinguish group-generalized and network-generalized exchange. Network-generalized exchange involves dyadic but not necessarily reciprocal interactions between members of the network. It therefore works through incentives from sanctions within the network—that is, through dyadic interactions. This is closely related in its structure to the communal norm of cooperativeness, although the most effective working of that norm depends on sanctions from virtually all members of the community. In group-generalized exchange, such dyadic enforcement is unavailable, because individuals contribute to the group's collective good rather than to one another individually. Hence, norm enforcement would suffer from free-rider problems. It is not typically in the interest of one of us to sanction a noncontributor, because the sanctioner gets little of the benefit from making the noncontributor contribute. In a group of moderate size, however, shunning a shirker, especially if several group members participate in the shunning, might cost the sanctioners less than it costs the shirker, so that the shunning might not be against the interests of the sanctioners.

The nature of group-generalized exchange fits Hardin's (1995, chapter 5) account of universalistic norms involving large-group benefits. Such norms are typically weaker than those governing dyadic interactions (Hardin 1995, 102–4). For example, as noted above, a norm against lying is dyadically enforced fairly readily, because if you lie to me, I will bear the cost of your deceit and will want to block you from gaining further through lying to me again. That is to say, it is directly in my interest to shun or otherwise sanction you; doing so does not entail a net cost to me, as is often assumed for sanctioners of normative misbehavior. Indeed, we may not even need a strong norm, that is, one which is deeply inculcated, against lying in many contexts. It will commonly not be in an individual's interest to lie, simply because the victim of the lie will have incentive to counter it and even to shun the liar for future interactions. It is only when such dyadic devices do not work that we might have a norm, the purpose of which is to add to the incentives individuals have to act cooperatively. Still, norms that serve collective interests are stronger when they are consistent with individual interests in sanctioning their violation and weaker when not (Hardin 1995, 140). The communal norms that we discuss here are collective but at the relatively small-group level of a small, close community, and they need not generalize to the much larger scale of an urban society just because sanctioning violators in such a diffuse context might not be in the interest of others.

Finally, Thomas Voss (chapter 4, this volume) discusses what is essentially a dyadic norm of cooperation that is enforced by sanctions not only from the person who suffers from a violation of it but also from others in the community through its multilateral reputational effects. Here he has in mind reciprocal cooperation, such as occurs in network trust relations, rather than the diffuse cooperativeness in small communities that we discuss. The trust relations that may govern networks in urban contexts are more nearly like the cooperative relations at the heart of Voss's account of the repeated-games approach to cooperation (which is also the approach to trust in the encapsulated-interest account). His brief discussion of "small, stable, and culturally homogeneous communities" and the norms of cooperation that are collectively enforceable in them might be analogous to our account of communal norms of cooperativeness if his norms do not depend on reciprocal exchange of benefits. Our norm of relatively general cooperativeness within a small community might often apply to members who primarily bear the costs of benefiting others without themselves being beneficiaries in return, either from those they specifically help or from anyone else in the community who might be subject to the norm of cooperativeness. That is to say, this norm applies even in contexts that do not have the structure of a prisoner's dilemma, which is the structure of Voss's norm.

## Notes

1. The most extreme sanction is to kill the violator, as in the Arab-Islamic practice of killing women who are thought to have committed adultery. The killing is commonly done by a male member of the woman's own family (see Douglas Jehl, "Arab Honor's Price: A Woman's Blood," *New York Times*, June 20, 1999).

2. There can, at least in principle, be a norm for virtually any behavior. Hence, there is no bite to the claim that there might be a norm of trustworthiness. The critical issue is whether trust relationships can work without any such norm, as apparently they can and commonly do.

3. "All loans must be repaid before anyone becomes eligible for a second, larger loan" (Holloway and Wallich 1992). In Miami in the 1960s, so-called character loans to Cuban immigrants were secured dyadically because anyone who failed to repay had no further prospects (Portes and Sensenbrenner 1993, 1334–35; Portes and Stepick 1993, chapters 5 and 6). See also Light 1972.

4. The bank's program has been replicated in fifty-eight nations.

5. Discussions with James Hsiung at New York University, October 29, 1997. Also see Boyer 1997 and Holan 1997.

# References

Aguilar, John. 1984. "Trust and Exchange: Expressive and Instrumental Dimensions of Reciprocity in a Peasant Community." *Ethos* 12(1): 3–29.

Amato, Paul R. 1993. "Urban-Rural Differences in Helping Friends and Family Members." *Social Psychology Quarterly* 56(4): 249–62.

Banfield, Edward C. 1958. *The Moral Basis of a Backward Society*. New York: Free Press.

Boyer, Peter J. 1997. "American Guanxi." *New Yorker,* April 14, pp. 48–61.

Coleman, James S. 1990. *Foundations of Social Theory*. Cambridge: Harvard University Press.

Cook, Karen S., and Richard Emerson. 1978. "Power, Equity, and Commitment in Exchange Networks." *American Sociological Review* 43(5): 721–39.

Cook, Karen S., Richard Emerson, Mary Gillmore, and Toshio Yamagishi. 1983. "The Distribution of Power in Exchange Networks: Theory and Empirical Results." *American Journal of Sociology* 89(2): 275–305.

Cook, Karen S., and Toshio Yamagishi. 1992. "Power in Exchange Networks: A Power-Dependence Formulation." *Social Networks* 14(3–4): 245–65.

Emerson, Richard M. 1962. "Power-Dependence Relations." *American Sociological Review* 27(1): 31–41.

———. 1964. "Power-Dependence Relations: Two Experiments." *Sociometry* 27(3): 282–98.

Fischer, Claude S. 1982. *To Dwell Among Friends: Personal Networks in Town and City*. Chicago: University of Chicago Press.

Fukuyama, Francis. 1995. *The Social Virtues and the Creation of Prosperity*. New York: Free Press.

Govier, Trudy. 1997. *Social Trust and Human Communities*. Montreal: McGill–Queens University Press.

Hamilton, Gary, and Xiaotong Fei. 1992. *From the Soil: The Foundation of Chinese Society*. Berkeley: University of California Press.

Hardin, Russell. 1991. "Trusting Persons, Trusting Institutions." In *The Strategy of Choice*, edited by Richard J. Zeckhauser. Cambridge, Mass.: MIT Press.

———. 1992. "The Street-Level Epistemology of Trust." *Analyse und Kritik* 14: 152–76. (Reprinted in *Politics and Society* 21 [1993]: 505–29.)

———. 1995. *One for All: The Logic of Group Conflict*. Princeton, N.J.: Princeton University Press.

Hardin, Russell, and Karen S. Cook. 1999. "Equality and Inequality: Micro and Macro Tradeoffs." Paper presented to the Thirty-fourth World Congress of the International Institute of Sociology. Tel Aviv (July 11–15, 1999).

Hirschman, Albert O. 1977. *The Passions and the Interests: Arguments for Capitalism Before Its Triumph*. Princeton, N.J.: Princeton University Press.

Holan, Frank. 1997. "Letter to the Editor." *New Yorker,* May 19, 1997, p.10.

Holloway, Marguerite, and Paul Wallich. 1992. "A Risk Worth Taking." *Scientific American*, November, 126.

Light, Ivan. 1972. *Ethnic Enterprise in America: Business and Welfare Among Chinese, Japanese, and Blacks*. Berkeley: University of California Press.

Lin, Nan. 1982. "Social Resources and Instrumental Action." In *Social Structure and*

*Network Analysis,* ed. Peter V. Marsden and Nan Lin. Beverly Hills, Calif.: Sage Publications.

————. Forthcoming. *Social Resources and Social Action.* New York: Cambridge University Press.

Lincoln, James R., Michael Gerlach, and Peggy Takahashi. 1992. "Keiretsu Networks in the Japanese Economy: A Dyad Analysis of Intercorporate Ties." *American Sociological Review* 57(5): 561–85.

Macaulay, Stewart. 1963. "Non-contractual Relations in Business: A Preliminary Study." *American Sociological Review* 28(1): 55–67.

Malinowski, Bronislaw. 1922. *Argonauts of the Western Pacific.* London: Routledge and Kegan Paul.

McIntosh, Elizabeth P. 1998. *Sisterhood of Spies: The Women of the OSS.* Annapolis, Md.: Naval Institute Press.

Portes, Alejandro, and Julia Sensenbrenner. 1993. "Embeddedness and Immigration: Notes on the Social Determinants of Economic Action." *American Journal of Sociology* 98(6): 1320–50.

Portes, Alejandro, and Alex Stepick. 1993. *City on the Edge.* Berkeley: University of California Press.

Putnam, Robert. 1995a. "Bowling Alone: America's Declining Social Capital." *Journal of Democracy* 6: 65–78.

————. 1995b. "Tuning In, Tuning Out: The Strange Disappearance of Social Capital in America." *PS: Political Science and Politics* (December): 664–83.

Rotter, Julian B. 1980. "Interpersonal Trust, Trustworthiness, and Gullibility." *American Psychologist* 35(1): 1–7.

Scharpf, Fritz. 1994. "Games Real Actors Could Play: Positive and Negative Coordination in Embedded Negotiations." *Journal of Theoretical Politics* 6: 27–53.

Stolle, Dietlind. 1998. "Bowling Together, Bowling Alone: The Development of Generalized Trust in Voluntary Associations." *Political Psychology* 19(3): 497–525.

Westacott, George H., and Lawrence K. Williams. 1976. "Interpersonal Trust and Modern Attitudes in Peru." *International Journal of Contemporary Society* 13(1–2): 117–37.

Westlake, Donald. 1998. "The Ladies Who Lied." Review of McIntosh 1998. *New York Times Book Review*, May 31, 1998, p. 44.

Williamson, Oliver E. 1975. *Markets and Hierarchies: Analysis and Antitrust Implications.* New York: Free Press.

Yamagishi, Toshio, and Karen S. Cook. 1993. "Generalized Exchange and Social Dilemmas." *Social Psychology Quarterly* 56(4): 235–48.

Yamagishi, Toshio, Karen Cook, and Motoki Watabe. 1998. "Uncertainty, Trust, and Commitment Formation." *American Journal of Sociology* 104(1): 165–94.

Yamagishi, Toshio, and Midori Yamagishi. 1994. "Trust and Commitment in the United States and Japan." *Motivation and Emotion* 18(2): 129–66.

Yunus, Muhammad. 1998. "Alleviating Poverty Through Technology." *Science*, October 16, 1998, pp. 409–10.

————. 1999. *Banker to the Poor: Micro-Lending and the Battle Against World Poverty.* New York: Public Affairs.

# 12

# RULE FINDING ABOUT RULE MAKING: COMPARISON PROCESSES AND THE MAKING OF RULES

## *Guillermina Jasso*

UMANS are rule makers. Every day, and in every area of life, they make rules—rules for themselves, rules for other individuals, and rules for groups and societies.[1] This intense rule-making activity may be a manifestation of a basic impulse to organize and systematize and simplify. Indeed, humans are not only *rule makers*, they are also *rule finders*. In understanding the world around them, humans find a wealth of rules—rules that summarize their views about the way the world works.

It is thus no accident that science and ethics—the fruits of the intellect and the will, to use classical words—both use the language of rules. There are laws of nature, and there are laws of states. There are rules for the swing of a pendulum, and there are rules for club members. Humans become scientists, and they become legislators. Humans discover the laws of nature, and they construct the laws of society.

If humans are trenchantly and pervasively rule makers and rule finders, then rule making and rule finding may be among the basic operations of the fundamental forces governing human behavior. My view, provisional as are all scientific views, is that, indeed, rule making and rule finding can be traced to fundamental forces of human nature.

The focus of this chapter is on rule making—specifically, the making of rules of conduct—and as this is scientific work, its aim is to find the rules about how humans make rules. Hence, this chapter is an exercise in *rule finding about rule making*.

There are in general two types of rule making and thus two types of rules. In the first kind of rule making, a spontaneous activity becomes a rule; let us call this a type 1 rule. In the second kind, a rule is deliberately devised to achieve an end; this we may call a type 2 rule. The two may not be wholly unrelated, for a rule may be devised to proscribe spontaneous activity, which has become normative for participants. Moreover, both types of rules may have to be unmade. Nonetheless, a distinction highlighting the genesis of a rule may prove fruitful in later work.

The type 2, or devised, rule, requires an end. The end may be individual or social, and the rule maker may devise the rule for him- or herself, and/or for individual others, for groups, or for any combination thereof. If sociobehavioral processes generate relationships between inputs and outputs, then these relationships may provide the content for rules. For example, if comparison processes generate links between gift giving and social welfare, then a rule maker may devise a rule about gift giving with the end of increasing social welfare (or, alternatively, with the end of reducing social welfare). Understanding type 2 rules is thus aided by systematic scrutiny of the operation of basic processes.

Of course, the same basic processes which generate connections between behavioral activities and social welfare, may also generate connections between the behavioral activities and the well-being of individuals. The consequences of the behavioral activities may not be uniformly beneficial for all individuals, and thus there will be both individuals who favor the activities and individuals who oppose the activities, as well as, perhaps, some individuals who are indifferent. Thus, type 2 rules have *constituencies*, and systematic scrutiny of the operation of basic sociobehavioral processes sheds light on the constituencies of particular rules.

My strategy in this chapter is to explore the emergence of type 2 rules from the operation of comparison processes, identifying likely rules, rule makers, and rule constituencies. Comparison processes have implications for many areas of the social life, and thus a framework for deriving rules from comparison theory may prove fruitful. In this chapter, I take the first step, laying the foundation for the framework and providing one illustration: the emergence of rules about theft. Of course, the procedures developed in this chapter will readily yield many more rule candidates when applied to other phenomena which are touched by comparison processes, beyond the theft phenomena used here as illustration. Moreover, future development of the framework would also explore the emergence of type 1 rules from comparison processes—a task that is beyond the scope of this chapter. As well, the procedures developed here may be fruitfully used to derive norm predictions from theories about many processes besides comparison processes.

The predictions of comparison theory are ceteris paribus predictions, and thus correct interpretation as well as testing of the implications for norm emergence require explicitly taking into account the possibility that other mechanisms, based on other processes beyond comparison processes, generate contradictory effects. Thus, the challenge is to assess the relative strengths of opposite effects. The difficulties associated with testing ceteris paribus predictions in a multifactor world, however, are mitigated by the abundance of predictions generated by comparison theory; testing can proceed across diverse fields of phenomena, not all of which will display the same configuration of effects.

# Studying the Making of Rules: First Principles
## Basic Premises

I begin with a simple summary of the four premises underlying this chapter. Space constraints do not permit fuller elaboration of these premises, yet delineating them is important in order to locate as precisely as possible the work undertaken in this chapter within the social science enterprise and thus to relate it to other work and to build upon it.[2]

First, following the view advanced by Isaac Newton for understanding physical nature, observed behavioral and social phenomena are viewed as the product of the joint operation of several basic forces. Put differently, the first premise holds that the world we seek to understand is a *multifactor* world, a view widely accepted in modern social science.[3] The scientific challenges are two, one theoretical, the other empirical. The theoretical challenge is to identify the basic forces governing human behavior, to describe their operation, and to derive their implications. The empirical challenge is to test the derived implications. The theoretical and empirical work jointly lead to the accumulation of reliable knowledge about human behavioral and social phenomena. (The second and fourth premises take up the theoretical and empirical challenges, respectively.)

Second, one cannot take seriously the Newtonian multifactor view without at least occasionally speculating about the identity of the basic forces governing human behavior, and the working sociologist, even when fully absorbed in a highly specialized piece of the sociobehavioral puzzle, is ever on the alert for clues. In that spirit, I offer four candidates for basic forces:

- to know the causes of things,
- to judge the goodness of things,
- to be perfect,
- to be free.

Though this is not the place for extended discussion of these candidate forces, I will make four remarks about them: All four candidate forces have been ascribed to humans as fundamental aspects of human nature.[4] All four refer to properties ascribed to God.[5] All four refer to things that play prominent parts in the discourse between humans and deities, both in what deities say they do for humans and in what humans pray for.[6] All four appear not only in what humans pray for but also in what they renounce in the spirit of sacrifice.[7] As both Émile Durkheim and Max Weber understood, the deepest aspects of human nature manifest themselves in religious phenomena, and thus the sociology of religion may play a prominent part in the methodology for unmasking the basic forces. Finally, note that it may someday be seen that the basic forces governing human nature are more than four or perhaps, at the other extreme, only one, the others being manifestations of a single more basic force.

Third, the point of departure for the work reported in this chapter is comparison processes, which, though basic enough to affect behavior in many areas of social life, are not at the level of fundamental forces; thus, this chapter works in the Mertonian middle range (Merton [1949] 1968). Of course, one may speculate that the operation of one or more of the four candidate forces leads to comparison processes, separately or jointly.

Finally, the multifactor view poses special empirical challenges, for the operation of two factors may lead to opposite effects, and hence isolating the two effects becomes the prime empirical objective. It may at first appear that one prediction is rejected, but in fact it may be that one of the two effects is stronger than the other. For example, suppose that mechanism A predicts that $y$ is an increasing function of $x$ and mechanism B predicts that $y$ is a decreasing function of $x$. The empirical finding that $y$ is an increasing function of $x$ does not constitute, in a multifactor world, evidence that mechanism B is not operating; rather, the finding would be consistent with the operation of both mechanisms such that the effect of mechanism A is stronger than, or "dominates," mechanism B. The converse would also be true. This is one of the reasons why the more fruitful a theory the easier it is to test.[8]

## Rule Making and the Basic Forces

Preliminary examination of the four candidate forces indicates the ubiquity of rules. The first candidate force, to know the causes of things, leads to rule finding. The second, to judge the goodness of things, leads to rule making. The third, to be perfect, leads to both rule making and rule unmaking. The fourth candidate force, to be free, leads to the unmaking of rules.

Careful study of the four candidate forces may reveal the precise ways in which their operation generates rules behavior. For example, operation of the second candidate force generates judgments of the goodness of alternative ways of organizing one's life as well as alternative ways of organizing society. Such perennial themes as "the good life" and "the good society" lead directly to rules designed to bring them about.

Thus, I am led to the view that humans are, by nature, rule makers. Fruitful questions for social science include those that address the processes by which norms emerge in the operation of basic forces; whether there are distinct classes of norms with distinct configurations, trajectories,

and sanctions; and the links between norms and other behavioral and social phenomena. In short, I take as given that norms are pervasive and ask
how norms work.

# Two Types of Rules

This chapter notices two types of rules, the first arising spontaneously, the
second deliberately devised to achieve an end. It may later prove useful to
distinguish more classes or to introduce dimensions along which to differentiate subclasses within these two; but for now these two broad classes
will suffice.

## Emergent Norms (Type 1 Rules)

In the case of type 1 rules, a spontaneous activity becomes a rule. What
was once a free and voluntary activity becomes an obligation; and sanctions follow. This is the type of norm about which Neil Smelser (1967, 7)
writes, "Other illustrations of norms . . . are found in informal, unwritten
expectations that grow up between two persons as they form a friendship."[9]
The process by which this occurs may be what Antoine de Saint-Exupéry
(1943) had in mind when he has the fox discuss "taming": "It would have
been better," the fox tells the Little Prince, "to come back at the same
hour. . . . One must observe the proper rites."

Type 1 rules often have to be unmade. For example, enthusiasm at the
start of a friendship or a courtship sometimes leads persons into activities
and habits that they cannot sustain after the initial glow fades. Joyously
playing tennis or cards every night at the start of the semester with newly
discovered like-minded dormitory mates quickly leads to a norm, which
then has to be unmade as the protagonists seek more time for other pur-
suits. In courtship, early habits can quickly become oppressive. Unmaking
these norms is not without trauma. Understanding the way type 1 norms
work involves both their making and their unmaking, together with the
process by which some type 1 norms are retained while others are discarded.

## Devised Norms (Type 2 Rules)

A type 2 rule is deliberately devised in order to achieve an end. The rule
maker may be an individual or a group. The rule maker may devise the
rule for himself or herself and/or for individual others, and/or for groups.
The end may be individual or social, positive or negative—that is, to increase and/or decrease well-being or social welfare.[10]

Coverage by a devised rule may be limited to members of a voluntary
association, or it may extend to all members of a society or, indeed, of the
world. For convenience, the former is called a "voluntary" rule, the latter

an "imposed" rule. Of course, the boundaries may be blurred. For example, an individual may be covered by the rules of the state of which he or she is a citizen, but citizenship may be relinquished and residence sought in a different state (as in cases of refuge and asylum). Examples of voluntary rules will be found in the by-laws of voluntary associations and in etiquette books. To illustrate, consider St. Benedict's *Rule for Monasteries* (1948). In the prologue to the *Rule*, Benedict (or the pseudo-Benedict) writes, "And so we are going to establish a school for the service of the Lord," whose end is to worship God.[11] In chapter 1, Benedict describes the four kinds of monks (then known), noting, "Let us proceed, with God's help, to lay down a rule for the strongest kind of monks, the Cenobites," so that the end is not merely to worship God but, more precisely, to achieve greater perfection in the worship of God (though not the "height of perfection," which requires more stringent practices, as Benedict notes in the final chapter of the *Rule*). But membership in the order was voluntary, and the *Rule* applied only to members of the monastery. Similarly, rules for social clubs and "polite society" apply only to members (and those seeking to become members—the aspirants).

In contrast, other rules are meant to apply to everyone (although particular individuals may construe themselves as not covered by the rule). When rules apply to everyone, there may be winners and losers. Norms acquire constituencies. There may be "outcasts" and "exiles."

Type 2 rules also have "patrons" or "sponsors" promoting the rule. When the rule is thought to benefit the whole of society—that is, when the rule is meant to promote the commonweal—the patron is called a "guardian." In other cases, the patron may have a personal stake or may be acting on behalf of individual others.

## Generating Rules from Comparison Processes: Theory and Method

Comparison theory yields both proactive and reactive implications, and it yields implications for both individuals, sets of individuals, and entire societies. It thus may be a useful arena for tracing out the process of rule making. As in all scientific work, there are two objectives, first, to achieve a faithful theoretical description of the operation of comparison processes, and, second, to detect empirically the operation of comparison processes and gauge the strength of their effects. In a multifactor world there are special challenges. For example, theoretical analysis may yield a derivation that appears on its face to differ from reality; the temptation to immediately discard the theory is strong, yet the effect may be real, only less strong than an opposite effect set in motion by a different set of processes.

There are two main strategies for deriving implications from comparison theory, known, respectively, as the micromodel and the macromodel strategies. Although both yield testable predictions at both individual and social levels, they differ in their starting points, the micromodel starting with the response of an individual to an event or a behavior, the macromodel starting with the distribution of well-being in a population. In general, there are more predictions for individuals and types of individuals in micromodel analyses and more predictions for groups and subgroups in macromodel analyses.

Note that while predictions involving behaviors such as theft and gift giving appear more quickly conducive to rule making, predictions involving reactions to external events, such as wars and disasters, may also lead to rule making. For example, the prediction that grief at the death of a loved one is attenuated by inheritance and the companion prediction that parental grief at the death of a child can be enormous because there is nothing to attenuate it could—in historical epochs when the productivity loss from grief needs to be curtailed—lead to devices like state compensation at the death of a minor child or life insurance for children.

The general approach, then, is to derive implications from the basic postulates of comparison theory, identifying possibilities for norm emergence. To provide depth, however, I restrict my attention here to implications obtained via the micromodel strategy. Moreover, to illustrate the approach, I restrict attention to a single domain, namely, theft.

## Basic Elements of Comparison Theory

The Mertonian starting idea for comparison theory is the idea that humans compare themselves to others and/or to previous or envisioned selves and thereby experience a variety of judgments and sentiments, including happiness, well-being, self-esteem, and the sense of justice. It is widely thought that comparison processes are pervasive and that their operation affects many areas of the social and behavioral life. The goal of a theory of comparison processes is thus systematically to trace out this operation—to draw out, and test, the myriad implications, including the nonobvious implications.

The first step in formalizing the starting idea shifts the comparison from a comparison of self to other or self to previous, envisioned self to a comparison of the actual levels of attributes and amounts of possessions to the levels and amounts expected or desired or thought just or appropriate (Jasso 1990). This shift has profound implications both for the mathematical formalization to follow (as shown in Jasso 1990) and also for the substantive coverage of comparison theory and correct interpretation of its assumptions and predictions. This shift implies, among other things, that individuals who never compare themselves to others are fully within the theoretical umbrella, as are individuals devoid of any concern for relative rank, provided they compare what they have to some standard or referent, whatever its source.[12]

Note that there is no presumption concerning the relative size of the actual condition and the comparison referent. Comparison theory covers both the overrewarded and the underrewarded.

Formalization of this fundamental idea of comparison yields a general relation, called the Axiom of Comparison:

$$Z = Z(A,C), \; Z_A > 0, \; Z_C < 0, \qquad\qquad 12.1$$

where $Z$ denotes the outcome, $A$ denotes the individual's actual condition, $C$ denotes the envisioned or desired condition, and subscript notation is used for partial derivatives. If the actual and envisioned conditions refer to an attribute or possession—for convenience termed "reward"—and, for simplicity, letting $Z$ refer to well-being, then the greater the actual reward, the greater the well-being, and the greater the comparison reward, the lower the well-being. The basic axiom applies to "bads" as wells as "goods," in which case the direction of the effects of the actual and expected rewards is reversed.

The specific form of the comparison function used in this chapter is the logarithmic-ratio form:

$$Z \propto \ln\left(\frac{A}{C}\right). \qquad\qquad 12.2$$

This form has been intensively studied since its introduction (Jasso 1978), and it is known, for example, that it is the only functional form that satisfies two conditions thought desirable in a justice evaluation function, a special case of the comparison function (Jasso 1990).[13]

In one version, the log-ratio form acquires a multiplicative constant, known as the Signature Constant and denoted $\theta$, which by its sign indicates whether the observer regards the reward as a good or as a bad and which by its absolute value indicates the observer's style of expression:

$$Z = \theta \ln\left(\frac{A}{C}\right). \qquad\qquad 12.3$$

In theoretical work, the Signature Constant is set at unity, whereas in empirical work it is estimated for each observer and for each of a class of situations. As in the general function, in the case of a good, $Z$ is an increasing function of the actual reward $A$ and a decreasing function of the comparison reward $C$. For example, the greater the actual amount of a valued good (wealth, say, or beauty), the greater the well-being, but the greater the desired amount of the valued good, the lower the well-being.

The logarithmic-ratio specification of the comparison function is the first postulate of comparison theory. Yet, as will be evident in the next section, if the log-ratio function were the only postulate, the micromodel approach to deriving predictions would be without teeth. The teeth, as it were, come from the third of the three individual-level postulates at the heart of comparison theory, a postulate with strong roots in the work of Robert Merton ([1949] 1968). By the third postulate, called the Identity Representation of the Comparison Holding, the comparison reward C is identically equal to, and can be expressed as, the product of the arithmetic mean of the actual reward in the collectivity and an individual-specific constant, denoted $\phi$, which captures everything that is unknown about how the individual chooses his or her own comparison reward. Further, because the arithmetic mean is itself equal to the total sum (S) of a thing divided by the population size (N), the comparison reward in the case of a cardinal reward can be written

$$C = \phi E(A) = \phi S / N.$$  \hfill 12.4

Thus, the Identity Representation postulate provides a way to incorporate into the basic comparison function in equation (12.3) two important factors: the group affluence $S$ and the group size $N$.[14]

Meanwhile, the second postulate of comparison theory provides a measurement rule whereby cardinal things are measured in their own units, denoted $x$, and ordinal things are measured as relative ranks. Thus, the comparison function for cardinal rewards becomes:

$$Z = \theta \ln \left( \frac{xN}{S\phi} \right),$$  \hfill 12.5

where $x$ denotes the individual's actual reward, $N$ denotes the population size, and $S$ denotes the total amount of the reward in the collectivity. Setting the Signature Constant to unity in preparation for the micromodel theoretical analysis yields

$$Z = \ln \left( \frac{xN}{S\phi} \right).$$  \hfill 12.6

(The micromodel strategy can also be used with ordinal rewards, but due to space constraints, I focus in this chapter on the cardinal case.)

*A Remark About the Inner Workings of Comparison Theory*    It may be useful to paraphrase the formal development of comparison theory verbally (though the price to be paid is a measure of imprecision). For simplicity, refer to *Z* as well-being. By the first postulate, well-being increases as the actual reward increases but decreases as the comparison reward increases. Individuals thus "care" about both the actual reward and the comparison referent. By the third postulate, the comparison reward, whatever it may be, can always be expressed as the product of the average actual reward in the collectivity and a person-specific parameter; for example, if an actor regards twenty thousand dollars as his or her just earnings and the average actual earnings are ten thousand dollars, this actor's just earnings can be represented by the quantity (2 × \$10,000). Usually, the theorist does not know and does not impute the just earnings and thus represents it by $\phi E(A)$, as in equation (12.4). Because the first postulate provides the logarithmic form of the comparison function, the phi parameter will be separable and, in many situations, as will be seen below, will drop out; thus, thanks to the first and third postulates, theoretical ignorance of the actor's just reward is no obstacle to predicting many comparison outcomes. Further, because the average is equal to the total amount of the reward divided by the number of persons, the operation of the total wealth and of the population size can be made explicit, as in equations (12.4), (12.5), and (12.6).

*A Remark About Comparison Theory and Justice Theory*    The question often arises what is the exact relation between comparison theory and justice theory. Comparison theory is both narrower and broader than justice theory. Comparison theory is broader than justice theory in that it covers all comparison processes, of which the justice evaluation is a special case. For example, the outcome *Z* in comparison theory can be the justice evaluation, or it can be self-esteem, or it can be happiness; similarly, the comparison referent *C* in the comparison function can be the just reward, or it can be an amount or level desired, expected, envisioned, thought appropriate, and the like. Concomitantly, however, comparison theory is narrower than justice theory in that, while comparison theory focuses exclusively on individuals' sentiments about their own situation (called the "reflexive" case in justice theory), justice theory covers as well individuals' ideas of the just reward for others and justice evaluations about whether others are justly or unjustly treated (the "nonreflexive" case). Justice theory accommodates mechanisms that differ across reflexive and nonreflexive situations; for example, individuals may be guided by different principles of justice for self and others, as discussed by Tom Tyler and colleagues (1997).[15] This leads to another point. While in comparison theory there are two major strategies for deriving predictions (the micromodel and the macromodel), in justice theory there is a third, called the matrixmodel approach, which uses all the justice evaluations that individuals make about both themselves and others (Jasso 1999).

## Protocol of the Micromodel Strategy

The micromodel approach begins with investigation of the effects of an event on an individual, where the event may be a human action (such as giving a gift or stealing a radio), or the outcome of a human action (such as receiving a gift or having a radio stolen), or an event not traceable to human agency (such as a natural disaster). The objective is to assess the effects of the event on a comparison outcome—such as well-being, self-esteem, or the sense of justice. The micromodel thus makes it possible to ascertain change in well-being, or in self-esteem, or in the sense of being justly or unjustly rewarded, establishing, for example, who becomes better off and who becomes worse off and by how much. The basic equation in the micromodel approach is an equation that compares the individual at two points in time:

$$CZ = Z_2 - Z_1,$$

12.7

where, as before, $Z$ denotes the comparison outcome (for example, well-being) and $CZ$ denotes change in $Z$.

Thus, the micromodel investigates the change in $Z$ between time 1 and time 2. If $CZ$ is zero, then whatever transpired between the two time periods has had no effect on the individual; if, however, $CZ$ is negative, then the individual has become worse off and, if positive, better off.[16]

Equation (12.6) is the basic expression that will be incorporated into the change equation (12.7). The events and actions whose effects on the individual's well-being can be investigated via the micromodel approach are not limited to events or actions that alter the individual's actual reward but encompass, as well, events and actions that affect the population size and the population's total amount of the reward—for example, the population's total wealth or total gross domestic product.

Because there are many events and actions that affect the constituent factors of $Z$ (that affect, for example, in the case of a cardinal good or bad, own wealth, population wealth, and population size), the micromodel procedure can be used for a wide variety of cases. To illustrate, theft affects own wealth $x$ and may affect group wealth $S$ (depending on whether the thief and victim are from the same group); murder affects population size $N$, may affect $x$ and $S$ (depending on bequests and relationship to the victim), and may affect the individual's rank $i$ in an ordinal good (or bad) regime. Similarly, giving and receiving a gift affects $x$ and may affect $S$, depending on whether giver and receiver are together or apart; and when a fellow group member gives or receives a gift, $S$ may be altered. Note that when $S$ or $N$ is altered, *all* group members experience a change in $Z$, not merely the protagonists in the situation (such as thief and victim, in the case of theft, or giver and receiver, in the case of a gift).

The basic equation for the change in well-being, in the case of a cardinal good, incorporating the more refined formula of equation (12.7), can now be written as

$$CZ = \ln\left(\frac{x_2 N_2 S_1 \phi_1}{x_1 N_1 S_2 \phi_2}\right). \qquad 12.8$$

The teeth in the micromodel approach are now fully visible in equation (12.8).

Table 12.1 outlines the protocol for the micromodel strategy, applied to a cardinal-good regime.[17] As shown, the micromodel approach begins with the formulas for $Z$ (step 1) and $CZ$ (step 2).

The goal is to systematically draw out the implications of basic comparison processes for a wide range of disparate domains. Accordingly, at the next step the theorist chooses a field of application (step 3). In general, any domain involving alterations in own wealth, population wealth, or population size is a candidate. After selecting the particular domain, the theorist identifies the kinds of actors involved and the kinds of situations and provides the pertinent special notation. The ensuing setup and analysis are referred to as "a model of _____ phenomena based on comparison theory," often abbreviated to "a comparison-based _____ model." Examples include the comparison-based theft model, the comparison-based gift model, and the comparison-based disaster model.

Using the basic $CZ$ formula and the setup for the particular application, the theorist next writes down the particular $CZ$ formula applicable to each actor-situation combination (step 4). The theorist then proceeds to the four main sets of questions, the answers to which constitute the predictions. The questions are as follows:

1. Has the event made the individual better off or worse off? (step 5)
2. In which situation is each kind of actor better off? (step 6)
3. Within situation, which actor experiences the greater change? (step 7)
4. For each actor-situation combination, what are the effects of each factor in the $CZ$ formula? (step 8)

To answer the first question (step 5), the task is simply to evaluate the sign of the $CZ$ formula for each actor-situation combination. To answer the second (step 6), the theorist evaluates, for each actor, the inequalities formed by the $CZ$ quantities across all situations. This step may lead to new relations, as will be seen in the theft model. To answer the third question (step 7), the task is to evaluate, for each situation, the inequalities formed by the $CZ$ quantities (or, more often, their absolute values) across

FIGURE 12.1     *The Micromodel Strategy for Deriving Predictions in Comparison Theory: Studying the Effects of an Event or Action in a Cardinal-Good Regime*

1. Write basic comparison-function formula in the cardinal-good case:

$$Z = \ln \frac{xN}{S\phi},$$

where $Z$ denotes the comparison-based response (for example, happiness or well-being), $x$ denotes the individual's own amount of the cardinal good (for example, wealth), $S$ denotes the total amount of the cardinal good in the collectivity, $N$ denotes the population size, and $\phi$ denotes the individual-specific parameter capturing idiosyncratic elements in the comparison standard used by the individual for himself or herself.

2. Express change in $Z$ from time 1 to time 2:

$$CZ = Z_2 - Z_1$$

$$CZ = \ln \frac{x_2 N_2}{S_2 \phi_2} - \ln \frac{x_1 N_1}{S_1 \phi_1}$$

$$CZ = \ln \frac{x_2 N_2 S_1 \phi_1}{x_1 N_1 S_2 \phi_2}.$$

3. Analyze the particular event or action.

4. Write the formulas for $CZ$ for each kind of actor in each situation or special case.

5. Is $CZ$ positive or negative? (This requires an assumption about $\phi$; for example, assume $\phi_1 = \phi_2$).

6. In which situation does each kind of actor have the higher $CZ$? (For each actor, evaluate the inequalities across all situations.)

7. Within situation, which actor has the higher $CZ$ and the higher absolute value of $CZ$? (For each situation, evaluate the inequalities across all actors.)

8. Obtain first- and second-order partial derivatives of $CZ$ with respect to each factor in the $CZ$ formulas.

9. The results obtained in steps 5, 6, 7, and 8 comprise the predictions.

*Source:* Author's compilation.

all actors. To answer the fourth question (step 8), the theorist obtains the full set of first- and second-order partial derivatives of the *CZ* formula.

The results obtained in these last four steps comprise the implications of the basic process for the domain to which it is being applied. Of course, depending on the phenomena under investigation, some steps may yield more interesting or more important predictions than others.

In comparison theory this simple protocol—using the micromodel strategy to derive predictions from the three individual-level postulates of comparison theory—has been applied, and is being applied, to a large and growing set of disparate domains. Predictions published to date include the following sets, classified by topical domain: theft (Jasso 1988); death and destruction (Jasso 1993a, 1993b, 1993c); gifts and bequests (Jasso 1993b, 1993c); migration (Jasso 1996a); and use of goods and bads to reward and punish (Jasso 1996b). A short sampler of the obtained predictions is presented in table 12.1. These predictions illustrate several features desirable in a theory: First, they span several disparate topical domains. Second, they represent a mix of intuitive and counterintuitive implications. Third, they include novel predictions. Note, moreover, that predictions are made for different social contexts and historical periods.[18]

Of course, other approaches to theoretical derivation yield many other predictions in comparison theory. For example, use of the macromodel strategy yields implications linking economic inequality with important societal outcomes, such as intergroup conflict, out-migration, and participation in religious institutions.

A useful feature of the theory is that it accommodates diverse social contexts while enabling precise attentiveness to each. For example, the situations highlighted in the protocol for the micromodel approach (figure 12.1, step 4) may in some topical domains refer to well-established groups and in other topical domains refer to transitory groupings. To illustrate, in the gift application, the situation may refer to whether the giver and receiver of a gift happen to be together, whereas in the theft application that follows the situation refers to less transitory groups. Moreover, the predictions apply to every level of analysis—family, neighborhood, ethnic group, professional association, and so on. The strength of their operation in each kind of situation depends principally on two features: the duration of time the actor spends in each kind of situation and the configuration of other factors and other mechanisms. In most cases, the theorist and/or empirical specialist will be able to judge which situations represent interesting application domains for the predictions. Sometimes these are so obvious that the predictions state them outright. The predictions in table 12.1 for disaster-related behaviors and for international migration are a case in point.

Finally, comparison theory, in addition to yielding predictions, also

TABLE 12.1    *Brief Selection of Predictions Obtained Using the Micromodel*
*Strategy*

| Application | Prediction |
|---|---|
| Gifts | 1. Parents of two or more nontwin children will spend more of their toy budget at an annual gift-giving occasion—such as Christmas—than at the children's birthdays.<br>2. The pleasure from receiving a gift is always greater in the giver's presence.<br>3. It is painful when a member of one's group receives a gift from someone outside the group. |
| Bequests and mourning | 1. If the parent who dies first leaves no bequest to the children, then in periods when wives tend to predecease husbands (for example, because of death in childbirth), mothers will be mourned more than fathers; however, in periods when husbands tend to predecease wives (for example, because of war), fathers will be mourned more than mothers.<br>2. The death of a child is mourned more than the death of a parent. |
| Theft | 1. The gain in well-being from theft is greater if a thief steals from a fellow group member rather than from an outsider; the extra gain is larger in poor groups than in rich groups.<br>2. Informants arise only in cross-group theft, in which case they are members of the thief's group. |
| Disaster and war | 1. If in a disaster there is no property damage but at least one death occurs, then all survivors will experience psychological distress.<br>2. If in a disaster there is property loss but no deaths, then nonvictims will experience a rush of energy and euphoria.<br>3. Post-traumatic stress is more severe for survivors of conveyance disasters than for survivors of natural disasters.<br>4. In disasters, property damage mitigates the ill effects of deaths.<br>5. The propensity to post-traumatic stress syndrome is greater among veterans of wars fought away from home than among veterans of wars fought on home soil. |
| International migration | 1. A necessary condition for origin and destination countries both to oppose, or both to favor, bilateral migration is that they have unequal wealth.<br>2. A necessary condition for origin and destination countries both to favor the migration is that the origin country be a poor country and the destination |

TABLE 12.1    *Continued*

| Application | Prediction |
| --- | --- |
| | country a rich country; a necessary condition for the origin and destination countries both to oppose the migration is that the origin country be a rich country and the destination country a poor country. |

*Source:* Author's compilation.

yields interpretations for nonrecurring events. For example, it provides an interpretation of the rise of the mendicant institutions in the thirteenth century (Jasso 1991) and of the invention of detective fiction in nineteenth-century England (Jasso 1986).[19] This feature may make the theory especially useful in the study of norm emergence.

## Protocol for Deriving Norm Predictions from Behavioral Predictions

Once the behavioral predictions have been derived, the next phase of the analysis consists of deriving predictions for norm phenomena. This phase has several steps, as follows:

First, arrange the behavioral predictions by the class of actors to whom the predictions apply, noting the direction of effects on the actors' well-being and noting as well whether the predictions are universal. An important aspect of universality refers to whether the prediction holds for all societies or only for homogeneous societies (societies consisting of a single group) or only for heterogeneous societies (societies consisting of two or more groups).

Second, construct potential norm candidates, noting the affected class of actors and whether their well-being is increased or decreased by each norm candidate. Third, construct a fourfold table to represent the norm candidates available to actors whose objective is to increase or decrease the well-being of self or others. Fourth, for each norm candidate, identify its constituencies, under the four scenarios represented by the fourfold table. Fifth, for each norm candidate and scenario, make a list of possible coalitions. Sixth, distinguish clearly between norm candidates for homogeneous societies and norm candidates for heterogeneous societies.

The predictions thus obtained are for norms that arise from an immediate situation—what we may call first-order norms. In the next stage of the protocol, scenarios are constructed for deriving second-order norms, norms that take into account the past and the future. For example, as will be seen in the theft illustration, an actor may suffer no loss in well-being when an acquaintance is robbed, and thus we would not predict first-order support for an antitheft rule; however, if this same actor fears that he or she may be a target of theft, second-order support for an antitheft rule would quickly arise.

To illustrate the framework, I derive norm predictions only for first-order situations and only for situations involving actors whose objective is to maximize their own well-being and guardians whose objective is to maximize the collective well-being. Finally, note that, like the behavioral predictions on which they are based, all norm predictions are ceteris paribus predictions.

## Illustration of the Framework: Predicting Theft Norms from Comparison Theory

I turn now to the theft illustration—first, deriving predictions from comparison theory, and, second, deriving theft norms from the behavioral predictions.

### Deriving Behavioral Predictions for Theft Situations

To derive behavioral predictions from comparison theory about theft phenomena, we use the micromodel strategy. As usual in the micromodel approach, we keep a step-by-step record of our work (shown in figure 12.2), consistent with the micromodel protocol (figure 12.1), and we begin by recalling the formulas for $Z$ and for $CZ$.

We now start the setup for the theft model, analyzing theft phenomena from the two vantage points of comparison theory and the micromodel strategy and introducing ingredients specific to the theft application. In the theft model, theft is the event that occurs between time 1 and time 2. Thus, $Z_1$ and $Z_2$ refer to each person's pretheft and posttheft well-being, respectively. Consistent with real-world theft, we let the social system contain one or more groups (each group described by its own $S$ and $N$), so that the full set of persons in the social system consists of thief, victim, members of the thief's group, and members of the victim's group, the two latter sets of actors collectively called "others." Accordingly, we define three theft situations. In situation T1, thief and victim are in the same group; there may also be others in the group. In situations T2 and T3, thief and victim are from different groups. T2 refers to the thief's group and T3 refers to the victim's group. In both T2 and T3, there are other members of the group. Situations T2 and T3 occur only in heterogeneous societies (societies containing at least two groups); situation T1 can occur in either a homogeneous (one group only) or a heterogeneous society.

Continuing with notation, let $t$ denote the amount stolen, where $t$ is measured in units of $x$. Finally, to simplify the illustration, let the group size $N$ in each group remain constant, and let the amounts of $x$ held by others also remain constant. These features specific to the setup for the theft application are recorded in figure 12.2 (step 3).

FIGURE 12.2   *Using the Micromodel Strategy to Derive Predictions from Comparison Theory for Theft Phenomena*

1. Write basic comparison-function formula in the cardinal-good case:

$$Z = \ln \frac{xN}{S\phi},$$

where $Z$ denotes the comparison-based response (for example, happiness or well-being), $x$ denotes the individual's own amount of the cardinal good (for example, wealth), $S$ denotes the total amount of the cardinal good in the collectivity, $N$ denotes the population size, and $\phi$ denotes the individual-specific parameter capturing idiosyncratic elements in the comparison standard used by the individual for himself or herself.

2. Express change in $Z$ from time 1 to time 2:

$$CZ = Z_2 - Z_1$$

$$CZ = \ln \frac{x_2 N_2}{S_2 \phi_2} - \ln \frac{x_1 N_1}{S_1 \phi_1}$$

$$CZ = \ln \frac{x_2 N_2 S_1 \phi_1}{x_1 N_1 S_2 \phi_2}.$$

3. Analyze the theft situation
   - There are three kinds of actors: Thief, Victim, and Others
   - Define three theft situations:
     (T1) Thief and Victim are in the same group; Others may be in the group
     (T2) Thief's group in outsider theft; Others are members of Thief's group
     (T3) Victim's group in outsider theft; Others are members of Victim's group
   - Let $t$ denote the amount stolen, where $t$ is measured in units of $x$
   - The simplest case has the following features: the group size $N$ remains the same, and the amounts of $x$ held by others remain constant.

4. Write the formula for $CZ$ for each kind of actor in each situation

| Situation | Thief | Victim | Others |
|---|---|---|---|
| T1 | $CZ = \ln \frac{(x + t)\phi_1}{x\phi_2}$ | $CZ = \ln \frac{(x - t)\phi_1}{x\phi_2}$ | $CZ = \ln \frac{\phi_1}{\phi_2}$ |
| T2 | $CZ = \ln \frac{S(x + t)\phi_1}{x(S + t)\phi_2}$ | — | $CZ = \ln \frac{S\phi_1}{(S + t)\phi_2}$ |
| T3 | — | $CZ = \ln \frac{S(x - t)\phi_1}{x(S - t)\phi_2}$ | $CZ = \ln \frac{S\phi_1}{(S - t)\phi_2}$ |

5. Is $CZ$ positive or negative? (Assume $\phi_1 = \phi_2$.)

| Situation | Thief | Victim | Others |
|---|---|---|---|
| T1 | + | − | 0 |
| T2 | + | NA | − |
| T3 | NA | − | + |

FIGURE 12.2    *Continued*

6. In which situation does each actor have the higher CZ?

| | | |
|---|---|---|
| Thief | $CZ^{T1}_{Thief} > CZ^{T2}_{Thief}$ | T1 (insider theft) |
| Victim | $CZ^{T3}_{Victim} > CZ^{T1}_{Victim}$ | T3 (outsider theft) |
| Others | $CZ^{T3}_{Others} > CZ^{T1}_{Others} > CZ^{T2}_{Others}$ | T3 (outsider theft, in victim's group) |

7. Is thief's gain greater than victim's loss?

Insider Theft

$$CZ^T \begin{Bmatrix} < \\ = \\ > \end{Bmatrix} \left| CZ^V \right| \text{ iff } t \begin{Bmatrix} > \\ = \\ < \end{Bmatrix} x^V - x^T$$

(Depends on relation between amount stolen and disparity between thief's and victim's pretheft wealth)

Outsider theft

$$CZ^T \begin{Bmatrix} < \\ = \\ > \end{Bmatrix} \left| CZ^V \right| \text{ iff } \frac{x^T x^V + t(x^V - x^T - t)}{S^T S^V + t(S^V - S^T - t)} \begin{Bmatrix} > \\ = \\ < \end{Bmatrix} \frac{x^T x^V}{S^T S^V}$$

(Depends on relation between amount stolen, disparity between thief's and victim's pretheft wealth, and disparity between thief's group's and victim's group's pretheft affluence)

8. Obtain first and second partial derivatives of CZ with respect to each factor in the CZ formulas. (First partial derivatives shown below)

| Derivative | Thief | Victim | Others |
|---|---|---|---|
| $CZ_x$ | T1 and T2: $-\dfrac{t}{x(x + t)} < 0$ | T1 and T3: $\dfrac{t}{x(x - t)} > 0$ | T1, T2, and T3: 0 |
| $CZ_t$ | T1: $\dfrac{1}{x + t} > 0$ | T1: $-\dfrac{1}{x - t} < 0$ | T1:  0 |
| | T2: $\dfrac{S - x}{(x + t)(S + t)} > 0$ | T3: $-\dfrac{S - x}{(x - t)(S - t)} < 0$ | T2: $-\dfrac{1}{S + t} < 0$ |
| | | | T3: $\dfrac{1}{S - t} > 0$ |
| $CZ_S$ | T1:  0 | T1:  0 | T1:  0 |
| | T2: $\dfrac{t}{S(S + t)} > 0$ | T3: $-\dfrac{t}{S(S - t)} < 0$ | T2: $\dfrac{t}{S(S + t)} > 0$ |
| | | | T3: $-\dfrac{t}{S(S - t)} < 0$ |

*Source:* Author's compilation.
*Note:* In insider theft, the problem of whether the thief's gain exceeds the victim's loss is equivalent to the problem of whether the expected value of Z—that is, the social welfare—increases.

The next step is to write the *CZ* formula for each of the three kinds of actors in each of the three situations in which they may find themselves (figure 12.2, step 4). It is now possible to eliminate all the temporal subscripts except those on $\phi$. Given that own wealth $x$ can change only for the thief and the victim, and given that it changes by the amount $t$, we let $x$ without a subscript denote its time 1 value; similarly, given that $S$ can change only by the amount $t$, we let $S$ without a subscript denote its time 1 value. Thus, there are seven refined formulas for *CZ*, corresponding to the seven possible actor-situation combinations; the formulas are reported in figure 12.2 (step 4). The *CZ* formulas express the change in well-being due to stealing or being stolen from or being in a group in which someone else has stolen or been stolen from. There are four main sets of questions to be addressed (corresponding to steps 4 through 7 in figure 12.1), each illuminating a different aspect of theft behavior and singly or in combination yielding a variety of predictions. These four main questions are:

1. What is the sign of *CZ*?
2. In which situation does each of the three kinds of actors have the higher *CZ*?
3. What are the differential gains and losses across actors?
4. What are the effects on *CZ* of own wealth, group wealth, the amount stolen, and the population size?

The sign of *CZ* indicates whether the individual is better off, worse off, or unaffected by the theft. As shown in figure 12.2 (step 4), all the formulas include the phi component; and thus it is not possible to know the sign of *CZ* without making an a priori assumption about phi. It is not unreasonable that phi, for a given individual, remains constant across the two time periods; that is, there is little a priori reason to suppose that stealing or being stolen from or witnessing such an event alters the individual's comparison reward. The most parsimonious assumption is that $\phi_1 = \phi_2$. It can also be argued that even if the comparison reward does change, it does not do so immediately; hence, there is an important period (of unknown duration) when $\phi_1 = \phi_2$. (The duration of this period when $\phi_1 = \phi_2$ becomes an interesting new question.) Figure 12.2 (step 5) reports the sign of *CZ*, assuming $\phi_1 = \phi_2$. As shown, *CZ* is always positive for the thief, always negative for the victim, and may be of any sign for the others.

This first set of results contains a mix of intuitive and counterintuitive implications. It is not unexpected that the thief experiences a gain and the victim a loss. The effects of theft on the others, however, are novel: While others are unaffected by insider theft, outsider theft changes their situation; members of the thief's group become worse off, and members of the victim's group become better off. Put differently, the "innocent bystanders" or "third parties" experience a gain from theft when the victim is a fellow group member, and they experience a loss when the thief is a fellow group member; however, they experience neither a gain nor a loss when both thief and victim are fellow group members. These results suggest that informants are likely to arise only in outsider theft and that they are likely to be members of the thief's group. Moreover, to guard against informants, thieves may choose to live alone or in bands of thieves—unless they share the booty with fellow group members.

These results also suggest two natural affinities in outsider theft: between the thief and members of the victim's group and between the victim and members of the thief's group. These affinities may lead to coalitions, possibly covert coalitions.

The second set of questions seeks to learn in which situation each of the three kinds of actors has the higher magnitude of CZ (step 6). To answer these questions, we set up and evaluate inequalities whose terms are CZ formulas specific to each actor-situation combination. In this case, it is not necessary to make any assumptions on the phi component, as the phi terms drop out. In general, the number of inequalities to be evaluated is equal to the number of relevant actors, and each inequality has as many terms as there are situations for that type of actor. In this application, there are three types of actors, so there will be three inequalities to evaluate. While the thief and the victim each appear in two situations (T1 and T2 for the thief, and T1 and T3 for the victim), there are other group members in all three situations; accordingly, there will be two two-term inequalities and one three-term inequality.

To begin, we ask whether the thief's gain is greater when stealing from an outsider (situation T2) or from a fellow group member (situation T1). Evaluating the inequality formed by the thief's CZ in T1 and T2, we conclude:

$$\ln \frac{(x + t)\phi_1}{x\phi_2} > \ln \frac{S(x + t)\phi_1}{x(S + t)\phi_2}$$

$$CZ_{\text{Thief}}^{\text{T1}} > CZ_{\text{Thief}}^{\text{T2}} .$$

12.9

Thus, stealing from a fellow group member is more advantageous than stealing from an outsider.

Next we ask whether the victim's loss is greater when the thief is a fellow group member or an outsider. In this case we conclude:

$$\ln \frac{S(x - t)\phi_1}{x(S - t)\phi_2} > \ln \frac{(x - t)\phi_1}{x\phi_2}$$

$$CZ_{\text{Victim}}^{\text{T3}} > CZ_{\text{Victim}}^{\text{T1}} .$$

12.10

Because the victim's CZ is always negative (according to step 4 of figure 12.2, the victim always experiences a loss), and a larger negative number is a negative number with a smaller absolute value, the victim is better off if the thief is an outsider than if the thief is a fellow group member. Thus, thief and victim are doubly at odds: Not only does the thief gain at the victim's expense, but also the situation in which the thief's gain is higher is the situation in which the victim's loss is greater.

What about the others? If they must live in a world with theft, would they prefer a theft involving two members of their group (T1), or a theft in which only the perpetrator is a fellow group member (T2), or a theft in which only the victim is a fellow group member (T3)? Because the sign of CZ differs across the three situations (step 4 of figure 12.2), the inequality can be stated immediately:

$$CZ^{T3}_{Others} > CZ^{T1}_{Others} > CZ^{T2}_{Others} . \tag{12.11}$$

Others are most well off when theft is cross-group and the victim is a fellow group member (T3); and others are least well off when theft is cross-group and the thief is a fellow group member (T2). As we know from step 5, others are unaffected by in-group theft (T1).

If thieves would rather target rich people than poor people, then an upright (nonthieving) poor person is better off among rich people (for example, buying the least expensive house in a gated community); the other gets the benefit of living in a group where fellow group members are theft victims but is not himself or herself at risk.

The existence of these differential gains and losses suggests the possible usefulness of directly investigating the "premiums." Consider the thief's greater gain from theft if the victim is a fellow group member. Let $P$ denote the positive difference between the thief's gains in T1 and T2:

$$P^{Thief} = \ln \frac{(x + t)\phi_1}{x\phi_2} = \ln \frac{S(x + t)\phi_1}{x(S + t)\phi_2}$$

$$= \ln \frac{S + t}{S} . \tag{12.12}$$

Because, as shown, the insider-theft premium, $P^{Thief}$, is itself a function of group affluence and of the amount stolen, we can establish exactly how the premium responds to changes in group affluence and in the amount stolen. The first partial derivative of $P^{Thief}$ with respect to $t$ is obviously positive, and it is no surprise that the larger the amount stolen, the greater the insider-theft premium. What is not immediately obvious, however, is the effect of group affluence. The first partial derivative of $P^{Thief}$ with respect to $S$,

$$P_S = - \frac{t}{S(S + t)},$$

12.13

is negative, indicating that the richer the thief's group, the lower the insider-theft premium. Thus, the thief's greater gain from insider theft is intensified in poor groups. If the thieving propensities respond to relative gains, then the preference to steal from a fellow group member is stronger in poor groups than in rich groups.

The victim, too, may have preferences. The victim always experiences a loss, but this loss is smaller in outsider theft. Define the victim's "premium" from outsider theft:

$$P^{\text{Victim}} = \ln \frac{S(x - t)\phi_1}{x(S - t)\phi_2} - \ln \frac{(x - t)\phi_1}{x\phi_2}$$

$$= \ln \frac{S}{S - t}.$$

12.14

The effect of the amount stolen is positive, and the effect of group affluence is negative. Thus, the victim's preference for an outsider thief is intensified by the magnitude of the amount stolen and is stronger in poor groups than in rich groups.

Both the thief's and the victim's premiums—that is, the thief's preference for insider theft and the victim's preference for outsider theft—disappear when their groups are very wealthy. In both cases, the limit of $P$, as $S$ approaches infinity, is zero. Formally,

$$\lim_{S \to \infty} P^{\text{Thief}} = \lim_{S \to \infty} \ln \frac{S + t}{S} = 0,$$

12.15

and

$$\lim_{S \to \infty} P^{\text{Victim}} = \lim_{S \to \infty} \ln \frac{S}{S - t} = 0.$$

12.16

The three inequalities—for thief, victim, and others—are collected in figure 12.2 (step 6).

Next we turn to compare the gains and losses of the different actors in each situation (step 7). In the theft application, the principal focus is on contrasting the thief's gain with the victim's loss. We again set up and evaluate inequalities. However, while the inequalities used to address the previous set of questions focused on each actor, asking in what situation each actor is better off, here we focus on within-situation, cross-actor inequalities. Accordingly, we ask the following question: given that the thief always gains and the victim always loses, does the thief's gain exceed the victim's loss? This question can be answered quickly for insider theft (T1) but less quickly for the case of outsider theft (and requires an assumption on $\phi$).

Evaluating the inequality formed by the thief's gain and the victim's loss in insider theft, under the assumption that for both thief and victim $\phi$ remains the same from time 1 to time 2, we find that the thief's gain exceeds the victim's loss if and only if the victim's pretheft wealth exceeded the thief's pretheft wealth by an amount larger than the amount stolen (step 7, figure 12.2). When the victim is wealthier than the thief and the thief steals exactly the difference between their pretheft wealth amounts, the thief's gain and the victim's loss are exactly equal. When the victim is poorer than the thief, the victim's loss always exceeds the thief's gain.

It should be noted that in insider theft, the question of whether the thief's gain exceeds the victim's loss is equivalent to the question of whether the expected value of Z—that is, the social welfare—increases. Thus, social welfare remains unchanged if the thief is poorer than the victim and the amount stolen is exactly equal to the difference in their pretheft wealth. This is a "trading-places" phenomenon. When the thief is richer than the victim, social welfare is always diminished. Social welfare increases only in the particular situation where the thief is poorer than the victim and the amount stolen is less than the entire difference between the thief's pretheft wealth and the victim's pretheft wealth.

The case of outsider theft is, as noted, more complicated. The results are presented in figure 12.2 (step 7), but we leave to future work the task of fully discussing them. Here we note only that in this case, whether the thief's gain exceeds the victim's loss depends not only on the relation between the amount stolen and the disparity between the thief's pretheft wealth and the victim's pretheft wealth (as it did in the case of insider theft) but also on the disparity between the affluence of the thief's group and the victim's group. This case will be especially interesting to investigate, as it may yield differential norms across the two groups as well as the possibility of the emergence of supernorms for the entire collectivity.

The final set of questions to be addressed involves the effects of each factor on the change function CZ. Figure 12.2 (step 8) reports the first partial derivatives for all the actor-situation combinations. Here we discuss only a few of the results. The effect of pretheft wealth is negative for the thief and positive for the victim, indicating that the richer the thief the smaller the gain from theft and the richer the victim the milder the loss from theft. Thus, richer people have both less to gain and less to lose from theft, ceteris paribus. Rich people, then, may be less likely to steal but also more likely targets of theft.

The results for the effects of the amount stolen on thief and victim are completely expected; the larger the amount stolen, the greater the thief's gain and the greater the victim's loss. Interestingly, in outsider theft, the effect of the amount stolen is the same for the victim and members of the thief's group—exacerbating the loss—and the same for the thief and members of the victim's group—intensifying the gain. Thus, again, there may be natural affinities between these actors, and may lead to coalitions, possibly covert coalitions.

Group affluence affects CZ only in outsider theft. It operates as an intensifier or attenuator. The richer the thief's group, the greater the thief's gain from theft, and the richer the victim's group, the more intense the victim's loss from theft. As for the others, group wealth attenuates their gains and losses; the richer the thief's group, the milder the loss experienced by members of the thief's group, and the richer the victim's group, the smaller the gain experienced by members of the victim's group. Thus, group affluence intensifies the thief's gain and the victim's loss and attenuates the gains and losses of their fellow group members. Again, these results would appear to have implications for the emergence of norms and sanctions.

The principal results for the change in well-being of the three kinds of actors are summarized in tables 12.3 and 12.4 for insider and outsider theft, respectively. Both tables indicate whether the actor experiences a gain or loss and summarize the conditioning factors, indicating whether the gain or loss is intensified or attenuated. Table 12.4 also reports the effect of outsider theft relative to that of insider theft. These tables will simplify the task of drawing out implications for norm emergence in the next section.

In this illustration we have followed the protocol for the micromodel strategy in the application to theft phenomena. We have obtained and reported all the principal mathematical results and have provided a flavor for their substantive interpretation. The reader will no doubt draw many further implications. Avenues of analysis that may prove fruitful include scrutiny of the connections between these implications and further implications for preference formation, coalition formation, and, as seen below, norm emergence. Of course, all the implications are ceteris paribus implications in a multifactor world, and thus testing them will require thoughtful research design.

## Deriving Norm Predictions for Theft Situations

*Norm Candidates and Constituencies in Theft Situations*   We turn now to inquire as to what kinds of rules might arise in theft situations and which actors form the constituencies for them. To do that, we begin by systematically inspecting the predictions, separately for each of the three types of actors, and asking what rules each actor would favor or oppose if the actor's end is to maximize his or her own well-being. We also explore norm emergence among guardians. Here we define a guardian as someone whose objective is to maximize the commonweal. We examine two aspects

TABLE 12.2    *Well-Being in Theft Situations: Insider Theft*

|  | Thief | Victim | Others |
|---|---|---|---|
| Change in well-being as a result of theft | gain | loss | — |
| Conditioning factors |  |  |  |
| Own wealth | attenuates | attenuates | — |
| Amount stolen | intensifies | intensifies | — |

*Source:* Author's compilation.

of the commonweal: first, the expected value of the well-being distribution, namely, $E(Z)$, which the guardian will seek to maximize; second, victims' losses, which the guardian will seek to minimize.

Note that the results obtained in the previous section can be used to derive implications for a diversity of situations, not only theft but also taxation and tribute, for example. Note also that in different contexts actors and guardians may have different ends. For example, a guardian in a society that is engaged in a protracted struggle against colonizers and is ruled by a dictator who demands payment of tribute may have as the objective to maximize the dictator's gain. We leave to the interested reader application of the results in the previous section to such contexts. Similarly, individuals may formulate rules whose end is not to maximize own well-being but rather to minimize own or others' well-being.

Note also that, as this chapter represents the first step in building a framework for deriving norms from comparison theory, the focus here is on rules that may be generated from the immediate situation, not from reflection about what the future might bring. For example, members of the victim's group are made better off by the theft, and we trace out their

TABLE 12.3    *Well-Being in Theft Situations: Outsider Theft*

|  | Thief | Victim | Members of Thief's Group | Members of Victim's Group |
|---|---|---|---|---|
| Change in well-being as a result of theft | gain | loss | loss | gain |
| Conditioning factors |  |  |  |  |
| Own wealth | attenuates | attenuates | — | — |
| Amount stolen | intensifies | intensifies | intensifies | intensifies |
| Group wealth | intensifies | intensifies | attenuates | attenuates |
| Effect of outsider theft, relative to insider theft | attenuates[a] | attenuates[a] | produces loss | produces gain |

*Source:* Author's compilation.
[a]Effect disappears as group wealth goes to infinity.

support for norm candidates based on their current situation, not on the fear that at a future time they may become victims. Similarly, members of the thief's group are made worse off by the theft, and we trace out their support for norm candidates based on their current situation, not on the hope that the thief will share the spoils with them. Thus, all the rules discussed here may be called first-order rules (although below we take a brief glimpse at second-order rules). Of course, future work will elaborate the framework to accommodate second-order rules.[20]

Tables 12.2 and 12.3 will be helpful as we trace out implications for norm emergence among thief, victim, and others in the case in which the objective is to maximize own well-being. In general, actors who gain from theft will oppose antitheft rules and actors who lose from theft will favor them; whatever intensifies the gain intensifies opposition to antitheft rules, and whatever intensifies the loss intensifies support for them. Similarly, the greater the gain from theft, the greater the support for leniency in punishment; and the greater the loss from theft, the greater the support for severity in punishment. As for guardian behavior, we inspect the results for the expected well-being and for victims' losses in order to derive the norm-related implications.

*Thief*   The thief's well-being always increases as a result of the theft (figure 12.2, step 5, and tables 12.2 and 12.3). Moreover, the magnitude of the gain is larger for poorer thieves, increases with the amount stolen, and, in outsider theft, increases with own-group affluence (figure 12.2, step 8, and tables 12.2 and 12.3). Additionally, the gain is larger if the victim is a fellow group member, and this premium is larger in poor groups than in rich groups (figure 12.2, step 6, and tables 12.2 and 12.3). Accordingly, a thief will favor the rules,

- Stealing is permissible (it may be called by another name, such as "demanding tribute" or "borrowing").[21]
- Be merciful to thieves.

And a thief will oppose the rule:

- Thou shalt not steal.

The thief's opposition to antitheft rules and advocacy of protheft rules and of leniency will be stronger, the greater the thief's gain. Thus, factors that intensify the thief's gain from theft (see tables 12.2 and 12.3) will promote opposition to antitheft rules. Accordingly, opposition to antitheft rules and advocacy of protheft rules and of leniency will be stronger among poor thieves and among thieves who steal large amounts. Additionally, in cases of outsider theft, opposition to antitheft rules and advocacy of protheft rules and of leniency will be stronger among thieves from wealthy groups.

In heterogeneous societies (societies with more than one subgroup), the thief's gain is greater in insider theft (figure 12.2, step 6, and tables 12.2 and 12.3), and thus thieves will also oppose the rule,

- Never steal from a fellow group member.

Opposition to the injunction against insider theft will be stronger, the greater the thief's gain from insider theft. Accordingly, opposition to the injunction against insider theft will be stronger among thieves in poor groups.

*Victim*    The victim's well-being always decreases as a result of the theft (figure 12.2, step 5, and tables 12.2 and 12.3). Moreover, the loss in well-being is larger for poorer victims, increases with the amount stolen, and, in outsider theft, increases with own-group affluence (figure 12.2, step 8, and tables 12.2 and 12.3). Additionally, the loss is larger if the thief is a fellow group member, and this difference is larger in poor groups than in rich groups (figure 12.2, step 6, and tables 12.2 and 12.3). Accordingly, a victim will favor the rule,

- Thou shalt not steal,

and will oppose the leniency rule,

- Be merciful to thieves.

The victim's support of antitheft rules and opposition to protheft rules and to leniency will be stronger, the greater the victim's loss. Thus, factors that intensify the victim's loss from theft (see tables 12.2 and 12.3) will promote support of antitheft rules. Accordingly, support for antitheft rules and opposition to protheft rules and to leniency will be stronger among poor victims and among victims from whom large amounts have been stolen. Additionally, in cases of outsider theft, support for antitheft rules and opposition to protheft rules will be stronger among victims from wealthy groups.

In heterogeneous societies, victim's loss is greater in insider theft (figure 12.2, step 6, and tables 12.2 and 12.3), and thus victims will also favor the rule,

- Never steal from a fellow group member.

Support for the injunction against insider theft will be stronger, the greater the victim's loss from insider theft. Accordingly, support for the injunction against insider theft will be stronger among victims in poor groups.

*Others*   In insider theft, others experience neither a gain nor a loss; in outsider theft, members of the thief's group become worse off, and members of the victim's group become better off (figure 12.2, step 5, and tables 12.2 and 12.3). In cross-group theft, members of the thief's group experience the same effects as the victim, and members of the victim's group experience the same effects as the thief except for the effects of group affluence (figure 12.2, step 8, and table 12.3). Accordingly, in homogeneous societies, others will neither favor nor oppose theft-related rules. In heterogeneous societies, members of the thief's group and members of the victim's group will favor and oppose different rules. Members of the thief's group will favor, and members of the the victim's group will oppose the rule,

- Thou shalt not steal.

Members of the the thief's group will oppose, and members of the victim's group will favor, the rule,

- Be merciful to thieves.

   Support of the antitheft norm and opposition to leniency among members of the thief's group will be stronger, the greater their loss from theft; and opposition to the antitheft norm and support for leniency among members of the victim's group will be stronger, the greater their gain from theft. Accordingly, support of the antitheft norm and opposition to leniency among members of the thief's group and opposition to the antitheft norm and support for leniency among members of the victim's group will *both* be stronger, the greater the amount stolen and the poorer their groups (table 12.3).
   The results in table 12.3 also lead to a punishment norm among others in cross-group theft. The larger the amount stolen, the greater the loss among members of the thief's group and the greater the gain among members of the victim's group (figure 12.2, step 8, and table 12.3). Thus, members of the thief's group will favor, and members of the victim's group will oppose, the rule,

- Punish the thief more severely, the larger the amount stolen.

   As for the injunction against insider theft,

- Never steal from a fellow group member,

it will be opposed by members of the thief's group, for whom outsider theft produces a loss, and supported by members of the victim's group, for whom outsider theft produces a gain (table 12.3).

*Guardians*   Meanwhile, the guardians care only about the commonweal. To begin, we represent the commonweal by $E(Z)$, the expected value of well-being, $Z$. We use the results in figure 12.2, step 7, to derive the implications based on the expected value of well-being. In homogeneous societies, guardians favor the rules,

- Never steal from someone poorer than yourself.
- If you steal from someone richer than yourself, never leave him or her poorer than you were before the theft.

In heterogeneous societies, the rules favored by guardians are quite complicated, as they involve relationships between the amount stolen, the disparity between the pretheft wealth of the thief and the victim and the disparity between the pretheft wealth of the thief's and the victim's groups.[22] The rules based on well-being lead to punishment norms. In homogeneous societies, guardians would favor the rules,

- If the victim is poorer than the thief, punish the thief more severely, the larger the amount stolen.
- If the victim is richer than the thief, punishment severity is non-monotonically related to amount stolen.

In heterogeneous societies, the well-being-based rules lead to a conditional punishment norm,

- Punishment severity depends on amount stolen and the disparities between the thief and the victim and between their groups.

Guardians may have different objectives than maximizing the expected well-being. They may, for example, seek to minimize the losses incurred by victims; or they may seek to maximize the gains achieved by thieves. Here, we examine one of these cases, the case in which the guardians seek to minimize victims' losses. The most basic way to minimize victims' losses is to reduce the incidence of theft. Accordingly, guardians will favor the rule,

- Thou shalt not steal.

Because the victim's loss is greater in insider theft, in heterogeneous societies the guardians will also favor the rule,

- Never steal from a fellow group member.

Another way to minimize victims' losses is to punish thieves more severely the greater the victim's loss. Again using tables 12.2 and 12.3, we see that the guardian would formulate punishment norms, as follows:

- Punish the thief more severely, the poorer the victim.
- Punish the thief more severely, the larger the amount stolen.

Additionally, in heterogeneous societies, the guardian would formulate the further punishment norms:

- In outsider theft, punish the thief more severely, the richer the victim's group.
- Punish the thief more severely, if victim is from thief's own group.

Note, however, that this rule disappears when the thief's group is very wealthy.

Holding constant the victim's pretheft wealth and the amount stolen, the severity of punishment, according to these norms, would be lowest in outsider theft when the victim is from a poor group, increasing with the victim's group's wealth. Severity of punishment would be greatest when the victim is from the thief's own group. (Severity of punishment when the victim is from the thief's own group is the limit approached by severity of punishment in outsider theft as the victim's group's wealth increases.)

Having systematically reviewed the support for norms likely to be found among thief, victim, others, and guardians, based on the operation of comparison processes, we now extract norm candidates and arrange them so that their constituencies can be gauged. Tables 12.4 and 12.5 present, for homogeneous societies and for cross-group theft in heterogeneous societies, respectively, matrices of selected norm candidates and their constituencies. These tables indicate support and opposition for norm candidates, together with the strength of support or opposition. A blank cell indicates the absence of a rationale for a first-order rule based on comparison theory.[23]

While some norm candidates engender both support and opposition, others have only support or only opposition (again based solely on comparison processes), as can be seen clearly from the tables. Immediately it is plausible that norm candidates with only support or only opposition will be the first adopted or discarded. Thus, all the "strong" candidates for norms are rules favored by guardians—such as, "Never steal from someone poorer than yourself," "Punish the thief more severely, the larger the amount stolen," and "In outsider theft, punish the thief more severely, the richer the victim's group." Not all rules favored by guardians are free from

TABLE 12.4    *Norm Candidates and Their Constituencies: Theft Situations in Homogeneous Societies, Based on Comparison Theory*

| | Constituency | | | |
| Norm Candidate | Thief | Victim | Others | Guardians |
|---|---|---|---|---|
| **General norms** | | | | |
| Thou shalt not steal | Oppose | Favor | Indifferent | Favor[a] |
| Never steal from someone poorer than yourself | — | — | — | Favor[b] |
| When stealing from someone richer than yourself, never leave him or her poorer than you were before the theft | — | — | — | Favor[b] |
| **Strength of constituency, by actor and situation characteristics** | | | | |
| Thou shalt not steal | Oppose more strongly the poorer the thief and the greater the amount stolen | Favor more strongly the poorer the victim and the greater the amount stolen | — | — |
| **Punishment norms** | | | | |
| Punish thief more severely, the poorer the victim | — | — | — | Favor[a] |
| Punish thief more severely, the larger the amount stolen | — | — | — | Favor[a] |
| If victim is poorer than thief, punish thief more severely, the larger the amount stolen | — | — | — | Favor[b] |
| If victim is richer than thief, punishment severity is nonmonotonically related to amount stolen | — | — | — | Favor[b] |

Source: Author's compilation.
[a]Guardian minimizes victims' losses.
[b]Guardian maximizes average well-being.

| | Constituency | | | | |
|---|---|---|---|---|---|
| Norm Candidate | Thief | Victim | Thief's Group | Victim's Group | Guardians |
| **General Norms** | | | | | |
| Thou shalt not steal | Oppose | Favor | Favor | Oppose | Favor[a] |
| Never steal from a fellow group member | Oppose | Favor | Oppose | Favor | Favor[a] |
| Conditional norm relating amount stolen, disparity between thief and victim and between their groups | — | — | — | — | Favor[b] |
| **Strength of Constituency, by Actor and Situation Characteristics** | | | | | |
| Thou shalt not steal | Oppose more strongly the poorer the thief, the greater the amount stolen, and the richer the group | Favor more strongly the poorer the victim, the greater the amount stolen, and the richer the group | Favor more strongly the greater the amount stolen and the poorer the group | Oppose more strongly the greater the amount stolen and the poorer the group | — |
| Never steal from a fellow group member | Oppose more strongly the poorer the group | Favor more strongly the poorer the group | — | — | — |

| Punishment Norms | | | | | | |
|---|---|---|---|---|---|---|
| Punish thief more severely, the poorer the victim | — | — | — | — | — | Favor[a] |
| Punish thief more severely, the larger the amount stolen | — | Favor | — | Oppose | — | Favor[a] |
| In outsider theft, punish thief more severely, the richer the victim's group | — | — | — | — | — | Favor[a] |
| Punishment severity depends on amount stolen, disparity between thief and victim and between their groups | — | — | — | — | — | Favor[b] |

*Source:* Author's compilation.
[a]Guardian minimizes victim's loss.
[b]Guardian maximizes average well-being.

opposition, however; examples include "Thou shalt not steal" and "Punish the thief more severely, the larger the amount stolen."

If protagonists in theft situations—thief and victim—are a tiny segment of the society, then the views of the others assume a critical importance. Tables 12.4 and 12.5 indicate that in homogeneous societies others are indifferent and in heterogeneous societies they are pervasively at cross-purposes, depending on whether they are members of the thief's or victim's group All the norm candidates in heterogeneous societies that engage others engender opposite reactions and thus will have a rocky history. Understanding their trajectory will require a systematic look at the proportions in each of the actor sets and the incidence of theft; moreover, more complete understanding may require invoking behavioral processes far afield from comparison processes, such as power and bargaining processes.

*Characterizing Theft Norms in Homogeneous and Heterogeneous Societies*   Will there be a general norm about theft? If yes, will theft norms notice offender characteristics, victim characteristics, and social context? How will theft norms differ across homogeneous and heterogeneous societies? Reasoning along the lines suggested above, we can form an image of the configuration of theft norms.

*Homogeneous Societies*   In homogeneous societies, thieves will favor a permissive rule, victims a proscriptive rule, and everyone else—except guardians—will be indifferent (table 12.4). Thus, homogeneous societies are likely to resort to private devices, such as dueling, the vendetta, and so on, to settle theft disputes. If, however, theft becomes widespread, so that the group of others is diminished, the first rules likely to be adopted will be those proposed by guardians and that have only support. These rules are:

- Never steal from someone poorer than yourself
- When stealing from someone richer than yourself, never leave him or her poorer than you were before the theft
- Punish the thief more severely, the poorer the victim
- Punish the thief more severely, the larger the amount stolen
- If the victim is poorer than the thief, punish thief more severely, the larger the amount stolen
- If the victim is richer than the thief, punishment severity is non-monotonically related to amount stolen.

If theft becomes even more widespread, the only recourse is for guardians to intervene and introduce the antitheft norm whose opposition comes only from thieves—that is,

- Thou shalt not steal.

*Heterogeneous Societies*    Heterogeneous societies are substantially more complicated than homogeneous societies. Not only might there be norms covering cross-group theft, but also there might be norms covering the differential propensity for insider and outsider theft.

As shown in table 12.5, the first great difference between heterogeneous and homogeneous societies is the absence, in the case of cross-group theft, of a group of others indifferent to theft. Cross-group theft affects everyone; there are no longer unaffected others. Heterogeneous societies thus immediately have a rationale, based on operation of comparison processes, for abandoning the private-justice traditions of a homogeneous past. Because everyone is affected by cross-group theft, there may be more legislation in heterogeneous societies than in homogeneous societies, even if there is less theft. As in homogeneous societies, the first rules adopted are likely to be rules proposed by guardians and which engender no opposition. Based on table 12.5, the first rules to be adopted are the following:

- Punish the thief more severely, the poorer the the victim.
- Punish the thief more severely, the richer the victim's group.
- Conditional norms—both general and punishment norms—relating the amount stolen, disparity between the thief's and the victim's pretheft wealth, and disparity between their groups' pretheft wealth.

Meanwhile, there will be debate about three further rules that engender both support and opposition, all three of which are favored by guardians:

- Thou shalt not steal.
- Never steal from a fellow group member.
- Punish the thief more severely, the larger the amount stolen.

If the incidence of theft increases, then guardians may impose these further rules or contrive to have a superguardian impose them.

*Universal Theft Norms*    A final task is to enumerate theft norms that may be found in all societies, whether homogeneous or heterogeneous. We begin with rules that are likely to arise. In this analysis, based on comparison theory, and focusing on first-order rules, there is only one candidate norm that immediately and unambiguously appears likely to arise in all societies, that is, to be proposed in all societies and to be without opposition (tables 12.4 and 12.5). That norm is,

- Punish the thief more severely, the poorer the the victim.

We can reason further that, to the extent that insider theft in heterogeneous societies is subject to the same mechanisms as theft in homogeneous societies, all societies may adopt the subset of homogeneous-society rules that do not have opposition in cross-group theft. These are the following:

- Never steal from someone poorer than yourself.

- When stealing from someone richer than yourself, never leave him or her poorer than you were before the theft.

- If the victim is poorer than the thief, punish the thief more severely, the larger the amount stolen.

- If the victim is richer than the thief, punishment severity is non-monotonically related to the amount stolen.

    Finally, in all societies guardians will propose the rule,

- Thou shalt not steal.

This rule is not without opposition, however, and may have to be imposed from above.

## How Do Norms Emerge? Speculations on the Road to Testing

I have argued that humans are by nature rule makers and that the characteristics of the norms they make grow out of the operation of the basic forces governing human behavior. Thus, the characteristics of norms—their polarity and conditionality, as well as their constituencies, configurations, trajectories, and the constituencies' strength of adherence and opposition—can in principle be explained by theories describing the operation of basic forces. At this stage in the development of sociobehavioral science, when the quest is to identify the basic forces, a feasible task is to work in the Mertonian middle range, deriving predictions for norm emergence from the operation of middle-range processes. To that end, I have reported development of a framework to derive predictions for norms from the theory of comparison processes.

    The framework has two parts. First, we derive behavioral predictions from comparison theory; second, we derive norm predictions from the behavioral predictions, for specific scenarios in which actors seek to increase or decrease the well-being of self or others. To illustrate, we derived a set of behavioral predictions that can be obtained using one particular strategy for deriving implications (that is, comparison theory may yield more behavioral theft predictions than the ones obtained here); these behavioral predictions predict which parties in a theft situation will become better off, worse off, or remain untouched by the theft and also how the characteristics of the theft situation and of the parties and groups involved intensify or attenuate the basic effects. For example, comparison theory predicts that the victim of a theft will become worse off and that the magnitude of the loss in well-being is smaller the richer the victim and the smaller the amount stolen. Next, we derived norm predictions, both for individuals and for the societal guardians, in scenarios in which the individuals seek their own well-being and the guardians seek the commonweal, and for both homogeneous and heterogeneous societies.

The question now arises, How to test the norm predictions? Testing the norm predictions, like testing the behavioral predictions, will require thoughtful design. As noted, all the predictions are ceteris paribus predictions, and we live in a decidedly multifactor world. In this section, we speculate briefly about two of the avenues for testing the norm predictions: testing in the historical record—in which often the best that can be achieved is an interpretation consistent with the predictions—and testing in the anthropological record. Of course, there are other testing avenues, such as in schools, small groups, and in the laboratory.

One of the strongest of the norm predictions derived from comparison theory is that the rule, "Thou shalt not steal," is not likely to arise unless it is imposed by guardians; in homogeneous societies, it does not arise because most of the population is indifferent, and in heterogeneous societies because there are strong factions both in support and in opposition. Other predicted norms are based on features of the theft situation—for example, the prediction that guardians will favor a penalty norm with stronger punishment the larger the amount stolen. In an initial reconnaissance expedition, we began a review of anthropological research on primitive societies, early Greek history, and biblical accounts. The evidentiary requirements are stringent: First, the society must be clearly identifiable as homogeneous or heterogeneous in one or more characteristics. Second, there must be narratives that describe group sanctions, group members' sanctioning behavior, and/or the sanctions' deterrent effects. That is, the evidence must show, for example, with respect to an antitheft norm in the homogeneous case either evidence of indifference or evidence of sanctioning behavior; and, if there is sanctioning behavior, the evidence must include a narrative about the emergence of the norm. Moreover, searching for evidence on theft norms presupposes the existence of private property; thus, societies in which theft cannot occur, because no one "owns" anything that can be taken without the owner's consent, must be excluded. Accordingly, the first task is to build a data base of societies with private property, coding them as homogeneous or heterogeneous on appropriate dimensions. Obviously, it will take much research to compile the evidence and to compare carefully all the predicted norms against the evidence. Here, we sketch some preliminary observations drawn from the initial review of potentially pertinent sources.

## Anthropological Research on Primitive Societies

The initial review produced one fascinating account of the emergence of an antitheft norm, K.N. Llewellyn and Adamson Hoebel's (1941) account based on work among the Cheyenne of the Great Plains of the United States. Llewellyn and Hoebel (1941) and Hoebel (1960) recount that traditionally the Cheyenne had a system of "borrowing" under which it was permitted to take someone's goods provided the borrower left a personal item both to identify himself or herself and to provide surety. This system began to break down with the introduction of horses by the Europeans, for horses could be taken long distances. Horse owners began to complain, and by 1850 the issue loomed large. Finally, a horse owner, Wolf-Lies-Down, whose horse had been borrowed and kept for more than a year, took the matter to his military society, the Elk Soldiers. The Elk Soldiers sent an emissary to the borrower's camp, whereupon the borrower returned, contritely, and not only returned Wolf-Lies-Down's horse to him but also gave him a second horse. Wolf-Lies-Down made peace with the borrower, and the Elk Soldiers with the borrower's group. The matter did not end there, however. The Elk Soldiers made a rule, which became a rule for the whole tribe: "There shall be no more borrowing of horses without asking. If any man takes another's goods without asking, we will go over and get them back for him. More than that, if the taker tries to keep them, we will give him a whipping" (Llewellyn and Hoebel 1941, 127–28).

To interpret this account from the perspective of the norm predictions derived from comparison theory, we begin by noting that the society was clearly heterogeneous in that there were distinct soldier groups and camps. According to the first-order predictions derived in this chapter, the members of the victim's group—the Elk Soldiers—should have opposed an antitheft norm. Perhaps they did, in the years between the introduction of the horse around 1760 (Hoebel 1960, 1–2) and 1850. Horse borrowing apparently became widespread, so that large numbers of Cheyenne were actual victims and larger numbers potential victims. The account does not describe individual sanctioning behavior; according to comparison theory, we would expect that in insider horse borrowing, everyone would be indifferent except the victim, and that in cross-group horse borrowing, members of the borrower's group would sanction the borrower. Indeed, perhaps the borrower's soldier society insisted that the borrower give the second horse in compensation to Wolf-Lies-Down. By 1850, after ninety years of horse borrowing, there would be both guardians looking out for the victims' well-being and, in a second-order twist, large numbers of actual and potential victims. Whether the Elk Soldiers made the new rule acting as guardians or as victims, the evidence does not make it possible to ascertain.

Elsewhere, Hoebel ([1954] 1968, 169) notes that among the Cheyenne, "a fair amount of petty pilfering took place in the camps, but theft was never made a legal issue. A known thief was publicly shamed with the remark, 'If I had known you wanted that thing, I would have given it to you.'" This account appears to refer to within-camp theft, but we cannot be sure. Only the victim sanctions the thief, which would be consistent with within-camp theft. Moreover, Hoebel's phrase "publicly shamed" is ambiguous in the absence of direct information about the behavior of persons other than the victim.

Among the Andaman Islanders, it also appears that theft is sanctioned only by the victim, who throws a tantrum, sometimes a ferocious tantrum, in response to being robbed (Hoebel [1954] 1968, 296). This would be consistent with the comparison-theory view of within-group theft.

## Early Greek History

As with the anthropological material, a chief challenge in looking at early Greek history is to discern sanctioning behavior. Initial review yielded some highly suggestive accounts.

We begin with Sparta. Aristotle in the *Politics* (1952c, book 2, chapter 9) and Plutarch ([early 2d century] 1952, 41) provide detailed accounts of the structure, customs, and laws of Sparta and of the lawgiver Lycurgus—although some of the material might be legendary rather than historical. The accounts suggest that there was no antitheft norm in Sparta. In fact, perhaps quite the opposite. In the elaborate system for educating boys to become warriors, stealing was part of the curriculum. Boys and young men had to learn to steal. If they were caught, they were severely punished—not for stealing but for getting caught. The situation at Sparta appears consistent with the predictions of comparison theory.

At Athens, Draco had made laws (the code dates to ca. 621 B.C.), which Solon (ca. 630 to ca. 560 B.C.) later reformed. Aristotle in *The Athenian Constitution* (1952a) and Plutarch ([early 2d century] 1952) provide accounts of these laws. Both codes include antitheft laws, so we must infer that an antitheft norm had already arisen in Attica by the seventh century B.C. For possible information into the norm's history, we have to rely on pre-Draco sources, especially Homer. Pending that search, we note that whereas Draco had a single punishment for most offenses—death—Solon prescribed differentiated penalties. The penalty for theft varied according to the value of the stolen goods (Gagarin 1986, 65). This is what comparison theory predicts, based on guardians' sympathy for victims, whose loss of well-being is greater the larger the amount stolen.

All accounts of the Athenian laws mention contemporaneous turmoil and strife. This is consistent with comparison theory's prediction that in heterogeneous societies—and Attica was already heterogeneous in the seventh century B.C.—there would have been factions favoring and opposing an antitheft norm. In such a situation, guardians would arise whose objective would be to safeguard the commonweal. In Athens, the guardian emerged in the person of the lawgiver, appointed by the state.[24]

## Biblical Accounts

The first two books of the Bible, Genesis and Exodus, provide an interesting account. In the first period after the Fall, there is no norm against theft, and theft disputes are handled privately. For example, when Jacob and his family leave Laban's household (Genesis 31), Laban, discovering that the household idols have been stolen, races after Jacob and accuses him of the theft. Jacob is innocent and knows nothing about it; his wife Rachel has stolen the idols from her father's house and hides them in a camel cushion. Time passes, and by the time Moses has led the Israelites out of Egypt we can discern a second period in which Moses, acting as guardian, settles private disputes and then, on the advice of his father-in-law, Jethro, appoints assistants to handle less important cases (Exodus 18). Our results suggest that the rules these early judges used may have been like the rules listed in tables 12.4 and 12.5, which are favored by guardians and are unopposed. Evidently, however, stronger intervention was required. In Exodus 20, the Lord Himself delivers the edict, "Thou shalt not steal." Note that no human guardian, not even Moses, makes a rule in the face of opposition. This requires a superguardian, and Moses finds the superguardian on Mount Sinai.

This preliminary reconnaissance of anthropological, historical, and biblical records provided accounts that both illustrate the evidentiary requirements for testing the norm predictions derived from comparison theory and also lend themselves well to special interpretation from the perspective of comparison theory. Additionally, our initial review is highly suggestive about the sociological importance of the lawgiver.

## Concluding Note

Humans are rule makers. The challenge for social science is to describe the content, configurations, and trajectories of the norms they produce. The objective of this chapter was to lay the foundation for a framework for studying the part played by comparison processes in the emergence of norms. My strategy, as a first step, was to explore the emergence of the first-order subset of type 2, or devised, rules, identifying the likely rules, rule makers, and rule constituencies. To illustrate, I focused on rule making in theft situations. The procedures I followed not only constitute the foundation of the framework but also can immediately be used to explore rule making in other domains touched by comparison processes, including domains amenable to analysis not only via means of the micromodel used to

study theft phenomena but also via using the other main prediction protocol, the macromodel.

Substantively, the theft analysis generated two initial sets of norm candidates, one for homogeneous societies, the other for the case of cross-
group theft in heterogeneous societies, including information about the
support or opposition among the major actors—thief, victim, others (and,
in heterogeneous societies, members of the thief's group and members of
the victim's groups), and guardians. We next considered special norms in
heterogeneous societies that concern the thief's choice of victim, whether
the victim is to be a fellow group member or an outsider. Finally, we dis-
tilled from the analysis of theft norm candidates in homogeneous and heterogeneous societies a subset common to both—the universal norms.

Future theoretical tasks include systematic mapping of second-order
rules, tracing out rules specific to the groups of heterogeneous societies as
well as the supernorms applicable to the entire society, and carrying out
analyses in other domains in which comparison theory has already been
fruitfully applied, including, for example, the domains of gift giving, disasters, migration, and war. Future empirical tasks include testing the predictions for norm emergence, taking into account the likely operation of other
factors, outside the purview of comparison processes, some of which may
generate effects in the opposite direction, at least a subset of which may
dominate the comparison effects.

Testable predictions obtained from the theft analysis used to illustrate
the framework in this chapter include: The rule, "Thou shalt not steal," is
not likely to arise unless it is imposed by guardians; it does not arise in
homogeneous societies because most of the population is indifferent, and
in heterogeneous societies because there are strong factions both in support
and in opposition. A homogeneous society quickly embraces the rules,
"Never steal from someone poorer than yourself" and "When stealing from
someone richer than yourself, never leave him or her poorer than you were
before the theft." The only rule quickly adopted in both homogeneous and
heterogeneous societies is, "Punish the thief more severely, the poorer the
victim." In heterogeneous societies, the rule, "Never steal from a fellow
group member," is proposed by guardians, but it engenders both support
and opposition from the population. In heterogeneous societies, in the case
of outsider theft, a rule, adopted is, "Punish the thief more severely, the
richer the victim's group." However, insider theft will be punished even
more severely.

# Notes

1. The ubiquity of rule making is illustrated by Descartes' observation, "Every
   problem that I solved became a rule which served afterwards to solve other
   problems."

2. For fuller discussion of the four premises underlying the work reported in this chapter, see Jasso 1988, 1996a, 49–51.

3. For example, see Parsons 1968 on Durkheim as a multifactor theorist.

4. For example, with respect to the first candidate force, Aristotle (*Metaphysics,* book 1, chapter 5) observes that "all men by nature desire knowledge." With respect to the third candidate force, Aquinas (*Summa Theologica,* book 2, part 1, question 5) observes that "humans seek their own perfection," desiring "a well-disposed body" and "keenness of wit and beauty of body" (ibid., question 4).

5. For example, the first candidate force is related to the property of omniscience and the fourth to the property of omnipotence. The second evokes the biblical account of the temptation that led to the Fall: "The moment you eat of it your eyes will be opened and you will be like gods who know what is good and what is bad" (Genesis 3:5). As has been often remarked, humans ascribe to God that which they most admire and desire.

6. To illustrate, the first and fourth candidate forces appear in the powerful words that John the Evangelist gives Christ, "You shall know the truth, and the truth shall make you free" (John 8:32).

7. The vow of obedience is a case in point, as freedom is relinquished.

8. As Arthur Danto (1967, 299–300), observes, "Indeed, it is by and large the ability of a theory to permit derivations far afield from its original domain which serves as a criterion for accepting a theory, for in addition to the obvious fruitfulness such a criterion emphasizes, such derivations permit an increasingly broad and diversified basis for testing the theory."

9. Incidentally, Smelser (1967, xv) provides an especially apt illustration of the transposition of this chapter's title: "Two principles guided me in organizing the headings and chapters." Smelser, in this instance, is *rule making about rule finding.*

10. Of course, type 2 rules may also have to be unmade, but the process of unmaking a devised rule will differ from that of unmaking a spontaneously emergent rule. A distinction based on the genesis of the original rule may prove fruitful.

11. It is believed that St. Benedict of Nursia formulated the *Rule,* combining earlier sources with parts he wrote himself, sometime between his founding of the monastery at Monte Cassino (ca. 529) and his death (ca. 547).

12. This shift also suggests an important further avenue for research—namely, to assess how the sources of people's ideas of what they deserve or would like to have differ across social contexts and/or change over the life course.

13. These conditions are scale invariance and additivity. As well, the logarithmic-ratio form quantifies the common idea that deficiency is felt more keenly than comparable excess. Because of these and other appealing properties, the logarithmic-ratio form was proposed as a general Law of Justice Evaluation. (Jasso 1978)

14. For an account of Merton's contributions to justice and comparison theory, see Jasso 2000.

15. In justice theory, all the quantities and mechanisms may differ according to five dimensions of the justice context. These five dimensions, conveniently

known by the mnemonic "brots," refer to the benefit or burden, the rewardee, the observer, the time period, and the society.

16.  Note that the change equation refers exclusively to one individual at two points in time. The individual may become better and/or worse off relative to his or her own situation at time 1.

17.  Space constraints do not permit presentation of the protocol for a micromodel analysis in the case of ordinal rewards.

18.  Among the predictions listed in table 12.1, all but one are deduced strictly from the three individual-level basic postulates of comparison theory. The exception is the first prediction—about parental gift giving—which requires an additional assumption. In this case, the strictly deduced prediction is that in families with two or more nontwin children, the children will be happier if they receive gifts at an annual gift-giving occasion rather than at their birthdays. The additional assumption implicit in this prediction, as stated in table 12.1, is that parents care about their children's happiness.

19.  In both cases, the new cultural "products" are seen as a response to the switch from valuing ordinal goods (like birth and nobility) to valuing cardinal goods (like wealth).

20.  A related issue concerns the enforcement of norms. The interplay between rule making, strength of adherence to norms, rule unmaking, and enforcement is critical to the trajectory of a given norm. For example, if a norm is not enforced, why unmake it? The task ahead is fourfold: (1) assess what comparison theory may imply about enforcement; (2) obtain predictions for enforcement based on other theories; (3) integrate the predictions of comparison theory and other theories; and (4) incorporate the integrated enforcement predictions into derivations for emergence of second-order rules.

21.  As St. Augustine (*City of God*, Book IV, chap. 4) observed, without justice, kingdoms are like giant robberies.

22.  These rules exemplify the conditionality property of norms studied by Jasso and Opp 1997.

23.  Note that the results collected in the tables can be straightforwardly applied to other cases; for example, the strength of the thief's opposition to the antitheft norm operates in the same way as the strength of a dictator's support for the rule, "Thou shalt pay tribute."

24.  For elaboration of the circumstances surrounding the appointment of lawgivers and their personal qualities, see Gagarin 1986, 58–61, and Greenberg 1996.

# References

Aquinas, St. Thomas. [1267–1273] 1952. *Summa theologica*. Two volumes. Translated by Fathers of the English Dominican Province. Revised by Daniel J. Sullivan. Chicago: Encyclopaedia Britannica.

Aristotle. 1952a. *The Athenian Constitution*. Translated by Benjamin Jowett. Chicago: Encyclopaedia Britannica.

———. 1952b. *Metaphysics*. Translated by W.D. Ross. Chicago: Encyclopaedia Britannica.

———. 1952c. *Politics*. Translated by Benjamin Jowett. Chicago: Encyclopaedia Britannica.

St. Augustine. [413–426] 1952. *The City of God*. Translated by Marcus Dods. Chicago: Encyclopaedia Britannica.

St. Benedict. *Rule for Monasteries*. 1948. Translated by Leonard J. Doyle from the 3d edition of the text edited by Dom Cuthbert Butler (1935). Collegeville, Minnesota: Liturgical Press of St. John's Abbey.

Danto, Arthur C. 1967. "Philosophy of Science, Problems of." In vol. 6 of *Encyclopedia of Philosophy*, edited by Paul Edwards. New York: Macmillan.

Descartes, René. [1637] 1952. Discourse on Method. Translated by Elizabeth S. Haldane and G.R.T. Ross. Chicago: Encyclopaedia Britannica.

Gagarin, Michael. 1986. *Early Greek Law*. Berkeley: University of California Press.

Greenberg, David F. 1996. "Rhetorics of Legitimation in Ancient and Modern Law." Paper presented to the Law and Society Meeting. Glasgow, Scotland (July 1996).

Hoebel, E. Adamson. 1960. *The Cheyennes: Indians of the Great Plains*. New York: Holt, Rinehart and Winston.

———. [1954] 1968. *The Law of Primitive Man: A Study in Comparative Legal Dynamics*. New York: Atheneum.

Jasso, Guillermina. 1978. "On the Justice of Earnings: A New Specification of the Justice Evaluation Function." *American Journal of Sociology* 83(6): 1398–1419.

———. 1986. "A New Representation of the Just Term in Distributive-Justice Theory: Its Properties and Operation in Theoretical Derivation and Empirical Estimation." *Journal of Mathematical Sociology* 12(3): 251–74.

———. 1988. "Principles of Theoretical Analysis." *Sociological Theory* 6(1): 1–20.

———. 1990. "Methods for the Theoretical and Empirical Analysis of Comparison Processes." *Sociological Methodology* 20: 369–419.

———. 1991. "Cloister and Society: Analyzing the Public Benefit of Monastic and Mendicant Institutions." *Journal of Mathematical Sociology* 16(1): 109–36.

———. 1993a. "Building the Theory of Comparison Processes: Construction of Postulates and Derivation of Predictions." In *Theoretical Research Programs: Studies in the Growth of Theory*, edited by Joseph Berger and Morris Zelditch Jr. Stanford: Stanford University Press.

———. 1993b. "Choice and Emotion in Comparison Theory." *Rationality and Society* 5(2): 231–74.

———. 1993c. "Using Abell's Narrative Method to Build a Theory: The Case of the Theory of Distributive Justice and Its Generalization to the Theory of Comparison Processes." *Journal of Mathematical Sociology* 18(2–3): 219–51.

———. 1996a. "Deriving Implications of Comparison Theory for Demographic Phenomena: A First Step in the Analysis of Migration." *Sociological Quarterly* 37(1): 19–57.

———. 1996b. "Exploring the Reciprocal Relations Between Theoretical and Empirical Work (Paper in Honor of Robert K. Merton)." *Sociological Methods and Research* 24(3): 253–303.

———. 1999. "How Much Injustice Is There in the World? Two New Justice Indexes." *American Sociological Review* 64(1): 133–68.

———. 2000. "Some of Robert K. Merton's Contributions to Justice Theory." *Sociological Theory* 18: 329–37.

Jasso, Guillermina, and Karl-Dieter Opp. 1997. "Probing the Character of Norms: A Factorial Survey Analysis of the Norms of Political Action." *American Sociological Review* 62(6): 947–64.

Llewellyn, K. N., and E. Adamson Hoebel. 1941. *The Cheyenne Way: Conflict and Case Law in Primitive Jurisprudence*. Norman: University of Oklahoma Press.

Merton, Robert K. [1949] 1968. *Social Theory and Social Structure*. New York: Free Press.

Parsons, Talcott. 1968. "Émile Durkheim." In vol. 4 of *International Encyclopedia of the Social Sciences,* edited by David L. Sills. New York: Macmillan.

Plutarch. [Early 2d century] 1952. *The Lives of the Noble Grecians and Romans*. The Dryden Translation. Chicago: Encyclopaedia Britannica.

Saint-Exupéry, Antoine de. 1943. *The Little Prince*. Translated by Katherine Woods. New York: Harcourt Brace.

Smelser, Neil J. 1967. *Sociology: An Introduction*. New York: Wiley.

Tyler, Tom R., Robert J. Boeckmann, Yuen J. Huo, and Heather J. Smith. 1997. *Social Justice in a Diverse Society*. Boulder: Westview.

# 13

# WHAT HAVE WE LEARNED ABOUT THE EMERGENCE OF SOCIAL NORMS?

## *Michael Hechter and Karl-Dieter Opp*

I N THIS final chapter, we consider the extent to which the empirical analyses in part II of this volume point the way to a theory of the emergence of norms.[1] First, we explore some of the principal points of agreement and disagreement that have surfaced in the volume. This prompts us
to reconsider the fundamental issue of how norms can best be defined. We
then proceed to a number of suggestions for future empirical research. The
chapter concludes with some observations about the ambiguity and muta-
bility of norms.

Because our contributors represent a wide variety of theoretical and
methodological perspectives, it is no surprise to discover that their views
about what norms are and how they may be explained are in some respects
disparate.

## Are Norms Given or Constructed?

The principal disagreement separates authors who view norms as clear
constraints on action from those for whom norms are more plastic social
constructions. This amounts to a distinction between a conception of norms
as given and "obeyed," on the one hand, and norms as negotiated and
"performed," on the other. Most of the contributors treat norms as consisting of clear guidelines for action to be applied in specific situations. This is
perhaps exemplified best in chapter 9. Satoshi Kanazawa and Mary Still
assume that once a marriage norm has emerged, it is recognized as such by
the members of a group and serves to regulate their behavior accordingly.
Each man knows full well that he cannot marry more than one woman at a
time, and the converse is true for each woman. In the rational choice theorist's world, norms provide common knowledge about the individual payoffs to particular courses of action. On this view, norms are readily con-

ceived as akin to relative prices. It is then a simple matter to analyze the consequences of shifts in norms for social outcomes.

Gary Alan Fine, in chapter 5, rejects this view and argues instead that norms are understandings that are recognized in situ. In the words of constructionist sociologists, one does not "obey" norms, one "does" (or "performs") norms. Yet, although norms are enacted, they are also capable of being reported, incorporated in various discourses, and, as a result, becoming general and constraining. Fine does not advance the extreme position that norms are generated entirely in situ. On the contrary, he recognizes that norms are guidelines to action that can be reported and transmitted in the process of socialization. Nonetheless, when it comes to their application, Fine insists that norms are "negotiated." In this regard, he seems to be making claims that

1. norms are conditional: people can only collect mushrooms under certain conditions.
2. norms are ambiguous: the norm that nature ought to be protected from human depredation is subject to interpretation.
3. norms are negotiated: if some actors believe that they are in a situation that calls for compliance to some norm and others disagree, then they discuss ("negotiate") the extent to which the norm holds in that situation.

These claims seem to be at variance with the view of norms subscribed to by most of our contributors. Yet it is doubtful that anyone would reject Fine's claims out of hand. Several of the case studies do emphasize both conditionality and ambiguity. Both play a large role in Michael Hechter and Elizabeth Borland's discussion of national self-determination (chapter 7). Michael Schudson (chapter 6) notes the conditionality of the norm of objectivity (reporting on sports events need not be objective—unlike reporting on politics), and Karl-Dieter Opp stresses conditionality in his study of the emergence of protest norms (chapter 8). When writers with different theoretical commitments reach similar conclusions, this lends these conclusions greater plausibility.

Consider the following norm, discussed by Kanazawa and Still: *A man must marry no more than one woman at a time.* This norm appears to be unconditional (it would be conditional if, for example, the norm did not apply to members of the aristocracy). It is also relatively unambiguous: "marriage" has a well-defined legal meaning, a person's sex is generally (if not always) self-evident, and the meaning of "at a time" is straightforward. Hence, this particular norm appears to provide relatively little leeway for negotiation or divergent interpretations.

Note how different the situation is for one of the norms held by Fine's mycologists: *The natural environment should be protected from human depreda-*

*tion.* Like many others, this particular norm appears to be both unconditional and straightforward. As chapter 5 reveals, however, the reality is
quite different. In fact, the norm is conditional and vulnerable to multiple
interpretations. Rather than defining them absolutely, it seems more fruitful
to regard any given norm as more or less conditional and ambiguous—
and, hence, subject to negotiation. These elements then can be studied empirically using a variety of qualitative and quantitative methods.

Disagreements about the givenness of norms are often ascribed to theoretical commitments. Symbolic interactionists and cultural sociologists
typically insist on the elusiveness of norms, whereas rational choice theorists see them as hard constraints. As this volume indicates, however, such
disagreement may owe less to theoretical commitments than to differences
in the substantive norms that different writers have chosen to study. Those
who are inclined to believe that norms are given should test this claim by
examining the ambiguity and conditionality of the norms they are studying. By the same token, those who believe that norms are elusive should
concentrate on finding situations in which norms are relatively unambiguous. Beyond this, the authors seem to agree about many other aspects
of norms.

## The Instrumentality of Norms

As noted in the introduction, the idea that norms emerge if they are instrumental commands the greatest scholarly consensus in the volume. We reconsider the instrumentality proposition in this conclusion and discuss
some further issues.

The validity of the instrumentality proposition cannot be determined
unless we distinguish between its individualist and collectivist versions.
Imagine a community that has no norms about protection of the environment. Now a number of technological innovations create new negative externalities in the form of increased pollution. Assume that the community
as a whole would be better off if some norm against pollution were to
develop. Will such a norm emerge? Different versions of the instrumentality principle make different predictions in this respect.

A functionalist might argue that the technological innovation leads to
a systemic disequilibrium that calls forth a new norm to reestablish equilibrium.[2] On this view, an environmental norm is instrumental for the survival
of the system. This kind of functional explanation is collectivist because it
ignores individual actors. Collectivist functionalism has been criticized so
extensively in the past that we need not reiterate its limitations here.[3]

A second kind of functionalist explanation does refer to individual
actors, however. On this view, a norm will tend to emerge if it increases the
welfare of the individual members of a group.[4] More specifically, if individual actors would prefer a situation S, and if a norm is instrumental for

achieving S, then they will choose actions leading to the emergence of the norm. Max Weber's ([1921–22] 1978) discussion of the advent of bureaucratic norms is a notable case in point. This kind of functionalist logic refers to individual interests, but in doing so it makes several strong assumptions. First, it stipulates that the actual—rather than the perceived—instrumentality of a norm motivates individual action. This presumes that actors' belief that the given norm will bring about state S is, in fact, correct. Second, it assumes that there is no free-rider problem. Third, it assumes that each individual knows how to contribute effectively to the establishment of the desired norm. Finally, it assumes that individuals have the same interest with respect to the norm—in this case, that the new technology imposes externalities on all the members of the community—and that everybody demands a norm that reduces or eliminates the externality. Because there is little reason to believe that all of these assumptions can be satisfied for every existing norm, it is unlikely that norms are entirely reducible to individual interest (Elster 1989, 150).

Norms may also emerge as an unintended consequence of individual behavior. For example, credible scientific evidence suggests that passive smoking causes lung cancer. This gives nonsmokers a personal interest in avoiding exposure to secondhand smoke. Once this evidence is promulgated, it is likely to spur the health conscious among them to ask smokers to desist from smoking even without an antismoking norm. Smokers as a whole will increasingly experience hostility, which will increase their cost of smoking. After some time an antismoking norm will emerge. As in the functionalist stories, the emergence of this antismoking norm makes nonsmokers better off, but note that their individual actions were not intended to establish a norm. Presumably, many customs arise on the basis of mechanisms of this sort. As William Graham Sumner (1906, 3–4) notes, "From recurrent needs arise habits for the individual and customs for the group, but these results are consequences which were never conscious, and never foreseen or intended." This is not necessarily inconsistent with an individual-level functionalist account, however. All it maintains is that if individual actors have certain interests, then a certain effect will ensue. In general, however, functionalist accounts are mute about the mechanisms responsible for producing norms.

The instrumental approach to norms leads naturally to questions about normative efficiency. As might be expected, economists have been particularly concerned with these kinds of questions.[5] The meaning of normative efficiency is quite contentious, however. Economists usually equate efficiency with Pareto superiority and optimality. Outcome X is Pareto superior to (or more efficient than) outcome Y if at least one person is better off, and no other person worse off, in X. If X cannot be altered so that at least one person is made better off while no one is made worse off, then X is Pareto optimal or maximally efficient.

Unfortunately, Pareto optimality hardly ever occurs in the real world of norms. This is because norms usually have differential effects on individuals. Even the appealing universal norm, "Thou shalt not kill," diminishes the welfare of killers; similarly, an antismoking norm reduces the welfare of smokers, and so on. To get around this problem, the efficiency of a norm can be defined on utilitarian rather than Paretian grounds. For utilitarians, norm X is more efficient than Y if it produces greater welfare for the greatest number of the group or society. Thus Robert Ellickson (1991, 167; see also 170–74) argues that "members of a close-knit group develop and maintain norms whose content serves to maximize the aggregate welfare that members obtain in their workaday affairs." Ellickson's argument has been criticized for being ad hoc and purely speculative. Economist critics of utilitarianism have long claimed that it is impossible to measure the impact of policy or normative interventions for the general welfare because of the impossibility of making valid interpersonal utility comparisons, and no one has yet succeeded in persuading them otherwise.[6] On this account, at least, the concept of the general welfare remains elusive.[7]

Despite these measurement difficulties, some norms (such as the norm of reciprocity) do seem more welfare enhancing than others (such as the vendetta). Whereas most of the chapters in this book treat norms—like those against smoking and for protest—as if they were self-evidently welfare enhancing, mention has also been made of disjoint norms (chapter 7, this volume). On the face of it, the effects of disjoint norms like honor killing and female genital mutilation are far from welfare enhancing, at least for the unfortunates who are subjected to them.

Do these difficulties in measuring efficiency suggest that welfare effects be ignored in future studies of norms? Not at all: suboptimal or exploitative norms might provide an incentive to launch processes that subvert or change the norm. In this way, ignoring welfare effects may preclude the explanation of whole classes of norms.

By any reckoning, the assumptions required to drive functionalist explanations of the emergence of norms are difficult to satisfy. People seldom have valid information about the side effects of norms. The free-rider problem is an obstacle to the provision of many public goods. It is far from obvious what individuals ought to do if they seek to establish a specific norm, and the members of groups usually have conflicting interests when it comes to many norms.

Instrumentality is only one of several factors that plays a role in the emergence of norms. Any account of the emergence of norms also must consider the quality of the actors' beliefs. If these are at odds with reality, then suboptimal norms may emerge. Moreover, incentives are also important. For example, actors may understand that a given norm is suboptimal but in the absence of the requisite positive incentives, it may be too costly to do away with it (Mackie 1996; see also chapter 3, this volume).

# The Role of Social Networks

Social networks are regarded as relevant for the emergence of norms in almost every chapter of this book. For example, the mycologists are a close-knit group, and the norms that Fine describes emerge, in part, because of the solidarity of this group. The subjects of Christine Horne's experiment were all college students at the same university and, at least in terms of age and interest, probably a close-knit group; her results might have been different in other types of groups. The thrust of the specific studies as well as of the general chapters is that norms are more likely to emerge when people are closely related.

Why is this so? Chapter 8 argues that networks produce incentives for the emergence of norms. Thomas Voss emphasizes this as well, when he writes, in chapter 4, that "norms of cooperation are enforceable in small, stable, and culturally homogeneous communities" and when social relations are "diffuse and multiplex." Hechter and Borland argue that a norm of self-determination emerged because it was promoted by a small network of powerful states in the international system.

Insofar as norms emerge through collective action, and networks facilitate collective action, this conclusion is not terribly surprising. More intriguing is the (very real) possibility that social networks might foster the emergence of norms that are at variance with those imposed by authorities. For example, the workers in a machine shop or the students in a class might establish output-restriction norms that counter overall firm or school norms. Similarly, people may appeal to friendship to press their claim to an office as a means of circumventing bureaucratic norms that appear to disfavor them.

That norms of all varieties are more likely to emerge in close-knit groups than in loosely structured networks seems to be so widely accepted that it might be a social law. Is this network principle really so plausible? Assume that a group of close friends meets regularly to produce some joint good, a good that can be produced only if the members routinely attend group meetings: absences are tolerated only under exceptional circumstances. Each member would, naturally, prefer to have maximum latitude to skip meetings. The group norm supporting production of the joint good could be established by enunciating normative statements advocating regular participation and by punishing absenteeism. However, punishing one's friends is costly. Because these costs are likely to be higher the more solidary the group is, certain norms might be *less* likely to emerge in highly solidary groups.[8] Yet Opp finds that protest norms are more likely to emerge in friendship groups and groups of colleagues than in less solidary groups. These ostensibly conflicting conclusions could be reconciled if there is a nonlinear relation between solidarity and the emergence of norms. A relatively low degree of solidarity might be conducive to the emergence of norms, but if solidarity exceeds some particular threshold, other kinds of norms may be precluded. Moreover, the relation between solidarity and the emergence of norms may differ for conjoint and disjoint norms, for example. For the emergence of conjoint norms, repeated interaction might suffice, whereas for disjoint norms some degree of closeness might be important. Although the network principle is plausible at first sight, many questions about it remain to be explored in further research.

## Other Factors

Four other factors that affect the emergence of norms are discussed in part II: culture, power, behavioral regularities, and normative systems.

### Culture

Fine claims that the legitimations or justifications that can be used to negotiate a norm are an aspect of a group's culture. He argues that the mycologists looked for justifications that changed the content of a norm. Hechter and Borland argue that legitimation mechanisms contributed to the spread of the norm of self-determination. In particular, legitimation may particularly favor the diffusion of benevolent norms. Voss argues that the emergence of norms may be promoted by "different cultures (groups, communities)" that may lead to differential enforcement of norms in similar situations.

To be sure, the concept of culture refers to legitimations and justifications. However, culture also refers to a multitude of other phenomena. For example, values, beliefs, and attitudes are all items of culture. What is seldom appreciated is that the very definition of an externality is rarely fixed in stone; rather, it often represents a movable boundary that is subject to cultural contention (Wildavsky 1993). This point has obvious implications for the instrumentality proposition about the emergence of norms. To the degree that externalities are social constructions, the instrumentality of a norm can no longer be regarded as self-evident. Further research should explore the effects that various aspects of culture have on the emergence of norms in greater detail.

### Power

The emergence of effective norms requires the support of a sufficiently powerful constituency. In this volume, power plays its most prominent role in chapter 7. Hechter and Borland emphasize the power of the United Nations, and particularly the United States, as an important factor for the emergence of the norm of self-determination. Power is related to resources or to the costs of punishing or rewarding others. It also plays a role in delimiting behavioral opportunities: Kanazawa and Still assume that the power of women to choose men is a condition for the emergence of the norms of polygyny or monogamy. These aspects of power are also emphasized in the chapters of part I. As has already been noted, differential power is likely to play a key role in the emergence of disjoint norms, those for which the beneficiaries differ from the targets (see chapter 7, this volume).

Admittedly, power is an elusive concept. In chapter 7, it refers to the resources that are at the disposal of individual or collective actors. This meaning of power concurs with that often used by exchange and rational choice theorists. The distribution of power in a group or society is likely to be an important determinant of the content of emerging norms. Similarly, it is particularly important for the emergence of disjoint norms. Power also plays a key role in selecting between multiple coordination equilibria. In situations in which several coordination equilibria are equally attractive (such as driving on the left or the right side of the street), how is a particular equilibrium arrived at? Actors with relatively high levels of resources may function as normative entrepreneurs who are able to influence the diffusion of one norm rather than another.

Evidently, power is imbricated in many normative phenomena. Further research is needed to clarify the conditions under which powerful actors can establish a norm that becomes accepted or internalized.

## Behavioral Regularities

Several chapters mention that a behavioral regularity can trigger the emergence of a norm. Fine shows how the intense preoccupation with collecting mushrooms—a behavioral regularity—instigated the search for justifications for this activity. Horne's experimental study addresses this question, as well. The idea that a behavioral regularity often leads to norms is not new, as chapter 1 reveals. Yet the conditions under which a behavioral regularity leads to a norm are also not well understood at this time.

## Systems of Norms

Norms do not exist in splendid isolation; instead they are linked in various ways to other norms. Fine's mycologists, for example, subscribe to a set of mutually inconsistent norms about environmental protection, on the one hand, and about the legitimacy of consuming the mushrooms they gather in the wild, on the other. Similarly, states are willing to grant independence to external colonies but not to internal ones.

This point can be readily appreciated by a common real-life example. You are traveling on a transcontinental flight in an overcrowded cabin. The infant seated directly behind you begins crying uncontrollably. All the passengers in the cabin are disturbed by the crying—it causes an unambiguously negative externality. If norms are instrumental, then there should be a strong norm that discourages children from crying on airplanes. In fact, such a norm probably does exist: parents, no doubt, feel some pressure to control their children's public behavior. Yet not all of them succeed in settling their unruly children. When they fail, no norm has emerged that permits other passengers to quiet the crying child or that allows them to sanction the incompetent parent. Why not? What does the absence of such a norm reveal?

Clearly, a system of norms is at work here. Whereas the instrumentality principle suggests that squalling children will be sanctioned, in this case more fundamental norms regarding the treatment of children trump it. The right to discipline children is firmly lodged with parents in all Western societies. Even when parental incompetence is perceived to be responsible for the crying, norms about the sanctioning of parents are very weak. Thus, other passengers might give the incompetent parents a disapproving look, but few people would ever engage in verbal sanctioning.

The degree to which norms in a given group, or society, are mutually consistent is, of course, highly variable. To the degree that norms are mutually consistent, social behavior will be regulated and predictable. Sets of relatively inconsistent norms allow for more idiosyncratic behavior (see Simmel 1955 on the web of multiple group affiliation). Although this topic is broached in the chapters in the volume, it is not analyzed sufficiently. Controversies surrounding multiculturalism in the United States and elsewhere raise this issue in a particularly potent fashion (Hechter 2000). Conflicts about bilingual education and the legitimacy of minority national cultures are responsible for much of the current political instability in the world. Invariably, the issue in these conflicts revolves around the social efficiency of normative diversity. It is striking that Robin Williams's (1968, 206) call for research "to ascertain whether norms combine into systems, and, if so, what conditions and reasons govern these combinations" remains unanswered, despite the passage of three decades.

## Some Guidelines for Further Research on Norms

There are several problems related to the explanation of norms that have not received sufficient attention, either in this volume or in the literature more generally. Resolving these problems is critical for future theory and research on the emergence of norms.

### Defining Norms

Although we have highlighted several questions about norms that deserve further research, little progress can be expected without a consensual definition of the concept. Truth to tell, there is no standard definition of the term. Eric A. Posner (1996, 1699) is one of the few scholars who concedes that his own definition of the term "norm" is arbitrary; rather than justify it, Posner merely admits that "this is a defect shared by all writings on this subject." We have to do better than this.

For some writers, a norm exists when people say that in a given circumstance a certain course of action is appropriate. A large literature on the relation between attitude and behavior, however, suggests that actions often do not follow words (see particularly Kuran 1995). For other writers—especially economists (see chapters 3 and 4, this volume)—norms are behavioral regularities supported by corresponding sanctions. Another view (expressed in chapters 5, 6, and 8, this volume) is that normative expectations by themselves constitute norms. Finally, Robert Sugden argues that norms consist of behavioral regularities in addition to normative and cognitive expectations. Thus, he comments, "I shall use the word 'norm' to refer to any regularity in behavior within a given community which is generally expected, not only in the empirical sense, but also in the normative sense" (Sugden 1998, 78–79).

Although the most common element in these definitions is "oughtness"—an expectation that is shared by the members of some group—most definitions in the literature combine several dimensions. Which of these different definitions is best? Economists often argue that norms are behavioral regularities backed by sanctions because they assume that behaviors are more readily measured than subjective phenomena like expectations. This is a questionable view, however: the direct measurement of some kinds of behaviors is well-nigh impossible. For example, sexual practices, drug use, and criminal activities—by their very nature—are hidden from public view and hence difficult to measure.

Of course, some behavioral regularities (especially those occurring in public) are highly observable. Yet norms cannot automatically be assumed to be responsible for these behavioral regularities. True, internalized norms (sometimes termed "values") can induce people to behave similarly because they share the belief that a given behavior ought (or ought not) to be performed. Thus observant Catholics will abstain from contraception; observant Jews and Muslims will not eat pork, and so forth. However, people having a common interest who face similar constraints will behave similarly even if they share no norms. Think of the marketplace, where consumers tend to purchase a standard good from that producer who offers it at the lowest price. In consequence, the most efficient producer will prosper at the expense of his competitors. Likewise, despite their sometimes considerable normative differences, Catholics, Protestants, Jews, and Muslims all open up their umbrellas when it begins to rain (see also Williams 1968, 205). Moreover, behavioral regularities can result from positive or negative sanctions. A sanction is a punishment (or reward) enacted on the basis of a social agreement that a given course of action ought (or ought not) to occur (Epstein 1968). In other words, sanctions, at a minimum, consist of punishments or rewards combined with the sense of oughtness. Behavioral regularities can exist in the absence of oughtness, and in the absence of sanctions, as well. Thus, behavioral definitions of norms conflate three elements—behavior, oughtness, and punishment (or reward).

How, then, should norms be defined? Evidently, when social scientists address normative phenomena they focus on some combination of behavioral regularities, oughtness, and punishment or reward. Because these elements are not necessarily covariant, however, it is preferable to decompose norms into their constituent elements. Behavior, punishment or reward, and oughtness can be considered separately; only by doing so can their mutual dependence be determined (much the same conclusion was reached by Jack Gibbs [1968, 208]). This will permit researchers to disentangle the complex relations between these elements, their causes, and their consequences (as Horne does in chapter 10). This discussion suggests that researchers should focus on three distinct elements of normness: behavioral regularities, oughtness, and sanctions (that is, rewards and punishments).

## Explaining the Oughtness of Norms

The "oughtness" of a norm rests ultimately on "some standard of value that is taken without further justification as valid by the individual or group in question" (Williams 1968, 205). This standard is not individually idiosyncratic but—to some extent—socially shared. If oughtness is one of the constitutive elements of norms, of just what does it consist? Consider the following norm N, presumably one that is held by Greens the world over: The environment ought to be protected from human depredation. What might it mean to explain the emergence of the oughtness of this norm? One way of explaining N is to discover the conditions under which people make statements to the effect that the environment ought to be protected. Not all such statements are sincere, however. If you live in Cuba, for example, you are well advised to exclaim "Viva la Revolución!" at the drop of a hat; but we would be naïve if we took your exclamation at face value.

To gain a deeper explanation of norms, we must understand why some norms are more accepted than others. To accept a norm is to have a positive attitude toward it. Thus, explaining oughtness may mean explaining the conditions under which the members of a given group have a positive attitude toward N. An attitude is "a psychological tendency that is expressed by evaluating a particular entity with some degrees of favor or disfavor" (Eagly and Chaiken 1993, 1). When it is accepted, a norm becomes this kind of an entity.[9]

It is common to distinguish between two kinds of attitudes toward norms: mere acceptance, on the one hand, and internalization, on the other. Let us say that you accept the need for traffic lights in your city. Even so, when you accidentally drive through a red light, you feel neither shame nor guilt. In contrast, the violation of other norms—for example, "Thou shall not kill"—is likely to cause you considerable anguish. In the latter case, the norm is internalized. Socialization research is concerned with determining the conditions responsible for normative internalization. In contrast, game theorists usually analyze norms—such as coordination or fairness—that elicit no shame or guilt when they are violated. Hence, oughtness may be explained by uncovering the conditions in which the members of a given group internalize a positive attitude toward N.

Rational choice theorists consider norms to be a (second-order) public good. For them, explaining a norm means understanding when individuals contribute to the establishment of this public good. Thus, people may join a social movement to pressure the government to liberalize abortion laws. By joining this social movement an individual thus helps foster a norm liberalizing abortion.

Although these various conceptions of oughtness are seldom distinguished in the current literature, they are likely to have crucial implications for the resilience of a norm. If oughtness merely refers to statements of N and the sanctions supporting N decrease—for example, because of the collapse of an authoritarian regime that once firmly upheld N—then utterances of N will sharply decrease, if not disappear altogether. If oughtness refers to the acceptance of a norm, however, then it should be more resilient. Clearly, oughtness is most resilient when it is internalized. In that case, oughtness is least vulnerable to shifting opportunities. To the degree that the norm against murder is internalized, then shifts in the punishment levied against murderers may not affect the murder rate. Thus, shifts in circumstances will have varying consequences for the resilience of different types of norms.

Furthermore, it is important to distinguish the various components of oughtness, for different theories may be required to account for the behavioral and subjective components of norms. Consider the typical rational choice theory of the emergence of norms. If, as this theory claims, norms are second-order public goods, then normative utterances might be regarded as helping to establish a norm, thereby leading to behavioral regularities. This particular norm, however, may be neither accepted nor internalized. A theory of attitude formation may be required to account for the various elements of oughtness. If so, then other questions soon arise. Which of the several theories of attitude formation best explains the acceptance or internalization of norms? Can a theory of attitude formation be fruitfully combined with rational choice theory? Such questions have seldom been raised.

## The Conditionality of Norms

Most norms—perhaps all of them—are conditional. For example, when people are asked if one should tell the truth, the great majority agree. In

some situations, however, telling a lie is justified; it may even be an obligation (Bok 1978). A physician who is convinced that her patient would commit suicide if told that he has a malignant cancer may feel obligated to
conceal the truth about his condition from her patient.

Many accounts of the emergence of norms fail to specify the conditions under which a norm holds, Thus Assar Lindbeck (1995, 488–90) attempts to explain the gradual attenuation of the norm of saving. He argues,
in brief, that the growth of the welfare state has made saving unnecessary
as a means for coping with illness and loss (surely he is thinking of
Sweden rather than the United States!). Yet the attenuation of the saving
norm may not be as general as Lindbeck asserts. People living in welfare
states still may accept a norm that one should save for the children's education or to purchase an expensive car. The point is that shifts in the saving
norm may be conditional. It is difficult to know just what is being claimed
by arguing that "the" norm of saving attenuates. Does this claim imply that
fewer people accept a norm of saving for all purposes? Does attenuation,
on the contrary, mean that the number of purposes for which saving is an
obligation decreases? Unless these questions are answered, the phenomenon to be explained is shrouded in mystery.[10]

To generalize the point, if researchers do not analyze the conditionality
of a norm, it is unclear just what they are explaining.[11] This is because
conditionality indicates the scope of a norm. Suppose, for example, that we
want to explain why antismoking norms are increasingly being accepted.
To a large extent, antismoking norms are conditional: for example, one can
smoke at a party if the host allows it. Consider what it means to claim that
antismoking norms are spreading. Assume there are four conditions under
which the antismoking norm holds (see table 13.1). Scenario 1 presents a
state-of-nature baseline in which there is no antismoking norm at all. Now,
for reasons that need not be delved into (but see chapter 2, this volume, for
an analysis), an antismoking norm emerges. This means that one of the
scenarios from 2 to 6 comes to pass. In scenario 2, for instance, 20 percent
of the population thinks one ought not smoke under conditions A and B.
Scenarios 3 to 6 have other distributions of the antismoking norm. The
statement that "an antismoking norm has emerged" fails to distinguish between these different scenarios. The same can be said for a situation in
which an existing norm attenuates. Without specifying conditionality, it is
difficult to know the meaning of claims that a given norm diffuses or attenuates.

## The Role of Path Dependence

Many of the contributions to this volume (especially chapter 8) take the
view that norms emerge instrumentally to serve the ends of a group. There
are, however, a number of ways to skin a cat. Thus a group may seek to

TABLE 13.1    *Conditionality of a Behavior Norm*

| Scenario | Popular Support for a Norm Proscribing Smoking Under Certain Conditions (Percentage) | | | |
|---|---|---|---|---|
| | Condition A | Condition B | Condition C | Condition D |
| Scenario 1 (no norm) | 0 | 0 | 0 | 0 |
| Scenario 2 | 20 | 20 | 0 | 0 |
| Scenario 3 | 20 | 20 | 20 | 0 |
| Scenario 4 | 20 | 20 | 20 | 20 |
| Scenario 5 | 30 | 30 | 30 | 30 |
| Scenario 6 | 40 | 40 | 0 | 0 |

*Source:* Authors' compilation.
*Note:* For example, in scenario 1, there is no norm. In scenario 2, 20 percent of the population thinks that smoking ought to be proscribed under conditions A and B.

improve its material welfare by adopting more (that is, socialist) or less (that is, capitalist) egalitarian norms. Even if the instrumentality principle is sound, therefore, it is insufficient to account for the particular features of any given norm. Evidently, the principle must be supplemented by other kinds of causal factors. Path dependence is one such factor.

The past often casts its shadow in the present, and present behavior is thereby to some degree path dependent (see chapter 4).[12] Consider the following example: In a given industry, 80 percent of all employees use Apple computers. Now imagine that a new start-up firm in this industry has to select a computer system. Odds are good that this new firm will also decide to buy Apple computers.[13] In this way, the present behavior of this firm is in part dependent on past decisions made by other firms in its industry.

To what degree does path dependence affect the emergence of norms? The Apple computer example suggests that the likelihood of compliance to a norm in a group is an increasing function of the proportion of members who have complied with that norm in the past.[14] Is this a plausible proposition? Consider a second example: Evidently, the number of people who comply with an antismoking norm has increased over the past twenty years or so. Is the diffusion of this norm path dependent? Note that if the number of those who hold an antismoking norm increases, then the cost of sanctioning smokers will fall. If only 10 percent of the population adheres to an antismoking norm, it takes more courage to sanction a smoker than if 80 percent of the population adheres to it. Thus, it does seem likely that the greater the proportion of those who hold a norm, the lower the average cost of sanctioning and the higher the likelihood that an antismoking norm will diffuse.

It is therefore plausible that the proportion of those who hold an antismoking norm at any given time will affect the rate of diffusion of an antismoking norm (see chapter 1, this volume, for more on diffusion processes). This function might look like curve A in figure 13.1.[15] The *x*-axis in the figure designates the proportion of members of a group (or a population) who accept a norm, and the *y*-axis indicates the likelihood that another member accepts the respective norm. The straight 45-degree line from the lower left to the upper right corner portrays the situation in which the proportion of those who comply with a norm is equal to the likelihood that another member complies. Curve A describes quite a different relationship. If the proportion of adherents to an antismoking norm is very low—in this example, less than 15 percent—an increase in the proportion of compliants has no spillover effect. Only when the compliant proportion is more than 15 percent of the group membership does the likelihood of diffusion increase. If more than 40 percent of the population complies, then the rate of diffusion increases steeply: if the proportion of adherents rises from 40 percent to 50 percent (that is, from .40 to .50) the chance that others adopt the norm increases from 14 percent to 55 percent. If about 50 percent of the group has adopted the norm, the curve becomes flatter: an increase in the proportion of those who comply with the norm lowers the rate of diffusion, because there is likely to be a hard core of "zealots" who are members of a counterculture of smokers.[16]

Many other functions might describe the relationship between the proportion compliant and the rate of diffusion (see also Marwell and Oliver 1993 for a discussion of critical mass models). Consider curve B. Assume that a certain percentage of people in a particular group pioneers a new fashion. Some fashion innovators (Ellickson's normative entrepreneurs) adopt and promulgate the style. However, as more and more people adopt the style, others turn away from it for this very same reason. Thus, it is cool to dress in a certain way, but only if not too many others are doing so. As in the previous example there is path dependence, but the function that describes this dependence is quite different.

If the proportion of those who comply with a norm has different effects on its diffusion, what accounts for these differences? These various functions describe the effects of a stimulus (the proportion of norm adherents) on a response (the likelihood that others follow suit). The effects of the stimulus depend on the processes set in motion when the stimulus occurs. In the smoking example, the increasing number of adherents to an antismoking norm lowers the costs of sanctioning. In the fashion example, the increasing popularity of the innovation reduces the status of the new fashion.[17] Thus, the diffusion of a norm depends on the incentives elicited when the proportion of adherents to a norm increases. This causal chain is depicted in figure 13.2.

Figure 13.2 assumes that some proportion of group members comply with a norm in the first place. Thus, compliance with a norm is to some

FIGURE 13.1    *Effect of Group Support for a Norm on the Likelihood That Others Accept the Norm*

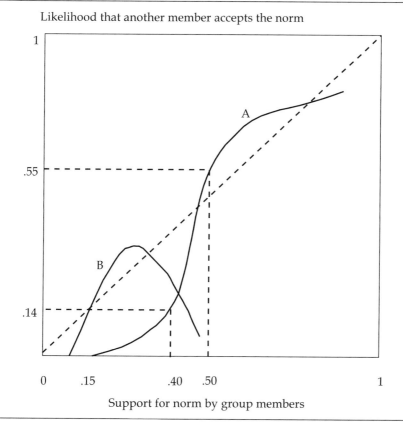

*Source:* Authors' compilation.

degree independent of the number of users. Even if path dependence holds, therefore, additional factors have an impact on the emergence of norms.[18]

Path dependence also occurs if preexisting norms have an effect on the emergence of other norms.[19] Which kinds of preexisting norms could have an effect on the diffusion of a given norm? Antismoking norms are clearly subsumed under a more general norm stating that one's actions should not cause harm to others. If the evidence shows that smoking, both active and passive, leads to cancer, then smoking in the presence of others becomes a negative externality. Thus an overarching norm against harming others helps an antismoking norm to diffuse. Similarly, there is a less general norm that one should refrain from taking drugs. When smoking is inter-

FIGURE 13.2   *Norm Adherents and the Likelihood of Diffusion*

| Proportion of adherents to a norm | → | Incentives | → | Likelihood that others adopt the norm |

*Source:* Authors' compilation.

preted, or framed (see chapter 5, this volume), as a type of drug taking, then an antismoking norm will diffuse more rapidly. Thus actors often relate general norms or values to more specific norms.

There is little doubt that the emergence of norms is path dependent: the diffusion of a norm depends on the number of individuals who accept a norm and on preexisting norms. Other conditions also affect the emergence of norms, however; these are poorly understood at the present time.

## Coda: On Normative Ambiguity

Several of the chapters in this volume highlight the ambiguity of norms and the strategic uses that actors make of this ambiguity. Mushroomers espouse norms on behalf of environmental preservation, but at the same time desire to eat the mushrooms they collect. Their solution to this dilemma is to tweak the environmental protection norm in such a fashion that it is not inconsistent with the eating of mushrooms. Many mushroomers claim that eating the fruit of the mushroom in no way damages the root structure of the plant and thus causes no environmental damage. The ambiguity of environmental protection norms makes such an interpretation plausible, at least to mushroom lovers.

Hechter and Borland show that the "self" referred to by the norm of national self-determination is inherently ambiguous. Whereas in principle the term "self" could be applied to all collectivities that are self-defined nations, in practice it has tended to refer only to colonial territories, rather than to internal colonies or other kinds of national minorities in sovereign states. This is strategic for powerful actors in the international system, because under this interpretation of the norm of national self-determination, shifts in international boundaries—a key cause of political instability—are minimized.

It would be hard to imagine a more graphic example of the ambiguity of norms than that offered by the United States Constitution. This document—a model for many other constitutions in the world today—is so ambiguous that it is the principal task of the Supreme Court to interpret the "constitutionality" of all laws enacted in the country. The Supreme Court has such great discretion in its interpretative capacity that its decisions are regarded as perhaps the most important single determinant of the future course of American social policy. For this reason, one of the greatest powers of the American presidency is the incumbent's right to nominate members of the Supreme Court.

Whereas norms often have been portrayed as constraints that channel individual behavior and thus are ultimately responsible for social order, an appreciation of their ambiguity leads to somewhat different conclusions. Rather than offering hard incentives or constraints, norms may perform the much less directive role of providing a framework that both permits contestation but limits its extent, as well. Whereas this insight has long been appreciated by legal scholars, social scientists tend to be much less aware of it.

Perhaps the most striking conclusion of the substantive chapters is that norms are more ambiguous than has been appreciated in much current social theory.[20] Much of this ambiguity stems from their conditionality, which inherently leads to measurement problems. Whenever we say that norm X holds in condition Y but not in condition Z, then difficult measurement issues often ensue. How are conditions Y and Z to be defined and measured? Because it is extremely costly to specify the relevant conditions in detail—this is one of the fundamental insights of transactions cost economics (Barzel 1982)—norms are always, to a greater or lesser extent, ambiguous. This is also a key insight that derives from symbolic interactionism. To the degree that norms are ambiguous, they are unable to regulate behavior.

This conclusion about the ambiguity of norms—and the consequent importance of interpretation and the negotiation of norms—should not be terribly surprising. Consider classical music, which lays down a score replete with notes, keys, tempi and a wide variety of directions about how loudly each measure is to be played. Despite this elaborate roadmap—one for which there is no analogue in social life—we are not surprised when two concert pianists perform quite different versions of the same Beethoven sonata. (Indeed, we are disappointed if they fail to do so.) One pianist's adagio is much slower than another's, one's forte is louder, one gives greater emphasis to the left hand part, and so forth. These different versions of the same score are referred to as interpretations, and the artist's role is explicitly understood to be that of Beethoven's interpreter. If classical music, which is so precisely scripted, is subject to rival interpretations, how can norms be any less subject to interpretation?

There are important reasons why norms cannot be totally constraining. If norms were highly specific, it is unlikely that they could command enough social support to become institutionalized in the first place. In part, normative flexibility is the result of the excessively high cost of specifying all the conditions under which a given norm would hold. The reasoning here is analogous to that lying behind analyses of implicit contracting in law and economics (see chapter 2, this volume, for some relevant citations).

To command support in a large, socially heterogeneous community, a norm must be at least somewhat vague. Just as the Downsian view of politics in a two-party system suggests that the successful candidate must provide an ambiguous platform (so as to maximize his or her electoral support), so an institutionalized norm must have sufficient latitude to maintain support in a group. For this reason, studying the conditions responsible for variations in normative ambiguity is perhaps one of the most critical tasks for future empirical research on norms.

## Notes

1.  As noted in the introduction, this book focuses on social rather than legal norms. Thus when we speak of "norms" in this chapter, we are referring to social norms. Despite this caveat, much of what is said in this chapter holds for social as well as legal norms. A detailed discussion of the relation between social and legal norms lies beyond the scope of this chapter.

2.  The functionalist proposition is discussed in Gibbs (1968, 212). For the best general critiques of functionalist arguments see Hempel (1965), chapter 11, and Nagel (1956). We assume that the disequilibrium is not so severe that the system will unravel.

3.  See, in particular, Hempel (1965) and Nagel (1956).

4.  The members may constitute a majority, but a minority of group members still may prevail if others are indifferent to the norm (for a critique, see Hardin 1980, and Opp 1983). Even so, many of the norms that we would like to see never manage to emerge. One anonymous reviewer of this book provided us with a list of such missing norms that includes the following: academic journals should send rejection letters on as promptly as they send acceptances; mail-order companies should stock the goods they advertise; airline attendants should not ask you to close your window shades so that you can look at half an hour of advertising; on classical music stations, the disc jockey should resist the temptation to talk all the time instead of playing music; and more than the minimum number of trash cans should be placed at picnic grounds so one is always nearby, and so they are not always full whenever there is warm sunny weather.

5.  See the discussion in chapter 3, this volume. James S. Coleman (1990, chapters 10 and 11) is one of the few sociologists who discusses the efficiency of norms.

6.  More than three decades have passed since Coleman (1966) pointed out that legislatures solve interpersonal comparison problems every day. Even though he was the one sociologist most known and appreciated by economists, and even though this paper was published in the *American Economic Review*, Coleman's observation has been ignored in subsequent discussions of the problem of interpersonal comparisons.

7.  In the absence of consensual measures of the general welfare, it is impossible to resolve arguments—such as those between Jon Elster (1990) and Russell Hardin (1995)—about the overall welfare consequences of norms such as the vendetta and the feud.

8. For a similar argument in regard to collective action, see Flache and Macy 1996.

9. As has already been noted, there may be conflicting norms. This means that there are positive as well as negative attitudes toward norms. In order not to complicate this discussion, we will ignore negative attitudes.

10. To be fair, Lindbeck does not pretend to offer a detailed explanation of saving norms. He invokes them merely as an example of effects of the welfare state on various types of social outcomes.

11. By implication, making unconditionality a defining characteristic of a norm (as Elster 1999 does) is unfruitful.

12. The strong version of path dependence asserts not only that present outcomes are conditioned by past actions but also that present equilibria are inefficient on this account.

13. Of course, the decision on what computer to purchase also depends on considerations of available software and price.

14. Note that institutionalists account for institutional mimicry through different mechanisms—for example, identification and legitimation mechanisms (see chapter 7, this volume).

15. For a more extensive discussion of this type of diagram see Dixit and Nalebuff 1991, chapter 9, and Arthur 1989. These authors do not address norms specifically, but they do discuss the extent to which a behavior of a proportion of a certain group of people affects the behavior of others. Avinash Dixit and Barry Nalebuff, for example, discuss the effects of the proportion of people who use the QWERTY keyboard ($x$-axis) on the likelihood that a new employee uses this keyboard ($y$-axis).

16. There are other circumstances in which it is conceivable that the number of adherents to a norm will reduce the likelihood of compliance to it. People may think that if everyone complies with a norm, little will be lost if someone fails to do so. Another way to interpret this is that widespread compliance with a norm may provide an extra incentive to free ride. If so, then such behavior would, of course, result in the attenuation of a norm.

17. A similar example is the use of wireless phones. When few people used wireless phones, it seemed to become a sort of duty for trendy people to possess a phone and show it. As the number of those who phone in public increases there is no longer any prestige awarded to those who phone in public. The likelihood of new users thinking that one has to use a wireless phone thus decreases.

18. For an example that addresses the effects of the number of those who comply with a norm and other factors, as well, on the attenuation of norms, see Opp (1990).

19. This question is addressed in a comment by N. Thomas Hakansson on the article by Jean Ensminger and Jack Knight (Ensminger and Knight 1997, 15–16). However, Hakansson's comment refers specifically to the norms that are addressed by Ensminger and Knight and not to norms in general.

20. Elster (1989) seems particularly oblivious to this point. For him, norms are distinguished by their ability to exercise a "grip on the mind." Although some norms may, indeed, grip the mind, by no means does this imply that they are

immune from differential interpretation. Albert Yee (1997) also stresses the importance of interpretation for the analysis of normative phenomena.

# References

Arthur, Brian. 1989. "Competing Technologies, Increasing Returns, and Lock-in by Historical Events." *Economic Journal* 99: 116–31.

Barzel, Yoram. 1982. "Measurement Cost and the Organization of Markets." *Journal of Law and Economics* 25(1): 27–48.

Bok, Sissela. 1978. *Lying: Moral Choice in Public and Private Life*. New York: Pantheon Books.

Coleman, James. S. 1966. "The Possibility of a Social Welfare Function." *American Economic Review* 56(5): 1105–22.

———. 1990. *Foundations of Social Theory*. Cambridge: Harvard University Press, Belknap Press.

Dixit, Avinash K., and Barry J. Nalebuff. 1991. *Thinking Strategically. The Competitive Edge in Business, Politics, and Everyday Life*. New York: Norton.

Eagly, Alice H., and Shelly Chaiken. 1993. *The Psychology of Attitudes*. Fort Worth: Harcourt.

Ellickson, Robert C. 1991. *Order Without Law: How Neighbors Settle Disputes*. Cambridge, Mass.: Harvard University Press.

Elster, Jon. 1989. *The Cement of Society: A Study of Social Order*. Cambridge: Cambridge University Press.

———. 1990. "Norms of Revenge." *Ethics* 100(4): 862–85.

———. 1999. *Alchemies of the Mind: Rationality and the Emotions*. Cambridge: Cambridge University Press.

Ensminger, Jean, and Jack Knight. 1997. "Changing Social Norms: Common Property, Bridewealth, and Clan Exogamy." *Current Anthropology* 38(1): 1–24.

Epstein, A.L. 1968. "Sanctions." In *International Encyclopedia of the Social Sciences*, vol. 14, edited by David L. Sills. New York: Macmillan.

Flache, Andreas, and Michael Macy. 1996. "The Weakness of Strong Ties: Collective Action Failure in a Highly Cohesive Group." *Journal of Mathematical Sociology* 21(1): 3–28.

Gibbs, Jack P. 1968. "The Study of Norms." In vol. 11 of *International Encyclopedia of the Social Sciences*, edited by David L. Sills. New York: Macmillan.

Hardin, Russell. 1980. "The Emergence of Norms." *Ethics* 90(4): 575–87.

———. 1995. *One for All: The Logic of Group Conflict*. Princeton: Princeton University Press.

Hechter, Michael. 2000. *Containing Nationalism*. Oxford: Oxford University Press.

Hempel, Carl G. 1965. *Aspects of Scientific Explanation and other Essays in the Philosophy of Science*. New York: Free Press.

Kuran, Timur. 1995. *Private Truths, Public Lies: The Social Consequences of Preference Falsification*. Cambridge: Harvard University Press.

Lindbeck, Assar. 1995. "Welfare State Disincentives with Endogenous Habits and Norms." *Scandinavian Journal of Economics* 97(4): 477–94.

Mackie, Gerry. 1996. "Footbinding and Infibulation: A Convention Account." *American Sociological Review* 61(6): 999–1017.

Marwell, Gerald, and Pamela Oliver. 1993. *The Critical Mass in Collective Action: A Micro-Social Theory*. New York: Cambridge University Press.

Nagel, Ernest. 1956. "Formalization of Functionalism." In *Logic Without Metaphysics*, edited by Ernest Nagel. Glencoe, Ill.: Free Press.

Opp, Karl-Dieter. 1983. *Die Entstehung sozialer Normen: Ein Integrationsversuch soziologischer, sozialpsychologischer, und ökonomischer Erklärungen.* Tübingen: Mohr Siebeck.

———. 1990. "The Attenuation of Customs." In *Social Institutions: Their Emergence, Maintenance, and Effects*, edited by Michael Hechter, Karl-Dieter Opp, and Reinhard Wippler. New York: Aldine de Gruyter.

Posner, Eric A. 1996. "Law, Economics, and Inefficient Norms." *University of Pennsylvania Law Review* 144(5): 1697–1744.

Simmel, Georg. 1955. "The Web of Group Affiliations." In *Conflict and the Web of Group Affiliations*, edited by Georg Simmel. New York: Free Press.

Sugden, Robert. 1998. "Normative Expectations: The Simultaneous Evolution of Institutions and Norms." In *Economics, Values, and Organization*, edited by Ben-Ner Avner and Louis Putterman. Cambridge: Cambridge University Press.

Sumner, William Graham. 1906. *Folkways: A Study of the Sociological Importance of Usages, Manners, Customs, Mores, and Morals.* Boston: Ginn and Company.

Weber, Max. 1978 [1921–22]. *Economy and Society.* Edited by G. Roth and C. Wittich. Berkeley: University of California Press.

Wildavsky, Aaron. 1993. "On the Social Construction of Distinctions: Risk, Rape, Public Goods and Altruism." In *The Origin of Values,* edited by Michael Hechter, Lynn Nadel, and Richard E. Michod. New York: Aldine de Gruyter.

Williams, Robin M. 1968. "The Concept of Norms." In vol. 11 of *International Encyclopedia of the Social Sciences,* edited by David L. Sills. New York: Macmillan.

Yee, Albert S. 1997. "Thick Rationality and the Missing 'Brute Fact': The Limits of Rationalist Incorporations of Norms and Ideas." *Journal of Politics* 59(4): 1001–39.

# Index